# Rebel Rank and File

# Rebel Rank and File

## Labor Militancy and Revolt
from Below in the Long 1970s

Edited by

AARON BRENNER, ROBERT BRENNER,
AND CAL WINSLOW

VERSO

London • New York

First published by Verso 2010
© the collection Verso 2010
© individual contributions the contributors

All rights reserved

The moral rights of the author have been asserted

1 3 5 7 9 10 8 6 4 2

**Verso**
UK: 6 Meard Street, London W1F 0EG
US: 20 Jay Street, Suite 1010, Brooklyn, NY 11201
www.versobooks.com

Verso is the imprint of New Left Books

ISBN-13: 978-1-84467-173-1 (hbk)
ISBN-13: 978-1-84467-174-8 (pbk)

**British Library Cataloguing in Publication Data**
A catalogue record for this book is available from the British Library

**Library of Congress Cataloging-in-Publication Data**
A catalog record for this book is available from the Library of Congress

Typeset in Bembo by Hewer Text UK Ltd, Edinburgh
Printed in the US by Maple Vail

# Contents

Foreword: Mike Hamlin      VII

Preface: Aaron Brenner      XI

Acknowledgments      xxi

1. *Overview: The Rebellion from Below, 1965–81*
   Cal Winslow      I

2. *The Political Economy of the Rank-and-File Rebellion*
   Robert Brenner      37

3. *Conflict, Change, and Economic Policy in the Long 1970s*
   Judith Stein      77

4. *Understanding the Rank-and-File Rebellion in the Long 1970s*
   Kim Moody      105

5. *The United Farm Workers from the Ground Up*
   Frank Bardacke      149

6. *Rank-and-File Movements in the United Mine Workers of America, Early 1960s–Early 1980s*
   Paul J. Nyden      173

7. *The Tumultuous Teamsters of the 1970s*
   Dan La Botz      199

8. *Militancy in Many Forms: Teachers Strikes and Urban Insurrection, 1967–74*
   Marjorie Murphy      229

9. *Rank-and-File Struggles at the Telephone Company*
   Aaron Brenner      251

10. *Rank-and-File Opposition in the UAW During the Long 1970s*
    A. C. Jones                                                    281

11. *American Petrograd: Detroit and the League of Revolutionary*
    *Black Workers*
    Kieran Taylor                                                  311

12. *"A Spontaneous Loss of Enthusiasm": Workplace Feminism*
    *and the Transformation of Women's Service Jobs in the 1970s*
    Dorothy Sue Cobble                                             335

13. *The Enduring Legacy and Contemporary Relevance of Labor*
    *Insurgency in the 1970s*
    Steve Early                                                    357


    List of Contributors                                           395

    Index                                                          399

# Foreword

## Mike Hamlin

In 1967, John Watson and I began publishing a revolutionary newspaper, *The Inner City Voice*, designed to educate, mobilize, and organize blacks under the leadership of black workers. This led to collaboration with General Baker and our subsequent involvement with factory workers at the Chrysler Dodge Main plant in Hamtramck, Michigan, including the formation of the Dodge Revolutionary Union Movement (DRUM) and the League of Revolutionary Black Workers in Detroit.

During that time, if any of the workers had revealed themselves as leaders of a militant movement such as ours, they would have been immediately fired or worse. As a result, I chaired the meetings and, with General Baker, became a principal spokesperson for DRUM. We were in the lead in 1968 during the two strikes DRUM led at Chrysler's Dodge Main and Eldon Avenue plants. The risks were great, the pressure enormous, but it was exhilarating, and the success impacted black workers not only at Chrysler but throughout the auto industry and workplaces of all types. It also brought back militancy to the working class and broke the shackles that had suppressed the class struggle during the McCarthy period. These strikes pointed to and paved the way for the rank-and-file movements of the seventies.

For blacks, and especially revolutionary blacks, this period is important to look at for a not so obvious reason. As we fought through the fifties and sixties, we had no practice model to guide us. We had to improvise and react spontaneously to events as they developed, which took an enormous toll on the participants, especially the leaders, and left them unable to participate in any process of consolidation or provide effective leadership in the organizations, institutions, and forms of struggle they had developed. Another result, almost universal in the black community, was that vanguard elements of black liberation and black workers' struggles were either in prison, dead, in hiding, mentally ill, exhausted, or in organizations not committed to mass action.

We therefore have a limited view of the rank-and-file struggles of the seventies. Now, as we deal with the impact of the current economy and the degradation of the working class, it is absolutely essential that we study the bold and powerful rank-and-file movements of the period. One reason it is important that black and white workers understand these struggles is that I can remember when leftists in this country argued that workers had no revolutionary potential. Our experience in the League of Revolutionary Black Workers should have put that notion to rest. Likewise, the rank-and-file efforts of the seventies were part of a class struggle that was guided by class consciousness. The great weakness of the time was the inability of the leadership of these movements to link up.

The essays collected here are important because they present many of the lessons that we learned in the course of the class struggle in the sixties and seventies. If there is one axiom for revolutionaries, it is that you must study history and learn from the mistakes of those who have gone before you. We failed to do this and paid a terrible price. Hopefully these essays will spark a dialogue within the working class, and I look forward to it.

*Venceremos!*

Mike Hamlin, Detroit

(Mike Hamlin was a founder of the Dodge Revolutionary Union Movement [DRUM] and the League of Revolutionary Black Workers.)

Union supporters, J. P. Stevens & Co, North Carolina

# Preface

## Aaron Brenner

Between the early 1960s and 1981, American workers engaged in an extraordinarily high level of workplace militancy, exhibiting a sustained rebelliousness not seen since the 1930s. The most obvious manifestation of their combativeness was one of the largest strike waves in U.S. history, during which workers twice set records for the number of strikes in a single year. Rank-and-file contract rejections, collective insubordination, sabotage, organized slowdowns, and wildcat strikes provided further evidence of workers' militant mood. Though the level and intensity of workplace agitation never reached the peaks of unrest achieved in 1877, 1919, the 1930s, or 1945, workers' bellicosity was great enough to provoke military intervention on several occasions and presidential action numerous times. It inspired dozens of anti-labor injunctions, thousands of arrests, numerous calls for anti-strike legislation, and ever more systematic and coordinated efforts on the part of corporate managers to organize against the labor movement.

Workers with a history of militancy, such as those in auto, mining, and construction, accounted for much of the unrest, but so too did flight attendants, teachers, communications workers, nurses, clericals, letter carriers, and farm workers. Their protests preserved and expanded wages and benefits, workplace prerogatives such as seniority rights, and workers' confidence and dignity. In the public sector, the militancy led to a massive expansion of government sector unionization. On a large scale, strikes such as those by Memphis sanitation workers to finally win real workplace equality, or by West Virginia coal miners to win passage of Black Lung legislation—the rare American political strike—represented historic achievements with lasting impact. On a smaller scale, thousands of wildcats addressed immediate grievances against the indignities of work, such as the guilty-until-proven-innocent nature of workplace disciplinary procedures, the arbitrariness of supervisors, or the horrendous pace of work.

Particularly striking about the new labor insurgency was the fact that union workers aimed so much of their activity not only at their employers, but at their union leaders as well. Rank-and-file members of many of the country's most powerful unions created dissident groups that organized collective action against employers on the job *and* mounted political challenges to incumbent union officials reluctant to take on the companies. Furthermore, these militants fought around more than the bread-and-butter issues of wages and working conditions. Drawing on the civil rights, Black Power, feminist, and antiwar movements, and on the labor movement's own traditions of militancy, rank-and-file self-organization, and workers' control, they advocated a more aggressive, inclusive, democratic, and politicized union movement that they believed could win greater rights for workers both on and off the job. They developed a broad agenda that stressed job control, worker welfare, and militant confrontation with management as the guiding principles of workplace activity. In their view, existing union organization and incumbent union leaders presented obstacles to the re-invigorated union movement they envisioned, so they demanded a range of union reforms, encouraged independent rank-and-file activism, ran candidates for union office, and filed lawsuits against union officials. Their activity disrupted the stable one-party rule that had governed most U.S. unions for the previous twenty years and ended the long reign of many entrenched union leaders.

Workplace militancy in the long 1970s is all the more remarkable because it took place when blue-collar workers, especially white male blue-collar workers, were often depicted as ignorant, passive, and conservative. Popular portrayals, such as the television series *All in the Family* and the feature movie *Joe*, painted them as beer-guzzling, tough-talking bigots. Pundits on both the political right and the liberal left generally concurred with these portraits, agreeing that blue-collar workers supported the war in Vietnam, despised student protesters, opposed the enforcement of civil rights laws, hated the counterculture, resisted gender equity, feared homosexuality, and detested liberals. A wide spectrum of observers concluded that workers were self-centered, that they cared little about local or national politics, and that they sought only more consumer goods and more leisure. They convinced themselves that working-class resistance and opposition to authority were unlikely, if not impossible.[1]

In fact, opposition to the Vietnam War, as registered in the polls, ran as

---

[1]  This portrait also dominates much of the literature on blue-collar workers since the early 1970s, even where such literature is sympathetic to the labor movement and labor liberalism. See, for example, T. B. Edsall and M. Edsall, *Chain Reaction: The Impact of Race, Rights and Taxes on American Politics* (New York: W.W. Norton, 1991) and J. Rieder, *Canarsie: The Jews and Italians of Brooklyn Against Liberalism* (Cambridge, MA: Harvard University, 1985).

high among blue-collar workers as it did among white-collar professionals. The core of support for right-wing politicians such as Joe McCarthy, Barry Goldwater, and George Wallace and the movements that grew up around them came from the middle-class suburbs and major corporations, not workers, although Wallace did attract significant working-class backing with his racist and populist appeals. Moreover, workers' pervasive and unshakeable backing for New Deal and Great Society programs obliged even Republican presidents Richard Nixon and Gerald Ford to support such liberal reforms as occupational safety and health, environmental protection, the earned income tax credit, and a historic expansion of social security as preconditions for their own electoral viability. But most importantly, workers' militancy put the lie to the portrayals of working-class conservatism. Reactionary loading-dock worker Archie Bunker may have topped television ratings when *All in the Family* debuted in 1971, but at the very same time real loading-dock workers and their truck-driving brothers and sisters in the International Brotherhood of Teamsters were challenging the status quo in their warehouses *and* their union halls with a series of strikes, wildcats, contract campaigns, and rank-and-file organizations that lasted from 1967 to 1976 and beyond. Their actions, mirrored by millions more workers across the economy, demonstrated that large portions of the working class were engaged, mobilized, connected to each other, and motivated not just by wages and working conditions but by belief in expansive versions of industrial and union democracy.

Significant sections of the white working class *did* identify with U.S. imperial adventures and responded strongly to racist appeals, most notably in the movements to keep black people out of white neighborhoods and against school busing. But it is remarkable how little the U.S. New Left tried to provide an alternative. The leading forces of U.S. radicalism of the period made little attempt to connect with the working class, especially its unionized sectors. Students for a Democratic Society (SDS), the vanguard organization of the student left, made a major contribution to the antiwar movement and to the society-wide radicalization taking place. However, nurtured on Baran and Sweezy's *Monopoly Capital* and Marcuse's *One-Dimensional Man*, the majority of SDS had been convinced that, thanks to state intervention, capitalism could expand indefinitely, that the working class had been largely bought off and domesticated, and that the main plausible social bases for a struggle against capitalism were to be found among marginal elements, black people, and in the Third World. Given SDS's roots in the social democratic Student League for Industrial Democracy, some members did take the working class and unions quite seriously, especially early on, as evidenced by the Economic Research and Action Projects in Chicago, Baltimore, and Newark. Yet within SDS, they were always in the minority, and their influence waned over time. Mesmerized by the Kennedy-Johnson boom and the military Keynesianism that lay behind it, the majority of SDSers shrugged off the deep recessions of the late 1950s and never registered the falling rates of profit and rising international competition plaguing the heartland of U.S. industry beginning in the late 1960s. Even more serious, they missed an ever more intense assault on workers by employers seeking to recover their profitability; this attack profoundly affected the living standards of supposedly bought-off workers and exacerbated the appalling working conditions under which they labored. The tragic result was that most new radicals of the time neglected the working-class insurgency running parallel to their own rebellions, distinguished, like their own, by mass direct action, resistance to hierarchy, and demands for democracy and self-determination.

With the collapse of SDS, a small but significant number of young radicals did make a "turn" to the working class. They "industrialized" by taking jobs in auto, trucking, post office, telephone, steel, and other industries, where they played an important role in the sustained militancy and rank-and-file organizations of the era. Representing different radical political tendencies—some seeing black workers as the vanguard of revolutionary change, others focusing on capturing union leadership, and still others trying to build grassroots groups—they found some receptivity among their fellow workers. While the New Deal liberal experience of the postwar era fostered high expectations for social and economic progress among many workers, New Deal institutions of labor relations were failing to deliver in the more challenging economic circumstances of the late 1960s and 1970s. Wildcat strikes, sabotage, collective disobedience, workplace self-organization and protest, and formal rank-and-file organizations illustrated workers' frustration with established institutions and procedures for workplace dispute resolution, including unions, grievance processes, collective bargaining, the National Labor Relations Board, and the courts. These institutions, in many ways the epitome of the New Deal liberal impulse, often failed to serve their interests and left them at a disadvantage vis-à-vis management. Indeed, as radicals pointed out, they were designed to channel power away from the rank and file on the shop floor and into more "responsible hands," leaving workers incapable of amassing the collective power necessary to take on the employers. As an alternative, radicals insisted on workers' rights and the necessity to shape the labor process directly through their own collective action. Millions of workers put that message into practice.

As we know, the rank-and-file rebellion of the long 1970s did not in the end halt the employers' offensive, transform the bureaucratic torpidity of the official labor movement, or reverse the downward trend in private sector union density. Perhaps the ultimate reason for this failure was simply the sheer power and ferocious opposition of capital, unparalleled elsewhere in the advanced capitalist countries. U.S. corporations never willingly accepted trade unionism—it had been forced upon them by the mass struggles of the 1930s. They had, moreover, a strong basis of political support in major sections of small business and the middle class, which always resented unions, taxes, and the welfare state. Nowhere else in the industrialized countries did government provide more blatant and consistent support for corporations. Even during the extended postwar period of liberal predominance, Democratic administrations with huge electoral majorities refused to press for the revision of the viciously anti-labor Taft-Hartley Act. Responding to downward pressure on profits over the long 1970s, U.S. corporations organized themselves ever more systematically against the labor movement. Individually, they implemented a panoply of strategies now well understood, including moving to non-union regions in the South, West, and abroad, hiring union-busting lawyers, running decertification campaigns, and promiscuously violating national labor law that provided no real sanctions. Collectively, they organized to expand their political power through such groups as the Business Roundtable and by promoting the rise of the far right within the Republican Party. In all these activities, they fought to win, with a ruthlessness rarely rivaled in the industrial world.

The rank-and-file insurgency failed, as well, because it could not overcome the bureaucratic business unionism that emerged during World War II, flourished during the boom of the 1950s, and then proved entirely inadequate to counter employers' rising assaults that started in the late 1950s. When, in 1978, United Auto Workers (UAW) leader Douglas Fraser rightly complained of "a one-sided class war against working people," he neglected to point out that this unbalanced struggle had been going on for at least two decades and that a fundamental reason it had been so one-sided was that so many labor officials had been reluctant to confront employers throughout the period. Indeed, a large portion of the union leadership pursued what amounted to concessionary bargaining after the late 1950s, evidenced in the sharp slowdown in wage growth and the deterioration of working conditions, and they often did so despite demands from the ranks that they fight. Their unwillingness to oppose employers often contrasted sharply with the determination they showed in repressing any opposition from the membership. The murder of mine worker leader Jock Yablonski and the frequent beatings of oppositionists in the Teamsters were the most notorious examples of union leaders' violent repression of resistance from below. But even an ostensibly progressive union, the UAW, assaulted the picket lines and maligned the politics of the League of Revolutionary Black

Workers in 1968 and 1969, and mobilized one thousand armed officials and loyalists in the summer of 1973 to physically attack and break a wildcat at Chrysler's Mack Avenue stamping plant in Detroit. And violence was only the most overt tactic used by union officials against rank-and-file militants. They stole union elections, engaged in bureaucratic maneuvers, red-baited, co-opted rank-and-file leaders, collaborated with employers to discipline or fire troublemakers, and simply refused to implement the demands of a majority of the membership. By the end of the 1970s, officials in every major union, with the notable exception of the United Mine Workers, had largely crushed their internal oppositions and faced no serious threats to their control. The sad irony of this success was that it disarmed unions in the face of the employers' continuing offensive.

The suppression of independent rank-and-file opposition to the employers reflected the inherent conservatism of union officials as a social layer. Their dual need to preserve both the unions as institutions and their own positions at the helm of those institutions drove them to accommodate employers' requirements for profits, on the one hand, and eliminate opposition from the membership, on the other. The rank-and-file rebellion threatened not only to dislodge highly paid, generously benefited, well-pensioned, and sometimes literally profitable individual officials from union leadership, but to incite the wrath of corporations and the government, which risked crippling or even destroying the union organization itself.

Similar logic lay behind the unions' failure to create and sustain an independent class-based political party and their embrace of the Democratic Party instead. This dependence on a party dominated by business and still heavily influenced by its largely racist and conservative Southern wing helps explain why the official labor movement failed to give much support to the mass social movements of the period, leaving both the labor and social movements weaker. Most unions, including the UAW, refused to oppose the Vietnam War, and even the few that did provided little material support to the antiwar movement. Assistance was more forthcoming for the civil rights movement and some of its offshoots, but not for the most militant, independent, and progressive manifestations of black people's struggles: SNCC, the Mississippi Freedom Democratic Party, the urban rebellions, or the League of Revolutionary Black Workers. Rather than support the most dynamic social movements of the period and push for widespread social change to transform the role of all workers in society, union officials chose to protect their own institutions.

The rank-and-file rebellion of the long 1970s had debilitating weaknesses of its own. Most crucially, militants most often confined their activity, and even their independent organizations, within the boundaries established by business unionism. As a result, their movements reflected its weaknesses and suffered from its limitations. Militants often focused on replacing union leaders, and in some locals and in one national union (the UMW) they succeeded. This did little, however, to alter the behavior of the unions. Newly elected officers remained subject to the same constraints as their predecessors, facing pressure from employers without the permanent self-organization of the rank and file that would provide strength and discipline to individual leaders in struggles against the companies. Where militants mobilized the ranks, they generally adhered to the jurisdictional boundaries imposed by the official labor movement. Each group remained confined within established jurisdictions, and while they often built intense solidarity within an industry, it rarely spilled from industry to industry or union to union, let alone to non-union workers or the unemployed. Nor did the militants squarely confront the racial and gender inequalities that limited access to employment and mobility on the job for black and women workers, as well as entry into the union hierarchies. Despite the substantial, but usually temporary, influence of black, feminist, and young radical workers, the rank-and-file struggles and groups that emerged in this period mostly failed to build material alliances with the era's social movements. Nor in most cases could they overcome divisions of geography, skill, religion, or politics.

The dissipation of the rank-and-file rebellion had profound consequences for the labor movement and, by extension, for the country as a whole. The epoch-making labor upsurge of the 1930s, as well as labor's continued political influence during the period of long boom, had made possible the rise and perpetuation of liberal dominance in the United States. Then the struggle for black liberation, as well as the antiwar movement, sustained the momentum for reform during the 1960s. But with the decline of the labor movement, following the disappearance of the antiwar and student movements and the repression and cooptation of the black insurgency, the field was open for Reagan and the new right. By contrast, in Europe, the parallel but much more powerful explosion of rank-and-file workers' movements against employers and entrenched union officials made significant economic and political gains, often through not only Social Democratic or Communist parties, but also in more independent parties of the revolutionary left. Though they failed to sustain a long-term political radicalization that at times seemed possible, these struggles from below did strengthen the region's labor movements, and union density throughout most countries in Western Europe continued to rise dramatically during the 1970s and 1980s. The persistent power of labor provided the key political force that held off the neo-liberalization that took place in the Anglo-Saxon countries in those years. It also underpinned both rising real wages and an impressive, ongoing expansion of the welfare state right through the turn of the century, at a time when both real wages and the welfare state stagnated or declined in the United States, especially for the poor. The rank-and-file rebellion of the long 1970s proved to be the last great effort, up to the present, to recreate a strong U.S. labor movement that could provide the necessary foundation for a more influential U.S. left. We will need another one if working-class power is to be rebuilt and progressive politics revived in the United States.

Despite its breadth and depth, and despite the plethora of literature on the civil rights, Black Power, feminist, student, and antiwar movements, the militancy and rank-and-file movements of the long 1970s have been ignored by all but a tiny group of historians, several of whom appear in this collection.[2] It has been said that history is written by the victors, and this no doubt helps to explain the dearth of attention to the rank-and-file revolt. Since 1980 and the end of the revolt from below, the labor movement has suffered a long-term decline, evidenced by a drop in membership, organizing activity, strikes, and political influence. Likewise, labor history, so vibrant during the period of the upsurge, is now marginalized in the academy. Today, with less than one in twelve private-sector workers in a union, organized labor flirts with irrelevance and, for the majority of historians, irrelevance in the present translates into irrelevance in the past. Yet recovering the rank-and-file rebellion of the 1960s and 1970s—the task of this volume—is a valuable project. Not only is the topic worthy in its own right, involving so many millions of workers in so many important battles, but perhaps more important, *Rebel Rank and File: Labor Militancy and Revolt from Below in the Long 1970s* recovers the successes and failures of the rank-and-file rebellion, which helps us understand the larger political shifts taking place from the 1960s to the 1980s and offers important lessons for the labor movement today.

*Rebel Rank and File* grew out of a conference sponsored by the Center for Social Theory and Comparative History at the University of California, Los Angeles. Over two and a half days in November 2005, historians, social scientists, and labor activists delivered papers and engaged in discussion and debate about the working-class upsurge of the long 1970s. Following the conference, a number of participants agreed to develop their papers for inclusion in this volume.

Cal Winslow opens the volume with an overview of the rank-and-file rebellion, rooting it in the social and political movements of the sixties.

---

2   See, for example, A. Brenner, "Rank-and-File Rebellion, 1966–1975" (PhD Diss, Columbia University, 1996); J. Brecher, *Strike!* (Cambridge, MA: South Press End Press, 1972); J. Green, *The World of the Worker: Labor in Twentieth-Century America* (New York: Hill and Wang, 1980); D. La Botz, *Rank-and-File Rebellion: Teamsters for a Democratic Union* (London: Verso, 1990); and K. Moody, *An Injury to All: The Decline of American Unionism* (London: Verso, 1988).

Two essays then explore aspects of the larger context for workers' struggle. Robert Brenner offers an analysis of the evolution of the labor movement, and the rank-and-file insurgency emerging from it, by situating it within the stages through which the postwar economy passed—from the high boom of the late 1940s and 1950s, to the first signs of difficulty in the late 1950s and early 1960s, to the boom and profitability crisis of the later 1960s and 1970s. Judith Stein traces the trajectory of U.S. economic policy over the period, bringing out its minimal place in the political consciousness of the left and labor, their limited contribution to its creation, and the high price they had to pay for their neglect, as the U.S. economy globalized without reference to the needs of U.S. workers.

The remaining essays focus on the rank-and-file rebellion itself. First, Kim Moody understands the ascent of the labor bureaucracy during wartime and the postwar period as a largely conscious political process, explains the adoption of business unionism in connection with bureaucratization and prosperity, and, against that background, offers an account of the rise of the rank-and-file movements. Next come a collection of case studies that flesh out the various forms taken by the rank-and-file revolt as it emerged in different sectors. Most of these concentrate on individual industries: Frank Bardacke on farm workers, Paul Nyden on miners, Dan La Botz on Teamsters, Marjorie Murphy on teachers, Aaron Brenner on telephone workers, and A. C. Jones on auto workers. Kieran Taylor examines the League of Revolutionary Black Workers, which tried to combine workplace militancy with the struggle for black liberation. Dorothy Sue Cobble reviews the rank-and-file militancy of women workers in three female-dominated service occupations: flight attendants, clericals, and domestic workers. The volume ends with an essay by Steve Early that demonstrates how the people and events of the rank-and-file rebellion of the long 1970s continue to shape workers' struggles today, and how the lessons of the era offer essential guidance for revitalizing the American labor movement.

# *Acknowledgments*

This volume derives from a conference on "Rank-and-File Movements of the Long 1970s," which took place in the fall of 2005 at the Center for Social Theory and Comparative History at UCLA. Steve Early and Cal Winslow originated the idea for the conference, and both helped organize this volume all the way to publication. Nelson Lichtenstein was instrumental in finding funding for and helping to plan the conference. Funding came from the All-UC Labor and Employment Research Fund, a unit of what is now the Miguel Contreras Labor Program, the UCLA Institute for Research on Labor and Employment, the UCLA Institute for Social Research, and the Center for Social Theory and Comparative History. We are grateful to the participants, all of whom offered stimulating insights. They included Frank Bardacke, Dorothy Sue Cobble, Jefferson Cowie, Mike Davis, Steve Early, Michael Goldfield, Mike Hamlin, Meg Jacobs, Dan La Botz, Nelson Lichtenstein, Tom Mertes, Kim Moody, Marjorie Murphy, Paul J. Nyden, Ken Paff, Mike Parker, A. C. Jones, Steve Shapiro, and Judith Stein, as well as the editors. Mike Davis and Ken Paff, both of whom championed the conference, provided inspiration at the conference's evening event, a Los Angeles–wide fundraiser for Teamsters for a Democratic Union.

Our greatest debt is to Tom Mertes, who made the conference happen with his organizational efforts and acted as traffic cop, taskmaster, and copy editor for the volume, offering indispensable discipline and leadership for an unruly rank and file.

## Photo Acknowledgment

The editors are very pleased to present a small collection of the extraordinary photos of Earl Dotter, who has been a photographer of America's working class since the 1960s. He chronicled the efforts of Miners for Democracy as a photographer for its paper, *The Miner's Voice*, and then worked for the *UMWA Journal* following MFD's successful election campaign to unseat the corrupt regime of Tony Boyle. He is the author of *The Quiet Sickness: A Photographic Chronicle of Hazardous Work in America*, and his photos have appeared in dozens of magazines and newspapers. The photos in this volume provide unique insight into the lives and struggles of American workers in the period of the long 1970s. We thank Dotter for making the photos available and encourage readers to visit www.earldotter.com.

# Overview: The Rebellion from Below, 1965–81[1]

## Cal Winslow

In October 1973, roving pickets shut down United Parcel Service (UPS) in Western Pennsylvania and Ohio, as part of an eight-week dispute in Pittsburgh. A "well-organized council" of workers directed the pickets. They were protesting the increased use of part-time employees inside UPS shipping centers. This strike, highlighted in historian David Montgomery's widely read *Workers' Control in America*, was just one of many in "a rebellion from below," a wave of strikes and conflicts that transformed industrial relations in the United States.[2]

The UPS pickets were wildcat strikers—in Cleveland they were met but not deterred by baseball bat–carrying officials of their union, the International Brotherhood of Teamsters (IBT), Local 407. "Wildcat strike" refers of course to an "unofficial," often spontaneous strike—one not sanctioned by the union, so often an illegal strike.[3] In the late 1960s and early 1970s, wildcat strikes accounted for more than a third of all strikes in the United States. Wildcat strikers were the shock troops of the "rebellions from below," and their strikes became all but routine elements in contractual disputes and grievance negotiations. These strikes were often repudiations of the union leadership and, implicitly, of the entire postwar system of industrial relations.

---

1 I would like to gratefully acknowledge the support of Steve Early and Iain Boal, comrades, collaborators, and co-conspirators, as well as my always patient and encouraging son, Matthew Winslow, himself much engaged in this project.

2 D. Montgomery, *Workers' Control in America, Studies in the History of Work, Technology, and Labor Struggles* (Cambridge: Cambridge University Press, 1979), p. 173.

3 A. W. Gouldner, *Wildcat Strike: A Study in Worker–Management Relationships* (New York: Harper, 1965). This 1954 study of wildcat strikes was, interestingly, reissued in 1965. It points to the "aggressiveness" of wildcat strikes and their "spontaneous" nature. It suggests that wildcat strikes are frequently about issues of "little interest" to "formal trade union leaders" and the "dilatory manner in which their grievances are dealt with, i.e., the 'runaround.'" pp. 89, 91, 95.

Increasingly, critics noted, wildcat strikes were examples of rank-and-file members taking initiative and responsibility. They indicated not just tests of economic strength but also new forms of protest.

Worker militancy, full-blown, thus returned to center stage in the United States. In these years, "the long seventies," by which we mean roughly the mid-1960s to 1981, there were strikes of all kinds. They included nationally significant conflicts in coal mining, longshore, auto, trucking, teaching, railroad, transit, and construction. In 1971, the strike of West Coast longshoremen threatened the flow of military goods and personnel to Vietnam. Richard Nixon, asserting that the strike undermined the war effort, invoked an anti-strike Taft-Hartley injunction, though this failed to deter longshoremen from conducting the longest waterfront strike in U.S. history.[4] The independent truckers' strikes of 1974 generated fears of chaos and anarchy in elected officials, leading Milton Shapp, governor of Pennsylvania, to warn Richard Nixon of the danger of "national economic collapse."[5] In the coalfields, between 1974 and 1975, there were nine thousand strikes, 99 percent of them wildcats.[6] In the 1978 national coal miners strike, the Carter administration also invoked the Taft-Hartley Act, but it only provoked the anger and defiance of miners ("Taft can mine it, Hartley can haul it, and Carter can shove it!"). Carter's threat to "seize" the nation's coal mines failed to stop the miners' strike, a conflict that ultimately lasted 110 days. [7]

In these years, worker militancy was an international phenomenon. This was the decade of the "Paris Spring," the massive 1968 movement and general strike of French students and workers. It was also the time of the Italian *autunno caldo* (hot autumn), the 1969 season of strikes and factory occupations during which 1.5 million workers struck, including workers at all the major metalworking factories in Italy.[8] In 1972, British workers celebrated a "Glorious Summer," the high point in the strike wave of 1969 to 1974, an insurgency that ultimately toppled the Conservative government.[9] Richard Hyman, the British industrial relations specialist,

---

4   "Nixon Accuses Congress of a Lag on Dock Strike," *New York Times*, February 3, 1972. D. Brody puts the anti-labor Taft-Hartley Act in context in *Labor Embattled* (Urbana: University of Illinois Press, 2005), p. 131.

5   M. Jacobs, "The Independent Truckers' Rebellion: The Energy Crisis and the Not So Silent Majority," CSTCH Conference Paper, UCLA, November 11, 2005, p. 73.

6   C. R. Perry, *Collective Bargaining and the Decline of the United Mine Workers* (Philadelphia: University of Pennsylvania Press, 1984), p. 209.

7   P. Nyden (see chapter 6).

8   P. Ginsborg, *A History of Contemporary Italy* (London: Penguin Books, 1990). See chapter 9, "The Era of Collective Action, 1968–73," pp. 298–347.

9   D. Lyddon, "'Glorious Summer,' 1972: The High Tide of Rank and File Militancy,"

called the 1970s in Europe "the decade of the unions."[10] In these years, unions in Europe grew dramatically in numbers and influence, advances with major implications in the evolution of national politics.

This was not exactly the case in the United States, where, by and large, the unions resisted change and maintained membership totals only by virtue of the rapid organization of public sector workers.[11] The union leaders, when not reactionaries, were disinterested in the great social issues of the day: racism, sexism, poverty, unemployment, and the concentration of economic and political power. The trade unions, the domain of these leaders and their bureaucratic cliques, were, most often, institutions far removed from the temper of the times. George Meany, president of the AFL-CIO, boasted: "I never went on strike in my life, never ran a strike in my life, never ordered anyone else to run a strike in my life, never had anything to do with a picket line . . ."[12] The unions saw themselves as partners, perhaps junior partners, with the Democrats, often the hawkish, Henry Jackson wing of the party. There existed no left-wing political current to speak of—there was, however, an ill-defined history of syndicalism, better described perhaps as a tradition of "direct action."[13]

We might, however, call the long 1970s in the United States the decade of the rank and file. These were strike-prone years. The year 1970 itself ranks toward the top of the table of strikes and strikers in any single year: there were 5,716 strikes involving more than 3 million workers. And 1970 was just one high point in a decade of strikes.[14] In these years, rank-and-file workers led wildcat strikes, rejected contracts, and forced official strikes; one strike alone, the nationwide wildcat strike of postal workers, involved 200,000 workers.[15] This explosion of strikes, lasting throughout the long seventies, coincided with the ending of the long postwar boom but took

---

in J. McIlroy, N. Fishman, and A. Campbell, eds, *British Trade Unions and Industrial Politics: The High Tide of Trade Unionism, 1964–79* (Aldershot, Hants: Ashgate, 1999), pp. 326–52.

10   R. Hyman, "European Unions Towards 2000," *Work, Employment & Society* vol. 5:4 (December 1991).

11   M. H. Maier, *City Unions: Managing Discontent in New York City* (New Brunswick, NJ: Rutgers University Press, 1987). "In a sudden and unexpected wave of organizing, public sector union membership jumped from slightly over 1 million in 1960 to over 3 million in 1976, accounting for over 80% of total union growth both public and private during that time period," pp. 8–9.

12   See L. Huberman, "Foreword," in H. O'Connor, *Revolution in Seattle* (Seattle: Left Bank Books, 1981), p. ix.

13   D. Montgomery, "What's Happening to the American Worker" (Boston: Radical America pamphlet, n.d., c. 1969), p. 19.

14   Historical Statistics Part 1, p. 179, Bureau of Labor Statistics.

15   A. Brenner, "Rank-and-File Rebellion, 1966–1975" (PhD Diss., Columbia University, 1996). See chapter 3, "The 1970 Post Office Strike," pp. 112–50.

place in economic conditions that greatly increased workers' confidence, even long after the crisis of 1973–4.[16] Combined with an unprecedented challenge to authority within the unions, these strikes make the decade an extraordinary era, one that ranks high indeed in the history of class struggle in the United States.

This workers' rebellion drew on deep working-class traditions. But the strikes of the 1970s were unique in the degree to which they fit in with the broader wave of protest in the period, that is, the degree to which they were a protest movement of the workers that shared much in common with the other protest movements of the 1960s and '70s—the black and women's movements, the anti–Vietnam War movement, and the student movement, each of which profoundly influenced the workers' rebellion. These movements were all simultaneously economic and political; they were all, each in its own way, responses to the "precipitous descent of the economy into a long term crisis of profitability."[17] The employers' main response to this crisis was a stepped-up attack on working conditions and living standards. Workers responded in self-defense, above all with the strike weapon, but also by challenging their trade union leaders to stand up to the employers' offensive, and defying them with wildcat strikes and rank-and-file movements when they would not.

The postwar years of near full employment and rising real wages had created confidence and combativeness among American workers. This confidence was fueled by the new politics of the 1960s. The strikes of the long 1970s were about money, working conditions, and the "narrow" issues of trade unionism, in particular in the years when inflation surged. But they were about much more as well. Montgomery called the strike movement a "new unionism."[18] The sight, he wrote in 1969, of "school teachers, hospital workers, and garbage men going off to jail for violating injunctions is becoming routine. The teachers are demonstrating that arbitrary authority is as common, and as intolerable, in educational hierarchies as it is in factories."[19] The movement was also an expression of the spirit of restlessness, the new militancy, and the rising expectations to be found everywhere. It represented, in New Left language, workers continuing "the march through the institutions," that is, "working against the established institutions while working within them," including the

---

16  R. Brenner (see chapter 2). D. Lyddon writes: "In the UK, the second half of the 1970s saw an unbowed working class, notwithstanding that its economic power was draining away—hence long strikes." Letter to author.

17  R. Brenner (see chapter 2).

18  Montgomery, "What's Happening to the American Worker," p. 21.

19  Ibid.

unions and workplaces of the country.[20] In the United States, the trade unions, as with so many institutions in those years, were deeply conservative and unresponsive to the demands of the era—hence the predominance of wildcat strikes and unofficial movements. A key element of the seventies revolt was the challenge to business unionism, the form of trade union leadership that thoroughly dominated the U.S. labor movement.[21]

Miners for Democracy (MFD) was by far the best-known organization in this dramatic revival of rank-and-file movements—the *New York Times*, reporting its 1972 victory, wrote, "nothing like it had ever happened in the labor movement before."[22] The MFD's roots, too, were in the 1950s and 1960s, first of all in the dictatorial regime of John L. Lewis. His betrayal of the miners resulted in the near collapse of the union, as a result of granting the companies a free hand to mechanize the mines—in 1950 there were 416,000 working miners; by 1959, Lewis's last year in office, only 180,000 remained at work in the coalfields.[23]

MFD's successful challenge followed the ill-fated campaign of Jock Yablonski, an oppositionist assassinated in 1969 by gunmen hired by the union's president, Tony Boyle. In 1972 Arnold Miller, a rank-and-file miner, was elected president. The following year, at the Pittsburgh convention, miners rewrote the union's constitution, guaranteeing rank-and-file rights, increasing district autonomy, and reorganizing the union's dues structure in favor of the districts and the locals and the right to ratify contracts. In an atmosphere of jubilation—worried reporters deplored "parliamentary permissiveness"—rank-and-file miners then set out to transform formal democracy into practical democracy, and the coal miners embarked upon a campaign to redo relations in the mines themselves.[24]

It was quite appropriate, then, for Paul Dietsch, a spokesperson for the Fraternal Association of Steel Haulers (FASH), to suggest that the steel haulers were the "Black Panthers of the Working Class."[25] Studs Terkel called the workers' rebellion the "new, new left."[26] Auto workers struck to

---

20    M. Watts, "1968 and All That . . ." *Progress in Human Geography* vol. 25:2 (June 2001), p. 178.

21    K. Moody, *An Injury to All: The Decline of American Unionism* (London: Verso, 1988), pp. 68–9.

22    *New York Times*, December 16, 1972.

23    P. Clark, *The Miners' Fight for Democracy: Arnold Miller and the Reform of the United Mine Workers* (Ithaca: Cornell University Press, 1981), p. 17.

24    "Mine Union Convention Action Lags Behind Schedule," *New York Times*, December 9, 1973.

25    P. Dietsch, interview with author.

26    S. Terkel, "The New Left: A Trucker Speaks Out," *New Times,* December 28, 1973, p. 20.

"humanize working conditions"; coal miners fought for an end to chronic poverty in Appalachia; black workers demanded access, integration, and equality; truckers and miners called for union democracy; UPS workers rebelled against "being treated like machines"—millions of workers clearly wanted something better in life. Blacks, Latinos, women, and young workers brought their movements into the workplace. With their demand for democracy in their unions, workers sought to make these institutions their own, recalling the students' demand for self-government—"participatory democracy."[27] They also fought for control on their jobs—and, as their signs so often said, for "dignity," a central demand, of course, of the Southern civil rights movement. Workers turned to direct action. Importantly, they did this in the context of a general challenge to authority, and in the shadow of the great spectacle of radical conflict: the Tet Offensive, the Paris Spring, the Black Panthers, Kent State, Jackson State, Attica.

Workers' demands were most often immediate, partial, and sectional. The workers were "economistic," but that wasn't the end of the story. The radical currents of the times, in the words of Nelson Lichtenstein, gave "a political edge to many shop floor struggles, especially after 1967."[28] Altogether they presented a significant challenge to American capital. The focus was the workplace, as it traditionally has been for American workers, in the absence of significant working-class political parties. The issues, in addition to wages, were, by and large, about control, and protests concerned speedup, work rules, the grievance procedure, the pace of work, job assignments, and health and safety. They challenged institutionalized racism as well as racist foremen, and fought for equal access to jobs and promotion, and the struggle was intense. The fact that this workers' protest movement was industrial and economic, rather than "political," is not evidence that it was less substantial than other movements. On the contrary, direct action has historically been a political trademark of American workers, at least partly because, as David Brody has suggested, "no other working class has stood so exposed to the market forces of modern capitalism; or concomitantly, been so reliant on its own collective efforts for achieving some measure of economic justice."[29]

In these years, new ideas combined with the old, including the all but extinct notion that the very system of capitalism required the suppression of vast parts of the human personality—and that nowhere was this clearer than

---

27    Watts, "1968 and All That . . ." p.181.

28    N. Lichtenstein, *Walter Reuther: The Most Dangerous Man in Detroit* (Urbana: University of Illinois Press, 1997), p. 397.

29    D. Brody, *In Labor's Cause: Main Themes on the History of the American Worker* (New York: Oxford University Press, 1993), p. 170.

in industry. There began a renewed search for alternatives, often with great optimism. Everything seemed possible, but, alas, the workers' movement was no more successful than its social counterparts; prescient minorities did not become majorities. Still, there were significant contributions, including the revival within the labor movement of the notion of industrial democracy, of the idea of ownership and control of industry and its democratic management in the interest of all the people, and of Rosa Luxemburg's great exhortation that humanity's "chains must be broken where they are forged."

The rebellion began in the 1960s, peaked in the years 1970–4, and then began to decline, though there were important conflicts, including the creation of rank-and-file institutions, right to the end of the decade. It didn't end until the air traffic controllers' (PATCO) debacle. This movement, the rank-and-file movement of the long 1970s, is, curiously, rarely celebrated, certainly not in the way that the black and women's movements are, and not in the way the "generation of 1968" has canonized itself. This volume is, then, a chapter in the history of an important decade. It is also a rescue mission, a history of the workers' movement in these years—from the bottom up.

## The Strike Wave

The long seventies is defined above all by the strike wave; hence the necessity to focus on strikes and related conflict. Strikes, of course, are central to understanding the development of the modern labor movement, key indicators of understanding industrial relations, and important signposts in assessing the balance of forces in the industrial world. They are also windows into the lives, beliefs, and aspirations of workers, especially in the United States, where workers are seen, if at all, as passive victims, obscuring, in the words of the late historian Edward Thompson, "the agency of working people, the degree to which they contributed by conscious efforts, to the making of history."[30] Thompson's highly influential writings in the 1960s, above all his *The Making of the English Working Class* (1963), were themselves expressions of the renewed interest in socialism from below, as well as an engagement with the revival of working-class struggle.[31]

The strike is an expression of the power of workers, a fundamental weapon in their conflict with the employers, a means of defense, and at times a way of forcing concessions. Strikes are basic points of resistance to capital.

---

30 E. P. Thompson, *The Making of the English Working Class* (Harmondsworth: Penguin, 1963), p. 13.

31 See also E. P. Thompson, with R. Williams and S. Hall, *The May Day Manifesto* (Harmondsworth: Penguin, 1968).

At best, strikes are also moments of education and even transformation for workers. Importantly, the strike is a collective activity, and as such is central to the creation of solidarity, working-class organization, and working-class consciousness. Strikes open new vistas for workers, thereby clearing the way for higher forms of organization and consciousness. The outcome of a strike is crucial, even when what is at stake, say a few cents or a work rule, is not so great. Strikes can have symbolic importance—a sign of strength or weakness can swing the initiative to the other side.[32]

Strikes were common in the fifties: 1952 and 1959 were peak years; in 1952 there were 5,117 strikes.[33] The number of strikes then plunged in the early sixties. Strike levels, however, rose as the decade advanced. But, importantly, they rose with a difference. Things were changing; defensiveness was giving way to aggressiveness and optimism. By the mid-1960s, increasingly, observers were reporting that they detected a new mood among American workers, in Stan Weir's words, "a labor revolt."[34] Weir, a veteran labor radical, wrote in 1967 of "natural on-the-job leaders" conducting "an insurgency from below," including "daily guerrilla skirmishes with the employers and often against their official union representatives." He called attention to several conflicts, including to the auto workers at the Mansfield, Ohio parts plant where a wildcat strike all but stopped General Motors (GM), idling 133,000 workers in twenty plants; the coal miners of Moundsville, West Virginia, who led an unauthorized strike that "in one week spread over West Virginia, Ohio and Pennsylvania"; and the five-week strike of airline mechanics in 1966 that grounded an estimated 60 percent of the nation's passenger service.[35]

Weir's account of this unrest went on to include the 1965 wildcat strike of truck drivers who shut down Philadelphia. The mayor, who called the strikers "hoodlums," held a press conference calling on Jimmy Hoffa, then General Secretary of the IBT, to come in and settle the dispute. As he spoke, "hundreds of striking Teamsters milled around City Hall, in defiance of a judge who threatened them all with jail," shouting that Hoffa

---

32  See R. Hyman, *Strikes* (London: Fontana, 1972), p. 19. Strikes can be manipulated by both management and trade union leaders. The huge 1970 auto strike, according to W. Serrin, "was a political strike, a strike not to win agreement but to win ratification." That is, it was a strike to cool off the workers. W. Serrin, *The Company and the Union: The "Civilized Relationship" of the General Motors Corporation and the United Automobile Workers* (New York: Vintage Books, 1974), p. 298. Strikes can also be reactionary; see the 1968 racist New York teachers' strikes.

33  Historical Statistics Part 1, p. 179, Bureau of Labor Statistics.

34  S. Weir, "U.S.A.: The Labor Revolt," *International Socialist Journal* vol. 4: 20 (April 1967), pp. 279–96.

35  Ibid., pp. 282, 287, 292, 294.

was not wanted. In the course of the strike, the truck drivers patrolled Philadelphia's streets and stopped all trucking, forcing out-of-town drivers to leave the city. They blocked highways with overturned trailers and fought pitched battles with police in a "guerrilla-type war that continued in the city for several days."[36]

Jack Barbash, an academic authority on labor, found evidence of a "new mood" in the multiplying "strikes, especially wildcat strikes . . . the eruption of new union or union-like militancy" and "pressures from below for changes in collective bargaining policies . . . for greater influence in union affairs." He pointed to the workers' "feeling of self-power" and the "protest direct action militancy model" of union groups. He singled out public sector workers where the teachers were "the most strike-prone" in 1966. "The vanguard place in union militancy," he wrote, "goes to the teachers. There were 54 teacher strikes in 1966 involving almost 45,000 teachers." He cited the comment in 1967 by a new National Education Association (NEA) secretary: "Strikes are illegal, yet teachers are calling them and making gains with them."[37] Philip Taft, Professor of Economics at Brown University, perhaps the best-known mainstream labor historian at the time, compared the "restiveness" of the late sixties to the strike years of 1919 and 1945, and viewed developments with some concern. He pointed to "the higher expectations of the work force, which leaders of unions cannot always moderate." But he was hopeful that "discontent among workers" would "remain isolated."[38]

These observations were well grounded, both the expectations and the fears. In the late sixties, strikes were increasing in the United States, and their character was changing. The *New York Times* called the International Longshoremen's Association (ILA) "a union in terror of its rank and file."[39] In 1968, in keeping with the *Times*' observation, East and Gulf Coast longshoremen carried out the first ever membership-initiated, all-union strike in their history; this 116-day work stoppage was the longest in longshore history until it was surpassed by the 123-day strike in 1971–2 on the West Coast.

The UAW, perhaps more than any other union, experienced the entire range of rank-and-file unrest, including wildcat strikes, grievance strikes, contract rejection, and extended local-issues negotiations, plus contested

---

36 "Teamsters Strike in Philadelphia," *New York Times*, June 22, 1965.
37 J. Barbash, "The Causes of Rank-and-File Unrest," in J. Seidman, ed. *Trade Union Government and Collective Bargaining, Some Critical Issues* (New York: Praeger, 1970), pp. 42–43, 45.
38 P. Taft, "Unrest in Historic Perspective," in J. Seidman, ed., *Trade Union Government and Collective Bargaining*, p. 102.
39 "Longshore Strike," *New York Times*, January 18, 1965.

local union elections, often initiated by "the restlessness of the younger union member."[40] In 1966, the UAW leader Walter Reuther expressed the view of this from the top: "Organizing the unorganized is less crucial than the task of unionizing the organized, educating these hundreds of thousands of young workers . . . they don't know where we came from. They don't know where we're going. They don't know what the American labor movement is about."[41] In 1966, one out of every three UAW members employed in the big corporations had less than five years of seniority. The 1972 strike at GM's gigantic new Lordstown, Ohio complex—where young workers, some long-haired and unshaven, fought to slow the world's fastest assembly lines—became emblematic of a youth rebellion in the factories. Gary Bryner, twenty-nine, was the president of Lordstown Local 1112, UAW. "Lordstown," he told Studs Terkel, was "the Woodstock of the working man."[42]

In 1970, the workers' rebellion reached a high point, and New York City, historically the center of the U.S. labor movement, became the "City of Strikes," according to the *Economist*.[43] Hundreds of thousands of workers participated in this wave of walkouts, becoming part of a movement that would peak the following year when 4.2 million work days would be "lost" in the city. Conflicts ranged from the "drawbridge strike"—when workers shut down bridges connecting the boroughs with Manhattan and walked off their jobs, taking with them electrical parts, handles, fuses, and keys, and leaving the drawbridges up—to the strike at New York Telephone, which, following the union's national contract ratification, continued in New York for another eight months.[44] New York City was the starting point of the 1970 national wildcat strike of postal workers. Beginning at midnight on March 18, letter carriers and clerks walked off their jobs in Manhattan and the Bronx. By morning, strikers had stopped postal service in most of New York, New Jersey, and Connecticut. This was a massive wildcat strike; it was also in defiance of federal law. By Saturday, the strike had spread to Chicago, Cleveland, Los Angeles, Detroit, San Francisco, Boston, Denver, Pittsburgh, Minneapolis, Philadelphia, and dozens of other cities. Rank-and-file workers organized the strike, and no mail moved in the country's major cities. The strike lasted eight days in New York, despite

---

40   Barbash, "The Causes of Rank-and-File Unrest," p. 48.
41   Quoted in ibid., p. 48.
42   S. Terkel, *Working: People Talk About What They Do All Day and How They Feel About What They Do* (New York: Pantheon, 1972), p. 187.
43   "City of Strikes," *Economist*, October 5, 1968, cited in Brenner, "Rank-and-File Rebellion, 1966–1975." See chapter 3, "The 1970 Post Office Strike," p. 140.
44   Maier, *City Unions*, p. 87. Brenner, "Rank-and-File Rebellion, 1966–1975." See chapter 4, "Rank-and-File Struggles at the Telephone Company," pp. 147–223.

the deployment of 30,000 national guardsmen. Across the nation, 200,000 workers participated in the largest wildcat strike ever.[45]

A national truckers' wildcat followed in April, originating in a contract dispute in Chicago. The *New York Times* called the strike "a revolt against the union leadership," as strikers rejected a contract that included a $1.10 an hour pay raise. Roving pickets spread the strike to sixteen cities, notably Los Angeles and Cleveland. Violence was widespread. According to a *New York Times* reporter in Cleveland:

> Strikers have set up a roving patrol system that they say can muster 300 men within an hour to stop any truck moving goods in the area. The strikers are allowing trucks carrying food, drugs and beer to continue, but they have become outraged when they have found food trucks carrying other cargo. There has been rock throwing, windshields have been smashed, tires slashed and air hoses cut.[46]

The United Press reported that 500,000 people were out of work as a result of the strike. The governor of Ohio ordered 4,100 national guardsmen into duty to combat what he called "open warfare" on the state's highways.[47] Among these soldiers were the guardsmen of the 145th Infantry, soon to be redeployed to Kent State University, where students were protesting the escalation of the war in Vietnam and the invasion of Cambodia. The truckers' strike lasted twelve weeks until the employers in Chicago capitulated, granting higher wage increases in a settlement that broke the Nixon administration's national wage guidelines. The truckers' rebellion stood out for what it revealed: the anger and frustration of workers; the ability of workers to spread the strike, despite opposition from both company and union; the violence of both the state and the workers; and the breadth of protest, from campus to workplace.

This wave of strikes marked a major shift in American industrial relations. In the 1950s and 1960s, the consensus of industrial relations specialists in the United States was that there existed a sort of modus vivendi between capital and labor, sometimes called the "New Deal formula of industrial relations."[48] The trade union hierarchy had become a social layer with interests of its own, separate from the rank and file. Politically, the unions were one-party organizations, dominated by "the

---

45   Brenner, "Rank-and-File Rebellion." See chapter 3, "The 1970 Post Office Strike," pp. 112–46

46   "Guard on Duty in Ohio as Teamster Strike Goes On," *New York Times*, May 1, 1970.

47   Ibid.

48   D. Montgomery, *Workers' Control in America.* See chapter 7, "American Workers and the New Deal Formula," pp. 153–80.

machine." Dave Beck, the 1950s IBT leader, bluntly declared, "Unions are big business."[49] And the business unionists of those years did indeed seek stable collaborative relationships with the employers. But this truce between business and business unionism was always partial and temporary. By the late 1960s, the postwar bargain between labor and capital was in tatters, in part as employers faced falling profitability and in turn transmitted this crisis to the workers. The Vietnam War had fueled economic expansion, but by the end of the 1960s growth was slowing and the escalation of military spending was sending prices soaring, foreshadowing the "stagflation" of the decade to follow. One result was that wage and benefit increases, common in the 1950s, were far harder for the unions to win.[50] The issue that stood out, however, was the "speedup." This was symbolized by the line speed at Lordstown, the stopwatch at UPS, the productivity drive in the coal mines, and the generalized attack on working conditions, all part of an "employers' offensive." Workers resisted, first with straightforward militant trade unionism, rooted in the 1950s and earlier. They also developed what can be called "movements." These strikes and movements reflected their efforts to counter this offensive, but also the depth of the frustration of rank-and-file workers with their unions.

## Movements

These movements and the new "restlessness" can also be seen in the actions of those sections of the working class left out of the postwar prosperity—particularly workers of color and women, hitherto excluded and disenfranchised—workers who had not enjoyed the "affluence" of the postwar boom. In 1965 the United Farm Workers (UFW) launched its long campaign—the years of strikes, boycotts, fasts, and demonstrations. It became a social movement in the fields, a trade union and a civil rights movement; millions of ordinary Americans contributed to its cause, most often by boycotting grapes.

Nowhere was the "new mood" of rebellion seen more clearly than in the emergence of a black movement in the workplace. First, the fact that Martin Luther King, Jr. was in Memphis in 1968 to support striking sanitation workers is well known.[51] What is less well known is that upon his assassination, workers throughout the country left their jobs. According to one report:

---

49   Quoted in Moody, *An Injury to All*, p. 57.
50   R. Brenner (see chapter 2).
51   W. H. Harris, *The Harder We Run: Black Workers Since the Civil War* (New York: Oxford University Press, 1982), p. 175.

in addition to work stoppages by meat cutters, retail clerks, East Coast longshoremen and seamen, dozens of auto assembly plants all over the country had to shut down at least for two shifts immediately following the assassination of Martin Luther King, Jr. because black workers walked off the job. It is also known that in at least several instances the blacks were accompanied by large numbers of whites.[52]

Black auto workers in Detroit left their jobs in the thousands, all but shutting down the city's auto plants.

The black workers' movement, following the pattern of the black struggle, began in the South and migrated north. According to William H. Harris,

> the actions of working-class blacks . . . the sacrifices and sufferings of working-class black people in both rural and urban areas throughout the South, people whose names we will never know, stirred the consciousness of the nation and made it possible for the Civil Rights Movement to succeed.[53]

The Negro American Labor Council provided much of the funding and leadership for the 1963 march on Washington. Major victories were won by Memphis, Tennessee sanitation workers and Charleston, South Carolina hospital workers. By the mid-1970s, according to historian Michael Honey, this spilled over into industry, so that "after decades of painful effort . . . black workers in a core of unionized factory jobs had torn down most Jim Crow barriers within their workplaces and unions."[54] According to Harris, "As in other sectors of American life, blacks were no longer willing to bear the brunt of economic oppression and to treat the situation as inevitable."[55]

"Black Power" also migrated north; in industry it represented a tactic to force both the employers and the unions to recognize the rights and demands of black workers. The automobile industry expanded in the boom years in the 1960s. In Detroit, then still the center of the automobile industry, the boom years' expansion continued, even in the aftermath of the 1967 Detroit Rebellion. The companies recruited thousands of new young workers, and a large proportion of these workers, particularly in Detroit, were black. The majority of the new recruits worked in unskilled,

---

52   C. Pierce, "Black Militants and the Unions," *International Socialist*, August 1968.
53   W. H. Harris, *The Harder We Run*, p. 149.
54   M. K. Honey, *Black Workers Remember: An Oral History of Segregation, Unionism, and the Freedom Struggle* (Berkeley: University of California Press, 1999), p. 322.
55   W. H. Harris, *The Harder We Run*, p. 160.

often dangerous jobs, performing the monotonous, nerve-wracking tasks that led to the high turnover and absentee rates for which the industry was notorious.[56] The origins of the black caucus movement are found in these conditions—in the automobile industry, it began in wildcat strikes and the development of a revolutionary union movement spearheaded by DRUM (Dodge Revolutionary Union Movement) at Chrysler's Dodge Main plant in Detroit. Other black auto workers followed, establishing revolutionary union movements at Eldon Road (ELRUM), Ford's River Rouge plant (FRUM), and Chrysler's Jefferson Avenue assembly plant (JARUM). Workers in other industries also joined in; hospital workers organized HRUM, newspaper workers NEWRUM, and United Parcel workers UPRUM, ultimately leading to the creation of the League of Revolutionary Black Workers.[57]

The revolt of black workers inspired many, including white workers. It did not lead, however, to the black/white unity many hoped for, certainly not in the automobile industry. When black auto workers, fighting the speedup, staged sit-in strikes in the summer of 1973 in Detroit at the Jefferson Assembly, Eldon Road, and Mack Avenue plants, they were not, for the most part, supported by whites, a few radicals excepted.[58] This alliance that did not happen, together with the 1974 crash in automobile production, resulted in the end of the rebellion in auto.

## Public Workers

The major breakthrough for workers in the postwar system of industrial relations was winning the right to organize by local, state, and federal government workers, and the subsequent organization of millions of these workers into trade unions. "The growth of US public sector unions" in the fifties and sixties was, according to Mark Maier, "analogous to the

---

56  D. Georgakas and M. Surkin, *Detroit: I Do Mind Dying: A Study in Urban Revolution* (Cambridge, MA: South End Press, 1998), pp. 27–8; M. Marable, *Race, Reform, and Rebellion: The Second Reconstruction in Black America, 1945–1990* (Jackson: University of Mississippi Press, 1991), p.116.

57  Georgakas and Surkin, *Detroit: I Do Mind Dying*, p. 69.

58  The rebellion of black workers, following the long civil rights struggle, inspired various theories of a "black vanguard." In 1969, D. Montgomery, for example, wrote, "Through black caucuses, revolutionary union movements like the one at Dodge, and introduction into collective bargaining of tactics developed on the civil-rights front this influence is already being felt. In such areas as Pittsburgh hospitals, black workers are clearly leading the way for whites to follow. It is safe to say that the more effective black workers are in these new organizing efforts the more the white workers will be tempted to join them rather than oppose them." Montgomery, "What's Happening to the American Worker," p. 22–3.

expansion of private sector unions during the 1930s."[59] Women entered the service and public sector sections of the labor force in the millions; they became the backbone of the new teachers' movements, in particular of the NEA, now transformed into a union. In the 1970s, public employee unions grew four times as fast as total union membership, and women made up a very large proportion of these new members. These union women were joined by office workers, telephone workers, nurses, and healthcare workers. In June 1974, 4,000 northern California nurses struck forty major Bay Area hospitals and clinics, demanding, among other things, increased pay, better pensions, and a guarantee of every other weekend off. In addition, the *New York Times* reported, many strikers agreed with Gail Dolson of Mount Zion Hospital that the nurses' increasing "feminist consciousness" led them to seek more equal authority with the hospitals' largely male administrative staff. [60]

The Coalition of Labor Union Women (CLUW), founded in 1974 in Chicago, was born in a moment of great enthusiasm and embodied a potential movement to support working women and their struggles. Three thousand trade union women attended the founding convention; nearly a third were reported to be young radicals.[61] These newcomers—trade unionism in the United States was well over a hundred years old—set out quite late to lay the foundations of public sector/service sector unionism. Their movements, developing in the midst of the transition from an industrial working class to one based on the public and service sectors, representing large numbers of women and workers of color, are, of course, of great importance. And their unions continue. These unions represent, according to labor historian David Lyddon, "even now, potentially a rising movement central to unionism in most countries."[62]

We consider here the experience of teachers, where, interestingly, the influence of the black movement was, again, highly influential. Teachers responded to these new conditions, in particular the NEA, which was already a large organization in the 1960s. Historically, it was a professional organization; unlike the American Federation of Teachers (AFT), it had no ties to the organized labor movement. In the 1960s, however, this began to change. "Within the NEA," writes historian Marjorie Murphy, "internal changes had made it clear that the mammoth organization was slowly but

---

59   Maier, *City Unions*, p. 8.

60   "Nurses on Coast Still on Strike," *New York Times*, June 12, 1974

61   A. Withorn, "The Death of CLUW," *Radical America* #10, (March–April 1976), pp. 50–1, quoted in D. Balser, *Sisterhood and Solidarity: Feminism and Labor in Modern Times* (Boston: South End Press, 1987), p. 188.

62   D. Lyddon, conversation with author.

inevitably restructuring itself into a union."[63] In the course of the 1970s, the NEA grew at a rate of nearly 100,000 new members each year, reaching the two million mark in 1980.[64] The AFT grew as well, though not nearly so dramatically. The AFT was organized as a trade union, and its roots were in the cities, above all in New York City; it was affiliated with the AFL-CIO. Membership in the two unions came to nearly match that of the Teamsters Union, the largest of the industrial unions.[65]

Both unions responded to changing conditions in the sixties with strikes and organizing drives. The NEA, however, quickly outpaced its rival. Of the thousands of teachers' strikes in the seventies, perhaps as many as 80 percent were led by NEA teachers; moreover, these teachers' strikes represented a grassroots movement, and the NEA was highly decentralized, certainly in comparison to the AFT. The NEA swept through the new districts, the small towns, the suburbs, and the West.[66]

The NEA had another advantage. In these years of extensive teacher activity, the AFT was embroiled in racial disputes—a legacy, in part, of its racist confrontations with black community activists in the New York teachers' strikes of 1968.[67] There were also conflicts with black parents in Youngstown and Newark, where black activists, including Amiri Baraka, challenged the union, even when led by black teachers. In September 1975, in Boston, 4,950 teachers, 90 percent of the workforce, struck in response to a bargaining impasse—their strike also, however, crippled the District's two-week-old, court-ordered desegregation program.[68] The AFT welcomed the anti–affirmative action Bakke decision (the Supreme Court ruling against racial quotas) and opposed NEA policies that implemented racial and gender quotas in its governing bodies.[69]

In the same years, the NEA, despite its conservative origins in the era of

---

63  M. Murphy, *Blackboard Unions: The AFT and the NEA, 1900–1980* (Ithaca: Cornell University Press, 1990), p. 252.

64  On NEA membership and strikes, see AFT President's Collection, Box 55, Walter P. Reuther Library, Wayne State University. Thanks to Dan Golodner for this.

65  The IBT had 1,946,000 members in 1976. See K. Moody, *US Labor in Trouble and Transition* (London and New York: Verso, 2007) p. 102.

66  "Teacher Groups End Unity Talks," *New York Times*, March 1, 1974. See also A. West, *The National Education Association: The Power Base for Education* (New York: The Free Press, 1980).

67  See S. Zeluck, "The UFT Strike: A Blow Against Teacher Unionism," in B. Hall, ed., *Autocracy and Insurgency in Organized Labor* (New Brunswick, NJ: Transaction Books, 1972), pp. 201–12.

68  "Over 90% of Boston Teachers Strike, Crippling Desegregation," *New York Times*, September 23, 1975; "Newark School Strike Splits Blacks," *New York Times*, February 14, 1971.

69  Murphy, *Blackboard Unions*, p. 270.

segregated schools—it organized biracial unions in the South—supported integration and affirmative action.[70] In 1964 it ordered that all its affiliates be merged, though in 1974 the Louisiana association remained segregated. In 1967, however, Elizabeth Koontz, an African American classroom teacher from North Carolina, became the NEA's first black president.[71] In 1972, when two black students at Southern University were shot and killed by police, the NEA joined students and black organizations in demanding an official investigation.[72] The NEA denounced a court ruling that would not require school authorities to readjust attendance zones to keep up with racial population shifts. According to an NEA officer, "We are convinced that our Board of Education in Pasadena [California] has the intention of going back to segregated schools in September."[73]

When the AFT and the NEA abandoned unity talks in 1974, the reasons were numerous, including simple organizational issues and the problems of professionalism, the latter strongest in the NEA. But when Helen Wise, NEA president, rebutted the charge that the NEA teachers were not trade unionists, she said, fairly, that there "are many liberals within the association who think of the AFL-CIO as too conservative." She continued, "The AFT, while paying lip service to minority involvement, opposed an effective way to assure it. There is no compatibility between the NEA commitment and the AFT laissez-faire attitude on this issue."[74] From the first, the NEA enthusiastically supported the Equal Rights Amendment (ERA) for women. In 1974 it won a Supreme Court case striking down mandatory leave for pregnant teachers.[75]

In addition, then, to aggressive organizing, including the use of the strike, the NEA, in Murphy's words, took "bolder, more progressive positions on a range of social issues."[76] The AFT and the AFL-CIO strongly supported the war in Vietnam—they no doubt believed that American workers did as well. This was not the case with teachers, however, and the AFT paid a price. In 1970–1980, the NEA grew by a million members.[77] The majority

---

70    E. Arnesen, "Biracial Unionism in an Age of Segregation," in C. Winslow, *Waterfront Workers: New Perspectives on Race and Class* (Urbana: University of Illinois Press, 1998), pp. 19–61.

71    Murphy, *Blackboard Unions*, pp. 205–6.

72    "Scattered Demonstrations Score Killings of 2 on Southern Campus," *New York Times*, November 18, 1972.

73    "NEA Chief Predicts More Strikes by Teachers," *New York Times*, June 30, 1976.

74    "Teacher Groups End Unity Talks," *New York Times*, March 1, 1974.

75    Murphy, *Blackboard Unions*, p. 261.

76    Ibid., p. 273.

77    On NEA membership and strikes, see AFT President's Collection, Box 55, Walter P. Reuther Library, Wayne State University.

of these new members were women, many were black and Latina; tens of thousands attended university in the 1960s. The factors that led to the teachers' successes were many. Certainly their movement was fueled by inflation, and then the fiscal crisis. The teachers were also, however, the products of their times. According to Murphy, "teachers complained about over-supervision, increasing bureaucratization, inappropriate assignments, and a lack of control over licensing, training and assignments."[78] Out of these conflicts emerged what was soon to be the nation's largest union—demonstrating that, given the right circumstances and the willingness to act, trade unions, even progressive trade unions, could still grow and succeed.

The year 1974 was the twin peak of the rebellion; strike statistics nearly matched those of 1970. Beginning in the winter, the gas crisis severely disrupted the economy. The shortage of fuel, the result in part of war in the Middle East, produced new strikes and new forms of conflict. West Virginia coal miners struck to demand that the state's governor roll back skyrocketing gas prices, citing the rising costs of long commutes to work.[79] Then truckers, the independent operators, who were considered by some an "aristocracy of workers" and by others small businessmen in overalls, emerged in an astonishing movement to challenge the Nixon administration and its energy policies. The truckers' spontaneous blockades and slowdowns first snarled traffic and then began to shut down industry. Thousands of big tractor-trailers jammed the turnpikes in Ohio and Pennsylvania and choked off the New York–Washington, D.C. corridor at the Delaware Memorial Bridge.[80] Just hours into the first blockades, GM management closed the Lordstown assembly plant, located adjacent to the Ohio Turnpike, fearing a shortage of parts. In Toledo, factory workers left their jobs to join truckers on the interchange of Interstate 75 and the turnpike. The truckers' strikes were met with fierce resistance from the authorities, including the National Guard. Interestingly, interviews with truckers on the Ohio Turnpike south of Cleveland invariably turned to Kent State University and the 1970 killings by guardsmen.[81] If these truckers failed to develop a winning strategy, their movements remain a striking example of the capacity of workers to organize—the truckers' blockades were in some ways analogous to the sit-down strikes of an earlier era. They took control of their own workplace: the highways. There have been few more dramatic examples of the power of American workers.

---

78   Murphy, *Blackboard Unions*, p. 222.
79   "Fuel Strikes Spread," *Workers' Power*, March 15, 1974.
80   "Ohio Protest Goes On," *New York Times*, December 6, 1973.
81   C. Winslow, interviews with truckers, winter 1973–4. In author's possession.

In March, four Service Employees International Union (SEIU) locals, representing hospital, clerical, maintenance, and social workers, rejected a wage offer from San Francisco's Board of Supervisors and struck. They were joined by teachers, who honored picket lines set up at the schools. The Municipal Railway's mostly black motormen and conductors joined in, as did transit drivers. Farm workers joined substitute teachers to shut down school bus barns. Governor Ronald Reagan threatened to send in the National Guard, but the strike continued to spread.[82] Only an early settlement by SEIU leaders prevented a much wider strike. In August 1974, *Workers' Power* reported, "Everywhere you turn, someone is on strike. Airline mechanics, bus drivers, copper miners, sanitation workers, firemen, hospital workers, painters, scattered Teamsters, auto workers, steelworkers and telephone workers. The American Federation of State, County, and Municipal Employees (AFSCME) voted to shut down the state of Ohio."[83]

On November 12, 1974, 120,000 coal miners walked off their jobs, honoring the tradition of "No contract, no work." This strike was the first for the new reform administration. The UMW leaders had quickly disbanded the MFD, the rank-and-file organization of miners, apparently considering it superfluous. They had not, however, established anything in its place. Now, with an executive committee dominated by the old guard still in place, they faced the Bituminous Coal Operators Assocation (BCOA) in a nationwide confrontation. Tony Boyle, John L. Lewis's successor, had exercised dictatorial control over contract negotiations, though with increasing difficulty. In 1964, 1966, and 1971, miners, anticipating gains in a reviving market for coal, responded to his settlements with wildcat strikes. Now the UMW leaders, in part as the result of their own efforts, were obliged to submit any agreement to the rank and file for ratification. And the rank and file entered the negotiations with very high expectations indeed. In 1974 there were 40,000 new miners in the union, many of them Vietnam War veterans. These miners—led by young militants (they referred to themselves as "radicals")—challenged the companies on all fronts: safety, productivity, job assignments, and the grievance procedure.[84] Spearheaded by the Miners' Right to Strike Committee, they demanded that the right to strike on these issues be written into the contract. They also wanted democratically elected, full-time safety committeemen and the right to strike on safety issues.

In these years of struggle, miners had improved their wages and benefits and lowered productivity: average output of miners per day in underground

---

82   "Labor Earthquake Hits San Francisco," *Workers' Power*, March 29, 1974.

83   "Strike Wave Grows," *Workers' Power*, August 1974.

84   Nyden (see chapter 6).

mines, which reached almost sixteen tons in 1969, fell to under twelve tons by 1974, and under eight tons by 1979, no small achievement.[85] They took issues of health and safety into their own hands—in each case using their power in the workplace, plus strike action, to do so. They were strengthened by their solidarity, the long tradition in the coalfields of honoring picket lines—a tradition so strong that a single picket, a "stranger picket," at the mine site was sufficient to close it.

The UMW leaders and coal operators succeeded in ending the strike, though the result was at best a stalemate. In the new agreement the miners won an improved wage package—10 percent the first year, followed by 4 percent and 3 percent in the remaining two years; they won five sick days, two additional vacation days and a national holiday, a cost-of-living allowance increased to 8 percent, and improved pensions. Still, 44 percent of miners voted to reject the settlement and stay on strike.[86] In Ohio's District 6, miners denounced Arnold Miller, the new president of the UMW, burned copies of the contract, and marched through Bellaire, Ohio, chanting, "No right to safety, no work!" Rank-and-file miners had demanded a revamped grievance procedure—they received instead an additional step in an already time-consuming and cumbersome process. They had wanted elected safety committeemen and the right to walk away from unsafe jobs: "You can't put production on a miner's life," said an angry miner.[87] Most importantly, despite near universal support for the right to strike over local issues—and the thousands of signatures collected by the District 29 (West Virginia) Committee to Defend the Right to Strike—the national union leadership refused in bargaining to even raise the issue.[88] This strike and the settlement exhibited the extraordinary militancy of the coal miners, as well as the impasse in the hierarchy of the union. In a fundamental way, the new leaders of the UMW considered the 1972 election the end of the story. For significant sections of the rank and file, however, 1972 was just the beginning.

## Recession

In 1974–5, the economy was in recession, the most severe since the 1930s. This new recession seemed to signal once and for all that the postwar boom was over. The country entered a new period of slowing expansion and severe cyclical crises. There were long lines at unemployment offices, and free food

---

85   Perry, *Collective Bargaining and the Decline of the United Mine Workers*, p. 28.
86   "Miners Back to Work," *Workers' Power*, December 12, 1974.
87   Ibid.
88   Ibid.

distribution began in the industrial centers. In the automobile industry, the workforce was reduced by a third. Jack Weinberg, a former leader of the Berkeley Free Speech Movement who had gone into industry as an organizer, was one of the auto workers fired in the aftermath of the 1973 Mack Avenue sit-in. He described the situation this way: "A month ago, under the impact of inflation, it was hard to get by on a forty hour paycheck. Already today, lay-offs make the forty hour paycheck look real sweet . . . With survival on the mind, it's sometimes hard to respond to questions of speed-up, health and safety, working conditions." Weinberg called the situation "a depression . . . A year or two from now we'll have another boom—and then another depression . . . Economic stability is a thing of the past."[89]

The economy did recover in 1975, but the decade ended as it had begun—in recession. Moreover, each downturn was sharper than the one that proceeded it. Yet, as we know now, this pattern did not continue indefinitely; we also know that these downturns, despite the depth of the 1974–5 recession, followed by the even deeper recession in Reagan's first years, did not produce a working-class upheaval. Still, while 1974 marked the high tide of the rank-and-file revolt, the rebellion was far from over. The movement in the automobile industry, however, did not recover; economic recovery resulted not in new conflict, but rather in working-class retreat, then in the 1979 Chrysler concessions crisis. Elsewhere, however, the struggle continued; there were still major—indeed, historic—battles ahead. The number of strikes in 1976, for example, was nearly as high as that in 1970.[90] Concluding this story in 1974, as some do, then, is a mistake; it conflates events and leaves out much that is important; it makes the outcome seem overly determined. It also ignores the significant confrontations to come, above all in the coalfields.[91]

The political-economic context in the United States, however, was changing. The 1970s witnessed the decline of 1960s radicalism in the course of a developing economic crisis. This decline occurred unevenly but steadily. In 1975 the Vietnam War was over at last; the student antiwar movement had vanished. The civil rights movement, the inspiration for so much of the resistance in the sixties and seventies, had come to an end; significantly, Martin Luther King, Jr.'s idea that a

---

89  J. Weinberg, "Detroit Auto Uprising, 1973," Network Pamphlet (Highland Park, MI, n.d., c. 1975), p. 1.

90  Historical Statistics Part 1, p. 179, Bureau of Labor Statistics.

91  Jeremy Brecher, a historian of U.S. strikes, concluded his chapter on this era in his book *Strike!* this way: "At the end of 1974, the economy entered a sharp recession . . . as in the recession of 1921, sudden mass layoffs took the steam out of the labor insurgency . . . the result was a period of decline for the labor movement that rivaled that of the 1920's." Brecher, *Strike!* (Cambridge, MA: South End Press, 1997), p. 270.

poor people's movement might fuse white and black labor had never materialized. By 1975, black nationalism was "splintered, repressed and removed from political discourse."[92] In some ways, of course, the black movement seemed a triumph: voting rights were won, Jim Crow was dead, and integration seemed an accomplished fact, in many ways a dazzling success. There were now, for example, black mayors in Chicago, Detroit, Atlanta, and Los Angeles. It was, however, another story for black workers. Both black and white workers experienced severe increases in unemployment during the recession of 1974–5, compounding the difficulties of workers who had not recovered from the recession of 1970–1.[93] This in turn was exacerbated by the fiscal crisis of the state; in New York, for example, in 1975 the leading financial institutions began refusing to lend the city money, demanding a program of austerity including "a freeze or cutback in the number of city workers, an increase in their productivity, reductions in capital spending, cutbacks in city services, and increased fees and taxes."[94] In the upturn in 1975, large numbers of white workers returned to work; large numbers of blacks did not. Between 1975 and 1977, unemployment among blacks actually increased by 700,000. By 1977, black unemployment stood at an all-time postwar high, with 14.5 percent of the black labor force out of work. Black people constituted one third of the nation's poor. William Harris concluded that for blacks this was "a depression."[95] This crisis also exposed the new divide between the success of the (small) black elite and the reality of black workers. This was nowhere clearer than in Atlanta. In 1977, black mayor Maynard Jackson fired nine hundred mostly black sanitation workers during a strike for higher pay. These workers, members of AFSCME, had been at the core of his support in his successful electoral campaign for mayor in 1973.[96] "Radicalism and militancy were defeated," according to Manning Marable. "Reform had supplanted rebellion."[97]

The women's movement had far from run its course, yet there were signs that its impact too, certainly on working women, would be limited. In September 1976, 2,500 Seattle nurses were on strike, a strike that lasted sixty-five days, the longest nurses' strike ever at that point, reflecting, according to the New York Times, "the new militancy of registered nurses

92   Marable, Race, Reform, and Rebellion, p.147.
93   Harris, The Harder We Run, p. 181.
94   J. B. Freeman, Working Class New York: Life and Labor Since World War II (New York: The New Press, 2000), p. 256.
95   Harris, The Harder We Run, p. 181.
96   Marable, Race, Reform, and Rebellion, p. 172–3.
97   Ibid., p. 147.

here and elsewhere." The issues were wages, staffing, and the agency shop. But there was also an "emotional issue" according to one doctor. "It used to be nurses could be yelled at and their opinions ignored . . . Now, they will challenge doctors and sometimes even substitute their judgment for his . . . This is the issue of parity, brought by the smart young nurses who have recently graduated and sparked by the women's movement that is making it so hard to end this strike . . ."[98]

CLUW, the organization of trade union women, seemed an ideal vehicle for uniting women's liberation with a movement of working-class women. CLUW also spoke to the vast increase in the numbers of working women, virtually all unorganized. Within two years, however, CLUW was essentially dead. The first constitutional convention of CLUW was held in Detroit in December 1975 to formally establish the organization. Yet as Ann Withorn reported in *Radical America*, this meeting "for all practical purposes, ended the struggle. The bureaucrats have gained solid control of the organization, although in order to gain their victory, they were forced to destroy CLUW as a widely based mass organization within the trade unions."[99] Olga Madar, a UAW careerist, was elected president. The radicals contested the election but were easily defeated. Madar, speaking for the majority, according to the *New York Times*, "expressed the hope that the leftist women might leave the coalition and turn their attention elsewhere."[100]

There were other troubling signs. In October 1975, pressmen struck the *Washington Post* in response to the paper's plans to automate production, replace workers, and, in publisher Katharine Graham's words, "eliminate archaic union practices."[101] It soon emerged that the *Post* was prepared to destroy the union and had spent two years planning to do so. It intended to publish without the unions. This was not altogether necessary; the majority of journalists crossed pressmen's picket lines or were flown in by helicopter. In the bitter and highly publicized dispute, the strikers were called criminals and Luddites; they were compared to "Belfast snipers" and "airline highjackers"—the 1975 equivalent of terrorists.[102] Fifteen pressmen were charged with felonies, the *Post* claiming the pressmen were

---

98   "Coast Nurses' Strike Enters 7th Week; Outlook Dim," New York Times, August 26, 1976.
99   A. Withorn, "The Death of CLUW," pp. 188–9.
100   Ibid., p. 187.
101   "Washington Post Firm Over Strike," *New York Times*, October 12, 1975; "The Plan that Broke Local 6," *Socialist Worker*, May 1977.
102   The use of the term "Luddite" is very interesting, especially in a period of rapid technological innovation. Raymond Williams wrote, "What is now called Luddism, or wildcat militancy, is very often, at root, a fight . . . to use machines rather than be used by them." Quoted in R. Hyman, *Strikes*, p. 172. "Working Class Defeat," *Socialist Worker*, May 1977.

responsible for millions of dollars of damage and a riot in the pressroom. In fact, the pressmen had done nothing more than temporarily disable the presses on which they worked, by removing key parts. The *Post* strike, which never officially ended, only concluded in April 1977 when the pressmen pled guilty to reduced charges.[103] This defeat inevitably assumed a larger significance. It took place, after all, just a short walk from the palatial headquarters of the AFL-CIO, minutes from the Capitol—and support was forthcoming from neither place.

In 1976 Jimmy Carter led the Democrats back to power in Washington, but his regime was, perhaps, the worst for labor in the postwar period. "Government," he declared, in a theme commonplace today, "cannot eliminate poverty, provide a bountiful economy, reduce inflation, save our cities, cure illiteracy, provide energy, or mandate goodness."[104] In the course of his tenure in the White House, Jimmy Carter attempted to impose wage restrictions, challenged the rights of public workers, forced striking railroad workers into a "cooling-off period," deregulated trucking and airlines, and invoked the Taft-Hartley Act in the miners' strike. Despite Democratic majorities in both Houses, labor law reform was defeated. While the 1978 Humphrey-Hawkins bill promised full employment, in fact it was designed to produce very little, relying, as Carter favored, overwhelmingly on the private sector.[105]

Still, by the middle of 1975, employment was nearly back to pre-recession levels, and the workers' insurgency remained very much alive, above all in the coalfields. In the summers of 1975 and 1976 there were nationwide wildcat strike movements in the coalfields—the first, of 80,000, for the right to strike, and the second, of 120,000 (virtually the entire workforce in the East), against the injunctions imposed on striking miners. This continued into the summer of 1977, when, in anticipation of a national strike, 85,000 miners struck.[106] In 1976, the number of major strikes (5,648) nearly matched that of 1970 (5,716), though the number of strikers was not so high.[107] In the years 1976–9, there were again strikes everywhere, that is, in every sector and throughout the country. At the same time, new movements emerged.

---

103    "8 More Indicted in Paper Strike," *New York Times*, July 22, 1975.
104    "Excerpts from President Carter's Message," *New York Times*, January 20, 1978.
105    Harris, *The Harder We Run*, p. 185.
106    Nyden (see chapter 6).
107    Historical Statistics Part 1, p. 179, Bureau of Labor Statistics.

## Rank-and-File Organization

If everything seemed possible in 1970, what was still possible in 1976? Two movements in the Teamsters illustrate that the rebellion continued. In 1976, Frank Fitzsimmons, IBT president, called an official nationwide strike of truckers in freight, under pressure from the rank and file, including the new organization Teamsters for a Decent Contract (TDC). The following October, TDC became Teamsters for a Democratic Union (TDU).[108] The same spring, the IBT struck UPS in the central states, this time pressured by UPSurge, the organization of the UPS rank and file. The settlement in freight was met with a wildcat strike in Detroit. UPSurge responded to the UPS settlement with wildcat strikes in eight Midwestern cities. In the Teamsters, still the largest union in the country, the "rebellion from below" provided the foundation for building a national rank-and-file movement within the union from the bottom up. In 1976, TDU was founded at Kent State University in Ohio; audaciously, activists set out to challenge the leadership of this corrupt, often brutal union with close ties to organized crime. TDU quickly grew to a movement of thousands; it was active in contract negotiations, promoted solidarity in strikes and among jurisdictions, sponsored by-law reforms, and exposed corruption and criminality. Its greatest achievements came in 1991 when it played a key role in the victory of Ron Carey, the UPS workers' leader, in his contest for the union's presidency. This in turn led to a successful challenge to the AFL-CIO old guard leadership in 1995. TDU then was instrumental in the 1997 national strike at UPS—an unparalleled victory and the single most important strike of the last decades of the twentieth century. Carey called the victory a "historic turning point," saying that "American workers have shown they can stand up to corporate greed."[109]

UPSurge, founded in Cleveland, also in 1975, was allied with the TDU but differed in that it was first of all organized to fight the company. Its initial focus was preparation for the 1976 central states contract negotiations. It began in the central states and was built on an informal shop stewards' network with roots in decades of militant activity. In the sixties and seventies there were continuous conflicts and strikes, official and unofficial, including the traveling Pennsylvania wildcat pickets in 1973.[110] In 1970, New York UPS workers struck, demanding that package drivers be allowed to wear American flag badges on their uniforms. The wildcat strike ended with the

---

108   D. La Botz (see chapter 7).
109   "Teamsters and UPS Agree on Five Year Contract," *New York Times*, August 17, 1997.
110   "Drivers Use Flying Squad Against UPS," *Workers' Power*, December 7, 1973.

ban on flags overturned and twenty fired drivers reinstated. But before it was settled, Ron Carey, the president of the New York local, was forced to add another issue to arbitration—the demand of black drivers to wear black liberation badges. The New York City United Parcel workforce was about 35 percent black at that time.[111] United Parcel led the trucking industry in hiring blacks and minorities, then women. Its workers were younger and more diverse than average in trucking.

In this period, UPS became the largest employer of Teamsters, as well as the largest transportation company in the world. The company was well known, even internationally, for its brown trucks, its military-style uniforms, and its ubiquitous supervisors armed with clipboards and stopwatches. In an industry still dominated by small and mid-sized firms, UPS became an innovator—it specialized in "Taylorism," a form of scientific management that took control of every detail in work, producing, in Harry Braverman's words, "the disassociation of the labor process from the skills of the worker."[112] UPS introduced new technologies, added airfreight, and brought in students and young workers as part-timers.

The founding "convention" of UPSurge was held in Indianapolis on January 31, 1976; it was astonishing. Six hundred and fifty UPSers gathered in a Holiday Inn in the western suburbs of the city. The meeting was part business, part protest rally, part celebration—it was certainly unparalleled in UPS history. Workers came from as far as Portland, Oregon, and Boston, Massachusetts, though overwhelmingly they came from the central states. A steering committee was elected, with representatives from eleven cities.[113] Ten contract demands were chosen, which focused on the following areas: part-timers (same pay rates, first bid on openings), appearance standards (uniform but no further restrictions), supervisors working (none), grievance procedure (innocent until proven guilty), overtime (voluntary and at double pay), health, welfare, and maternity leave (length of leave set by doctor, not company), unsafe equipment (right to refuse to operate), sick days (twelve

111   "United Parcel Strike Is Ended by Lifting Ban on Flags," *New York Times*, August 11, 1970.

112   H. Braverman, *Labor and Monopoly Capital: The Degradation of Work in the Twentieth Century* (New York: Monthly Review, 1974). See introduction, pp. 3–41. On "Job Dissatisfaction in the 1970s," Braverman writes, "The apparent increase in active dissatisfaction has been attributed to a number of causes, some having to do with the characteristics of the workers—younger, more years of schooling, 'infected' by the new-generational restlessness—and others having to do with the changing nature of work itself. One reporter cites the belief that 'American Industry in some instances may have pushed technology too far by taking the last few bits of skill out of jobs, and that a point of human resistance has been reached,'" p. 35.

113   UPSurge, Monthly UPS Workers Paper #5 (February 1976).

per year), holidays (the day after Thanksgiving), and radios (no restrictions on CBs and personal equipment). UPSurge made no economic demands but endorsed the appeal of Vince Meredith, the Louisville chief steward: "Vote the first [offer] down; the second one is always better!"[114]

While UPSurge existed, from 1975 to 1979, it exposed the depth of rank-and-file unrest, this time in a powerful, national, highly profitable company. The UPSurge steering committee was, in essence, a central states' shop stewards' movement, that is, nearly every member was a working, elected, recallable, shop-floor leader. UPSurge joined these leaders into an organization of local activists, representing dozens of workplaces spread across thousands of miles—but independent of the union's leadership— in a remarkable display of workers' democracy. The UPSurge campaign emphasized the inhumanity of the working conditions at UPS and exposed the company's reliance on coercion in its drive for profits.[115]

## Steel

The steel industry once dominated U.S. industry, its scale gigantic. In the Pittsburgh region alone, a dozen great mills lined the banks of the Monongahela River. Nationally, hundreds of thousands worked in basic steel. In 1959, 519,000 steelworkers struck for 116 days, at that point the largest single strike in U.S. history.[116] In the seventies, however, steelworkers were losing jobs; they faced stagnant and declining incomes and witnessed increasing numbers of plant closings. The industry and the union blamed foreign competition, but just as important was over-capacity in an aging, capital-intensive industry. The steel companies used the crisis to combine jobs, intensify "discipline," and increase productivity, at the same time replacing older facilities with new technology. In 1973 the companies and the union agreed to the Experimental Negotiating Agreement (ENA), a national no-strike pledge, that exchanged the right to strike in national bargaining for cash bonuses, cost-of-living adjustments, and widened access to arbitration. Steelworkers retained the right to strike on local issues, and in 1977 there were more than a hundred strike votes, compared to just seven in 1974. All this produced a rebellion within the union, first and foremost in District 31, the United Steelworkers' (USW) largest, based in the Chicago-Gary area.[117] There

---

114 UPSurge, Monthly UPS Workers Paper, #10 (May 1976).
115 UPSurge, Monthly UPS Workers Paper, #1 (September 1975).
116 J. P. Hoerr, *And the Wolf Finally Came: The Decline of the American Steel Industry* (Pittsburgh, PA: University of Pittsburgh Press, 1988), p. 101.
117 P. W. Nyden, *Steelworkers Rank-and-File: The Political Economy of a Union Reform Movement* (South Hadley, MA: Bergin and Garvey, 1984), p. 69–70.

Ed Sadlowski, a local official, defeated the incumbent for the position of district director. In other districts, Youngstown and the Iron Range, reformers won control in important local unions.

The insurgents proposed to end the 1973 ENA, demanded the right to ratify contracts, and sought to elect a new national leadership to mobilize the rank and file. In 1975, dissidents and local militants formed Steelworkers Fight Back, a national network of oppositionists. The decision was made to run Sadlowski for USW president with Fight Back as the campaign organization, even then a controversial decision.[118] Nevertheless, the 1976–7 campaign developed a crusading spirit focusing on issues like the ENA, opposition to a dues increase, and the right to ratify contracts. This spirit was supported by the fact that Sadlowski himself had been outspoken on broader social issues, such as the Vietnam War and civil rights. In the end Sadlowski lost, though he received 43 percent of the votes, including a majority in the largest locals, which were mostly in basic steel. In defeat, Fight Back soon disappeared; the promising network of oppositionists dissolved. This tragedy for steelworkers, in ways similar to the disbanding of the MFD, left workers with no organizational framework and, in Kim Moody's words, "with no place to discuss strategy, train new leaders, or recruit in other jurisdictions. The reform movement remained confined to basic steel—and that industry was on the verge of a precipitous decline."[119] Domestic steel plummeted sharply following 1979, as steel corporations carried out drastic rationalizations. Two hundred thousand steelworkers lost their jobs. In early 1980, steelworkers in Youngstown, Ohio, occupied the district headquarters of U.S. Steel in a bold but desperate, abortive attempt to stave off shutting down their mill. The sit-in was quickly abandoned on orders from the local union officers and their advisers.[120]

In the late 1970s, strikes continued to be the order of the day. The example of successful UFW strikes and boycotts of grapes and lettuce was followed by strikes and consumer boycotts in clothing and textiles at Farah and J.P. Stevens, as well as at Coors Brewing. These boycotts involved considerable numbers of supporters, other workers, as well as the general public.[121] In September 1976, cannery workers near Toledo struck, then occupied the Morgan Packing Company facilities. The strikers erected barricades, held off the authorities, and won, in a crucial early victory for the

---

118   Ibid., p. 72.
119   Moody, *An Injury to All*, p. 226.
120   S. Lynd, *The Fight Against Shutdowns: Youngstown's Steel Mill Closings* (San Pedro, CA: Singlejack Books, 1982), pp. 157, 225–6.
121   "Labor Opens Boycott Drive Against J.P. Stevens," *New York Times*, July 26, 1977.

Farm Labor Organizing Committee (FLOC). Founded by former student activist Baldemar Velasquez, FLOC began organizing in the tomato fields of northeastern Ohio. FLOC, now affiliated with the AFL-CIO, continues as a trade union and a social movement, organizing cannery workers, migrants, and immigrant workers nationwide.[122]

In the 1975–6 school year, there were 203 strikes, overwhelmingly called by the National Education Association (NEA). In Seattle, 17,000 Boeing machinists struck. In bitter strikes of miners in Stearns, Kentucky, and factory workers in Elwood, Indiana, strikers were beaten, shot at, and arrested. The conflict in Elwood left Carol Frye, a striker, with a bullet in her back—the strikers' slogan, coined by the poet grandmother Georgia Ellis, was "Essex = 4 B's: Barb Wire, Bullets, Blood, Brutality. We Demand Justice!"[123]

In January 1978, when teachers struck the Canton, Ohio schools, four hundred were arrested, including 230 in one swoop at Timken High School. That same year, firefighters struck in Memphis, Tennessee, a wildcat strike, as well as in Normal, Illinois, and Dayton, Ohio. In September 1978, 20,000 members of AFSCME walked off their jobs in Philadelphia. Safeway was shut down in Northern California in a bitter confrontation with Teamsters—in August a picketing striker was killed. Railroad workers, in defiance of federal interventions, turned an eighty-one-day dispute with the Norfolk Western into a national railroad strike. Fifteen thousand pulp and paper workers used mass picketing and traveling pickets in a near-general strike in the Pacific Northwest. In 1979, there was a wildcat strike of steel haulers in Youngstown. Car haulers wildcatted in Linwood, New Jersey, and Lordstown, Ohio; postal workers at the Richmond, California bulk mail center. Nuclear workers walked out at Goodyear's Piketown, Ohio plant. Steelworkers won recognition in the shipyards at Newport News, following a two-year strike. Faculty struck at Boston University and the University of Cincinnati. And again, there were the school teachers. There were 199 teachers' strikes in 1979, matching the previous high in 1975–6. Teachers struck for more money, reduced class sizes, additional preparation time, and, in some places, student discipline. Finally, there was the 1979 strike of California farmworkers.[124]

The final great conflict of the decade came in the coalfields, the 110-day strike that culminated a decade of rank-and-file insurgency. This conflict came to a head when the union called its second consecutive

122  www.floc.com.
123  Reports of these strikes can be found in the *New York Times* and other national papers.
124  F. Bardacke (see chapter 5).

national strike at the end of 1977. The strike of 160,000 miners lasted 110 days, continuing despite the Taft-Hartley injunction issued by President Jimmy Carter.[125] Twice, rank-and-file miners defied UMW leaders and rejected concessionary contracts. It was a "classic" strike, the "industrial equivalent," Hyman suggests, "of war between nations."[126] The operators wanted what miners called a "1930's-style contract" with the right to fire strikers, big health deductibles, and punitive absentee controls.[127] Critics contended that the union called the strike in the worst possible circumstances; there were months of coal stockpiles on the ground. Critics also felt the union leadership had no intention of winning the strike.[128] Nevertheless, the rank-and-file miners did, and they fought the companies—all subsidiaries of giant energy corporations—to a bloody standstill. They also fought state troopers, national guardsmen in Indiana, and thousands of company guards and goons. Three miners were shot and killed on picket lines, hundreds were arrested, and thousands were fined. There was widespread sympathy for the striking miners, including solidarity rallies, food collections, and caravans, but no other union took action in their support. The miners fought alone, nevertheless, and they defeated the companies on many issues. Only hunger forced them back. Even then, 40 percent of the miners voting rejected the settlement, preferring to fight on. The miners were exhausted in 1978, but not defeated. Neither, however, were they prepared for what was to come— the wholesale removal of coal mining to the West.[129]

In this brief account of the rank-and-file rebellion of the long seventies, I have pointed to the inherent strength of workers, their capacity to organize, and the potential for democracy in their movements, that is, of a real "participatory" democracy—in contrast to the passive, formal, cash democracy of our times. I have emphasized the importance of the workplace—the heart of corporate capitalism—and the struggle there for control. The conflicts of the 1970s were widespread and intense. It was in the 1980s that the annual average of major strikes collapsed to eighty-one

---

125   Nyden (see chapter 6).

126   Hyman, *Strikes*, p. 20.

127   Nyden (see chapter 6).

128   Perry, *Collective Bargaining and the Decline of the United Mine Workers*. See pp. 231–3 for a critique of the union leadership.

129   An interesting pamphlet published in the late 1970s by David Greene and signed by a group of local officers, including future UMW president Cecil Roberts, warned of the danger of western coal and called for, among other things, "People before profits . . . a rational, humane development of western coal with the guarantee of protecting our jobs, our hospital cards and our pensions." It also called for "nationalization of the energy industry." D. Greene, "The Threat of Western Coal," (Racine, WV: n.d. c. 1978).

strikes in 1983 (involving one thousand workers or more), then in 1999 to just seventeen.[130]

Why, then, did workers not win more? Why were they defeated?

First of all, it is important to stress that there *were* victories; not all was lost. And the end of the "rebellion from below" was not the end of trade unionism. There were still 20 million members in the AFL-CIO in 1980.[131] The public sector unions had grown by millions and have since held their own. The importance of staying power was demonstrated in the IBT, where victories in the nineties were the direct consequences of events of the seventies. The same can be said, indirectly, for the 1997 victory at UPS. Today the NEA is by far the largest labor organization in the United States, representing more than 3 million members, though it remains independent of the AFL-CIO.[132] With official support, as in the case of the teachers, there was much that could be achieved. The UMW, the union that bankrolled the CIO in the thirties, remained, in 1980, unbowed, a force.

Why was there defeat? We should begin with the raw power of American capital; the power and resources of corporations such as General Motors and U.S. Steel were staggering, even in times of crisis. Moreover, large U.S. corporations never really accepted trade unionism—it had been forced upon them by the rebellions of the 1930s. Therefore, in their offensive of the 1970s, they fought to win, with ruthlessness rarely rivaled in the industrial countries. They routinely took every opportunity to undermine workers' collective power and extend management control in the work process. And almost nowhere, at least in the industrialized countries, was government more supportive of these corporations. When Douglas Fraser complained of the one-sided class war against labor, he was right; the problem was that he left the "class war against capital" to the rank and file. The trade union leaders in the United States lamented the passing of the era of collaboration but did nothing to replace it.

The unions, for the most part, were obstacles in the paths of rank-and-file workers. This was first of all the result of inaction—sticking to business as usual in a tumultuous decade. Union officials stubbornly clung to bureaucratic practices, hoping to preserve the institutions of collective bargaining upon which they depended for their existence. Yet these were increasingly inadequate in the face of the changed circumstances

---

130    www.bls.gov/news.release/wkstp.to1.htm. Accessed July 1, 2007. After 1981, the Bureau of Labor Statistics reported only strikes of one thousand or more workers.

131    See Moody, *US Labor in Trouble and Transition*, p. 100. Membership in U.S. unions reached its high point in 1980 at 20,095,000, though trade union density was rapidly falling, from a high in 1953 of 32.5 percent to 23 percent in 1980. Today the figures are 12 percent for all unions, and 7.4 percent in the private sector.

132    The NEA claims 3.2 million members. www.nea.org.

of the employers' offensive. In the major unions, only the miners were successful in overthrowing an established leadership, and even then, just temporarily.

## Results and Prospects

What of the larger demands? The demand for "workers' control," the ownership and control of industry and its democratic management by the workers in the interest of all the people—these must now seem utterly utopian. The fight for democratic unions, for unions capable of withstanding the corporate offensive, must also seem utopian. Today there are academics and activists who argue that strikes are obsolete and that democracy just holds unions back. And for some time now, historians, even historians of labor, have seen the 1970s not as a decade of great hope, but rather as a time when labor, big labor, was defeated—big labor, one supposes, being better than no labor. The seventies are commonly seen as the beginnings of the backlash and the new majority, of the conservative consensus of the late twentieth century, with workers—in particular, white male workers—as a core constituency of the new right. Of course there is truth in this, but only if one chooses to ignore the very real alternatives posed at the time. In the 1970s, the United States was contested terrain, and the struggle for the allegiance of workers was central. Many turned to the right, and this was a great tragedy—we live with the consequences.

Still, this is not the end of history, and, following Michael Watts, in his reflection on 1968, this volume should "not be read as a hymnal" for the long seventies. He writes that from the struggles of 1968, "the enlargement of the field of the possible . . . emerged . . . It is a measure of the conservatism of our era and the capacity to silence the past that such innovations are now seen to be so retrograde as to be almost an embarrassment to articulate in public."[133] What were the "innovations" of these "rebellions from below"? I will just suggest the reinvention of direct action, the assault on racism in the workplace, the smashing down of barriers to women and the demand for dignity ("human rights") on the job, as well as the right of the rank and file to dissent, to challenge the leadership, to organize independently. They include the revival of workers' councils and roving pickets. The shop steward, in the fifties and sixties too often reduced to a policeman on a beat, was redefined as fighter, organizer, and leader. The tradition of popular participation in the most basic of institutions, industry and the unions, was reborn. Also, I might add, the lived experience, however limited, of autonomy, self-government, and the taste of workers' control. Is this of

---

133   Watts, "1968 and All That . . ." p. 182.

any significance? Were these causes in vain? The world remains on the path of industrialization, corporate power reigns virtually unchecked, and never have the stakes been higher—in this phase the fate of the earth itself is the issue. We must hope that others will find insights in these movements.

Finally, what were the weaknesses of the rank-and-file rebellion? The workers' movements inevitably reflected the unions, the institutions in which they developed. They were not, for the most part, able to transcend the limitations this imposed upon them. The movements reflected the deep racial and gender divides in the United States. American workers never overcame these divides, and class solidarity remained illusive—white racism prevented the fusing of the civil rights movement, the Black Power movement, and the working-class movement.

The strikes and rank-and-file movements overwhelmingly remained confined to single industries and unions, and while there was often intense solidarity within individual industries and unions, it rarely spilled from industry to industry or union to union. Certainly there was widespread sympathy for workers in struggle, but there was no organized way of expressing such support.

The rank-and-file revolt produced no center, no coordinators, and no recognizable leaders. The movement developed no coherent ideology—no conscious, generalized mission. This problem was compounded by the very geography of the country—the great distances between industrial centers, the isolation of important groups, like black workers in the inner cities, coal miners in Appalachia, farmworkers in the California valleys.

While intimately connected to the social movements of the time, the rank-and-file movements developed separately, in time as well as space—in the early seventies the student antiwar movement was a thing of the past, and the radical black movement had been crushed. The rank-and-file rebellion of the 1960s and 1970s had debilitating weaknesses of its own. It replicated the hierarchies of existing industrial structure and union organization—telephone operators were divided from telephone repairmen. Most crucially, militants confined their activity, and even their independent organizations, within the boundaries of bureaucratic business unionism. They often focused on replacing union leaders, and in some locals, including one national union (the UMW), they succeeded. This did not, however, alter the fundamental structural conservatism of the trade unions and their officialdom.

Repression, both by the employers and from the state, played a significant role, and striking workers, in particular in the absence of official union support, were often defenseless in the face of violence. The employers increasingly contemplated a union-free workforce. Individually, they implemented a panoply of strategies that are now legendary, including hiring union-busting lawyers, running decertification campaigns, and moving to non-union regions in the South and abroad. The level of violence in the 1970s did not match that of 1919 or the 1930s; nevertheless, workers routinely faced armed guards, police, and national guardsmen, as well as strike-breakers and union goons. When not collaborating, the unions were also enforcers. The IBT was known for its violent repression of dissent, but other unions followed suit, as when the UAW mobilized one thousand armed officials and loyalists to break the 1973 strike at Chrysler's Mack Avenue stamping plant in Detroit.[134] The murder of mine worker leader Jock Yablonski and the beatings of oppositionists in the Teamsters were the most notorious examples of union leaders' violent repression of dissent.

Finally, the strikers of the 1970s never faced up to an essential problem: as Richard Hyman has written, "the only real solution to the strike problem lies in a transformation of the status of labor and the whole structure of control in industry: replacing minority domination and the pursuit of profit by democratic control and the satisfaction of human needs."[135]

In conclusion, the labor movement in the United States, we should repeat, remained at end of this decade a potentially powerful force. The exhaustion of the rank-and-file rebellion was not the defeat of the labor movement. This came—and it was decisive—not in 1974, and not in 1978, but in 1981, when the new president, Ronald Reagan, fired the striking air traffic controllers and decertified their union, the Professional Air Traffic Controllers Organization (PATCO).[136]

The air traffic controllers represented a small number of workers; their union, in terms of the labor movement, was peripheral. The conflict was, then, symbolic. But in this case, the symbols represented life and death for trade unionism in the United States. Lane Kirkland, president of the AFL–CIO, responded to the new Reagan administration's aggressive anti-union stance by organizing "Solidarity Day" in Washington, D.C.—September 19, 1981. Hundreds of thousands of workers responded, PATCO prominently among them, marching in massive battalions through the Capitol, in a spectacular display of trade union power. This demonstration dramatically symbolized the possibility of stopping Reagan, saving PATCO, and rescuing what remained of trade union strength and organization, all of which was still considerable in 1981.

It was not to happen. Solidarity Day came and went. Support for PATCO was not forthcoming; indeed, the AFL-CIO privately undermined any

---

134   Weinberg, "Detroit Auto Uprising, 1973," p. 40.
135   Hyman, *Strikes*, p. 171.
136   See A. B. Shostak and D. Skocik, *The Air Controllers' Controversy: Lessons from the PATCO Strike* (New York: Human Sciences Press, 1990).

possibility of practical solidarity, and the air traffic controllers' union was lost. After that there was no coming back; the floodgates of concessions and systematic retreat were opened, and union membership collapsed. The 1980s were a catastrophe for the labor movement. "The chickens came home to roost." The rest of the story is well known.

# The Political Economy of the Rank-and-File Rebellion

## Robert Brenner

The conditions making for the emergence of the rank-and-file movements of the 1960s and 1970s were constituted in three successive phases corresponding to three successive stages in the evolution of the postwar economy. The first phase, extending from the end of the 1940s to the end of the 1950s, might be viewed as a honeymoon for labor, made possible by the somewhat unexpected onset of the long upturn of the American economy. This expansion, which was already petering out after mid-decade, made for tight labor markets, high levels of militancy, and a relatively restrained approach to workers on the part of employers, opening the way for historic economic gains for American working people.

The second, and in retrospect decisive, phase was marked by a sudden and profound toughening on the part of U.S. manufacturing employers toward labor, from the last years of the 1950s through the middle 1960s, at both the bargaining table and on the shop floor. This employers' offensive was driven by a sharp fall in profitability and a half-decade of economic stagnation resulting from the only straightforward wages-productivity squeeze of the postwar epoch in the United States. The short-term crisis was exacerbated by a rising wave of U.S. investment overseas and the initial appearance on world export and U.S. import markets of formidable overseas rivals. Especially because the employers' "new hard line" was met, after some initial resistance, by the acquiescence of labor's officialdom, it brought a radical reduction in the growth of compensation and a harsh intensification of labor for much of the manufacturing working class, which made for a speedy and impressive revival of the manufacturing rate of return between 1961 and 1965. For the same reasons, it also incited the first stirrings of rank-and-file resistance, in the form of a rising tide of shop-floor struggles, contract rejections, wildcat strikes, and the overthrow of long-entrenched union leaders.

In the third and final phase, between 1965 and 1973, U.S. employers rewarded the aid and succor of union officialdom with a further turning of the screws on their employees—downward pressure on compensation, deterioration in working conditions, defiance of NLRB labor law, and stepped-up resistance to union organizing. This constituted the obligatory response on the part of capital to the sudden, precipitous descent of the economy into a long-term crisis of profitability between 1965 and 1973. The combination of intensifying employers' assault and bureaucratic complaisance provided the precipitating conditions for an explosion of working-class self-activity from below just after the middle of the decade. The latter not only galvanized official union resistance, but issued in widespread unofficial actions on the part of the membership independent from labor's officialdom, leading, in a number of unions, to the formation of autonomous rank-and-file organizations.

Nevertheless, because the crisis of profitability turned out to be not cyclical but secular, it soon put a definitive end to the postwar boom. It thereby deprived an inherently weak American labor movement of the extended draft of economic prosperity that had long been the indispensable condition for its reasonably good health. The deep recession of 1974–5, the worst since the Great Depression, delivered a knock-down punch from which neither the unions nor the rank-and-file organizations that had grown up within them were ever able to recover. As the economy sank into an extended period of low rates of return and slowed growth, the level of employer organization and the intensity of employer offensive continued to rise, but the breadth and depth of the union retort shrank correspondingly.[1]

## The Dissipation of Working-Class Power, 1937–48

At the end of the 1940s, there seemed little reason to look forward to a new period of union vigor or sustained improvement in the working class's material condition. The titanic burst of energy that had dynamized the labor movement during the 1930s had been largely dispersed. The CIO had emerged from an ascending wave of mass strikes, which, by transforming the activity of the working class, brought about a historic increase in its power and an epoch-making alteration in its consciousness. Mobilized in the process was the indispensable force that underpinned New Deal social reforms, as well as the sociopolitical base for the longer term ascendancy of the Democratic Party. The new industrial unions were created by means

---

1   For definition and data sources on profit rates and their components, as well as investment, productivity, wages and benefits, and employment, along with international trade, see R. Brenner, *The Economics of Global Turbulence* (London: Verso, 2006), Appendixes I and II.

of a series of militant mass-organizing struggles, emanating from the factory floor, which, thanks especially to the leadership provided by political radicals in the shops—Communists, Trotskyists, and socialists of several sorts—were pursued by way of a "rank-and-file strategy" of class independence, direct action, and expanding solidarity.[2] This strategy broke decisively from the tactics of avoiding strikes, conciliating the employers, relying on mediation, and calling in the state that had been pursued with such disastrous and demoralizing results by the AFL "federal unions" during the defeat of the more or less spontaneous drive of industrial workers for industrial unions from 1933–4, notably in auto, steel, and rubber. It called instead for reliance on mass mobilization against the employers, avoidance of the courts and the government, autonomy from the existing official union leaderships, and the fullest internal union democracy. It also entailed the search for those ever broader alliances—across union and geographical boundaries, with urban communities, and with the unemployed, not to mention the push for a party of labor—that were indispensable for transcending the initially parochial character of workers' resistance and amplifying workers' power.

These efforts would never have borne fruit if they had to depend on the initiatives and strategic counsel of the leadership group that made the indispensable break from the AFL to create the CIO. In the grip of a bureaucratic mentality formed through long years at the peak of their unions, John L. Lewis, Sidney Hillman, and Philip Murray sought, as they always had, iron-fisted control of the movement from the top, with no pretense of union democracy. They did everything in their power to contain the impetuous, autonomous, and unruly mass offensives from below which, nonetheless, by time and again confronting the corporations against the better judgment and advice of the CIO leadership, turned out to provide the ultimate key to the CIO's success.[3] The struggles that brought industrial unionism into being were detonated in 1933–4 by the miners' huge self-generating rank-and-file movement to reform the United Mine Workers union and to begin to extend union organization to the so-called captive mines owned by the steel corporations. They were highlighted

2   For this and the following three paragraphs, see in general A. Preis's pioneering book *Labor's Giant Step* (New York: Pioneer Publishers, 1964), especially Part I; and Mike Davis's fundamental *Prisoners of the American Dream* (London: Verso, 1986), specifically chapters 2 and 3, as well as Staughton Lynd's path-breaking essays, "The Possibility of Radicalism in the Early 1930s: The Case of Steel," *Radical America* vol. 6 (November–December 1972) and "The United Front: A Note," *Radical America* vol. 8 (July 1974).

3   See L. L. Cary, "Institutionalized Conservatism in the Early C.I.O.: Adolph Germer, A Case Study," *Labor History* 13:4 (Fall 1972); and Lynd, "The Possibility of Radicalism in the Early 1930s."

by the victorious city-wide general strikes of 1934 in Minneapolis, San
Francisco, and Toledo, led in each case by revolutionaries, as well as by the
monumental, if ultimately defeated, general strike by textile workers in the
same year. They were dramatically reignited in the first half of 1936 by a
huge wave of sit-down strikes in the rubber industry, following the model
established by rubber workers at General Tire in 1934, which opened
the way to the breakthrough triumphs of the United Rubber Workers
in Akron at Goodrich and Goodyear. They reached their zenith with the
classical rank-and-file movement, led primarily by Communists and other
radicals of various stripes. The CIO won union recognition for the auto
workers, first by way of a series of groundbreaking local organizing efforts
between 1934 and 1936 that broke the grip of the AFL officials and formed
the UAW, and ultimately leading to the great sit-down strikes, especially
at Flint, in the winter of 1936–7. By forcing the world's largest and most
powerful corporation, against its will, to recognize it, the UAW opened
the way to a new era of industrial unionism and, for a time, working-class
power.[4]

Nevertheless, the ink had barely dried on the epoch-making GM
contract when the ascending wave of working-class resistance began
to ebb, thanks in no small measure to the Herculean efforts to subdue
it by the emergent CIO officialdom, reactionary initiatives in which the
hitherto oppositional Communist Party, and especially its powerful trade
union wing, played an indispensable part.[5] The first fruits of the CIO's
bureaucratic counter-offensive were to prove decisive, as they included the
following decisions: not to press the much weaker Chrysler corporation
for a better contract than had been extracted from GM in early 1937; to
try to repress rather than amplify the rising tide of wildcats and sit-down
strikes that, inspired by and gaining confidence from the victory over GM,
had naturally broken out throughout the auto industry and beyond in the
winter and spring of 1937; to attempt to organize Little Steel on the basis of
the dubious, and ultimately disastrous, strategy of trusting in state and local
Democratic politicians, as well as Roosevelt himself; and to give up even
a propagandistic commitment to the necessity of a third-party alternative
to the two capitalist parties, after the UAW had initially refused to support

---

4   J. Irons, "The Challenge of National Coordination: Southern Textile Workers and the
General Textile Strike of 1934," in S. Lynd, ed., "*We are All Leaders*": *The Alternative Unionism
of the Early 1930s* (Urbana: University of Illinois Press, 1996); D. Nelson, "Origins of the Sit-
Down Era: Worker Militancy and Innovation in the Rubber Industry, 1934–38," *Labor History*
23:2 (Spring 1982); R. R. Keeran, "Communists and Auto Workers: The Struggle for a Union,
1919–1941" (PhD Diss., University of Wisconsin, 1974), chapters 3, 4, and 5.

5   See C. Post, "The Popular Front in the US: The Only Option?" *Against the Current* #66
(July–August 1996).

the Democrats and Roosevelt at its founding convention in 1936. The implementation of the CIO's top-down approach quickly culminated in the decisive defeat of its Steelworkers' Organizing Committee (SWOC) at Little Steel in May 1937 and was soon followed, in the second part of the year, by the deep "second depression" of the 1930s. The rocketing unemployment that ensued profoundly undermined the unions' position across industry, short-circuited an initial CIO attempt to organize the South by unionizing the textile industry, and opened the way to a powerful counter-offensive by the employers, aided and abetted by a resurgent AFL, not to mention congressional witch-hunters.[6] A very great part of the extraordinary momentum coming out of the remarkable series of victorious struggles by labor over capital between 1933 and 1937 was thus quickly squandered and irrevocably lost.

What followed was an accelerated, if classical, process of trade union bureaucratization, whose underlying dynamics have long been evident. On the one hand, trade union officials are obliged to confront the discouraging reality of the uneven and discontinuous character of working-class resistance, which leaves them no choice, most of the time, but to try to craft viable responses to the continuous pressure from capital, in the face of the diminishing self-activity of their members, the reduction in the number of rank-and-file activists or leaders that they can count on, and the increasing narrowness of actual struggles, particularly in the wake of the exhaustion of the mass strike dynamic. On the other hand, they find themselves separated in their condition from workers on the shop floor in finding their material base, so to speak—their salaries, their careers, their whole form of life—to be constituted by the union organization itself. Composing a distinct social layer that is neither proletarian nor capitalist, but lies in socioeconomic and political terms between the employers and their employees, these paid officials have managed to escape dependence on the corporations for employment and compensation, as well as the miseries of work under the aegis of capital in factory, office, or farm. They have, as a result, ceased to rely, as most union members must continue to do, on extracting gains and defending their working conditions and their compensation through the always-dangerous process of confronting the employers. Since the officials' well-being depends instead on whatever it takes to secure the trade union's health and prosperity, their overriding tendency is to confuse the defense of the organization with the defense of the membership, with the former taking precedence over the latter and tending to become an end in itself, rather than simply a means to further the goals of the rank and file. Their

---

6  S. Fraser, "The 'Labor Question,'" in S. Fraser and G. Gerstle, eds, *The Rise and Fall of the New Deal Order, 1930–1980* (Princeton: Princeton University Press, 1989), pp. 72–6.

bottom-line concern for the reproduction of the union organization per se decisively differentiates their interests from those of the membership. Given the power of the employers, the strategic approach of the trade union officialdom standardly entails the adoption of a series of strategies designed to pursue the concerns of the membership while prioritizing the defense of, by minimizing the risk to, the union organization itself.

The point, it should be stressed, is not at all that labor officials never lead struggles in which the union is obliged to test its strength against the employers, for obviously they do. It is rather that they cannot be counted on to defend the interests of the membership, for the reason that, under virtually all conceivable circumstances, they not only have self-evident routes to defend themselves and their organizations against the employers that do not require or involve defending the rank and file, but also possess powerful material interests in availing themselves of these channels. The bottom line is that the organization and its paid officials can survive, and prosper, even while the members suffer the serious deterioration in their condition. This is not to say that the union membership is always self-activated and desirous of confronting the employers but held back by the leadership. But it is the conclusion that, on those occasions when the rank and file do set themselves autonomously in motion against the boss, they can expect, as a matter of course, that the union officialdom, especially beyond the local level, rather than nurturing their struggles as the only way to enhance the union's actual power, will tend to want to sidetrack if not derail them. This is not asserted simply as a theoretical deduction, but as an empirical proposition, holding—and ever increasingly so—for the entirety of the postwar epoch. It is this reality—one not obviously confined to the postwar United States but familiar across the capitalist world throughout the twentieth century—that has accounted for the periodic emergence, at different times and places, of rank-and-file organizations having as their raison d'être to counter the systematic tendency of the union officialdom to repress rather than attempt to build outbreaks of worker resistance that they do not control, so as to force the union to fight.

The foregoing political sociology has implications for the interpretation of the actual strategies pursued by the emerging layer of CIO officials in the wake of the decline of mass working-class action, and therefore mass working-class power, from 1937. As a substitute for risking open-ended confrontations with management, the emerging CIO bureaucracies tended to pursue a two-pronged policy aimed at stabilizing the union's position. At the level of industry, they sought state-sanctioned collective bargaining. At the level of politics, they took the electoral road by way of the Democratic Party. In pursuing both these strategies, they sought from the start, but with only minimal success, to secure the support of the state for formal or informal tripartite arrangements among capital, labor, and the government that would contain and regularize the class struggle in the interest of social stability and union security. But the tendency to depend ever increasingly on the institutions of collective bargaining, particularly the grievance procedure, and on the Democratic Party to realize their own and their members' interests turned out, over time, to be profoundly self-undermining.

In order to survive in the competitive struggle, corporations were obliged to put the highest priority on achieving surplus profits via securing in any way they could lower costs than their rivals. They were thus obliged to pursue "productivity increases" indifferently by way of either technical improvement or the intensification of labor. As a result, every individual corporation had little choice but to seek systematically to appropriate the lion's share of the gains resulting from the growth of productiveness, and to devolve upon their employees a disproportionate share of the costs, whether in the form of reduced employment growth, increased layoffs, speedup, or deteriorating working conditions. This was, as the labor officialdom well knew, the essence and payoff of the so-called "right to manage" upon which the corporations insisted as the condition for granting steady gains in compensation. The outcome, however, was endemic, intense conflict at the point of production in which the union officials found themselves in the middle, having to arbitrate between the demands for equitable treatment on the part of the rank and file and for competitive production on the part of the employers. Especially in view of the system of bargaining-by-company that prevailed in the United States, it was a foregone conclusion that the union officials would choose the latter over the former, unless prevented from doing so by an aroused membership. Standing up for the rank and file on the shop floor might undermine the profitability and thus the viability of the company. It might at the same time call forth reprisals from the company that could threaten the security of the union itself.[7] Nevertheless, the implied costs were enormous, especially over time. This was because, in seeking as they did to repress the autonomous self-activity and self-organization of the membership as it spontaneously arose out of shop-floor conflicts on the basis of primary work groups, the union officialdom could not but undermine and destroy what was ultimately the only viable source

---

7   As Lichtenstein succinctly puts it vis-à-vis the auto industry, after 1946, the UAW "tied its fate ever more closely to the industry and increasingly subordinated the endemic shop-floor struggle over working conditions and production standards to the UAW's national bargaining program . . . Just as liberalism increasingly came to define itself as largely concerned with the maintenance of economic growth and an expansion of the welfare state, so too the UAW redefined its mission in these same terms." N. Lichtenstein, "UAW Bargaining Strategy and Shop Floor Conflict," *Industrial Relations* vol. 24 (Fall 1985), p. 363.

of the union's own strength relative to the corporations—i.e., the power of the organized, educated, and self-activating membership itself.

The dependence on the Democratic Party set in motion analogously self-defeating processes, not only for the unions but also for the party itself, especially as a vehicle of liberal aspirations. To the extent that they sought to substitute the electoral struggle, in which workers as individual citizens ostensibly fought the class war in the relative safety of the voting booth, for the much more perilous processes of collectively confronting employers in industry and on the shop floor, the trade unions eroded their power independent of the Democratic Party. The unavoidable result was to forfeit their ability to exert leverage over the Democrats, and to become increasingly reliant upon them for gains for their members. The Democratic leadership could therefore count ever more securely on the unions' services and support for ever less in return, especially in the area most vital to the labor movement (and the employers), that of union rights, where the Party was, throughout the postwar epoch, conspicuous for its indifference to union interests. The Democrats were thus left ever freer to move, in accordance with purely party-political calculus, to broaden their legislative, electoral, and financial base by consolidating the support of forces on the right, notably their traditional supporters in the South and, of course, business. But in so doing, the Democrats, like the union officials, furthered the disintegration and political dispersal of their own most powerful and most reliable social base.

As most of the new layer of officials well understood, the fundamental premise of their whole approach was the shaky notion that the economy could be made to expand more or less continuously. Only such perpetual growth would provide the growing pie that could dissolve the threat to capitalist profits represented by growing workers' compensation, let alone improved working conditions. Only such ongoing expansion could make it possible for the employers to find it in their interest to pursue stable industrial relations with the goal of securing uninterrupted production through the avoidance of disruption from below, and thus to continue to absorb the costs of routinized unionization as preferable to paying the costs of confrontation. In sum, only permanent prosperity would allow the trade union officials to continue to extract gains from the employers for the membership, while continuing to erode the independent power of the rank and file. The whole perspective would come to naught with the advent of falling profit rates and economic slowdown, when the employers would have little choice but to sacrifice stability and continuity in production to take on the unions in order to gain a larger share of the slower-growing pie by securing more intense work for lower pay. Under such conditions, the union officials would see little choice but to help the corporations recover their profits, as the precondition for pursuing material gains for their membership, not least because they had already overseen the long-term disintegration of the power of the union rank and file.

World War II turned out not only to rescue the new unions, but also to bring about an otherwise inconceivable acceleration of the process of bureaucratization, while simultaneously strengthening the dynamics of decline of labor that would prevail increasingly throughout most of the postwar era. The unions secured huge gains in membership and security for their organizations, but only, all too characteristically, on the condition that their officials would honor and enforce the pledge not to strike for the duration of the hostilities, while also implicitly agreeing to sacrifice rank-and-file interests and powers at the level of the labor process to the needs of stable production. Meanwhile, business achieved a stunning revival—of profits, prestige, and political influence—leading to a major shift of the balance of forces against labor. The consequence was that, when World War II came to an end, the union leaderships failed to extract from the employers the industry-level bargaining that was so critical to effectively taking labor costs out of competition, let alone the continuation of the tripartite corporatism, however watered down, that had prevailed while the nation was at war. Instead, the unions were left on their own to face a rising assault by revanchist employers aiming to recover the power in politics, industry, and on the shop floor that they had been compelled to cede to an aroused, self-mobilized working class during the 1930s upsurge.

The great postwar strike wave of 1946 did win significant wage gains for workers and established the unions as here to stay. But it largely failed to realize union hopes to begin to make the labor movement a more credible representative of the working class as a whole, specifically by obliging management to accept wage increases without imposing compensating increases in prices. The resulting disillusion and demoralization across much of the working class, and the mass abstention from voting that ensued, opened the way for a huge Republican victory in the 1946 Congressional elections and, in the longer term, the consolidation of the conservative alliance between Republicans and southern Democrats that brought the effective end of union hopes for the construction in the United States of the sort of far-reaching welfare state that would emerge in postwar Europe. The unions were left to attempt to wrench health, pension, and unemployment benefits directly from the employers. But in thereby falling back on what turned out to be a "private welfare state," the union membership increasingly separated itself from an ever-growing unprotected, or less protected, section of the working class, giving it, over time, ever more the appearance of the special interest group that its enemies claimed it was.[8]

---

8   See J. Boylan, *The New Deal Coalition and the Election of 1946* (New York: Garland

Perhaps most destructive for working-class power in the longer run, union attempts to organize the Southern working class ended in abject failure. The union officialdom could not begin to contemplate unleashing the sort of wide-ranging, confrontational, and disruptive social struggles that had been indispensable for winning industrial unions in the 1930s. As a consequence, Operation Dixie went down in humiliating defeat, setting the stage for serious union-busting efforts in the following decade. As union density in the South fell by half between 1945 and 1960, from 20 percent to 10 percent, the region was opened up for an epoch-making wave of industrialization beyond union influence, the first phase of the great postwar process of globalization. As the flip side of the same coin, union membership was left concentrated in the older industrial areas of the Northeast, Midwest, and West Coast, with two-thirds of all union members living in just ten states, decisively limiting union power, not just economically but also in the national political arena.

Carrying the postwar corporate offensive and Cold War right-wing reaction to its culmination, in 1947 Congress passed, over President Truman's veto, the Taft-Hartley Act, which further reduced the arsenal at the unions' disposal. A key weapon of solidarity, the secondary boycott, was declared illegal. Perhaps most devastating, much of the white-collar workforce was ruled ineligible for union membership/representation under the National Labor Relations Act. Meanwhile, an enormous government-led red-baiting assault on the trade-union Left and the unions in general further weakened the labor movement by setting it against itself and precipitating the expulsion of the Communist-led unions, which constituted the labor movement's most militant and politically progressive wing, not least on the crucial question of race.[9]

After exploding upward at an average annual rate of 8 percent between 1940 and 1944 during the exceptionally favorable conditions of the wartime boom, average annual real wage growth for manufacturing production and non-supervisory workers fell slightly below zero for the mainly recession years between 1944 and 1948. To all appearances, the employers were back in the saddle. With the economic situation looking uncertain, union prospects seemed murky at best.

---

Publishing, 1981); N. Lichtenstein, "From Corporatism to Collective Bargaining: Organized Labor and the Eclipse of Social Democracy in the Postwar Era," in Fraser and Gerstle, eds, *The Rise and Fall of the New Deal*.

9   M. Goldfield, "The Failure of Operation Dixie: A Critical Turning Point in American Political Development?" in G. E. Fink and M. E. Reed, eds, *Race, Class, and Community in Southern Labor History* (Tuscaloosa: University of Alabama Press, 1994); N. Lichtenstein, *State of the Union: A Century of American Labor* (Princeton: Princeton University Press, 2003), pp. 110–4; J. Stein, *Running Steel, Running America: Race, Economic Policy, and the Decline of Liberalism* (Chapel Hill: University of North Carolina Press, 1998), pp. 16–8; J. Stepan-Norris and M. Zietlin, *Left Out: Reds and America's Industrial Unions* (Cambridge: Cambridge University Press, 2003).

## The Postwar Boom and the Regeneration of the Unions, 1948–58

The fact remains that, notwithstanding the series of devastating reversals that overtook the labor movement during the second half of the 1940s, over the decade that followed there took place a very major turnaround, which was little expected at the time. Unions continued to win a very high percentage of National Labor Relations Board (NLRB) union-recognition elections, and thereby further increased the proportion of the labor force that was unionized. Union density in the private sector reached its historic peak in 1953–4, at around 35 percent.[10] Unions also came to display a higher propensity to strike than they would do at any other time in the postwar epoch after 1946. Taking either the decade 1946–56 or the half decade 1949–54, a greater *proportion* of total workdays was lost to work stoppages in this era than in any other comparable intervals after 1946.[11] The outcome was that, during the business cycles between 1948 and 1959, the average annual growth of real wages for production and non-supervisory workers in manufacturing leaped to 3.4 percent and was roughly matched by the non-farm sector as a whole. Leaving aside World War II, this was the highest rate of wage increase for any comparable period during the twentieth century. The 1950s was the true golden age for the American worker.

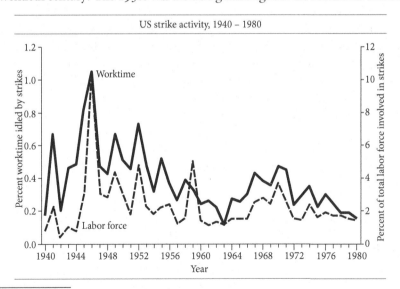

US strike activity, 1940 – 1980

10   For data on union-certification elections and levels of unionization, see the fundamental work by M. Goldfield, *The Decline of Organized Labor in the United States* (Chicago: University of Chicago Press, 1987), pp. 10, 90–1. My thanks to Mike Goldfield for many very helpful discussions of the U.S. economy and labor movement, and for providing me with much useful data.

11   "Work Stoppages in the United States, 1927–1980," table supplied by the U.S. Bureau of Labor Statistics, Office of Compensation and Working Conditions, Division of Development in Labor–Management Relations.

The factors enabling such major—and unexpected—gains for the labor movement and the working class as a whole are not hard to discover. They are the same ones that made possible the onset of the two-decade-long postwar boom, and more specifically its very favorable opening phase. The fundamental underlying condition for the expansion was achieved during World War II, when corporations secured an extraordinary recovery of their rate of profit in the wake of the Great Depression.[12] The recession of 1948–9 proved unexpectedly mild. Then, from 1949–50, under the enormous stimulus provided by rearmament and the Korean War, the growth of the GDP, which had languished at −2.2 percent per annum for the business cycle between 1944 and 1948, suddenly shot forward at 4.9 percent per annum for the business cycle between 1948 and 1953, while the rate of growth of non-farm employment jumped up by one-third over the same interval. As a consequence, the rate of unemployment fell from an average of 5.6 percent for 1949 and 1950 to an average of just over 3 percent for 1951, 1952, and 1953 inclusive. In view of the ensuing flood of demand, employers had every reason to trade increases in compensation for stability of production, and this obviously provided workers with a powerful lever. Since U.S. producers had, moreover, during the immediate postwar period, dramatically improved their already dominant position on the world market, organized labor had little reason as yet to take account of international competition in making its demands. The unions were therefore free to flex their muscles, revive some of the militancy displayed at the close of World War II, and exploit the favorable climate for struggle of these years.

It was thanks to the high boom conditions of the first half of the 1950s that the "classical" (if, in retrospect, short-lived) system of postwar labor relations could be consolidated—the long-term contract, regular wage gains in accord with productivity growth, and the cost-of-living escalator, as well as the rise of pension, health, unemployment, and vacation benefits. Even so, it required the unions' capacity and willingness to strike core industries with regularity to confirm this arrangement. The United Steelworkers of America (USW) engaged in national strikes against the steel companies in 1949, 1952, 1955, and 1956, before the great strike of 1959, and, between 1949 and 1960, there was at least one "major work stoppage" (involving one thousand or more workers) each year, which annually involved, on average, one-third of all production workers in the industry. The UAW was similarly obliged to strike at least one of the big three companies to settle virtually every contract during the same period.[13]

---

12   G. Dumenil, M. Glick, and D. Levy, "The Rise of the Rate of Profit During World War II," *Review of Economics and Statistics* vol. 57:2 (May 1993).

13   R. Betheil, "The ENA in Perspective: The Transformation of Collective Bargaining in

Of course, the high frequency of strikes around contract negotiations had as its counterpart union officials' ever more systematic efforts to repress rank-and-file resistance at the point of production and channel discontent through the grievance procedure. This trade-off resulted from the unions' recognition of the bosses' "right to manage" as the condition for securing steady gains in compensation for the membership. The landmark settlement between the auto companies and the UAW of 1950, the so-called "Treaty of Detroit," thus won high praise in business circles because it was understood to obligate the union to cooperate with management in rationalizing the labor process to raise productivity, including by intensifying labor. *Fortune* estimated that "in planning freedom alone the contract is worth fifteen cents per man hour to the corporation," an amount that almost entirely offset the estimated nineteen cents per hour increase in labor costs that the corporation had to shoulder in the contract's first year. The upshot, in Lichtenstein's words, was that "the UAW came increasingly to resemble a combination of political machine and welfare bureaucracy, which 'serviced' the membership and 'policed' the contract." The Reuther administration's ever greater acquiescence over the following decade to the companies' demands at the point of production was evidenced, among other ways, in its growing reluctance to approve locals' requests for work stoppages over work standards, and by the corresponding build-up of no less than 11,000 unresolved grievances between the 1955 and 1958 contracts.[14]

Nevertheless, at the level of the shop floor in union strongholds, workers remained able to resort more or less routinely to direct action to defend and improve their working and living conditions. Despite Walter Reuther's promises to secure the opposite, unofficial walkouts at Ford rose by more than 20 percent during the first half of the 1950s, compared to the second half of the 1940s, centered on the 63,000-worker River Rouge plant, long a fortress of radicals and militants. When the 1955 Ford settlement left hundreds of shop issues unresolved and about three quarters of the Rouge plant negotiating committee dissatisfied, more than 114,000 of Ford's total of 140,000 workers shut down eighty-nine plants and parts depots across the system, almost before Reuther and his counterpart at the corporation could finish shaking hands. At Chrysler, where shop stewards, uniquely within the Big Three, were able to perpetuate their

---

the Basic Steel Industry," *Review of Radical Political Economics* vol. 10:2 (1978), p. 2.

14  N. Lichtenstein, *The Most Dangerous Man in Detroit*, (New York: Basic Books, 1995) pp. 288–92, 296–8; N. Lichtenstein, "UAW Bargaining Strategy," *Industrial Relations*, p. 365 (quotation); N. Lichtenstein, "Auto Worker Militancy and Factory Life, 1937–1945," *Journal of American History* vol. 67:2 (September 1980), pp. 349–53; S. Flaherty, "Mature Collective Bargaining and Rank and File Militancy: Breaking the Peace of the 'Treaty of Detroit,'" in P. Zarembka, ed., *Research in Political Economy* vol. 11 (1988), pp. 249–50 (quote from *Fortune*).

power at the point of production well into the postwar era, there was after 1950 a true explosion of wildcat strikes in response to the company's rationalization efforts. Astoundingly, between 1954 and 1959, the number of unauthorized walkouts rose to nearly double the average annual level that they had reached during the turbulent wartime years between 1941 and 1945, insuring that the company's shop-floor regime would remain by far the most lax among the Big Three and its unit labor costs the highest.[15]

In the steel industry, the Murray leadership of the United Steelworkers Union sought from the end of World War II not only to continue the no-strike pledge, but to forge an explicit productivity deal with management. But an aroused rank and file stopped both of these initiatives in their tracks and went on to construct a maze of work rules that fettered corporate efforts at intensifying labor. In 1955, in the largest of many wildcats in the steel industry during the first half of the decade, 400,000 steelworkers went out on an unauthorized strike over management's refusal to grant a supplementary unemployment benefit plan that would have given workers a minimum annual income regardless of available work or demand. By 1956, to secure the long-term contract that it believed it needed for achieving labor peace and stable production, steel management was obliged to grant a veritable bonanza of improvements in wages, insurance, and pensions to the USW that brought the rate of increase in steelworkers' compensation above that of auto workers for the first time in the postwar era. Even then, the steel corporations were unable to challenge the famous section 2-B of the contract, introduced in 1947, which denied management the right to make any changes in work rules that were not directly the result of the introduction of new machinery or a change in the process of production and which thereby provided steelworkers a shield against speedup probably unmatched in any other industry.[16] The success of industrial workers and their unions in pressuring the corporations, even in the face of the declining productivity increase and slowing GDP growth that came to plague the economy after mid-decade, brought about, in the space of just a few years, a stunning fall-off in the corporate rate of return, putting paid, for the foreseeable future, to any realistic hopes for a sustainable capital-labor equilibrium.

15   Lichtenstein, "UAW Bargaining Strategy," p. 370; Flaherty, "Mature Collective Bargaining," p. 256, Table 1a, "Authorized and Unauthorized Strike Activity at the 'Big Three,'" 1942–59."

16   Betheil, "ENA in Perspective," pp. 2–4; J. D. Rose, "The Struggle over Management Rights at US Steel, 1946–1960: A Reassessment of Section 2-B of the Collective Bargaining Contract," *The Business History Review* vol. 72 (Autumn, 1998), pp. 446–77.

## Economic Stagnation, Employers' Offensive,
## Bureaucratic Complaisance, 1958–65

From the end of the Korean War, the U.S. economy experienced a palpable loss of dynamism. In the business cycles between 1953 and 1959, GDP grew at an average annual rate of only 2.7 percent, substantially below the average annual rate of 4.9 percent between 1948 and 1953, let alone the 5.9 percent average annual rate between 1937 and 1948. Over the course of the 1950s, unemployment remained ominously higher after the completion of each successive cyclical downturn than it had during the previous one.[17] Above all, in the later years of the decade, the manufacturing sector entered into a major crisis of investment growth. Whereas the increase of the manufacturing capital stock averaged 3.3 percent between 1949 and 1957, between 1957 and 1963 it averaged just 1.9 percent. As a student of the economy of the 1950s put it at the time, "Looking at the decade as a whole, most persons would judge the growth rate of output as rather sluggish. If the latter part of the decade is made the reference point, the rate would be judged unsatisfactory, particularly when compared with the 1920s or the long-run performance of the economy prior to the Great Depression of the 1930s."[18]

At the source of the economy's problems was a decline in the manufacturing profit rate, which resulted, most immediately, from a slowdown of manufacturing productivity growth that was not matched by a reduction in wage growth. During the years between 1953 and 1959, manufacturing productivity growth declined by almost 40 percent, compared to that of the Korean War boom between 1948 and 1953, from 3.7 percent per annum to 2.3 percent per annum. But the growth of compensation failed to adjust accordingly. In particular, the generous long-term contracts granted by auto, steel, and electrical employers in the mid-1950s in the interests of stable, uninterrupted production proved to have been based on unrealistic expectations as to the vitality and longevity of the expansion. The outcome was that the manufacturing product wage—that is, the nominal or money wage adjusted for manufacturing product prices—rocketed, making for a big hit to the manufacturing profit share. As a result, the manufacturing rate of profit fell by about one-quarter between

---

17   H. G. Vatter, *The US Economy in the 1950s* (New York: W.W. Norton, 1963), p. 120; A. Hansen, *The Postwar American Economy: Performance and Problems* (New York: W.W. Norton, 1964), pp. 7–12.

18   Hansen, *Postwar American Economy*, p. 8. Compare B. G. Hickman, *Growth and Stability of the Postwar Economy* (Washington, DC: Brookings Institution Press, 1960). Hansen sees these years in terms of "semistagnation," p. 9.

these two intervals. Surprisingly, labor's pressure and wage increase actually squeezed capital's profits, the *only* time this happened during the entire period since World War II.

The wage-productivity squeeze of the later 1950s was exacerbated by the rise of over-capacity. This resulted from an enormous wave of industrial (over-)investment in the middle years of the decade, which, from the close of 1957, came up against the most severe decline in business activity since World War II, itself made worse by the Eisenhower administration's insistence on reducing spending and imposing tighter credit. Symptomatically, from 1956 through 1959, in the steel industry at the heart of the industrial economy, capacity increased by 20 million tons while production fell by 22 million tons. Capacity utilization in the steel industry thus declined from 90 percent to 63 percent, and steel employment plunged by 200,000 workers, with another 300,000 working fewer hours. Meanwhile, by early 1958, auto unemployment had rocketed to 300,000, and nearly 900,000 unsold cars were sitting in factory lots.[19]

The profitability decline and ensuing slide into recession was made much more serious by the emergence of a problem unprecedented in the U.S. economy during the twentieth century—the increasing capacity of manufacturers to produce more profitably abroad than at home in an increasing number of industries. This led to a decline in U.S. manufacturing competitiveness, making for a fall in exports and a rise in imports that ultimately affected profitability itself. At the same time, it further discouraged investment at home, thereby exacerbating the slowdown in productivity growth and profitability. The U.S. economy enjoyed far higher absolute levels of productivity than did its closest rivals, Germany and Japan. But this advantage was more than cancelled out by the relatively higher real wages enjoyed by U.S. workers, an expression of both the historic strength of the U.S. economy and the successes of the U.S. labor movement. In 1950, U.S. manufacturing unit labor costs in dollar terms were, on average, 41 percent higher than Japan's and 37 percent higher than Germany's, and the gap widened over the course of the decade, as productivity growth relative to wage growth in both places increased much faster than in the United States.[20]

---

19  J. Stein, *Running Steel, Running America* (Chapel Hill: University of North Carolina Press, 1998), pp. 21–2; Lichtenstein, *The Most Dangerous Man in Detroit*, p. 295.

20  D. J. Daly, Japanese Manufacturing Competitiveness: Implications for International Trade, University of Toronto–York University Joint Center for Asia Pacific Studies, Working Paper Series, no. 53, August 1988, pp. 35–9.

| Manufacturing Unit Labor Cost Levels, 1950–1960 | | |
|---|---|---|
| (index: United States 1977 = 100) | | |
| | 1950 | 1955 | 1960 |
| United States | 41.8 | 48.9 | 58.7 |
| Germany | 26.2 | 26.9 | 31.1 |
| Japan | 24.6 | 26.6 | 25.0 |
| Source: D. J. Daly, *Japanese Manufacturing Competitiveness* | | |

The relatively high rate of growth of costs was reflected in deepening difficulties for trade. The unit value of manufacturing exports over the course of the 1950s rose by 15 percent in the United States, rose by only 5 percent in Germany, and *fell* by 11 percent in Japan. Between 1950 and 1959, the United States' share of advanced country manufacturing exports declined sharply from 27.1 percent to 21.0 percent.[21] Meanwhile, from 1953 through 1960, manufactured imports (current prices) grew at an average annual rate of 8.4 percent, and exports just 3.1 percent. Especially in the latter part of the decade, when the U.S. economy experienced an initial bout of inflation as employers sought to pass on large nominal wage increases in the form of price increases, U.S. producers had to confront major challenges from their overseas rivals in the economy's core manufacturing industries. In auto, which witnessed the initial invasion of small cars from abroad, in electrical equipment, and especially in steel, where U.S. prices rose well above those of Germany, foreign producers seized startlingly increased shares of the American market in the brief period from 1956 through 1959.[22] The rising pressure in the world market increased manufacturers' disincentive to invest and increase employment within the United States beyond that already resulting from the falling rate of return.

As a powerful expression—and, to a growing degree, a cause—of the stagnation of capital accumulation in the United States, from the mid-1950s U.S. private direct investment overseas grew at the spectacular average annual rate of 10.2 percent, more than twice as fast as domestic investment was growing.[23] Foreign direct investment never represented

21   E. Sohmen, "The Dollar and the Mark," in S. E. Harris, ed., *The Dollar in Crisis* (New York: Harcourt, Brace & World, 1961), p. 194; GATT, Trends in United States Merchandise Trade 1953–1960 (Geneva, July 1972), p. 4, Table 2; A. Maizels, *Industrial Growth and World Trade* (Cambridge: Cambridge University Press, 1963), p. 220.

22   Sohmen, "The Dollar and the Mark," pp. 190–3, where data on relative prices at this time for these industries is presented; H. R. Northrup, "Management's 'New Look' in Labor Relations," *Industrial Relations* vol. 1 (October 1961), p.12, Figure 1, for import figures for core industries.

23   W. H. Branson, "Trends in United States International Trade and Investment Since

more than a small fraction of total investment by U.S. private business
as a whole, but for the U.S. manufacturing sector, led by the great U.S.
multinationals, overseas investment was very significant, and increasingly
so. Between 1957 and 1965, manufacturing investment in new plant and
equipment overseas by majority-owned foreign affiliates of U.S. companies
grew at an astonishing annual average rate of 15.7 percent, compared to 5.6
percent domestically. In just this eight-year period, the ratio of foreign to
domestic investment in new plant and equipment made annually by U.S.-
based manufacturing corporations doubled, growing from 11.8 percent to
22.8 percent.[24] Just as U.S. manufacturing corporations were deterred from
investing in the U.S. domestic economy by downward pressure on the
profit share resulting from the failure of wage growth to adjust downward
to productivity growth, they were increasingly attracted to the superior
opportunities for profit-making overseas, especially in Europe, where they
could combine relatively cheap labor with relatively advanced technology
and produce against relatively weak competitors in rapidly growing
markets.[25]

Ratio of foreign to domestic manufacturing investment by US Corporations. 1957–93

World War II," in M. Feldstein, ed., *The American Economy in Transition* (Chicago: University
of Chicago Press, 1980), p. 238.

24   M. Fahim-Nader, "Capital Expenditures by Majority-Owned Foreign Affiliates of US
Companies," *Survey of Current Business* vol. 74:9 (September 1994), p. 59.

25   As the opposite side of the same coin, by the early 1960s, Europeans were complaining
of the spectacular growth of foreign direct investment by U.S. multinationals, the so-called
"American Challenge." See J. J. Servan-Schreiber, *Le Défi américain* (Paris: Denoël, 1967).

During the last years of the 1950s, the U.S. economy—plagued, it appeared, by "continuing stagnation"—entered into something of a crisis, with two successive cyclical downturns complicated by the sudden deterioration in the U.S. international economic position.[26] In just the two years between 1957 and 1959, while U.S. merchandise imports continued their decade-long accelerating ascent, U.S. merchandise exports *fell* from $19.3 billion to $16.2 billion, the U.S. trade balance decreased from $6.1 billion to only $988 million, and the U.S. share of world exports declined from 19.3 percent to 16.2 percent. The export decline would have come sooner and been more severe had the Suez Crisis not hurt the exports of U.S. allies in 1956–7. As it was, the balance on the current account did go negative in 1959. The problem was particularly acute in trade between the United States and its rising competitors. As late as the mid-1950s, the United States had enjoyed a substantial trade surplus with both Germany and Japan. But by 1959 the trade balance had fallen to $50 million with Japan and had actually gone into the red by $40 million with Germany.[27]

In response to their burgeoning problems of productivity, profitability, and competitiveness, manufacturing employers had little choice but to seek control of production costs, and they did so in standard fashion. Firms reduced their placements of new capital, so investment stagnated from the later 1950s through the early 1960s, while the growth of non-farm employment was cut in half, from 2.4 percent to 1.1 percent. The resulting rise in joblessness, which saw the average unemployment rate in the period of 1957–63 increase more than 50 percent compared to the years 1948–57, softened up the labor market. Against this background, firms unleashed a powerful across-the-board assault on workers and their institutions, and achieved what turned out to be a fundamental shift in the balance of class power and in the character of labor–management relations. In the process, they demonstrated in practice why workers cannot, as a rule, impose a squeeze on capitalist profitability for very long and thereby, on their own, cause a sustained crisis.

There has never been, in the postwar United States, anything like a capital-labor accord. Nevertheless, during the boom years that marked the period from the later 1940s through the end of the Korean conflict, employers intent on reaping high profits by maintaining uninterrupted

---

26  Phrase in quotation marks is from Sohmen, "The Dollar and the Mark," p. 195.

27  Vatter, *US Economy in the 1950s*, pp. 262–7; Maizels, *Industrial Growth and World Trade*, p. 220; T. Liesner, *One Hundred Years of Economic Statistics* (New York: Facts on File, 1989), Table US15; V. Argy, *Postwar International Money Crisis* (London: George Allen & Unwin, 1981), pp. 33–4.

production to meet elevated demand took an approach to labor that could be described as relatively accommodating.[28] But facing a major wage-productivity profit squeeze during the later 1950s and confronting simultaneously an unprecedented threat from international competition, employers reversed direction and took up what was immediately recognized at the time as a "new hard line," and found major support at the level of the polity.[29] The Republican right unleashed a series of efforts to pass right-to-work laws, making the union shop illegal in the emerging Sunbelt. But much more problematic for labor, the Eisenhower, Kennedy, and Johnson administrations, with effectively no opposition from massive Democratic Party majorities in Congress, imposed ever more systematic wage-price guidelines. These were, in the first instance, intended to keep prices from rising, especially in the face of a Kennedy-Johnson experiment in military Keynesianism, driven, as it would be later under Ronald Reagan, by tax cuts for corporations and expenditure increases for the armed forces. But, especially following Kennedy's humiliating back-down from his 1962 confrontation with the steel owners, the guidelines were directed in practice only at labor and wages, with the aim of backing up the efforts of capital to restore its profits and increase its international competitiveness, while government deficits pushed the economy forward.[30]

Big corporations in manufacturing, especially in those industries where international competition had increased most, confronted and defeated the labor movement in a series of battles between 1958 and 1961. In auto, the 1958 stalemate in bargaining brought the union unusually small gains, compared to the early postwar period. In steel, the great 163-day strike of

---

28  For this generalization, see, for example, T. A. Kochan and M. J. Piore, "US Industrial Relations in Transition," and J. A. Klein and E. D. Wanger, "The Legal Setting for the Emergence of the Union Avoidance Strategy," both in T. A. Kochan, ed., *Challenges and Choices Facing American Labor* (Cambridge, MA: MIT Press, 1985).

29  Around 1960 there was a sudden spate of literature on the employers' new hard line. In this and the following two paragraphs, I depend especially on two lengthy symposia, "The Employer Challenge and the Union Response," *Industrial Relations* vol. 1:1 (October 1961), and "The Crisis in the American Trade-Union Movement," *The Annals of the American Academy of Political and Social Science* vol. 350 (November 1963)—particularly H. R. Northrup, "Management's 'New Look' in Labor Relations," in the first of these, and G. Strauss, "Union Bargaining Strength: Goliath or Paper Tiger?" in the second. I also draw upon D. J. B. Mitchell, "Recent Union Contract Concessions," *Brookings Papers on Economic Activity* #1 (1982), p. 174, and D. J. B. Mitchell, *Unions, Wages, and Inflation* (Washington, DC: Brookings Institution, 1980), pp. 45–7. Cf. G. Strauss, "The Shifting Power Balance in the Plant," *Industrial Relations* vol. 1:3 (May 1962). For a penetrating overview of the employers' offensive and ensuing conflicts, see M. Davis, *Prisoners of the American Dream* pp. 121–4.

30  Stein, *Running Steel, Running America*, pp. 26–30.

1959 won the United Steelworkers virtually nothing, though they were able preserve section 2-B of their contract. In aircraft, the United Auto Workers and the International Association of Machinists lost a strike against the United Aircraft Corporation when the company managed to operate throughout the dispute. Finally, there was the ill-advised General Electric strike of 1960 in which the International Union of Electrical Workers struck some fifty plants, but was forced to accept the widely publicized terms the company had offered before the start of the work stoppage.

Management's new look was also evident in its increasing, and increasingly successful, resistance to the extension of unionization, particularly in newly constructed plants, many of them "runaways" relocated in the South and Southwest. The National Labor Relations Board appointed by Eisenhower aided this process by handing down a series of pro-business interpretations of the already fiercely anti-labor Taft-Hartley Act. Firms were thus able to interfere with union organizing efforts much more openly and powerfully than at any time since the passage of the Wagner Act in 1935. Beginning in the mid- to late 1950s, the number of illegal actions committed by management in the course of union recognition campaigns, after declining for years, began to soar, and unions found it significantly harder to win recognition.[31] The proportion of union victories in NLRB elections fell from 73.5 percent in the years 1950–5 to 63 percent in the years 1955–60 to 56 percent in the years 1960–5. Unions had been able to organize 2 percent of all private wage and salary workers in the year 1950 and 1 percent in the year 1955, but by the year 1960 only 0.7 percent. Between 1953 and 1965 the percentage of the private sector labor force that was unionized fell from its peak of 35.7 percent to 30.8 percent—from 42.4 percent to 37.2 percent in manufacturing.[32]

Employers also stepped up their efforts to control the shop floor. Urged on by a phalanx of newly hired, college-trained labor-relations professionals, employers sought to reverse a relatively loose regime of supervision on the shop floor, under which foremen had been allowed considerable leeway in keeping the peace with the rank and file. At the same time, employers suddenly began to stand firm against unofficial strikes.[33] These trends only

31   Klein and Wanger, "The Legal Setting for the Emergence of the Union Avoidance Strategy"; R. B. Freeman, "Why Are Unions Faring Poorly in NLRB Representation Elections?" in Kochan, ed., *Challenges and Choices Facing American Labor*, pp. 46, 53.

32   Goldfield, *Decline of Organized Labor*, pp. 10, 90; R. B. Freeman, "Contraction and Expansion: The Divergence of Private Sector and Public Sector Unionism in the United States," *Journal of Economic Perspectives* vol. 2 (Spring 1988), p. 64; L. Troy and N. Sheflin, *Union Sourcebook* (Trenton, NJ: Industrial Relations Data and Information Services, 1985).

33   Lichtenstein, "UAW Bargaining Strategy," pp. 376–7.

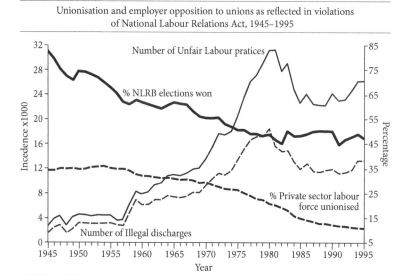

Unionisation and employer opposition to unions as reflected in violations
of National Labour Relations Act, 1945–1995

became more pronounced over time, suggesting that in postwar relations between capital and labor, the decade from the mid-1950s to the mid-1960s marked a turning point.

The material gains employers accrued from their new hard line were dramatic. They turned the tide on wage growth, especially in manufacturing. From 1959 to 1965, the rate of growth of manufacturing real compensation fell by almost half, to only 2.1 percent, compared to 3.6 percent for the years between 1948 and 1959, despite the fact that accelerating economic growth was bringing about a reduction of unemployment in these years, from 6.8 percent in 1958 to 4.5 percent in 1965. Employers were also able to secure striking gains in productiveness. Labor productivity in manufacturing grew at the impressive average annual rate of 3.8 percent, higher than in any other comparable period after 1950 (before the 1990s). More rapid technological advance was perhaps partly responsible for this increase. Nevertheless, management appears to have extracted the greater part of it directly from workers themselves. Between 1958 and 1965, the amount of plant and equipment per worker-hour grew very slowly, as the net capital-labor ratio increased far less rapidly than in any other comparable period in the postwar epoch. Between 1958 and 1965, the average annual rate of growth of the net capital-labor ratio was only 0.6 percent, compared to 3.5 percent between 1950 and 1958 and 3.9 percent between 1965 and 1973. Much of the gain in productiveness registered in this new era of employers' offensive was thus evidently achieved by a combination of shedding less productive plant equipment and impelling workers to labor more intensely, otherwise known as speedup.

Labor officials did little to respond to the employers' pressure on their members' wages and shop-floor conditions, implicitly accepting the corporations' need to increase their competitiveness and rates of return as the precondition for further gains for their memberships. While employers recovered their cost position at the expense of workers during the first half of the 1960s, the official union leadership accepted with barely a murmur both the major reduction in the growth of compensation in manufacturing and employers' moves to rationalize production via labor intensification. Union resistance to the employers fell to a postwar low, as the official leaderships increasingly eschewed the strike weapon and cut back on efforts to organize new workers. Whereas the loss of total work time resulting from official work stoppages had averaged 0.23 percent during the years 1950–8, it averaged 0.16 percent during the years 1958–65. Whereas the proportion of the labor force involved in official work stoppages had averaged 4.44 percent during the years 1950–8, it averaged 2.63 percent during the years 1958–65. Twenty major unions had spent $1.03 and $1.02 per non-union employee on organizing in 1953 and 1955 respectively, but that figure fell to $0.95 in 1960 and just $0.83 by 1965.[34]

Union officials across the manufacturing sector were not content to accede to employers' demands, but went out of their way to assist the restructuring of operations. Perhaps the most striking instance was in steel. Here, even as the brutal strike of 1959 was at its most confrontational, the companies were calling for a new, more collaborative bargaining structure, and the union, under the leadership of its president, David McDonald, was responding favorably, ultimately headlining its own report on the settlement reached at the end of the bitter conflict, "Strike-Free Industry Seen as Next Steel Worker Goal." That contract established a new labor–management Human Relations Committee, and beginning in spring 1960 and continuing through the first half of the 1960s (and beyond), the union leadership and the company settled their differences virtually entirely through joint participation on this body. The Human Relations Committee met more or less continuously behind closed doors, preventing the rank and file from participating in or scrutinizing negotiations, and offered contracts to the membership as faits accomplis. The results were stunning. The union gave up the so-called annual improvement factor and ceded Cost-of-living adjustments (COLA), while accepting 2 percent and 2.5 percent wage increases for 1962 and 1963, respectively, which barely matched the rate of inflation. Meanwhile, the union leadership and companies moved in incremental fashion to bring about changes in job classification, seniority, and work rules that management had long desired but which had hitherto

---

34   Freeman, "Why Are Unions Faring Poorly?" p. 51, Table 3.2.

been ruled off the table by the militancy of the membership. Whereas real wages in steel had increased at an average annual rate of 3.76 percent in the years 1949–60 inclusive, they rose at an annual average rate of just 0.44 percent in the years 1961–70 inclusive. In the words of the *New York Times*, the steel industry had "passed into a new era of accommodation."[35]

The trajectory in the auto industry during the same period was not all that different. With unemployment soaring in early 1958, the Big Three automakers seized the moment to stand firm against significant gains in wages, benefits, and job security in the 1958 contract, and to impose significant work rules changes. Chrysler, long the least competitive among the Big Three, saw its chance to close the gap between itself and GM and Ford with respect to both production costs and shop-floor discipline by moving to disperse the powerful shop stewards organization at the company, which, since the later 1930s, had been a bulwark of workers' control over the labor process. In response, the UAW's big Detroit Chrysler locals demanded strike authorization. But Walter Reuther and his executive board acceded to company demands. Fearful that Chrysler might go bankrupt, they stalled, giving the company "the chance to grind down the opposition, set new production standards, and suppress the wildcat strike tradition."[36] Reuther repeated the pattern at GM in 1961 and 1964. When in 1961 the UAW's GM council voted for a company-wide shutdown to support striking locals in their unresolved bargaining demands, Reuther refused to go along, and, within a week, the union's executive board had rescinded strike authorization for those locals still out on strike.[37] In 1964, despite placing at the top of his negotiating agenda working conditions, speedup, and "dignity and humanity on the job," and despite being forced to strike by the UAW's top negotiating team, Reuther intervened directly to force a settlement, confronting, local by local, the most steadfast shop-floor militants, for whom the ubiquitous bumper-sticker "Humanize Working Conditions" had become a rallying cry. Tellingly, the *New York Times* applauded Reuther for letting his rank and file "blow off steam" to avoid a real rebellion.[38]

Given their unions' cooperative strategy, rank and filers who wished to

---

35  Betheil, "The ENA in Perspective," pp.1–3, 5–10 (quotation).

36  Lichtenstein, *The Most Dangerous Man in Detroit*, pp. 289–90, 295–6 (quotation). See also W. Serrin, *The Company and the Union: The "Civilized Relationship" of the General Motors Corporation and the United Automobile Workers* (New York: Vintage Books, 1974), pp. 231–2.

37  S. Flaherty, "Mature Collective Bargaining and Rank and File Militancy," pp. 261–2 (quotation).

38  Lichtenstein, *The Most Dangerous Man in Detroit*, pp. 397–401 (Reuther quote, p. 397); Flaherty, "Mature Collective Bargaining," pp. 262, 277, n.17.

defend their living and working standards against the employers' "hard line" had little choice but to take matters into their own hands.[39] Between 1960 and 1966, workers resorted to wildcat strikes with increasing frequency, the percentage of strikes during the term of the agreement rising from 22 percent of all strikes in 1960 (the first year of reporting) to 36.5 percent in 1966. They also increasingly voted down the contracts negotiated by their leaders, with the percentage of rejections growing steadily and increasing by more than 60 percent between 1964 and 1967, with leading industrial unions like the machinists, the auto workers, and longshoremen especially affected.[40] At the same time, to try to secure a more militant and effective union leadership, rank and filers supported a series of successful campaigns to replace insufficiently militant local officers, as well as long-entrenched top union bureaucrats. In the single year 1963, more than one-third of the top officials in UAW production locals were voted out of office.[41] In the years that followed, long-ruling arch-bureaucrats in steel, electrical, rubber, and, later, coal were all forced to go. Still, well past mid-decade employers were having their way and the passivity of the unions and their conservative bureaucratic leaderships was apparent. This was implicitly acknowledged even by the chair of the Council of Economic Advisers, Gardner Ackley, when, in May 1966, he said, "labor cannot be expected to continue honoring the [administration's voluntary wage-price] guidelines as well as it has when it sees prices and profit margins continually rising."[42]

Despite the initial expressions of rank-and-file self-organization during the first half of the 1960s, employers succeeded in repressing wage growth and increasing measured output per hour and per unit of capital, opening the way to a significant recovery of competitiveness. After experiencing mounting pressure from abroad for almost a decade, U.S. firms turned the tables and put the squeeze on their overseas rivals. Between 1960 and 1965, unit labor costs (expressed in dollars) in manufacturing in the United States actually *fell* by 5.2 percent, while those in Germany and Japan rose

---

39 See S. Weir, "USA: The Labor Revolt," *International Socialist Journal* vol. 4:20–21 (April–June 1967), for an incisive analysis of the nascent rebellion from below.

40 J. Barbash, "The Causes of Rank-and-File Unrest," in J. Seidman, ed., *Trade Union Government and Collective Bargaining* (New York: Praeger, 1970), pp. 41, 45, 51–3; W. E. Simkin, "Refusals to Ratify Contracts," *Industrial and Labor Relations Review* vol. 21 (July 1968), p. 520. There are no statistics on unofficial strikes per se, so data on strikes during the period of the contract—not the same thing, but hopefully a decent surrogate—are used to stand for them.

41 N. Lichtenstein, "The Treaty of Detroit: Old Before Its Time," paper presented at the American Historical Association Annual Convention, January 1995. I wish to thank Nelson Lichtenstein for allowing me to make reference to this paper.

42 *Business Week*, May 12, 1966. I owe this reference to Dean Baker.

by 24.7 percent and 22.9 percent, respectively. In turn, U.S. export prices grew at an average annual rate of only 1.3 percent between 1960 and 1965 (only 0.6 between 1960 and 1964). This was only slightly more slowly than Germany's 1.4 percent over the same period, and still not as slowly as Japan's 0.3 percent (0.5 percent between 1960 and 1964). But, in view of how much more rapidly unit labor costs in Japan and Germany grew in this period than in the United States, it is evident that producers in both countries were obliged to accept reductions in profitability to keep their export price increases so very low.

On the basis of capital's renewed capacity to control costs, the economy achieved a new export boom. Between 1958 and 1965, the average annual growth of exports increased to 7.1 percent, from 4.4 percent between 1950 and 1958. The U.S. merchandise trade balance had drifted downward during the 1950s to an average of slightly under $3 billion for the years 1958–60. But it increased to $7 billion by 1964 and was still at $5.3 billion in 1965, and it had recovered particularly well in relation to Germany and Japan. As a result, the current account, which had gone negative in 1959, reached a peak of $5.8 billion in 1964, and remained at $4.3 billion in 1965.

The upshot was a major economic turnaround, led by the manufacturing sector. Between 1959 and 1965, GDP jumped up at an average annual rate of 4.6 percent, almost as fast as the 4.9 percent average annual rate achieved between 1948 and 1953, when the Korean War was pushing the economy forward, and far faster than the average annual rate of 2.8 percent between 1953 and 1959. At the same time, manufacturing output grew at an average annual pace of 5.5 percent, more than double the 2.3 percent achieved between 1949 and 1959. These improvements were part and parcel of a simultaneous takeoff in the rate of profit. Between 1960 and 1965, the level of the profit rate in manufacturing rose by 50 percent, in the private business economy by 45 percent. Thanks especially to the assault on a largely undefended industrial labor force, American capital seemed to have regained its equilibrium.

## Descent into Crisis, Class Struggle, and the Rank-and-File Rebellion

Nevertheless, the U.S. economic recovery of the first half of the 1960s proved very short-lived. Between 1965 and 1973 the rates of profit in the manufacturing and private business sectors fell by 40.9 percent and 29.3 percent, respectively. Put another way, from the business cycle that marked the height of the long postwar upturn, which ran from the second quarter of 1960 through to the third quarter of 1969, to the first business cycle of the long downturn, which ran from the fourth quarter of 1969 through to the third quarter of 1973, the average rates of profit in the manufacturing and private business sectors fell by 31 percent and 18.5 percent, respectively. Profitability in the U.S. economy thus began a downward trajectory that would not bottom out until the early 1980s and that profoundly affected the labor movement and working-class resistance.

### Was Intensified Labor Resistance Behind the Fall in the Rate of Profit?
It has become something of an accepted argument that an increase in workers' power and militancy, conditioned by rapidly falling unemployment, was responsible for the squeeze on profit rates that took place in this period. This mechanism is said to have operated through one or both of two channels, either a "wage explosion" expressing stronger workers' organization or a "productivity crisis" reflecting stepped-up on-the-job resistance. But this perspective does not cohere with the actual economic trends.[43]

The average annual growth of real compensation in manufacturing actually fell steadily, in both the long run and the short run—from 3.6 percent between 1948 and 1959 to 1.95 percent between 1959 and 1965 to 1.9 percent between 1965 and 1973, when profitability first fell. In the private economy as a whole, the trend was similar, as the rate of growth of real compensation registered 3.3 percent, 2.2 percent, and 1.9 percent, respectively, for the same intervals. The tendency of real wages offers little evidence of either increasing workers' power or growing wage pressure on profits.

The notion of a "productivity slowdown" has equally little basis in fact. In manufacturing, labor productivity growth actually sped up to 3.3 percent during the period of falling profitability between 1965 and 1973, over and against 2.9 percent between 1948 and 1965. In the private business economy, labor productivity growth averaged 2.7 percent between 1965 and 1973, compared to 2.8 percent between 1948 and 1965. These numbers cannot support a case for increasing shop-floor power translating into rising costs for employers.

Indeed, the notion of a wage-productivity squeeze on profits, resulting from the increased power of and pressure from labor, entirely disintegrates when the forces that actually brought down profitability between 1965 and 1973 are delineated. This is accomplished by comparing trends within the manufacturing sector to those in the rest of the economy outside it. The

---

43   For left versions of this position, see the works of the American Social Structure of Accumulation School and the French Regulation School. For a joint and fully elaborated statement of the position, see A. Glyn, A. Lipietz, A. Hughes, and A. Singh, "The Rise and Fall of the Golden Age," in S. Marglin and J. Schor, eds, *The Golden Age* (Oxford: Clarendon Press, 1990). For an interesting center-left version, see J. Sachs, "Wages, Profits, and Macroeconomic Adjustment," *Brookings Papers on Economic Activity* #2 (1979). For a sophisticated presentation of the interpretation from the right, see A. Lindbeck, "What Is Wrong with the West European Economies?" *The World Economy* vol. VIII (June 1985).

basic point is that almost the entirety of the decline in the rate of profit that took place in the private economy between 1965 and 1973 occurred in the manufacturing sector, where the profit rate dropped by 41.9 percent, compared to just 13.1 percent in non-manufacturing (leaving aside the impact of changes in indirect business taxes). This occurred despite the fact that cost pressures resulting from the movements of productivity and wages were much *lower* in manufacturing than in non-manufacturing. Thus, because, between 1965 and 1973, productivity increased at a rate of just 2.4 percent in non-manufacturing, compared to 3.3 percent in manufacturing, and because the rate of increase of the nominal wage was 7.2 percent in non-manufacturing, compared to 6.4 percent in manufacturing, unit labor costs rose at a rate of 4.7 percent in non-manufacturing, compared to just 3.05 percent in manufacturing. But, again, it was manufacturing that was the scene of most of the fall in the profit rate. Whereas the average rate of profit in manufacturing in the business cycle between 1969 and 1973 was a full one-third lower than in the business cycle between 1959 and 1969, it was less than 7 percent lower in the non-manufacturing sector.

| Net Profit Rates: Average Levels, 1948–1990 (percent) | | | | | | |
|---|---|---|---|---|---|---|
| | 1948–1959 | 1959–1969 | 1969–1973 | 1973–1979 | 1969–1979 | 1979–1990 |
| Manufacturing | 25 | 24.6 | 16.6 | 14 | 15.05 | 13 |
| Non-Manufacturing | 11 | 11.1 | 10.4 | 10.3 | 10.3 | 9.1 |
| Total Private | 19.9 | 20.8 | 18.3 | 16.3 | 17.1 | 15 |
| Source: See R. Brenner, *The Economics of Global Turbulence*, Appendix 1 | | | | | | |

Since cost pressure was so much greater in non-manufacturing than in manufacturing, yet profitability fell so much further in manufacturing than non-manufacturing, it is evident that rising costs—attributable to rising workers' power or anything else—were *not* at the root of the profitability decline. The source of the problem lay elsewhere, not in costs per se, but the *capacity to absorb them* through increasing prices. It was because manufacturers were so much less able to raise their prices vis-à-vis costs than non-manufacturers—manufacturing prices rose at 2.1 percent per annum compared to 4.4 percent per annum in non-manufacturing—that they were obliged to accept the huge decline in profitability that their counterparts outside of manufacturing largely avoided.

The question that thus imposes itself is why?

| | Manufacturing | Non-manufacturing |
|---|---|---|
| **The Growth of Costs, Prices and Profitability in the United States, 1965–73 Manufacturing versus Non-Manufacturing (Percentage Rates of Change)** *Not adjusted for indirect business taxes* | | |
| Net profit rate | −6 | −1.7 |
| Net profit share | −2.8 | −0.7 |
| Real wage | 1.9 | 2.7 |
| Product wage | 4.2 | 2.7 |
| Labor productivity | 3.3 | 2.35 |
| Nominal wage | 6.4 | 7.2 |
| Unit labor costs | 3.05 | 4.7 |
| Product price | 2.1 | 4.4 |
| Output-capital ratio | −3.4 | −1 |
| Real output-capital ratio | −0.4 | 0 |
| Capital stock price | 5.2 | 5.6 |
| Source: See R. Brenner, *The Economics of Global Turbulence*, Appendix II | | |

## The Onset of Over-capacity in International Manufacturing

From the start of the 1960s, in the wake of the establishment of currency convertibility throughout most of the advanced capitalist world at the end of the 1950s and the initiation of the movement to reduce trade barriers, the growth of world trade accelerated, with far-reaching though contradictory consequences for the international economy. Between 1963 and 1973, with the volume of both world exports and world manufacturing exports increasing 42 percent faster than between 1953 and 1963, the growth of exports began to outrun the growth of domestic production in a truly radical fashion. Already growing 50 percent faster than world manufacturing output between 1953 and 1963, world manufacturing exports were suddenly increasing almost twice as fast. Between 1960 and 1974, in the advanced capitalist economies, the average annual rate of growth of manufacturing exports was two-thirds faster than that of manufacturing output—9.9 percent compared to 5.9 percent.[44]

---

44   Glyn et al., "Rise and Fall of the Golden Age," p. 111.

| World Exports and World Output | | | |
|---|---|---|---|
| | annual growth rates | | ratio of annual growth rates |
| | 1953–63 | 1963–73 | 1963–73/1953–63 |
| World Exports | 9.2% | 13.1% | 1.42 |
| World Output | 6.7% | 8.0% | 1.19 |
| Exports/Output | 1.4 | 1.63 | |
| World Mfgr. Exports | 12.7% | 18.0% | 1.42 |
| World Mfgr. Output | 8.5% | 9.7% | 1.14 |
| Mfgr.Exp./Mfgr.Out. | 1.49 | 1.86 | |
| Constructed from Van Der Wee, *Prosperity and Upheaval*, p. 260 | | | |

Part and parcel of the same development, from the early to mid-1960s, exports as a proportion of output (the export share) for the OECD as a whole, as well as for its component parts, was suddenly growing at twice the pace it had previously. The export shares of the OECD as a whole, and of its European and U.S. components, thus grew the same amount in the eight years between 1965 and 1973 as in the fifteen years between 1950 and 1965. The increase in the rate of growth of Japan's export share began a bit earlier, and was equally sharp.

| Percentage Growth of Export Shares of GDP (constant prices) | | | | | | |
|---|---|---|---|---|---|---|
| | 1950 | 1965 | Increase | 1965 | 1973 | Increase |
| OECD Total | 09.0 | 12.4 | 37.7 | 12.4 | 16.8 | 35.4 |
| OECD Europe | 12.7 | 18.1 | 42.1 | 18.1 | 25.6 | 42.9 |
| United States | 04.3 | 05.1 | 35.0 | 05.1 | 06.9 | 36.0 |
| | | | | | | |
| | 1950 | 1960 | Increase | 1960 | 1973 | Increase |
| Japan | 04.7 | 05.6 | 19.0 | 05.6 | 07.9 | 38.0 |
| Source: Glyn et al., *The Rise and Fall of the Golden Age*, p. 43 | | | | | | |

The rapid increase in the growth of trade from the early 1960s had a dual effect on the economic evolution of the advanced capitalist economies. On the one hand, it had just the impact it was supposed to have: in classical fashion, it helped make possible the accelerated economic expansion of the advanced capitalist economies by means of the growth of the international division of labor. Between 1965 and 1970, as world trade grew faster, the

G-7 capitalist economies *outside* the United States reached the zenith of their postwar boom, with manufacturing output, labor productivity, and investment increasing substantially faster than over the previous decade, and manufacturing profitability enjoying something of turnaround from its major downward drift between 1960 and 1965.

On the other hand, due precisely to the precipitous growth in world trade in these years, new producers, without warning, began to supply radically increased fractions of the world market, challenging long-ensconced incumbents, with severely disruptive consequences. Despite the rapid growth of trade from the start of the postwar boom, economic development into the early 1960s in the advanced capitalist countries was actually characterized by relatively separate development on the part of the three main economic blocs—the United States, western Europe, and Japan—paralleled by a relatively high level of diversification within regions and nations. The technologically following, later developing, and fast-growing economies of western Europe and Japan were thus producing bundles of goods that were *quite similar* to those already being produced by the technologically leading, earlier developing economies, namely the United States (and to some extent the United Kingdom). It was therefore inevitable that they would develop their export potential by increasing the output of such goods. As the OECD explained, "the industrial countries' patterns of trade and output tended to converge, with most countries increasingly producing and exchanging similar commodities."[45] Indeed, later entrants into the world market had every reason to increase their exports of goods that they were already producing for the domestic market, since they could often do so at a lower cost than could the earlier developing incumbents. The newer, lower-cost producers—notably Germany and, above all, Japan—thus expanded their exports largely by invading markets hitherto dominated by producers of the leader regions, especially the United States and the United Kingdom. This made for the growth of output that was *competitive and redundant, rather than complementary*, with respect to the output that was already being produced. The trend had, of course, already been evident to some extent during the 1950s and early 1960s, but now it was radically accelerated.

During the second half of the 1960s, taking advantage of slowdowns in the growth of costs that had been brought about by unusually severe mid-decade recessions in both countries, the German and Japanese economies were able to sharply increase their vitality. In these years, the Japanese economy in particular reached the apogee of its postwar growth, achieving unprecedented increases in investment and productivity, and on that

---

45   OECD, *Structural Adjustment and Economic Performance* (Paris: OECD, 1987), p. 269.

basis posing a wide-ranging challenge to U.S. manufacturing supremacy. Between 1960 and 1965, the ratios of Japanese and German to U.S. annual average labor productivity growth in manufacturing were about two to one and 1.5 to one, respectively (8.7 percent and 6.2 percent to 4.4 percent); between 1965 and 1970, these ratios grew to about five to one and three to one, respectively (12.4 percent and 5.9 percent to 2.6 percent).

U.S. manufacturing's problem of increasingly slow productivity growth *in relative terms* was exacerbated by the renewed outbreak of inflation after 1965, provoked by the rapid rise of government deficits and accommodated by easy money. The sharp increase in the rate of growth of the nominal wage that took place did not cause the increased growth of prices; indeed, it was insufficient to prevent real wage growth from falling slightly. Nevertheless, in attempting (unsuccessfully) to keep up with the increase in the rate of growth of the consumer price index brought on by government fiscal and monetary policies, workers raised the nominal wage so as to create a rising floor on prices and thereby helped to further fuel inflation, undermining competitiveness.

Between 1965 and 1970, the growth of manufacturing unit labor costs in the United States in dollar terms, at 4.2 percent, was roughly double that in Japan, at 2.25 percent, and more than triple that in Germany, at 1.3 percent (between 1965 and 1969). The recovery of export price competitiveness that had been achieved by U.S. manufacturers during the first half of the 1960s thus turned out to be only temporary. Between 1965 and 1970, export prices grew at an average annual rate of 3.2 percent in the United States, compared to 0.9 percent in Japan and 1.7 percent in Germany (between 1965 and 1969), obviously with serious negative consequences for U.S. producers' competitive position and in turn their profitability.

A comparison of cost *levels* in U.S. manufacturing with those of Germany and Japan indicates the sort of competitive pressures to which U.S. producers were being subjected. According to data provided by the U.S. Bureau of Labor Statistics, by 1970 average labor productivity in Japanese and German manufacturing had only reached 50 percent and 75 percent of the U.S. level, respectively. But since manufacturing wages in Germany and Japan were 60 percent and 25 percent, respectively, of those in the United States, manufacturing unit labor costs in Germany and Japan turned out to be, respectively, 80 percent and less than 50 percent those in the United States.[46] In their comparative study of the

---

46  Daly, "Japanese Manufacturing Competitiveness," pp. 35, 37, 39. These figures may exaggerate the average manufacturing productivity gap between the United States and Japan. According to the Japan Productivity Center *Report on International Comparison of Labor Productivity* (Tokyo, 1981), in 1974 U.S. labor productivity was just 38 percent higher

evolution of costs in the United States and Japan, Jorgenson and Kuroda were able to conclude that:

> in 1970, on the eve of the Smithsonian Agreements . . . almost all Japanese industries were more competitive internationally than their US counterparts. By this we mean that they could provide products to the international marketplace at prices below those available from their US competitors.[47]

It is no wonder that already by 1969—even before the recession of 1970 registered its substantial additional impact on profitability—the rate of profit in the U.S. manufacturing sector had already fallen no less than 33 percent below its level in 1965, when it had reached its peak, whereas the rate of profit outside manufacturing had fallen by a scant 5 percent below its level in 1965 (and had actually *increased* each year between 1965 and 1968).

As a consequence of U.S. manufacturers' growing inability to match the costs of their chief overseas rivals, the United States experienced a true crisis of trade in the later 1960s and early 1970s. Having stabilized itself at around 24 percent over the years 1958–65, the U.S. share of the manufacturing exports of the main industrial countries fell sharply by a third, to around 18 percent, from 1965 to 1973.[48] Simultaneously, there was a massive invasion of manufactured imports, as foreign-made steel, autos, machine tools, machinery, consumer electronics, and the like quickly grabbed a significant share of the U.S. market. Until this point, the twentieth-century U.S. economy had been remarkably self-enclosed, a reflection of its superior productiveness and competitiveness, as well as the costs of trans-oceanic transport. But change came suddenly and dramatically from the mid-1960s. Between 1965 and 1970, manufacturing imports grew at an average annual pace of 19.1 percent, twice as fast as during the comparable period of the 1950s. The manufacturing import penetration ratio, still averaging only 6.9 percent over the years 1959–66, grew to an average of 11.9 percent in 1966–9 and to an average of 15.8 percent in 1969–73.[49]

---

than that in the Japan. (M. Bronfenbrenner, "Japanese Productivity Experience," in W. J. Baumol and K. McLennan, eds, *Productivity Growth and US Competitiveness* [New York: Oxford University Press, 1985], p. 71.)

47   D. W. Jorgenson and M. Kuroda, "Productivity and International Competitiveness in Japan and the United States, 1960–85," *The Economic Studies Quarterly* vol. 93 (December 1992), p. 314.

48   B. R. Scott, "US Competitiveness: Concepts, Performance, and Implications," in B. R. Scott and G. C. Lodge, eds, *US Competitiveness in the World Economy* (Cambridge, MA: Harvard University Business Press, 1985), p. 27.

49   Scott, "US Competitiveness," p. 22; Krause, "US Economy and International

Of course, U.S. manufacturers' loss of markets abroad and at home represented only the tip of the iceberg, and provides only a partial indication of the decline in U.S. manufacturing competitiveness in this era and of the damage visited by declining competitiveness on the economic health of U.S. manufacturers. To the degree that they avoided ceding market share, and *as a condition for retaining it*, U.S. manufacturers had to refrain from raising prices as much in proportion to costs as they had been accustomed to doing, with unavoidable consequences for profitability. It is the accelerated injection of lower cost, lower priced, *redundant* manufacturers onto the world market—making for the rise of over-capacity and over-production on an international scale—that therefore constitutes the key to the puzzle of the relatively slow growth of manufacturing prices in this period, and therefore to the resulting fall in the manufacturing rate of profit. Because its output was composed largely of tradables, the manufacturing sector was highly exposed to intensifying international competition. In contrast, despite sustaining increases in unit labor costs and capital costs that, taken together, were substantially higher than those in manufacturing, the private business economy outside of manufacturing, which was largely immune from international competition, experienced a very much more limited fall in profitability because its firms could raise prices in line with much faster growing costs almost as easily as before.

## Rank-and-File Revolt

Against this economic background, we can better specify the significance of action by labor in the years of declining profitability between 1965 and 1973. A major eruption of labor militancy did certainly take place in this period. But that outbreak should be understood much more as an indirect effect of the fall in the rate of profit than a significant cause. It represented, in part, an effort on the part of organized labor, pressured by an increasingly restive rank and file, to counter an employers' offensive, dating back to the end of the 1950s, which was now becoming even more severe in response to the reverses suffered by capital as a consequence of the rise of over-capacity on a system-wide scale, as well as declining U.S. competitiveness. It represented, beyond that, the frustration of rank-and-file workers across the economy with their unions' failure to defend their condition, either on the shop floor or at the bargaining table, and their attempt to take matters into their own hands, not only by compelling their unions to strike on a

---

Trade," p. 395; T. Weisskopf, "Sources of Profit Rate Decline in the Advanced Capitalist Economies: An Empirical Test of the High-Employment Profit Squeeze Theory," unpublished manuscript, University of Michigan (December 1985), Table 10.

scale and scope not seen since the early 1950s, but by organizing wildcat strikes and constructing their own rank-and-file organizations to oblige the unions to make a more aggressive and more effective retort to the employers.

Employers had, as has been seen, originally unleashed their onslaught in order to hold down wages and to increase shop-floor discipline so as to both reverse the wage-productivity squeeze on profits that had overtaken manufacturing in the early and mid-1950s and to respond to the onset of international competition in manufacturing. Though successful in the first half of the 1960s, the employers faced an even more serious challenge in the years that followed. They were therefore impelled to reduce wage growth even further, while accelerating their attempts to raise output per hour by increasing the pace of work. Apparently reflecting the additional speedup, between 1965 and 1970 the industrial accident rate rose almost 20 percent above its level between 1960 and 1965.[50]

To prevent workers from interfering in their stepped-up campaign to cut costs, employers intensified their resistance to unionization. Between the early 1950s and 1965, employers had consistently voluntarily accepted about 42 percent of all petitions to hold union representation elections; but from 1965 on, their willingness to agree to such petitions dropped precipitously. The proportion of petitions voluntarily accepted fell to 26.5 percent by 1970 and 16.3 percent by 1973. Meanwhile, there was a phenomenal increase in employers' illegal efforts to interfere with union organizing. Between 1965 and 1973, the number of charges against employers that involved firing workers for union activity rose by 50 percent, the number of workers awarded back pay or reinstated to their jobs after having been illegally fired almost tripled, and the number of all unfair-labor-practice charges against employers doubled.[51]

The union membership, for their part, was in no mood for further concessions. Thanks especially to the complaisance of their union officials, they had suffered, with rising anger, the profoundly unequal distribution of the gains provided by the reviving economy during the first half of the 1960s. During this same period, moreover, they found themselves in an increasingly more powerful position to resist, due to the rising employment provided by the recovery. Unemployment fell from 6.8 percent in 1958 to 4.5 percent in 1965 and to 3.5 percent in 1969. Still, the economy's rapid growth was a double-edged sword. While it brought rising job

50 U.S. Department of Commerce, *Historical Statistics of the United States*, p. 182.

51 R. L. Seeber and W. N. Cooke, "The Decline in Union Success in NLRB Representation Elections," *Industrial Relations* vol. 22 (Winter 1983), pp. 42–3; Freeman, "Why Are Unions Faring Poorly in NLRB Representation Elections?" p. 53.

opportunities, it also came with accelerating inflation, threatening to undermine workers' hard-fought wage gains. Whereas the consumer price index had increased at an average annual rate of 1.3 percent between 1959 and 1965, it leaped up at an average annual rate of 4.35 percent between 1965 and 1969. Increasingly frustrated by their inability to get their proper share of the fruits of prosperity, increasingly confident in their ability to confront the employers, and increasingly insecure about their economic prospects, American workers were on the warpath.

Squeezed between an accelerating employers' attack from above and mounting unofficial resistance from below, the official union leaderships by mid-decade had little option but to overcome their passivity and take action, if only for the sake of appearances.[52] Beginning in 1966 and 1967, they organized a major waves of strikes, with the result that, in the years between 1966 and 1973, the percentage of total work time lost due to work stoppages grew to 0.23, compared to 0.18 for the years between 1958 and 1965, while the proportion of the employed labor force annually involved in work stoppages rose to 3.6 percent, compared to 2.6 percent, an increase of almost one third. These figures represented a very major increase in labor resistance. Nevertheless, the magnitude of the revolt should be kept in perspective. Greater numbers of workers were annually involved in strikes in this period than at any other time in the postwar period. But, in terms of the *proportion* of days lost through strikes and the *proportion* of the labor force annually involved in strikes—not to mention economic gains—the militancy of this period fell notably short of that of the late 1940s through the mid-1950s.

Judging from its results, the rise of union militancy in the private economy appears to have represented less the flexing of muscles of an increasingly powerful labor movement building its strength on tight labor markets than a defensive struggle for survival provoked by the assaults of an increasingly well-organized and aggressive class of capitalist manufacturing employers and catalyzed by an angry rank and file. Real wage gains in this period were the lowest up to that point after 1950. Perhaps even more telling, despite the increased number of strikes, unions were decreasingly able to hold their place within the labor force. During the years 1965–73, the proportion of union victories in NLRB elections fell to 56.4 percent, compared to 60.4 percent in the early 1960s, and the proportion of the private sector labor force that was unionized fell by 5 percent, from 32 percent in 1966 to 27 percent in 1973.[53]

---

52  See, for example, Serrin, *The Company and the Union*.
53  Goldfield, *The Decline of Organized Labor*, pp. 90–1; Freeman, "The Divergence of Private Sector and Public Sector Unionism," p. 64.

Unions' declining leverage against employers, even when they took militant action, is illustrated by the fact that, between 1964 and 1971, union workers secured wage gains that were at best equal to, and probably a bit less than, those won by non-union workers. Union clout did once again begin to make a difference around 1971, after which point non-union workers saw their real wage growth plummet to near zero under the impact of inflation. Still, while union workers began to do much better in these years in relative terms than did their non-union counterparts, they were able to do no more than maintain their real wage growth at the level of the later 1960s, at which point it had fallen substantially compared to the 1950s and early 1960s.[54] Perhaps most striking was the shift in the balance of forces that the employers' offensive in manufacturing appears to have brought about. Though less unionized and for the most part less militant than their counterparts in manufacturing, between 1965 and 1973, non-manufacturing workers achieved significantly faster average annual wage growth—at 6.4 percent in manufacturing, compared to 7.2 percent in non-manufacturing (before adjusting for inflation). In the absence of pressure from labor made possible by intense working-class militancy, real wage growth would certainly have fallen significantly faster than it actually did, and the fall in profitability would have been correspondingly reduced. But to argue that increased labor resistance prevented a better adjustment by capital than otherwise to the downward trend in its profitability is a long way from seeing it as at the source of that decline.

### Afterword

As late as 1972–3, forced forward by Nixon's hyper macroeconomic stimulus and benefiting hugely from the breakdown of Bretton Woods and the devaluation of the dollar, the U.S. economy enjoyed a brief indian summer. But with the oil crisis striking an economy already weighed down by an enormous fall in profitability, the postwar boom came to an end with the deep recession of 1974–5. The rest of the 1970s saw an additional major decline in manufacturing profitability that was severe enough to bring down, on its own, the private economy profit rate even more, which culminated in the worst crisis of the postwar epoch between 1979 and 1982. The official labor movement had functioned creditably under conditions of high prosperity during the Korean War boom and for a few years thereafter, but it was profoundly dependent upon those conditions. It revealed its feet

---

54 D. J. B. Mitchell, *Unions, Wages, and Inflation* (Washington, D.C.: Brookings Institution Press, 1980), p. 40, Table 2-4, as well as pp. 48–53.

of clay in the wake of the 1950s stagnation, when employers began to find it worth their while—indeed necessary—to risk disrupting production in order to secure the potentially larger benefits that might accrue from assaulting their workers' living standards and working conditions. The offensive that capital unleashed at this juncture only intensified as time went on, but without accomplishing that restoration of profitability and stability that most of the union leadership was banking on to make possible a return to their all too brief golden age. From the mid-1960s, rank-and-file workers across many industries, inside and outside manufacturing—facing employers who were themselves confronting deepening crisis and raising the stakes of class struggle—sought to take their organizations into their own hands and fashion them into more effective weapons for combat with their bosses. But once the last glimmer of the postwar prosperity disappeared after 1973, they found, for the most part, that it was too much to fight not only employers who stepped up their assault still another notch, and entrenched union leaderships quite unwilling to risk union organizations that offered them a relatively secure material base, whatever the outcome of the interaction of those organizations with the employers, however unsuccessfully they defended their memberships. It was perfectly indicative of the long-standing divergence of the trajectory of the union officials from that of workers on the shop floor that it was only during the later 1970s that UAW chief Doug Fraser made his famous complaint over the "one-sided class war" now being waged by the employers against labor. The ironies could hardly have been greater. Given that that class war had been taking place with increasing intensity for, charitably speaking, two decades, what had Fraser been waiting for? Maybe more to the point, given his own leading position in the labor movement, why had he allowed it to be so one-sided for so long?

BLACK LUNG KILLS
BLACK LUNG KILLS
BLACK LUNG KILLS
BLACK LUNG KILLS
BLACK LUNG LAW NOW

# Conflict, Change, and Economic Policy in the Long 1970s

## Judith Stein

Between 1973 and 1975, the long period of postwar economic growth ended. The Bretton Woods fixed currency regime collapsed, oil prices quadrupled, and the global economy entered the worst recession of the era. These system-shaking events brought in their wake an extended period of slower growth, higher unemployment, and reduced technological progress, putting an abrupt end to 1960s talk that the problems of regulating capitalism had been solved and that the business cycle was a thing of the past. The ensuing downturn could not and did not determine its own policy responses. But it unquestionably did demand new forms of economic regulation, different from those that had governed the economy in its golden age. The left, broadly speaking, and in particular the labor movement and its rank-and-file oppositions, was woefully unprepared for the policy challenges posed by the sudden economic shift. This was most generally because its approach to politics, and to economic policy in particular, had been premised upon the perpetuation of the long postwar boom. During the period of prosperity, there was little concern about what was needed to maintain the marriage between modernization and working-class progress that was the essence of New Deal liberalism. As a consequence, the left failed to develop forms of state intervention that addressed the changing needs of industries and the industrial labor force in a world of ongoing technical change and increasing economic integration and competition.

After World War II, U.S. state intervention was largely confined to the management of demand. Successive administrations—most notably the Democratic administrations of this era—relied on fiscal policy, and in particular tax rates, to manage growth and business cycles, and even the problems of particular industries. Presidents Kennedy, Johnson, and Carter—not to mention Nixon and Ford—thus stood consistently against policies that addressed particular economic sectors or systematic efforts at educating and retraining the labor force. Meanwhile, internationally, they pursued free trade and free capital movements—opening the U.S. market, subsidizing direct investment overseas, and creating ever expanding realms of freedom for finance—while the United States' overseas rivals in Europe and Japan were doing pretty much the opposite: protecting the domestic market, imposing controls on capital, taming finance, and pursuing various industrial and active labor market policies. When boom gave way to crisis and the cushion hitherto provided by a fast growing economic pie disappeared, these differences became more salient. Yet Keynesian perspectives were not immediately traded in for free-market ideology, which did not actually triumph in the United States until the Reagan presidency of the 1980s. The long 1970s constituted an interregnum, a period of experiment between the eras of state intervention and of neo-liberalism, in which statist and social democratic alternatives remained on the agenda. But the fact remains that already during the golden age of capitalism, important U.S. industries and their labor forces were already finding themselves at a disadvantage vis-à-vis their European counterparts as a consequence of the nation's limited management of the domestic economy and the government's international policies of openness in the face of what turned out to be the first great wave of globalization. When the crisis struck during the mid- and late 1970s, neither liberals in government nor the U.S. left and labor more generally could mobilize sufficient strength to reverse what was a well-established policy stance.

## Golden Age Economics

Keynesian objectives—industrialization, full employment, and social welfare—were the legacy of the Great Depression and World War II. They were, moreover, realized to a historically unprecedented degree in the United States and throughout the industrial world during the subsequent quarter-century. The average rate of unemployment in Europe during the 1960s was 1.5 percent. The United States reduced the figure to below 4 percent. Each nation had its own mix of policies, but all believed that government could promote growth and employment. Europeans managed their economies more than the Americans. As the *Wall Street Journal* quipped in 1972, "When things don't go well, the response in the US is to regulate, in Western Europe to nationalize."[1] American Keynesianism meant manipulating spending and taxes and allowing the market to determine the resulting levels of output and employment. Government macro-policy

---

1   *Wall Street Journal*, July 15, 1972.

aimed to reduce the risk and raise the rewards for business investment. As economist James Tobin said, "No one is to be ordered to grow."[2] Incentives, not compulsions, and grants, not specific plans, were the methods of the Americans. Microeconomic policies to encourage sector-specific investment, technical change, labor-force upgrading, rationalizing industries, reallocating production, and labor were outside the repertoire of the American government.

Other nations used Keynes, but he often took a backseat to Karl Marx or Frederick List. Whatever the inspiration, European and Japanese governments nurtured national industries, using import restraints, currency controls, income policies, and direct government assistance to enhance national wealth. France employed industrial planning and state ownership, and its budgets were always very balanced. Germany and Japan in different ways emphasized supply, not demand, and were also fiscally frugal. In Great Britain, Keynesian demand stimulation was more prevalent, but still took a backseat to nationalization. In all of these cases, governments concluded that the state must act deliberately and according to plan where markets feared to tread. The stunning results were mirrored, among other places, in Italian film. In 1949 Vittorio De Sica's hero in *The Bicycle Thief* was a man looking for a job in postwar Italy. Already by 1960, the hero of Federico Fellini's *La Dolce Vita* was one who had a very good job and life, but was dissatisfied with it, alienated from it.

Had capitalism changed? Whatever you call it, the mixed economy flourished. Political leaders concluded that the catastrophe of the 1930s should not be allowed to return, and that the Great Depression had been caused by the failures of the unrestricted free market. Markets would have to be managed by the state so unemployment would not return. Persons with sterling capitalist credentials like W. Averell Harriman said that "People in this country are no longer scared of such words as 'planning' . . . people have accepted the fact that government has got to plan as well as individuals in this country."[3] But the fact remains that postwar U.S. governments not only proved reluctant to go beyond the Keynesian manipulation of aggregate demand to actually plan economic life, but applied different lessons internationally than they did domestically, with portentous implications for America's industrial trajectory and that of the entire capitalist world.

Since rising tariffs and competitive devaluations had closed off national

---

2  R. King, *Money, Time, and Politics: Investment Tax Subsidies and American Democracy* (New Haven: Yale University Press, 1993), p. 246.

3  C. S. Maier, *In Search of Stability: Explorations in Historical Political Economy* (New York: Cambridge University Press, 1987), p. 129.

markets and exacerbated the Great Depression, U.S. policymakers stressed the free flow of goods in order to buttress postwar economic dynamism. They were confident that, in view of the huge productivity advantage enjoyed by U.S. producers, that the nation would prosper in such a world. From the time of the Bretton Woods conference in 1944, the United States took the lead in the construction of three new international institutions—the World Bank, the IMF, and the GATT—to create an open global economic order. Nevertheless, the case for the free flow of commodities and investment internationally is ultimately the same as the case for laissez-faire domestically: The market knows best. The United States thus entered the postwar world with contrasting visions: On the one hand, the market needed the firm hand of government to produce full employment; on the other, laissez-faire should be the rule internationally, and goods and services should flow according to market principles.

The United States' commitment to free trade posed a direct challenge to its regulation of the economy through Keynesian demand management. The case for freer trade privileges consumption. It is claimed that the consumer will benefit from the cheapest widget, whether it is produced at home or abroad. By the same token, policies making for easier consumer credit highlighted the importance of consumption. But most consumers are producers, too. And no economy was separable from the society it served. The economic fluidity associated with the decline of supposedly "uncompetitive" products imperiled social stability. As a consequence, some states subsidized production in the interest of employment. Should imports of such goods be allowed to freely compete with unsubsidized domestic products? This question was not hypothetical because Keynesian deficits in a U.S. economy that was more open than that of its rivals tended to draw in imports, actually subsidizing the industries of its competitors at the expense of its own and putting downward pressure on the balance of trade. The U.S. combination of Keynesianism at home and laissez-faire abroad turned out to be an unstable recipe for progress. Its limitations were initially masked by the overwhelming superiority of American producers vis-à-vis their competitors, but once the Europeans and Japanese had rebuilt their economies and the U.S. trade surplus disappeared, its incongruity would be exposed.

In 1945, most nations other than the United States, whether they were rich or poor, eschewed free trade, and this was especially the case for America's leading rivals in Europe and Japan. According to the principle of comparative advantage, advanced by the British economist David Ricardo in the early nineteenth century, certain countries specialize in cloth and others wheat, and both benefit from producing one and buying the other. But the doctrine that seemed so obvious to economists was shunned by political leaders and ordinary people. As Japanese trade delegate K. Otabe observed in 1955, "If the theory of international trade were pursued to its ultimate conclusion, the United States would specialize in the production of automobiles and Japan in the production of tuna."[4] Japan rejected such trade, on the principle that "each government encourages and protects those industries which it believes important for reasons of national policy." Like some of its European counterparts, Japan systematically integrated its trade policies within a state-led approach to industrial development that put the emphasis on supply, productivity, and international competitiveness, subordinating consumption to investment and exports. Unlike the United States, other nations did not view the GATT as an instrument to create a liberal international order, but only a body to provide a civilized common law to govern relationships among mercantilist states.

Although the United States aimed to impose the principles of free trade and free capital flows, it was forced to yield. Faced with the difficulties of restoring European economies and aware of the lure of Soviet models, the Americans stepped back from pushing the open economy on its allies, as well as offering the Marshall Plan. In the interest of solidifying opposition to the Soviet Union, the United States thus looked the other way as Europe and Japan protected domestic markets. The American tolerance for measures that discriminated against its own producers was sustained by overwhelming U.S. economic dominance. In 1945, the United States contained 60 percent of all the capital stock of the advanced capitalist countries and produced 60 percent of all output. American leaders expected that protectionism would be temporary, as the GATT provided a structure for reducing trade barriers by periodic bargaining.

But the evolution of international trade did not follow the pattern foreseen by Ricardo. Trade grew most rapidly among countries with similar economies. In 1953, the industrial countries sold about 38 percent of their manufactured exports to each other; in the early 1970s this figure rose to 75 percent. This meant that the industrial countries were producing very much the same kind of goods as their partners and rivals, making for a pattern of intensifying competition, not complementary production. In this context, it was understandable that America's rivals viewed free trade skeptically. When Japan joined the GATT in 1955, fourteen nations, including the UK, France, and Belgium, invoked Article 35, which permitted them to waive a most-favored nation relationship with Japan. They refused to allow the entrance of Japanese goods into their markets on the same basis as the goods

---

4   A. Eckes, Jr., *Opening American Markets: US Foreign Trade Policy Since 1776* (Chapel Hill: University of North Carolina Press, 1995), p. 301.

of other GATT members. Japan was a low-wage country, which could disrupt domestic markets through dumping cheap goods; also, Japan's own trade liberalization was puny. The United States did not invoke Article 35 and even gave special access to its market to countries that permitted the entrance of Japanese goods. Building up Japan in the wake of the Communist victory in China was a crucial battle in the Cold War. This early action partly explains why so many Japanese cars ended up in the United States and not Europe. The Americans looked the other way, too, when the Europeans created their common market, which lowered internal tariffs but raised those for non-members like the United States. That was one reason why President Kennedy initiated a new round of trade talks in 1962. But George W. Ball, the president's Assistant Secretary of State, admitted that negotiators operated on the premise that "we Americans could afford to pay some economic price for a strong Europe."[5] The results of the Kennedy Round showed that that price was being paid. Imports rose 311.8 percent from 1962 to 1974, compared with a 51.7 percent gain in the GNP. Exports did not match such figures, and trade deficits were the result.[6]

This toll on American production and employment was tolerable only with rapidly expanding global markets, all the more so because U.S. policy, intentionally and unintentionally, promoted globalization, particularly foreign direct investment by its multinationals. After World War II, the typical multinational was no longer involved with raw materials, such as oil, copper, or agricultural commodities in the Third World, as it had been during the first part of the twentieth century, but in manufacturing in Europe. There were many reasons for this: Senator Jacob Javits of New York claimed, "You have to have these enterprises to hurdle the stupidities and parochialism of the nationalities of the world or the world will go bust and become a large version of the Russian model, a dull gray prison."[7] Translated, Javits argued that multinationals brought with them technology and up-to-date management. But what was in it for the corporations themselves? In the 1950s and 1960s, most places, including Europe, had lower production costs. Producing in country X also eliminated the transport costs to sell in country X. Also, locating in another country clothed a foreign company in native garb. But perhaps the most important impetus for American firms was the formation of the European Economic Community (EEC) in 1957. The EEC reduced restrictions among its members but erected trade barriers

---

5  G. W. Ball, *The Past Has Another Pattern: Memoirs* (New York: W.W. Norton, 1983), pp. 191–2.

6  J. Goldstein, *Ideas, Interests, and American Trade Policy* (Ithaca: Cornell University Press, 1993), pp. 163, 168.

7  "Senate Foreign Relations Subcommittee on Multinational Corps," record of first hearings on OPIC, p. 318.

for outsiders who wanted to export into Europe. Because exporting became more difficult, American companies set up new plants in Europe, behind the high tariff walls. The new European mercantilism violated a postwar vision of free trade, and possibly the GATT itself. It also made for the transfer of much new US investment abroad. The American government only encouraged this development, offering preferential tax treatment on the multinationals' overseas profits.

A manager from Caterpillar Tractor, which made earth-moving machinery, explained, "We originally went abroad with plants primarily to protect markets where competitive problems, monetary problems or political problems (such as import quotas or other restrictions) prevented us from selling direct from our US plants."[8] The effect of diverting investment that would otherwise have occurred in the United States for export to Europe and elsewhere was to reduce U.S. employment, output, and productivity. By 1965, new investment abroad accounted for 33.9 percent of overall net American investment in rubber manufacturing, 25.4 percent in the manufacture of transportation equipment, 25 percent in chemicals, 22.1 percent in non-electrical machinery, and 21.4 percent in electrical machinery. By 1970, new investment in manufacturing in oil, mining, and smelting abroad totaled almost 35 percent of domestic investments in the same sectors. A Commerce Department official feared that foreign subsidiaries operated as "a vacuum pump that sucks our new technology out as soon as it's created."[9] Still, it was a mark of the times and of the prevailing attitudes that American policymakers downplayed the negative economic effects of these developments on the U.S. domestic economy, not least their devastating impact on American workers, both directly in terms of jobs lost and indirectly in terms of their reduced leverage against the employers. They also convinced themselves that only the richer Less Developed Countries (LDCs)—Mexico, Brazil, and India—would benefit and only the domestic textile industry would be hurt by the emerging trend toward "runaway shops." But those closer to the problem reached a different conclusion. Already in 1968 the *Wall Street Journal* was sounding the alarm on increasing imports of "unsophisticated electronics" for teenagers coming from U.S. companies in Taiwan, and in less than a decade what was then still pretty much a trickle would become a torrent.[10]

---

8   *Wall Street Journal*, February 13, 1971.
9   *Wall Street Journal*, October 26, 1970.
10  *Wall Street Journal*, November 11, 1968.

## The Kennedy and Johnson Years

The United States could confidently pursue the combination of Keynesianism and openness, because it operated on the premise that the boom would persist and that its industries would remain world beaters. Postwar affluence in the United States was real. Rising employment and productivity advanced GNP 37 percent in real terms, and the wage component of national income rose slightly. Whereas during the depression of the 1930s unemployment had ranged from 14 to 25 percent, it averaged just 4.6 percent during the 1950s. Nevertheless, from 1957 through 1963 the nation suffered from recession or low growth, accompanied by elevated levels of unemployment. Heavily focused on foreign policy, and particularly the threats from the Soviet Union, President John F. Kennedy refused initially to deal with joblessness. He told all who would listen that a 7 percent jobless rate meant that 93 percent were content.[11] Pushed by a Democratic majority in the Senate, Kennedy did sign a $900 million public works bill in 1962. But Kennedy would not speak to the longer-term problems of technological and structural unemployment that affected agriculture and manufacturing alike. Senate liberals wrote the Manpower Development and Training Act in 1962, but the compromises necessary to obtain the law left manpower programs fragmented and partial, and thus ineffectual. The president did see the dangers of the mercantilism of the EEC and sought to open up European markets to U.S. goods. But Cold War priorities meant that sustaining the alliance took precedence over creating opportunities for U.S. exporters. Because he insisted that freer trade would only increase economic activity at home, Kennedy would approve only the weakest possible version of a provision put forward by Senate liberals to compensate workers, communities, and firms hurt by tariff reduction and foreign competition. As it turned out, the U.S. Tariff Commission would find not a single worker to be eligible for assistance under this provision until 1969.[12]

Kennedy was ultimately moved to act on the sluggish economy not because of employment but because he understood the relationship between a strong economy and a strong foreign policy. In the end, tax cuts for business were the cure for everything. The investment tax credit and liberalization of depreciation schedules would make investment more

---

11   R. Reeves, *President Kennedy: Profile of Power* (New York: Simon and Schuster, 1993), p. 295.

12   J. Stein, *Running Steel, Running America: Race, Economic Policy, and the Decline of Liberalism* (Chapel Hill: University of North Carolina Press, 1998), p. 225.

profitable. These changes required business to invest, but they were untargeted and as available to firms that had sufficient capital as those that did not. They were as available to owners of racetracks as to owners of steel mills. In addition, fearing an actual recession in 1962, Kennedy agreed to a general tax reduction—lowering the rates of both individuals and corporations. Signed by President Lyndon B. Johnson in February 1964, the law reduced government revenue by $11.6 billion for 1965. It seemed to work, at least in the short run. By December 1965, the unemployment rate had fallen to 4.1 percent. Investment rates of 16 and 17 percent as a percentage of GDP equaled those of the boom of the mid-1950s. By adding Keynesian demand stimulus by way of tax cuts to the older commitments to spur competition and see to the dispersal of industry across regions, the nation seemed to have found the formula for industrial efficiency and working-class prosperity.

The long economic expansion of the 1960s, which appeared to be produced by Keynesian deficits, nurtured an economic complacency among American elites and intellectuals and activists on the left, who, believing the problem of economic growth to have been solved, contemplated the social, rather than the economic realm.[13] Telltale signs were ignored. Labor productivity, the mother's milk of growth, began falling in the late 1960s. Real wages for manufacturing workers fell by 82 cents an hour from 1965–9. Over-capacity in manufacturing began to grip the global system.[14] But if the conflict between liberal internationalism and managed national economies seems obvious in retrospect, living actors did not find it so. The combined commitment to free trade and Keynesian economics continued to constitute the unquestioned premise of economic policy. Nixon's election in 1968 did not change that.

## The Nixon Years

Pundits commonly claim that conservatism triumphed with Nixon in 1968. One year later, Kevin Phillips published *The Emerging Republican Majority*, predicting a cycle of GOP power, ending the Democratic era begun by Franklin D. Roosevelt in 1932. Phillips alleged that the desertion from Democratic ranks by Southern whites, urban Catholics, and affluent migrants to the suburbs and the West in 1968 was permanent and marked a growing conservatism in American life. Similarly, Democrats Richard

---

13   H. Brick, "The Postcapitalist Vision as Theory and Ideology," unpublished paper at OAH convention, Boston, March 27, 2004.

14   R. Brenner, "The Economics of Global Turbulence," *New Left Review* 229 (May–June, 1998).

Scammon and Ben Wattenberg hectored their party to attend to a majority anxious about crime, militants, and the new permissive values.[15] Conservatives did note with pleasure the Democratic strife. But the king of right-wing Republicans, the *National Review*'s editor William Buckley, believed that it was not yet the time for conservatives. Richard Nixon himself thought the right-wing Young Americans for Freedom were "nuts and second-raters."[16] And Howard K. Smith, a principal commentator for the ABC news network, remarked in 1971, "No matter how often we reporters pronounce the old FDR Coalition dead—the blacks, the poor, labor, and so on—every election it seems to pull together enough to keep the Democrats the majority party."[17]

One way to clarify what was happening is to distinguish social from economic liberalism. Whatever the people concluded in 1968 about the values question, they did not reject Keynesian economics, which was not contested at all in the election. People often comment upon President Nixon's supposed Paul-like conversion in 1971 when he said, "I am now a Keynesian in economics."[18] Alan Matusow, the historian of Nixon's economic policies, claimed that Nixon, the ultimate political opportunist, adopted the idea only because of its political potency. But there is little evidence that he had rejected Keynesianism, any more than had Eisenhower before him. In any case, the prior question is: Why was it politically opportunistic to turn to Keynesian economics in 1971 when it would not be today? What is important is the content of the well from which leaders drink, and the political well in 1971 was Keynesian.

Despite Nixon's small-town, Quaker upbringing, his service in the uptight, button-down Eisenhower administration, and his 1968 campaign against the hippies, he also embraced elements of the 1960s counterculture. In his first inaugural address, Nixon surveyed the nation's troubles and invoked Franklin Roosevelt's great speech of 1933. Roosevelt had concluded that the nation lacked, "thank God, only material things." The American spirit was intact and could be marshaled to produce the plenty, absent from the American larder. Nixon declared that "our crisis is in reverse. We find ourselves rich in goods, but ragged in spirit . . . We see around us empty lives, wanting fulfillment. We see tasks that need doing, waiting for hands to do them. To a crisis, we need an answer of the spirit." At the end of the year he told a group of businessmen that the key questions

---

15   R. M. Scammon and B. J. Wattenberg, *The Real Majority* (New York: Coward, McCann & Geoghegan, 1970).

16   D. J. Kotlowski, *Nixon's Civil Rights: Politics, Principle, and Policy* (Cambridge, MA: Harvard University Press), p. 23.

17   Presidential Papers of Richard Nixon, March 22, 1971, p. 460.

18   *New York Times*, January 7, 1971; *Business Week*, January 16, 1971.

were not material but rather "what has happened to the America idea?"[19] Nixon was practicing the politics of affluence, and this politics colored his views even of taxation and government, the key elements in all American political ideologies.

In the late 1960s and early 1970s, liberal tax reformers were seeking to shift more of the burden to the wealthy and business, not shrink the government and cut taxes altogether. Tax equity, not tax cuts, was the slogan. Nixon's tax proposals actually fit easily in this tradition. As the president put it in 1969, "We can never make taxation popular but we can make taxation fair." He accepted the Alternate Minimum Tax, embodying the idea that high-income persons should pay something. He also recommended removing the 7 percent investment tax credit for expanding plant and equipment, which had been part of John F. Kennedy's tax package in the early 1960s. Explaining why a Republican administration supported repeal of the credit that business wanted retained, Nixon's economic adviser and future chairman of the Council of Economic Advisers Herbert Stein said, "it seemed . . . that there were more important things at this juncture in history to do . . . than to make even more rapid a rate of growth that is already very rapid or making larger a gross national product in 1975 or 1980 which already in any case is going to be a staggering size."[20] John Kenneth Galbraith could not have said it better.

Nixon and most of the nation concluded that economic growth had become self-generating. The consumer demand created by the economy, supplemented when necessary by deficit spending, would be sufficient incentive for industrial modernization. In 1969, as in the Democratic 1960s, there appeared to be no conflict between consumption and investment, labor and capital, equity and growth. Business did not need subsidies to produce, and government needed revenue to regulate and compensate. Thus Nixon was for tax reform, not reduction. Still, Nixon was no Democrat. Nixon was critical of aspects of Lyndon Johnson's Great Society. But he proposed to mend them, not end them. "We are the richest country but need to modernize our institutions . . . We face an urban crisis, a social crisis—and at the same time, a crisis of confidence in the capacity of government to do its job." The answer was not to contract out government functions to private institutions, but "to make government effective." A young Donald Rumsfeld did just that with the poverty program. Rumsfeld called himself a "modern Republican," meaning one who accepted the mixed economy plus elements of the welfare state. It was not an accident that Nixon approved laws expanding Social Security and Medicare. He set up

---

19   Presidential Papers of Richard Nixon, 1969, pp. 2, 960.
20   *New York Times*, April 25, 1969.

the Environmental Protection Agency (EPA) and signed the Occupational Safety and Health Administration (OSHA), a Clean Air Act, and numerous other pieces of environmental legislation. All these reforms were evidence that liberal hegemony had not ended in 1968.

But it would be wrong to portray Nixon or the nation as obsessed with the economy or even domestic issues. That is the point. After the Kennedy-Johnson tax cut and the subsequent fine-tuning by the Federal Reserve, it appeared as if Keynes had repealed the business cycle. Nixon saw the most urgent problem facing the nation as foreign policy, and of course Vietnam monopolized his attention. Although attentive to his party's business constituencies, Nixon, unlike Robert Taft or even Gerald Ford, did not rise in politics on the basis of his service to industry. He built his career on anti-Communism, and although this ideology had domestic uses, it was the big stage of foreign policy that attracted him and provoked the opposition of the left.

## Things Fall Apart: Money, Trade, and Oil

What ended the economic complacency and challenged Keynesian practices was the sudden emergence of economic conflict both among the advanced capitalist countries and between the Western world and what was then known as the Third World. Between 1971 and 1973, the international monetary system devised at Bretton Woods disintegrated. Then, in late 1973, oil prices quadrupled. The collapse of fixed currencies and the disappearance of cheap commodity prices placed severe pressure upon the international arrangements set up after World War II to facilitate economic expansion. U.S. policymakers had little choice but to re-examine their assumptions about the workings of the open international economic order.

A dreary statistic, the merchandise trade deficit in 1971, the first one since 1893, catalyzed the process of crisis and conflict. The deficit sent off alarm bells among government officials, if not the populace. For it revealed three tectonic effects of globalization that blunted Keynesian forms of managing the economy and U.S. adherence to laissez-faire internationally. First, U.S. imports had been growing much faster than exports. A dollar of Keynesian stimulus was thus yielding fewer jobs because some of the demand it created was being satisfied by imports. Second, the trade deficit, along with military spending abroad and the buildup of foreign investment by multinationals, was producing piles of dollars in what was called the Eurodollar market, a sphere of unfettered money and credit. The rise of the Eurodollar market undermined Fed's ability to control business expansions by setting interest rates, as it enabled corporations to borrow dollars abroad. It also meant that financial operators could freely convert the dollar into, say, German marks, if there was belief that the dollar would fall, or buy German bonds if interest rates in Germany were higher than elsewhere. A new element of instability and speculation thus entered each ordinary economic transaction. Third, the emerging trade deficit put the spotlight on the export of jobs out of the U.S. economy as a consequence of fast rising foreign investment. The adjective "multinational" entered Webster's dictionary only in 1971, when the placement of plant and equipment overseas by American firms began to affect the U.S. economy. As Paul Volcker, Undersecretary of the Treasury for Monetary Affairs, noted, business's "approach to foreign markets has been to put plants abroad instead of direct selling of US products," and this was one obvious source of the trade deficit.[21] Unlike today's elites, Volcker did not assume that such behavior was economically efficient, necessary, or inevitable

Volcker did not connect the multinational with U.S. trade policy. But throughout the postwar epoch, as we have seen, trade negotiators opened the U.S. market, but failed to open foreign ones. In this way, they not only encouraged foreign competition in the domestic market and weakened exports in overseas markets, but encouraged the building of U.S. factories abroad. Like his predecessors in the Kennedy and Johnson administrations, Henry Kissinger made certain that Nixon was aware that to protect American shoemakers would jeopardize military bases in Spain and play into Communist hands in Italy.[22] Shoes were left dangling in the wind. Like most Cold War strategists, Kissinger was uninterested in economics. His aide Fred Bergsten quipped, "Working as an economist for Kissinger was comparable to being in charge of the military for the Pope."[23]

Sacrificing domestic industries in order to realize foreign policy goals had been tolerable in the days when the U.S. competitiveness was unmatched and global markets expanding. In the shrinking and turbulent economy of

---

21  P. Volcker, "Memorandum of Conversation," May 3–5, 1970, Foreign Relations of the United States, 1969, III, Foreign Economic Policy, 1969–72; International Monetary Policy, 1969–72 (Washington, DC: GPO, 2001).

22  "Memorandum From the President's Assistant for National Security Affairs (Kissinger) to President Nixon," January 2, 1971, NSC Files, Agency Files, Box 196, Agriculture vol. 2, 1971—president's handwritten comments; "Action Memorandum From the President's Assistant for National Security Affairs (Kissinger) to President Nixon," July 8, 1970, NSC Files, Subject Files, Box 401, Trade General vol. 2 4/70–12/70. Confidential, Nixon Presidential Materials, National Archives. Ford, too, rejected help for the industry on the same strategic grounds. R. B. Porter, *Presidential Decision Making: The Economic Policy Board* (Cambridge: Cambridge University Press, 1980), pp. 159–69; Alan Greenspan, "Memorandum for the President," April 7, 1976, Box 2, Folder April 1976, Council of Economic Advisers Papers, Ford Library.

23  *New York Times*, September 30, 1982.

the 1970s, the economic and political costs of such policies became much more difficult to absorb. Nixon told Kissinger, "we cannot continue to sell out US interests for State's foreign policy considerations."[24] In 1971, this was a bipartisan conclusion. In the words of the Democratic-controlled Senate Finance Committee, "throughout most of the postwar era, US trade policy has been the orphan of US foreign policy. Too often the Executive has granted trade concessions to accomplish political objectives." Peter Peterson, chair of Bell and Howell, told Nixon that "other industrialized nations have been more vigorous in pursuit of their economic interests," and he should give precedence to the nation's economic over its diplomatic interest. Instead, the president created a blue ribbon commission headed by the CEO of IBM. As it was composed of the heads of major international companies like IBM, its recommendation—that the United States simply continue to "eliminate barriers to international trade and capital movements"—could have surprised no one. The commission's two labor members, I. W. Abel of the steelworkers union and Floyd Smith of the machinists, dissented, calling attention to the sharply rising foreign investment and its costs.[25]

The thinking of Abel and Smith was embodied in the Foreign Trade and Investment Act, the Burke-Hartke bill, proposed by the AFL-CIO at the start of the 1970s. This law would have imposed across-the-board import quotas and changes to international tax laws so sweeping that most foreign direct investment would have become unprofitable for U.S. companies. The bill also proposed to create a tripartite commission with strong powers to regulate imports and capital flows. The law constituted what was in effect the first critique of and alternative to the international economic arrangements of the affluent society. Senator Vance Hartke from Indiana had earlier been critical of the Kennedy Round trade treaties. Even though the unemployment rate was falling in the late 1960s, he argued that the influx of foreign steel was depriving U.S. workers of the good jobs that the War on Poverty was promising. Congressman James Burke from Massachusetts was aiming, among other things, to respond to the problem of his state's textile workers. George Baldanzi, head of the textile workers union and a strong supporter of the bill, was worried about the fate of American textile workers, and especially African Americans now seeking to enter the industry in the wake of the passage of Title VII of the Civil Rights Act. On the one hand, the U.S. government was encouraging black

---

24  Nixon's comments on "Information Memorandum from Kissinger to Nixon," November 13, 1970, box 322, WXM vol. 1 1969–70, Nixon Presidential files, National Archives.

25  Stein, *Running Steel, Running America*, pp. 202–3.

employment, but on the other it was promoting the export of jobs that blacks could fill.[26]

Nixon was able to ward off the Burke-Hartke challenge because of the overwhelming opposition by American business, led by the multinationals assembled in the Emergency Committee for American Trade (ECAT). ECAT was created in 1967 by David Rockefeller to make sure that the Kennedy Round of tariff cuts were ratified and remained the leading proponent of global free trade. But the business mobilization might not have been successful had not labor-liberal forces been so distracted and divided. The internal division within the Democratic Party between the McGovern liberals, uninterested in the issue, and the AFL-CIO was worsened by another, between the AFL-CIO and UAW, which had left the federation in 1968. The UAW did not support Burke-Hartke because it hoped to create a global auto union and because auto jobs were not yet threatened in the way they would be from the mid- to late 1970s. UAW support for trade adjustment assistance instead of managed trade allowed liberals to do the same without feeling they had abandoned the working class. Moreover, few liberals opposed multilateral corporations on anything but anti-imperialist grounds, for the most part neglecting their impact on the domestic working class.

Nonetheless, the threat of Burke-Hartke forced the Nixon administration to do something about the problem of international competition. As it turned out, the related currency crisis offered a more palatable way to address the issue. So long as U.S. productivity was far ahead of the others, the Bretton Woods system had worked fine. But after the recovery of Europe and Japan, the value of their currencies should have risen or the value of the U.S. dollar should have fallen. Neither happened. The overvalued dollar made U.S. exports more costly, putting downward pressure on the United States' trade balance.[27] Germany and Japan were in no hurry to revalue their currencies because their undervalued mark and yen cheapened exports. Moreover, threatening the hegemonic currency could backfire. The dollar was not just the nation's currency but the world's, so an unstable dollar would rattle not just the American but the global system of finance. The Federal Reserve long sustained the currency's value by buying up the dollars accumulating in Europe. But to do so, it had to draw down the U.S. reserves of gold and foreign currency. This could not go on forever. As countries like Germany and Japan increased their surpluses, they demanded gold from the United States in exchange for their

---

26 Ibid., pp. 219–21.

27 J. S. Gowa, *Closing the Gold Window: Domestic Politics and the End of Bretton Woods* (Ithaca: Cornell University Press, 1983), p. 110.

dollars, and in the end the Nixon administration had little choice but to close the Treasury gold window in August 1971, abandon the special gold-exchange obligation assumed at Bretton Woods, and reduce the dollar's exchange value. The president also placed a temporary 10 percent surtax on imports, as a bargaining tool to get other countries to raise the value of their currency, and instituted a temporary wage and price freeze to dampen inflation.[28] By 1973, the United States formally renounced its obligation to sustain the fixed exchange rate, and the dollar floated, its value determined on the free market. Nixon sold the package as a way to increase U.S. exports and decrease its imports. Devaluation could provide a quick fix and hold off more radical changes in international economic policy. In 1971, to demonstrate its concern to make the U.S. economy more productive in the longer term, the administration brought back the investment tax credit, which it had disposed of in 1969.

In his elation, the president told Secretary of Treasury John Connally that the economic program would be like the China thing, totally unexpected. It surely was. To this day, the Japanese refer to it as the Nixon shock. The president was not very interested in economics, but he liked big, bold moves. However, these big, bold moves—the economic package, the opening to China, and détente with the Soviet Union—were grounded in more than personality. They reflected the diminished economic and strategic power of the United States in the 1970s.

## Oil

Shortly after the currency deliberations ended in early 1973, the onset of the oil crisis sent the system spinning again. This conflict between the developed countries and the underdeveloped world, represented now by the Organization of Petroleum Exporting Countries (OPEC), shifted resources from industrial to oil powers, produced a wave of global inflation, created new distributional and regional struggles, and fragmented relations among developed states as each tried to cut the best deal with the oil producers. To moderate these inter-capitalist rivalries, the first economic summit of what would be known as the G-7 nations met in 1975. Secretary of State Henry Kissinger acknowledged that "the bipolar world was dead, replaced by a new world of multiple centers of power. Consciousness of global interdependence was the basis of the ultimate fulfillment of national objectives." In plain English, United States prosperity was dependent upon global relationships, which it could not always command. The best example was oil. In 1970, 90 percent of the nation's energy needs were supplied

---

28   Ibid., pp.135–75.

domestically. By 1980, only 50 percent would be. Europe and Japan were even more dependent on foreign sources of energy.

In the early 1970s, "third-world" nations were only in the process of becoming important manufacturing competitors of domestic producers, but they were already suppliers of strategic commodities, which now took on a new role when prices rose in response to the extended boom of the 1960s and early 1970s. The success of the oil producers in 1973, after the Arab-Israeli war, and then in 1979, in the wake of the revolution in Iran, shaped global politics in two ways. First, the siphoning off of funds from oil importers to oil exporters, mainly Middle East nations, produced new centers of wealth and power. Second, by demonstrating the vulnerability of industrial nations, the oil cartel emboldened "third-world" producers of other vital commodities—bauxite, tin, copper. Although no other commodity was able to command as oil did, that conclusion is more obvious today than in 1975. It is not unreasonable to assume that a more confident and prosperous United States would have taken a harder line on the OPEC action in 1973 and against Iran in 1979. The United States had effected regime change in Iran in 1954 after the government threatened to nationalize the oil industry. But in 1973, most of the oil was in the hands of states, not Western oil companies, a mark of the new third-world power. After Vietnam, military action was out of the question.

The global economy of the 1970s was thus inflected by inter-capitalist rivalries and North-South conflicts, which complicated and at times overshadowed Cold War politics. The North Vietnamese united the nation in 1975, and Communist victories in Laos and Cambodia followed the Vietnamese win. The United States could not be everywhere, so Nixon and Kissinger had designated regional surrogates, like the Shah of Iran, to manage a turbulent world, and struck deals with the Soviet Union and China to limit its overseas commitments. By the end of the decade, both political parties were practicing a more sober foreign policy, under the pressure of the defeat in Vietnam and economic decline. If Lyndon Johnson thought he could have guns and butter, Richard Nixon, Gerald Ford, and Jimmy Carter knew they could not. The new international tensions inevitably affected the way the United States resolved its domestic troubles.

The trade, currency, and oil crises of the early 1970s did not replace the Keynesian ideas of the mixed economy with pro-market ideologies. Given the dangers, it seemed that states had to do more. The international banker David Rockefeller concluded that "nothing less than serious economic planning on an international scale" was required.[29] Most Americans were

---

29 Trilateral Commission meetings, October 15–16, 1973, January 1974, Trilateral

slow to recognize the new challenges because of the Watergate crisis. Nixon and the rest of the country were preoccupied with the scandal from the middle of 1973 through August 1974 when the president resigned. His successor, Gerald Ford, and his chief economic adviser Alan Greenspan were obsessed with inflation but were blind to the encroaching recession. Neither man knew that from October 1974 through March 1975 the nation would experience its deepest economic downturn since the 1930s. Their initial prescription of tax increases was thus good old-fashioned Republican medicine for inflation—but badly out of touch with reality.

The president switched gears in late December. With criticism coming from all quarters, he reduced taxes, tilting toward the lower and middling population, those who would spend. He had already agreed to the Earned Income Tax credit, which removed millions of the poorest working Americans from the rolls and supplemented their income. Nevertheless, in May 1975 unemployment peaked at 9 percent. Dollars that would have bought appliances went to oil companies and other countries to pay for costly gasoline and heating oil. Factories in the north faced with higher energy costs escaped to the Sunbelt and increasingly abroad, where lower wages might keep them in the black. Urban crises like the near bankruptcy of New York City littered the land.

Fierce disagreements arose between the Republican president and Democratic Congress over consumption and investment, labor and capital, equity and growth. But although the consensus of the affluent society had ended, it was still a Keynesian world, with political liberalism very much alive, if not entirely well. President Ford was interested in corporate tax cuts to revitalize industry. But he ended up accepting the interclass equity of the Keynesian era, refusing to support the plan of his Secretary of Treasury William Simon to end the double taxation of dividends, which would become the centerpiece of President G. W. Bush's tax cut legislation of 2003.[30] For Ford, the simplification of the tax system could not justify the handout to the rich.[31]

In 1976, with unemployment still at 7.7 percent, it still seemed possible that the most effective challenge to the Keynesian world might come from the left, rather than the right. Believing that deficit spending had proven

Commission papers, Rockefeller Archives; Mike Duval to Jim Cannon, August 28, 1975, Cannon Box 13, file Energy-Independent Authority, June–September 1975, Cannon Papers, Gerald Ford Presidential Library, Ann Arbor, Michigan.

30  W. E. Simon, "Memorandum for the President" nd, f. Capital Formation, July 1975, Box 45, William Seidman Papers; Leach, "Tax Reform: Outlook and Options," May 19, 1975, f. "Tax Reform Act, December 1975," Box 18, Leach Papers, Ford Library.

31  R. L. Dunham for the president, March 27–28, 1975, f. Economy-Meeting, March 28, 1975, Box 12, Cannon Papers, Ford Library.

itself inadequate and that the government had to do more, Democratic Senator Hubert Humphrey and Republican Senator Jacob Javits introduced legislation that would require planning for full employment and growth.[32] Alan Greenspan feared that what the two senators were really after was "mandatory planning," which he vehemently opposed.[33] The masses were not rallying in the streets for Humphrey-Javits in 1975, but they had not rallied for the National Recovery Act in 1933. The difference was that in 1933 key White House officials—Adolph Berle and Rexford Tugwell, to name two—and then-President Roosevelt himself supported NRA. Humphrey-Javits had no such luck in 1975, but prospects seemed to brighten the next year when the country elected a Democratic president.

## Carter and the Democrats Tackle the New World Order

By giving the Democrats a narrow victory in the race for the presidency and overwhelming control of Congress, the elections of 1976 offered them an opportunity. The *Wall Street Journal* asked whether the GOP would survive and urged the Republican big four—Gerald Ford, Nelson Rockefeller, Ronald Reagan, and John Connally—to step back and let younger people come to the fore.[34] If conservatism was the wave of the future, the *Journal* did not see it in 1977. As longtime Republican economic adviser Herbert Stein concluded, "we are left now with accumulating criticism of the kind of fiscal policy we have been practicing for the last twenty years but with no substantial support for any alternative to it. The result is that we shall go on playing the old game of fine-tuning functional finance, not because it is a good game but because it is the only wheel in town."[35]

On the other hand, Alan Greenspan's fears of a new era of industrial planning were much exaggerated. The Democratic Party's resurgence sprang from the electorate's revulsion with Watergate, not their embrace of a Democratic alternative. The scandal both distracted Democrats and made

---

32  The Ford administration took Humphrey-Javits seriously. See R. Hormats for Economic Policy Board, March 19, 1975, f. EPB March 1975 (2), Box 58; D. Metz for B. Weidman and B. Gorog, March 23, 1975, f. Humphrey-Javits bill, Box 46, Council of Economic Advisers Papers, Ford Library. The Chamber of Commerce and National Association of Manufacturers also took it seriously. See Report of Task Force on National Economic Planning, October 13, 1976, Board of Directors of Chamber of Commerce, "Meeting," November 11–12, 1976, Box 1D, Chamber of Commerce Papers; File Richard C. Kautz memo, March 24, 1976, Box 24, National Association of Manufacturers Papers, Hagley Library, Wilmington, Delaware.

33  A. Greenspan, "Memorandum for L. William Seidman," June 26, 1975, f. Humphrey-Javits Bill, Box 46, Council of Economic Advisers Papers, Ford Library.

34  *Wall Street Journal*, January 14, 1977.

35  *Wall Street Journal*, May 31, 1977.

them complacent, as they harvested the votes of suburban Republicans outraged at the president's behavior. The Democrats had forgotten how to think about the economy. That too had a history. If conservatives viewed the era of affluence as a triumph of free enterprise, liberals saw it as the down payment on a socialized future to be built upon a welfare state that they expected to continue to expand into the indefinite future. The environmental and consumer movements had also emerged from the booming economy of the 1960s and early 1970s, and they too operated on the assumption that the economy's health was now assured. Based in a new middle class employed in education, government, and social services, they had only loose ties to American industries or the labor movement, and they often made their arguments about the costs of growth, over-consumption, and the manipulation of the consumer without acknowledging the economy's growing difficulties and the way these were affecting the citizenry. As a result, after 1974, their issues competed for the Democrats' attention with declining incomes and vanishing jobs. Environmental regulation does not have to conflict with economic growth. But the early environmental legislation was written with the assumptions of the affluent society—all things were possible. The Clean Air Act of 1970 mandated strict standards independent of cost, and such a law guaranteed trouble. Moreover, the early activists were often contemptuous of industry. One member of Carter's Environmental Protection Agency concluded that "the steel industry should die."[36] Such adversarial and self-righteous behavior made it difficult for the Democratic Party to harmonize with the interests of its constituents. Even when there was no direct conflict, priorities differed. In 1978, a member of the Congressional Black Caucus, concerned about rising black unemployment, complained, "black causes rank 50th, behind the snail darter," a fish on the endangered species list.[37]

To rekindle the economy, the Democratic Party had to shift gears and figure out how, in a period of deepening economic problems, to promote the production and consumption that many of its intellectuals and activists had derided. Yet the Humphrey-Hawkins law, guaranteeing full employment and proposed by the Democrats, was, again, premised on perpetual prosperity. Strong on symbols but weak on blueprints, it offered at best an ancillary source of jobs for a healthy economy. But the economy was not healthy, and the left did not engage the issue.

Translating the idea of full employment into policy would have been

---

36  Lloyd Cutler, "Memorandum for the President," August 26, 1980 [1], C-201, Staff Secretary Papers, Jimmy Carter Library, Atlanta, Georgia.

37  J. Malkin to J. Douglas, October 12, 1978, f. 6, Box 3, Records of the Washington Bureau of the National Urban League, II, Library of Congress, Washington, DC.

difficult for a Democratic president possessing the political skills and intellectual ability of a FDR. As it turned out, the man given the job had none of them. President Jimmy Carter initially continued the Keynesian tradition—raising spending and reducing taxes. But many believed that Keynes did not address the kind of inflation the nation was experiencing. It was not a case of too much demand for too few goods, but inadequate or too costly supplies. Most of the inflation of the 1970s was caused by the rising prices of commodities—oil, grains, and beef. (Everyone remembers the Clinton scandal over Whitewater, but few recall the scandal over Hillary Clinton's participation in the beef price boom.) Because these were onetime developments, not patterns reflecting excessive wage increases, solutions required supply-side measures addressing each sector, larded by consensual measures between labor and capital. This was the recipe employed successfully in Germany and Japan.

But Carter was elected as an anti-Washington, anti-Watergate candidate. As governor of a small Southern state, he never had to deal with a powerful labor movement; he had wooed business, not bargained with it. His great successes were bringing Georgia's benighted state government into the twentieth century and accepting the changes produced by the civil rights movement. Taking Washington for Atlanta, he stressed the need to rationalize government. When his reform efforts failed, he fell back on the anti-Washington themes of his campaign and blamed the nation's problems on a bloated federal bureaucracy and recalcitrant Congress. During his 1976 campaign, he promised a government as good as the people; now the people were the problem, and he prescribed fewer demands on government and less selfishness. He pointed to the deficit as the source of inflation and spending fueled by selfish interest groups as the cause of the deficit, an analysis that only amplified his anti-government themes. But the leader of the Democratic Party, a diverse coalition that since the 1940s had argued for the goal of full employment and the expansion a mélange of federal programs, could not succeed politically on such principles.

The international situation didn't help. Carter's foreign policy was informed by the new internationalism of the Trilateral Commission, founded by David Rockefeller in 1973, both as a response to the unilateralism of Nixon and Kissinger and as an alternative to the universalism of the United Nations. Carter had been a trilateralist, and sixteen Trilateral Commissioners populated his administration. Their core belief was that the United States, Japan, and Europe had to cooperate in order to manage the new global situation of the 1970s. Carter thus stimulated the U.S. economy for both domestic and international reasons, hoping to make the United States "the locomotive" for a teetering global economy. But Europe and Japan, more fearful of inflation, attempted to export themselves out of trouble, rather than turn to public deficits to increase domestic demand, with the result that a torrent of manufacturing imports entered the United States from Germany and Japan. Between 1975 and 1978, U.S. imports more than doubled while exports increased less than one third.[38]

Declining productivity growth, especially in relative terms, also contributed to the rising U.S. trade deficits. After 1973, productivity increase fell in all of the developed countries. Having averaged 5.3 percent for the industrialized world as a whole between 1969 and 1973, it averaged just 2.8 percent between 1973 and 1979, but with the U.S. rate the lowest of all at less than 1 percent.[39] Yet the U.S. government lacked many of the best tools to enhance productivity. American Keynesianism commanded by manipulating budgets and taxes. It allowed the market to sort out the fate of different sectors. The United States did subsidize the home building industry, but homes are not tradable goods and did little for the balance of payments. The United States also planned and subsidized agriculture to good effect, the agricultural export surplus helping the nation's trade balance significantly during the 1970s. Unfortunately, agriculture supplied fewer and fewer jobs. Meanwhile, the Europeans and Japanese were closing off many of the best markets for American commodities.

So what could Carter do? He did not pick up the Humphrey-Javits initiative or any other kind of industrial planning when he first took office. His attacks on government and special interests made it difficult for him to bargain with business and labor on prices and wages. The growth of imports, the exodus of jobs and capital, and the fluidity of money blunted the old Keynesian tools, and the United States had no others in the kit. The president's insistence that deficits caused inflation limited whatever room to maneuver even the Keynesians still had. Carter did not fully understand the implications of his own appointment of the austerity-minded Paul Volcker in 1979 to head the Federal Reserve Board. He chose Volcker "to reassure the markets" about the dollar, in the words of *New York Times*

---

38   I. M. Destler and N. Mitsuyu, "Locomotives on Different Tracks: Macroeconomic Diplomacy, 1977–79," in I. M. Destler and Hideo Sato, eds, *Coping with US-Japanese Economic Conflicts* (Lexington, MA: D.C. Heath, 1982); Z. Brzezinski, *Power and Principle: Memoirs of the National Security Adviser, 1977 1981* (New York: Farrar, Straus & Giroux, 1981), pp. 314–5; S. Eizenstat and B. Ginsburg, "Memorandum for the President," August 12, 1977, 5 (Treasury opinion); R. Cooper to Z. Brzezinski, n.d.(Oct. 1–Dec. 31, 1977), WHCF, TA, C-TA-1; A. W. Wolff, "US International Trade Policy," March 21, 1977, International Trade, CF O/A 243, C-227, Eizenstat Papers, Carter Library.

39   A. Lindbeck, "The Recent Slowdown of Productivity Growth," *The Economic Journal* vol. 93 (March 1983), p. 14.

columnist Leonard Silk.[40] Inflation had shot up from 7.6 percent in 1978 to 13.5 percent in 1980, mainly because of the second oil crisis in the wake of the Iranian Revolution and rising food prices. But Carter's pollster Pat Cadell warned the president that it was the elites, especially the financial community, that were most concerned about inflation, not the people.[41] In fact, elite industrialists knew that there was no necessary relationship between inflation and growth,[42] and the Business Roundtable argued that the only solution to inflation was to "improve productivity."[43] It wanted tax changes, not austerity.

The Fed began its radical tightening on October 6, 1979, just after Volcker returned from an IMF meeting in Europe, where European bankers, who held many dollars that were losing value, gave Volcker an earful about U.S. inflation. It was a sign of the growing power of financial interests within the American polity that, unlike the price rises that accompanied the first oil crisis, those that accompanied the second one of 1979 would be met with deep austerity measures.[44] But the Fed went overboard, producing a short but sharp recession and instability everywhere. Carter's chair of the Council of Economic Advisers, Charles Schultze, told him in September 1980, "the Fed has made us all prisoners of its own rhetoric; monetary policy is driven much more by mechanics (short-term fluctuations in the money growth) than by consideration of what is going on in the economy itself."[45] Nothing worked for Carter. The Fed's sky-high interest rates, combined with elevated oil prices, pushed the economy into a sharp recession in 1980 without reducing inflation, preparing the ground for the advancing of new, radical economic solutions by the Right, even though the economy was in better shape than it had been in 1975, or would be

---

40 L. Silk, *New York Times*, July 27, 1979, D-2.

41 P. H. Caddell, "Memorandum for the President," March 1, 1980, CF O/A, Box 1, file Caddell, Pat 7/773/-80, Eizenstat Papers, Carter Library.

42 For inflation rates below 20 percent a year, relations between growth and inflation are not statistically significant. See R. Barrow, "Inflation and Economic Growth," Bank of England Quarterly Bulletin vol. 35:2 (May 1995), p. 12. J. E. Stiglitz makes the same point in his *Roaring Nineties: A New History of the World's Most Prosperous Decade* (New York: W. W. Norton, 2003).

43 "Statement of L. Stanton Williams on behalf of the Business Roundtable," submitted to the Joint Economic Committee, Congress of the United States, June 18, 1980, copy in possession of the author.

44 C. Schultze, "Memorandum for the President," September 25, 1979 [2], C-148, Staff Secretary Papers, Carter Library; H. Stein, *Presidential Economics: The Making of Economy Policy from Roosevelt to Reagan and Beyond*, 2nd rev. ed., (Washington, DC: American Enterprise Institute, 1988), pp. 229–31.

45 Schultze, "Memorandum for the President," September 18, 1980, p.2, f. 9/1980 [4], Box 206, Staff Secretary Papers, Carter Library.

during the recession of 1982. But everything appeared out of sorts and out of control in 1980. Old answers looked feeble, and supply-siders offered a seductive alternative, one which proposed to cure the country's problems without economic pain.

As the election approached, some of Carter's political advisers finally concluded that his program of budget cuts and high interest rates offered no prospect of economic revival, and was politically suicidal at a time when Ronald Reagan was offering broad tax cuts for individuals and businesses. So, in August 1980, the president proposed a semi-public corporation to mobilize private, pension, and public funds to finance critical industries. The bank would have tripartite management. Initially proposed by Lane Kirkland, the new leader of the AFL-CIO, the initiative assumed that industry needed new funds but that the tax cuts proposed by Reagan would not, any more than earlier ones, necessarily result in investment where it was needed or even at home. Even though Carter's embrace of this proposal for industrial policy was weak, the proposition created a firestorm within the Democratic Party. Charles Schultze declared there was "no evidence that we needed a new and vastly enlarged federal role in channeling investment among industries or locations."[46] Liberal Keynesians were not the only opposition. The proposal produced a mini-war between two tendencies in post-New Deal liberalism. The first was the anti-government strain that originated within the New Left. Ralph Nader's anti-corporatism led him to oppose all forms of tripartite governance. His politics substituted consumers, represented by activist lawyers like himself, for the traditional working class. Empowering unions was not part of his program. The second was the social democratic strain that had constituted a minor trend within the labor movement during the era of affluence, but now assumed an important role at a time when unions were concluding that the U.S. economy faced structural, not simply cyclical problems, and the more worldly Lane Kirkland replaced George Meany as head of the AFL-CIO.

The past weighed heavily on the present. There was no tradition of industrial planning. Acting reluctantly in response to short-term problems and political pressures rather than in accord with a long-term vision of domestic economic development, governments of both parties offered import relief sporadically, and usually only after the industry was hit by severe or unfair import competition.[47] Meanwhile, foreign investment

46   Schultze, "Memorandum for the President," August 24, 1980, f. 8/28/80 [4], Box 202, Staff Secretary Files, Carter Library.

47   In the 1980s, government spent five times more on R&D for commercial fisheries than for steel, and provided $455 million in tax breaks for the timber industry but none

abroad filled the gap opened up by the absence of an industrial policy. Multinational companies like Caterpillar Tractor solved their immediate problems by buying foreign parts abroad that went into domestically assembled products, while it made plans to build plants in countries where costs were lowest. The outcome was the rise of transnational production, based in international supply chains. Electronics producers were already globalizing during the mid-1960s, even though this form of production would fully mature in the late 1970s and 1980s, when corporations felt intensifying pressure on costs, due especially to rising oil prices and emerging competition from state-led, newly industrializing economies, especially in East Asia.

Even had Carter been more committed to industrial policy, he had run out of time. Neither traditional Keynesianism nor the Fed's new monetarism improved the economy, and their failures empowered groups who proposed alternatives. Ronald Reagan was aided by a newly mobilized business community. Through associations like the Business Roundtable (1973) and richly funded think tanks, such as the American Enterprise Institute (1970) and the Heritage Foundation (1973), American business, which had traditionally lobbied to advance the interests of individual businesses or a single business sector, now ended its parochialism and used its combined power to influence broad areas of public policy—labor, taxation, energy, and regulation. Business now openly repudiated the mixed economy of enterprises regulated by the state and labor. Government and unions, and in some instances democracy itself, were seen as fetters on investment and production. Reagan gathered the support of the new industries of the South and West, especially energy, defense, and financial services, which had never been enthusiastic about the mixed economy, along with traditional manufacturing, which now disengaged from it. Even so, most who voted for Ronald Reagan were unfamiliar with the new coalitions and the new economic theories. They had simply lost faith in Jimmy Carter. Only 11 percent of those who voted for Reagan did so because they believed he was a conservative; 38 percent because they thought it was time for a change.[48] The electorate repudiated Carter, but it was a decision based upon his performance, not any particular ideology.

Power allows those with ideas to implement them. After Ronald Reagan won, he acted to weaken unions and government regulation and promote business and market solutions. But this recipe for economic governance did not triumph in the 1970s, or even 1980, but only in 1983, when the president convinced the nation that his policies of tax reduction and

---

for semiconductors. R. B. Reich, *Tales of a New America* (New York: Times Books, 1987).
48   *New York Times*, November 9, 1980.

deregulation had produced the upturn, reducing the unemployment rate from 10.8 percent in January 1983 to 7.5 percent by January 1984. In the meantime, the 1982 recession had reduced inflation to 3.2 percent, and at the beginning of 1984 it was still only 4.3 percent. So the president went into the 1984 election year with employment rising and inflation falling. Ironically, the president had to destroy the economy in order to save it, his government s policies producing the worst economic slump since the 1930s in 1982, when GNP fell 2.1 percent. But Reagan blamed the recession on Carter and then took credit for the upward turn in 1983, claiming that his supply-side policies and the free market had done it. The Reagan way was not the only way to resolve the conflicts of the 1970s. But the Democrats put forward no alternative to the classical Keynesianism of the postwar years, and the Fed's austerity, helped by falling oil prices and the recession, ended the inflation, while Reagan's tax cuts and defense spending boosted consumption. Reagan's promises of increased productivity and investment were unkept, the trade deficit grew, now accompanied by a huge budget deficit. Nevertheless, because it was a recovery, its methods—tax cuts, deregulation, and privatization—were enshrined as the new bipartisan consensus, replacing the Keynesianism of the postwar era.

# 4

# Understanding the Rank-and-File Rebellion in the Long 1970s

## Kim Moody[1]

"The rank-and-file union revolts that have been developing in the industrial workplaces since the early 1950s are now plainly visible. Like many of their compatriots, American workers are faced with paces, methods and conditions of work that are increasingly intolerable. Their union leaders are not sensitive to these conditions." So wrote trade union activist and longtime socialist Stan Weir in his classic 1967 article, which offered an initial interpretation of the rank-and-file labor rebellion.[2] Employers were exerting stepped-up pressure on the labor force, especially on the shop floor, but the trade union leadership was dragging its heels in mounting a defense. The workers therefore found themselves with little choice but to take matters into their own hands, the ensuing struggles often as much against the labor officials as against the bosses. As he presciently concluded, "the United States faces a period in which the struggles of the unionized sections of the population will have a direct and visible effect on the future of the entire population,"[3] and over the next decade and a half, the country was indeed gripped by a working-class upheaval that came to encompass not only the CIO manufacturing unions that still constituted labor's big battalions, but also farm laborers, teachers, professionals, and government service workers, all constituencies left largely untouched by the great labor upsurge of the 1930s.

From the mid-1960s to the 1980s, wildcat strikes once again became

---

1   Parts of this essay are adapted from the author's *An Injury to All* (New York: Verso, 1988).

2   S. Weir, "U.S.A.—The Labor Revolt," *International Socialism Journal* vol. IV:1 & 2 (1967). This and other works by Stan Weir are now available in G. Lipsitz, ed., *Stan Weir: Singlejack Solidarity* (Minneapolis: University of Minnesota Press, 2004), for which page references below.

3   Weir, "U.S.A.—The Labor Revolt," p. 294.

common, official work stoppages reached historic levels in absolute terms, rank-and-file caucuses emerged in union after union at both the local and national levels, black and Latino workers built their own organizations within the unions, working-class feminism exploded onto the scene as a new creative force, and public workers organized themselves on a broad scale for the first time, led by militants in schools, hospitals, post offices, and city services. The labor upsurge of the 1960s and 1970s was thus profoundly influenced by, and also helped to influence, the great social movements that shaped the era, above all the historic black movement for civil rights. Like Latinos, women, gays, and, indeed, the growing mass of American citizens against the Vietnam War, rank-and-file workers imitated the black struggle's rights consciousness, mass mobilizations, and direct-action tactics. When the civil rights movement moved north and gave rise to urban rebellions and radical political trends like Black Power, it powerfully influenced the consciousness of rank-and-file workers, particularly of course black workers in factories and offices who often led the workers' revolts.

The industrial upsurge reflected and contributed to the decline of authority across much of society and the spirit of cultural, political, and social rebellion of the era. Its working-class cultural icons included the black militant strikers of DRUM (Dodge Revolutionary Union Movement) at Chrysler's Dodge Main plant in Detroit in 1968, on the one hand, and the young, long-haired white workers at General Motors' (GM) brand new assembly plant in Lordstown, Ohio, in 1972. Whether they knew it or not, these young worker rebels were following in the footsteps of the black women domestic workers who refused to ride the buses of Montgomery, Alabama, in 1955, the coal miners who struck for Black Lung benefits in the late 1960s, the urban rioters from Harlem in 1964 to Detroit in 1967, and the countless Vietnam War protesters of every age, race, and class. What set them on this journey of rebellion, however, was not simply inspiration or imitation; it was a qualitative shift in the functioning of the U.S. economy and the way in which U.S. businesses, and in turn the leaderships of their unions, responded to it.

Toward the end of the 1950s, for the first time since the Great Depression, the U.S. economy was hit by a serious downturn. Two recessions in quick succession ushered in a half-decade of stagnation. American corporations succeeded for the time being in transcending this slowdown; nevertheless, even while enjoying a new wave of expansion across the 1960s, from the middle of the decade they faced an even more formidable threat— what turned out to be a very major, long-term fall in their profitability. Faced with these increasingly difficult problems, the corporations had little choice but to unleash an ever more far reaching offensive against their employees, aiming to cut costs so as to revive their rates of return. The union leaderships, for their part, had believed that they had secured during the prosperous 1950 a modus vivendi with the employers, albeit one in which they were obliged to sustain a high level of strikes in order to secure steady gains for their members. But they were now confronted, suddenly and without warning, with their greatest challenge since the 1930s.

## The State of the Unions

The unions that sustained the employers' heightening attacks from the late 1950s on were hardly the same organizations that took shape in the 1930s labor upsurge and led the huge wave of industry-wide and local general strikes of 1945–6. The dynamic, often highly democratic, internal life that had characterized many of these unions had been suppressed, if not entirely eliminated, as authority was centralized, the Communists expelled from the CIO, McCarthyism and Cold War ideology imported into union culture, and the internal labor press turned into self-congratulatory propaganda for the leadership. The material basis of this growing bureaucratization was strengthened by increasingly complex contracts (the "private welfare state"), which called forth squads of lawyers and armies of "reps" and business agents loyal to the regimes that hired them. On this widening social layer was nurtured the ideology of modern business unionism.[4]

In academic thought, the development of bureaucratic rule within labor organizations has long tended to be seen as a natural process associated with the increasing maturity of labor relations. Unions, the theory has it, proceed from their turbulent organizing phase, during which the labor leader is an agitator, to a more fully evolved relationship with management when the labor leader becomes an administrator. Perhaps the classic formulation of this theory appears in Robert Michels's 1911 study of German Social Democracy, *Political Parties*. Viewing the evolution of the trade union leader from the early days of the union through its development as a mass organization, Michels argued that "The great complexity of the duties which the trade union has now to fulfill and the increasing importance assumed in the life of the union by financial, technical, and administrative questions, render it necessary that the agitator should give place to the employee equipped with technical knowledge."[5] The growth of bureaucracy was nothing less than an "Iron Law of Oligarchy." It was not simply a tendency, but an inevitability.

In the 1950s a similar theory emerged within American academia and was given a textbook formulation by the labor economist Richard Lester in his 1958

---

4   Moody, *An Injury to All*, pp. 41–69.

5   R. Michels, *Political Parties: A Sociological Study of the Oligarchical Tendencies of Modern Democracy* (New York: Collier Books, 1962), p. 280.

book with the telltale title *Unions Mature*. Lester describes the maturation process much as did Michels:

> As a union's growth curve begins to level off, subtle psychological changes tend to take place. The turbulence and enthusiasm of youth, the missionary zeal of a new movement, slow down to a more moderate pace. Increasingly, decisions are made centrally, as a political machine becomes entrenched, as the channels of union communication are more tightly controlled from the top, and as reliance on staff specialists grows.[6]

Like Michels before him, Lester includes "the good life on a sizable salary" among a group of potentially corrupting influences on the modern labor leader and ventures that "with increasing size," "democratic checks may have weakened." But these are at best contributing factors to the process of bureaucratization. For Lester and most other academic labor theorists writing before the 1960s, bureaucracy is the gradual and inevitable result of an almost biological process.

This scenario did of course have a certain descriptive resonance, especially from the vantage point of the later 1950s. The labor movement had settled down, and all-powerful administrative machines had emerged in control of the unions. Union members did appear to have become more complacent as their wages rose. Bureaucracy therefore seemed to go hand in hand with unionism's very success and its acceptance by society and the employers. Nevertheless, this view, derived from a snapshot in time, confused cause and effect in the actual evolution of postwar industrial relations. Bureaucracy in the CIO did not evolve gradually and peacefully; it had to be fought for and imposed against enormous resistance where it did not already exist, as in the UAW, and aggressively defended and expanded where it did, as in the Steelworkers. Far from the natural outcome of the rise of the system of collective bargaining, bureaucratic rule had to consolidate itself before labor–management relations could be stabilized. The onset of wartime conditions was crucial in enabling the initiation and acceleration of this process, but it would not be completed until well into the postwar era.

A decade before American economists and sociologists were concluding that union bureaucracy was an inevitable product of mature labor relations, an earlier generation was hailing it as a desirable if not necessary precondition. In a Brookings Institution study published in 1941, economist Sumner Slichter extolled the advantages of bureaucratic authority in labor relations. From the premise that top officials are better able to grasp the consequences and long-term results of bargaining, Slichter concluded that "unions are more successful in adjusting themselves to technological and market changes when the officers

---

6   R. Lester, *When Unions Mature* (Princeton, NJ: Princeton University Press, 1958), pp. 160–7.

are permitted to make policies and negotiate agreements without ratification by the rank and file."[7] More likely than not, this observation was based on the experience of such prominent and highly bureaucratic unions as Sidney Hillman's Amalgamated Clothing Workers and John L. Lewis's United Mine Workers of America (UMWA). Indeed, Hillman, Lewis, and Philip Murray, who like Lewis came to the CIO and the Steelworkers from the UMWA, brought with them nearly two decades of bureaucratic experience. All three shared Slichter's view that authoritative leaders were better placed to deal with constantly changing conditions than the membership. All three were separated by decades from their roots in industrial work. In the 1920s both Hillman and Lewis had ruthlessly suppressed opposition within their respective unions. Their disagreement with the old-line leaders of the AFL was not over union democracy or how to relate to the employers, but over industrial organization. The new organizations they built, the national CIO and the Steel Workers Organizing Committee, predecessor of the United Steelworkers, reflected their bureaucratic outlook.

Hillman was the prototype of the bureaucratic labor statesman. According to labor historian Irving Bernstein, "Hillman addressed himself to the acquisition and manipulation of power." C. Wright Mills singled out Hillman as a leader among those seeking recognition in national ruling circles: "His lead during the early war years, his awareness of himself as a member of the national elite, and the real and imagined recognition he achieved as a member signaled the larger entrance . . . of labor leaders into the power elite." Even before the war, Hillman had become an emissary of the Roosevelt administration, working hard to end strikes at defense-oriented plants. When this role became embodied in official government agencies with broad powers to intervene in management-labor relations, Hillman, along with other top AFL and CIO leaders, was enabled to achieve a hitherto inconceivable control over previously autonomous unions.[8]

So long as the CIO's individual member organizations retained the power to conduct bargaining on their own on an industry-by-industry basis, the fact that the CIO at the federation level was bureaucratic did not much affect their structure or functioning. Aside from SWOC and the CIO itself, most of the new CIO unions were built up from the grassroots in militant struggles against the employers, and, until the war, they maintained the highly democratic organizations, at both the national and local levels. Against this background, bureaucracy could begin to

---

7 Quoted in D. Montgomery, *Workers' Control in America: Studies in the History of Work, Technology, and Labor Struggles* (Cambridge: Cambridge University Press, 1979), pp. 165–6.

8 I. Bernstein, *The Turbulent Years: A History of the American Worker, 1933–1941* (Boston: Houghton Mifflin, 1969), p. 74; I. L. Horowitz, ed., *Power, Politics and People: The Collected Essays of C. Wright Mills* (New York: Oxford University Press, 1962), p. 97; D. Milton, *The Politics of U.S. Labor: From the Great Depression to the New Deal* (New York: Monthly Review Press, 1982), pp. 130–1.

consolidate itself only when the state's wartime labor policy shifted bargaining between the unions and management away from the shop floor and the local union to the level of the federal government. Since the primary consideration of the negotiators was war production, not the needs of workers as they arose from employer-employee conflict at the point of production, the War Labor Board (WLB), composed of representatives of the corporations, the unions, and the government, viewed rank-and-file resistance in a hostile manner and sought to repress it, opening the way for Hillman, Lewis, and Murray to fashion a new relationship with their affiliated unions.

The WLB lost little time in making national policy of Sumner Slichter's wish for more bureaucratic control. In a 1942 case involving a strike at a small New England steel fabricating plant, the WLB ruled: "If this union is to become a responsible organization acting through its leaders, it is necessary that it have some powers over its members." A year later, when asked if the WLB recognized the right of union members to organize against the policy of their union leadership, WLB member William Davis replied that the board did not. In 1943 the board encouraged the leadership of the United Rubber Workers (URW) to control its locals and shop-floor organizations, and shortly thereafter the WLB upheld URW president Sherman Dalrymple when he expelled seventy-two members and fined several hundred others for their rebellious activity.[9]

Nevertheless, the struggle to establish bureaucratic power in the CIO unions was inevitably difficult, long, and politically complex. In virtually all the new unions, administrations that upheld the no-strike pledge in practice or moved to discipline locals faced opposition. Unauthorized strikes involving literally millions of industrial workers, unofficial shop-floor bargaining by strong stewards' organizations, rebellions by locals, and factionalism at union conventions constituted business as usual throughout the war and well into the postwar era. The economists' dream of a docile union membership led through the turbulent, ever-changing marketplace by an unchallenged leadership, always a myth, was simply out of the question under the conditions of rapid union growth, increasing workers' power, and rising expectations that prevailed during the war.

To consolidate bureaucratic rule so as to put into place the postwar system of labor relations, the emerging CIO officialdom had to take power and authority away from the workplace and the local union, while at the same time monopolizing communications at the national level by weakening the direct connections among locals. This required, in the first instance, bringing the great majority of issues negotiated with management under a national contract, most prominently including issues hitherto thought of as local, such as production standards and line speed. Locals would be left with less to bargain over and the power of top

---

9   N. Lichtenstein, *Labor's War at Home: The CIO in World War II* (Cambridge: Cambridge University Press, 1982), pp. 180–2.

officials extended. But such centralization would have been difficult to achieve had sophisticated political means not been found to concentrate decision-making power at the top and to weaken the unions' shop-floor organization, always the center of resistance to bureaucratization.

Here again, the federal government took the first step, establishing what Lichtenstein termed "industrial jurisprudence," with the full approval and support of the CIO leadership. This was the four-step wartime grievance procedure, which concluded with arbitration and which barred strikes and other forms of direct action. The new formalized structure, accepted by the CIO in 1942, was intended to replace the old, largely informal system of workplace negotiations, in which the outcome was determined in the final analysis by the threat of confrontation and the balance of power, an arrangement from which the shop stewards derived their strength. As Lichtenstein explains, "The system shifted disputes from the shop floor, where the stewards and work groups held the greatest leverage, to the realm of contractual interpretation, where the authority of management and the value of orderly procedure weighed more heavily."[10]

Nevertheless, the attempt to remove power from the shop floor did not really succeed during World War II, especially because high levels of employment and the demands of production for the war effort endowed workers with so much leverage. Management could not yet secure the clear legal or contractual right to discipline rebellious workers in the face of intervention by the stewards or direct action by informal work groups. The precedents defining what was grievable or not were insufficient to establish universally accepted norms. Nevertheless, in the years following the war, a body of such norms was indeed amassed, as grievance procedures were incorporated into the increasingly complex labor contracts negotiated throughout industry. In the 1946 Ford and Chrysler contracts, for example, the UAW granted "company security" no-strike clauses that gave management the contractual right to discipline workers who wildcatted. What would especially weaken workplace organization in subsequent years was the inclusion of the steward representation system in the contract itself. This gave the company the right to bargain over the extent of workers' shop-floor representation . . . and the union officialdom the right to accede to its diminution. From the one steward for every foreman that initially prevailed in many CIO-organized industries, the ratio of stewards to the shop-floor labor force declined dramatically; by the 1950s each steward was obliged to represent hundreds of workers and to confront ever more numerous company supervisors.

In building the power of the bureaucracy, the weakening of workplace union organization was one side of the equation. The other entailed translating the power that the officials derived from negotiating national contracts into control over the union's internal affairs. Despite how far-reaching the advance of bureaucratic

---

10   Ibid., pp. 179–80.

power was during the war, the authority of top officials still largely depended on the role of the WLB in centralizing control over wage determination. If the nascent system of labor relations constructed during the war was to survive the transition to a peacetime economy and evolve further, the leaderships would have to concentrate power in their own hands within the union organizations themselves by constructing viable political machines that extended from the national headquarters down to the local. But to make this happen in the turbulent conditions of the 1940s, union officials had to defeat oppositional political trends within the union, as well as recalcitrant militants on the shop floor.

Walter Reuther—who was head of the UAW's GM Department in 1945 when he advanced his innovative idea of wage increases with no price increases—was a master of maneuver. His brother Victor Reuther remembered years later that "the GM strike [of 1945–6] was designed to take the ball out of the hands of the stewards and committeemen and put it back in the hands of the national leadership." Reuther's willingness to put forward a radical program and to strike GM for a long time paved the way for his election as president of the UAW in 1946.[11]

The wartime CIO was alive with rank-and-file-based political trends, factions, and caucuses. Communists, socialists of all kinds, Democrats, organized Catholics, and just plain militant trade unionists formed organizations within their unions that debated policy and contended for power. This ongoing political contest was a powerful source of union democracy. No matter how much authority they had accrued over the bargaining process, the top leaders of most CIO unions still had to contend with opponents whose roots among workers and support within the ranks were very real and who had the ability to organize on a nationwide basis, often with the help of national left-wing political groups or parties with whom they were allied.

In examining the growth of bureaucracy in unions in the years following World War II, C. Wright Mills, by analogy with the urban political machine, wrote, "Between the democracy of the town meeting and the discipline necessary for militant action, there is a tension which the labor leader has resolved in the way of formal democracies everywhere—by the political machine."[12] In fact, the labor officialdom increasingly eschewed militant action in favor of routinized collective bargaining. Nevertheless, the tension was still very real, especially as a consequence of the ongoing pressure from below. The top union officials were able to deal with it by

11   Lichtenstein, *Labor War at Home*, p. 226; W. Serrin, *The Company and the Union: The "Civilized Relationship" of the General Motors Corporation and the United Automobile Workers* (New York: Vintage Books, 1974), pp. 135–8.

12   C. Wright Mills, *The New Men of Power: America's Labor Leaders* (Urbana: University of Illinois Press, 2001), p. 5.

constructing their own machines, not least by making use of the increasing patronage at their disposal, the ever greater number of full-time union offices that they had the right to fill.

Bureaucratization requires the building up of organization that is increasingly insulated from "outside"—i.e., rank-and-file—influence. So the growth in the number of full-timers appointed by top officials in the unions' various headquarters, departments, and so on was key. Writing in the late 1950s, Sidney Lens told of how the "business agents" had taken over the older craft unions years before, and he described in much the same terms the rise and political impact of the International Representatives who came to patrol the contract for the newer industrial unions. As hired guns for the leadership, these "reps" no longer spoke for internal factions, much less the rank and file. As Lens wrote, "The 'reps' speak as one voice with the top leadership. They often pay regular 'dues' to their top official's caucus, usually checked off their salaries, and they speak in favor of official 'policy' at meetings of the local unions they service, whether or not they personally agree with it. They are now part of the 'team.'"[13]

In the UAW, for example, not including office and maintenance employees or those employed by local unions, the full-time staff grew from 407 in 1949, already well above what it had been before the war, to 780 in 1958. After an economy drive it was reduced to 660 in 1960. This still added up to 60 percent growth over a decade, triple the 21 percent growth in union membership. Except for the eighteen-member International Executive Board, none of the full-time International staff was elected. By 1961, the average staffer had worked full time for 10.5 years. It had become a career. By 1964, U.S. unions employed 13,000 people in their national headquarters alone.[14]

Accelerating the process of bureaucratization, key struggles by militants to strengthen the union had the unintended and ironic result of enhancing the power of the machine, notably the fights for full-time committeemen and automatic dues check off. The former was aimed at better representation of the rank and file on the shop floor, the latter a greater union security. But both ended up by expanding the material base for the bureaucracy, the number of full-timers it could appoint and money flowing into its coffers, and further insulating it from control by the membership.[15]

13 S. Lens, *The Crisis of American Labor* (New York: Sagamore Press, 1959), pp. 46–69, 222–3.

14 J. Stieber, *Governing the UAW* (New York: John Wiley & Sons, 1962), pp. 92–4; Moody, *An Injury to All*, p. 64.

15 For this point, see G. Perusek, "Classical Political Sociology and Union Behavior," in G. Perusek and K. Worcester, eds, *Trade Union Politics: American Unions and Economic change, 1960s–1990s* (Atlantic Highlands, NJ: Humanities Press International, 1995), p. 68.

Democracy above the local union level was reduced to a formality in most of the major unions, including the most "progressive," like the UAW. The leadership and its army of experts and "reps" was transformed into a distinct social layer, based in the union organization itself, which controlled the process of collective bargaining and contract administration and represented the union as institution. While historically the machine begat the social layer, it now became an expression of that layer, which had its own self-interest to protect and extend. It did not hurt in this respect that the union leaderships could offer ordinary workers well-paid full-time employment away from the shop floor, mill, or assembly line—a powerful temptation not just to opportunists but to dedicated activists.

The ability of the leaderships in most unions to establish and sustain their increasingly elaborate bureaucratic administrations, as well as their own positions within them, ultimately rested on at least the acquiescence of the membership, and, during the first postwar decades, this was secured, to a large extent, by way of their successful practice of modern business unionism, conditioned in turn upon the prolonged economic boom. If the old business unionists of the AFL had operated on the principle that "unions are big business," to quote Teamster president Dave Beck, the business unionists of the CIO did the same, but gave the phrase a new social meaning by building a "private welfare state" by bargaining for increased benefits to supplement gains in wages. Having seen their political hopes for an American social democracy along European lines ignominiously collapse in the late 1940s, unions turned to negotiating directly with the employers for longer vacations, pensions, and health insurance.

"Social unionists," like business unionists more generally, saw the protection of capitalist profits as a top priority and the precondition for gains for the membership, and, thanks to the maintenance of high corporate rates of return through much of the 1950s, workers lucky enough to hold on to jobs in the leading industries enjoyed rapidly rising living standards. But the fact was that the union leaderships had little choice but to nurture the goose that laid the golden eggs, as the benefits that came to define their own success had to be purchased by way of their explicit commitment to help increase the company's productivity and thus profitability, even though this might mean the loss of jobs and/or more intense labor on the shop floor. John L. Lewis set the trend in a dramatic way in the 1950 coal industry agreement with the BCOA. In return for increased wages and benefits, the coal operators would be allowed to produce coal "at the lowest possible cost permitted by modern technology." As a result, employment in the industry plummeted over the next decade, the surplus army of unemployed in the coal regions reached historic proportions, and the UMWA left in a profoundly weakened state vis-à-vis the employers.[16] In 1957, paving the way for his signing the Modernization and Mechanization Agreement of 1960, Harry Bridges spelled out the arrangement even more clearly when he asked his members, "Do you want to continue our present policy of guerrilla resistance to the machine, or do we want to adopt a more flexible policy in order to buy specific benefits in return?"[17] The workplace was thus surrendered to management in hopes that increased productivity would continue to underwrite increased compensation and thereby counteract worker dissatisfaction with the layoffs and/or deteriorating working conditions that were the inevitable by-product of increased output per person.

In order to enforce the fundamental trade-off of working conditions and union control of the shop floor for increasing wages and benefits, top officials continued to centralize the bargaining process ever increasingly in their own hands. Ever more unions adopted the practice of having the International sign all agreements, local as well as national—the Rubber Workers in 1947, the UAW and the Steelworkers in 1950. Contracts that had been renegotiated annually were lengthened to three years in the 1950s, which not only spoke to the companies' requirements for longer-term planning, but the bureaucracies' own preference for minimizing the communication with and among the members that was required at contract time. The contradictions that spurred the revolt from below emerging in the early 1960s were thus built into the very structure and functioning of bureaucratic business unionism, even as it succeeded in its own terms.

### Workforce Change: Youth, Race, and Gender

For one thing, a new generation of workers, many of them Vietnam veterans, entered the workforce with a new set of attitudes. One retired auto worker noted that "the younger generation is not going to take the crap that we had to take. They got more sense." A UAW local union president, pointing specifically at black workers, said, "Young people . . . won't accept the conditions their fathers accepted. It's much harder to tie young black guys to the assembly line than it was thirty years ago."[18] A Steelworker official remarked in a similar vein, "Most of the older workers in my area are immigrants. They're somewhat afraid of authority. When a foreman pushed them around they take it. The young generation coming in now won't take that."[19]

---

16   P. Nyden, below, pp. 173–199.
17   Moody, *An Injury To All*, p. 67.
18   W. Serrin, *The Company and the Union*, p. 233.
19   J. Brecher, *Strike!* (Cambridge, MA: South End Press, 1997), p. 251.

Perhaps the most important changes were the mass entry of married women and African Americans into the workforce of the nation's major private industries and its growing public sector. The American working class has always been different from that of most other industrial nations in that it has experienced almost constant demographic change. In the years of the formation of the industrial workforce, from 1870 to 1920, over 26 million immigrants entered the country, while in the same period the non-agricultural workforce grew from about 6 million to just over 23 million.[20]

During both World Wars, large numbers of African Americans migrated from the rural South to the industrial North, again changing the complexion of the working class. In the years following World War II, some 4 million African Americans moved north, raising the proportion of the black population in the Northeast and Midwest from 5.5 percent in 1950 to 9.2 percent in 1970. In these years, industrial cities like Detroit and Gary moved toward becoming majority black cities. The auto plants and steel mills of these and other cities saw a dramatic rise in the proportion of black workers. Of the 9 million African Americans in the civilian workforce by 1970, 2.7 million were in basic industry.[21] By 1972 there were a quarter of a million African Americans in the auto industry. At GM and Chrysler, 25 percent of the hourly workforce was black, while at Ford it was 35 percent.[22] The percentage in steel was much lower, but in U.S. Steel's Gary Works it was about 25 percent in 1974.[23] Everywhere they went into northern industry, black workers met discrimination and racism. They found it in the workplace, where few were admitted to skilled jobs and hostility could be intense. Despite entering heavy industry in the North, the median family income of African Americans improved in relation to white income only slightly, from 53 percent in 1945 to 58 percent in 1973.[24]

The other major demographic change that took place just prior to and during the upsurge was the large-scale entrance of married women into the workforce. Stephanie Coontz notes, "Wives and mothers first started to work in great numbers in the 1950s in order to supplement their families' purchasing

20   J. Jones et al., *Created Equal: A Social and Political History of the United States, Vol. II* (New York: Longman, 2003), p. 550.

21   P. Foner, *Organized Labor and the Black Worker, 1619–1973* (New York: Pra Publishers, 1974), p. 425.

22   B. J. Widick, "Black Workers: Double Discontents," in Widick, *Auto Work and Its Discontents* (Baltimore: Johns Hopkins University Press), p. 57.

23   E. Greer, *Big Steel: Black Politics and Corporate Power in Gary, Indiana* (New York: Monthly Review Press, 1979), p. 103.

24   Greer, *Big Steel*, p. 101.

power . . ."[25] As Johanna Brenner has pointed out, they were taking these jobs not when the children had left home, but during childhood when family expenses were greatest, and that mostly among working-class women.[26] From 1950 to 1970, women went from 29 percent of the workforce to 38 percent, while married women grew from 52 percent of those workers to 63 percent in 1970.[27] From 1960 through 1974, 1.3 million women joined unions, accounting for 37 percent of union growth in those years. They went from 18 percent of the all union members to 21 percent during that period, and by 1980 women composed 30 percent of union membership.[28] These new women workers poured into the growing public sector unions like AFSCME and the AFT, but also led some of the independent unions of that era. Notable was the trend-setting Social Service Employees Union, in the New York City Welfare Department, which conducted a ground-breaking strike in 1965, led by socialist Judy Mage.[29] In the 1970s, airline flight attendants won autonomy, in the case of the Association of Flight Attendants, or gained independence from male-dominated unions, creating some of the first female-led national unions.[30] In the same years, African American woman Lillian Roberts led the organization of the city's public hospital workers through a series of strikes, following black and Latino women who began pouring into Local 1199 in the private hospitals in the late 1950s.[31]

The entry of married women into the workforce and of African Americans into heavy industry in the North was met with silence on the part of the major unions of the AFL-CIO. The growing insularity of business unionism's industry-by-industry, company-by-company focus on wages and benefits, along with the racism and sexism that dwelt in the house of labor, blinded it to the potential of the new workers. Labor ignored the growing proportion of minority and women workers in the workforce, even when many of them were entering the bastions of industrial unionism. The AFL-CIO's legislative department usually supported civil rights legislation, but only if it did not threaten existing labor practices or institutions (like limiting apprenticeships to white males)—and then only after demonstrations, civil disobedience, and even violence had made some reform

---

25  S. Coontz, *The Way We Never Were: American Families and the Nostalgia Trap* (New York: Basic Books, 1992), p. 38.

26  J. Brenner, *Women and the Politics of Class* (New York: Monthly Review Press, 2000), p. 68.

27  Statistical Abstract 1972, pp. 216, 219.

28  Statistical Abstract 1976, p. 384; Moody, *An Injury to All*, p. 272.

29  M. Maier, *City Unions: Managing Discontent in New York City* (New Brunswick, NJ: Rutgers University Press, 1987), pp. 62–72.

30  G. P. Nielsen, *From Sky Girl to Flight Attendant: Women and the Making of a Union* (Ithaca: Cornell University Press, 1982), pp. 3, 117–34.

31  Maier, City Unions, pp. 53–4; Leon Fink and Brian Greenberg, *Upheaval in the Quiet Zone: 1199SEIU and the Politics of Health Care Unionism* (Urbana: University of Illinois, 1989).

unavoidable. No John L. Lewis stood up to demand the organization of these new millions of workers. Unions might organize the new workers in their jurisdictions, but there was no coordinated strategy or pooling of resources like those that had launched the CIO. The barrier was not financial but ideological. In effect, business unionism disarmed itself rather than prepare for the struggles to come.

Black and women workers did not suffer quietly the indignities of union racism and sexism for long. First to mobilize were African American workers. By 1960, A. Philip Randolph, already in the midst of a fight with AFL-CIO leader George Meany, pulled together a network of pre-existing local committees and caucuses of black trade unionists to form the Negro American Labor Council (NALC).[32] The NALC took a militant stance against segregation in the labor movement, but most of its activity was focused on union politics, not the problems of black workers on the shop floor. Eventually the group made its peace with the leadership of the AFL-CIO, causing more militant African American labor activists to found the Coalition of Black Trade Unionists (CBTU) in 1972.[33] Like the NALC, however, the CBTU was based on black union officials, which explains its focus on the development of black leadership within the union hierarchy and its inability to lead more than a handful of black rank-and-file workers in more than a few effective campaigns. The NALC and CBTU were quite different from a more radical set of groups based among black rank-and-file workers that arose in the late 1960s, including most spectacularly the Revolutionary Union Movements in Detroit. Though built to address racism on the job and in the unions, these groups were part of the broader rank-and-file revolt of the 1960s and 1970s, which is discussed in more detail below.

Like black workers, women workers also built their own caucuses and committees to fight discrimination and press for gains within the labor movement. The best-known were Union WAGE (Union Women's Alliance to Gain Equality) and the Coalition of Labor Union Women (CLUW). Both groups combined the concerns of feminists and unionists, though not without conflict. Founded in 1971, Union WAGE developed demands that became common in the working women's movement, including equal pay for equal work, affirmative action, employer- and government-supported childcare, greater female participation in union leadership, and the organization of unorganized women workers. Uniquely, Union WAGE, with much of its base in California, played a central role in the passage of legislation requiring a number of protections to men that had previously been limited to women, including limitations

---

32   Foner, *Organized Labor and the Black Worker*, pp. 332–4.
33   Ibid., pp. 433–5.

on hours, premium overtime pay, and rest and meal periods.[34] CLUW was founded in 1974 as a national organization with a more mainstream feminist program. While it attracted many local union activists in its early years, it was always dominated by officials seeking to promote women into higher union office. There were many other groups, either local or specific to an industry or union. Looking back on the decade in 1979, *Labor Notes* asked the question, "What's Happening in the Working Women's Movement?" In an article based on a questionnaire, it answered by noting the existence of both official and unofficial organizations of women union activists, many fighting for entrance into "nontraditional" jobs in auto, steel, coal mining, and construction. Among those mentioned were the USWA District 31 Women's Caucus, Women in Steel in the Pittsburgh area, the UAW Region 1 Women's Council, Women in the Skilled Trades in Detroit, Hard-Hatted Women based in Pittsburgh, the Coal Employment Project, and Working Women or 9to5 in Cleveland, which attempted to organize clerical workers. Along with CLUW, many of these groups joined the fight for the Equal Rights Amendment, helping to push their unions and the AFL-CIO to support it.[35] These were only some of the more visible currents of working-class women's organization in the upsurge, and women's rights consciousness among working-class women was far broader and deeper. As Karen Nussbaum of 9to5 observed in 1979, "The ideas of equality for women have seeped down and affected the lives of working women who were not involved in the women's movement."[36]

Together and separately, the massive entrance of African Americans and women into the workforce starting in the 1950s shaped the working-class upsurge of the 1960s and 1970s, first by the mere presence of these workers with very different work and union experiences, and second by their involvement in the major social movements of the era. The existence of the civil rights/Black Power and women's movements gave the labor upsurge as a whole a broader political consciousness that it would not otherwise have had. Indeed, it is hard to imagine the rank-and-file upsurge of the 1960s and 1970s without the migration of African Americans to the industrial North and the entrance of married women into paid work. The independent social movements that each group spawned shaped the consciousness of the entire upsurge.

---

34  D. Balser, *Sisterhood and Solidarity: Feminism and Labor in Modern Times* (Cambridge, MA: South End Press, 1987), pp. 87–149.

35  *Labor Notes* #7 (August 1979), pp. 8–9; Moody, *An Injury to All*, pp. 272–81.

36  Quoted in J. Green, *The World of the Worker: Labor in Twentieth Century America* (Urbana: University of Illinois Press, 1998), pp. 240–1.

## The Origins of the Rebellion

The arrival of African American and women workers was not the only change to which the official American labor movement failed to respond. By the later years of the 1950s, the ability of bureaucratic business unionists to secure a certain working relationship with the employers, however tense, *and* to deliver the goods to their rank and file, however incompletely, conveyed a look of stability, even permanence. It was the seeming inevitability of the emerging system of industrial relations that gave rise in these years to theorizations of the labor movement in terms of evolutionary maturation and the functionality of bureaucracy.[37] But the appearance of finality would quickly prove illusory. This was because the relative amelioration of the ongoing conflict between capital and labor in this era had been premised on continuing economic expansion. When profits fell, growth subsided, and employers suddenly refused to hold up their side of the bargain, the union leaderships found themselves in an entirely new situation. It was the inability of the entrenched union officialdom to mount an effective response to an accelerating employers' offensive that assumed ever greater breadth and intensity from the end of the 1950s, which provoked a rebellion of the rank-and-file that refused to accept either the untrammeled authority of management or the practices of business unionism.

Even at the peak of prosperity, the economy was plagued by contradictions and rent by class struggle. The rate of profit was certainly quite high *on average* from the late 1940s through the late 1960s, but it was nonetheless also very volatile, the boom punctuated by a series of cyclical downturns/recessions, which left employers in the grip of uncertainty and in no position to take a relaxed attitude toward their employees.[38] On the contrary, from the morrow of World War II, the corporations sought, as they had from the moment of their recognition of the industrial unions and their acceptance of the NLRA, to roll back what they saw as illegitimate incursions on their right to manage imposed by the great workers' struggles of the 1930s and early 1940s. But the unions were in no mood to capitulate. With the unexpected onset of the postwar boom, especially in the wake of rearmament and the Korean War, they exploited tight labor markets to unleash a counter-offensive against management of sufficient potency to induce the corporations to grant consistent, impressive gains to their

---

37   See, for example, W. E. Simkin, "The Trend to Maturity in Industrial Relations," *Industrial Relations* vol. III (February 1964).
38   R. Brenner, *The Economics of Global Turbulence* (London: Verso, 2006), p. 101–17.

employees in order to secure continuous production. Labor resistance to capital, marked by major strikes at the expiration of virtually every contract in many major industries, not to mention the regular outbreak of wildcats, was thus intense throughout the 1950s, indeed the necessary precondition for the misleadingly termed "capital–labor accord" that came to prevail during the course of the decade.

For both management and workers, control of the labor process represented the critical pressure point. The upheavals of the 1930s and 1940s had bequeathed to the industrial working class "a regime of 'factional bargaining' on the shop floor whereby work-groups, abetted by restrictive work rules, used the grievance process to extract additional, extra-contractual concessions from lower management."[39] During the subsequent era, despite the limits imposed by no-strike and management's-rights clauses, the clumsy jurisprudence of grievance procedures, and the willingness of top labor leaders to tolerate increased speedup in exchange for higher wages and improved benefits, workplace organization and resistance remained strong and active. In this situation, "management would . . . not have been fulfilling its obligation to maximize profits for its stockholders, had it not exhausted every possibility for smashing the maze [of shop-floor work rules], breaking holes in it, or eliminating it altogether to restore its 'right to manage.'"[40]

Immediately after World War II, corporations sought to loosen labor's stronghold at the point of production by relocating production away from the old centers of dense unionization and effective workplace organization. Taking the lead in what would become an ever broadening process of globalization, the electrical manufacturing companies moved their operations out of older, larger factories and into newer, smaller facilities in the border states, the South, the Pacific Coast, rural sections of New England, Puerto Rico, and ultimately abroad to other countries.[41] Moving production, stage-by-stage, to ever cheaper, more union-free locations disrupted established workplace-community networks and systems of solidarity.[42] Meatpacking, auto, rubber and tire, and other industries followed this same pattern, much abetted by the new Interstate Highway system. Manifesting the depth and breadth of the geographical shift in production, from 1947 to 1972, value added in manufacturing in the South grew by 383 percent, but

---

39  M. Davis, *Prisoners of the American Dream*, (London: Verso, 1986), p. 122.

40  J. Metzgar, *Striking Steel: Solidarity Remembered* (Philadelphia: Temple University Press, 2000), p. 107.

41  R. Schatz, *The Electrical Workers: A History of Labor at General Electric and Westinghouse, 1923–1960* (Urbana: University of Illinois Press, 1983), pp. 232–6.

42  J. Cowie, *Capital Moves: RCA's 70-Year Quest for Cheap Labor* (Ithaca: Cornell University Press, 1999), pp. 1–11.

in the United States as a whole by just 186 percent. By 1972, no less than 27 percent of the total U.S. manufacturing labor force was located in the eleven states of the old Confederacy.[43]

But capital-intensive industries could not, and did not, change locations overnight, so, in their older plants, still the great majority, employers had little choice but to place ever increasing pressure on labor to remain competitive. Yet the situation changed qualitatively after the mid-1950s, when corporations found themselves quite unexpectedly confronting sharply declining productivity growth, as well as the runaway increase of compensation, which had been allowed to get out of hand during the mid-1950s. As the economy stagnated and foreign competition intensified, employers were suddenly inviting brutal industrial confrontations in one industry after another in order to gain stepped-up control of both the labor process and the growth of wages and benefits, and revealing in the process a trade union leadership decreasingly prepared to hold the line and all too willing to make concessions to restore the financial health of the corporations.[44]

The underlying raison d'être of bureaucratic business unionism was of course to deliver regular improvements in living standards for the membership by insuring, to the extent possible, rising profits by way of rising productivity by delivering a disciplined labor force to the corporations. It had accomplished this, on the one hand, by facilitating technical advances and the transformation of the labor process in aid of rising output per person, and, on the other, by undermining, over the longer run, the capacity of the rank and file to battle management at the point of production. But the combination of productivity decline and unaffordable benefits that suddenly gripped industry left the labor leaderships disarmed. Having long accepted the priority of profits and having corroded, over the long term, the capacity of their memberships to fight back, they appeared to lack either the will or the capacity to launch a counterattack. As one close observer concluded, "Unions have lost much of their vitality and forward motion; they are playing an essentially conservative role in the plant community, seeking to preserve what they have rather than make gains."[45]

The outcome was a crescendo of concessions in one industry after another. In steel, the David McDonald leadership of the USW turned to

43    D. Dodd, *Historical Statistics of the United States: Two Centuries of the Census, 1790 to 1990* (Westport: Greenwood Press, 1993), p. 442–60.

44    H. Northrup, "Management's 'New Look' in Labor Relations," *Industrial Relations* vol. 1:1 (May 1961), pp. 13ff. For a helpful overview of the "management offensive of 1958–63," see Davis, *Prisoners*, pp.122–4.

45    G. Strauss, "The Shifting Power Balance in the Plant," *Industrial Relations* vol. 1:3 (May 1962), pp. 65–96.

so-called Human Relations bargaining, which not only brought real wage gains practically to a halt, but allowed the corporations to dramatically erode work rules long protected by the famous Section 2-B of the contract. Reuther's UAW undermined struggles that Reuther himself authorized in 1961 and 1964 to finally confront long-deteriorating shop-floor conditions; rather it allowed Chrysler to effectively destroy the strongest bulwark for the defense of those conditions within the auto industry, the shop stewards organizations in the Chrysler plants.[46] The Harry Bridges–led ILWU on the West Coast, long known for its militancy and left-wing traditions, joined management in embracing new containerization and automation technology, opening the way to disunity within the ranks, and weakening the union's hold on employment through its hiring hall and the erosion of wage gains.[47] A similar story was played out at the point of production across much of the industrial sector, while, at the same time, the impressive rate of wage increase of the 1950s golden age was suddenly reduced by nearly 50 percent.

Faced at once with a sudden sharp slowdown in the growth of compensation and a profound deterioration of their working conditions, often under the guise of, or in connection with, the introduction of "automation," the rank and file was obliged to organize in its own defense. But the fact is that the practice of business unionism over the previous decade and a half, not to mention the provisions of the Taft-Hartley Act, had gone a good distance in depriving militants of their most important weapons of self-defense, destroying the class solidarity that had not that long ago made for an actual labor *movement*. In the 1930s, the labor movement was at the very least the CIO as a whole. Workers routinely came to one another's aid and reached out to the surrounding communities and the unemployed, who often responded in kind. Against that background, the great strike wave of 1945–6 was viewed by many as the first bargaining round of a re-emerging movement, and the outbreak of city-based general strikes in 1946 revealed the potential for the broadest forms of solidarity.[48] But, as things turned out, as Metzgar retrospectively observes, "For the purposes of working class memory . . . the CIO

---

46 See chapter 2, pp. 60–1

47 H. Mills, "The San Francisco Waterfront: The Social Consequences of Industrial Modernization," in A. Zimbalist, ed., *Case Studies on the Labor Process* (New York: Monthly Review Press, 1978), pp.146–7, 151–3; D. Wellman, *The Union Makes Us Strong: Radical Unionism on the San Francisco Waterfront* (New York: Cambridge University Press, 1995); R. Boyden, "Why the ILWU Strike Failed," *New Politics* vol. x:1 (Fall 1972), pp. 61–4.

48 G. Lipsitz, *Rainbow at Midnight: Labor and Culture in the 1940s* (Urbana: University of Illinois Press, 1994), pp. 99–154.

was gone by 1946, disappeared among its constituent parts, lost in the confusion of different leaders and organizational initials that only the most astute rank and filer could keep straight."[49] The negotiation of the private welfare state on a strict union-by-union, company-by-company basis, by a union officialdom largely alienated from its own membership, replaced and further undercut direct workers' solidarity beyond the individual corporation or even factory floor. The unions' electoral mobilization and lobbying for a Democratic Party in which labor was always at best a junior partner—and that increasingly took working-class support for granted—substituted for a party of labor, permanently limiting working-class political action.[50] With anything remotely approaching class-wide activity largely a thing of the past, working-class consciousness continued to persist for the most part only in watered-down forms. Nor would the movement from below that now began to emerge, and which would reach its zenith between the middle 1960s and middle 1970s, ever overcome the particularisms and localisms that were the legacy of bureaucratic business unionism.[51]

Lacking vital connections with workers beyond their workplaces, the militants who now sought to build resistance to the employers' attack were left, as always, to fall back on the informal work groups that grew naturally and directly out of their cooperation at the point of production. This phenomenon, perpetually rediscovered by researchers in industrial relations—from Taylor in the early twentieth century to the Hawthorne experiments of the 1920s to the industrial sociologists of the 1940s and 1950s—constituted the fundamental building block of solidarity on the job. Harvey Swados noted it in the auto plants of the 1950s, and Stan Weir among shop stewards in many industries.[52] Even when class resistance was at a low ebb, informal work groups could be found mounting active and passive defense against the employer. When these informal groups became part of informal networks, they could vote down unacceptable contracts,

---

49   Metzgar, *Striking Steel*, pp. 30–1.

50   For the early failure of the CIO political strategy, see, for example, R. Zieger, *The CIO, 1935–1955* (Chapel Hill: University of North Carolina Press, 1995), p. 212; and S. Amberg, "The CIO Political Strategy in Historical Perspective: Creating a High Road Economy in the Postwar Era," in K. Boyle, ed., *Organized Labor and American Politics 1894–1994: The Liberal-Labor Alliance* (Albany: State University of New York Press, 1998), p. 173.

51   For the separation between the union as an "institution" and what remained of the union as a "movement," see S. Cohen, *Ramparts of Resistance: Why Workers Lost Their Power and How to Get It Back* (London: Pluto Press, 2006), pp. 149–73.

52   P. Thompson and D. McHugh, *Work Organizations* (New York: Palgrave, 3rd edition, 2002), pp. 47–8; H. Swados, *A Radical's America* (Boston: Little, Brown and Company, 1962), pp. 111–20; Weir, *Singlejack Solidarity*, p. 28.

launch quickie strikes, or even help to oust entrenched union officials. When conditions on the job drove the informal networks to repeated action, they could create a movement.

## Contract Rejections

The collective dissatisfaction of the rank and file with their union leaderships first began to show up in the rising number of rejections of contracts negotiated by their officials with management. Before 1962, according to the Federal Mediation and Conciliation Service (FMCS), contract rejections were so rare that the government did not bother to track their occurrence. Workers' growing disapprobation, however, led the FMCS to begin counting the number of contract rejections on a yearly basis, and the number of rejections rose steadily throughout the 1960s and into the early 1970s.[53] In 1964, the first year in which FMCS statistics are available, 8.7 percent of the total the rank and file rejected. Workers rejected 10 percent of such contracts in 1965, 11.7 percent in 1966, and 14.2 percent in 1967, leading FMCS director William E. Simkin to report that, "obviously, the rejection problem is widespread."[54]

Unionists who sent their officials back to negotiate better contracts in these years included machinists, as well as those in the electrical equipment, communications, trucking, steel, construction, and paper industries.[55] Most of the time, workers who rejected contracts won more money in the next settlement, leading Ronald Haughton, federal mediator and professor at Wayne State University, to tell *Business Week*: "Our society rewards groups that put the pressure on. The rank and file have learned this. Usually, when they reject a contract, the company offers something better."[56]

---

53  "Dissent in Unions Believed on Rise," *New York Times*, May 16, 1962, p. 30.

54  W. E. Simkin, "Refusals to Ratify Contracts," *Industrial and Labor Relations Review* vol. 21:4 (July 1967), p. 520; US Federal Mediation and Conciliation Service, Annual Report 1977 (Washington, DC: 1978), p. 26. The agency tracked contract rejections only for those labor negotiations with which it was involved on an "active basis," where an FMCS mediator was physically present at the bargaining table.

55  A. A. Imberman, "Labor Relations: Dealing with the Rank-and-File Rebellion," *Personnel* vol. 44:6 (November–December 1967), p. 27; FMCS, Annual Report, various years.

56  Approximately 67 percent of the time, contract rejections later led to better contracts for workers. Simkin, "Refusals to Ratify," pp. 536–7. Haughton quoted in R. Armstrong, "Labor 1970: Angry, Aggressive, Acquisitive," *Fortune* vol. 80:5 (October 1969), p. 94.

## Election Campaigns

As the labor upsurge took form and gathered momentum, union members inevitably sought to replace union officials whom they believed had failed adequately to represent them. These overturnings resulted from a "growing restiveness that is threatening the former invulnerability of union leaders. Only a few years ago, union leaders were rarely challenged at elections. Most clung to office as long as they lived or were able to serve—or thought they were able. Some still do. But this is true in fewer and fewer unions."[57]

The leaders ejected by their rank and file reads like a catalog of officials who had become too understanding of management's needs in the face of the companies' new hard line. David J. McDonald of the USWA fit the profile. Although he had led the 116-day strike in 1959 which preserved the past practice clause (2-B), he had been committed to "effective teamwork between union and management" since the mid-1950s. As a result, he faced his first opposition at the 1956 convention. His subsequent acquiescence in the formation of a joint union–management Human Relations Committee in 1960 made for the precipitous loss of rank-and-file power on the shop floor and sharply deteriorating results at the bargaining table. Already by 1963, one disgruntled official, who would subsequently join the union opposition, could sum up the results of Human Relations bargaining as follows: "two of the cheapest contracts in our union's postwar history," real wage cuts, bypassing the union's Wage Policy Committee, secret dealings, and the "determined non-usage of . . . the threat to strike."[58] By 1964, the union's executive board was split, and in 1965 its secretary-treasurer, I. W. Abel, mounted a campaign against McDonald and defeated him for union president by a little over 10,000 votes.[59] Nevertheless, Abel himself, a staunch business unionist, would carry on pretty much where McDonald left off, setting the stage for a rising tide of rank-and-file resistance during the decade that followed.

Following the exit of the United Electrical Workers from the CIO at the end of the 1940s, the remaining CIO leaders had hastened to set up a new union, the International Union of Electrical Workers (IUE). Its new leader was James Carey, president of the UE until his erstwhile Communist allies

---

57  "Winds of Change Ruffle Unions' Top Executives," *Business Week*, September 17, 1966.

58  J. Herling, *Right to Challenge: People and Power in the Steelworkers Union* (New York: Harper & Row Publishers, 1972), pp. 96–9.

59  Ibid., pp. 95–109.

deposed him in 1941. In NLRB elections held to replace the UE at the big electrical companies, the two unions took an almost equal number of locals, but the IUE came out with a majority of members. From the start, the IUE faced internal factionalism and inter-union jurisdictional rivalry as several unions staked out a place in the industry. Carey had already led a pair of disastrous walkouts in 1950 and 1952, when in 1960 he insisted on striking a General Electric (GE) corporation clearly out for blood. The outcome was "the worst setback any union has received in a nationwide strike since World War II."[60] Especially as many officials and local leaders had, before the strike, expressed strong doubts about the wisdom of a showdown with the electrical companies, a good number of them now turned on Carey, running Paul Jennings, a local official from New York. Carey twice attempted to steal the ballot, but in the end a Labor Department decision put Jennings in office.[61]

Electoral revolts also brought down established leaders in the Oil, Gas, and Atomic Workers and the United Rubber Workers. In the Oil Workers, President A. O. Knight retired early rather than face ousting. In the Rubber Workers, President George Burdon was attacked for losing touch with the ranks, abstaining from negotiations, and paying his wife's traveling expenses. In an unusual move, he confessed to "serious mistakes" and withdrew his nomination for re-election. Vice President Peter Bommarito was elected unanimously.[62] Similar overturnings hit the biggest public sector unions as well. In AFSCME, Jerry Wurf and Victor Gotbaum, both district-level officials, organized the Committee on Union Responsibility and, in 1964, tossed out the old-guard president Arnold Zander, introducing a more aggressive brand of trade unionism.[63]

These electoral overturnings emanated for the most part from the ranks of the unions' secondary leaders, who themselves faced mounting pressure from an increasingly restive rank and file. The new leaders had in most cases been dissident or "soft" members of the top leadership. Their campaigns reflected rank-and-file dissatisfaction and depended upon rank-and-file votes, but were not themselves grassroots rebellions nor carriers of rank-and-file demands. Whatever gains they were ultimately able to achieve in terms of wages and benefits, the new leaders virtually without exception accepted no less than their predecessors the companies' "right to manage," rarely if ever addressing the worsening working conditions that were the

---

60    Schatz, *The Electrical Workers*, pp. 225–8; Zieger, *The CIO*, p. 257.

61    Weir, "USA: The Labor Revolt," pp. 299–300.

62    Ibid., p. 300.

63    J. Bellush and B. Bellush, Union *Power & New York: Victor Gotbaum and District Council 37* (New York: Praeger Publishers, 1984), pp. 108–9.

overriding concern of their memberships. As a consequence, many of them were soon themselves having to deal with new, more vigorous opposition from below.[64]

## Wildcats

Obliged to mount their own defense, rank-and-file workers turned to direct action. The nascent rebellion of the rank and file was, above all, a wildcat strike movement, and the rise in the number and scope of wildcat strikes was perhaps their most dramatic expression. In 1964 alone, wildcats broke out among members of the UAW, USWA, IUE, the International Longshore Association (ILA), and the Oil and Atomic Workers.[65] Generally brief and motivated by on-the-job grievances as opposed to wages or benefits issues—and often taking place during the life of the contract— wildcats bypassed the grievance process and formal union strike procedures, defying the labor contracts, employer regulations, union rules, and usually union officials. Wildcats rejected management's unrestricted rights over the production process and denied the authority of union officials to speak for the ranks. They were also usually illegal. As such, they represented perhaps the most threatening challenge to the established system of labor relations, and union officials usually opposed them even if they were sympathetic to workers' demands.

Although no official record of wildcat strikes exists, strikes recorded by the Bureau of Labor Statistics as lasting three days or less and taking place during the life of the contract constitute a good proxy.[66] From the early 1960s through the mid-1970s, the number of unofficial strikes (wildcats) taking place each year more than doubled, from about six hundred to approximately fourteen hundred, and came to constitute a rising proportion of all strikes. In 1972, there were more than one thousand strikes among mine workers, 90 percent of which were unofficial. That year about half of all strikes by construction workers and one third of those by electrical workers were wildcats. In 1972, 1973, 1975, and 1976, wildcats made up one quarter of all strikes, whereas they had hovered between 15 and 18 percent of strikes during the previous seven years.[67]

---

64   "Winds of Change Ruffle Unions' Top Executives."
65   Weir, *New Era of Labor Revolt* (Berkeley: Independent Socialist Club, 1966), p. 3.
66   See P. K. Edwards, *Strikes in the United States, 1881–1974* (New York: St. Martin's Press, 1978), p. 180; R. Fantasia, *Cultures of Solidarity* (Berkeley: University of California Press, 1988), p. 64.
67   Calculated from U.S. Department of Labor, Bureau of Labor Statistics, Analysis of Work Stoppages, 1965–1976 (Washington, DC: GPO, 1967–1978). BLS Bulletin numbers as follows: 1525 (1965); 1573 (1966); 1611 (1967); 1646 (1968); 1687 (1969); 1727 (1970);

Miners and construction workers were particularly prone to walk out without official sanction, as were auto and electrical workers. Wildcats usually involved only one plant or a group of workers, but several major strikes involving tens of thousands of workers or more were unofficial, including those by Teamsters in 1970, postal workers in 1970, and telephone workers in 1971, as well as miners on many occasions.[68] Symptomatically, most wildcats involved job security and plant administration, as opposed to wages and benefits.[69]

## The Great Strike Wave

The rising tide of rank-and-file resistance expressed in increasing contract rejections, electoral ousters of top officials, and wildcat strikes was aimed at giving new life to the unions and creating more effective organizations to fight the employers. But during the first half of the 1960s, the nascent revolt could not begin to slow the accelerating offensive of the employers, which won major gains for the corporations at the direct expense of working people. These years witnessed one of the fastest economic expansions in American history, but labor and capital shared unequally in the prosperity. Largely as a consequence of management's concerted speedup campaign, average annual manufacturing productivity growth between 1959 and 1965 reached its highest level of the postwar period up to that point. Meanwhile, due to employers' stepped-up resistance to union demands, the growth of compensation in manufacturing and the private sector as a whole fell by nearly half. Thus the profit rate for manufacturing, and the private sector as a whole, achieved a dramatic revival.[70]

---

1777 (1971); 1813 (1972); 1877 (1973); 1902 (1974); 1940 (1975); 1996 (1976).

68  BLS, Analysis of Work Stoppages, 1972, pp. 18–9; BLS, Analysis of Work Stoppages, 1971, p. 25. On miners' wildcats, see "Wildcats' Reward," *The Economist*, March 22, 1969; T. O'Hanlon, "Anarchy Threatens the Kingdom of Coal," *Fortune* vol. 83:1 (January 1971), pp. 78–85; J. M. Brett and S. B. Goldberg, "Wildcat Strikes in Bituminous Coal Mining," *Industrial and Labor Relations Review* vol. 32:4 (July 1979), pp. 465–83. Other wildcat examples include: "Walkouts Hurt the USW," *Business Week*, November 4, 1967; *Wildcat: Dodge Truck*, June 1974, pamphlet (Detroit: Red and Black, n.d.); "Strikes' Spiral," *The Economist*, April 18, 1970, p. 48; M. Brockway, "Keep on Truckin'," in Root & Branch, eds, *Root & Branch: The Rise of the Workers' Movement* (Greenwich, CT: Fawcett, 1975), pp. 39–48; C. Denby, "Black Caucuses in the Unions," in B. Hall, ed., *Autocracy & Insurgency in Organized Labor* (New Brunswick, NJ: Transaction Books, 1972), pp. 137–46.

69  P. K. Edwards, *Strikes in the United States, 1881–1974* (New York: St. Martin's Press, 1978), pp. 183–4.

70  Brenner, *The Economics of Global Turbulence*, pp. 61–6.

The threat posed to workers by their declining ability to share in the country's growing prosperity during the first half of the 1960s was rendered significantly more serious around mid-decade by the suddenly accelerating inflation. Price stability had been one of the more remarkable aspects of postwar prosperity, and inflation was particularly low between 1960 and 1965, averaging just 1.2 percent per year despite increasing economic growth. Beginning around 1965, however, prices began to rise, at first slowly and then more rapidly, from 1.6 percent in 1965, to 3.1 percent in 1967, to 5.5 percent in 1969, and to 5.7 percent in 1970, even though the last was a recession year. Workers could not but fear the further erosion of their living standards and make protection against inflation a top priority.[71]

If, in the middle years of the 1960s, union workers were increasingly resentful of their inability to share equitably in the country's growing prosperity, and were ever more concerned about the resurgent threat of rising prices to their wage packets, they were also demonstrating growing resolve to turn the tables on the employers, their confidence swelled by the fast-improving employment situation. As the economy continued to expand, the rate of unemployment fell from 4.5 percent in 1965 to 3.5 percent in 1969. As *Business Week* recognized, "The union member in September 1966 is militant, confident, and loaded for bear. He intends to press for substantial wage increases—as a matter of justice, to match booming profits, and as a matter of need, to compensate for rising living costs. He is remarkably well informed about both these phenomena." In the words of Walter Dorosh, president of UAW Local 600 at Ford's enormous River Rouge complex outside Detroit, auto union workers "know all about companies' high profits and the large salaries of top executives. They bring me clippings. I don't have to tell them; they tell me." Discussing workers' anger toward the Johnson administration's recently announced 3.2 percent wage guidelines for non-inflationary raises, William Garnes, UAW Local 647 representative at General Electric's jet engine plant in Cincinnati, protested:

> To hell with the guideline! Don't talk to the guy in the factory about 3.2% when profits are up 30% and 40% and productivity has increased 5.5% and 6%. Why should workers be asked to accept something less than what industry can pay? . . . Workers feel that some of this [high

---

71 "The Push Is On for Fatter Pay Envelopes"; "What Will Strife Cost?" *Business Week*, April 8, 1967, p. 27; Council of Economic Advisers, Economic Report of the President 2007, p. 303.

profits] should be passed along to them. If this requires a strike, I think they're in a frame of mind to have one.[72]

Something of the atmosphere of the period was conveyed in August 1966, during a lengthy strike by the International Association of Machinists (IAM) against the country's five largest airlines. After four weeks on the line, the union's president came back with a settlement that would have increased the wage by more than 20 percent over the next three years—by about $.70 per hour over their existing average wage of $3.25 per hour. But the membership rejected the contract by a three-to-one vote. As Jack Barry, a member of IAM Lodge 1487 in Chicago, explained, "Anyone knows this wage package won't mean a thing if the prices on everything start jumping. A cost-of-living escalator is what we really want."[73] Added Pat Magarelli of IAM Lodge 1056 in New York City, "The people down there in Washington have got to face reality. The average working man has obligations to meet. You just can't tell him 3.2 percent is all he can get, when the companies are making 200 percent."[74]

Unfortunately for union workers, at precisely the moment when they were stepping up their effort to make up the ground they had lost during the first half of the decade and to cope with the new wave of rising prices, the trend toward rising corporate profit rates of the early 1960s was going into reverse, especially in the industrial sector. Between 1965 and 1969, the rate of profit in U.S. manufacturing fell by 33 percent, and in the non-financial corporate sector as a whole by 22 percent. Manufacturing employers were especially hard hit, as they faced a new, more threatening round of foreign competition and, more generally, the onset of over-capacity on a system-wide scale.

As corporations saw the recovery of profitability in the first half of the 1960s come increasingly under threat, they saw little choice but to toughen the hard line that had been contributing so signally to their economic well-being. As early as August 1966, *Business Week* noted that:

The bargaining attitude of employers in 1967 will be more cautious. Economic indicators worry many of them. They look for a tighter squeeze on profits next year and perhaps a decline in business. Under the circumstances,

---

72  All three quotes from "The Mood Is Militant," *Business Week*, September 24, 1966, p. 47. See also M. Gart, "Labor's Rebellious Rank and File," *Fortune* vol. 74:6 (November 1966), p. 150; "The Blue-Collar Revolution," *Forbes* vol. 99:2 (January 1967), p. 13; and "Boom Gives Labor Its '67 Leverage," *Business Week*, May 14, 1967, pp. 40–1.

73  "Airline Terms, and Why They Were Rejected," *The Machinist*, August 11, 1966, p. 3.

74  Ibid.

operating costs will be scrutinized more closely. Union demands will be resisted more strenuously than in recent years.75

One route in employers' quest for reduced costs was, of course, to concede only slower (and eventually zero) real wage growth. But alterations in the labor process, especially through the elimination of unions' hard-won work rules, remained at the heart of their offensive, especially as those rules served not only as barriers to labor efficiency but bastions of unionists' shop-floor power. Auto companies continued to automate their plants, increase the speed of their assembly lines, and cut the number of workers, forcing the remaining employees to do more. GE ignored workers' grievances, introduced job-replacing machinery, lowered piece rates, and demanded more work. Construction firms attempted to reduce skill levels by standardizing tasks and increasing specialization; others went non-union. Mining and steel companies eliminated jobs through technological innovation and violated health and safety rules. The US Post Office Department continued to use decrepit facilities, while telephone companies imposed new work rules and automated away jobs.[76]

As corporations' financial room for maneuvering contracted and unionists' resolve to reverse their deteriorating position increased, tensions around the country's collective bargaining tables began to rise, and agreements acceptable to both sides grew more difficult to reach, all the more so in view of the intensified pressure upon union officials being exerted by increasingly well-organized rank-and-file militants. The resulting stalemate could not but usher in a major increase in strikes, especially because, as the decade wore on and the business cycle reached record lengths, declining unemployment further improved workers' bargaining position, and the

75    "The Demand Is: 'More—Much More,'" *Business Week*, August 6, 1966, p. 118.
76    Auto: D. Georgakas and M. Surkin, *Detroit: I Do Mind Dying: A Study in Urban Revolution* (New York: St. Martin's Press, 1975); Green, *World of the Worker*, p. 219; "Vega Speedup Revolt," *Workers' Power* 51 (February 18–March 2, 1972); J. Single, "Lordstown, Woodcock and the Reuther Tradition," *Workers' Power* 54 (March 31–April 13, 1972). GE: J. Matles and J. Higgins, *Them and Us: The Struggles of a Rank-and-File Union* (Englewood Cliffs, NJ: Prentice-Hall, 1974), chapter 17; "Why the Rank and File Say No," *Business Week*, December 17, 1966; "GE Strikers Back Their Leaders," *Business Week*, November 8, 1969. Construction: J. Freeman, "Hardhats: Construction Workers, Manliness, and the 1970 Pro-War Demonstrations," *Journal of Social History* vol. 26:4 (Summer 1993), p. 733; "Open Shops Build Up in Construction," *Business Week*, July 1, 1972. Mining: Nyden, "Miners for Democracy," chapters 6 and 7; M. Stewart, "Hyden: Government Murders Miners," *Workers' Power* 28 (January 15–28, 1971). Steel: P. W. Nyden, *Steelworkers Rank-and-File: The Political Economy of a Union Reform Movement* (New York: Praeger Publishers, 1984), pp. 45–7.

increasing likelihood of recession increased employers' concerns about profits. Strike activity had declined from their early 1950s peak to a postwar low in 1963. But from that point on, the number of strikes, the number of days lost to strikes, the proportion of union workers on strike, and the proportion of time lost to strikes all rose steadily, and at times dramatically.

Labor negotiations were occurring inside a pressure cooker, and in its October 1969 issue *Fortune* worried about the possible consequences: "Just as the companies begin to prepare for an expected slowing in the economy, and an expected crunch on profits, they will be met with wage demands that are rocketing upward along with inflation. Such a combination of events is unusual, and dangerous."[77] *Fortune*'s fears were fully borne out the following year, 1970, when 66 million work days were lost during 5,716 walkouts (the most ever at the time), and more than 17 percent of union members (one in six) went on strike. The strikes of 1970 turned out to represent the crest of a decade-long strike wave and a culmination of the mounting rank-and-file militancy in the late 1960s. Thirty-four major work stoppages involving 10,000 or more workers took place, the most in eighteen years. Included among these were a 197-day strike by 27,000 construction workers in Kansas City, two strikes by 13,000 teachers in Philadelphia, a wildcat of 25,000 coal miners, a sixty-four-day walkout of 23,000 rubber workers, a stoppage by 13,000 longshoremen in New Jersey, a one-day walkout of 35,000 airline workers, and a strike by 42,000 New York taxi drivers. Five of the biggest and most dramatic national strikes were those by 133,000 electrical workers against General Electric in January, 152,000 postal workers wildcatting against the U.S. government in March, 110,000 Teamsters in an unauthorized walkout against the nation's interstate trucking companies in May, 355,000 auto workers versus General Motors in September, and 360,000 railroad workers against the country's railroads in December.[78]

But the fact remains that, for unionized workers, the great strike wave of the late 1960s and early 1970s turned out to be less than meets the eye, with wage increases won in collective bargaining agreements running not much more than a percentage point ahead of inflation.[79] Even the 1970 explosion was only partly successful, with pay packages averaging close to 9 percent per year for three-year contracts for unionized workers in

---

77  Armstrong, "Labor 1970: Angry, Aggressive, Acquisitive," p. 94.

78  BLS, *Analysis of Work Stoppages, 1970*, Bulletin 1727 (Washington, DC: GPO, 1972), pp. 1, 15–18. Note that the electrical workers strike actually began in 1969 and is therefore not counted in BLS statistics for 1970.

79  Department of Commerce, *Statistical Abstract of the United States 1970*, p. 233; Council of Economic Advisers, *Economic Report of the President 2007*, p. 303.

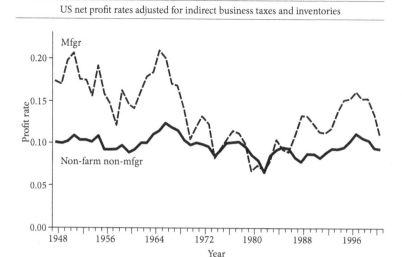

US net profit rates adjusted for indirect business taxes and inventories

the economy as a whole and only 6 percent for those in manufacturing, compared to a 5.7 percent increase that year in the consumer price index.[80] For some of the most powerful unions, the strike wave actually brought major concessions. The UAW agreed to severe limits on cost-of-living adjustments (COLA) after striking against Ford Motors in 1967, receiving only a 3 percent nominal wage increase in return.[81] In 1970, the Teamsters gave up one of their most powerful levers against their employers, the right to strike for twenty-four hours over any grievance, which they traded away for a pay raise. In 1973, the United Steelworkers sold off the right to strike (even after contract expiration) in exchange for a COLA and a productivity-driven wage increase.

The meager results of the late 1960s strike wave are understandable not only in terms of employers' increasing intransigence, but also to an important degree as a reflection of the officials' bureaucratic accommodationism. As an anonymous economist from the Bureau of Labor Statistics suggested to *Fortune*, strikes could be part of the officials' conflict-avoidance strategy: "A strike is not just economic, but political as well. Union leaders do not find it advisable to say so publicly, but perhaps they need a round of strikes to blow pressure and pull the membership together."[82] This is precisely what happened in the 1970–1 GM strike, one of the largest of the period. UAW officials believed the strike was necessary not to squeeze greater economic

---

80 Statistical Abstract 1978, p. 423.
81 "Reuther Delivers the Goods," *Business Week*, November 4, 1967.
82 Armstrong, "Labor 1970: Angry, Aggressive, Acquisitive," p. 94.

concessions from GM but to exhaust the membership so as to win their acquiescence to the contract. William Serrin pointed out, "General Motors would have signed the same agreement in September [before the strike] if the UAW had made it known that it was prepared to settle." And as Eunice Williams, one of the UAW negotiators, admitted, "If we had brought that settlement [the one eventually ratified] to the rank and file on September 15, they would have told us to go to hell." Emil Mazey, UAW secretary-treasurer, summarized the strategy, "I think strikes make ratification easier."[83]

## Independent Organization

The strikes of 1970 and the limited gains they were able to secure reflected the problems faced by workers forced to function according to the rules of modern business unionism. Even as union leaders mounted ever greater numbers of official work stoppages in response to the pressure from below, rank-and-file militants were finding it necessary, and increasingly possible, to organize ever more widespread, and large-scale, unofficial actions (wildcats) on their own, as we have seen. Nevertheless, although wildcat strikers managed to step outside the legal framework of U.S. industrial relations, they had a difficult time forcing their concerns onto official union agendas, even when they went out en masse. Control of the bargaining process was, of course, a major factor in allowing the international unions to ignore the demands of their members. But of equal importance was the ability of top officials to exploit their tight control of national organizations to keep the centers of local and regional opposition at the root of the strike movements isolated and fragmented. The only really effective way to get beyond the domination of the union officials was to build a union-wide organization based in the rank and file to force the hand of the leadership and, ultimately, to replace it.

This was not something new in the American labor movement. Rank-and-file movements in American unions could be traced back to the years just following World War I, if not before. Up to that time, the major conflict within organized labor was an openly political one between socialists and the "pure-and-simple" trade unionists led by Samuel Gompers, a struggle which remained endemic within the AFL right up through the war.[84]

---

83  W. Serrin, *The Company and the Union* (New York: Vintage Books, 1974), p. 298, Williams quoted on p. 299, Mazey quoted on p. 4. See also B. J. Widick, "Black City, Black Unions?" *Dissent* vol. 19:1 (Winter 1972), pp. 141–2.

84  P. Foner, *History of the Labor Movement in the United States, Vol. 2* (New York: International Publishers, 1975), pp. 292–4.

But with the Russian Revolution, the explosion of labor militancy and radicalism on the morrow of World War I, the split in the world socialist movement, the emergence of the CPUSA, and the rapid decline of the Socialist Party, opposition within many unions took the form of rank-and-file caucuses, often led by radical left-wingers at the head of broader formations of less politicized workers.

The rise of rank-and-file movements within the unions occurred in the context of the biggest labor upsurge in U.S. history up to that time. As in Europe, shop stewards and factory committees formed in many industries in efforts to get around the conservative craft unionists who dominated most unions. In 1920, there were 253 unauthorized (wildcat) strikes, and they involved over half of all those who participated in work stoppages in that year, as dissatisfaction with business union leadership ran high. Opposition movements emerged within the unions of miners, garment workers, railroad workers, metal workers, and many more, and out of this ferment there arose a coalition of more militant unions opposed to the old-line leaders within the AFL. Progressive influence reached the "high-water mark" in 1921 and, within this context of rising internal opposition, syndicalist and soon to be Communist William Z. Foster took the lead in forming the Trade Union Educational League (TUEL). Though not formed as an opposition group per se, the TUEL nevertheless assumed the function of one in several unions. Its main demands were for amalgamation with the goals of industrial unionism, union democracy, and an independent labor party. Even after the decline of TUEL, other rank-and-file-based opposition movements would arise, most notably the "Save Our Union" movement in the Mine Workers, which unsuccessfully challenged John L. Lewis in 1927.[85]

By the end of the 1960s many wildcatters and militants concluded that they needed to build their own national organizations if they were going to have a chance to take control of, or at least influence, their unions. In virtually every major union during the 1960s and 1970s, these militants, often led by political radicals from socialist groups of one kind or another, launched some type of rank-and-file organization that challenged both employers and union officials. Groups were formed in the AFT, the CWA, the ILWU, the National Maritime Workers Union, the Painters Union, the URW, and the USWA, to name a few.

The most impressive of the rank-and-file organizations was Miners for

---

85   D. Montgomery, *The Fall of the House of Labor: The Workplace, the State, and American Labor Activism, 1865–1925* (New York: Cambridge University Press, 1989), pp. 399–428; S. Lens, *Left, Right, and Center: Conflicting Forces in American Labor* (Hinsdale, IL: Henry Regnery Company, 1949), pp. 173–85.

Democracy (MFD), which formed in 1970 shortly after the December 30, 1969 assassination of opposition candidate Jock Yablonski. Yablonski's candidacy had grown from the Black Lung strike in February 1969, when 45,000 miners successfully refused to mine coal until the West Virginia legislature passed a pension law to compensate miners with pneumoconiosis (black lung), the largest political strike in modern U.S. labor history. Riding a wave of workplace militancy and political mobilization in the coal towns, MFD went on to win control of the UMW in 1972, the only rank-and-file group to do so during the 1970s. Despite the democratization of the union that followed, MFD leaders had no vision beyond business unionism and developed no effective response to the employers' offensive, which included technological change, runaway pits, and cutting corners on health and safety. As a result, rank-and-file militancy, including numerous and massive wildcats and the 110-day official strike in 1978, continued in the mines throughout the 1970s.[86]

Teamster militants produced several rank-and-file organizations in the 1960s and 1970s. Most of these were local and short-lived. The Fraternal Order of Steel Haulers (FASH), launched in 1967, and Teamsters United Rank and File (TURF), begun in 1970, were national groups that capitalized on Teamsters' frustration with their union's indolence, but lacked the organizational capacity to survive union and employer attacks or cooptation. The most enduring of the rank-and-file organizations of the 1970s was the Teamsters for a Democratic Union (TDU). The reign of President Frank Fitzsimmons, who replaced the jailed Jimmy Hoffa, was a disaster. The proportion of freight handled by union members under the NMFA tumbled by 20 to 25 percent between 1967 and 1977. The union, furthermore, was granting more and more "special riders" to regions, undermining work standards.[87] In 1973, Fitzsimmons, a Republican, agreed to a poor settlement under pressure from his friend Richard Nixon. So, in August 1975, a group of about thirty-five activists, mostly veterans of the 1970 strike, TURF, and a number of local rank-and-file newsletters, met in Chicago to discuss what might been done about the NMFA that would expire in 1976. They formed Teamsters for a Decent Contract (TDC), which distributed thousands of leaflets demanding a long series of improvements, including COLAs for wages, pensions, and health, a two-year contract (instead of three), separate votes on all supplements and riders to the national contract, and restoration of the right to strike for twenty-four hours. In November it held its first national meeting. Along with an allied group of UPS workers called UPSurge, TDC adopted the slogan "Ready to Strike." Fitzsimmons was forced to call strikes over both the NMFA and UPS

86   See chapter 7.
87   Moody, *An Injury to All*, p. 231.

contracts, both of which were followed by brief local wildcats. At the June
1976 IBT convention, TDC activists were harassed, and one, Pete Camarata,
was beaten. This only helped put TDC on the map.[88]

The success of TDC led its activists to believe the time had come for a
permanent rank-and-file reform organization. On September 18 and 19,
in Kent, Ohio, the founding convention of TDU attracted 250 Teamsters.
For its first decade or more, TDU was not primarily an electoral movement
like Steelworkers Fight Back or the MFD. There was little room for such
a focus in the Teamsters at that time, rather it was on the workplace, the
local union, and the various national contracts. It put out its own national
newspaper, *Convoy*, and began to spread its influence. In 1979 it merged
with the Nader-inspired Professional Drivers Council (PROD). In that same
year it organized the Car Haulers Contract Committee. By the 1980s it had
chapters around the United States and Canada and counted its membership
in the thousands. In 1983, it would organize the overwhelming rejection of
IBT president Jackie Presser's first NMFA agreement. In 1986, it would lend
crucial support to the Latina cannery strikers in Watsonville, California. At
the end of the 1980s, it would lay the groundwork for the first one-member-
one-vote national election in 1991.[89] Unlike most of the other rank-and-
file organizations of the upsurge years, TDU would become a permanent
feature of Teamster politics and an inspiration to union reformers across the
movement up to today. Key to its survival were the commitment of radicals,
the decentralization and division of the IBT leadership, the dispersed nature
of trucking operations, and the ability to hold on to a core of activists in a
series of struggles around workplace issues, contracts, and union democracy.
By surviving, TDU was able to play a key role in the democratization of the
union and the election of a reform union president.[90]

Black workers played outsized roles in several rank-and-file groups, particularly
those in auto and steel. The most famous of these were the DRUM and the other
Revolutionary Union Movements (RUMs) formed by black workers in the auto
factories of Detroit. Others included the United Black Brothers at the Ford plant
in Mahwah, New Jersey, and the Black Panther caucus at the General Motors
Fremont, California plant. At North American Aviation, black UAW members
put out a mimeographed newsletter called *The Protester*. Unlike MFD or TDU,
these black caucuses saw themselves as politically radical and part of a broader

88   D. La Botz, *Rank-and-File Rebellion: Teamsters for a Democratic Union* (London: Verso,
1990), pp. 50–65; A. Brenner, "Rank-and-File Teamster Movements in Comparative
Perspective," in Perusek and Worcester, *Trade Union Politics*, pp. 126–7.
89   Moody, An Injury to All, pp. 233–6; La Botz, *Rank-and-File Rebellion*, pp. 77–80, 177–80,
314–27; K. C. Crowe, *Collision: How the Rank and File Took Back the Teamsters Union* (New
York: Charles Scribner's Sons, 1993), passim.
90   See chapter 7.

movement for black liberation and, in some sense, international revolution. Yet they also focused on workplace issues, forwarding practical demands and leading wildcat strikes to cope with miserable conditions in the plants, while at the same time publishing political manifestos. Political radicals played key roles in these caucuses and in Detroit tried to bring them together in the League of Revolutionary Black Workers.[91]

Black auto workers also had a disproportionate role in the United National Caucus, especially after the RUMs declined in the early 1970s. Begun in 1968, the UNC brought together a number of single-issue pressure groups, including the 30-And-Out movement for early retirement and the Dollar-An-Hour-Now movement among skilled tradesmen. It advanced economic demands, some of which were adopted by the politically sophisticated officials of the UAW, and it tried to relate to the rising militancy of black auto workers, including the RUMs. Its co-chair was Jordan Sims, an African American worker, who became president of Local 961 at Chrysler's Eldon Gear and Axle plant. UNC activists were involved in three wildcat strikes at Chrysler in July and August 1973 that protested health and safety violations and the combination of racist supervision and brutal speedup that the RUMs dubbed "niggermation." During the last of these strikes, the UAW's Chrysler division chief Douglas Fraser led a two-day assault of one thousand UAW officials from all over the area, some carrying baseball bats and other weapons, on the strikers in an effort to drive them back to work. The event demonstrated how far the UAW had come from the glory days of the 1930s, when it had led "industrial slaves" in the great sit-down strikes to break auto company tyranny at the point of production. The union now organized to break, rather than build, a factory occupation of the most oppressed workers in the industry.

There was a long history of black self-organization in steel, including the Committee for Equality at the Sparrow's Point works of Bethlehem Steel and the national Ad Hoc Committee for Concerned Black Steelworkers, though the latter was quickly co-opted by the union leadership.[92] African Americans and Latinos had a sizeable role in the Rank and File Caucus of USWA Local 1010, which was at the heart of the Steelworkers Fight Back campaign formed in 1975 to vie for power in the union. Oliver Montgomery, a black rank-and-file leader, was the group's candidate for one of the vice presidential slots.[93] Led by Ed Sadlowski, who had been elected director of USWA District 31 in 1974, Steelworkers Fight Back was essentially a Sadlowski election campaign, albeit one rooted in rank-and-file mobilization. The group proposed to end the 1973 Experimental

91  See chapter 11.
92  C. Denby, "Black Caucuses in the Unions," in Hall, *Autocracy and Insurgency in Organized Labor*, pp. 137–46; Nyden, "Miners for Democracy," pp. 50, 88.
93  Nyden, "Miners for Democracy," pp. 65–6, 72–82, 88.

Negotiating Agreement, under which the union agreed to a seven-year contract and pledged not to strike in national bargaining in return for a $150 bonus for each worker.[94] Other planks of the platform included mobilization of the union to resist, rather than embrace, productivity committees, and the right of rank-and-file members to ratify contracts. The Steelworkers Fight Back campaigned had a crusading spirit, despite organizational shortcomings, but, in the end, Sadlowski won just 43 percent of the vote, largely because the campaign failed to address the concerns of members outside basic steel.

All the rank-and-file groups originated in workplace resistance and came together in an effort to mobilize beyond an existing activist layer. They combined on-the-job struggles with union political activity in varying combinations. The black caucuses, however, saw themselves as political radicals, part of a broader movement for black liberation and in some sense international revolution. Like the other groups, they forwarded practical demands and led wildcat strikes to cope with the miserable conditions in their plants, while at the same time, unlike most of the others, publishing political manifestos. Although the black revolutionary caucuses proposed joint action with white workers, racial polarization within the plants and the union limited the sort of interracial coalition that they envisioned. As happened in other unions, the UAW leadership undermined the revolutionary caucuses by sponsoring more moderate black candidates in local union elections, a process that was eased considerably by the broader decline of the black movement, physically repressed by law enforcement at various levels and torn apart by internal factionalism, often itself abetted by the spies of government agencies.[95]

With the exception of MFD, no rank-and-file group during the 1970s was able to take control of a national union. A few won local union office. Some, like TDU and United National Caucus, managed to mobilize enough support to wield political influence that translated into tougher negotiations by union officials, some strikes, and better contracts. But in the end they all failed to transform their unions, let alone the labor movement. Symptomatic of the limits of the rank-and-file upsurge was the virtual absence of any contact or cross-fertilization between the groups. Almost as a given, the leaders and activists of these movements accepted the isolation that went along with business unionism. Such outside support as came, for example, to MFD did not include mutual aid between various groups or strikes. This was, in part, a reflection of how successful the American labor bureaucracy had been in abolishing the practice and even

---

94   R. Betheil, "The ENA in Perspective: The Transformation of Collective Bargaining in the Basic Steel Industry," *Review of Radical Political Economics* vol. x (1978), pp.16–18 (quotation on p. 17). I have appropriated several phrases from Betheil's article.
95   J. A. Geschwender, *Class, Race and Worker Insurgency: The League of Revolutionary Black Workers* (Cambridge: Cambridge University Press, 1977) pp. 83–126, 153–61; H. A. Thompson, *Whose Detroit?: Politics, Labor, and Race in a Modern American City* (Ithaca: Cornell University Press, 2001)..

legitimacy of labor solidarity and of any active conception of a labor movement. As a result, the various forms of rebellion never became a single movement like the civil rights, women's, or antiwar movements. The "private welfare state" created by the union contract further divided activists by keeping their attention primarily on their own employers rather than the state, which was the focus of most of the other movements of the time. There were exceptions, such as the Black Lung strikes by miners, and at least by implication, the 1970 postal workers strike, but these remained exceptions. The upsurge lacked a centralizing organization, political tendency, or institution that could concentrate and magnify the activity of disparate rank-and-file groups.

## Conclusion

The failure of independent rank-and-file organizations and other manifestations of the upsurge from below to transcend the framework of business unionism left the movements unarmed when economic and political conditions changed for the worse in the mid-1970s. The first major blow was the recession of 1974–5, the deepest since the 1930s. Manufacturing capacity utilization collapsed from 83 percent in 1973 to 65 percent in March 1975, while indices of industrial production plummeted. Reflecting the slump in production, unemployment rose from 4.9 percent in 1973 to 8.5 percent in 1975, by far the highest rate of the postwar era. For black workers, the unemployment rate rose from 8.9 percent to 13.9 percent, for blue-collar workers from 5.3 percent to 11.6 percent, for factory operatives from 5.7 percent to 13.2 percent, for white-collar employees from 2.9 percent to 4.7 percent.[96] For workers from Lordstown to the coalfields, from the steel mills to the telephone company, the 1974–5 recession was a quick education in the downside of capitalism and a blow to the confidence of youth. For workers to win wage gains, greater shop-floor control, and increased benefits under such conditions would have required a far more massive movement than the rank-and-file upsurge. More specifically, it would have required a decisive break from business unionism, akin to the rebellion of the 1930s.

The shock of the recession did not, however, put a complete end to the upheaval. Until the close of the decade, the number of strikes, which peaked in 1974, remained above the levels of the early 1960s. Militancy declined in some industries, such as auto and post office, but it carried on in others, such as trucking. Miners remained extraordinarily active throughout the decade, participating in dozens of wildcats and a 110-day national strike that defied President Carter's invocation of the Taft-Hartley Act in 1977–8. Public

---

96   E. Mandel, *The Second Slump: A Marxist Analysis of Recession in the Seventies* (London: New Left Books, 1978), p. 26; Council of Economic Advisers, Economic Report of the President 1986, pp. 231–2; BLS, Handbook of Labor Statistics 1980, pp. 61, 73.

workers, especially teachers, remained strike-prone, too. The second half of the 1970s also saw the emergence of significant rank-and-file organizations, including Steel Workers Fight Back and TDU. The labor upsurge of the 1960s and 1970s did not sputter to an end with a whimper, but collapsed with a bang in the brief interval between two major government assaults on the labor movement—the Chrysler bailout in the fall of 1979, which opened the floodgates of concessionary bargaining, and Ronald Reagan's firing of striking Professional Air Traffic Controllers and decertification of their union at the end of 1981. The sudden decline in militancy is expressed in the nearly 50 percent drop-off in the number of strikes between 1979 and 1981, from 4,827 to 2,568. During this same period, organizing efforts in the private sector also collapsed, with the number of NLRB elections dropping from nearly eight thousand in 1980 to half that in 1981.[97] Union membership dropped by almost 2 million members between 1979 and 1983, never to recover. In fact, the eight largest unions lost 2.2 million members between 1976 and 1983.[98] Much of this could be attributed to the recession of 1980–2, if it were not for the fact that the significantly deeper recession of 1974–5 failed to have such an impact, as in its wake strikes held up, NLRB elections barely decreased, and membership continued to grow, albeit largely due to public sector growth.

It is true that unions had been losing momentum for a very extended period, held back by bureaucratic inertia and business unionist accommodationism. Wage-deflated union organizing expenditures per non-union worker fell by 9 percent between 1953 and 1960, and another 21 percent between 1960 and 1970. Union organizing drives produced declining increases in the proportion of the non-agricultural labor force signed up each year—from 0.8 percent in 1955, to 0.6 percent in 1960, to 0.5 percent in 1970, to 0.3 percent in 1975. Union density fell continuously from the mid-1950s, and from 1970 onward both the density and the absolute numbers of unionized workers in the private sector declined.[99] From 1972 onward, negotiated wage settlements over the life of the contract shrank in real terms more or less continuously.[100]

---

97    H. Farber and B. Western, "Round Up the Usual Suspects: The Decline of Unions in the Private Sector, 1973–1998," Working Paper #437, Princeton University, Industrial Relations Section, April 2000, p. 9.

98    See K. Moody, *U.S. Labor in Trouble and Transition: The Failure of Reform from Above, the Promise of Revival from Below* (London: Verso, 2007), chapter 6.

99    L. Troy, "The Rise and Fall of American Trade Unions: The Labor Movement from FDR to RR," in S. M. Lipset, ed., *Unions in Transition: Entering the Second Century* (San Francisco: ICS Press, 1986), p. 81; T. Ferguson and J. Rogers, *Right Turn: The Decline of the Democrats and the Future of American Politics* (New York: Hill and Wang, 1986), p. 63.

100   Statistical Abstract 1978, p. 425; 1986, p. 423.

Several new trends of the 1970s changed the rules of the game. First, capital got organized, as symbolized by the emergence of the Business Roundtable in the early 1970s. Second, business resistance to the unionization of new workers grew ever fiercer, leading to the virtual collapse of organizing efforts in 1980–1. Third, there was a sharp move to the right in national politics as a whole, and in particular in the Democratic Party, manifested in the failure of President Jimmy Carter and huge Democratic majorities in Congress to support even mild labor law reform.[101] In the background, of course, were the deepening difficulties of the economy, manifested in reduced profit rates and intensifying international competition, which led to the profound restructuring of a series of major industries, such as auto and steel, that began toward the end of the 1970s and confronted unions and the working class as a whole with unprecedented challenges.

Still, as important as all of these factors were, it was ultimately the response of the labor leadership across the board—not just their vacillating response to the employers, but above all their implacably repressive response to the revolt from below—that brought resistance to such a low point so very rapidly, opening the way to the years of concessions and decline of the 1980s. Rather than nurture energies mobilized by rank-and-file organizing and resistance, and channel them toward the struggle against the employers, labor officials systematically dispersed them, decisively undermining their own power and that of the labor movement as a whole. Some of the more dramatic moments in this ongoing effort to isolate and destroy militancy were the UAW's breaking of the three Chrysler wildcat plant occupations in the summer of 1973, the surrender of the New York public sector unions during that city's 1975 fiscal crisis, and the Steelworkers' 1973 Experimental Negotiating Agreement that banned strikes. In fact, it is difficult to specify a single instance where top union officials welcomed, rather than sought to smash, autonomous rank-and-file organizing and militancy, and the costs turned out to be very high—the dispersal of the unions' greatest source of potential strength.

The union officials' very success in subduing their own "militant base" in the struggle to secure their own power and material base was thus a fundamental factor in weakening many of the labor movement's strongest unions—notably the UAW, the USWA, and the IBT. Precisely to the degree they succeeded in wearing down the resistance of the ranks, they also wore down the ability of the union as an institution to fight back in the face of increased employer aggression.

Of course, the success of bureaucratic business unionists in sustaining their dominance expressed the weakness and ultimate failure of rank-and-file organizing and, beyond that, working class consciousness. For all

---

101 See, for example, Moody, *An Injury to All*, pp. 127–46.

their oppositional character and independence of action, the rank-and-file rebellions of the period remained prisoners of the business union institutions they sought to change and reflected its own limitations, above all its fragmentation and disunity. Perhaps most striking, the maze of jurisdictional boundaries that defined the union movement was implicitly accepted, left unchallenged. The 1970s saw massive strike movements across industries, but there was virtually no contact among them, despite the presence of significant organization from below. Nor did the leading rank-and-file organizations of the era, like TDU, MFD, UNC, or Steelworkers Fight Back, make serious attempts to relate to one another, let alone organize umbrella organizations that might help them to provide mutual support. Almost as a given, the leaders and activists of these movements accepted the isolation that went along with business unionism. Such outside support as there was, as for example in the miners' strike of 1977–8, did not include, or lead to, mutual aid between various groups or strikes, a reflection of just how successful the labor bureaucracy had been in abolishing the practice and even legitimacy of labor solidarity and of any active conception of a labor movement.

Unlike the other social movements of the 1960s and 1970s, there were no nationally recognized leaders or organizations that straddled the movement as a whole. Nor was there the sort of radical core of organized leftists that had provided so much of the indispensable grassroots leadership, at the shop-floor level and across the movement as a whole, as there had been in earlier labor upheavals. Socialists and other radicals played important roles in some rank-and-file organizations—in the Teamsters, the UAW, Steelworkers, and a few others—but their numbers were few, and none of their organizations were strong enough to provide anything like national leadership and direction to the movement as a whole, with perhaps the exception of TDU in the IBT. Strike movements and internal union oppositions in different unions possessed their own rhythms and timing, so, without outside support to sustain them during the periods when activity inevitably dropped off, they could not but ultimately run their course. While these movements again and again pointed beyond the limits of business unionism, they lacked the power and the vision to transcend it, which only comes from greater organization and broader activity leading to greater class consciousness.

Especially in the context of usually localized rank-and-file activity and organization, racial division played a significant part in exacerbating fragmentation, and the possibilities for doing more to bring about greater unity were further limited by the somewhat disparate timings of the black freedom movement and the rank-and-file revolt. There can be no question that rank-and-file initiatives within the unions were not only inspired by the example of the black movement, but were directly strengthened by the disproportionate role in most of them of black and Latino workers, especially as the struggle for black liberation maintained momentum into the later 1960s. But by the early 1970s, as the rank-and-file rebellion faced its biggest challenges—to find ways to achieve greater permanence and breadth—virtually all wings of the black freedom movement were in sharp decline, as the civil rights movement confronted implacable resistance as it went north, and Black Power and black nationalist movements faced isolation and repression. As a result, the rank-and-file rebellion was deprived of a central source of dynamism. The fact that, as the obverse side of the weakening of the black struggle, the "white backlash" gathered increasing momentum across much of the industrial "heartland" in the late 1960s and throughout the 1970s only added to the challenge. And working-class votes for Wallace and then Nixon were just the tip of the iceberg. The size and influence, however temporary, of the highly interracial rank-and-file movements in the UMWA, UAW, USWA, IBT, and others is remarkable in this context. But they were going against the stream.

The upsurge of the 1960s and 1970s shared many of the characteristics of previous labor rebellions in twentieth-century America. Like the strike waves during and after World War I or the rise of the CIO in the 1930s, the upheaval of the 1960s and 1970s was a revolt from below, characterized by the collective militancy of tens of thousands of workers pushing and sometimes moving beyond the boundaries of existing union organization. In all three eras, workers' militancy challenged the tyranny of employers on the shop floor and the bargaining table, seeking to win for workers not just "bread and butter" demands, such as better wages and benefits, but moral and ethical demands, including dignity, respect, and equality. Political radicals played key roles in each era, providing cadre, experience, vision, direction, and inspiration. But the impact of the labor unrest of the 1960s and 1970s failed to match that of the earlier upsurges.

In the Progressive and New Deal Eras, the demands of the labor movement found echoes in other social movements and, more importantly, in the political process. The labor question was at the center of public policy debates at every level of government. Separately or in conjunction with the labor movement, many Progressive Era reforms, including anti-trust, consumer protection, and protective legislation, sought to limit the destructive power of corporations. And of course the New Deal established workers' right to join unions and provided a state-sanctioned process for the exercise of those rights. While workers' militancy played a central role in many of these transformative political victories, the same cannot be said of the rank-and-file rebellion of the 1960s and 1970s. Rather, in the later era, the civil rights, Black Power, antiwar, and feminist movements had the greatest impact on American society. Class was no longer a central issue; indeed, to many Americans the labor question appeared answered. In this sense, the rank-and-file upsurge was a victim of earlier success, particularly that of the 1930s, when the New Deal established labor as a permanent, albeit second-class, institution of the American political economy. The institutionalization of the labor movement provided great gains for workers, but it circumscribed the possible paths for working-class collective action when those gains were threatened by economic and political shifts. The rank-and-file upsurge of the 1960s and 1970s proved that the labor question remained open. But, stuck inside a sclerotic labor movement, it did not succeed in providing a definitive answer.

# 5

# The United Farm Workers from the Ground Up

## Frank Bardacke

It is not just that the struggle of California farm workers is generally unknown, it's worse than that: much of what is known is either wrong or irrelevant. I begin this essay, therefore, with a couple of corrections, in an attempt to disabuse the readers of some ideas they might have about farm workers. Once that is done, and not until then, I can deliver my own version of the roller-coaster history of the California farm workers' union, the UFW.

The union itself is responsible for a good deal of the confusion. Semi-official UFW history portrays California farm workers as powerless and defeated—until César Chávez came along to organize them. Here are two prominent UFW voices delivering that message. In *Conquering Goliath*, Fred Ross's 1989 account of how he tutored César Chávez in organizing, Ross described Oxnard farm workers as "meek, self-effacing people whose lifestyle had been one of being pushed around by authorities without a peep . . ." In 2004, LeRoy Chatfield, directing the "UFW Documentation Project" that now appears on the official UFW website, described the essential problem of UFW history like this:

> Without doubt, future academics and readers will ask the question: how did Cesar Chavez overcome the obstacles he faced in order to build the first farmworker union in the history of California (and the US)? There were two obstacles: (1) California agribusiness, (2) California farmworkers.

Chatfield goes on to explain that California farm workers[1] were an obstacle

---

1  Chatfield and others spell farm workers as one word, "farmworkers." This is a bad habit, as it suggests that farm workers are some special category of workers, perhaps more like peasants than rural proletarians. Let's be clear: the people who made up the

to Chávez's achievement for many of the oft-cited reasons: they were debilitated by their dependency on the growers, trapped by low wages and the ineffectiveness of farm worker strikes, pitted against each other on the basis of race and ethnicity, and without the protection of labor laws.

Ross and Chatfield are not insignificant figures; what they have to say counts.[2] Their view of California farm workers is standard UFW fare, a product of several interlocking and reinforcing ideological, economic, and political influences and imperatives: the Alinskyite[3] view of the central position of the organizer in politics, the attitude of Catholic Social Action toward the flock, the UFW's promotion of the genius of César Chávez, and, most importantly, the UFW's desire to win sympathy and support for farm workers from its boycott constituency: liberal and radical students, middle-class consumers, trade union officials, and Democratic Party politicians.

Despite its prominence, the idea of the powerless farm worker is, at best, misleading and incomplete. As long as this picture of the hat-in-hand peasant waiting dutifully before his all-powerful patron is imprinted on the retina of the mind's eye, the story of the UFW's rise and fall will remain fuzzy, out of focus, a mystery, a subject for all manner of bizarre explanations.[4]

In arguing against the idea of the meek, powerless farm worker, I do not invoke the general proposition that where there is oppression, there will

---

membership of the UFW were workers, selling their labor power to bosses, not small proprietors or sharecroppers, or peons tied to the land and indebted to the patron. Furthermore, I did not insert a "sic" in the midst of the Chatfield quote; the UFW was not the first farm worker union in the history of California or the United States. There were many that were successful for a while, some, like the Filipino Agricultural Labor Association, that were quite strong in the fields for several years before they lost their power and influence, much as has the UFW, which currently has but five thousand members.

2   Fred Ross, in the Alinskyite phrase which became a UFW standard, "organized" César Chávez. He brought him into politics, supervised him for his first ten years as a professional organizer, and later became the chief architect of the UFW's successful 1965–70 table grape boycott. Chatfield, a former Christian Brother, left the order in 1966 to become Chávez's chief of staff, where he remained until 1972, and now he serves as the in-house guardian of early UFW history.

3   Alinskyism has been the dominant theory of community organizing in the United States since the publication of Saul Alinsky's first book, *Reveille for Radicals*, in 1946. What defines the approach is the central role of the outside organizer who transforms a divided neighborhood, city, or region into a united community fighting for its interests. Today there are scores of Alinskyite or neo-Alinskyite training centers, and hundreds of Alinsky-inspired community organizations, of which ACORN is only the most prominent.

4   A fair number of ex-UFW staffers, for example, believe that after César Chávez built the UFW he went crazy and destroyed it. This view can be gleaned from the above-mentioned "UFW Documentation Project."

be struggle. Nor the idea that the exploited always find the means to fight back, but in ways that are usually missing from standard historical narratives. Those propositions are generally true, but I am arguing something more: that periodic farm worker power is built into the nature of fresh fruit and vegetable production, and that the particular way vegetables were harvested in the period of UFW ascendancy produced a strata of skilled, militant farm workers who were at the heart of UFW power.

Even in California, where farming most closely resembles an industrial enterprise, the rhythms of nature still govern the pace of production. Before you can reap, you must sow. Before growers can realize a profit (before they can get to "Department Three," for you careful readers of *Capital*), they must pay land rent, cultivate and prepare the soil, irrigate, thin, weed, fumigate, and often weed again. Moreover, the reaping that follows the sowing does not last; the harvest is intermittent, and is replaced by another long period of investment when growers once again have no product to sell.[5] To make matters worse, fruits and vegetables have to be harvested within a few days of when they are ready, with the actual number of days depending on the crop and the vagaries of the weather. What is not harvested is lost, along with all the money that was invested prior to the harvest. If growers can't settle a strike in time, they do not have the option of warehousing their fields or shutting down their assembly lines for a while, and then working people overtime once the work stoppage is over.

All of this gives farm workers considerable power, as California growers have been saying for more than a hundred years. When workers strike in the midst of the harvest, they start to be effective almost immediately. In a couple of days or weeks, depending on the crop, striking workers may be able to ruin a growers' entire season. This power is augmented by the periodic shortages of labor associated, once again, with the peculiarities of agricultural production. The growers' demand for labor varies greatly during a calendar year, and often there is not enough work in a particular area to promote an extensive settlement of agricultural workers—which is another way of saying that farm workers are often migrants. But migratory trails are occasionally disrupted, and sometimes enough farm workers don't arrive when needed, especially at the beginning of a harvest. These periodic labor shortages, rooted in the cycles of agricultural production, have been seized upon by farm workers to temporarily drive up wages.

---

5   The periodic nature of Department Three in agricultural production is why credit is so important in rural communities and why the small Midwestern and Southern farmers who formed the backbone of the populist movement made "democratic credit" their central demand. See L. Goodwyn, *The Populist Moment: A Short History of the Agrarian Revolt in America* (New York: Oxford University Press, 1978).

Finally, as California growers have discovered in numerous strikes, and all ideology to the contrary, the harvesting of fresh fruit and vegetables is skilled work that cannot be done efficiently by inexperienced scabs. This skill is not only embodied in the dexterity, strength, and endurance of the individual worker with a tool in his or her hands, but also resides in the piece-work crews which were particularly important after the end of the Bracero Program in 1965, in the period of rapid UFW growth. These crews, especially the lettuce crews, were made up of people (mostly men) who were often related to each other (brothers, cousins, fathers, and sons) and worked closely together for long periods of time, each earning an equal split of their collective pay. Their work is physically exhausting, and takes years to learn to do well. Only the most determined and skilled could put up with it for very long, despite the relatively high wages. Over time, these crews developed an intense measure of internal solidarity, their own leaders, a great deal of collective pride, and a tradition of on-the-job independence and militancy.

The people on these crews had very little in common with the powerless farm workers made popular by the UFW. They were masters of harvest strikes, slowdowns, and various kinds of agricultural sabotage. They often refused to enter a field until a wage was renegotiated on the spot. Their *paros* (short work stoppages), *planes tortugas* (turtle plans, or slowdowns), *planes cochinos* (pig plans, or sabotage), and *planes canguros* (kangaroo plans, where the workers skip over vegetables ready to be cut) were all part of the farm worker arsenal before the UFW ever came around. Farm workers taught these ideas to UFW staff, not the reverse.

California farm workers also had a long history of conventional strikes before the arrival of the UFW in the mid-1960s. They struck in massive numbers in the 1920s and 1930s, prompting the U.S. government, in league with the largest growers, to introduce contracted Mexican labor into Texas and California, starting in 1941. In the early years of the Bracero Program, the number of strikes slowed down, but farm workers resumed their characteristic militancy in the late 1950s and early 1960s, in a series of strikes which helped end the entire bracero operation. By some measures, the level of unrest among agricultural workers was greater than that of their industrial counterparts. In 1933, for example, nearly 50,000 people went on strike in the California fields, about 25 percent of all California farm workers. In comparison, in 1936, at the height of strike activity among U.S. industrial workers, only 10 percent of the workforce went on strike. Moreover, more than 80 percent of the 1933 strikes won higher wages and improved benefits, as the growers scrambled to get their workers back on the job before the harvest was over.

But if California farm workers had so much power and such a tradition of militancy, why weren't they able to build a lasting union? The main answer is that farm worker power, like the harvest, was periodic, and largely disappeared after the harvest was over. Growers may have been forced to raise their wages in order to get farm workers to harvest their crops, but the long period between harvests and the large turnover in the migrant labor force meant that the workers' power was short-lived. After the harvest, the growers had plenty of time to sabotage and destroy most of the unions they had earlier recognized in order to get their crops cut and packed. Every year, therefore, the workers had to begin anew.[6]

Another factor, almost as important, is the isolation of farm workers from their natural allies in the rest of society, especially the industrial working class. Let's look back again at 1933, when a quarter of all California farm workers went out on strike but were unable to secure lasting union contracts. The next year, 1934, saw the victorious strikes of truckers in Minneapolis, longshoremen in San Francisco, and tire builders in Toledo. In each of these cases, the strikers won when their particular strikes became general strikes, that is, when they won the support of other nearby workers and the communities in which they all lived. Farm workers, however, migrated in and out of small rural communities where there were no other large groups of workers who supported them. They were isolated spatially from their potential allies in the cities, and by race, language, and culture from other rural Californians. They may have been skilled and militant, with periodic power at harvest time, but they were isolated, without powerful allies, and easy to defeat once the harvest was over.

One way to understand the history of the UFW, then, is that the table grape boycott of 1965–70 ended the isolation of California farm workers, linked them up to their allies in U.S. cities, and helped establish a union structure which added long-term institutional power to the periodic power of farm workers at harvest time. Once the UFW established itself as a significant presence in urban America, farm worker militants no longer stood alone. They now had the economic and political support of unions, churches, liberal and radical students,

---

6 The Industrial Workers of the World (IWW) has been famously criticized for refusing to sign union contracts in the hopes that the lack of a contract would force workers to maintain a high level of vigilance and class consciousness. IWW critics point out that the Wobblies ignored the need to form a stratum to defend partial victories, and the periodic nature of mass movements and mobilizations. Therefore, they undervalued the benefits of contracts and regular union officials. I am not an expert on the Wobblies, but since so many of them were farm workers, I think it is possible that their view about contracts was not an idea the IWW imposed on workers, but rather an idea that grew out of the reality of periodic harvests and the actual power relationship between farm workers and their bosses. The Wobblies demanded that which they could win.

liberal foundations, Democratic Party politicians, and consumers. It was a heady combination, but not without its contradictions.

## The UFW Grape Boycott

I have done my best to correct the notion of the hat-in-hand farm worker whose "meek, self-effacing" ways were an "obstacle" that César Chávez had to overcome before he could build a union. But now, as I begin my story of the UFW, it is time to acknowledge the political brilliance of César Chávez, and the indispensable role he played in UFW history. It was Chávez (and a few people around him, most prominently Protestant minister Jim Drake) who chose not to accept the verdict of a 1965 losing strike, but rather chose to keep that strike symbolically alive, popularize it throughout the country, and initiate a boycott that leveraged the union's support in other areas against the seemingly victorious table grape growers. Today that may not seem to have been such a remarkable choice. That is but a trick of time. In the mid-sixties, the boycott was a stroke of genius.

Let's review. At the time of the 1965 table grape strike, boycotts were not a popular weapon in labor struggles. They amounted to little more than "Don't Buy" lists on the back pages of rarely read union newspapers and magazines. The UFW brought boycotts back into fashion; the Farah boycott, the Nestlé boycott, and all the various boycotts that followed were inspired by the success of the UFW's boycott of table grapes. Now, when a local struggle is defeated, people almost automatically think of boycott possibilities. The UFW opened that door in 1965. César Chávez turned the handle.

In retrospect, we can see that conditions were ripe for a boycott in the 1960s. Delano was a lot closer to San Francisco and Los Angeles (where the table grape boycotts began) in 1965 than it had been in 1933, or even in the 1950s when farm workers tried unsuccessfully to mount a boycott of the table grape potentate Di Giorgio Corporation. Improved roads and cars made the country smaller. Students and labor activists from California's coastal cities could drop by Delano for a weekend. Farm workers could make the same trip in the opposite direction. New, relatively inexpensive airplane travel made it possible for UFW leaders, especially César Chávez, to personally promote the boycott in Midwestern and Eastern cities. The introduction of the handheld video camera in the early sixties allowed television newsmen to bring images of distant struggles into the nation's living rooms and made long-distance solidarity easier.

As important as these physical changes were, however, they took second place to the new political opportunities of the sixties, opened up by the civil rights movement. Southern blacks changed the meaning of U.S. race relations. Among many other accomplishments, they established that race didn't have to divide and isolate people from one another, but could be a basis of support and solidarity. The most immediate precursors of the table grape boycott were the picket lines in front of northern Woolworth stores in support of southern lunch-counter sit-ins. The northern liberal, church, student, and union support for the southern civil rights movement was the rough model that César Chávez had in mind at the beginning of the grape boycott. He expanded on it and adapted it, most significantly by sending farm workers to live in U.S. cities to help staff and promote the boycott effort. But the political configuration of UFW support between 1965 and 1970 was a replica of northern support for the early civil rights movement.

More than a replica, it was almost a substitute. In 1966, as the UFW boycott was getting under way, there was a crisis in the civil rights movement. The liberal betrayal of the Mississippi Democratic Party in 1964, followed by Stockley Carmichael's endorsement of Black Power, the split in SNCC, and the riots in northern U.S. cities, taken together broke the connection between liberal support and the black struggle. Unable to find a comfortable home among the new advocates of Black Power and estranged from the radical student opposition to the war in Vietnam, liberals were distant from the most important social movements of the day. The farm worker movement gave them another opportunity. Walter Reuther is the emblematic figure. He orchestrated the 1964 betrayal in Atlantic City, was instrumental in cutting off northern money to SNCC in 1965, and was the first national figure to come to Delano to support the grape boycott in 1966.

Did César Chávez understand all this when he threw most of the resources and energies of his tiny farm labor association into a campaign for a national grape boycott? Of course not. This is a reconstruction made possible by the passage of time, a historical perspective. But he understood some of it, and he jumped at an opportunity that only a few other people around him could see. And then he stubbornly stuck by his decision during the four long years when the outcome was far from clear, when others were filled with doubt, and some proposed alternative strategies or gave up the battle entirely. Finally, in 1970, when the grape boycott had convinced millions of people to stop buying grapes and thereby forced almost all of the California grape growers to sign three-year contracts with the UFW, the union had not only won a great victory, but César Chávez had earned his place in U.S. history.

There is no final conflict. Political victories are rarely complete, and always have their troublesome consequences. The table grape boycott was no exception. As it was primarily the power of the farm workers' supporters which won the first big contracts, the organization tilted toward the cities and away from the fields. The UFW became a twin-souled organization: a combination of a farm worker advocacy group and a farm workers' union. That is not just a manner of speaking: full-time boycotters who lived and worked together in major U.S. cities became members of the union, with voting rights at the union's national conventions. Thus the UFW membership became an amalgam of mostly Mexican farm workers who were covered by UFW contracts, and primarily middle-class, white boycotters, many of whom were on leave from religious orders, who ran the boycott and became the principle staff of the union. This peculiar hybrid worked for a while, but it also intensified some of the disputes that usually exist between union staffers and rank-and-file workers.

The successful table grape boycott reinforced the idea among the UFW leadership that the essential power of their union was among its supporters in the cities rather than among the workers in the fields. In the wake of that first boycott victory, and influenced by the disdain for rank-and-file power inherent in both Alinsky's organizer-centered politics and in Catholic Social Action's commitment to hierarchy, Chávez and the people around him established a union structure which blocked the full development of farm worker power within the union. Most dramatically (and, as it turned out, disastrously), the union leadership even rejected the idea of forming union locals. Instead of locals, the UFW established field offices whose staff was appointed by César Chávez. Often these staffers were people who had been recruited to the union through the boycott, or were former field workers who had proved their loyalty to the UFW leaders through years of boycott activity. The farm worker members of the union did not have the right to elect anyone to union office, except at the twice-yearly national conventions, where they routinely affirmed the official slate for Executive Board. Farm workers could vote for their own ranch committees, but people who served on these committees continued to work in the fields and did not have the time to take over the business of the union. In general, the ranch committees—the only bodies that directly represented farm worker opinion inside the union—did not set union policy; they followed it.

Equally serious in its long-term implications for democratic power inside the UFW, the union staff had its own source of income, separate from union dues. In the period between 1970 and 1985, union dues were usually less than 50 percent of UFW income; the rest of the union's money was generated by boycott events or from donations by wealthy individuals, other unions, and church groups. In addition, in the midst of the grape boycott, the UFW established a network of charity organizations, under its effective control, which received money from private foundations and government grants, as well as payments from growers that were stipulated in UFW contracts. Thus, by the early 1980s, when the union staff and the rank-and-file farm worker leadership were in the middle of a battle over the direction of the union, the staff did not depend upon farm worker dues for its continued existence.

A last consequence of the boycott victory and the undemocratic union structure that partially flowed out of it was the distinct ethnic difference between the farm worker membership of the union and UFW officialdom.[7] The UFW's original founders—César and Helen Chávez, Dolores Huerta, and Gilbert Padilla—were all Chicanos, that is, people of Mexican heritage who were born and raised in the United States. Moreover, the table grape workers around Delano, who were the UFW's original base among California farm workers, were largely people whose families had come to the United States in the 1920s, rather than recent immigrants. These were the farm workers that the UFW sent out on the original boycott and brought on to the UFW staff. Thus, the early staff, formed in the crucible of the boycott, was Chicano and white. That remained true, even though by the late seventies the majority of the membership of the union were not grape workers but vegetable workers, who were not Chicanos but transnational Mexican immigrants. Unable to elect anyone to full-time union office, these Mexican farm workers remained unrepresented on the union staff. This added one more tension between the staff and the rank and file, and mattered in the final battle between them.

## Farm Workers' Strikes

What generally passes for the history of the UFW is but the history of the UFW leadership and staff. Journalists and academics have recorded only one soul of the union, that chamber of its two-chambered heart that beats in the nation's cities, among the wide coalition of farm worker supporters. The other chamber, the one that beats in the fields, has gone unrecorded, its story unknown. In the rest of this essay, I provide but a glimpse into this second soul of the union by giving a very brief account of five of the six strikes that formed the backbone of UFW history, and a slightly longer description of the UFW's last great strike, the 1979 vegetable strike. This final, eight-month struggle, the most successful strike in California agricultural history, promised to secure the UFW's place in the California fields but instead set up the union for its ultimate demise.

These six strikes are but the backbone of the UFW's story. Countless others make up the rest of the skeleton. I do not use the word "countless"

---

7    I do not mean to argue that the boycott was entirely responsible for the undemocratic structure of the UFW; there is ample precedent for anti-democratic structure, culture, and practice among U.S. unions that never gained any of their power from boycotts.

irresponsibly. Some of the other strikes between 1960 and 1979 have been counted: the nearly annual melon strikes between 1971 and 1979; the 1974 Yuma and the 1978 Oxnard lemon strikes; the various McFarland rose strikes between 1964 and 1978; the Sacramento tomato strikes, not annual events in the mid-seventies, but nearly so. These strikes, and others, were among those big enough to be recorded. Many, however, were not big enough, and were known only to farm workers and their supervisors; they were uncounted, recorded by neither journalist nor historian. These "countless" small strikes, coupled with the larger recorded battles and multiple on-the-job fights, made the California fields in the 1960s and 1970s a place of nearly constant struggle, as farm workers, conscious that the presence of the UFW strengthened their hand, used what power they had to significantly drive up their wages and improve their working conditions in the fields.

But here I can give only a sketch of the backbone, and must leave the rest of skeleton off the page, still hidden in oblivion. Also, my discussion of the first five strikes is highly limited: I offer only a brief description of their importance, and of the relationship between the UFW staff and the rank and file in the various battles, as it is that relationship which is a chief topic of this essay. Finally, I do the sixth strike more justice.

**The 1960–1 Imperial Valley Vegetable Strike.** Piece-rate lettuce crews, angry because their employers had unilaterally declared that henceforth they would be paid by the hour (which would have reduced their wages significantly), initiated this strike. They went to the offices of the AFL–CIO-sponsored Agricultural Workers Organizing Committee (AWOC) and persuaded the local organizers to call a strike meeting. At that meeting, and a subsequent one, workers overwhelmingly endorsed the strike, which lasted nearly two months. To counteract the extended walkout, the growers had to restore piece rates, as well as raise hourly wages. But as was usual in farm worker struggles, the strike did not force growers to sign with AWOC, and George Meany, who had financed the operation, removed the main AWOC organizers and cut its funding.[8]

At a crucial moment in the strike, braceros who cut most of the lettuce in the Imperial Valley joined a sit-in of strikers in front of a bracero camp. This was an act of great courage: the braceros had to climb the fence of their camp, in full view of U.S. police officials, in order to cast their lot with the striking sit-inners. Climbing that fence opened two decades of struggle

---

8   Meany had reluctantly established AWOC in response to complaints that the AFL–CIO was neglecting farm workers. But when the new Kennedy administration, speaking through Labor Department chief and prototypical Cold War liberal Arthur Goldberg, complained that the unruly Imperial Valley strike was complicating relations with Mexico, Meany temporarily shut AWOC down. He then re-opened it with new, more conservative leadership.

in the fields, in the same way that the 1955 Montgomery Bus Boycott and the 1959 San Francisco demonstration against HUAC opened the African-American and student movements. The braceros who joined the strike, coupled with a few others who had been joining AWOC strikes for the last two years, put the entire Bracero Program in jeopardy.[9] After the strike, California Senator Clair Engle declared that the Congress would soon end the entire program. The most farsighted grower, Bud Antle, agreed, and concluded that unionization in the fields was therefore inevitable. A few months after the strike ended, he signed a contract with the Teamsters to protect himself from a more militant union that he feared might come.

Working through the local Imperial Valley Community Service Organization (CSO), an Alinskyite-style community group of Mexican Americans, César Chávez had a firsthand view of the strike. Two years later he resigned from CSO because it would not make organizing farm workers a main priority, and founded the National Farm Workers Association, which eventually became the UFW.

**The 1965 Table Grape Strike.** Initiated by Filipino workers in the Coachella Valley and reluctantly endorsed by the new, more conservative leadership of AWOC, this strike successfully raised wages in Coachella and then moved north to Delano, the center of California table grape production. Faced with the choice of scabbing on a Filipino strike or joining what they considered a doomed effort, César Chávez and the leadership of the National Farm Workers Association decided to join the strike. Helped by the shortage of labor due to the closing down of the Bracero Program, the strike was quite strong for a couple of weeks, but after the strikers won their wage demands, most of them went back to work. The NFWA, unrecognized by the growers, refused to admit defeat. With some of the most militant strikers newly recruited to its staff, and with the help of students from Los Angeles and San Francisco, the NFWA kept their small picket lines alive and began a national boycott of table grapes. Four years later, after a series of small strikes in the fields meant to, in the words of the UFW, "legitimize the boycott," enough people had stopped buying grapes to force almost all of the California table grape growers to sign with the UFW.

---

9 The end of the Bracero Program, like most everything else in life, was over-determined. The introduction of the cotton machine in Texas, the complaints of the Mexican government, years of liberal agitation, and the progressive Congresses of the civil rights era all played their parts. But history has robbed the braceros of their own role in the drama. The increasing participation of braceros in farm worker strikes starting in the late 1950s, although well known in the fields, is barely noted in published works. Accounts of braceros climbing the fence to join the 1961 sit-in are found only in the contemporary Imperial Valley newspapers, and in the memories of surviving farm workers.

**The 1970 Salinas Vegetable Strike.** Frightened by the capitulation of the table grape growers, Salinas Valley vegetable growers finally saw the wisdom of Bud Antle's 1961 maneuver and signed a contract with the Teamsters Union. But what had served as a shield in 1961 had become a target in 1970, and the UFW leadership moved immediately from the table grape signing ceremony in Delano to the scene of the backdoor Teamster agreement in Salinas. There they met the leadership of the already self-organized piece-rate crews, who quickly aligned with the UFW and began to agitate for a strike. After weeks of delay partially caused by the UFW officials' fear that a strike would be quickly defeated, the union finally endorsed the walkout. Thousands of workers struck for three and a half weeks, reducing the valley's production by two-thirds in the first two weeks, and by half in the strike's closing days. In Salinas in 1970, the union's potential boycott power and its strength in the fields meshed smoothly. Under the threat of the boycott and unable to get enough scabs to harvest their crops, three large national corporations with agricultural holdings in Salinas repudiated their Teamster contracts and signed with the UFW. One large local company also signed. The UFW had won a small foothold in the fresh vegetable industry.

**The 1973 Grape Strike.** Aided by the Nixon administration, which had close ties to California agriculture, enabled by the Teamsters Union, which had a long history on the West Coast as an alternative to more militant unionism, and taking advantage of the UFW's failure to democratically integrate its new table grape membership into the union, the table grape growers refused to re-sign the contracts that the boycott had forced them to sign in 1970. In response, the union called a statewide grape strike (and a limited melon strike), which extended from Coachella in the south to Fresno in the north. Thousands of workers, loyal to the UFW, responded with a remarkable campaign of civil disobedience, in which many hundreds were arrested for breaking unreasonable and unconstitutional court orders that put severe limits on picketing. Many workers were arrested more than once, and some were arrested multiple times—in all there were more than three thousand arrests—which served to overwhelm several rural county jails and nearly bankrupt a few county governments. The successful civil disobedience campaign, however, did not cause a serious fall in table grape production, as there was a large group of grape workers (especially Filipinos, but not exclusively so) who remained alienated from the union during the three years that the UFW held the table grape contracts. Finally, after one of the UFW strikers, Juan de la Cruz, was shot dead while standing on a UFW picket line, the UFW leaders called the strike off and sent hundreds of strikers back out on a renewed grape boycott. The new boycott, however, never took hold. A few table grape growers eventually signed new contracts for a few years in the late 1970s, but after 1973 the UFW had lost its grip on the table grape industry. In the space of a few months, UFW membership fell from about 50,000 to less than 6,000.

**The 1974 Strike Tsunami.** Large numbers of California farm workers who had never worked under UFW contracts were worried about the UFW's defeat in the table grapes. They had benefited from the industry-wide rise in wages and improved working conditions that was a consequence of the end of the Bracero Program and the growers' subsequent attempt to contain the UFW. Many feared (quite reasonably) that if the UFW were defeated those gains would be reversed. Having lost most of its membership, and with its boycott failing to thrive, the UFW turned to these workers for help. More than 10,000 struck in lemon and apple orchards, strawberry and tomato fields, and mushroom sheds. From February to September the battle raged, with workers demanding higher wages, better benefits, and the Teamsters out of the fields. The UFW encouraged the individual strikes, many of which were initiated and run by rank-and-file workers. The union also brought several contingents of strikers to Sacramento, where they jammed the chambers in which the state solons were considering farm worker legislation. California editorial pages bemoaned the "chaos" in the fields, and agricultural trade journals argued that California growers would soon have to accept some form of agricultural labor law. In November, with UFW support, Jerry Brown became Governor of California; the next spring he negotiated a compromise between the growers and the UFW, the California Agricultural Labor Relations Act (ALRA). The new law was, and is, the most union-friendly legislation in the United States. The union's early struggles in Delano and Salinas, the civil disobedience campaign of 1973, the widespread strikes of 1974, and the latent threat of a resumed boycott had forced a historic concession from California agribusiness.

In the four years between the passage of the ALRA and the beginning of the 1979 vegetable strike, the trajectory of the UFW was generally consistent with its earlier history, but with some surprising twists and curlicues. As the growers had hoped, the new law sharply decreased the number of strikes on California farms. For two years, California farm workers typically voted in the fields rather than walking out of them. The elections verified what the earlier strikes had already demonstrated. The UFW lost most of the table grape elections up and down the Central Valley, but won in most every other crop, especially in the vegetable industry, centered in the Salinas and Imperial Valleys. With plenty of problems of their own, and disappointed by the elections results, Teamster chiefs pulled their union out of the fields. The growers lost a major ally; the UFW lost its competition among farm workers.

The election campaigns focused the UFW's attention on the fields, but not exclusively so. The elections were run by a farm labor board established by the ALRA; UFW leaders spent much of their time pressuring Governor Brown and other Democratic Party politicians in Sacramento to make sure that the board was adequately funded and that its appointees and policies continued to reflect the law's original pro-union language and intent. Rapidly, the boycott/advocacy soul of the union got enmeshed in Sacramento politics and, despite the farm worker election campaigns, remained generally out of touch with what was happening in the fields among the rank and file.

Life among the top UFW officers and their administrative staff did get a bit bizarre. They lived and worked together at La Paz, an ex-tuberculosis sanitarium in the Tehachapi foothills, not physically far but culturally distant from the farm workers who lived and worked in the valleys below them. Prodded by Chávez, they tried to become not only the administrative center of the union but a semi-religious intentional community that would be a model of group living, cooperation, and sacrifice for others. No longer having to compete with the Teamsters, separated from the concerns of ordinary farm workers, this "experiment," as Chávez called it, suffered from the usual deformities of such efforts. Open debate was discouraged, dissent was defined as disloyalty, leftists were purged, and the community turned even more in upon itself. For about eighteen months—from the spring of 1977 to the fall of 1978—the community spent much of its time and energy attacking each other in a form of aggressive therapy developed by Synanon, one of the nastier cults that flourished in the California counterculture of the 1970s.

All of these shenanigans at the top were unknown to the union membership, another measure of the extraordinary distance between the two souls of the UFW. What farm workers did notice, however, was that many of the UFW's administrative functions were badly managed. Workers were especially annoyed by the union's medical plan, run out of La Paz, which was consistently late in paying its share of the members' medical bills. In the late 1970s, the complaints from the valleys about the medical plan were so loud and so numerous that they were heard even in the foothills of the Tehachapis. Eventually the medical plan would be one of the main terrains on which the final battle between the two souls of the union would be fought.

In the 1979 vegetable strike, the growers and the workers battled where the UFW was strongest, in the vegetable fields of the Imperial and Salinas Valleys. But even in the vegetables, UFW strength was precarious, as the union still had less than half of the industry under contract. The highly competitive business of fresh vegetables could not last long being half union and half union-free. Although the non-union firms had to raise their wages to union standards in order to recruit workers and keep the UFW out, they did not pay nearly as much for benefits, and therefore they paid less for labor. Moreover, at the union farms the crews had more control over the pace of production, which added to its costs. It all promised a dangerous future where the lower-cost non-union companies would thrive and grow, and the union firms would be in jeopardy.

The strike affected only the union companies, whose contracts expired in January 1979. The growers went into the strike hoping to keep their labor bill down, so as to minimize their disadvantage versus their non-union competitors. They also proposed getting rid of the union hiring hall, which protected union seniority and had significant control over the hiring of new employees. Finally, the growers demanded several changes in the work rules designed to give the foremen and supervisors more control over the crews. On the union's side, the workers wanted significant raises, as much of what they had gained since the end of the Bracero Program and the emergence of the UFW had been eaten up by the rampaging inflation of the Carter years. The union officials were initially willing to give up the hiring hall and to grant new contract language to strengthen the foremen's power in the fields. But in a series of pre-strike meetings, the workers adamantly refused to make those concessions and went into the strike determined to maintain their control over production.

The union struck twelve of the twenty-eight vegetable companies that held UFW contracts. They did not initiate a general strike because they hoped to apply enough economic pressure to make one of the more vulnerable companies capitulate, after which they intended to force that agreement on the rest of the unionized firms. Their chief target was Sun Harvest, a subdivision of the transnational corporation United Fruit, which had been renamed United Brands. Although Sun Harvest was a major player in the California vegetable industry, it was a very small part of the parent corporation, making up about 2 percent of its total sales. Union strategists figured that by threatening to boycott United Brand's Chiquita Bananas, which accounted for more than 20 percent of its sales, the union could force the company to quickly agree to most of the union's demands at its relatively inconsequential Sun Harvest subsidiary.

Two weeks into the strike, in his first visit to the Imperial Valley picket lines, César Chávez was forthright about his own role in the struggle. He congratulated a rally of three thousand farm workers for their early success in stopping scabs and urged them to continue doing their job, which was to "strike, strike, strike." "My job," he said, "is in the cities . . . among large churches, labor unions, and student groups . . . to bring food and money in here, medical aid, all the things people need." The two-chambered heart was beating in lovely syncopation. The strikers would take care of the fields, César and the union staff would take care of the cities.

The strike was lead by a strike committee, representatives from each union company who had been appointed by the ranch committees. Many of the people on the strike committee were the ranch committee presidents themselves, most of whom were longtime leaders of their crews, including a core group of militants who had been active in the union for years: Mario and Chava Bustamante, Cleofus Guzman, Aristeo Zambrano, Berta Batres, Sergio Reyes, and Hermilo Mojica.[10] The entire committee was made up of transnational Mexican immigrants, as were the overwhelming majority of people who worked in vegetables. The committee was organized and directed by Marshall Ganz, the son of a rabbi, a refugee from the breakup of SNCC in 1965, the UFW Director of Organizing, and the executive board member closest to the rank and file.

In the third week of the strike, companies tried to bring in skilled farm worker scabs to harvest the crops. As they have done in California farm worker battles since the 1920s, the strikers rushed the fields in massive numbers in a largely successful effort to intimidate the scabs and get them to stop working. In response, in the midst of one of these charges into the fields, two foremen and a truck driver simultaneously fired at the unarmed strikers, killing one of them, Rufino Contreras. After the massive, emotional funeral and a one-day general strike, César Chávez announced the boycott of Chiquita Bananas and replaced Ganz with Frank Ortiz, another member of the executive board. Ortiz ordered the workers to stop running into the fields and restricted other mass strike activities.

Large strikes are not so easy to ratchet down, and workers continued periodic charges into the fields, but without the union's implicit support, they quickly became less effective. Most of the strike committee was furious at Ortiz but not yet capable of carrying out mass activities on its own. For the last three weeks of the Imperial Valley harvest, some five hundred skilled scabs harvested the fields, and a few of the original strikers returned to work. As the lettuce season moved on to the Salinas Valley, prospects seemed bleak.

Believing that victory depended on a successful boycott and could not be won in the fields, Chávez put strict limits on the strike in the Salinas Valley. Twelve companies had struck in Imperial; La Paz permitted only

---

10   Some of these people came out of the Mexican tradition of left agrarianism; others were brought into politics by the Mexican student movement of the late 1960s. Hermilo Mojica is the great-nephew of General Francisco Mújiga, the leftist in Lazaro Cardenas's cabinet most associated with the nationalization of Mexican oil. Collectively, they are another example of the impact of leftist immigrants on U.S. politics, especially union politics.

six to strike in Salinas, including Sun Harvest, the United Brands/United Fruit subsidiary. Chávez was still enthralled by his first great boycott victory and was using the Delano table grape campaign as a model for the vegetable strike: he intended to keep a small, limited strike alive in the fields and use it to animate and legitimize the boycott. Chávez began to tour U.S. cities, rebuilding the union's urban apparatus and promoting the anti-Chiquita campaign.

Back in the Salinas Valley, the strike committee had a very different point of view. They believed that in order to win, the strike had to be enlarged, extended to the other union companies, and perhaps even to the non-union ones. The limited strike was ineffectual, they thought, and demoralized both the strikers and the union members who stayed on their jobs. They argued that in a larger battle, with more strikers, they could more easily control the scabs, who were now fairly numerous at the six struck companies.

Standing in the middle of this widening breach was Marshall Ganz, whom Chávez had put back in charge of the strike in hopes of reviving it in Salinas. Ganz knew the arguments and positions of both La Paz and the strike committee. He understood the depth of the disagreement, and he tried to keep it from breaking out into an open fight. He did not fully report Chávez's point of view to the strike committee, nor did he report the opinion of the strike committee to Chávez. He hoped that he could finesse the difference, and that over the course of the strike new possibilities would open up and a strategy which most could agree on would emerge.

But the strike committee could not long be held back, and Ganz did not passively wait for that strategy to evolve. Together they devised what they called the *pre-huelga*, the pre-strike, as a way of remaining within Chávez's limits while extending the strike. The *pre-huelga* was based on the unity and discipline of the piece-rate vegetable crews and their long tradition of militant on-the-job action. The *pre-huelga* was a combination of the one-day *paro*, and the plans *cochino*, *tortuga*, and *cangaru*. Splendidly organized and carefully coordinated, workers at the non-struck firms would periodically leave their jobs after a few hours and then drive in caravan to join the picket lines of the firms that were officially on strike. Or they would work very slowly, cutting less lettuce or broccoli than the company had already sold on the day's market. Or they would work sloppily, cutting and packing a box of produce that would be hard for their bosses to sell. Or they would skip over vegetables that were ready to be cut, leaving them to rot in the fields. Or they would put in a regular day's work, as if nothing unusual were happening.

The *pre-huelga*'s success depended on the growers' unwillingness to fire their regular crews. If they fired those workers, they would have to find scabs to replace them, which was difficult and expensive, especially for the smaller companies. So the growers put up with the *pre-huelga* and accepted the periodic disruptions. They hoped to get as much product out of the fields as they could without being added to the list of companies that were officially on strike, and all the trouble that entailed.

There have been many on-the-job campaigns in the history of the U.S. working class. Often they have been more myth than substance, as worker unity has disintegrated under the pressure of laboring under the boss's roof. The *pre-huelga* was the real thing, made possible by the unique internal solidarity of the piece-rate crews and the special characteristics of agricultural production. Very widespread, it severely tried the patience of the growers; among the workers there were many stories of foremen and supervisors going slightly berserk under the pressure of the *pre-huelga*. But it couldn't be overused or go on forever, and the strike coordinators were quite aware of that. Eventually the growers wouldn't be able to take it anymore and would fire or suspend the *pre-huelgistas*. That was all right with the strike committee: it would be a perfect transition into the extended strike they were all hoping for.

The UFW executive board and the strike committee finally met face to face in mid-August, seven months into the strike. The Salinas Valley companies were gearing up for the last six weeks of the harvest, and it was no longer possible to finesse the differences over strike strategy. The confrontation came late at night, at the conclusion of two marches into Salinas: one coming from San Francisco, made up of about a hundred union supporters; the other coming up the Salinas Valley, in which thousands of farm workers participated. Chávez flew back and forth in a small plane so that he could appear at the rallies of both marches, but there was no doubt as to which one he belonged in. He had come to Salinas with the intention of further de-emphasizing the strike, officially mounting a major boycott campaign, and recruiting hundreds of strikers to go to U.S. cities to staff the boycott offices.

At the midnight meeting, Chávez tried to convince the strike committee to endorse his strategy.[11] He argued that they were not going to win the current strike, and that the union did not have the funds to expand it. Even if it did, he said, expanding the strike would be a wild gamble, a "throw of the dice" into an "unknown future." He said the surest way to win was to keep the strike small and to put all of the union's efforts into the boycott. The strike committee politely but vehemently disagreed. They argued that the scabs had not been able to do even a halfway decent job and that

---

11    Luckily, this meeting was taped. The rest of my account of this strike comes from contemporary newspapers and interviews with many of the participants.

the companies were close to signing. Also, they reminded the executive board, they had already promised the workers that the strike was going to be expanded once the marches were over, and if they backed out now the strike and the union would lose all credibility. An extended strike was the surest road to victory, they said. The boycott would take too long, and they personally didn't want to move to the cities. Better to win or lose the fight right here at home in the fields and accept the consequences.

The meeting broke up without agreement. At the next day's convention the executive board introduced a resolution that called for an all-out boycott effort and said nothing about the strike. Mario Bustamante, of the strike committee, offered an amendment to the resolution that called on the workers to expand the strike. Chávez chose not to contest the amendment in the open convention, and it passed unanimously. Later that day, however, as the convention was coming to a close, the executive board's sentiments became clear. A tomato company that had been bargaining with the union gave in and signed a contract on the UFW's terms. After this first strike victory was announced to the delegates, they began snake dancing through the aisles, chanting, "*Huelga, huelga, huelga!*" The executive board and a few invited guests sitting on the stage answered with a chant of "Boycott, boycott, boycott!" Those who used to sing in harmony were now in a discordant war.

After the convention, Chávez returned to La Paz without contacting either Ganz or the strike committee. He told the press that the union was going ahead with its boycott plans and that the strike would not be expanded in the immediate future. By the time his statement was released to the press, it was irrelevant. The strike committee, acting on its own, had already expanded the strike. Three hundred and fifty workers at a mid-sized lettuce company, West Coast Farms, had joined the strike, as well as a couple of hundred others at another tomato farm.

The strike committee had expanded the strike without consulting Marshall Ganz. He now had to make a choice. Was he going to join the committee and help with the unauthorized strikes, or was he going to side with Chávez and do what he could to keep the strike limited and small? Ganz sided with the strikers. César Chávez never forgave him.

After two weeks of the extended strike, West Coast Farms signed, again accepting all of the union's basic demands. In the immediate wake of that victory, the strike committee put out leaflets calling for a general strike throughout the Salinas Valley. One week later the big prize, Sun Harvest/United Fruit, capitulated. Immediately the non-union firms raised their wages to the new standard, or slightly above, and the other union companies lined up to sign the new agreement so that they could get their crews back to work. All but one, Bruce Church Inc., eventually signed.

The strike committee had defied César Chávez, extended the strike, and won. Chávez did not take it gracefully and was in no mood to make peace. He refused to return to Salinas to celebrate the final victory.

## From Union to NGO?

Again, the apparently healthy victory contained the germ of the next defeat. This time it would be fatal. One of the union demands that had been accepted by the companies was that the workers could elect full-time representatives, paid by the growers, who would help administer the contracts. Modeled on UAW committeemen, these "paid reps" were the first people in the history of the UFW elected by the rank and file into full-time union positions. As the elections came soon after the glorious 1979 strike victory, many of the most militant leaders of that strike, people who had served on the strike committee, became the paid reps. The very people who had defied Chávez and gone on to win the strike were now the first people on the UFW staff who owed their jobs not to the people above them, but to the ranks below.

The paid reps understood that the strike victory had intensified the competitive disadvantage of the union companies. They knew that the industry could not continue to be half union and half non-union. Although their job descriptions did not authorize them to do so, they began to spend some of their time organizing among the non-union companies. In addition, whereas La Paz had hoped that the paid reps would take care of enforcing the contracts and thereby reduce the grievances from the fields, nearly the reverse happened. The reps did enforce the contracts, but they also carried the complaints of the workers to the administrative center of the union at La Paz. Their major concern was the poor administration of the medical plan. When La Paz failed to adequately improve the plan, the paid reps continued to clamor about it. Rather than softening the attack on La Paz, they sharpened it.

With no history of locals or elected union officers, and without a tradition of democratic debate, La Paz could not handle its differences with the paid reps and the active rank and file who supported them. César Chávez and Dolores Huerta interpreted the dispute as an attempt by Marshall Ganz and top union officials Jessica Govea and Jerry Cohen to use the paid reps as a vehicle to take over the union, or to break away a Salinas local that they would control. It was easy enough to force those three out, along with UFW cofounder Gilbert Padilla, who had also built close ties with some of the newly elected representatives.

But that did no good at all, as the paid reps were not being manipulated by anyone and were acting out of their own political instincts and convictions. They did want some power within the union, commensurate with their authority among the rank and file. They were willing to fight for it, but they did not conceive of their fight as anti-union or even, at the beginning, anti-Chávez. Chávez, however, disturbed by the challenge to his power in the union, did not seek an accommodation. Believing that the reps were forming a union of their own, he blocked their efforts to organize the non-union firms. He also dragged his feet on fixing the medical plan, to demonstrate to the rank and file that the paid reps could not solve their problems.

In response, the paid reps decided to run a partial, alternative slate at the 1981 union convention. The slate was readily defeated. Enraged by an executive board maneuver that prohibited them from voting for their own candidates, some of the paid reps led a walkout of the convention. Chávez responded by sending Dolores Huerta to Salinas to organize their recall. That attempt failed, and Chávez fired nine of them, the very people who had led the 1979 strike.

Despite an adverse legal ruling, Chávez made the firings stick. But the battle ate up the union from the inside, divided the rank and file in Salinas, and ended all attempts to spread the union to non-union companies. In 1982, as the internal fight was cooling but while its consequences were still red hot, Republican George Deukmejian was elected Governor of California. He butchered the farm labor board, allowing the growers to develop various legal ways of leaving the union. Other growers, including Sun Harvest and West Coast Farms, unable to compete with the non-union companies, went out of business. The workers, their militant leadership destroyed, were in no position to regroup and fight back. The farm worker soul of the union, already mortally wounded, was finally killed off. All that remained was the advocacy soul, fully ensconced in La Paz, materially supported by their handsomely endowed string of non-profit organizations, and spiritually sustained by their warm memories of earlier triumphs.

What to make of this sad story? In some respects it fits snugly into the history of California agriculture, where several unions have had their moments of glory and then collapsed. What is different here is that the UFW continues on, not so much as a union, but as a cross between a farm worker advocacy group and a family business, whose primary capital is the story of César Chávez. On the other hand, the UFW's defeat as a labor union was not inevitable. The end of the Bracero Program and the temporary shortage of farm workers it produced, coupled with social movements of the sixties and seventies which provided significant support for the young union, allowed the UFW to get its foot in the door—nay, to move into the living room of California's fresh vegetable industry and secure a position from which it might have been able to establish a lasting presence in the

California fields. That didn't happen—not because it couldn't have, but because the leadership of the UFW overvalued the strength of its supporters and neither appreciated nor nurtured the power and political abilities of the skilled vegetable workers whose periodic militancy in the fields had been essential to most everything the UFW had won.

Perhaps the story of the UFW can also provide a small correction to the standard account of the defeat of social movements of the sixties and seventies. So often we are told that those movements were done in by their extravagant demands, their dreams of revolutionary change, their failures to scale back their hopes to the real political opportunities of the time. That may not be entirely wrong, but it is not what happened to the farm worker movement. There it was the realists in command of the UFW who tailored its strategies to what was acceptable to its supporters, who purged the left from the union, who built an anti-democratic union structure, who thwarted the larger ambitions of its militant rank and file, and who thereby were largely responsible for the union's defeat.

# 6

# Rank-and-File Movements in the United Mine Workers of America, Early 1960s–Early 1980s

## Paul J. Nyden

On March 4, 1978, members of United Mine Workers Local 6608 at Armco Steel's No. 7 mine gathered in their union hall in Sundial, West Virginia, to vote on the second contract proposal from the Bituminous Coal Operators Association. Running against the tide in the Appalachian coal fields, they ratified it. A few days later, after 69.6 percent of the miners across the country voted it down, Local 6608 met again. This time, after discussing Jimmy Carter's invocation of the Taft-Hartley Act, they voted unanimously to defy both Carter and Taft-Hartley. There was no better indication of the resolution of coal miners to remain united against both the companies and the government. Now, from the narrow hollows of southern West Virginia to the rolling hills of western Pennsylvania and the pine woods of northern Alabama, miners echoed: "Taft can mine it, Hartley can haul it, and Carter can shove it!"

The dramatic 110-day coal strike of 1977–8 reflected the militant traditions of American coal miners. It also represented the culmination of a historic wave of rank-and-file resistance to both the mining companies and the leadership of the UMW, extending for almost two decades. After offering a brief account of the miners' socioeconomic condition and the history of their struggles, this chapter examines the revolt of the long 1970s and analyzes its consequences. It follows the ascending trajectory of militancy that began around 1963, creating the conditions for the founding of the Miners for Democracy (MFD) in 1970, the insurgent organization that took over the union in 1972 with the election of Arnold Miller. It outlines the counterattack launched by the coal companies and sections of the old Tony Boyle officialdom that immediately ensued, seeking to undermine and overthrow the new administration and disperse the movement behind it. It discusses the fatal weakness of the Miller leadership that diluted the victory of the miners, manifested practically from the moment it took office in its compromises with both the companies and old-line bureaucrats. Finally, it traces the new explosions of rank-and-file militancy that developed between 1972 and 1977 in response to the assaults by the mine owners, as well as the Miller leadership's failure to defend the membership. The chapter concludes with an analysis of the great strike of 1977–8, a struggle that represented at once the high point of the mine workers' rebellion and the beginning of its decline.

## A Rich History of Struggle, A Postwar Trajectory of Decline

The solidarity of miners in the United States and around the world was forged both by the dangerous nature of mining itself and by the kinds of communities in which miners live. In the United States, more than 100,000 soft-coal miners have been killed since 1900, and more than 1.5 million have suffered disabling injuries since 1935. Any oversight could cost lives. As John Brophy wrote in *A Miner's Life*, "Loyalty to his fellow workers required a very alert awareness of danger every minute that he spent in the mine. Careless or selfish actions that endangered lives were unthinkable, and any miner who broke the safety rules was quickly made aware of the other man's disapproval."[1]

Coal miners lived in what have been termed "isolated masses," or "occupational communities," separated geographically from the rest of the working class. The most strike-prone groups of workers have generally lived and worked in the same sorts of places: miners in coal towns, sailors on ships, longshoremen in waterfront districts, loggers in logging camps, and textile workers in textile towns. Workers in such communities have found themselves and their families constituting most of the population, experiencing the same multiple grievances at the same time at the hands of the same people, and cut off in important respects from the rest of the world.[2] Appalachian miners were isolated in mountainous regions, which were basically one-industry fiefdoms ruled by outside corporations, in which the vast majority of personal income came from mining.[3] Living in company towns, they and their families faced the same individuals as

---

1  J. Brophy, *A Miner's Life* (Madison: University of Wisconsin Press, 1964), p. 41.
2  C. Kerr and A. Siegel, "The Interindustry Propensity to Strike—An International Comparison," in A. Komhauser, R. Dunn, and A. M. Ross, eds, *Industrial Conflict* (New York: McGraw-Hill, 1954), pp. 189–212; also see S. M. Lipset, M. Trow, and J. A. Coleman, *Union Democracy* (New York: Free Press, 1956), pp. 29, 77, 159, 257–60, 413–8.
3  In 1976, of total personal income earned in the West Virginia mining counties of McDowell, Wyoming, Boone, Barbour, Nicholas, Upshur, and Logan, 84 percent, 80 percent, 75 percent, 64 percent, 63 percent, 58 percent, and 55 percent, respectively, came from mining. See West Virginia Coal Association, *West Virginia Coal Facts '77* (Charleston, WV: WVCA, 1977), p. 28.

employers, landlords, and grocers. They were delivered by company doctors and buried in company cemeteries. Their children learned from company-paid teachers, their families worshipped under company-hired preachers, and they all obeyed laws enforced by company policemen and gun thugs. Class relationships were thus especially clear, all the more so because the middle and professional classes in the region were so underdeveloped, with West Virginia ranking forty-ninth in 1970 among all states in the percentage of its population holding a college degree.[4]

The collectively shared experiences of fighting to organize unions and struggling to achieve some economic security forged a loyalty among miners, both to their union and to each other, surpassed by no other group of workers. The danger of underground work produced an ironclad tradition among miners never to cross a picket line, which required nothing more to be effective than a single miner pouring water out of his lunch bucket and walking out of the portal. The nature of the work process did not, moreover, inhibit spontaneous strikes, as it did in many other industries, such as steel. If steelworkers walked off their jobs, molten steel would freeze, ruining molding and casting machinery, and blast furnaces would blow sky-high unless they were banked, a process which took several days. But if miners left work, they could return the next day, week, or month and begin mining again, so long as a couple of people stayed behind to keep water from flooding the workings.

Irish anthracite miners in eastern Pennsylvania were among the first industrial workers to organize. Coal miners were the only workers who established lasting union locals in the Deep South before 1900. The United Mine Workers (UMW) was founded in 1890 and was for many decades the country's largest industrial union. Coal miners were the first industrial workers to win an eight-hour day, in 1898. They waged many strikes of national importance, such as those on Cabin and Paint Creeks in 1912 and 1913, and they lent key organizational and financial support to the first national steel strike in 1919. In 1921, in Logan and Mingo Counties, 15,000 union miners and gun thugs hired by the non-union coal operators engaged in the largest armed confrontation in American labor history, with the miners winning until the companies brought in federal troops.

During the 1920s, which saw a series of defeats for organized labor and the virtual disappearance of the UMW, coal miners organized the largest left-led union of the period, the National Miners Union (NMU). The NMU, led by Communist Party militants, kept unionism alive in coal fields

---

4   US Bureau of the Census, *County and City Data Book 1972* (Washington, DC: US Government Printing Office, 1973). Miners generally could not buy their own houses until after World War II.

from western Pennsylvania to eastern Kentucky and central New Mexico between 1928 and 1933.[5] When the UMW was reorganized between 1933 and 1935, it became the driving force behind the formation of the Congress of Industrial Organizations (CIO). Between 1935 and 1941, the CIO organized the nation's basic industries for the first time. During World War II, when the no-strike pledge was in effect, coal miners were one of the few groups of workers to openly fight their employers, this to guarantee safe working conditions. The federal government seized the mines half a dozen times during wartime strikes. Between 1946 and 1950, when miners sought to restore wages and fringe benefits frozen during the war, the government seized the mines another half-dozen times.

The years between 1945 and 1950 witnessed an explosion of class struggle throughout the coal fields, focused on establishing a health and retirement fund under union control. Begun in 1946, the Welfare and Retirement Fund was financed with royalties paid by the companies on every ton of union coal mined. In 1950 and 1952, the Fund was put on a firm fiscal basis with the negotiation of the first national bituminous coal wage agreements. But in exchange for the coal owners' agreement to provide these royalties, Lewis and the UMW leadership agreed to collaborate with industry in mechanizing the mines. This hugely increased corporate profitability but brought massive economic hardship and poverty to the coal towns.

The coal operators were essentially granted a free hand in pressing for increased productivity. As John L. Lewis would later boast:

> The United Mine Workers not only cooperated with the operators on that—we invented the policy. We've encouraged the leading companies in the industry to resort to modernization in order to increase the living standards of the miner and improve his working conditions . . . It is better to have half a million men working in the industry at good wages and high standards than it is to have a million working in the industry in poverty and degradation.[6]

But the price paid by the mining population for Lewis's high standards was staggering. Between 1948, when continuous mining machinery was first introduced, and the mid-1960s, when production began to rise again, more than 300,000 miners lost their jobs, with the consequence that well over a million people—most of them in Appalachia—were deprived of

---

5   For an excellent account of the development of the National Miners Union, and its differences with the UMW, see L. Nyden, "Black Miners in Western Pennsylvania, 1925–1931: The NMU and the UMW," *Science and Society* 41:#1 (Spring 1977), pp. 69–101.
6   P. Clark, *The Miners' Fight for Democracy* (Ithaca: Cornell University, 1981), p. 17.

their means of support, forced to retire early and live on public assistance, or to move out of the region to find work. Over roughly the same period (1950–67), weekly wages for an average miner rose from $67 to $153. Nevertheless, due to the gains in productivity and the reductions of the labor force that took place simultaneously, the companies were able to increase coal output by 36 million tons, for which they paid in aggregate $310 million less in total wages, a seventeen-year decline of more than 20 percent in wage payments (without adjustment for inflation).[7] Where three men worked in the late 1940s, only one was left by the late 1960s.

For more than fifteen years the companies did almost no hiring, and by the late 1960s, many mines employed no one under forty. In every Appalachian coal town, there could be found a surplus of experienced miners, vastly strengthening the hand of the employers. Miners lucky enough to retain their jobs lived in constant fear of losing them. If any miner complained, his boss could tell him, "Pick up your lunch bucket and get the hell out. There's a barefoot man down the road just waiting for your job." A well-qualified replacement could be found the next morning. Nor did the UMW do much to defend the miners in these years, as Lewis abandoned the progressive and militant stances he had often assumed between 1933 and 1950. Safety in particular deteriorated, especially because the union did so little to protect militant Safety Committeemen against the owners. During the 1960s, Tony Boyle, Lewis's hand-picked successor, climbed into bed with the bosses even more eagerly than had his larger-than-life predecessor, and with considerably less style.

During the 1950s and early 1960s, the market for coal labor weakened as a consequence of not only increasing productivity secured by way of mechanization and layoffs, but also the rise of competition from substitute fuels, as railroads converted locomotives to diesel fuel and as home heating was taken over by oil and natural gas. It was only from the mid-1960s that demand for coal began to increase again, thanks to the sudden precipitous rise of electricity consumption. For fifty years, the share of total electric power generated in coal-fired plants had remained relatively constant, but electricity production doubled and doubled again during the following two decades. After having fallen to its nadir in the late 1960s, at between 125,000 and 135,000 workers, mining employment began a rapid upward climb to reach 215,000 workers in 1977. By the late 1960s, the oversupply of miners had disappeared, and for the first time in a generation, companies began complaining of difficulties in hiring and keeping a stable, skilled workforce.

---

7   US Bureau of Labor Statistics, Employment and Earnings Statistics for the United States, 1909–1968, *BLS Bulletin* no. 1312-6 (Washington, DC: US Government Printing Office, 1968), pp. 20–1.

It was in this new context of increasing employment security that anti-company sentiment once again began to be expressed more openly and workers' activity to increase.

The return of stable employment, not the worsening of hardship, was thus the decisive determinant in opening the way to a new era of class conflict in the mines, but the changing political climate in the nation was also a factor. The ascendancy of Cold War thinking in the late 1940s and early 1950s, with its anti-labor, anti-black, and anti-Communist components, had put progressive political movements on the defensive, not least in mining country. But with the emergence of the civil rights struggle and then the rise of the mass movement against the war in Southeast Asia, the reactionary political atmosphere was reversed. Many young people coming into the mines for the first time in the late 1960s had themselves served in the military, and many had fought in Vietnam. Indeed, it was no accident that impoverished West Virginia contributed proportionally more of its young men, and saw more of them killed, than any other state in the country. Men who escaped death or injury in Vietnam had little inclination to be maimed or killed in a coal mine once they returned home.

## The Rise of Rank-and-File Resistance, 1963–73

In 1963, Tony Boyle took office, and militancy exploded upward almost immediately thereafter, as miners raised the level of struggle over the next decade and a half to levels unmatched in any other industry in the United States. Lewis had maintained personal and total control over the bargaining process; in the 1950s his method came to be known as "mystery bargaining," in reference to the clandestine character of the process. According to Paul Clark,

> talks consisted of two-man sessions, Lewis and the operator's representative, conducted in strict privacy. Since agreements reached after 1950 were open-ended, having no expiration date, and since the parties allowed no publicity when contract talks began, no one except the men negotiating knew when a new contract was being formulated. When Lewis and the operators' representatives reached a new agreement, the wage policy committee quietly assembled to give it their seal of approval. Not until the pact was final and binding did Lewis inform the membership of its provisions.[8]

Boyle attempted to continue this tradition but with less success. In 1964, 18,000 miners struck, protesting the contract signed by Boyle and the

---

8   Clark, *The Miners' Fight for Democracy*, p. 10.

coal companies. Strikes followed the 1966 contract as well, with 40,000 miners walking out in protest. The strike movement escalated dramatically in January 1968, when 60,000 miners in five states struck to protest the arrests of pickets by state police in Pennsylvania. In October, 66,000 miners were involved in a wildcat strike movement. The miners' mood turned to anger in the aftermath of the explosion at Consol No. 9 in Farmington, West Virginia, in November 1968, which left seventy-eight men dead. This disaster spurred the formation of the Black Lung Association (BLA) in January 1969 and the Black Lung strike of February and March 1969, in which 45,000 West Virginia miners walked off their jobs. This walkout was the most important political strike in modern labor history. It forced passage of the first compensation law for Black Lung in West Virginia's history in March 1969 and accelerated the passage of a new federal mine health and safety act in December of that year. There was, then, a very significant and growing movement of rank-and-file miners on the ground when Joseph "Jock" Yablonski declared his candidacy against the pro-company Boyle machine in May 1969.

Yablonski was a careerist in the union, a faithful servant of the UMW leaders. He had served in the leadership since 1942 and as a district president for eight years. He had not been an active miner for twenty-five years when he challenged Boyle in 1969. Still, he seemed to reflect coal miners' discontent when he denounced the UMW leadership for sitting " . . . on their backsides for so long they've let the fat come up between their ears and they don't know what the coal miner's problems are anymore." Yablonski was also expressing a new mood when he denounced the Vietnam War. Speaking to a 1969 May Day rally at the University of Pittsburgh, he concluded, " . . . there's one more thing we need to do in this country, and that's to get the hell out of Vietnam." Yablonski's campaign, aided by Washington liberals such as Americans for Democratic Action (ADA) lawyer Joseph Rauh, called for the involvement of the union in the transformation of Appalachian society and began an electoral struggle that ultimately led to the ouster of the Boyle machine three and a half years later. The miners' wives and widows, the activists in the Black Lung Association, the wildcat strikers, and above all the young miners who were dramatically reshaping the composition of the UMW constituted the backbone of the movement. Nevertheless, Yablonski lost the contested election in December 1969. On New Year's Eve, three weeks after the balloting, gunmen hired by Tony Boyle murdered Yablonski, his wife, and his daughter in their beds.

Miners for Democracy was founded at Yablonski's funeral in January 1970. Supported by the Black Lung Association and the Disabled Miners and Widows, the MFD channeled the spontaneous militancy arising throughout the Appalachian coal fields into an electoral crusade. In

December 1972 they succeeded in ousting one of the country's most corrupt and deeply entrenched union bureaucracies with a slate of rank-and-file workers. Arnold Miller, the new president, was the son of a coal miner; a partially disabled repairman, suffering from black lung and arthritis, he had been president of the Black Lung Association. Mike Trbovich, the new vice president and the pre-convention favorite, was a working miner from Clarksville, Pennsylvania. He had been Yablonski's campaign manager and had served for twenty years as a local union officer. Harry Patrick, who became secretary-treasurer, was a mine mechanic from Barrackville, West Virginia, and, at forty-one, he was the youngest of the new leaders.

At the first UMW convention following the MFD electoral triumph, held in Pittsburgh in December 1973, the rank-and-file movements that had made that victory possible were finally able to express themselves. For the first time in decades, working miners dominated convention business, writing several major reforms into the union constitution. The convention restored autonomy to every union district, enhancing union democracy and the possibilities for the development of leaders with the experience and exposure to run for International office. It also gave working miners the right to vote on their contracts for the first time in the UMW's eighty-four-year history. The importance of this innovation would become especially clear during the great 1977–8 strike. Pensioners had traditionally constituted a power base for the incumbent UMW machine, but now the assembled membership restricted the officers for whom they could vote. The convention also enlarged and strengthened both the safety and organizing departments, while the new UMW leadership forged alliances with other progressive unions, especially by way of invitations to address the UMW Convention to César Chávez of the United Farm Workers, Albert Fitzgerald and James Matles of the United Electrical Workers, and David Livingston of the Distributive Workers. However, the convention made no special efforts to combat company racism and its reflections within the union, nor did they abolish the UMW constitution's anti-Communist clause, which had been frequently used against dissidents within the union, including the MFD leaders themselves.

## The Coal Companies' Counter-Offensive

The increasing pressure from ever more powerful and well-organized rank-and-file miners anxious to improve their conditions ran sharply up against the growing desire of the coal corporations to exploit to the utmost the demand for their product, which rose skyward throughout most of the 1970s. With employment leaping up by nearly 100,000 over the course of the decade, production broke records in both 1975 and 1976, at 648 million tons and 679 million tons, respectively, climbing above the previous high of 631 million tons reached back in 1947. At the same time, beginning in 1970, prices soared, with the average value per ton nationally, which had fluctuated between $4.39 and $5.08 between 1948 and 1969, jumping up to $22 per ton in 1977, while the average value of coal mined in West Virginia rose from $7.93 in 1970 to $32.50 in 1976. According to the *Keystone Coal Industry Manual*, the value of coal mined annually by each miner rocketed from $10,973 in 1957 to $61,460 in 1976. In 1977, major companies were making profits of up to $15 a ton, according to *Business Week*. In 1976, Pittston, the nation's largest independent, made only 53 percent of its total sales in coal, but 91 percent of its profits.[9] Coal was in these years becoming increasingly critical to the economy, essential to the operation of electric utilities, steel mills, and a variety of other manufacturing processes. It had also become indispensable to the well-being of many corporations with mining investments, as profits from coal were frequently used to bolster other operations. Standard Oil of Ohio, for example, transferred Old Ben Coal profits to finance the Alaska pipeline, and Occidental Petroleum used Island Creek money to expand oil-producing facilities in the North Sea and Libya. Steel companies had a special interest in maximizing profits by blunting rank-and-file unionism within the UMW. Nearly 100 percent of their mines were in the Appalachian coal fields, where the UMW was strongest. Since high-quality metallurgical coal was found primarily in Appalachia, they could not easily augment eastern production with western coal, as some other companies had been doing.

The companies that faced off against the emergent rank-and-file movements in the mines were an increasingly imposing force. The American coal industry had become ever more concentrated following World War II, with the top fifty coal-producing companies raising their share of total production from 44.1 percent in 1945 to 64.5 percent by 1976. But the fact remains that none of the coal companies dominated their market in the same way as did a handful of major producers in the auto, steel, and electrical industries. Still, the coal companies were able to vastly enhance their power in this era through a route other than concentration, by way of the sale of most of them to huge companies from other industries. This trend began in the mid-1960s, with the takeovers of the three largest coal producers: Consolidation Coal by Continental Oil in 1965, Peabody Coal by Kennecott Copper in 1968, and Island Creek Coal by Occidental Petroleum in 1968. By 1976, of the top fifteen coal companies, only three were independent; four were now owned by petroleum companies, three

---

9 A major compilation of coal industry statistics is Bituminous Coal Data, issued annually by the National Coal Association (Washington, DC).

by power companies, two by steel companies, two by metal-mining companies, and one by a conglomerate. The third-largest producer had become Amax, owned by American Metal Climax, which in turn was 20 percent controlled by Standard Oil of California.

The mine owners' counter-offensive against the UMW had two major thrusts: to prevent the spread of the UMW to newly opened mines, especially in eastern Kentucky and the West, and to encourage the internal dissension that was brewing within the UMW officialdom in the wake of the MFD takeover. In 1950, when the first national coal wage agreement was negotiated, more than 80 percent of all coal was union-mined; by 1972, after ten years of Tony Boyle, it had dropped to 70 percent. This was accomplished partly by rapid expansion of production in the West, where most miners did not belong to the UMW. In 1970, only one out of every seventeen tons was mined west of the Mississippi, but, by 1975, this figure had risen to one out of every seven tons. But this erosion of union density was also made possible by the increase of non-union operations in the old UMW heartland. By 1977, more than a third of all coal produced in District 2 in central Pennsylvania, District 6 in Ohio, District 28 in Virginia, and District 31 in northern West Virginia was scab. More than 70 percent of coal from eastern Kentucky and Tennessee was run non-union, where powerful corporations like Duke Power and St. Joe Minerals took an increasingly important role. By the time of the national strike in December 1977, nearly 50 percent of all coal mined was being dug in non-UMW pits.

Meanwhile, the coal owners were seeking to turn to their own advantage divisions that had arisen among the miners, especially by encouraging forces within the union that came to oppose the new Miller leadership. This was a task made significantly easier by the weakness and incompetence of Miller himself. Hardly had the Miller administration been installed than it came under attack from Vice President Mike Trbovich, who opened fire on many of the most progressive aspects of the UMW's new program. Trbovich had been a top leader of the reform movement. In view of how much authority he carried within the UMW, his defection was a hard blow for the new administration. Between 1973 and 1976, the UMW organized 120 mines and put an additional $50 million into the Welfare and Retirement Fund annually.[10] But in June 1975, when the operators were trying to block further UMW successes in the West, Trbovich blasted Miller for "wasting" union funds on organizing drives. At the same time, Trbovich publicly charged that International staff members were "masterminding" wildcat strikes in West Virginia, a statement that could have opened the union

---

10   United Mine Workers of America, "UMWA: It's Your Union", Officers' Report to the 1976 Constitutional Convention (Washington, DC: UMWA, 1976), p. 53.

to company lawsuits. In September 1975, Trbovich urged miners not to support efforts by the Black Lung Association, and the union itself not to back a stronger black lung bill in Congress, claiming there was no chance of its passage. Trbovich also aligned himself with the pro-company I. W. Abel leadership against insurgents in the United Steelworkers Union (USW) and attacked "reds" in both unions. At the 1976 UMW convention in Cincinnati, Trbovich announced that he was trying to "prevent the internal infiltration of the Socialistic, Revolutionary, and Communistic elements which may soon threaten to destroy this union." By the time that convention opened, Trbovich was openly supporting the candidacy of Lee Roy Patterson, a Boyle henchman who became leader of the old machine still active within the UMW.[11]

To make matters worse for the new administration, the Boyle machine had never been destroyed, this in large part because Miller himself had done so little to mobilize active support for MFD district slates running in late 1973. Boyle supporters were elected to several positions at that time, and, as they regrouped, they also began to win to their side some MFD figures on the International Executive Board (IEB). By mid-1975, this coalition held the balance of power on the board. By the end of 1976, with support from Trbovich and Vice President for Pensioner Affairs George Vranesh, they were able to field a slate for the upcoming June 1977 elections.

While the Boyle forces were reorganizing, the Abel administration in the USW began blasting Miller's administration. In May 1975, Abel's IEB passed a vituperative resolution condemning the UMW for supporting Ed Sadlowski in his successful race for the district directorship in the Chicago-Gary area and Walter Bachowski, an anti-Abel leader in northwestern Pennsylvania. Criticism from both the USW and the AFL-CIO became more public during 1976. By 1977, the Steelworkers' staff was openly intervening in UMW affairs, supporting Lee Roy Patterson for UMW president and pumping in 20 percent of all the funds Patterson used during his campaign. Behind the scenes, the USW Abel leadership and UMW Boyle-Patterson forces talked of merging the UMW into the 1.4-million-member USW. According to their plans, the Steelworkers would swallow up the UMW the same way they'd taken over the militant hard-rock miners' Mine, Mill and Smelter Workers Union in 1967.

It did not help that, during these years, union wreckers of all kinds began rearing their heads in the Appalachian coal fields in response to the MFD victories. Racist groups, especially the Ku Klux Klan, began public

---

11   See full accounts in *Miner's Report* no. 10 (November–December 1975) and no. 12 (September–October 1976), esp. pp. 8–9. Trbovich's convention quote comes from the text of the speech distributed to the press, September 24, 1976, p. 1.

activity. During the historic Brookside strike of 1973–4, the Klan began to organize in Harlan County against black people, welfare recipients, and the UMW. Actively opposed by both local miners and the UMW, however, they made little headway. Their most dramatic effort was to support the Kanawha County, West Virginia "book boycott" in 1974. While this campaign did express some legitimate anger at high-handed methods and elitist attitudes of the local school board, the thrust of the boycott was directed against books written by black and progressive writers. Not only the KKK and John Birch Society, but a dozen other right-wing hate groups came into the Kanawha Valley to spread their propaganda. The Heritage Foundation, which was bankrolled by the union-busting Coors beer family and the Mellon Scaife fortunes, both at the heart of the emerging American far right, financed speakers and provided legal expenses for those arrested for violent activities connected with the boycott.[12] Unity between black and white miners had been critical to the success of the MFD: the first presidents of both the Black Lung Association and the Disabled Miners and Widows of southern West Virginia were black miners. Any spread of racist feeling in southern West Virginia would benefit only the coal operators.

At the same time, extreme leftists also migrated into the coal fields after the MFD takeover. The most disruptive of these was the Miners' Right to Strike Committee (MRTSC), led by the Maoist Revolutionary Union, later the Revolutionary Communist Party. They had done nothing to elect rank-and-file candidates to UMW office or to back up UMW organizing drives. Their publications criticized the companies only in the most abstract and rhetorical terms and focused their attacks on UMW leaders, especially the most progressive ones. In June 1977, they labeled UMW presidential candidates Patrick, Miller, and Patterson all "company stooges" and told coal miners to vote for no one, just as they had instructed steelworkers to boycott their international elections in February 1977, when Sadlowski was running against I. W. Abel's successor Lloyd McBride. During the 1977–8 strike, the MRTSC said little about the mine owners, expending their energies denouncing Miller and demanding his removal in the middle of the strike, a tactic rejected by the vast majority of Miller's other critics within the union. The major impact of this splinter group was not to organize miners to accomplish anything, but to disorganize and disorient people. By presenting their outlandish and provocative statements as those of "communists," they also served to discredit the serious and pro-union left.

---

12   For a detailed analysis, see "The Kanawha Fight Is About More Than Textbooks," *Daily World Magazine* 22 (February 1975), pp. M4–5.

## A New UMW Bureaucracy: The Dismantling of the MFD and the Re-emergence of Rank-and-File Resistance, 1972–7

In spite of the wide-ranging rank-and-file program passed at the 1973 convention that the MFD victory made possible, the new UMW leaders displayed little commitment to rank-and-file unionism. Their intent was not to reorganize the union with the goal of strengthening rank-and-file power from below, but to serve the membership as personal vehicles of reform. The union officials that led the MFD were, at bottom, traditional union reformers. As early as November 1972, well before their election victory, MFD leaders were discussing dismantling their organization if they won. One of their campaign ads stated: "The name Miners for Democracy won't be necessary the day we elect Arnold Miller because we will have democracy in our great union." After a series of district election victories in May and June 1973, several newly elected officers proclaimed the end of MFD. District 17 President Jack Perry announced in Charleston, "it got what we wanted—the right to elect our people . . . But we are United Mine Workers and not Miners for Democracy." Kenneth Dawes, new president of District 12 in Illinois, put it bluntly: "Forget the MFD." As Lou Antal was inaugurated District 5 president in Pittsburgh, he claimed, "The need for MFD has ceased to exist and we now must devote our time to rejuvenating the union that we all want to serve and must improve."[13] But the *Pittsburgh Post-Gazette* was able to see through this line. As it responded in an editorial, "True, one could argue, as Mr. Antal does, that now that the MFD is in the saddle, it hardly can be a rebel outfit against itself. But this actually points to a continuing need in the labor union for opposition."[14] Some rank-and-file miners also felt that the MFD should continue in existence, both to provide organized support for the newly elected leaders in implementing the MFD program, and to remain as a watchdog in case they should depart from their promises. But in the euphoria of reformers' victory—something which had taken so many years to win—the majority went along with MFD's abolition.

There was one attempt to revive MFD. This was launched in District 5 in late November 1973, and a new set of MFD officers was actually chosen during a meeting in Cokeburg. But at the reorganization meeting no program was articulated, and the group soon withered away. The Disabled Miners and Widows of southern West Virginia continued to meet

---

13   *UMW Journal*, November 15, 1972, p. 27; *Charleston Gazette*, June 1, 1973; *Pittsburgh Post-Gazette*, July 2, 1973.

14   *Pittsburgh Post-Gazette*, July 10, 1973.

sporadically but played little public role after the December 1972 election. The Black Lung Association was the only exception. They elected new officers and continued to fight on behalf of disabled miners, retirees, and widows, both within the union itself and before state legislatures. The BLA consistently played an actively progressive role throughout the central Appalachian coal fields but never tried to organize working miners to influence union policies. (The effectiveness of BLA leader Bill Worthington was however recognized by Westmoreland Coal when, in 1977, they offered him a position as their top troubleshooter. Worthington, of course, refused the offer.)

In the course of the negotiation of the 1974 contract, the evaluation by many miners of the group of reformers that they had catapulted into office less than two years previously began to change radically. Miller conducted his first negotiations behind the scenes, just as Boyle and his cronies always had. At a time when company profits were skyrocketing—up an average of 180 percent for the top ten producers during the first half of 1974—many miners believed Miller could have won a much larger pension increase, more fringe benefits, and higher wages. Miller, moreover, publicly promised the operators and government mediators that he would sell the contract to his membership, before he had even shown the agreement to them. Placing his prestige behind the contract, Miller actively campaigned for its adoption. When the votes were tallied in early December, 43.9 percent of the miners had voted against it (65.4 percent of those eligible cast votes). It seemed that no sooner had the membership installed in office what had been their own opposition slate, they discovered that they would have to oppose it, a conviction that only grew over time as Miller failed, again and again, to support their efforts against the companies.

Of course, in important respects, Miller's trajectory was all too typical. During the 1960s and 1970s, a series of union insurgencies benefiting from rank-and-file support overthrew a succession of top leaders across the labor movement. But in not one single case did the newly elected reform officials subject themselves to rank-and-file control or nurture independent rank-and-file militancy. The result was, in most instances, the longer-term weakening of rank-and-file activity. What stands out about the miners is the depth of the rank-and-file uprising, a bottom-up movement that not only preceded the organized reform movement and brought it to power but carried itself forward through the disappointing results of the 1974 contract and beyond.

Having failed to install a new leadership responsive to their needs, rank-and-file miners were left with no option but to go back to dealing with their problems by way of direct action. What perhaps provoked the miners most was the widespread company stratagem of refusing to settle grievances at the mines and forcing them all the way through the five-step grievance process into arbitration. This left the miners to wait months, or even years, for the elimination of practices that they felt could lead to death or permanent injury. In the period covered by the 1974 UMW-BCOA contract, miners therefore organized approximately nine thousand wildcat strikes that sought to bypass the grievance machinery, especially in the realm of health and safety. In a probably not unrelated development, between 1969 and 1979, a period in which mining employment was doubling, production per man per day fell from almost 20 tons to 13.5 tons.[15]

When wildcat strikes erupted, the companies rushed into court for injunctions. The miners responded by spreading the strikes. But UMW president Arnold Miller consistently ordered the miners back to work, claiming that a small group of "troublemakers" was behind the resistance. But the fact is that no fewer than 80,000 miners went out on strike in the summer of 1975 in the "right to strike" strike, and another 120,000 the following summer in the "anti-injunction" strike. Just about every union miner east of the Mississippi took part in these uprisings. It is true that to protect the UMW from company suits, Miller did have to pay lip service to contract enforcement; nevertheless, he went far beyond what was legally required of him in providing cover for the companies. This was made crystal clear in August 1976, when the coal miners made history by obliging federal judges in Charleston, West Virginia, to withdraw all fines, injunctions, and threatened jail terms imposed during the strikes.

During the period that followed the 1974 contract, distrust of the Miller leadership grew precipitously, especially in the wake of its traitorous response to the massive summer wildcats of 1975 and 1976, which had mushroomed into national confrontations with the operators. During the next International convention, held in Cincinnati between September 23 and October 2, 1976, in a stunning expression of direct rank-and-file democracy, the 1,883 delegates present literally wrote their proposed contract word-for-word on the convention floor, expressing how little faith they had in Arnold Miller's judgment. At the top of their list of demands was the right to strike during the term of the contract, which was passed unanimously. A proposal by Miller's administration to institute disciplinary procedures against leaders of wildcats foundered when not a single delegate was willing to second. Possessing no organization of their own independent of the UMW leadership, convention delegates knew that this would be their only opportunity to press forward their views in a collective manner prior to the opening of the 1977 negotiations.

---

15    C. R. Perry, *Collective Bargaining and the Decline of the United Mine Workers* (Philadelphia: University of Pennsylvania Press, 1984), p. 28.

The new administration contributed to its own undoing by its failure to maintain sufficient distance with politicians and company representatives. Most flagrant in this respect was the behavior of Miller himself. Miller had long boasted of his personal friendship with John D. Rockefeller IV, who came to the state as a VISTA worker in the late 1960s and was elected governor in 1976. The Miller-Rockefeller relationship had already developed by 1970, by which time many of the more sophisticated coal operators—among whom the Rockefeller family certainly ranked high—had undoubtedly concluded that Boyle's days were numbered and that it would be fortunate if his replacement was not too anti-company. In December 1976, columnist Jack Anderson published, in a devastating report, that "While 80,000 miners were out of work during a West Virginia strike in August 1975, Miller was lounging part of the time at Pocahontas estate of John 'Jay' Rockefeller, now governor elect." Anderson went on: "Miller admits he spent time at Rockefeller's home," and "Rockefeller spokesman said the home is always open to Miller."[16] The Miller-Rockefeller relationship would draw national attention when Miller used Rockefeller's private jet to shuttle between Charleston, West Virginia, and Washington, D.C., during the national contract negotiations, and when he appeared jointly with Jay Rockefeller on February 6 to laud the first version of the 1978 contract.

On June 14, 1977, Miller was re-elected UMW president, with 39.8 percent of the vote. Harry Patrick received 24.9 percent, running especially well among younger miners, with the remaining 35.3 percent going to Patterson. Patterson's 1977 showing represented a decline of 9.2 percent from Boyle's own vote in 1972. Many miners voted for Miller rather than Patrick because they did not wish to risk the return of Boyleism and believed Patrick lacked a realistic chance to win. It was Patrick, however, who most effectively exposed Patterson's pro-company policies, his racism, and his red-baiting. Miller ran a hollow public-relations campaign, rather than grappling with basic issues. It was all too symptomatic that Miller's running mate for Vice President for Pensioner Affairs was James E. Blair, a campaign coordinator for George Wallace in western Kentucky in 1968. Blair ran against the black candidate on Patterson's slate.

A few days after Miller's re-election, UMW members received letters announcing cutbacks in their hospitalization benefits, reductions planned with Miller's approval but intentionally concealed by him until after the voting. This lowered his popularity still further and provoked another large wildcat strike centered in southern West Virginia. Miller condemned this strike, too. Many of his liberal staff members had begun drifting away,

---

16   J. Anderson, "UAW leader's reputation fades," *Pittsburgh Press*, December 9, 1976.

beginning in 1974; after the Cincinnati convention, Miller began removing any still left who were critical of his rightward drift. In November 1977, Miller proposed not only the expulsion of all "Communists" from the union, but their deportation from the United States as well. "They ought," he told the *Charleston Gazette*, "to go to some other country. They ought to get the hell out. They ought to be thrown out."[17] From being a target of red-baiting while he was BLA President, MFD candidate (MFD, according to Boyle, stood for "Moscow Fire Department") and newly elected UMW president Miller had become a red-baiter himself.

### The 1977–8 Strike

During the 110-day strike, which began at midnight after work on December 6, 1977, upon the expiration of the 1974 agreement, the miners demonstrated a greater degree of unity than they had for years. The seriousness of the confrontation was made clear by the Bituminous Coal Operators Association (BCOA) during the first negotiating session on October 6, at which time they warned that the forthcoming "agreement must restore stability and improved productivity in coal." Otherwise, "we . . . will see the decline and possible extinction of the United Mine Workers as a force in the national collective bargaining."[18]

Despite the fact that the UMW represented only slightly more than half of all bituminous tonnage mined, miners shut down many non-union mines as well as their own, and threatened to cripple American industry with power shortages. After nearly four months of negotiations, Miller summoned the union's thirty-nine-man Bargaining Council to Washington on February 2, 1978, to discuss a tentative agreement he had worked out. But when, on February 6, he tried to gain the council's approval without showing them anything but a fifteen-page summary, they demanded the full text. When details of the proposed agreement leaked out, it was widely denounced, and hundreds of miners traveled to Washington to demonstrate in front of the UMW's headquarters. On February 12, with the strike sixty-seven days old, the bargaining council formally rejected the tentative accord, refusing to send it down to the membership by a vote of thirty to six. At this point, Miller needlessly inflamed the miners when he defended the contract and attacked the council. The contents of a letter sent from the officers of the Eccles, West Virginia local, which had given Miller 73.8 percent of their votes in June 1977, typified the membership's reaction:

17   *Charleston Gazette*, November 21, 1977.
18   "Statement of the Bituminous Coal Operators Association," Washington, DC, October 6, 1977, pp. 1, 10.

The members of Local Union 5770 feel that you have made a grave mistake when you publicly berated the Bargaining Council for voting down a contract that was not fully explained . . . You were instrumental in setting up the Bargaining Council in order to have a system of checks and balances on the International officers . . .so the desires of the rank-and-file members would be served. All of us made mistakes and we feel no one should be punished for making one. But to make a mistake and then try to justify it is unforgivable.[19]

The rejected agreement was a comprehensive attempt to roll back fringe benefits and working conditions. It did provide for a wage increase but eliminated the cost-of-living escalator. Pressured especially by U.S. Steel, the BCOA proposed to scrap the UMW's Welfare and Retirement Fund and turn healthcare over to private insurance carriers. The working miners would have to pay up to $500 annually in deductibles, and retirees up to $250.20.[20] Pensions were not raised substantially. Nor was the huge disparity between pension payments to pre- and post-1976, one of the miners' leading grievances, seriously addressed. Perhaps most galling to the membership, the proposed agreement not only failed to contain the right to strike over unresolved local grievances, but gave management the right to fire or penalize anyone organizing, walking on, or honoring a picket line. It mandated a $20 fine per day and eliminated health benefits for the families of these miners after ten days. Miners wanted a shorter work week, but the operators rejected this demand, as well as their proposal for a daily maintenance shift. The BCOA also asked that the mines be run seven days a week, in a break with tradition. A repressive program against absenteeism was laid out, providing for the firing of miners in a six-step process.

The first proposed contract also included productivity incentives encouraging speedup at the expense of safety. It allowed arbitrators to rule on safety disputes and permitted mine management to remove any Safety Committeeman for the life of the contract if his judgment in shutting down a section or entire mine was later overruled by an arbitrator. The training period for new miners was reduced from ninety to forty-five days, despite the elevated accident rate for miners with less than one year's experience. The tentative agreement also specified

---

19   *Beckley Post-Herald*, February 16, 1978.
20   On the role of U.S. Steel, see *Coal Age* (April 1978), p. 17; *Time*, March 20, 1978, p. 16; and personal interview with Louis Antal in Arnold, Pennsylvania, on December 31, 1977.

that an arbitrator could rule on a miner's "ability to perform work" in disputes arising from company refusals to promote the most senior person bidding on a job, disputes often provoked by company retaliation against more militant employees. Finally, the proposed settlement established a thirty-day probationary period for newly hired miners, during which they would be without the protection of union membership, a method already in use by steel companies to weed out "troublemakers" in their mills.[21]

After the bargaining council rejected this first contract, a new national agreement was drawn up along the lines of a separate contract that had been reached with Gulf Oil's Pittsburg and Midway Coal on February 20. This second version contained several improvements: only organizers of wildcats were to be disciplined, work incentives were eliminated unless local unions agreed to them, the cost-of-living escalator was reinstated, Sunday work was eliminated, and health and safety provisions were strengthened somewhat. The council approved the Pittsburg and Midway contract, twenty-five to thirteen. On February 24, the BCOA agreed to a similar contract, which was then sent to 160,000 BCOA-employed miners without another council vote. As it was being distributed to BCOA miners, however, Pittsburg and Midway employees were in the process of turning it down by a 356 to 163 margin, despite the fact they were considered more moderate than the bulk of UMW members. Miners around the country organized and demonstrated against the second version of the contract. District 29 miners took out full-page newspaper ads; their "Message to the BCOA" began: "We demand a contract for the future and not a return to the past."[22] When the BCOA voting ended on March 5—despite the fact that Carter was already threatening to invoke Taft-Hartley and cut off food stamps to families of striking miners—miners in 794 locals had turned the second contract down, 77,292 to 33,751.

On March 7, the *Wall Street Journal*'s lead editorial, entitled "The Miners Have a Point," read in part:

UMW President Arnold Miller, the mine owners and the federal mediators can begin by apologizing for not following instructions in the first place. Before the negotiations began last year the miners were

21 See partial text of contract in the *Raleigh Register*, February 8, 1978, p. 5; ad from Miners Support Committee, *Beckley Post-Herald*, February 18, 1978, p. 8: and P. Siegelbaum, "The Coal Strike: A Victory of Rank-and-File Miners," *Political Affairs* vol. 57:4 (April 1978), pp. 10–8.
22 *Beckley Post-Herald*, February 16, 1978, p. 16.

surveyed on their demands, and cited health benefits first, pension benefits second and wages third. Yet their union boss went the other way. The 37% package breaks down to 31% in wages and only 6% in fringe benefits. And Mr. Miller negotiated away the all-expenses health plan the miners have had for 30 years.

The editorial went on to criticize the operators for maximizing the proportion of the 37 percent increase that would go to the government, by stressing that wage increases are taxable. It concluded that "it is not the workers but the negotiators who need a 'cooling off' period." Referring to the punitive measures coal operators were seeking against picketing, business publications such as *Business Week*, as well as the *Wall Street Journal*, criticized the operators for attempting to reverse long-standing traditions in the Appalachian coal fields in a single blow. In their February 24 article, subtitled "The Companies Want It All," *Journal* reporters warned, "It is difficult to force suspicious and obstinate miners to accept a contract that, in their view, would shatter the traditions of their union, especially the time-honored practice of refusing to cross any picket line regardless of its legality." They added that it was also "difficult to force an innovative labor bargain with weak leaders."

On March 6, the day after the miners rejected the second contract, President Carter invoked the anti-strike provisions of the Taft-Hartley Act; the formal federal order was issued three days later. In West Virginia, fewer than one hundred of the state's 60,000 miners returned to work. Carter had considered a government seizure of the mines, a step that most miners favored both because the government would set the terms of work during the seizure and because they felt the government was more subject to pressure than the companies during the negotiating process. But he ultimately capitulated to pressure from operators such as John Higgins, vice president of Eastern Gas and Fuel Associates, who argued that "nationalization of the mines would set a dangerous precedent. We'd be heading down the road toward socialism." [23] Nevertheless, Carter's dramatic attempt to force a settlement upon the miners proved a total fiasco, ending up demonstrating both the power of the miners and the impotence of Taft-Hartley. When the temporary order issued under Taft-Hartley expired after a week, the federal judge actually refused to renew it. After the strike was over, a *Fortune* analysis commented, "This section [of Taft-Hartley] has now been made a dead letter—not only by the almost universal contempt shown for the law by the miners but

---

23   *Wall Street Journal*, February 22, 1978.

even more by the lack of stomach both the executive and the judicial branch exhibited for even the feeblest attempt at enforcement."[24]

One of the most memorable aspects of the strike was the wide support that the miners were able to mobilize, especially within the trade union movement, support more extensive than that given any other strike since the late 1940s. Gifts of $2 million came from the United Auto Workers, of $1 million each from the United Steelworkers and Communication Workers of America, and of $500,000 from several other labor unions. Perhaps even more politically significant were the support rallies held in dozens of cities throughout the country, which were sponsored by AFL-CIO central labor councils and unions—including the Amalgamated Clothing Workers, Textile Workers Union, International Longshoremen's and Warehousemen's Union, United Electrical Workers, Teamsters, and Local 1199 of the Hospital Workers—and which raised tens of thousands of dollars. Caravans brought food from auto workers in Detroit and hospital workers in Washington, D.C., to miners in southern West Virginia, from electrical workers in Pittsburgh to miners in western Pennsylvania, and from striking farm workers in the West to miners in Kentucky. Miners Support Committees—including union, church, community, and professional organizations and leaders—functioned in many cities, including Pittsburgh, Cleveland, Cincinnati, Chicago, and New York. A free clinic was established in Beckley, West Virginia, where several doctors and health professionals donated their services.[25] At the time when the contract was ultimately ratified, the West Coast longshoremen had just decided to conduct a one-day sympathy strike in protest of Carter's use of Taft-Hartley.

Backing for the miners' cause also found expression in popular culture. Red Sovine, one of the nation's leading country-and-western performers and known for his songs about truck drivers, recorded a hit celebrating the struggles of miners and farmers:

The farmer and the miner—they're a special breed of men,
Their roots are deeply buried, let's not wear their patience thin;
They got busted backs and calloused hands from work that took its toll,
Lord, the farmers and the miners got a long, hard row to hoe.
With our bellies full and our furnace stoked, we fail to realize,

---

24   A. H. Raskin, "Coal Dust Darkens the Bargaining Table," *Fortune*, April 24, 1978, p. 58.
25   See D. Stanley, "The Mine Strike: How One Community Organized," *Southern Fight-Back* vol. 3:2 (May 1978), p. 4.

But with our freezers bare and our houses cold, that'll open up our eyes.
They're the backbone of the nation, so let's not let 'em down,
That long, hard row with our support can be dug in softer ground.[26]

The strike itself made Sovine's point to millions of people—that coal is essential to the functioning of the country, that miners deserved support from everyone who benefits from the product that they produce, and that, in resisting an employer's offensive that was accelerating all across the economy, the miners' struggle was in the interests of all working people.

The rejection of the second contract, coupled with the miners' massive refusal to obey Taft-Hartley, derailed the operators' effort to roll back the gains won by miners over many years. The operators themselves became divided as the strike progressed. In March, the hardliners from U.S. Steel, Peabody Coal, and Consol were displaced as negotiators by more moderate executives from Island Creek Coal and Pittston, a change supported by the smaller operators within the BCOA.[27] When the third contract was sent down to the miners by a twenty-two to seventeen bargaining council vote on March 15, most of the measures most threatening to the miners had been taken out. Radical plans of the corporations to dismantle the BCOA and revert to company-by-company or district-by-district bargaining had been scrapped. The money value of the settlement had crept up from $4.72 per hour in the first proposal to $4.75 in the second and $4.97 in the third. The third contract also increased pensions for pre-1976 retirees and based eligibility for pensions on 1,000 hours worked per year, rather than the 1,450 hours proposed in the earlier versions.[28] This contract was accepted by miners on March 24, by a vote of 58,802 to 44,457, a majority of only 56.9 percent (with about 65 percent of those eligible voting). The miners returned to the pits on March 27, but few were happy with the new agreement, especially its dismantling of the health plan (despite the reduction of deductibles to $200 annually in the third contract) and continuance of unequal pensions.

## The Aftermath of the Strike

In many respects, the strike was a victory for the rank-and-file coal miner. It also discredited nearly totally the leadership of Arnold Miller, who had gone so far as to openly discourage the formation of Miners' Strike

---

26   R. Sovine, "Farmers and the Miners," written by J. Lockwood and F. Carlo, released by Gusto-Starday Records, 1977.

27   *Coal Age*, April 1978, p. 17; *Time*, March 27, 1978, p. 15.

28   *Coal Age*, April 1978, p. 11.

Committees and to block the distribution of funds for strike relief in his efforts to force miners back to work. The miners ended the strike not so much because they were satisfied with the contract as because they were exhausted from a struggle constantly undermined by Miller leadership. Faced with foreclosures and repossessions, they had little hope that Miller would be willing to fight for more in still another trip to the bargaining table. As *New York Times* reporter Ben A. Franklin aptly concluded as the miners were returning to work:

> Looming through the gritty Appalachian mist was one stirring fact. Although its leadership and its reputation and its treasury have been ruined, the rank and file of the United Mine Workers have emerged as unexpectedly, stubbornly, even heroically strong men and women. They overcame their own inept hierarchy and, to an extent that Mr. Miller obviously never believed possible, humbled the operators.[29]

But the new contract represented a partial victory not only for the miners, but also for the coal operators, and it was evident to virtually everyone acquainted with the mining industry that the resulting stalemate had laid the basis for three more years of intense conflict. This point was brought home with crystal clarity when, with the ink barely dry on the 1978 contract, two new Virginia mine tragedies, taking place on April 4 and April 13, took the lives of a total of eight miners and sparked the first large wildcats under the new agreement. The determination of the miners had set an example for all American labor. As veteran labor writer A. H. Raskin observed in *Fortune*, "Some union leaders have a large new problem in the wake of the miners' demonstration that 'anarchy pays.'"[30]

Internal dissension within the UMW intensified. Opponents of Arnold Miller had already collected more than 20,000 signatures on recall petitions by the end of the strike, enough to initiate the recall process. They now called for a special International convention to order a new election. During the strike, Miller had attacked Cecil Roberts, a popular Vietnam veteran who was vice president of the union's largest district, for speaking out against the contract. He had similarly criticized Donald Nunley, a District 6 executive board member who had been especially effective in organizing pickets to block the shipment of scab coal, and was soon asking the FBI to investigate whether Nunley had violated any federal laws by crossing state lines to incite violence. District officials in eastern Kentucky

---

29  B. A. Franklin, "In the Bitter Aftermath, Whither the U.M.W.?" *New York Times*, March 26, 1978, p. E5.
30  Raskin, p. 58.

and Tennessee, who had opposed all three contracts, also found themselves under assault by the beleaguered UMW president. Miller even began to threaten to revoke the autonomy of some districts. His announcement in July that the next UMW convention would be held in Miami represented a betrayal of his own platform, which recalled the policies of Tony Boyle.

Plagued by ill health and beaten down by infighting within the union, Arnold Miller resigned on November 16, 1979. Of his original MFD-backed administration, he alone had remained. Mike Trbovich had long since defected to the anti-Miller faction. Harry Patrick, secretary-treasurer, who had run third in the voting in the 1977 elections, had left the union, taking a job as a federal mediator. Sam Church, originally an electrician in southwestern Virginia, who had been elected vice president of the UMW in 1977, was sworn into office as president the day Miller retired. Church had supported Tony Boyle in Miller's 1972 election challenge to Boyle but had risen rapidly, with Miller's support, on the International staff.

But the bottom line was that no movement emerged from below to carry the union forward. A new organization of the rank and file might have helped contain the demoralization many miners felt in the aftermath of the strike. The UMW health plan had been eliminated; miners' clinics were closed in Pennsylvania, West Virginia, and Arkansas; organizing drives were stalled; and non-union miners were mining more and more coal. The Black Lung Association did continue its work, and its national president and state and chapter leaders did call for a new rank-and-file organization that would project a militant program to fight the companies. The West Virginia Miners' Wives and Widows Association, led by two black women—Anise Floyd of Charleston (before she was shot and killed in May) and Helen Powell of Beckley—also persisted with the struggle. The miners desperately needed a program that would address the problems of organizing new members, of safety in the mines, of equalizing pensions, as well as racist and sexist discrimination in hiring and union education.

The Bituminous Coal Operators Association had failed to accomplish most of its bargaining goals in 1978, but put the same reactionary demands on the table once again in 1981. In the meantime, the companies had been able to take advantage of new anti-union arbitration rulings to blunt the effectiveness of the UMW. Arbitration Decision 108, handed down on October 10, 1977, in a case where Consolidation Coal was attempting to fire picketers, posed an especially profound threat to miners. Recognizing that one known union member standing at the entrance to a mine "can and does furnish ample signal to cause a work stoppage," the Arbitration Board, which had been established in 1974, ruled that, "until this begins to be turned around, the passing-out of information relating to a dispute even in public places near an affected mine cannot realistically be viewed as the exercise of constitutionally protected freedom of speech and must be viewed, instead, as a contractually improper act of work-stoppage inducement."[31] Under ARB 108, companies could fire any miner who did no more than pass out material relating to a labor–management dispute.

In the meantime, the expected expansion of the industry had failed to materialize. In the recession year 1980, more than 20,000 miners were laid off and many mines were closed. At the same time, the shift to western coal, as well as to surface mining generally, continued apace, ultimately threatening the very existence of the union. In the face of such trends, a rank-and-file movement that had any hope of success would have had to go beyond defending and strengthening the membership. During the strike, miners had indeed begun to consider the nationalization of the mines and public ownership of the industry more seriously than they had for years.[32] But unless and until alternatives such at this one are discussed and realized, miners will continue facing massive problems every day on the job and at home. Life in Appalachia—in many respects like life in a colony—can never be changed until profits from production are used to benefit the people living in the region. Today, Appalachians continue to have some of the worst schools, hospitals, sports facilities, cultural opportunities, and roads anywhere in the country. Appalachia, along with the Deep South, continues to be the poorest region in the country. But it cannot be denied that the coal miners, organized into rank-and-file movements that created a strong union, made a fundamental effort to change the face of their whole region. The example of their challenge and their unity during the long 1970s, culminating in the 1977–8 contract strike, will endure.

---

31  Arbitration Review Board Decision 108, October 10, 1977, pp. 17, 21.

32  During the strike, Cecil Roberts and several local union officers had issued a statement which read, in part, "As a longer range target, we raise the demand for the nationalization of the energy industry. That the fuel, oil, gas, and power companies would be taken away from private owners and be run by government in a humane way, with people coming before profits." See also David Greene, "The Threat of Western Coal" (Racine, West Virginia Pamphlet, 1977), p. 9.

# 7

# The Tumultuous Teamsters of the 1970s

## Dan La Botz

The late 1960s and 1970s were tumultuous years for trucking industry workers and their union, the International Brotherhood of Teamsters (IBT). Trucking companies were rapidly consolidating, introducing new technologies, and asserting greater control over their workers, trends that gathered steam over the decade and accelerated to lightspeed with industry deregulation in 1978. In the face of these changes, workers' militancy increased. Teamsters rejected contracts negotiated by their union leaders, forcing several major strikes that involved hundreds of thousands of workers, paralyzed truck traffic in dozens of states, and brought other industries to a halt. In some states, there were shoot-outs and street battles between strikers and union officials, police, or National Guard troops. Rank-and-file Teamsters also engaged in unofficial work stoppages, several of which mobilized tens of thousands of workers in what became virtual general strikes of the freight industry in a city or region, one of them a national wildcat.

Teamsters did not confine their militancy to the workplace. Rank-and-file activists and union dissidents created several different reform organizations or movements of regional and national significance. One of them, Teamsters for a Democratic Union (TDU), became a permanent opposition party within the IBT, continually revitalizing a grassroots movement for democracy that still survives today. TDU and its predecessors launched their efforts at union reform as a direct outgrowth of industrial action against the employers. They fought management on the job, campaigned against sell-out contracts, challenged union leaders, elected reform slates, revised union by-laws, and fought for reform of union health, welfare, and pension funds. In a historic overturning of the old guard, they ultimately elected a reform leader president of the Teamsters. In these activities, leftist activists played a significant role, offering local, regional, and national leadership and helping to change both the Teamsters and the AFL-CIO.

The rise of Teamster militancy in the 1960s and 1970s and beyond was fundamentally a response to employers' attacks on workers' living standards and workers' power in the workplace, the central thrust in trucking company efforts to maintain profits in the more challenging conditions of slower growth, higher inflation, and increased competition that characterized the industry in the 1970s. Simply put, as employers pushed for concessions at the bargaining table and control on the job, rank-and-file Teamsters fought back.

Teamster union reform sentiment had various sources: concerns about truck safety, Mafia control of union pension funds, the centralization of power in the hands of Jimmy Hoffa, and the loss of local union autonomy. But the reform *movement* grew out of workers' struggles against the employers and was primarily a response to the failure of IBT officials to protect the wages, benefits, and job control won by rank-and-file Teamsters during and after the original organization of over-the-road trucking in the 1930s and 1940s. When Teamster leaders in the late 1960s and 1970s negotiated weak contracts and acquiesced to work rule changes, rank-and-file Teamsters concluded that their union needed changing. They organized on the job and off, turning to traditions of local union autonomy to build reform organizations that fought employers in the workplace and demanded democracy in the union. They drew especially on the Teamster tradition of job control, the defense of which motivated the struggle and the reliance on which organized the struggle. The freedom on the job that Teamsters continued to enjoy was indeed a critical factor in enabling them to create successful workplace organizations. Low unemployment also helped, since it boosted workers' confidence. The social movements of the period, particularly the student antiwar, civil rights, and Black Power movements, and the New Left provided inspiring examples of successful collective struggle, as well as an important source of experienced political activists for the reform movements. The International Socialists (IS), in particular, a small organization of the far left, played an indispensable role in founding TDU and keeping it alive by providing ideas, organizational resources, and political cadres. High levels of Teamster militancy failed to survive beyond the 1970s, due mostly to the recession, deregulation, the ebb of the social movements, and the growth of conservative political power. Nonetheless, the struggle continued at a lower level, sustaining a thrust for reform that eventually brought about a dramatic transformation of the IBT, if only temporarily.[1]

---

1   In writing this paper, I have benefited from the comments of three longtime socialist activists in the Teamsters Union who prefer to remain anonymous. I have also appreciated comments on the paper from Steve Early of the Communications Workers of America and

## Prosperity and Power

The background to the Teamster militancy of the 1970s was provided by the long period of prosperity following World War II. It was a golden age for trucking. Between 1948 and 1968, the number of intercity ton-miles (one ton of cargo moved one mile) moved by truck increased by a factor of six. The industry's gross operating revenue increased from $867 million to $12.4 billion, a fourteen-fold increase before inflation.[2] Trucking benefited particularly from the expansion of manufacturing and retail trades, two of its largest customers. Federal subsidies by way of the Interstate Highway System literally paved the way for trucking's expansion, while national regulation, in the form of the Motor Carrier Act of 1935, virtually eliminated competition. Under this act the state limited new entrants, distributed routes, and controlled freight rates, thereby stabilizing the industry by insuring employer profitability, restraining competition, allowing small carriers to persist, and buttressing employment. All these conditions facilitated union organization, as guaranteed profits and reduced competition allowed carriers to pass the cost of labor contracts on to customers.

Still, the Teamsters had to undertake militant strikes, mass picketing, and pitched battles for union recognition, contracts, and some control over the industry. Between 1934 and 1963 Teamster leaders Farrell Dobbs, Dave Beck, John M. Sullivan, and Jimmy Hoffa Sr. built local union solidarity and employed militant leapfrog tactics, which entailed organizing key points and threatening to or actually acting to interrupt interline shipments. Through boycotts, slowdowns, and strikes at key points, the union brought employers to the table and created city-wide, regional, and national contracts in the freight industry.[3] During the 1950s, Hoffa extended Teamster organization into the South, making the IBT

---

from Ken Paff, TDU's National Organizer. Thanks to Katie Laux, a graduate student in the Department of History of Miami University, who helped me with research.

2   American Trucking Association, American Trucking Trends 1969 (Washington, DC: American Trucking Association, 1969), pp. 8–9.

3   The story of Teamster organizing in the 1930s can be found in C. R. Walker, *American City: A Rank-and-File History* (New York: Arno & New York Times, 1971, 1937); F. Dobbs, *Teamster Rebellion* (New York: Monad Press, 1972) and *Teamster Power* (New York: Monad Press, 1973); D. Garnel, *The Rise of Teamster Power in the West* (Berkeley: University of California Press, 1972); and P. Korth, *Minneapolis Teamsters Strike of 1934* (East Lansing: Michigan State University Press, 1995). I summarize this period in my book *Rank-and-File Rebellion: Teamsters for a Democratic Union* (New York: Verso, 1990), pp. 83–192.

one of the few national unions to succeed in Dixie. By 1964, when Hoffa negotiated the first National Master Freight Agreement, the IBT was the one truly national, private-sector union in the United States. It was also the most powerful entity in the trucking industry, a single organization, with 2 million members at its peak, against dozens of small carriers with far fewer resources.[4]

Industry stability and unionization encouraged long-term, permanent, full-time employment.[5] The union's typical three-year contracts, with their regular wage increases and, by the 1950s, their health-and-welfare and pension plans, led workers to stay with one company in order to build seniority, earn higher wages, and protect their retirement. After three decades of economic prosperity and something near national full-employment (at least for white workers), many Teamsters had little fear of being fired. A Detroit Teamster freight worker told me, "We didn't care if the boss fired us, we'd just go next door and get a job." Teamsters in the freight industry could expect job security, high wages, and good benefits, and came to feel entitled to them.

Teamster control of truck transportation gave the union remarkable power in the economy. Perhaps more than any other union, the IBT supported organizing drives and work stoppages of other unions through solidarity strikes and boycotts. By refusing to cross the picket lines of Teamster or other unions, IBT locals and individual members regularly stopped the delivery of raw materials, parts, machinery, or finished goods. By refusing to deliver coal or fuel oil, Teamster drivers could bring a plant to a cold, still halt. The cooperation of Teamster rock-sand-and-gravel drivers was particularly important to building trade unions of the AFL-CIO.

From the 1930s to the 1970s, Teamsters' shop-floor and local union action commonly disciplined employers. Teamsters often had the power to set the work pace and establish their own production standards. Dock workers determined how many pieces or tons they would move in a night; truck drivers made only so many deliveries and pickups per day. This sort of control preserved jobs, increased overtime work, and protected workers' health and safety. In some of the larger barns (terminals), union stewards or other workers frequently solved grievances by "pulling down the doors," that is, shutting down the terminal briefly in order to get the attention of the terminal manager.

---

4   R. D. Leiter, *The Teamsters Union: A Study of Its Economic Impact* (New York: Bookman Associates, Inc., 1957); R. James and E. James, *Hoffa and the Teamsters: A Study of Union Power* (Princeton: D. Van Nostrand Company, Inc., 1965).

5   When in 1974 I was hired on as a truck driver at F. Landon Cartage, a Chicago-area trucking company, the top-seniority worker had been there since 1934, and others had been hired in 1930s, '40s, and '50s.

Sometimes Teamster truck drivers "got caught in traffic," "got lost," or "broke down" in order to punish the dispatcher or supervisor who refused to attend to grievances over wages or working conditions. Dock workers could "lose" or misdirect cargo to pressure foremen and terminal managers. Teamster contracts gave the local union the right to strike over grievances for twenty-four hours, and some locals used it regularly, a powerful weapon in the hands of local officials. Local Teamster unions also used their power to strike individual companies. Their long-standing traditions of solidarity and militancy endowed rank-and-file Teamsters with considerable confidence in their ability to confront their bosses, and their experience of years of rising wages and benefits, combined with their long-term job security, only reinforced the feeling.

## Crime and Politics

Teamster involvement with organized crime stretched back to its founding in 1903 and compromised union traditions of solidarity and militancy. The Mafia used its control of Teamster locals in cities like New York, Chicago, Cleveland, and Detroit to move contraband, for extortion, and as a source of jobs for common soldiers of the Cosa Nostra. While most Teamsters and their union officials were hard-working, honest people, the significant presence of organized crime became a real blight on the union, especially after 1957, when Hoffa became president and brought the Mafia into the very heart of the organization. His Mafia associates assumed influence over the union's increasingly large pension funds and took jobs on the International union's payroll as organizers and business agents.[6] Mafia involvement led to Congressional investigations, Robert Kennedy's obsession with "getting Hoffa," criminal prosecutions, the expulsion of the IBT from the AFL-CIO, and eventually Hoffa's imprisonment in March 1967.[7]

---

6   On Teamster corruption there are many books, some quite sensationalist. The best of these "exposés" are: W. Sheridan, *The Fall and Rise of Jimmy Hoffa* (New York: Saturday Review Press, 1972); J. Neff, *Mobbed Up: Jackie Presser's High-Wire Life in the Teamsters, the Mafia and the F.B.I.* (New York: Atlantic Monthly Press, 1989); and A. Friedman and T. Schwartz, *Power and Greed: Inside the Teamsters Empire of Corruption* (New York: Franklin Watts, 1989). A study prepared by the IBT itself is: Stier, Anderson & Malone, LLC, *The Teamsters: Perception and Reality: An Investigative Study of Organized Crime Influence in the Union* (N.P.: Stier, Anderson & Malone, LLC, 2002). A thoughtful treatment is D. Witwer, *Corruption and Reform in the Teamsters Union* (Chicago: University of Illinois Press, 2003).

7   M. J. Goldberg, "The Teamsters' Board of Monitors: An Experiment in Union Reform Litigation," *Labor History* vol. 30:4 (Fall 1989), pp. 568–84.

The IBT's mob ties gave the government a good excuse for seeking to limit its power. The Taft-Hartley Act of 1947 had already targeted the Teamsters and railroad unions with its prohibition on "hot-cargo" strikes, in which workers refuse to handle goods from companies involved in a labor dispute. In 1959, the Landrum-Griffin Act (Labor–Management Reporting and Disclosure Act), which grew from Congressional hearings into IBT-Mob ties, led by Senator John McClellan, imposed further restrictions on unions, and particularly on the Teamsters, by further limiting secondary boycotting as well as organizational and recognition picketing (i.e., picketing of companies where a rival union is already recognized). At the same time, the Landrum-Griffin Act's labor bill of rights guaranteed workers access to information, free speech in the union, and regular union elections, making it an important tool of union reform movements in the 1960s and '70s.

During the 1950s, the Teamsters Union came to represent a rather more corrupt, often more militant, but astonishingly successful version of American business unionism. The IBT was a business union in two senses. The union cooperated with the largest employers in the industries it organized to maintain a set of arrangements that benefited both the employers and union officials, often at the expense of the union's majority of lower-paid members. At the same time, union officials ran the union itself as a business, which provided them with high salaries, magnificent benefits packages, and such perquisites of office as luxury automobiles and expense accounts, as well as investment opportunities and political connections.

## The Teamsters on the Eve of Upheaval

By the late 1960s, the Teamsters was the largest union in the country, with about 2 million members. It was a sprawling, complex organization with a particularly high-profile public image. It had a well-deserved reputation for power based on its history of class struggle, solidarity, and shop-floor militancy, but its Mafia connections and the associated threat of violence made it something of a pariah within the union movement. Many workers came to both admire and fear the IBT, and some came to identify with its macho image of head-bashing, bone-crunching bruisers who struck terror into the hearts of employers, other union leaders, and ordinary workers.

Inside the organization, the union had a social pyramid much like that of the country as a whole. At the top were a small number of white men running the union who had high salaries, often had investments in Teamster-organized businesses, and sometimes had ties to organized crime. Under them was the International union's bureaucracy, hundreds of paid staff and 20,000 full-time officials, nearly all of them white men as well, who oversaw the union's organizing campaigns and helped to service and often supervise approximately eight hundred local unions.[8] Below the union officialdom and bureaucracy were the members themselves, who fell into two separate social groups. The first group included freight, car haul, rock-sand-and-gravel, and beverage drivers, almost all white men who earned the highest salaries and enjoyed the best health and pension benefits. These workers constituted the most political section of the Teamsters, those who dominated local unions and sent delegates to international conventions. Under them was a second group, composed of lower-paid truck drivers and dock workers, as well as food processing and manufacturing workers, many of them African American and Latino. These members of the union had less power, sometimes even in their own local unions, and were politically less significant in the International union. The Teamsters had begun to recruit women in the 1940s. Most of them worked either as clerks in the freight section or as factory workers in food processing or manufacture. But women had little role in the union.[9]

Unlike most other old AFL unions, the Teamsters did organize African American workers and accepted them as members of the union, but they were for the most part confined to food processing, manufacturing, and driving metal scrap or garbage trucks.[10] Those African American workers employed by freight companies mostly worked on the docks and were generally excluded from jobs as drivers. Under federal court orders, companies began to hire African American drivers around 1970, beginning the integration of the motor freight industry. Teamster locals and white workers often objected, and protested having to work with African Americans. No African Americans were found in the top leadership of the union, virtually none in the joint councils, and only a few in local union leadership positions.[11] African American workers, some bringing civil rights experience, demonstrated in

---

8   M. Rinaldi, "Dissent in the Brotherhood: Organizing in the Teamsters Union," *Radical America* vol. 11:4 (1977), pp. 43–55, gives the 20,000 figure.

9   L. F. Vosko and D. S. Witwer, "'Not a Man's Union': Women Teamsters in the United States during the 1940s and 1950s," *Journal of Women's History* vol. 13:3 (Autumn 2001), pp. 169–92.

10   D. Witwer, "Race Relations in the Early Teamsters," *Labor History* vol. 43:4 (November 2002), pp. 505–32, explains that in the very early years of the century, the IBT had organized black workers in the North and South. The Teamsters on the West Coast also had a record of racism against the Japanese during World War II. See C. W. Romney, "The Business of Unionism: Race, Politics, Capitalism, and the West Coast Teamsters, 1940–1952," (PhD Diss. UCLA, 1996), chapter 3, "War Against the Japanese," pp. 97–145.

11   R. D. Leone, The Negro in the Trucking Industry (Philadelphia: University of Pennsylvania, 1970), pp. 94–132. At the same time, there were some extraordinary African American leaders in the Teamsters. See, for example, B. Cawthra, "Ernest Calloway: Labor, Civil Rights, and Black Leadership in St. Louis," *Gateway Heritage* (Winter, 2000–1), pp. 5–15.

Los Angeles to protest their exclusion from union in leadership.[12] Some also participated in rank-and-file organizations in the 1970s.

The Teamsters Union under Hoffa and his successor Frank Fitzsimmons remained highly authoritarian, corrupt, and undemocratic. Union officers commonly held several offices and took home multiple salaries, often amounting to hundreds of thousands of dollars a year, ten or twenty times the wages of the workers they represented. The Teamster General President held enormous power, both constitutionally and in practice, though the union was never as centralized as the UAW or USWA. As in most U.S. labor unions by the 1950s, neither Teamster national conventions nor local union meetings saw much discussion and debate, nor did the composition of the convention, made up as it was of elected officers and staff members, reflect the union's membership. A good number of Teamster local unions were dominated by dictatorial leaders who ruled with a heavy (and sometimes violent) hand. Union stewards were often appointed from above rather than elected from below. Collective bargaining agreements negotiated by union leaderships could be rejected only if there was a two-thirds majority against, making it difficult for the membership to reject them. While some Teamster locals were democratic, many gave rank-and-file members no voice in the union or vote on their contract.[13]

The IBT was not monolithic, however; historically, it was highly decentralized, tending after the fall of Beck and Hoffa to be dominated by regional barons such as William Presser in Ohio. Long-established traditions of local union autonomy persisted, even as Hoffa began in the 1950s to impose greater International staff control over the local and regional bureaucracies. Numbers of freight locals resisted centralization and rebelled against attempts to bring them into the National Master Freight Agreement (NMFA). While these movements for local control often had a parochial and conservative character, they sometimes also advanced notions of rights, participation, and local union democracy, and they eventually fed into the revolts of the late 1960s and 1970s.[14]

---

12   W. B. Gould, *Black Workers in White Unions: Job Discrimination in the United States* (Ithaca: Cornell University Press, 1977), pp. 365–71.

13   Many of these problems with the union are laid out in A. Fox II and J. C. Sikorski, *Teamster Democracy and Financial Responsibility* (Washington, DC: PROD, 1976).

14   Discussions of the Teamsters local autonomy movements can be found in: D. Witwer, "Local Rank and File Militancy: The Battle for Teamster Reform in Philadelphia in the Early 1960s," *Labor History* vol. 41: 3 (August 2000), pp. 263–78, which discusses the Teamster Voice; R. Bussel's "'A Trade Union Oriented War on the Slums': Harold Gibbons, Ernest Calloway and the St. Louis Teamsters in the 1960s," *Labor History* vol. 44:1 (February 2003), pp. 49–67, discusses in passing Rank-and-File Teamsters (RAFT), an opposition in Gibbons's local in St. Louis; Sheridan, *The Fall and Rise of Jimmy Hoffa*, discusses several of the local autonomy movements of the early 1960s.

The imprisonment of Hoffa in 1967 did not change the nature of the IBT, but it did expand the fissures in the union's officialdom. Hoffa's successor Frank Fitzsimmons was a weak leader, incapable of enforcing his will on the vast bureaucracy. Local and regional leaders gained considerable freedom to build their own structures of power, and quite a few, in important locations like Detroit, Chicago, and New York, increased their involvement with the Mafia. The resulting rise in corruption and abuse provided rank-and-file activists an additional set of issues to organize around, while internal incoherence and local or regional union autonomy opened some space for them to act.

## Employers' Offensive

With or without Hoffa, the leadership of the IBT was unprepared for the industry's productivity push that accelerated from the mid-1960s right through to the 1980s. Many of the changes implemented by the employers threatened Teamsters' traditions of workplace control. Automation began to alter the work process. From the 1930s to the 1960s, most motor freight had been composed of loose boxes, but beginning in the 1950s more and more companies used pallets and forklifts. Truck trailer lengths grew to forty and eventually forty-five feet, and some companies began to use double, and later triple, trailers. Intermodal operations grew with trains hauling truck trailers; later came intermodal containers that could be moved by ships, trains, and trucks.

Stoking technological change was the trend toward the merger of local trucking companies into interstate and eventually national corporations, and the management of the much larger companies that emerged introduced greater and more systematic control of production as they brought in the most modern plants and machinery. Truck terminals and UPS hubs grew into massive facilities, some with hundreds of dock workers. UPS, which developed the nickname Big Brown Machine, introduced complex mechanized systems of conveyor belts called "carousels to distribute packages." The larger size of freight terminals and the use of machinery were accompanied by the introduction of time-and-motion study and production standards (pieces or pounds moved per hour or shift). Radio dispatch increasingly directed drivers, while some companies installed machinery to track their direction, speed, and stops. All of these innovations were designed to reduce workers' control over their work and push them to greater productivity by eliminating certain jobs, changing the organization of work, and disrupting what had become traditional freight-handling methods bequeathed from the horse-and-wagon days of the industry. Teamsters thus worked harder and under worse conditions as new equipment and new management techniques eliminated jobs while forcing those still employed to pick up the slack.

Companies realized that two Teamsters doing the work of three and paid overtime to do it still cost less, since the third would have to be paid health and pension benefits. Increased use of casuals, which cut the number of full-time Teamsters and companies' overall wage bill, produced similar results. But cutting corners made the work more hazardous. Larger loads, longer hours and distances, and quicker safety checks increased the likelihood of accidents and injury. The institution of flextime in place of regular schedules kept Teamsters guessing as to when they would have to work, forcing them to sit by the phone without pay. Flextime also meant the loss of overtime pay for working before 8:00 a.m. or after 5:00 p.m., and shift starting times were staggered, breaking up social networkers in the barns.

Sophisticated labor relations went along with sophisticated operations. Many trucking companies were large and smart enough to employ full-time experts, quite a few of whom were retired IBT business agents, who used their experience to teach employers how to exploit the contract. Employers also learned from the IBT the advantage of cooperation. Led by the larger firms, they began to strengthen associations among themselves during the 1960s. While unity had initially been foisted upon them by Hoffa's drive for an NMFA, the employers quickly adapted it to their own purposes. In April 1967, after the union negotiated a new NMFA, rank-and-file Teamsters protested its skimpy wage increase by launching wildcat strikes. In retaliation, fifteen hundred trucking companies shut down more than two-thirds of the nation's freight for three days.[15] This increase in employer cohesiveness at precisely the moment when the IBT leadership was splintering shifted the balance of power at the bargaining table, and the bosses took advantage. Wage growth slowed and the rising inflation of the period exacerbated the problem.[16] With the union leadership ever more ineffectual, corrupt, and in bed with the employers, the rank and file was obliged to fashion its own fight back.

---

15  "Tough Test for Labor," *Business Week*, April 15, 1967, pp. 33–5; S. R. Friedman, *Teamster Rank and File: Power, Bureaucracy, and Rebellion at Work and in a Union* (New York: Columbia University Press, 1982), pp. 120–3.

16  A. Brenner, "Rank-and-File Teamster Movements in Comparative Perspective," in G. Perusek and K. Worcester, eds, *Trade Union Politics: American Unions and Economic Change, 1960–1990s* (Atlantic Highlands, NJ: Humanities Press International, 1995), explains the political economy behind the Teamster rebellion of the 1970s with an emphasis on the decline of profitability and the trucking employers' offensive aimed at recouping control of the workplace and reducing labor costs.

## The Origins of Teamster Reform: FASH, TURF, and PROD

In fashioning a response to the employers' offensive, Teamster militants and reformers drew inspiration from the social movements of the period, particularly the African American civil rights movement of the 1950s and 1960s and the anti–Vietnam War movement from 1965 through 1975, even if, as is probable, relatively few actually participated in them. These movements legitimized dissent, protest, civil disobedience, and direct action, while making more conceivable a revitalization of the labor movement from below and providing a vision of what a revitalized labor movement might look like. Just as they shook up political parties and opened up space in society for critical thinking in all areas of life, they led workers, Teamsters included, to contemplate collective action to address their problems, and, by exposing the hypocrisy and violence of government, corporations, unions, and other institutions, they provoked many to question authority.

The social movements also offered positive alternatives to the established order—visions of equality, democracy, civil rights, and community participation that reverberated throughout American society, even into the labor movement. The African American civil rights movement popularized the view that American citizens had certain rights to equality and justice that had to be respected. Social and political movements such as Students for a Democratic Society, the Black Panthers, and the Puerto Ricans' Young Lords Party raised notions of participatory democracy and community control that challenged and enriched traditional ideas of representative government. Such conceptions were broadly disseminated and popularized not only in the mass print, radio, and television news media, but also in widely watched television situation comedies and dramas, and in motion pictures.

Barely a month after Hoffa entered prison in March 1967, opposition erupted in the IBT over the NMFA, stoked by old pro-Hoffa elements in the union. After Fitzsimmons announced a settlement of the national contract, leaders of Locals 705 and 710 in Chicago, who were not covered by the national contract, took their members out on picket lines demanding more money. Though their motivation was largely political—they wanted to demonstrate Fitzsimmons's lack of control over their unions—rank-and-file Chicago Teamsters enthusiastically joined the strike. Members in several other cities also wildcatted in support of higher wage demands. After twelve days, Chicago employers agreed to ten cents more per hour, forcing Fitzsimmons to renegotiate the national agreement to meet the new terms. But that did not end the dissension.

Most steel haulers were also disappointed with the NMFA. Steel haulers owned their own rigs and contracted to work for licensed carriers. As owner-operators who were also employees of a sort, they had joined the IBT. But the union had little interest in their grievances. Said Hoffa, "We represent you as a worker and a worker only. Don't come to us asking us to negotiate a profit on your equipment."[17] Dissident steel haulers had circulated demands to be included in the NMFA, including a pay increase to 79 percent of total hauling costs (up from 72 percent), pay for covering their loads with chains and tarps, and fifteen dollars an hour after the first two hours of waiting at steel mills to load or unload, as well as separate ratification of the steel haul NMFA supplement and a separate IBT steel haul division. When, at the end of May, the union ratified the NMFA, steel haulers were angry, since it contained none of the improvements they had demanded.[18]

Over the next several months, the steel hauler dissidents, led by Jim Leavitt of Detroit, Tom Guilt and John Hack of Gary, and William Kusley of Hobart, launched a series of protests, featuring several wildcat strikes that caused havoc in the Great Lakes steel region. One of the walkouts lasted two months, involved 20,000 steel haulers, and resulted in considerable violence.[19] Governors mobilized the National Guard in several states. But the combined opposition of the union and the employers weighed heavily on the strikers, and their rank-and-file leadership began to splinter. Eventually, Fitzsimmons negotiated waiting time pay of ten dollars per hour, allowing the strikers to claim a small victory. The steel haulers returned to work, but within days dissidents met again to form the Fraternal Association of Steel Haulers (FASH), a rank-and-file group with the purpose of promoting cooperation among steel haulers, exchanging information, and advising steel haulers of their rights.

Over the long term, FASH hoped to achieve the goals that went unrealized in the 1967 strike, especially the right to separate representation within the IBT. In 1969, the group initiated another strike, but this time the union responded by organizing dozens of officials and goons to attack pickets and crush the strike. Shooting broke out, killing one striker and

---

17  D. Moldea, *Hoffa Wars: Teamsters, Rebels, Politicians, and the Mob* (New York: Paddington Press, 1978), p. 193.
18  D. R. Jones, "Few Defy Strike of Steel Haulers," *New York Times*, October 8, 1967, p. 82; D. R. Jones, "Striking Steel Haulers Grimly Vow to Fight On," *New York Times*, September 24, 1967, p. 72; Moldea, *Hoffa Wars*, p. 195.
19  "Teamsters Seek Parley on Strike," *New York Times*, September 19, 1967, p. 39; "Haulers' Strike Spurs Violence," *New York Times*, September 21, 1967, p. 52; "Mills Feel Impact of Haulers' Strike," *New York Times*, October 6, 1967, p. 43; D. R. Jones, "7-Week Strike by Steel Haulers Spreads Disruption in Industry," *New York Times*, October 9, 1967, p. 54; Moldea, *Hoffa Wars*, pp. 197–202; La Botz, *Rank-and-File Rebellion*, p. 25.

wounding several more people on both sides. The home of a FASH leader was firebombed. The IBT's implacable hostility led FASH leaders to conclude that they had no choice but to secede from the union as soon as possible, and they began to organize with that objective. But FASH was unable to create an independent union; the strategy failed. The steel haulers were too big and important a part of the Teamsters Union to be permitted to leave by either the union or the employers, who naturally preferred the business-minded Teamsters to the FASH wildcatters. FASH activists, however, went on to play a role in other movements, and later some of them became founders of TDU.

Negotiations for the 1970 NMFA were almost a repeat of 1967. Once again Chicago local leaders refused to accept the $1.10-per-hour raise negotiated by Fitzsimmons, and they called a strike demanding $1.70.[20] The official Chicago strike called by Louis Peick, head of Local 705, and William Joyce, head of Local 710, encouraged unofficial wildcat strikes by Teamsters in cities across the country, from New Jersey to California. In Los Angeles, the strike involved thousands of workers and lasted fourteen weeks.[21] Across the nation, tens of thousands of Teamsters joined the walkout, which in some places involved violent clashes with employers, scabs, police, or National Guard troops and, begun on April 1, continued on and off in one city or another until July 3. FASH took advantage of the wildcats to launch a strike of its own. As in 1967, rank-and-file action proved somewhat successful. Chicago Teamsters won raises of $1.65 per hour, and Fitzsimmons had to renegotiate the NMFA for $1.85 per hour, which was then also extended to the Chicago locals.

As in 1967, the 1970 walkouts inspired Teamster dissidents to form a new organization, and on July 25, 1971, a year after the strike, a group of Teamster activists met in Toledo to found Teamster Union Rank and File (TURF). TURF was different from FASH in that its concerns were broader and of interest to the members of the entire union. But it never reflected the thrust from below of militant rank-and-filers in the way that FASH had. From the beginning it involved local union leaders of some stature, was constituted on the basis of an emerging movement of local union reform caucuses, and included a pension reform group; but it in no way broke from the norms of business unionism. While many local TURF activists were truck drivers in search of a more militant and

---

20   The Chicago Truck Drivers Union (CTDU), also known as the Independent, was an independent Teamsters union, not part of the IBT. However, it negotiated with IBT locals in Chicago. I was a member of the CTDU between 1974 and 1980.

21   On the 1970s wildcat in Los Angeles, see Friedman, *Teamster Rank and File*, chapter 7, "Apolitical Activism Ambushed: The 1970 Wildcat," pp. 136–68.

democratic union, in the end TURF functioned as a de facto vehicle for the aspirations of ambitious out-of-office bureaucrats, some of whom had risen quite high up in the union hierarchy. In the late 1960s Andrew Provenzino had formed the Unity Committee in Detroit Local 299 as a local political party representing a more reform-minded faction in the union. The Unity Committee concept spread to other Teamster locals in the Midwest. Provenzino brought them to the Toledo meeting, where they were joined by Don Vestal, a leader of Nashville Local 327, and his followers. (Once a Hoffa supporter and a trustee of the Central States Pension Fund, Vestal had had a falling out with Hoffa, with the result that Hoffa and then Fitzsimmons had pursued a long-term vendetta against him, having his office shot up and his house subject to armed attack. When Vestal attempted a failed counterattack by mounting a candidacy against Fitzsimmons's re-election at the 1971 convention, the International finally succeeded in its longstanding effort to throw his local into trusteeship, leaving Vestal with no office in the union.) A final key participant in TURF's initial meeting was "Curly" Best, founder and leader of the "500 at 50 Clubs" based in Los Angeles, a pension reform movement within the Teamsters seeking five hundred dollars per month for retirement at fifty years of age.

TURF had some experienced leaders, each with a following in different parts of the country, and was still benefiting from the sense of power that pervaded the union's rank and file after the 1970 strikes. TURF chapters rapidly spread throughout the Midwest and in some other areas of the country. Local activists used the organization as a way to run for office. As an expression of genuine grievances arising out of the ranks, the organization was attractive. However, TURF never organized militant struggles against the employers, and the aspirations of most of its leaders were no greater than to place themselves as good officials in union positions occupied by bad officials. Some of its leaders rapidly went over to Fitzsimmons, and within a year or so, TURF had faded from the scene.

The Professional Drivers Council (PROD) was formed at about the same time as TURF, but was very different in character. Where TURF became a vehicle for out-of-office bureaucrats, PROD functioned more like a traditional political pressure group. In 1971 Ralph Nader, the consumer advocate and safety watchdog, called a Professional Drivers Conference on Truck and Bus Safety in Washington, D.C., at which most of those in attendance were over-the-road drivers from the East Coast and the South. At the time, Nader was a good-government reformer seeking to pressure Congress mainly through lobbying. The conferees not only called for government action on safety, but also criticized the Teamsters Union for failing to fight for it and went on to form a new union reform organization,

PROD. The name said it all: they wished to *prod* the Teamster leaders and government officials to bring about reform.

Rank-and-file Teamsters working with local union reformers in Cleveland and Indianapolis sponsored meetings of PROD. They soon discovered, however, that PROD generally wanted nominal members, not activists. Moreover, PROD, created by a consumer advocate, was reluctant to call for higher wages, as this would raise costs and, most likely, also prices. That position fatally undermined PROD's usefulness as a vehicle for a workers' movement.[22] Nevertheless, under the leadership of attorney Arthur Fox, hired by Nader, PROD worked closely with Teamster road drivers and, in collaboration with his assistant John Sikorski, provided some important weapons for the struggle for Teamster reform, notably the pamphlet "Teamster Democracy and Financial Responsibility," a devastating critique of the Teamster bureaucracy, published in time for the June 1976 Las Vegas Teamster Convention.[23] PROD's modus operandi was, in the style of Nader, to bring about reforms though pressuring the government and the IBT by way of education, court cases, and lobbying. PROD called local meetings, held discussions on truck safety, circulated questionnaires to garner drivers' views, trained some PROD members as local leaders, and brought them to testify at Congressional hearings. PROD did not, however, contemplate militant collective action against the companies.

## The Teamsters for a Democratic Union

Teamsters for a Democratic Union (TDU) represented a radically distinct alternative for the union. What made it qualitatively different was that it sought not only a change in leadership and the democratization of the union, but also to constitute a permanent organization of the rank and file in order to compel the union leadership to carry the fight to the employers. The idea of creating union power from the bottom up, by starting from the shop floor where rank-and-file power was ultimately based and building outward, was a truly radical one for the Teamsters Union, and indeed for the highly bureaucratized and business-unionist labor movement as a whole. Bringing it into the IBT was the signal contribution of the International Socialists (IS), which played a central role in much of its subsequent history.[24]

---

22  Interview with anonymous former IS and TDU activist, September 2005.

23  Fox and Sikorski, *Teamster Democracy and Financial Responsibility*.

24  At the same time, IS employees at United Parcel Service (UPS) worked with IBT union activists in the UPS locals to create UPSurge, a union reform organization concentrating

The IS strategy grew from its political analysis of the nature of the period and the character of U.S. labor movement. The group argued that U.S. and international capitalism had entered an era of crisis, marked by a fall in the average rate of profit for business. In order to respond to their profitability problems, the corporations would find it necessary to unleash an offensive against labor, opening the way for intensifying class struggle. In the view of the IS, 1968 in France and Italy's "hot autumn" of 1969 were harbingers of the new epoch. At the same time, drawing on the work of Leon Trotsky, Max Shachtman, Hal Draper, Stan Weir, Sidney Lens, C. Wright Mills, Herman Benson, and Burton Hall, the IS offered its own view of the labor officialdom, which entailed a particular approach to the unions that itself went back to the Communist-led Trade Union Educational League of the 1920s. According to the IS, union leaders had become a social caste within the unions, with an interest in preserving their power and position at all costs and a concomitant reluctance to challenge the employers. The officials' failure to respond to the employers' challenge would create the need for an alternative. Radicals would therefore have an opening to organize a class-struggle tendency within the labor movement by organizing rank-and-file caucuses within the different unions. The caucuses would lead workplace struggles over grievances, contract fights, and other collective actions, which were seen as key to changing workers' consciousness—of their relationship to the employers, as well as to the state—and to developing their sense of power and self-confidence. Through such struggles, workers would become open not only to more militant action and the fight for democracy in their unions, but also to socialist ideas. These caucuses, as they became stronger, would challenge the bureaucracy, pushing it forward or pushing it aside. Working along these lines in several different unions, the IS hoped to pull together a layer of union activists, shop stewards, and local union officers recruited to its idea of socialism from below. These union activists would form the core of a revolutionary socialist party.[25]

In their thinking about the strategy for building workers' power in the unions, IS members were very much affected by the very mixed experience

---

its efforts on UPS workers. For a brief period, UPSurge organized large meetings and some demonstrations, but it later collapsed. On the IS role in the Teamsters, see M. Fisk, *Socialism From Below in the United States: The Origins of the International Socialist Organization* (Cleveland: Hera Press, 1977); R. Fitch, "Revolution in the Teamsters," *Tikkun* vol. 8:2 (March–April 1993), pp. 19–24; A. Brenner, "Rank-and-File Teamster Movements in Comparative Perspective."

25   For the IS experience, see Fisk's *Socialism From Below in the United States*, part VI, "The International Socialists in the Early Seventies," online at www.marxists.de/trotism/fisk/ch6.htm, and part VII, "The Mid-Seventies to the Founding of the International Socialist Organization," at www.marxists.de/trotism/fisk/ch7.htm.

of Miners for Democracy (MFD), the caucus that had led the struggle against the Tony Boyle regime in the UMW. During the 1960s and early 1970s, militant miners had engaged in a long series of job actions and wildcat strikes, created reform groups such as the Black Lung Association, used the Landrum-Griffin Act to win fair elections, and then supported the successful MFD campaign to overthrow the Boyle machine. Nevertheless, immediately upon coming to office in 1972, the MFD had dissolved, its members and leaders convinced that now that honest men had been elected to office, they would carry the struggle forward. The IS believed that the dissolution of the MFD had been a mistake, that reformers had to create permanent organizations inside the unions that would continue to represent the ranks even after new leaders took power, this both to provide the necessary power to back up these leaders against the employers and to make sure that they continued to represent rank-and-file interests.

From the end of the 1960s, the IS began to encourage its members to seek jobs in certain industries—steel, auto, telephone, and trucking—to implement its rank-and-file strategy. Over the following years, IS sent about two dozen of its members into the trucking industry in the Bay Area, Seattle, Los Angeles, Cleveland, Chicago, Pittsburgh, and other cities. As early as 1970, they had made contact with Teamster activists on the West Coast, while some worked with Curly Best's 500 at 50 Club and with TURF. The relationships with Teamster rank-and-filers in Los Angeles were originally forged at the time of the U.S. incursion into Cambodia and the shootings at Kent State and Jackson State in late spring 1970, when mass protests shut down a number of universities in the area. A handful of Teamsters seized the moment to make contact with campus radicals, notably at UCLA, to get student support for their national wildcat strike, which was going on at that very moment. Hundreds of students were soon picketing at local trucking barns to counter an injunction preventing Teamsters from posting more than five picketers at any location, and they continued to do so until the walkout ended. Out of this collaboration, some of the campus radicals formed a local collective that put out a citywide labor newspaper, *Picket Line*, to provide rank-and-file workers throughout the city the opportunity to get out their message to their fellow employees. Through participating in this collective and its newspaper, ISers made their initial contacts with Los Angeles–area rank-and-filers, and relations solidified during the strike.

In the Bay Area, IS members made the acquaintance of Dennis Dalton, who published a rank-and-file newspaper called *The Fifth Wheel* (named after the device that connects a truck tractor to a trailer). Dalton, assisted by IS members, used the paper to attempt to build a caucus of the Bay Area Teamsters. This exclusively Teamster paper became the model for future IS attempts to build rank-and-file groups in local unions throughout the country.

Though IS members made only a few contacts with Teamsters in L.A. and the Bay Area, the relationships they developed were invaluable. They provided IS members with a basic understanding of the trucking industry, the politics of the IBT, and the ideas and language of Teamsters. With these relationships, the IS members, most of whom were in their late twenties, initiated local Teamster reform organizations in several cities, each of which published its own rank-and-file newspaper. In the Bay Area there was *The Fifth Wheel*, in Seattle *The Seattle Semi*, in Los Angeles *The Grapevine*, and in Pittsburgh *From the Horse's Mouth*.[26]

In 1974, at the suggestion of IS members in the local reform groups, these organizations and some others came together to launch a national campaign around the upcoming NMFA. Distributing tens of thousands of brochures throughout the country, the campaigners, who called their organization Teamsters for a Decent Contract (TDC), soon came to the attention of many Teamsters, including a group of rank-and-file Hoffa supporters in Detroit who had been set adrift by the disappearance of their leader.[27] The affiliation of the Detroit Teamsters activists gave TDC some real numbers and power in the heart of the most important local union in the nation, Hoffa's home, Local 299.

As the 1976 contract expiration date approached, TDC organized a series of escalating demonstrations in cities throughout the United States. The largest, in Detroit, attracted two thousand Teamsters, but there were also rallies in Los Angeles, Cleveland, Pittsburgh, and many other cities. Under pressure from TDC's "no contract, no work" movement, Fitzsimmons was obliged to call an official strike that lasted three days. TDC activists and members of UPSurge led wildcat strikes at freight terminals in Detroit, and briefly at UPS terminals in eight cities in the Central States region. It was the first national IBT strike in freight, and it secured for the members a significantly improved contract.

The success of TDC led its leaders to create a national rank-and-file organization in the union, and on June 5, 1976, thirty-five TDC and UPSurge activists decided to transform TDC into Teamsters for a Democratic Union (TDU). Ten days later, several TDU members headed out to the Teamsters International Convention in Las Vegas.

---

26  Socialists, both men and women, worked in the trucking industry. Most women worked at UPS as package car drivers, though the IS also had one woman freight driver and one woman dock worker, a forklift driver. Women socialists also participated in TDU as Teamster wives, since TDU encouraged Teamster spouses (men or women) to join as full members, as permitted in the TDU constitution.

27  J. R. Hoffa and D. I. Rogers, *The Trials of Jimmy Hoffa* (Chicago: Henry Regnery Company, 1970); L. Velie, *Desperate Bargain: Why Jimmy Hoffa Had to Die* (New York: Readers Digest Press, 1977); Moldea, *Hoffa Wars*.

There TDU's lone delegate, Detroit Teamster Pete Camarata, introduced resolutions, written by PROD, calling for union reform. Speaking at the convention, Fitzsimmons told TDU to "go to hell," and Teamster officials beat up Camarata and other TDUers. Its presence at the Las Vegas convention brought TDU to national attention. It was able to constitute itself as a viable opposition in the union by virtue of its having led militant rank-and-file action in the freight and UPS contract fights, and having stood up to the bureaucracy in the name of reform at the IBT convention, as well as its ability to inspire already existing local groups to come together in a national organization. TDU held its founding convention at Kent State University on September 18, 1976, with more than one hundred Teamsters from forty-four local unions in fifteen states.

The initial success of the militants who formed TDU elicited wide attention, both wanted and unwanted. In the mass media, there was a small outpouring of newspaper and magazine articles, and even books. But at the same time, the International began to accuse TDU of being a socialist or Communist-led movement, with no legitimate place in the Teamsters. From day one, IS members in TDU had to deal with red-baiting and attempts to discredit the group because of the role of socialists in its founding. While IS members did hope to recruit Teamster activists to the cause of socialism, they never intended TDU to be a socialist organization.[28] When challenged about the role of socialists, they frequently said, "TDU is an organization of rank-and-file Teamsters committed to reforming the union and fighting the employers. We have Democrats in TDU, we have Republicans in TDU, and we have some socialists in TDU, because TDU is open to all Teamster members." The idea that all Teamster members (and their spouses) should have the right to participate, regardless of their political views, generally quieted the critics.[29]

The IS was not trying to create a socialist caucus in the union, but rather, by way of TDU, to construct a much broader rank-and-file organization dedicated to enabling the IBT membership to fight the companies, as well as the Teamster bureaucrats who stood in the way. But IS members were nonetheless committed to having some sort of socialist presence in TDU and in the IBT, though how to do so was always a subject of keen debate. There was always the fear that an emphasis on socialism might drive away

---

28   As it turned out, the IS recruited very few members from its TDU work.

29   M. Rinaldi, "Dissent in the Brotherhood," pp. 43–55, has an interesting discussion of the IS members' handling of their socialist identity and politics in the Teamsters Union. He argues that the IS members abruptly announced that they were socialists in the union and thereby jeopardized their work.

Teamster activists, but the flip side of the same coin was the worry that a single-minded focus on activism and reform might lead to the neglect of socialism, which was after all the ultimate goal. IS arrived at a modus operandi, though it varied somewhat from city to city. At TDU and local meetings, non-Teamsters sold *Workers Power*, the IS newspaper, and other IS pamphlets. IS members discussed their socialist convictions and their IS membership with their closest collaborators, if only to insure that Teamster rank-and-filers would not be taken by surprise if employers, the union, or the government were to identify the IS, its members, and their role. In general, because they respected the IS members' work in the union, these close collaborators accepted the new information with good will and kept it in confidence. In some cases, IS members also invited TDU activists to socialist meetings.

A small number of TDU members from working-class backgrounds joined the IS. But of the score or so of Teamsters who were recruited between 1976 and 1978, most had left by 1979 or 1980.[30] The changes in the national economy, politics, the labor movement, and the left, as well as a factional struggle within the IS, led the new members to leave. They had joined the group when they thought it could lead; they left it when it seemed too divided to succeed.

The IS had set out around 1970 to create rank-and-file caucuses in several major unions, but only in the Teamsters Union was the group successful. The United National Caucus, which IS backed and which worked within the UAW, failed largely because it was unable to cope with the power and sophistication of the Reuther's leadership or the National Caucus. The IS members in the USWA found themselves in the midst of a complex and sophisticated opposition within the union that included Ed Sadlowski and his Communist Party advisers, along with the independent pro-Sadlowski Steelworkers Fight Back and its Maoist organizers. Rather than creating an independent caucus in the USWA, the IS members became absorbed into the Sadlowski/Fight Back milieu and eventually left the organization. After playing a role in the 1971 telephone strike, IS members led caucuses in the CWA in New York City and occasionally in other places, but the group never became a factor in the union on a national basis.

Why the IS proved so much more able to build a rank-and-file opposition in the IBT than elsewhere is not entirely clear. Whereas in other industries and unions various left groups competed for leadership, most of the time in

---

30    There were about twenty IS members in the Teamsters in 1975, and as many as fifty very briefly in 1978, some of whom were college youth who took Teamster jobs, often at UPS, others of whom were longtime Teamsters who became socialists. By 1980 there were less than twenty, perhaps only a dozen.

the Teamsters the IS was the only left group in the union, and its leadership role in the rank-and-file reform movement was crucial. It no doubt helped as well that in freight and the other constituencies organized by the Teamsters, workers were up against companies that were much smaller and less well organized than the corporate behemoths in auto, steel, or telephone. That the IBT, largely an association of regional baronies, was itself so much more decentralized and disorganized than the core CIO industrial unions also facilitated the growth of dissidence. The survival of strong rank-and-file organization within the IBT at the level of the workplace, especially in freight, as well as truck drivers' continuing freedom on the job, may have been the most important factors of all. In any case, the IS's very success in the Teamsters Union had the paradoxical result of provoking bitter debates among IS members and Teamster collaborators about the correct strategy for building the movement in the IBT. Within the IS, differences over socialist strategy in the unions, focusing especially on TDU, became intense, leading to a series of faction fights that affected IS work in the Teamsters and ultimately devastated the political organization itself.

The closely related issue that caused the greatest controversy was whether, under what conditions, and in what way TDUers should run for office and work with local elected officials. Some IS members feared that if TDU members were elected to office without the backing of a sufficiently active and conscious base, they might succumb to the inherent pressures of the union's bureaucratic structure, the employers' blandishments or bludgeoning, or to government laws and regulations that constrained and inhibited unions' power.

Three different positions associated with three different factions inside the organization emerged. The first group argued that the IS, with its emphasis on union work in prioritized industries and its collaboration with union reformers whose politics was often far from radical, was giving up on doing necessary propaganda work and neglecting the task of building a socialist party. After an acrimonious internal fight, the IS majority expelled that faction, about one-third of the total three hundred members, in 1977.[31] The second group also attacked what it saw as the tendency toward reformism, but from a different angle. They argued that IS union or TDU members who ran for union office, as they often had to, without the support of a large, active, and class-conscious base, risked becoming mere union reformers and eventually simply union bureaucrats. The risks were similar in working with local officials, whom TDU had no way to discipline. For this group the emphasis had to be on leading shop-floor and workplace conflicts and linking them to other social movements, with

---

31    The group expelled in 1977 became the International Socialist Organization (ISO).

the hope that as the struggles deepened and broadened, it would become more feasible to successfully put forward socialist ideas to workers. That group left in 1978, also taking about a hundred members.[32] Having been reduced by the two splits to just one hundred members in many fewer branches, the International Socialists continued the policies of industrial priorities, building rank-and-file caucuses, and attempting to build a socialist organization within the Teamsters and other unions.

The crisis in the IS coincided with a precipitous decline in union activism across the American economy. Within TDU, the IS soon abandoned virtually all efforts at socialist propaganda and gave up attempts to recruit new members to socialism. The IS no longer had the capacity to send new recruits to get jobs in certain local unions or as workers for specific companies. Nor did it have the personnel or resources to simultaneously play a leading role in TDU and a role in building the IS. The IS leaders in TDU therefore lowered their expectations and focused on maintaining TDU as a militant pole of attraction within the IBT. Workplace struggle continued within the industry, but after the 1975–6 recession it began to decline, and after 1979 work stoppages and wildcat strikes virtually ceased everywhere. Union activism on a national scale declined, though struggle still broke out from time to time in different Teamster jurisdictions. The result was a certain shift in TDU activity, from a focus on workers' struggles against the employer at the local level to an emphasis on national contract campaigns, organizing within the union around democratic issues, and elections for local office.

TDU work became ever more organized, professional, and effective. Within two years of its founding, it had created a national steering committee, opened a national office, hired a national organizer (Ken Paff of Cleveland Local 407), and began to publish a national newspaper, *Convoy*.[33] After PROD joined TDU in 1979, the organization established a Washington, D.C. office to conduct lobbying on legislation of importance to Teamsters and to take legal action in defense of union members' rights and interests, such as pensions. The national organization provided stability and continuity, and coordinated activity around the major events of the union: three-year contracts and five-year conventions. In between, local TDU activists organized around workplace issues, such as productivity standards on the docks, and union reform issues, such as by-laws changes

---

32  The group that left in 1978 became Workers Power, which created *Against the Current* magazine. In 1986 the International Socialists and Workers Power joined with former Socialist Workers Party (US) members to form Solidarity: A Socialist, Feminist Organization, later just Solidarity.

33  After the merger with PROD, the paper became *Convoy-Dispatch*, adding the name of the PROD paper.

to allow for elected stewards. TDU supported a few candidates running for local office, and those candidates won in some local union elections. On the basis of this work, TDU soon built a number of effective networks of activists, notably at large freight companies, such as Roadway, and among certain crafts such as brewery, car haul, and later cannery workers. In 1979, TDU's agitation helped force Fitzsimmons to call an eleven-day national freight strike. Car haulers and steel haulers also struck, and all three groups of workers won better agreements than they otherwise might have. TDU seemed, to some observers, poised to take power in one or two large local unions, and it looked as if, within a couple of years, TDU might elect a substantial number of delegates to the IBT convention.[34]

## The End of the Upsurge, In for the Long Haul

Rank-and-file Teamster militancy peaked roughly from 1967 to about 1979, and then entered into serious decline as the social, political, and economic context was rapidly transformed. The end of the Vietnam War in 1975 meant the end of the antiwar movement. The decline in roughly the same period of the African Americans' struggle, as well as the movements of Latinos, women, and gays and lesbians, quickly reduced both activism and social criticism, and the possibilities of major social or political change began to seem remote. In 1974–5 and again in 1979–83, the U.S. economy passed through deep recessions, detonating several waves of plant closings in auto, steel, and other industries, in which tens of thousands of industrial workers saw their jobs eliminated. Many were forced to take non-union jobs for much lower wages and benefits. Levels of union density declined dramatically. In this economic climate, unions and workers were reluctant to strike for fear of losing their jobs, and management took advantage of the situation to open an era of concession bargaining, demanding give-backs of wages and benefits from unionized workers that threatened to roll back the epoch-making gains of the postwar era.

---

34 TDU does not hold delegated annual conventions. The TDU national organizer and steering committee work to bring TDU members involved in the most important movements in the union to conventions, which are open to all members. TDU conventions do not revolve around resolutions. They involve a testimonial session, a report from the national organizer, panels of speakers discussing important union issues, workshops for training members in dealing with contracts, elections, or other issues, and meetings of Teamsters by craft or division, such as car haul or UPS. TDU conventions focus on the Teamsters Union and seldom take up general issues of concern to the labor movement or social issues, though those broader issues are sometimes discussed. Such social or political issues sometimes come to the membership through the guest speakers. Partisan political debates are discouraged, and an attempt is made to work toward consensus on Teamster issues.

The 1980s were dark days for Teamsters. Already in the last years of the Carter administration, Congress, led by such liberal Democrats as Senator Ted Kennedy, had passed the deregulation of the trucking industry with the basic goal of reducing costs, above all labor costs.[35] As intended, new non-union trucking firms swarmed into the industry, union firms went bankrupt en masse, and a series of buyouts and mergers pushed the industry toward oligopoly. Part and parcel of the same processes, the IBT lost tens and eventually hundreds of thousands of unionized truck drivers and dockworkers, and within a decade the Teamsters Union had been obliged to cede its long-standing position as the dominant force in American over-the-road truck operations.[36] Since the freight industry had been the heart of the union and freight workers the most political and active union members, the cost to the union as a fighting organization went far beyond mere numbers, and the impact was equally great on TDU, since its strongest base was in the freight sector.[37]

Meanwhile, aided by union presidents Frank Fitzsimmons, Jackie Presser, and Roy Williams, as well as regional Teamster barons, employers systematically assaulted the working conditions and living standards that had long been assured by IBT's principal contracts—in freight, UPS, and car haul. They began to "double breast," that is, open new non-union subsidiaries and move much of the work to the non-union company. They pushed for two-tier wage scales, with lower wages for new hires, dividing the workforce and putting older workers under pressure from younger, lower-paid workers. They expanded the use of casuals to avoid hiring workers entitled to full benefits. Everywhere TDU kept Teamsters informed of these disastrous developments, and at many local workplaces and in local unions it organized resistance, but it was difficult to get much traction. Nevertheless, as the decade progressed, Teamsters began to fight back, at both the local and national levels, offering TDU new opportunities to aid in the resistance. When Yellow Freight in Los Angeles pushed for

---

35   Ralph Nader, who inspired PROD, had contributed to this drive for deregulation with "The Ralph Nader Study Group Report on the Interstate Commerce Commission and Transportation," published as: R. C. Fellmeth, *The Interstate Commerce Omission: The Public Interest and the ICC* (New York: Grossman Publishers, 1970). See also T. G. Moore, "Trucking Deregulation," in *The Concise Encyclopedia of Economics* at www.econlib.org/library/Enc/TruckingDeregulation.html

36   M. Belzer, "Collective Bargaining After Deregulation: Do the Teamsters Still Count?" *Industrial and Labor Relations Review* vol. 48, no. 4 (July 1995), pp. 636–55. He argues that, at least for a while, the Teamsters lost bargaining power in the truckload sector but retained it in the less-than-truckload sector.

37   M. Belzer, *Sweatshops on Wheels: Winners and Losers in Trucking Deregulation* (New York: Oxford University Press, 2000).

more productivity and began to harass workers, TDU members in Local 208 organized sick-ins, work-to-rule campaigns, and slowdowns until the company fired its terminal manager.

Similar fights against the employers' productivity push took place in terminals across the country under TDU's leadership. In 1983, IBT president Jackie Presser tried to push through a secret contract rider that would have substantially cut workers' wages, but TDU got wind of it, took the information to the members, and defeated the Teamsters by a vote of nearly 9 to 1. *Business Week* called it "a slap in the face for Jackie Presser." During the 1985 contract fights, Presser succeeded in rushing through a poor UPS contract, but TDU won wide support, if not a victory, when it urged Teamsters to vote no to the freight contract. In car haul, where TDU was a leading force, 81 percent of the workers voted against the contract proposed by the International. TDU also played a role in the Watsonville Canning and Frozen Food Company strike of 1985, where Latino workers eventually stood strong against an attempt to destroy the contract there. And by the 1990s, TDU was well ensconced among Latino and immigrant workers in Teamster meatpacking plants.

Meanwhile, there were also major fights over workers' rights. When employers began to introduce drug testing, TDU took the lead in organizing opposition, charging that the programs violated workers' civil rights, while failing to provide rehabilitation instead of summary firings. After a two-year campaign by TDU, the IBT virtually conceded that TDU had been right and forced employers to end the testing.

During this same period, TDU was also working to overturn undemocratic, corrupt, or pro-company union leaders and replace them with local TDU activists or coalition slates supported by TDU. TDU members were elected local leaders in a variety of unions, from Denver to Atlanta. TDU also campaigned for the right of all union members to vote for the International president and executive board members. Finally, TDU challenged the Teamsters in the International elections, running Pete Camarata for president in 1981, Sam Theodus for the top office in 1986, and supporting reformer Ron Carey in 1991 and 1996.

At the end of the 1980s, the Justice Department brought suit against the IBT under the Racketeer Influenced and Corrupt Organizations Act (RICO), and the federal government threatened to take over the union. After a long debate within TDU over how to handle the RICO suit, TDU intervened, asking the federal government to do what it had done in the United Mine Workers Union, that is, oversee fair elections. When the federal government agreed to oversee elections, TDU staff and leaders proposed to Ron Carey, head of a UPS local in New York, that he run for International president. While Carey had never been a TDU member, he was seen as a reformer, honest, hardworking, and willing to fight the employers.[38]

In the 1991 election, TDU's national organization functioned as Ron Carey's campaign organization. TDU's national organizer, steering committee and staff, and local chapters insured that Carey's campaign reached local unions throughout the country, and his victory would have been unimaginable without that support. Twenty-five years of rank-and-file activism and union reform struggle came to fruition with the election of reformer Ron Carey as president in 1991.[39]

The combination of the U.S. government purge of Mafia-linked officials from the union and Carey's victory led to significant structural, procedural, and cultural changes in the union. Within this context, some union locals, like Local 705 in Chicago, underwent their own processes of reform.[40] Carey, still supported by the TDU reform movement, pushed democratic changes in the union, organized campaigns for improved contracts, and moved the union from backing Republicans to support for the Democratic Party. Carey, however, did not embrace TDU and did not put TDU's leaders into key spots in his organization, preferring instead former UMW/MFD leaders and leftist consultants with links to the Communist Party and to the Democratic Party.

TDU members on Carey's executive board represented the most progressive wing of the Carey coalition, and while they did not function as a bloc, they did represent watchdogs for democracy within the leadership. Some TDU leaders or pro-TDU staff members played an important role in certain offices, particularly in the Communications Department. They came to serve as an important link between Carey, TDU, and rank-and-file workers in the union, and functioned as a counterweight to old guard or do-nothing officials. When in some locals old guard officials attempted to sabotage Carey's reforms or campaigns, Communications could reach the ranks through TDU.

Carey also had an important impact on the labor movement at large. He helped to change the AFL-CIO when the Teamsters Union voted for the election of reformer John Sweeney as AFL-CIO president in 1995. And Carey's leadership of the 1997 UPS strike represented the most important victory not only in the Teamsters, but in the entire labor movement in more than twenty years.[41]

---

38   Carey had been praised as a potential savior of the union in S. Brill, *The Teamsters* (New York: Simon and Schuster, 1978).

39   The best account of this period is K. C. Crowe, *Collision: How the Rank and File Took Back the Teamsters* (New York: Charles Scribner's Sons, 1993).

40   R. Bruno, *Reforming the Chicago Teamsters: The Story of Local 705* (DeKalb: Northern Illinois University Press, 2003).

41   M. Witt and R. Wilson, "The Teamsters' UPS Strike of 1997: Building a New Labor

Cary and TDU reformers faced difficult problems in attempting to reform the Teamsters. While the Mafia-connected officials were purged, other conservative, bureaucratic, or corrupt officials remained. The reform movement had never really penetrated most of the non-freight locals, and many of them were corrupt or moribund. Carey decided to put some locals in trusteeship, but in other cases he decided that he had to coexist with the local leaders. He could not find enough honest, reform-minded, and experienced leaders for the trusteeships, and TDU did not have enough leaders to carry out reform campaigns in all the locals that needed renovation. Reform made significant strides, though much remained to be done.

Carey's removal from office, which came after aides used union funds for his re-election campaign, dealt the reform movement a heavy blow, leading to the election of James Hoffa Jr. to head the union. While the reform movement faltered in the late 1990s, it revived to face new challenges in the new century.[42]

TDU continued to be narrowly focused on Teamsters' economic issues and question of union democracy. TDU's newspaper *Convoy* seldom commented on other social movements and virtually never mentioned other unions. TDU conventions did not take up questions such as the wars in Kosovo, the Persian Gulf, Afghanistan, and Iraq, and would not discuss partisan political issues. Yet TDU's rank-and-file approach could have radical implications. During the Battle of Seattle in 1999, when environmentalists joined labor unions to oppose the World Trade Organization, it was a TDU-led Teamster local that played a leading role in the famous alliance of "Teamsters and Turtles." The IS members who helped to found TDU, however, did not merely intend to lead a struggle for union reform, democracy, and militancy, nor merely to build alliance with other social movements; they wanted to recruit out of activist rank-and-file movements the cadres of a revolutionary socialist party. The decline in the social movements of the 1960s and '70s, the recessions of 1975 and 1979, and the collapse of most of the revolutionary left organizations by 1980, together with the faction fights within the IS and the organization's reduced resources, meant that the building of an American revolutionary socialist party was postponed for at least another generation.

---

Movement," *Labor Studies Journal* 24:1 (Spring 1999), pp. 58–72; D. La Botz, "The Fight at UPS: The Teamsters' Victory and the Future of the 'New Labor Movement'" (Detroit: Solidarity, 1997), at www.solidarity-us.org/teamster/teamster.htm.

42   It would be impossible in this paper on the 1970s to deal with the 1980s and 1990s, and these broad brush strokes do not do justice to the complexity of the situation. For more, see the articles of J. Larkin and S. Early that appeared in *In These Times*, *The Nation* and *The Progressive*, which represent the best analysis of Ron Carey and his administration.

More than thirty years since its founding, TDU remains a force for change in the IBT, a kind of opposition political party that is also a grassroots movement. Today TDU still leads fights to defend workers' pensions, to win better contracts, and above all for democracy in the Teamsters Union. TDU's staying power derives in large measure from the founding notion that the organization was created not merely to lead particular struggles or to elect new leaders, but to lead workers in a fight for workers' power on the shop floor, in the union, and in society.

# 8

# Militancy in Many Forms: Teachers Strikes and Urban Insurrection, 1967–74

## Marjorie Murphy

Public school teacher militancy appeared suddenly in the late 1960s, though the movement for teacher unionism was quite mature, dating to the early twentieth century. Like the rank-and-file militancy in other sectors, teacher activism drew some of its strength from a new, younger workforce, very much dedicated to the social issues of the day, including desegregation and ending the Vietnam War. The examples of civil rights activists, student antiwar demonstrators, feminists, and other social movement protesters inspired teachers to confront school boards, mayors, and state legislatures in a wave of strikes and protests demanding better wages, improved working conditions, and more funding for schools. Unlike most workplace militants in other sectors, teacher activists mobilized in an environment—the public school system—that was the locus of struggle for another powerful social movement, namely that of African Americans. Inevitably, teachers and their unions would encounter African American public school activists fighting for desegregation and greater community control over their schools. What was not inevitable was the shape of this encounter.

Often, across the country, teacher unions and civil rights leaders could find common cause, or at least avoid conflict. In several large urban settings, however, the rise of Black Power, particularly its separatist tendency, led to a series of complicated confrontations between African American activists and militant teachers, with tragic results. In New York City's Ocean Hill-Brownsville section and in Newark, New Jersey, these confrontations weakened the teachers' unions and undermined the potential for meaningful community control of the schools. They bitterly divided the American Federation of Teachers (AFT), and what had been a very progressive union grew more conservative, a shift that made it easier for its rival, the National Education Association (NEA), to recruit the growing number of teachers interested in unionism. The reasons for the AFT's shift have much to do with the rise to national leadership of Albert Shanker as AFT president; it was his neo-conservative approach to education that most alienated teachers and weakened the union.[1]

## The Rise of Teacher Militancy

The number of work stoppages by public workers in the years after World War II added up to no more than a handful until the 1960s. In most states, legislation prohibited public workers, including teachers, policemen, and firemen, from striking. The prohibition was so strong that many unions, as a matter of course, adopted anti-strike pledges; others, however, clung to the right without ever using it. In 1962, President John F. Kennedy, advised by New York City Mayor Robert Wagner, issued Executive Order 10988, establishing collective bargaining rights for federal government workers. Four years earlier, Wagner had issued a similar Executive Order of his own, number 49, known as the "Little Wagner Act," which allowed collective bargaining for the city's workers. Other cities and states enacted similar legislation.

While most jurisdictions still prohibited strikes by public employees, the more accommodating legal environment encouraged public sector worker militancy, including work stoppages. Many of these strikes were recognition and first-contract strikes, because, despite the new laws, public sector workers still had to mobilize to convince local and state authorities to bargain. By the mid-sixties, there had been 142 work stoppages by public workers nationwide. The number grew to 169 in 1967 and 254 in 1968, compared to 15 in 1958. This rise in militancy accelerated in the late 1960s, with 411 public worker strikes in 1968 and 412 in 1969. The number dropped slightly in the early seventies and averaged about 375 for the rest of the decade. After 1981, the number of strikes fell dramatically.[2]

---

1  The author wishes to thank Cal Winslow and Marty Goldensohn, Aaron Brenner, and Carole Mackenoff for their comments and encouragement. On teacher militancy, see D. Selden, *The Teacher Rebellion* (Washington, DC: Howard University Press, 1985), pp. 75–80; M. Murphy, *Blackboard Unions: The AFT and the NEA, 1900–1980* (Ithaca: Cornell University Press, 1990), p. 226; S. Aronowitz, *From the Ashes of the Old: American Labor and America's Future* (Boston: Houghton Mifflin Co., 1998); T. W. Kheel, "Strikes and Public Employment," *Michigan Law Review* vol. 67:5 (March 1969), pp. 931–42; and P. Buhle, *Taking Care of Business: Samuel Gompers, George Meany, Lane Kirkland, and the Tragedy of American Labor* (New York: Monthly Review Press, 1999), pp. 146–203.

2  US Department of Labor, Bureau of Labor Statistics, Handbook of Labor Statistics 1966–82.

Teachers were some of the most militant public sector unions. They engaged in more than 300 teachers' strikes during the sixties, and in 1967 alone teachers nationwide walked out at least 105 times. David Selden, former AFT leader, calculated that at least 1,000 school districts experienced a strike or threatened strike during the hard-fought representation struggles of the 1960s, and another 2,000–3,000 districts saw job actions of one kind or another, short of a strike.[3]

The teachers union in New York City, the United Federation of Teachers (UFT), was one of the oldest teachers unions in the country. In the fall of 1960, it engaged in a one-day walkout aimed at winning union recognition. With more than half the teachers walking picket lines at hundreds of schools throughout the city, the demonstration had its effect; the city agreed to a union election for the following spring, which the UFT won. Teachers demanded a pay raise, sick pay for substitutes, a fifty-minute break for lunch, and binding arbitration, but when negotiations dragged on into the spring of 1962, the union called another strike. It lasted only one day, but convinced the state to provide the funds to meet the teachers' demands. They won the first comprehensive collective bargaining contract for teachers in the country.[4]

New York City teachers were not alone in growing more determined and militant. The success of union organizing and mobilization in the Big Apple led the AFT (of which the UFT was the largest local) to send organizers around the country, and the results were immediate. Detroit teachers won collective bargaining rights in 1964, and the next year, in neighboring Hamtramck, teachers, like the auto workers of the 1930s, held a two-week sit-down strike. Teachers in Pittsburgh walked out a few years later, and when they were arrested, the public outcry led a judge to release them. Teacher militancy helped establish the political clout of their unions. During several strikes by teachers in Gary, Indiana, the city's first African American mayor, elected with support of the black teachers, mediated favorable settlements. Nationwide, the AFT's efforts led to skyrocketing growth as the union expanded from 60,000 to 200,000 members between 1960 and 1970.

---

3   Selden, *Teacher Rebellion*, pp. 109–10. See also www.aft.org/about/history.
4   J. B. Freeman, *Working Class New York: Life and Labor Since World War II* (New York: New Press, 2000), pp. 49, 203; C. Carson, *In Struggle: SNCC and the Black Awakening of the 1960s* (Cambridge, MA: Harvard University Press, 1981); W. C. Hogan, *Many Minds, One Heart: SNCC's Dream for a New America* (Chapel Hill: University of North Carolina Press, 2007), Part Two; and T. Hayden, *Reunion: A Memoir* (New York: Random House, 1988), pp. 129, 161–4.

## Teacher Militancy Confronts Urban Unrest

The arc of teacher militancy coincided with rising urban unrest and escalating protests against the Vietnam War, but it was no coincidence. Teachers in the nation's big cities had watched as their chronically underfunded schools deteriorated. They held their employers, the boards of education, responsible for the terrible conditions and saw their militancy as a means to force the cities and states to improve the schools. They took a further step by connecting the conditions in the schools to larger issues of war, crime, unemployment, and racism. Such links were obvious to teachers, many of whom, for example, found themselves teaching young African American men of draft age who used high school to avoid the draft much as middle-class young white men used college. The inequalities of the draft and the American education system were manifest in the classroom. As teachers increasingly made these connections, they made the struggles of their communities part of their own struggles for better schools.

The AFT had considerable credibility in these efforts, because it was one of the most progressive unions in the country. Despite a substantial loss of membership in the South equaling some 18 percent of total membership, the union began desegregating in 1956 by combining its African American and lily-white locals a full fifteen years before the NEA did likewise. Teachers and AFT leaders funded and joined civil rights demonstrations, desegregation marches, and struggles for greater school funding in African American districts. Richard Parrish, an African American teacher and vice president of the UFT and AFT, led an integrated group of teachers to Prince Edward County, Virginia, in 1963 to start what later became known as Freedom Schools in the African American community. As a result of this type of activity, the AFT had strong relationships with local and national civil rights organizations, particularly around efforts to integrate the schools, and it won to its ranks thousands of African American teachers who saw the union as a means to fight racism.[5]

Relationships between the AFT and African American leaders were not without their tensions, and those tensions grew, especially in New York City, as both teacher militancy and the African American struggle accelerated in the late 1960s. Signs of growing conflict emerged in 1967 during the UFT's bargaining for a new contract in New York City. In

---

5   L. Buder, "City Stands Fast in School Dispute," *New York Times*, September 5, 1967, p. 1; "Another Opinion, Why the Teachers Are Not Teaching," *New York Times*, September 17, 1967, p. E15.

addition to a wage increase, the union had a series of demands related to the classroom. The teachers asked for more control over the curriculum, professional preparation time, paraprofessionals in the classroom, and the power to remove disruptive children. The union also demanded the expansion of its More Effective Schools (MES) program. This program, which the Board of Education adopted first in 1965 for about a dozen schools, called for smaller schools, a radical reduction in class size, the introduction of pre-K classes, and the use of teams of psychologists, social workers, and other specialists to work with students and their parents to address the impact of poverty and prejudice. In 1967, the UFT demanded that more schools be included in MES and that the city commit to lobbying the New York State Legislature to match its funding for MES. As part of the campaign, the union pointed to the false promises made by the Board of Education in Harlem, Bedford-Stuyvesant, and Ocean Hill-Brownsville. UFT leaders invited reporters to photograph the dilapidated schoolrooms in those areas and highlighted the rise in the crime statistics in the city's schools. After a two-week strike in the fall of 1967, the UFT won most of its demands, including, remarkably, the city's commitment to petition Albany for greater funding.[6]

With this victory, UFT leaders thought they had successfully combined the social progressivism of unionism with the push to reform education and save the city's poorest schools. "We thought [the union] was a vehicle for social change," one teacher leader recalled.[7] On the contrary, during the strikes the teachers found themselves excoriated in the community and the press. One *New York Times* columnist remarked, "Working teacher turned against non-working teacher, Negro parents (who three years ago had boycotted the schools with UFT support in protest against de facto segregation) charged the union with callousness toward slum children." Behind the criticism was a shift in the political context in New York

---

6  R. Teilhet, Oral History, American Federation of Teachers Oral History Project, Walter Reuther Archives, Wayne State University; Buder, "City Stands Fast in School Dispute," *New York Times*; Murphy, *Blackboard Unions*, pp. 232–51; B. Carter, *Pickets, Parents, and Power: The Story Behind the New York City Teachers' Strike* (New York: Citation Press, 1971); D. Ravitch, *The Great School Wars: New York, 1805–1973: A History of the Public Schools as Battleground for Social Change* (New York: Basic Books, 1974); J. A. Gordon, *Why They Couldn't Wait: A Critique of the Black-Jewish Conflict over Ocean Hill-Brownsville, 1967–1971* (New York: RoutledgeFalmer, 2001); C. Taylor, *Knocking at Our Own Door: Milton Galamison and the Struggle to Integrate New York City Schools* (New York: Columbia University Press, 1997), pp. 176–207; J. E. Podair, *The Strike That Changed New York: Blacks, Whites and the Ocean Hill-Brownsville Crisis* (New Haven: Yale University Press, 2002).

7  R. Teilhet, Oral History, American Federation of Teachers Oral History Project, Walter Reuther Archives, Wayne State University; Buder, "City Stands Fast in School Dispute." *New York Times*.

City and nationwide. The negotiations and strike had taken place against the background of major urban riots in the summer of 1967 in Tampa, Cincinnati, Atlanta, Newark, northern New Jersey (East Orange, Jersey City, Englewood, Plainfield, New Brunswick), and Detroit. Cities were in flames, dozens killed, and the turmoil lasted through the fall and winter.

The urban unrest accompanied and encouraged the emerging Black Power movement, which shifted the emphasis of the African American struggle from integration to empowerment. The Student Non-Violent Coordinating Committee became an exclusively African American organization, as Stokely Carmichael declared that "integration is irrelevant." Community-based organizations, such as the Black Panthers and the Congress of Racial Equality (CORE), rose to prominence. When it came to schools, these organizations were more interested in community control than desegregation. They wanted a thoroughgoing transformation of education that would address the specific needs and culture of African American children, including an Afro-centric curriculum. As they saw it, such an education was part and parcel of the larger social transformation they advocated for their communities and American society generally. In carrying out their activity, these community-based African American organizations differentiated between "the establishment" and "the community," and they usually identified teachers and their unions with the establishment.

The new breed of African American activists, which in New York City included most prominently Robert Sonny Carson of CORE, opposed many of the teachers' demands during the 1967 round of bargaining. As they saw it, demands to remove disruptive children and spend more time on class preparation illustrated teachers' racist disinterest in African American children. Contrary to the UFT slogan "Teachers want what children need," Carson and his followers viewed the strike as further evidence of the teachers' greed. Already skeptical of the union's commitment to the African American community, they dismissed MES as an effort to reinforce a racist curriculum and prevent more community control over what African American children would be taught. Many African American teachers, who had joined the union as a vehicle for civil rights, agreed with Carson, at least when it came to the strike, and for the first time large numbers of them refused to support the UFT and crossed the picket lines.[8]

---

8   "Athens Steps Up Its Loyalty Purge," *New York Times*, September 24, 1967, p. 20; J. Anderson, *Bayard Rustin: The Troubles I've Seen* (Berkeley: University of California Press, 1997). The Gotbaum-Shanker feud begins with this strike; see Freeman, *Working Class New York*, p. 225; J. Bellush, *Union Power and New York: Victor Gotbaum and District Council 37* (New York: Praeger, 1984).

The divisions between the UFT and the African American community, and within the UFT itself, remained muted during the 1967 strike, but the conflicts sparked by the strike set the terms of the much larger conflagration that took place the next year in the Ocean Hill-Brownsville section of Brooklyn.

## Ocean Hill-Brownsville

As in 1967, the conflict between the UFT and African American activists in Ocean Hill-Brownsville in 1968 took place against a backdrop of urban unrest, this time following the assassination of Martin Luther King, Jr. The assassination proved particularly tragic for Ocean Hill-Brownsville, because it ended an incipient movement for economic justice led by King that might have provided an alternative to the conflict that developed between labor and community. The alliance King envisioned at the time of his death would have rested on the two legs of an integrated civil rights organization and a more progressive labor movement. King's last speech, which took place in Memphis during the strike of predominantly African American sanitation workers, spoke to the possibility of such a coalition, the outlines of which he developed as he worked on the strike with William Lucy, secretary-treasurer of the American Federation of State, County, and Municipal Employees (AFSCME). While King had originally seen his work in Memphis as a distraction from his work on the anti-poverty campaign, with its march scheduled for that summer, the discussions in Memphis led him to believe that the movement could go forward with help from the trade unions where new black leadership was emerging.[9]

King's assassination on April 4, 1968, and the resulting urban unrest ended all such possibilities. Cities all over the country exploded in violence. Virtual insurrections took place in Chicago, Washington, D.C., Baltimore, Cambridge, Delaware, Cincinnati, Youngstown, Buffalo, Trenton, Newark, Jersey City, Kansas City, and Boston. Just six blocks from the White House, SNCC leader Stokely Carmichael urged his followers to "go home and get your guns." It took 21,000 troops to calm the streets of the nation's capitol, more in Chicago. The Pentagon set up a riot control unit and estimated that over 75,000 soldiers had been out on the streets enforcing citywide curfews, with orders to "shoot to kill" in some cities. In New York City, the poor community of Brownsville was burning. Firemen and police were met by young African Americans throwing stones

9  M. K. Honey, *Going Down Jericho Road: The Memphis Strike, Martin Luther King's Last Campaign* (New York: W. W. Norton, 2007), pp. 169, 200; D. Appleby, A. Graham, and S. J. Ross, *At the River I Stand* (San Francisco: California Newsreel, 1993).

and shouting "Kill whitey, out of our community!" One fireman thought his unit should comply. "If they want to burn up their neighborhood, it's their business," he said.[10]

Against this background, the UFT faced off against African American activists in Ocean Hill-Brownsville in the spring of 1968. That these two groups could become direct adversaries was the result of a complicated process that mixed school reform, philanthropy, racial politics, and class struggle. A year earlier, in the spring and summer of 1967, while the UFT negotiated its contract with the Board of Education, McGeorge Bundy, president of the Ford Foundation (and former Kennedy adviser who encouraged United States involvement in Vietnam), committed to fund and promote independent community school boards in new "experimental" school districts in New York City. This move toward "decentralization" grew out of Bundy's belief that plans to desegregate were inadequate. He declared an admiration for "legitimately militant black leaders . . . and their properly angry black words." Embracing the Black Power declarations of SNCC and CORE, Bundy asked, "Who can deny the right of young black students to have a part of their lives kept black? And who can be surprised that many of them exercise that right?" In a press conference, he said he did not expect to agree with community activists on all of the public questions concerned, but he believed they could use the money to help channel the black rage in the urban north. Continuing with this line of reasoning, Bundy thought "a little Black Power in the classroom would make the schools more responsive and more relevant to students and perhaps their reading and math scores would improve."[11]

The New York City Board of Education accepted the Ford Foundation's money and Bundy's proposal for community control of schools by agreeing to establish experimental school districts. With this move, the board sidestepped the pending decentralization proposals in the state legislature, thereby hampering the UFT's ability to shape the implementation of decentralization and community control. Because UFT officials disagreed

---

10   T. Johnson, "12 Arrested Here; Sporadic Violence Erupts in Harlem," *New York Times*, April 5, 1968, p.1, 26; N. Sheehan "Army Has 15,000 For Riot Control," *New York Times*, April 6, 1968, p. 25; D. Janson, "7 Die as Fires and Looting Spread in Chicago Rioting," *New York Times*, April 6, 1968, p. 1; R. Semple, "Capital's Police Using Restraint," *New York Times*, April 7, 1968, p. 62; J. Flint, "4,000 Guardsmen Stay in Detroit As City Keeps Curfew in Effect," *New York Times*, April 7, 1968, p. 63; F. P. Graham, "Police Restraint in Riots," *New York Times*, April 13, 1968, p. 16; "Long Wants Police to Shoot Looters," *New York Times*, April 14, 1968, p. 56; B. Colliers, "Jersey Guard Tightens Its Rules on Riot Control," *New York Times*, April 14, 1968, p. 56.
11   N. M. Rooks, *White Money, Black Power: The Surprising History of African American Studies and the Crisis of Race in Higher Education* (Boston: Beacon Press, 2006), pp. 81, 83–4, 90.

with both their exclusion from the decentralization process and the details of the Bundy proposal, they were hostile to the experiment. By accepting the Ford Foundation plan, the board succeeded in weakening the UFT politically and pitting it against the community.[12]

The first experimental school district started in Ocean Hill-Brownsville. An old industrial community nestled in Brooklyn just south of Bedford-Stuyvesant, Brownsville had been a blue-collar Jewish neighborhood until after World War II. As manufacturing declined in New York City in the 1960s, the new, largely African American and Latino migrants into the area suffered high unemployment and struggled with the decaying housing stock. The situation was similar in Ocean Hill, Brownsville's much smaller neighbor to the northeast.[13] To get the new school district off the ground, the Ford Foundation turned to CORE, which it had funded for years. Sonny Carson led the effort. Born and bred in Brooklyn, he was, by his own description, something of a gangland thug in his teenage years. He served in the Korean War with the 82nd Airborne division, an experience that radicalized him and motivated him eventually to join CORE. With a fluid set of politics that some labeled opportunist, he was a Black Nationalist in the late 1960s, and one of the most vocal critics of the UFT. He promised after the union's 1967 strike to prevent the teachers who struck from returning to "his" school district.[14]

From the spring of 1967 through the spring of 1968, Carson, CORE members, and other community activists organized elections for the new Ocean Hill-Brownsville district school board. The election results and the composition of the new local school board reflected their educational politics. Led by District Superintendent Rhoady McCoy but influenced heavily by CORE and Carson, the new board denounced the historic racism of the educational system both in the classroom and in the administration of schools. As they saw it, the existing system discriminated against African American teachers in examinations and licensing. Racist white teachers undermined African American children with their low expectations, colonialist mind-set, and Euro-centric curriculum. In contrast to the existing system, the board believed the schools could serve the community, give African American children a positive self-image, teach them the lost history of African American struggles, and lead them to believe in themselves as the arbiters of their own destiny.

---

12   M. Mayer, "The Full and Sometimes Very Simple Story of Ocean Hill, The Teachers' Union and the Teachers Strikes of 1968," *New York Times* Magazine, February 2, 1969, p. 18.

13   W. Pritchett, *Brownsville, Brooklyn: Blacks, Jews and the Changing Face of the Ghetto* (Chicago: University of Chicago Press, 2002), pp. 132–3.

14   Sonny Carson, *The Education of Sonny Carson* (New York, n.p., 1972), pp. 141–3; P. Kihss, "School Leaders See Bias to Oust Principals," *New York Times*, May 22, 1967, pp. 1, 24; Murphy, *Blackboard Unions*, pp. 237–43.

To accomplish its goals of transforming the schools, the board insisted on the right to hire teachers committed to its vision and fire those who did not share its predilections. However, the zeal with which it sought independence had its contradictions: the teachers who first went into the Harlem schools and turned teaching around for young African American children, who were educational pioneers in celebrating Black History Week, were turned away from the Ocean Hill-Brownsville school district because now parents and community leaders suspected their sincerity in developing the minds of African American children. This suspicion arose from the black nationalism fast becoming the dominant perspective in Brooklyn's African American community and found some justification in the UFT's opposition to school decentralization as it was being implemented by the city's Board of Education. There was also the simple issue of power.[15]

On May 7, 1968, the experimental Ocean Hill-Brownsville school board tested the limits of its power by dismissing thirteen union teachers, five assistant principals, and one principal on the grounds that they opposed the board's plan of community control. The teachers received no hearing and no alternative assignment, violations of the union contract and past practice of the central Board of Education. The dismissals sparked a series of strikes that spilled over from one school year to the next.[16] The entire debacle might have been avoided had the board waited just a few weeks until the summer, when the teachers could have been eased out of the district. In fact, all during the summer break, Albert Shanker, president of the UFT, Reverend Milton Galamison, a city civil rights leader, and Superintendent McCoy met for lunch once a week. All agreed that objectionable teachers would be quietly transferred. Galamison and Shanker thought that the issue had been settled when school started again in the fall.[17] McCoy, however, insisted upon the mass dismissals, and the strike began again on September 9.

The next two and a half months witnessed several long citywide teacher strikes, numerous community protests, bitter negotiations, accusations

---

15   M. L. King, Jr., *Where Do We Go from Here: Chaos or Community?* (New York: Harper & Row, 1967); Kihss, "School Leaders See Bias," *New York Times*, May 22, 1967; H. Bigart, "Negro School Ousts 19, Defies City," *New York Times*, May 10, 1968, p. 1; P. Hoffman, "Ousted Teachers Get Mixed Advice; Donovan and Union Favor Work—Supervisors Say No," *New York Times*, May 13, 1968, p. 39; l. Buder, "Parents Occupy Brooklyn School as Dispute Grows," *New York Times*, May 15, 1968, pp. 1, 44.
16   L. Buder, "8 Brooklyn Schools Boycotted by 6,000," *New York Times*, April 11, 1968, pp. 1, 36; H. Bigart, "Negro School Ousts 19," pp. 1, 38; L. Buder, "11 Teachers Defy Local Dismissals," *New York Times*, May 11, 1968, pp. 1, 29; Buder, "Parents Occupy Brooklyn School."
17   Parrish, "Teachers Strikes."

of racism and anti-Semitism, and near-violent confrontations. Increasing racial polarization characterized the conflict. McCoy fired an additional 350 teachers who walked out in support of their dismissed colleagues. He then hired replacements, including many young militant teachers who supported community control of the schools. On several occasions when UFT teachers tried to return to work, Carson led protests of students, parents, and replacement teachers against the returning strikers, personally blocking their entrance to the schools. These confrontations were characterized by shouting, jostling, and other forms of intimidation, despite the presence of police. At one community meeting in Ocean Hill-Brownsville, militants surrounded Shanker and refused to let him leave the room. From then on, he used a bodyguard.

The UFT's unstinting defense of union rights regardless of the community's needs was interpreted as racist not only by black nationalists. Many militant teachers were growing disillusioned with the UFT. Shanker insisted on strict union discipline during the strike, leaving teachers who supported community control and the idea of self-determination little room to maneuver. One of those teachers was Dick Parrish, a lifelong educator, who, as vice president of the national union, had made sure the AFT was one of the few AFL-CIO unions that had honestly desegregated by the late 1950s. He had played key role in making the UFT an important part of the school desegregation projects in New York City that began in 1964. Like other teachers who supported community control, Parrish had grown increasingly uncomfortable with the UFT's unwillingness to support the new militancy of the African American community. Through the strikes in 1967, the spring of 1968, and finally the fall of 1968, Parrish and other African American teachers grew increasingly angry with the union's exclusive focus on bread-and-butter union issues and its disregard for the community's educational interests. By the final strike, Parrish was urging teachers to cross the picket lines and teach African American children.[18]

Shanker contended that the strikes were about teachers' procedural

---

18   William Simon, Oral History Collection, AFT papers, Walter Reuther Archives, pp. 80, 101. See also Richard Parrish Papers, Box 1 additions; Parrish called the affair "a blow to education and a boon to racism"; R. Parrish, "The New York City Teachers Strikes," *Labor Today* (May 1969); D. Golodner, "The Integrating of the AFT Locals," delivered at the Midwest History of Education Society Conference, October 21–22, 2005. The ATA, the City Teachers' Association, and the United Parents Association all called for volunteers to keep schools open during the strike; T. A. Johnson, "Negro Teachers Give School Plan," *New York Times*, September 20, 1967, p. 37; L. Buder, "Lindsay Proposes a 26-Month Plan for School Peace," *New York Times*, September 20, 1967, pp. 1, 26.

rights, about preventing a precedent that would undermine the union's ability to protect teachers from the arbitrary power of the administration. He insisted that the UFT was not opposed to community control or decentralization. But his demand for complete union discipline polarized the situation by brooking no compromise between the union's rights to protect teachers and the community's right to decide its curriculum. He further stoked the conflict by exaggerating the anti-Semitism of the African American community-control movement. Despite the fact that they had no connection to the Ocean Hill-Brownsville Board, CORE, or any known organization, Shanker distributed 50,000 copies of anonymous anti-Semitic leaflets found in the mailboxes of several Ocean Hill-Brownsville teachers. These actions were designed to pit teachers against the community-control movement, especially Jewish teachers, and isolate the large minority of young, militant teachers, both black and white, who supported the African American struggle and wanted to push the UFT to take a more militant stance in favor of community control. Shanker's tactics worked to some degree, but not entirely. Of the teachers who crossed the picket lines in the fall of 1968 to teach African American children, 70–80 percent were white, and half of them Jews.[19] Thus, Shanker's willingness to polarize the conflict arose in part from his need to consolidate control over the union and suppress internal dissent.[20]

It took an outsider, the state commissioner of education, to convince all sides to settle the dispute. The union won the transfer issue, though most of the teachers fired by the local board were no longer in the district by the end of the strikes. The community experiment continued, but without the funding of the Ford Foundation, which also stopped supporting CORE. Dick Parrish remained a vice president of the AFT, but as William Simon, another African American vice president of the AFT at the time, recalled, "Dick differed with the leadership in New York in the Ocean Hill-Brownsville strike, [and as a result of his experience he] was crushed as a union person, as a human being . . . it's a sin and a shame."[21] Parrish was not the only one affected. The strike cast a long shadow over subsequent teachers rebellions.

---

19   Podair, *The Strike That Changed New York.*
20   King, *Where Do We Go from Here?*
21   William Simon, Oral History Collection, AFT papers, Walter Reuther Archives, pp. 80, 101. See also Richard Parrish Papers, Box 1 additions; R. Parrish, "The New York City Teachers Strikes." D. Golodner, "The Integrating of the AFT Locals."

## Newark: Ocean Hill-Brownsville Redux

Big teachers strikes in Philadelphia, Chicago, Los Angeles, and Newark in 1969 and 1970 followed the Ocean Hill-Brownsville conflagration. The strikes in the Midwest and West involved many issues, including union recognition, contract negotiations, decentralization, and community control. Many of these were large strikes, involving tens of thousands of teachers. Only in Newark did the conflict take similar form as in Brooklyn, only this time it was a revolution.

Teachers in Newark had long struggled for union recognition, as they followed the successes in nearby New York City. Newark had always been a blue-collar industrial city, but in the late sixties it was divided between the large Italian community in the North Ward and the largely African American and Puerto Rican community in the South and Central Wards. Recognizing the potential for working-class community organizing in the slums of Newark, Tom Hayden and SDS's Economic Research and Action Project (ERAP) moved into the city in 1964 to organize, much in the way that SNCC had in the South. By providing a left alternative to liberalism, the Newark ERAP project, dubbed the Newark Community Union Project (NCUP), hoped to challenge the Democratic machine politics of Mayor Hugh J. Addonizio and North Ward leader Anthony Imperiale, and to make Newark an example of how this kind of class-based organizing could encourage new leadership.

A city of 400,000 working people at the time, Newark had extraordinarily high rates of crime, maternal and infant mortality, tuberculosis, and venereal disease. A third of the housing was substandard. The unemployment rate was 15 percent and rising. Most importantly, the schools were in shambles. With one of the highest dropout rates in the nation, less than 10 percent of students achieved normal reading levels, and crime in the schools was rising. Worse still, the political establishment was so bankrupt that it preferred to appoint a white high school graduate as secretary of the Board of Education rather than an African American accountant with a master's degree. Leaders of the local CORE chapter were so incensed by the appointment that they took over the Board of Education meeting, but it only justified the anger of the reactionaries, while NCUP stood helplessly by. Hayden's project was running out of time in July of 1967 when the riot broke out.[22]

In five days of rioting, twenty-six people were killed, a thousand were

---

22  Hayden, *Reunion: A Memoir* pp. 114–32, 151–64; F. R. Harris, T. Wicker, comp., *The Kerner Commission Report: The 1968 Report of the National Advisory Commission on Civil Disorders* (Washington, DC: GPO, 1968), p. 60.

injured, fourteen hundred were arrested, and $16 million worth of property went up in flames. It took six thousand police, state troopers, and national guardsmen from two city armories to quell the storm. In Hayden's own words: "It was an urban Vietnam." Out of this cauldron came an uncanny alliance between Anthony Imperiale, the vigilante North Ward leader and racist nemesis of NCUP, and Amiri Baraka (formerly LeRoi Jones), the urban poet and playwright who was arrested during the riot for carrying guns. Both appeared on a radio show blaming the "so-called radical groups" for the city's problems. Imperiale and Jones established a "hotline" with each other so that they could patrol their own neighborhoods in case of racial trouble. The government offered them funding for "local police patrols" in the city, a way to arm the racial divide that Hayden and his group had hoped to avoid. The rhetoric of violence combined with the politics of separatism to transform Newark into an armed camp. Hayden left the city in despair, but Jones claimed his hometown as something that would now become a black city, representing the black majority, with a black mayor and a black Board of Education. Although it took him another three years to do it, Jones would now lead the Black Power movement, and the conflict in Newark would make Ocean Hill-Brownsville look like a picnic.[23]

The teachers union in Newark had been lead largely by an Irish Italian group that had benefited from the rising power of their New York City compatriots. They had won a new contract after their successful 1966 strike, but the New Jersey anti-strike laws meant one year of probation for thirty-one teachers and bankruptcy for the local. But in 1968, a new union alliance was formed under the leadership of Carole Graves, the first African American to head the union and one of the most important African Americans in the AFT. Meanwhile, Amiri Baraka formed a coalition of politicos that very explicitly meant to take over the city; in fact, during the King riots, Baraka assured reporters that there would be no riots in his town, as vigilante groups roamed the streets. "We've come to the conclusion that the city is ours anyway, that we can take it with ballots," he said. The teachers union was one of the last integrated groups left in the city.[24]

Even as 200,000 students missed the first day of classes in the fall of 1969 due to teachers' strikes in other cities, the Newark teachers were hoping for a settlement. They finally struck on February 3, 1970, and although their strike was 90 percent effective, the opposition was strong. Baraka

23 "Mayor Convenes New Peace Talks in School Strike," *New York Times*, September 29, 1968, p. 1, 78; Hayden, *Reunion: A Memoir*, p. 160. Harris, Wicker, comp., *The Kerner Commission Report*, pp. 60–9.
24 L. Buder, "Pressure by Boycott for Local Control," *New York Times*, April 14, 1968, p. E13; S. Golin, *The Newark Teacher Strikes: Hopes on the Line* (New Brunswick, NJ: Rutgers University Press, 2002).

conducted meetings throughout the South and Central Wards urging the black community to take over the schools. He argued that the teachers' fear of school violence was racist, that the teachers' demands for salary raises and release time for school preparation were attempts to evade the children who needed them. Three union leaders were arrested a few days later: Carole Graves, head of Local 481; Frank Fiorito, the executive vice president; and Donald Nicholas, a member of the union executive board. By the end of the week, thirty-nine teachers had gone to jail, and by the next week the number had risen to ninety-one. When the three-week strike ended, many teachers faced exorbitant fines and jail. The union victory had been bitter.[25]

That spring, the mayor, Hugh J. Addonizio, was under indictment for corruption, and a new face, Kenneth A. Gibson, emerged in urban politics to challenge the incumbent in a run-off where "race is going to be the issue." Gibson was the first black mayor of an eastern seaboard city, and immediately upon becoming mayor he appointed three new members of the school board, two African Americans and one Puerto Rican community leader. Imamu Amiri Baraka immediately set up an experimental classroom at the Robert Treat School, a rundown building in the Central Ward, as part of the African Free School, a plan to change the nature of classroom teaching. The certified teacher and four aides were dressed in the colors and costumes of Africa (green turbans, long black skirts, and red beads). They were called "mamas" and taught "collectively," with Baraka frequently visiting the classroom and joining in the pledge of allegiance to the red, black, and green flag of black nationalism.

Critics accused Baraka of having too much power, claiming that he was running a regency under the Gibson administration where he and his coalition, Committee for a Unified Newark, dictated educational policy. Baraka denied it, saying, "I'm being painted as some kind of shadowy figure controlling the action behind the scenes, but this is not true." But his Africa Free School closely mirrored some of the same characteristics of the training given to black teachers in the Ocean Hill-Brownsville area, where he and H. Rap Brown, head of SNCC, had toured in the summer of 1967 and 1968 to promote self-determination in education. Unlike the situation in New York City, where the union was more powerful and the city less polarized, the Newark case was about to become far more violent and extreme in the next teachers' strike.[26]

---

25   Golin, *The Newark Teacher Strikes*, pp. 72–80; "23 Arrested at Newark March Held to Back Teachers' Strike," *New York Times*, February 14, 1970, p. 25; M. A. Farber, "Teachers Ratify Pact in Newark," *New York Times*, February 26, 1970, p. 1.

26   "Dr. King's Mural Sets Off Melee," *New York Times*, January 17, 1970, p. 32; R. McFadden, "George Washington High Results in Arrests of 13 Students," *NYT*, April 11, 1970, p. 33.

The 1970 Newark teachers contract ran only one year. As it expired in February 1971, the new Board of Education decided that if it did not negotiate at all, it would not have a teachers union and, hence, there could be no strike. Exposing the inanity of that logic, the teachers walked out. Then, when ordered to negotiate, the Board of Education announced that all union demands, including recognition, were on the table, and that they would roll back teacher gains to before the 1966 contract. That just prolonged the strike.

As the union executive board dispersed in front of its headquarters on the first evening of the strike, twenty-five men dressed in paramilitary uniforms, armed with baseball bats and knives, attacked the teachers. First they beat the men, then the women union leaders. Of the fifteen victims, five were treated at the hospital; one was kept overnight. As the strike went on, the violence continued. Teachers were attacked and beaten on picket lines; their cars were smashed and bombed. Carole Graves, the president of the union, had a bomb hurled into her home.[27] Though the paramilitary groups were never identified or brought to trial, they were most likely extreme black nationalists. Some observers attributed the violence to the newly organized Organization of Negro Educators (ONE), which went about the city trying to break the strike and whose members were seen in paramilitary outfits. Nevertheless, their president denied involvement. ONE, like other nationalist groups, condemned the strikers for abandoning the African American children of Newark.

The strike continued for ten weeks, and, while the labor movement embraced the teachers, the black community was split between two factions. Even the teachers were divided. ONE had members in the union. As Carole Graves insisted, "This is just a labor–management fight. Jesse Jacob [president of the school board] and Amiri Baraka interject this racial business because it's a good way to break the union and get control of the schools." Graves went to jail that spring for six months, and her temporary replacement was attacked while the struggle continued. After ten weeks of striking, mediation, and arbitration, the school board rejected a settlement in a raucous meeting and finally settled in the eleventh week.[28]

---

27  R. Johnson, "Teachers Beaten in Newark Strike; Group Attacks 15 Leaving Meeting," *New York Times*, February 3, 1971, p. 1, 41; R. Johnson, "Ocean Hill Fund Nearing Its End; Unrest Feared if Education Center Cannot Continue," *New York Times*, February 3, 1971, p. 41.

28  F. Butterfield, "Newark School Strike Splits Blacks," *New York Times*, February 14, 1971, p. 45; F. Butterfield, "Newark Teachers Reject Pack," *New York Times*, April 16, 1971.

## The End of Integration and Militancy

The tragedy of the Ocean Hill-Brownsville and Newark teachers' strikes was that one of the few institutions that had fought racial segregation in the union movement, the American Federation of Teachers (AFT), became the very symbol of that racism. The project of integration had belonged to the AFT. Its leaders included African American teachers trying to transform the labor movement as a whole. But these strikes destroyed that possibility by forcing the African American leaders out of the AFT, demoralizing African American teachers, and reinforcing the conservative Shanker leadership. Nationally, the integrationist movement was over, and the teachers union, especially in Newark, would suffer the consequences. "Perhaps the real tragedy of the strike is that it makes it look like reason and racial integration won't work in Newark. The teachers union, for all of its own militancy, is one of the very few really integrated organizations around here," a local Democratic Party leader concluded.[29]

Despite the bitterness it instilled, the racial divide did not end teacher militancy. Instead, economic crisis finally drew the era of teachers' strikes to a close. Again, developments in New York City were emblematic. In the fall of 1974, Mayor Abraham Beame announced a fiscal crisis in the city, when his budget for 1974–5 was running $420 million short, in part because the city had to spend 11 percent of its budget servicing its $11 billion debt, including $3.4 billion in short-term notes. Beame blamed his predecessor John Lindsay, whom he accused of negotiating overly generous contracts with more and more public workers unions. Albert Shanker, who had become president of the AFT and remained leader of the now statewide UFT, had a hard time coming to terms with the crisis. Two months after Beame's lament, he asked the city for $2.78 billion for school improvements. By January 1975, however, the Board of Education was cutting seven hundred jobs and forcing new economies on the teachers. The banks were asking for 9.5 percent interest on a $500 million loan, and city bonds were selling at two-thirds of face value. The causes were readily identified: the decay of the city center, white flight, unionization of public employees, expansion of social services, inflation, and the doldrums of the financial industry. But the unions took the brunt of the blame.[30]

At first the unions refused to budge, but as the commercial banks refused to lend money to the city, the fiscal crisis deepened and the unions were

---

29  F. Butterfield, "At Root of Newark Teacher Strike: Race and Power," *New York Times*, April 8, 1971, p. 50.

30  M. H. Maier, *City Unions: Managing Discontent in New York City* (New Brunswick, NJ: Rutgers University Press, 1987), pp. 170–86; Freeman, *Working Class New York*, pp. 256–87.

drawn into negotiations to save the city. All of the municipal unions agreed to defer contractual demands, giving up billions of dollars in benefits and offering their pension funds to capitalize the city. "In terms of going deep into the pocketbook," AFSCME head Jerry Wurf explained, "we did a hell of a lot more than any of the banks. Yet we still ended up the villains." Shanker claimed that education took the brunt of the cutbacks, "22 per cent cuts while other city services averaged about 11 per cent."[31] The teachers' disproportionate burden grew in part from Shanker's alienation from other New York municipal union leaders, especially AFSCME District Council 37 leader Victor Gotbaum, who did the bulk of the negotiating with the city and the banks. Shanker claimed that teachers relied on the state legislature, not the city, for school funding, but it was his hostility to Gotbaum and sanitation union leader John DeLury that kept him from participating in the negotiations until October 1975. The teachers also paid for the failure of their strike in September 1975.

Ostensibly, the strike protested the large class sizes and poor school conditions teachers faced on opening day. Schools had opened with a "lack of textbooks and desks, programs were in confusion, teacher assignments and reassignments went well into October." The real reason for the strike was the fiscal crisis and the Board of Education's demands for a new contract that would eliminate most of the gains teachers had made, especially those won in the late 1960s. Included in those gains was a limit on class size of thirty-two, now routinely violated as the Board of Education cut back the number of teachers while the number of students remained the same. The Board demanded an additional thirty minutes of teaching per day and cuts to preparation time. In a disingenuous move, the board offered to keep to the limits on class size if the teachers would give up their prep time, arguing that they were only asking to increase teacher productivity, as if preparation had nothing to do with quality in education. Some 55,000 teachers struck that September, but they found little support from other municipal unions, who viewed the teachers as selfish for not agreeing to the same cuts they had taken. Not surprisingly, many in the African American community also thought the teachers selfish, seeing the strike and its demands to protect preparation time as further evidence that the teachers did not care about their children.[32]

In the end, the teachers took the same cuts as the other municipal unions.

---

31  J. C. Gouldin, *Jerry Wurf: Labor's Last Angry Man* (New York: Simon and Schuster, 1982), pp. 235–40; "AFT Crisis Report," December 29, 1975, Box 11, Albert Shanker Collection, Walter Reuther Archives, Detroit.

32  "AFT Crisis Report," December 29, 1975, Box 11, Albert Shanker Collection, Walter Reuther Archives, Detroit.

The Board of Education saved between $4.5 and $5.5 million each of the eight days the teachers were out, but the city won much more. Teachers worked longer days, but the students' days were shortened by forty-five minutes. African American parents were furious. Teachers gave up two of their preparation hours weekly. Class sizes stayed the same. Still the teachers remained the villains. They hated the contract, but they swallowed it. Even worse, prompted by the fiscal crisis, the Board of Education made drastic cuts that reduced or eliminated guidance counselors, crossing guards, sports programs, adult education, and summer school. From 1974 to 1976, the teaching workforce shrunk by nearly 25 percent, with most of the layoffs hitting young teachers. African American and Spanish-surnamed teachers were also hurt, and their percentage in the teaching workforce shrank to 3 percent from 11 percent. The impact was dramatic. Morale plummeted and union strength ebbed. The teachers' days of militancy were over.[33]

## Dream Deferred

In remembering the heady days of teacher militancy during the late sixties and early seventies, it is easy to forget what was attempted while remembering who succeeded and who failed. In Memphis, the sanitation workers and the African American community built something significant with lasting implications. In other cities, African American municipal workers organized unions and brought civil rights struggles and labor struggles together. Community control was not always met with union hostility. Martin Luther King, Jr. recognized the significance of going on with the struggle. "Nothing would be more tragic than to stop at this point in Memphis," he said the day before he was shot. And it would only add to the tragic side of the story if we stopped analyzing school struggles yesterday or today.

Consider, for example, the fact that urban schools still suffer from terrible inequality, with suburban white children receiving well-funded public education while urban African American children attend badly funded charter (private) schools. The origins of school choice and its complement, privatization, go back to 1968. As African Americans demanded control over their schools, many conservative pundits and politicians quickly realized that such demands could be accommodated without much cost or

33 Freeman, *Working Class New York*, p. 271; "AFT Crisis Report," December 29, 1975, Box 11, Albert Shanker Collection, Walter Reuther Archives, Detroit; L. Buder, "Tally 10,651–6,695, Relatively Close Count Reflects Bitterness—2,400 to be Rehired," *New York Times*, September 17, 1975, p. 1; L. Dembart, "A Familiar Accord: Teacher's Settlement Parallels Those Other Unions Accepted Without Strikes," *New York Times*, September 17, 1975, p. 28.

inconvenience to their core constituents in the lily-white suburbs. Instead of busing to achieve integration, African Americans could control their neighborhood schools, which were doomed to underfunded status given the urban tax base. Suburban schools, meanwhile, would prosper free of the burden of educating the city's children. It is no coincidence that school choice and privatization are most often touted for urban schools, not the suburbs.

Consider, too, that African American leaders in the teachers unions were ready to lead their unions in a new direction. Many observers remember the names of LeRoi Jones and Sonny Carson; few remember that there were also leaders like Dick Parrish, Carole Graves, and William Simon in the AFT, who were real classroom teachers fighting to reform the schools and the union they helped build. The narrative of teacher militancy is a complex one, but it helps to explain how public employee unionism in this period cannot be separated from the urban rebellion, and how the inability of the two to come together played a key role in breaking apart the labor–civil rights coalition King dreamed about.

# 9

# Rank-and-File Struggles at the Telephone Company

## Aaron Brenner

The struggles of rank-and-file workers at American Telephone and Telegraph (AT&T) in the late 1960s and early 1970s were part of the national, and even international, wave of working-class militancy that characterized the period.[1] In the United States, this widespread militancy had its roots in the economic dislocations of the 1960s and 1970s. Economic adversity, which took different forms as the period proceeded, produced an employers' offensive in which companies sought to maintain or restore their profitability by attacking workers' wages, benefits, working conditions, and job control. This offensive ignited a response by workers that grew increasingly militant and angry. But if the employers' offensive stoked the flames of rank-and-file rebellion, rising expectations and confidence gained over two decades of prosperity made the workers combustible. Then, the period's social movements and the workplace radicals they produced provided kindling for the blaze. And finally, ineffective union leadership just threw fuel on the fire. The result was not just one of the country's largest and longest strike waves; the combination of employers' offensive and ineffective union leadership produced rank-and-file organizations that mobilized collective action against employers on the job *and* mounted political challenges to incumbent union officials. In the end, however, rank-and-file militancy fizzled, undermined by rising unemployment, more determined employer and union opposition, splintering social movements, and simple exhaustion.

The rank-and-file struggles at the telephone company exhibited virtually every aspect of this national pattern of militancy. After rapid postwar growth, AT&T faced a productivity challenge in the late 1960s. Though its

---

[1]  On the breadth and character of the militancy in the United States, see A. Brenner, "Rank-and-File-Rebellion, 1966–1975," (PhD Diss., Columbia University, 1996), chapter 1.

problems never matched the profitability crisis suffered by manufacturers, the advent of competition, rising inflation, higher interest rates, and the growing hostility of state and federal regulators impelled the company to hold down costs at a time when demand for its products and services required the investment of billions of dollars in new equipment and labor. Bell System managers initiated an increasingly coherent set of policies to reduce expenses and meet demand. Their new approach undermined the workplace prerogatives and living standards of telephone employees, especially the plant workers who installed and maintained the phones, cables, and switches that constituted the phone system.

These mostly white and male workers had developed considerable power on the job and, with their union, the Communications Workers of America (CWA), had won rising wages and benefits over the postwar decades. Increasingly, younger African American and Latino men and women joined these more experienced craftsmen, and female operators, working on the poles, "frames," and switchboards of the phone system. These workers brought with them the general rebelliousness of the period and specific experiences in the antiwar, student, civil rights, Black Power, and women's movements. Together and apart, these groups of workers fought to protect their job rights and maintain their incomes in the face of inflation. Continuing demand for their labor bolstered their confidence. In many cases, CWA aided their struggles with aggressive action in collective bargaining, contract enforcement, and workplace organization. But the union's long-term inability to mount sufficient opposition to management's offensive sparked the emergence of local rank-and-file groups seeking to organize their own job actions and to challenge the union leadership.

Confined to a largely marginal existence in the face of company and union opposition, these groups found their greatest influence during a seven-month strike at New York Telephone in 1971–2. Along with other union dissidents, they were unable, however, to prevent the strike from becoming a decisive defeat that severely constrained effective opposition to management control over the labor process at AT&T. The strike was not a total disaster, however. It led to national bargaining for the first time, giving the national union much more bargaining power. Additionally, the strike experience unified one of the most important CWA locals in the country, making it much more effective in protecting workers' rights and improving their wages and benefits. A few rank-and-file activists maintained their organization and continued to push the union toward more militancy, but over time they either integrated into the union apparatus or joined the ranks of the apathetic.

## Workplace Power

When Charles Corris first went to work at the New Jersey Bell Telephone Company in 1966, he was an "outside plant" worker, laying and splicing cables, operating heavy machinery, and installing telephone equipment. He helped lay cables under the Delaware River and contributed to other major communications projects all over southern New Jersey. Young and recently out of the Navy, Corris liked the work and his workmates. "It was kind of a man's outfit," he recalled nearly thirty years later. "It was exclusively male . . . The men were strong and strong-minded and it was great. It was great for me. I enjoyed it as a young guy. I liked the camaraderie." He also enjoyed the freedom he and his fellow workers had on the job.

> They [the supervisors] allowed us to work at our own speed, which was maybe four times as fast as they expected, and then if we were finished with our work they didn't bother us. They allowed us to relax because we were turning in four times the amount of required work points that they wanted. We knew how to do the job really fast and safe, and correctly, too.[2]

Two years later, Corris moved to New York City, where he landed a job with AT&T in the Long Lines Department. There he worked "inside," maintaining telephone switching equipment at the company's office at 811 Tenth Avenue in Manhattan. Though the building had twenty stories, it had no windows, and "no matter how many cheap prints they hung on the walls," Corris felt like he was "working in a basement." Stuck inside and working under closer supervision, he still enjoyed the job for many of the same reasons. He liked the technical nature of it, he got along with his workmates, and he continued to control the pace and method of his work.[3]

Into the late 1960s, plant workers all over the Bell System enjoyed a level of freedom on their jobs like that of Charles Corris. Many held jobs that took them away from company offices and beyond the reach of management control. Outside plant workers, such as linemen and splicers, worked alone or in small crews, underground in manholes and aboveground on telephone poles, installing and maintaining phone cables and remote equipment. Installers and repairmen performed similar tasks, but on the cable and equipment at customer sites. Either way, they were on their own for most of their working day. "In my job they pretty much did leave you

---

2    Charles Corris, interview with the author, October 28, 1994, New York, NY.
3    Ibid.

alone," remembered Brent Kramer, a repairman who started at New York Telephone in 1970. "You'd get a bunch of repair orders and you'd just go do them. Presumably as quickly as you could, but in fact no one was looking over your shoulder, unless you tried to break their chops."[4]

By contrast, inside plant craftsmen, who worked under direct supervision, had to rely on other means to establish their job control. These framemen and switching technicians worked in the Bell System's myriad central offices, maintaining the complex of metal, cable, and machinery that performed the switching functions of the phone network. Their work involved thousands of intricate splices, circuits, and switches that required close attention and continual ingenuity. The electro-mechanical equipment required so much care and underwent so many repairs that only the craftsmen who nursed it from day to day truly understood every detail of its operation. This knowledge came only from experience with the system, and from discussion with fellow workers, not from formal company training or supervisors, as Corris discovered when he arrived at 811 Tenth Avenue: "The old guys were cranky but knowledgeable, and they had a lot to tell and a lot to teach, and in the old days we were proud of the tradition of teaching each other and helping each other. But the way the company acts and the way that they behave, they devalued what we knew and they insisted on teaching their way, which really didn't give you the experience that you needed. You didn't get right down to the wire, so to speak. It was a lot of theoretical stuff that really wasn't practical."[5]

Plant workers exploited their knowledge of the phone system to control the pace and method of their work. Despite the company's imperious attitude toward its workers' skills, supervisors had no choice but to defer to the judgment of their subordinates for the simple reason that they usually knew more about the job. And plant workers took advantage. One middle manager who began work as a frameman at New York Telephone in the 1960s described just how much power they exercised: "The craftsman for the most part ran the job. If I was a frameman today and behaved like that, *I'd fire me*. Things were routinely done that were unacceptable. Craftsmen'd look at a job and say, 'That's overtime.' So they'd go slow during the day and finish the job on time and a half."[6]

Plant workers' job control had a relatively brief history, made possible by unionization in the late 1940s and the rapid growth of the phone company thereafter. During the 1950s and early 1960s, AT&T

---

4  Brent Kramer, interview with the author, November 22, 1994, Brooklyn, NY.
5  Corris, interview with the author.
6  S. P. Vallas, *Power in the Workplace: The Politics of Production at AT&T* (Albany: SUNY Press, 1993), p. 105.

introduced its new electro-mechanical switching equipment. To handle the installation, maintenance, and repair of the new switches, the company had to hire more plant workers. From 124,000 in 1950, the number of craftsmen at AT&T grew to 163,000 in 1960, and nearly 280,000 in 1980.[7] Protected against unemployment by the corporation's growing demand for their labor, plant workers enjoyed more room to challenge management. Meanwhile, prosperity reduced the company's incentive to fight. Workers developed the confidence to resist the company's long-practiced twin labor-relations strategies of scientific management and paternalism. They used the organization of plant work and the nature of plant technology to forge control over the pace and methods of work. The union then enhanced and safeguarded that power. The CWA won contractual guarantees, such as seniority rights, which limited the power of management, and it organized a steward system and instituted grievance procedures that protected workers from arbitrary or vindictive supervision. Plant workers rewarded the union by becoming the backbone of its support and using their job control to make the union effective on the shop floor. The union's power and plant workers' job control mutually reinforced one another, and the two expanded quickly in the hothouse atmosphere of corporate prosperity.[8]

In contrast, telephone operators, who were exclusively women under management policy, had lost most of their job control before the turn of the twentieth century. Managers (both male and female) in the "traffic" department dictated every aspect of their job, including the words they uttered, how fast they processed calls, how they sat at their switchboards, what movements they made, when they visited the toilet, and which shifts they worked. To make matters worse, while AT&T was hiring plant workers, it was laying off operators. From a peak of about 185,000 in the early 1950s, the number of operators fell to 120,000 in the early 1960s, when the pace of decline slowed, leaving 100,000 operators in 1980. The CWA did nothing to stop the loss of operator jobs, though it did try to protect the rights of operators who remained. According to one operator with twenty-one years on the job in the 1950s, "Well, [the union] got us better working conditions . . . The supervisors are not allowed to yell at the girls like they used to be able to do. They used to tell the girls off, but now a girl has a right to turn around and tell her, and if she is dissatisfied she can go to the union

---

7 Ibid., pp. 99–100.
8 On the history of labor relations at AT&T, see Vallas, *Power in the Workplace*; S. Norwood, *Labor's Flaming Youth: Telephone Workers and Worker Militancy, 1878–1923* (Urbana: University of Illinois Press, 1989); T. R. Brooks, *Communications Workers of America: The Story of a Union* (New York: Mason/Charter Press, 1977).

and complain about it, and the union will make an adjustment."[9] Despite the union's efforts, operators remained second-class citizens within the union. In part, this reflected the difficulties of organizing them, since they did not have the same job power as the plant workers. The union did not win a union security clause until the 1970s, and a higher portion of operators, especially in New York City, remained outside the CWA. Equally important was the sexism and craft-bias of the union. CWA leaders were mostly male plant workers, and they put their interests before those of the operators.[10]

This division between traffic and plant workers persisted into the 1980s, and it proved to be one of the weaknesses the company could exploit as it sought to recapture control of the workplace from plant workers in the late 1960s and early 1970s.

## Ma Bell's Meltdown

In the spring and summer of 1969, the New York Telephone Company faced a severe service crisis. The company could not deliver the most basic phone service of all: a dial tone. It was not unusual for a telephone customer in New York City to pick up the receiver and hear silence, even after a wait of several minutes. Customers also had trouble completing calls, receiving directory assistance, and reaching a long-distance operator. False busy signals were common. Installation and repair was backed up for weeks, in some cases months.

The erosion of basic phone service led businesses to complain. Some quit paying their bills, and others took out full-page advertisements in the *New York Times* to protest the deterioration of service.[11] Residential customers also suffered from New York Telephone's service problems, and they took their complaints to the state's Public Service Commission (PSC). The Commission received 4,317 complaints from New York City during the first two hundred days of 1969, up from 1,316 during the same period in 1968, and 1,047 in 1967. Complaints upstate increased, too, some 200 percent.[12] Politicians joined the parade of witnesses before PSC hearings

---

9    Quoted in Brooks, *Communications Workers*, pp. 194–5.
10    Catherine Conroy, interviewed by Elizabeth Balanoff, The Twentieth Century Trade Union Woman Oral History Project, Institute of Labor and Industrial Relations, University of Michigan-Wayne State University, 1976; V. Green, "The Impact of Technology Upon Women's Work in the Telephone Industry, 1880–1980," (PhD Diss., Columbia University, 1990); Brooks, *Communications Workers*, pp. 166–7.
11    See, for example, E. Perlmutter, "Dial-Tone Delays Reported in City," *New York Times*, April 10, 1969, p. 34; G. Smith, "Two 'PL8' Customers Use Other Means to Signal Their Anger Over 'Busies,'" *New York Times*, July 14, 1969, p. 22; Advertisement by Association of Telephone Answering Services, *New York Times*, July 23, 1969, p. 28.
12    T. Brady, "Witnesses Score Phone Rate Rise," *New York Times*, August 22, 1969, p.

and threatened to turn New York Telephone's service problems into a corporate financial disaster by halting the company's rate increases.[13]

AT&T management faced additional problems beyond those at New York Telephone. Citing service failures in New York, Florida, and elsewhere, the FCC launched an investigation seeking information on the status of service nationwide. Around the country, state public service commissions followed the FCC's lead, which threatened to make it harder for AT&T and its operating companies to win rate increases.[14] Perhaps more frightening was the increased competition AT&T faced. Independent telephone companies were putting in new phones and reaping revenue growth at a faster rate than AT&T. In the telephone equipment market, AT&T's Western Electric faced a new wave of competition after the FCC's 1968 Carterfone decision allowing Bell System customers to attach non-AT&T equipment to their phone lines. These developments, and rumblings in Washington, convinced top AT&T management that the company would face stiffer competition throughout its businesses in the future.[15]

Whether or not the Bell System could compete in new markets, it was also having difficulty in the old ones. Economy-wide developments, including inflation, slowing growth rates, rising interest rates, and higher taxes, began to hurt the company's profit picture. From 1969 to 1971, earnings per share at the company remained stagnant at four dollars and "showed no signs of breaking out of a pattern of stagnation at that level." Rising interest rates were particularly troublesome for a company borrowing billions to finance the expansion it desperately needed to keep up with demand. Even though AT&T's debt ratio was quite low, and even though it financed a considerable portion of its expansion from retained earnings, the higher cost of expansion capital cut into its earnings. In turn, stagnant earnings made it harder to attract low-cost capital, catching the company in a vicious circle. New York Telephone exemplified this problem when its interest bill rose 37 percent in 1969, while its return on capital fell from 7.1 percent to 6.2 percent.[16]

---

32; P. Millones, "P.S.C. to Investigate Phone Service, Too," *New York Times*, August 7, 1969, p. 1; see also R. Phalon, "P.S.C. To 'Consider' 10.4% Phone Rise," *New York Times*, March 2, 1970, p. 1.

13  D. Bird, "City Aide Would Cut Bill If a Phone Fails," *New York Times*, August 16, 1969, p. 1; "Nickerson Appeals for Action by State Over Phone Service," *New York Times*, July 19, 1969, p. 27.

14  R. L. Madden, "F.C.C. Seeks Data on Phone Service," *New York Times*, August 16, 1969, p. 1. Quote from "Why You Hear a Busy Signal at AT&T"; A. von Auw, *Heritage and Destiny: Reflections on the Bell System in Transition* (New York: Praeger, 1983).

15  G. Smith, "'Ma Bell' and Children Pressing Rates Rises," *New York Times*, April 13, 1969, III, p. 1; Von Auw, *Heritage and Destiny*, Part Two; AT&T 1968 Annual Report, p. 7.

16  Von Auw, *Heritage and Destiny*, p. 11. See also "Long Lines Management Report," AT&T Long Lines Department, June 29, 1971, Box 14, Folder 11, Communications

Bell System managers responded to their dilemma in logical fashion. Though never coherently expressed as such, their efforts eventually coalesced into a two-pronged agenda. First, they invested huge sums in the physical expansion of the telephone system, paying billions of dollars for the installation of more equipment and the employment of thousands of new workers. Second, they extended their control over wages and the work process by introducing new technology, increasing their supervision of workers, and more strenuously resisting union demands. Ultimately, both strategies worked, but only after AT&T managers defeated the workers' rebellion their actions provoked.

### Winning Grievances with Strikes

On Friday, January 19, 1968, operators in AT&T's Long Lines Department in New York City walked off their jobs to attend a "twenty-four-hour union meeting" at St. Alphonsus Hall in Manhattan. At the meeting, called by CWA Local 1150, "the girls unanimously voted to strike for their rights—700 strong," and immediately set up picket lines which were "manned around the clock by the girls," according to the local's leaflets. The following day, four thousand telephone workers joined the strike as technicians from the Long Lines plant section, Western Electric installers, and New York Telephone technicians honored the operators' picket lines at three Manhattan locations. Managers in the Long Lines Department traffic section had provoked the work stoppage when they unilaterally, and in violation of seniority, switched several operators from their "basic tours" on the night shift to the day shift in order to train them to fill out "mark sense tickets" (new telephone call logs). The operators, many of whom had scheduled childcare and other family commitments around their basic tours, opposed the shift changes. They also had other grievances, but as one union leaflet put it, "this is the issue that has brought to a head the plight of the over-worked and under-paid operators." The strike lasted four days, until the two sides agreed to submit the shift dispute to arbitration.[17]

The operators' strike was a small example of the many conflicts created by the Bell System's management strategies during the late 1960s and early 1970s. Seeking to increase productivity through the introduction of new

---

Workers of America, Local 1150 Collection, Robert F. Wagner Labor Archives, Tamiment Library, New York University (hereafter CWA 1150).

17 "Emergency Traffic Meeting," leaflet, January 18, 1968; "Attention All Traffic Employees," leaflet, January 19, 1968; "An Invitation From Local 1150," leaflet, n.d.; "To All Local 1150 Members," leaflet, January 22, 1968; all in CWA 1150, Box 2, Folder 9; "Local 1150 Newsletter," January 24, 1968, CWA 1150, Box 15, Folder 9; "Phone Operators Stage a Walkout," *New York Times*, January 21, 1968, p. 60; "Operators End 4-Day Strike Against Telephone Company," *New York Times*, January 24, 1968, p. 55.

technology, in this case mark sense tickets, and through the reorganization of work, in this case training and shift changes, managers ran roughshod over the prerogatives and expectations telephone workers had acquired over the previous twenty years, in this case seniority-based scheduling. Virtually all of the conflicts in this period followed the same logic. Pressed to meet the challenges of rising costs and growing demand, managers implemented changes that adversely affected most areas of telephone workers' employment. Confident from past success, taking advantage of the demand for their labor, and well-organized at the workplace, workers fought back.

Even before its service problems had become a topic of public debate, the Bell System embarked on an enormous building campaign to expand the capacity of the telephone network. Bell spent over $4.3 billion on construction in 1967, $4.7 billion in 1968, and over $6 billion in 1970. At New York Telephone, the pace of expansion was frantic.[18] Desperate, the company requested the service of fifteen hundred telephone technicians from other companies in the Bell System. These workers, on top of the three thousand technicians hired over the previous year, would supplement the 23,000 technicians already working in the New York City area.[19]

The service crisis, the expansion program, and the arrival of out-of-state workers created an atmosphere of urgency throughout phone operations in New York City. Operators and plant craftsmen felt the pressure and responded.[20] In the plant department, supervisors desperate to finish their projects often ordered forced overtime, leading to several walkouts. Though many workers wanted *voluntary* overtime because they earned extra money, they deeply resented *forced* overtime. Under the contract, however, managers could order forced overtime as long as they provided advance notification. In their rush, many supervisors waited too long. Charles Corris and two other AT&T Long Lines technicians received word from their supervisor at 4:00 p.m. one Friday afternoon that they would have to work overtime that night. When they refused they were suspended, causing the rest of the building to walk out. The following Monday when they returned to work, all but the original three workers were suspended for the day. That sparked a local-wide strike of CWA Local 1150 that lasted several days before management finally agreed to reverse the suspensions.[21] A

---

18  AT&T Annual Reports, 1968, 1970; advertisement by NY Telephone, *New York Times*, July 23, 1969, p. 24; S. Fox, "Phone Aides See No Relief in Sight," *New York Times*, July 29, 1969, p. 43.

19  W. Borders, "1,500 Phone Men Being Sent Here," *New York Times*, July 28, 1969, p. 1.

20  "Overseas Phone Operators End Wildcat Strike Here," *New York Times*, June 29, 1969, p. 17. See also "Traffic Section Walkout," handwritten notes, June 26, 1969; Stewards Grievance Form, June 25, 1969; and "Local 1150 Newsletter," June 30, 1969, all in CWA 1150, Box 15, Folder 10.

21  Corris, interview.

similar strike occurred when Richard Ranzall, a shop steward at New York Telephone's central office at 228 East 56th Street, refused forced overtime and received a suspension. Seven hundred fellow workers walked out until the union, CWA Local 1101, negotiated his reinstatement.[22]

The success of wildcats and quickie strikes bred confidence in workers and led to more and bigger walkouts. Nevertheless, management was determined to impose its will. Discussing the situation many years later, New York Telephone's director of labor relations at the time confirmed that management's attitude reflected an attempt to take back shop-floor power lost to workers in previous years: "Management said, 'We're not gonna stand for this. We can't continue down this path. *We're* gonna run this business!' There was a strong anti-union feeling at the time, a feeling that the workers were taking advantage of us."[23]

Bell managers took a similar attitude at the negotiating table, where they strenuously resisted workers' rising wage and benefit demands. The result was a series of national and regional strikes that pitted management's cost-containment goals against workers' efforts to stay ahead of inflation and reap the rewards of productivity improvement. The disputes included the first national telephone strike in twenty-one years in the spring of 1968, and another national strike three years later. In between, several significant local strikes took place, including a couple at New York Telephone. But the strikes did not resolve the essential conflict.[24] Wages continued to fall behind inflation and profits continued to stagnate, especially during the 1970 recession. Both sides became increasingly frustrated. At New York Telephone, managers accelerated their productivity drive. And in response, the workers introduced a new weapon of resistance: the rank-and-file organization.

### Wringing Ma's Bell

*Strike Back!*, volume one, number one, appeared on December 21, 1970. Consisting of only two pages and four articles, the broadsheet nonetheless put forward a program for the Bell Workers Action Committee (BWAC), a recently formed group of rank-and-file telephone workers from the various units of the Bell System in New York City. Though the first issue listed several complaints about the corporation, including its disregard for

---

22   "700 Phone Workers Protest Suspension of a Union Aide," *New York Times*, January 29, 1970, p. 41.
23   Vallas, *Power in the Workplace*, 110; CWA Job Pressures Study Committee, Local President Survey, March 1969, CWA 1150, Box 17, Folder 29.
24   These strikes are described in Brenner, "Rank-and-File Rebellion," pp. 183–93.

workers' safety, its dictatorial workplace control programs, and its sexual and racial discrimination, much of the newspaper concentrated on a critique of the unions that represented telephone workers. As the BWAC saw it, "The problem at N.Y. Tel (AT&T) is that we don't have a union to fight for our interests and defend us from the crap the company hands down." The Communications Workers of America (CWA), the Telephone Traffic Union (TTU), and the United Telephone Workers (UTW) were not "real" unions because: "a real union isn't white shirts sitting in cushy offices telling us, the workers, what to do from outside"; a real union "does not sell out the majority of workers for some privileges for a minority"; and real unions are not "dominated by company collaborators" who "always put personal security ahead of the security of all workers, personal gain ahead of real unity."[25]

To illustrate its argument, the BWAC cited a recent Equal Employment Opportunity Commission filing with the FCC that charged AT&T with "pervasive, system-wide and blatantly unlawful discrimination." The group asked, "Why was it an *outside* government agency that had to blow the whistle on Ma Bell? Why haven't any of 'our' unions attacked AT&T and its N.Y. puppets N.Y. Tel and Western Electric?" The paper also discussed a wildcat strike by New York Telephone operators, criticizing their union, the TTU, for doing nothing to aid them, and the CWA for ordering its workers to cross their picket lines. Another short article criticized the CWA for not acting fast enough to prevent the dismissal of a ten-year veteran caught sleeping on the job. Luckily, according to the BWAC, a wildcat by his fellow workers saved his job in a matter of minutes. Other targets of the BWAC's critique were the union's "no strike" clause and its grievance procedure, which meant that "the company and the union are together *making us work* no matter how bad things get."

The BWAC finished its first issue of *Strike Back!* by describing the organization it hoped to build: "A real union never leaves the workplace. It never stops fighting for all the workers all the time . . . A union is an organization of workers that fights the company by any means necessary— slowdowns, overtime bans, work stoppages, strikes, plant takeovers, pulling people together, exposing BAD the company is doing, keeping everyone informed. We want to build a union like that. So we can say we stick with our sisters and our brothers even if they work in a different job or even a different company or even if they live in a different part of the world."[26]

---

25  "No Union," "Racist-Sexist Profit," and "Leaking Gas," *Strike Back!* 1:1 (December 21, 1970) Brent Kramer Collection.
26  "Racist-Sexist Profit," "Our Power," and "No Union."

Telephone workers in New York City built several rank-and-file organizations similar to the Bell Workers Action Committee during the late 1960s and early 1970s.[27] With names like Telephone Revolutionary Union Movement, New York Telephone Worker, Final Warning, and United Action, these groups, like the BWAC, arose from the combination of two simultaneous developments. On the one hand, they filled a vacuum created by the inability of existing telephone unions to mount adequate resistance to the Bell System's productivity drive. Made up of workers frustrated with the conditions at work and angry at the union leadership, they encouraged rank-and-file telephone employees to organize resistance on the shop floor and to mount political challenges within the union. On the other hand, the groups were also a product of changes among telephone workers. As the Bell System hired tens of thousands of new employees to facilitate its expansion efforts and cope with a very high quit rate, the workforce grew increasingly younger and contained a larger proportion of African American workers, especially in urban centers like New York City. These workers brought different experiences, expectations, and agendas to the job, and provided the backbone of support for rank-and-file groups.

In the mid-1960s, less than half the operators at New York Telephone in New York City were African American or Puerto Rican. By 1970, more than 80 percent were. Demographic trends, including marriage rates and suburbanization, may have played a role in this transformation, since white women who got married or moved out of the city often left their telephone jobs. But this doesn't explain why the company didn't hire more white women to replace them. Instead, the answer lies in the racial structure of the female labor market in New York City and the personnel policies of the New York Telephone company. The company paid its operators very low wages, for which white women increasingly refused to work. Unlike African American and Puerto Rican women, they could get higher paying jobs elsewhere. As Venus Green, a former telephone technician and writer of telephone labor history, has shown, New York Telephone clearly understood that it could pay African American and Puerto Rican operators less than white operators, and so the company consciously structured its wages and hiring procedures accordingly. By 1969, nine out of ten operators hired in New York City were African Americans. And since 80 percent of New York Telephone's African American workers were women, the company's rigid gender division of labor also translated into a rigid racial

---

27    Note that rank-and-file groups also sprung up in Los Angeles and the San Francisco Bay Area. See "The Bell Wringer," CWA 1101 TF—Bell Wringer; Militant Action Report, Yellow Pages, CWA 1101 TF—Rank and File Activity.

division of labor. The plant workforce was not only 99 percent male, but it remained predominantly white.[28]

The second alteration in the telephone workforce in the late 1960s was less dramatic, but nonetheless significant. No available statistics document the change, but anecdotal evidence makes it clear that the proportion of younger workers grew considerably at the Bell System. New York Telephone experienced very high turnover rates during the period, 68 percent among operators and 40 percent among craftsmen, meaning a large proportion of the workforce was new to the job and therefore more likely to be young. The crash expansion program, which brought thousands of new workers, also reinforced this trend toward youth. Joe Dunne, then assistant to the CWA Long Lines National Director, described the situation among the workers in his department, a large proportion of whom worked in New York City. "In Long Lines right now, for example, we've got fifty-three percent of the people who are what they call 'progression'; and that means that they have under five years' service, so they are young. The telephone company hires young. Anywhere from eighteen years old, or seventeen, if he graduates from high school, and almost the cut-off point [is] if you're over twenty-three or twenty-four. So we have a tremendous amount of young people." The often-raised demand for shorter progression schedules further suggests the growing influence of young workers, as they would have been the most likely beneficiaries of any acceleration along the road to top pay.[29]

The influx of African American workers and young workers constituted a significant challenge for the union, and officials worried about their ability to meet the needs of these new members. Joe Dunne said, "I think we're going to really face some challenges because the whole group of telephone people are changing today. We have a large influx into almost what was a lily-white company, of blacks and minority groups, not only blacks but

---

28  L. Van Gelder, "Information Operators Learn About City," *New York Times*, December 6, 1970, p. 16A; C. Lydon, "Job Bias at Bell Charged by Panel," *New York Times*, December 2, 1971, p. 1; L. Ledbetter, "Witness Ties Proposed Move of Bell System Offices to Bias," *New York Times*, May 13, 1972, p. 62; Green, "The Impact of Technology Upon Women's Work in the Telephone Industry," chapter 11; CWA-University of Iowa Oral History Project, interview by John Schacht with George Miller, August 6, 1969 and July 7, 1970. See also Vallas, *Power in the Workplace*, pp. 90–3; Rose Veviaka, "How Pa Bell Oppresses Women," *Workers' Power*, December 24, 1971–January 20, 1972, p. 8.

29  CWA Local 1101, untitled leaflet, n.d., CWA 1150, Box 15, Folder 12; CWA Local 1150 Telephone Tape Transcript, March 25, 1969; Box 20, Folder 2; Van Gelder, "Information Operators"; Lydon, "Job Bias"; W. Greene, "Can Ma Bell Really Be Sexist?" *New York Times*, December 5, 1971, IV, p. 3; CWA-University of Iowa Oral History Project, interview by John Schacht with Joe Dunne, Assistant to CWA Long Lines National Director, May 19 and 21, 1970.

Mexican Americans, some Indians, Spanish Americans; and you can see a rapid change. We are also getting the people who are no longer going along with the establishment, so I guess we're caught, like with everyone else, and I'm afraid that if we don't watch it, we're not going to keep up with this situation." The situation was particularly tense in New York City, according to George Miller, CWA District One vice president. "New York is a powder keg, and while we're supposed to be liberal in the East, I think there's really more hidden animosity than there is in the South, and it's very bitter animosity among some of the people in New York."[30]

Given the racial, sexual, and generational divisions among telephone workers, and given that white male workers dominated the Communications Workers of America, the major union, it is not surprising that young, African American, and female telephone workers made up the bulk, though not the entirety, of the membership of the rank-and-file groups. The racial and gender inequalities at the company and in the union provided one focal point for their activity. These issues were public news as the company came under a series of attacks from the Equal Employment Opportunity Commission for its discrimination against women and minority workers. Complaints against AT&T constituted 7 percent of the EEOC's total, though the corporation accounted for only 1 percent of the nation's employment. These figures and a long investigation led the EEOC to conclude that AT&T is "without doubt the largest oppresser [sic] of women in the United States," and that it relegated its black workers to "the lowest paying, least desirable jobs." Making matters worse, as the BWAC had pointed out, the CWA had done little to change this state of affairs, and when AT&T and the EEOC finally came to an agreement under which the company would implement an affirmative action plan, the union opposed the consent decree in court. These facts, combined with the period's mobilizations of women and African Americans for equal rights, kept the question of gender and racial equity at the Bell System in the forefront of many telephone workers' minds. Many of these workers gravitated to telephone rank-and-file organizations.[31]

---

30  CWA-University of Iowa Oral History Project, interview by John Schacht with Joe Dunne; CWA-University of Iowa Oral History Project, interview by John Schacht with George Miller. See also CWA-University of Iowa Oral History Project, interview by John Schacht with Richard Hackler, Assistant to the President of CWA, October 4, 1971.
31  P. Delany, "U.S. Agency, Charging Job Bias, Opposes Rate Rise for A.T.&T.," *New York Times*, December 11, 1970, p. 1; Greene, "Can Ma Bell Really Be Sexist?"; Green, "The Impact of Technology Upon Women's Work in the Telephone Industry," chapter 11. See also H. R. Northrup and J. A. Larson, *The Impact of the AT&T-EEOC Consent Decree* (Philadelphia: University of Pennsylvania Press, 1979).

The two most successful telephone rank-and-file groups, the Bell Workers Action Committee and United Action, made their opposition to discrimination an important part of their agenda. Another group, the Telephone Revolutionary Union Movement (TELRUM), made discrimination its central focus. Modeled after the Revolutionary Union Movement organizations formed by auto workers in the late 1960s in Detroit, New Jersey, and Oakland, TELRUM espoused the ideas of black and third-world nationalism and concentrated its energies on eliminating racist and sexist discrimination on the job and in the union. To that end, it tried to build an "independent struggle with a militant and revolutionary direction that fully represents the interests of Third World workers." Never well organized, TELRUM had trouble attracting telephone workers and lasted only a few months. Nevertheless, TELRUM provided one example of how the influx of African American workers and the influence of ideas from other struggles of African Americans stimulated the formation of telephone rank-and-file organization.[32]

In similar fashion, the BWAC and United Action were influenced by the ideas and experiences other young, African American, and female workers brought to their employment in the Bell System. Brent Kramer worked with both groups after getting a job as a repairman at New York Telephone in 1970. After growing up in a working-class New Jersey suburb, he went first to MIT for two years, and then to the University of Chicago, where he became an antiwar activist and a founder of Students Against the Rank, a group protesting the ranking of male students for the Selective Service. He also joined Students for a Democratic Society and refused to join Phi Beta Kappa in protest against its faculty adviser who had voted to expel several antiwar protesters. After graduation, he moved to New York City, worked for the New York City Welfare Department, and participated in Movement for a Democratic Society, a group of SDS alumni. He left the Welfare Department after a few months and decided to try the phone company, but not just because it offered steady employment. "The primary motivation was political," he said in an interview twenty-five years later.

> I had come to believe . . . [in] the need to get together and change the society, structure, political nature of the society . . . I did not have a big grounding in classic Marxist stuff, but I must have had enough to see working people as the motive force for change . . . I thought that somehow I could, with the power of my ability to suggest the possibility of change, sway workers to a more radical view of politics, for a major

32 "TELRUM—Black Workers Congress," leaflet, n.d., Brent Kramer Collection; Newman, interview; Kramer, interview.

change in the way the country was organized. I don't know that I would have defined it as working class power, as such, but certainly at least as more democratic and anti-imperialist.[33]

Kramer's experiences on the student left were not unique among newly hired telephone workers at the time.

Dave Newman, another telephone rank-and-file activist, had participated in the antiwar and civil rights movements while in high school in Manhattan and then at the City College of New York, where he studied industrial sociology. He had been a member of SDS and had fought for open admissions at the City University system. In an interview two and a half decades later, he described how he wound up applying to work at the phone company in 1970:

> I was involved in social justice issues and as an outgrowth of that I thought it was important for progressives to be in the labor movement, so there I went . . . I came in because I needed a job, but I came in motivated. I came in because I thought this would be a good job, a good union job, in which to effect some change, hopefully . . . I didn't really have any strategy with my life, or strategy with the job. It just seemed like the thing to do, like the natural outgrowth of where I had been and where I was going.

Within a few weeks on the job, Newman was branded a troublemaker "for asking questions and wanting to know why things were the way they were and trying to find out who my steward was. That was a very radical act, trying to find out who your steward is."[34]

Workers with the ideas, if not necessarily the backgrounds, of Newman and Kramer formed the core of the BWAC and United Action. These activists, like those in TELRUM, saw their telephone work as part of a larger political project of radical change. They hoped not only to organize resistance to the Bell System and telephone unions, but to convince telephone workers of the need for broader political mobilization around such large questions as black liberation, feminism, anti-imperialism, and socialism. A few were members of revolutionary organizations that proliferated during the period, including the Progressive Labor Party and the International Socialists, who sought to recruit new members from the telephone workforce. Others, like Kramer, were members of antiwar and civil rights groups who hoped to draw telephone workers to their activities

---

33   Kramer, interview.
34   Newman, interview.

and views. Most had no outside organizational affiliation.[35] At times, these differences led to arguments over ends and means, and prevented some activists from working with others. Generally, however, telephone activists shared concerns for racial and sexual equality and economic justice, which led them to find common cause against the phone company and phone unions. They also shared certain organizational priorities, including rank-and-file self-organization, internal democracy, and mass mobilization, which they tried to implement within their own organizations and within the unions in which they worked. Their best chance to do just that came during the thirteen months from January 1971 to February 1972, when telephone rank-and-file activism reached its highest peak and then suffered its worst defeat.

## Blowing Off Steam

On January 4, 1971, one thousand telephone technicians from various parts of the country arrived in New York City to begin work at New York Telephone. The group represented the second wave of reinforcements for the company's expansion drive, the first group having left the previous spring. The presence of the new arrivals upset local craftsmen, members of CWA Local 1101. To entice the out-of-towners, who were also members of the CWA, the company paid a small wage premium and living expenses, and guaranteed them twelve to sixteen hours of overtime every week. Local craftsmen, averaging only eight hours of overtime each week, resented the guarantee, and, on January 11, fifteen hundred of them walked off their jobs, demanding that the out-of-towners be sent home. The company refused and, as in the past, sought and won legal aid in court, where a judge issued a back-to-work order and levied fines against the local and its president, Howard Banker. Instead of going back to work, however, more workers joined the pickets, and the strike spread throughout the state until nearly 50,000 workers were off their jobs.[36]

The strike exposed divisions between the various levels of the union. Banker and other local leaders throughout the state, under pressure from the rank and file, supported the strike and refused to order a return to work. They appeared to believe the strike would force the company to capitulate. International officials, including President Joseph Beirne and

---

35  On the presence of revolutionaries and other activists from the political left, see "To Win—Phone Workers Need Unity!" Progressive Labor Party leaflet, January 1970, CWA 1150, Box 7, Folder 2; Kramer, interview; articles by B. Mackenzie and R. Veviaka in *Workers' Power* 1971–2.

36  CWA Local 1150 Telephone Tape Transcript, January 6, 11, and 12, 1971, CWA 1150, Box 20, Folder 4; "48,500 in State on Strike," *New York Times*, January 16, 1971, p. 1.

District One Vice President Morton Bahr, displayed ambivalence. They supported the workers' cause but not the tactic. They denounced the company in the press and demanded that the out-of-state craftsmen be sent home, but they also argued that the strikers should return to work since the union faced fines that would, as Bahr said, "put us in hock for the rest of our working lives." In an advertisement in the *New York Times* they detailed the company's responsibility for the overtime dispute and offered negotiation, mediation, or arbitration as the best means to settle the disagreement. Within the union they ordered a return to work, and Bahr sent telegrams to all New York State local presidents which said, "I direct you to direct your members to report to work at the beginning of the next shift."[37]

There was another organized voice among telephone workers, that of the rank-and-file groups. United Action argued that much more was involved in the strike than overtime.

THE OUT-OF-STATE MEN ARE HERE TO SAVE MA BELL IN THE UPCOMING STRIKE. That is the real issue in the strike. That is why this strike is in the interests of all telephone workers—including the out-of-staters and operators, whose contracts are coming up this summer also. Victory this time means getting all the out-of-state men sent home, now! THAT WAY WE PROTECT OUR OVERTIME *AND* PREPARE FOR THE BIG STRIKE.[38]

As United Action saw it, the Bell System imported the out-of-state workers to "get everything in working order so they will be able to hold out longer" during a possible strike in July, when the contract was set to expire.[39] Whereas the union officials viewed the strike as nothing more than a dispute about overtime, the rank-and-filers related the overtime issue to the larger question of union strength, seeing the strike as an opportunity to reinforce the union's power not just through the expulsion of the out-of-towners, but with the recruitment of operators who still belonged to the

---

37  P. L. Montgomery, "Phone Talks Fail; Dispute Spreads," *New York Times*, January 17, 1971, p. 1; "Telephone Test," editorial, *New York Times*, January 21, 1971, p. 34; "The Other Side of the Telephone Strike—A Response," CWA advertisement, *New York Times*, January 23, 1971; Morton Bahr to CWA Member, January 15, 1971, Morton Bahr to All NY Plant Local Presidents, January 19, 1971, Joseph Beirne to Joseph McNiff, telegram, January 22, 1971, all in CWA 1150, Box 15, Folder 12.
38  "The Strike Is Still On," Militant Rank & File leaflet, n.d., CWA 1101 TF—UA Caucus. Note that Militant Rank & File became United Action after only a few weeks.
39  "Operators: It's Your Strike Too," unsigned leaflet, n.d.; "Operators: Organize!" unsigned leaflet, n.d., CWA 1101 TF—UA Caucus.

TTU. To win the strike, United Action proposed several resolutions for passage at a CWA Local 1101 union meeting. In addition to insisting upon complete victory in the form of written guarantees from the company, the resolutions stressed rank-and-file involvement in decision making, no return to work without a membership meeting vote, the inclusion of other CWA locals in an effort to recall their out-of-towners, and financial and legal support for the operators to encourage them to join the strike and the local.[40]

The rank-and-filers attracted some support with their leaflets, but the strike ended without a union meeting. Instead, top union officials settled the dispute and convinced the local leaders to return to work. The two sides resolved to send the dispute to an arbitration panel. Meanwhile, the out-of-town craftsmen would not work. Banker and one other local president opposed the deal because it did not provide protection for several workers arrested during the strike, but they went along under pressure from Beirne, Bahr, and the others. The strike ended after thirteen days, and a week later the arbitrators returned a split decision. The out-of-town technicians could stay, but only for a limited time and only if overtime for all technicians was equal.[41]

Despite the ambiguous outcome, the overtime strike energized the rank-and-file groups and their supporters. Over the next several months, the BWAC and United Action began producing leaflets and periodic newspapers and holding regular meetings. Their literature and activity focused on the developments affecting telephone workers, everything from racist and sexist company practices to the grievance process, the moves of the union leadership, and the rulings of regulatory agencies. They participated in and chronicled the rising number of wildcat strikes, slowdowns, and any other challenges to management, seeing in them the seeds of their own success.[42] Like other rank-and-file groups in other industries during the period, they developed a contract campaign, aimed at influencing the upcoming contract negotiations between the CWA and the Bell System. This campaign included a set of bargaining demands and a program with which to win them. In the activists' view, the union made little effort to involve its members in collective bargaining, so the activists demanded

40  "Win the Strike!" Militant Rank & File leaflet, n.d., CWA 1101 TF—UA Caucus.

41  "Phone Union Warns of Widening Strike," *New York Times*, January 22, 1968, p. 43; CWA 1150 Telephone Tape Transcripts, January, 22, 24, 28, February 2, 1971, CWA 1150, Box 20, Folder 4; Joseph Beirne, "Press Release," January 21, 1971, CWA 1150, Box 7, Folder 3.

42  See United Action 1–5 (February 8, March 8, April 12, April 26, May 5, 1971), PF—United Action (CWA Local 1101), Tamiment Institute Library; various leaflets, CWA 1101 TF—United Caucus, Tamiment Institute Library; *Strike Back!* 1:1 (December 21, 1970), BK; *Strike Back!* 1:3 (n.d.), BK; *Strike Back!* 1:5 (May 1971), BK.

more union meetings at which the inclusion of the membership could begin. Under the bylaws of CWA Local 1101, a union meeting had to be called if enough members signed a petition demanding one, so United Action initiated a petition drive and then came up with resolutions to be passed at the meeting. They demanded the right to strike, an innocent-until-proven-guilty grievance system, a single union for all telephone workers, monthly shop meetings, abolition of the company's control plans, equal pay for equal work, and an end to job discrimination. These gains, they said, would help workers secure the higher wages, paid sick days, vacations, and retirement benefits they wanted and deserved.[43]

Recognizing the agitation among the membership, the CWA leadership went into the 1971 round of collective bargaining determined to win the largest wage and benefit increase in its history.[44] Negotiations began in April, but the parties reached no agreement before the expiration of the contracts at the two pattern-setting companies, Western Electric and Chesapeake & Potomac Telephone. Still, the union did not strike, preferring to wait for contracts at other Bell System units to expire. In May, CWA president Beirne held a nationally televised union meeting at which he asked members to authorize a strike and promised to lead a walkout if three fundamental demands were not met: 1) movement toward equalizing differentials between male and female pay scales, and between geographical areas, 2) better pay, retroactive for all units to the date of contract expiration, and 3) a union security clause requiring non-members to pay union dues. He also promised that the strike would not end before a vote of the membership. After members overwhelmingly authorized a strike in a mail ballot, the union chose Bastille Day, July 14, for the strike date, and bargaining continued.[45]

---

43  Newman, interview; "What We Want—What We Believe," *Strike Back!* 1:6 (June 1971); "Negotiations Update," *United Action* 2 (March 8, 1971); "25% Isn't Enough," *United Action* 3 (April 8, 1971); "Get in Shape for a REAL Fight," *United Action* 4 (April 26, 1971); "We Need a Union Meeting Now," "Resolutions for the Next Union Meeting," *United Action* 5 (May 10, 1971); "Let's Talk About Contract Demands 1st," Strike Back–United Action leaflet, n.d., CWA 1101 T—UA Caucus; "1101 Members—Come to the Membership Meeting and Fight for These Resolutions," United Action leaflet, n.d., Dave Newman collection (hereafter DN).
44  "CWA Is Serving Notice—Our Members Deserve More Income," CWA Advertisement, CWA 1150, Box 5, Folder 1, which ran in *New York Times*, March 29, 1971, p. 26; "CWA President Beirne calls 25% Wage Raise Proposal 'Reasonable and Justifiable' in Light of Economic Trends, Charges Nixon Administration Economic Policies Have Failed," CWA Press Release, March 23, 1971, CWA 1150, Box 5, Folder 1. See also "Is the Bell System Planning a Strike Against CWA?" CWA Advertisement, CWA 1150, Box 5, Folder 1, which ran in *New York Times*, May 16, 1971, p. 16.
45  BLS, *Wage Chronology* 5–6; "Bell System Strike Voted by Workers; Talks Said to

In New York City, rank-and-file agitation grew throughout the spring. In early June, the CWA Local 1101 finally held a membership meeting, at which United Action and the Bell Workers Action Committee were well organized. Eight of their resolutions passed. The local went on record in support of financial and legal aid to eighteen members arrested during the January strike, abolition of the "no strike" clause in the contract, abolition of the company's control plans, a commitment to organize New York Telephone operators into the local, a pledge to support operators in their job actions even if they did not join the local, union efforts to get food stamps for members during the strike, local investigation of how dues were spent, automatic upgrade for clerks, and a 50 percent wage increase. The rank-and-file groups also began distributing information for the upcoming strike. They detailed where to go for unemployment, welfare, and food stamps, and made suggestions for demonstrations, phone bill boycotts, picketing, and other types of strike support. In short, they did what they thought the union should do to prepare for the strike.[46]

The walkout began on July 14, but it was not designed to pressure the company. Instead, it was meant to blow off the steam of rank-and-file agitation. The company and the union were only 1 percent apart on wages and .75 percent apart on pensions when the strike started, and it took them only four days to reach agreement. As the editors of the *New York Times* stated, from the start, union and management were "less concerned about any real differences between them than about how to fashion an agreement that would satisfy the inflated expectations of a restless union rank and file." Beirne essentially confirmed this assessment when he ordered members back to work before giving them the chance to ratify the agreement, a clear violation of his previous commitment. He did promise to resume the strike should the members reject the accord, but by ending the walkout before the vote he reduced the level of militancy and thereby the possibility of rejection. The strategy worked, for the most part. Beirne announced that the deal amounted to a gain of 33.5 percent in wages and benefits over three years, the largest in union history, and included a 3 percent cost-of-living adjustment, some pension improvements, big city allowances, and a modified agency shop. The membership approved the contract by more than a two-to-one margin on August 14, 1971. But the strike did not end in New York.[47]

---

Lag," *New York Times*, June 15, 1971, p. 35; "Phone Strike Date Is Set For July 14," *New York Times*, June 17, 1971, p. 31; Joseph Beirne, "Task Force Report #3," May 10, 1971, CWA 1150, Box 14, Folder 11.

46 "CWA Union Meeting," *Strike Back!* 1:7 (July 1971); "1101 Meeting—Ranks Begin to Move," *United Action* 7 (June, 21, 1971).

47 P. Shabecoff, "Phone Strike On Across Nation; Impact Is Slight," *New York Times*, July

While the national vote was 196,877 yes and 71,456 no, the vote at New York Telephone was 9,734 for and 11,405 against. Even before the results came in, many workers and their local union presidents at New York Telephone, Western Electric, and AT&T Long Lines refused to endorse the accord and remained on strike against Beirne's back-to-work order. Workers also remained out in Pennsylvania, Florida, and New Jersey. The dissidents felt that Beirne had broken several promises and that the accord was not as good as he had claimed. After demanding an immediate 25 percent wage increase, the union had settled for 12.8 percent in the first year, and despite promising to hold out for progress on wage equality, the tentative contract had no provisions on this issue. They were also angry that Beirne concluded the strike before they had voted. For supporters of United Action and the BWAC, the contract also failed to address many of their other demands, particularly discrimination, upgrades, and "critical" local issues like the control plans. As workers outside New York State returned to work, the only unit officially still on strike was New York Telephone, though workers from Western Electric and Long Lines, as well as the operators' union, continued to honor the picket lines for some time.[48]

Though CWA district and international officials endorsed the strike at New York Telephone, they were reluctant to carry it out. A significantly better contract in New York would undermine the agreements made elsewhere and embarrass Beirne within the union. Before two meetings of New York local presidents, he argued that they should accept the national contract. President Nixon's August 15 announcement of wage and price controls added to the force of his arguments. Since the national agreement was ratified before August 15, 1971, its wage increase would not be subject to approval by a government-appointed Cost of Living Council. Any wage increase in a new contract would require approval and would not take effect until November 12.

Despite the obvious government hostility toward large wage increases, the New York local presidents voted to continue the strike and endorsed a set of demands that now included time and a half for Sunday, an improved wage offer, better COLA, three weeks of vacation after five years, full

---

15, 1971, p. 1; Philip Shabecoff, "Accords Reach in Phone Strike and Postal Talks," *New York Times*, July 20, 1971, p. 1; "High Price for Labor Peace," editorial, *New York Times*, July 21, 1971, p. 34.

48   CWA Press Release, August 14, 1971, CWA 1150, Box 5, Folder 1; E. Perlmutter, "90,000 Phone Strikers Defy Back-to-Work Orders of Leaders," *New York Times*, July 22, 1971, p. 17; Joseph F. McNiff, President CWA Local 1150, to Membership, July 29, 1971, CWA 1150 Box 14, Folder 11; "Stop the Sellout," UA leaflet, July 1971, CWA 1101 TF—UA Caucus; Joseph Nabach, "The Telephone Strike: Frozen Militancy," *New Politics* 9:4 (Winter 1972), pp. 40–6.

union shop, increases in city allowances, improved medical benefits, and changes in the contract's language concerning absence control, contract labor, transfers, and grievances. Beirne, while still expressing his disapproval, agreed to endorse their demands and support the bargaining committee's negotiations with the company.[49]

New York Telephone, however, refused to improve its offer, citing the wage and price controls. Though faced with a growing backlog of installation and repair orders, the company had a large number of supervisors to keep telephone service humming along, which reduced the impact of the strike. Beirne's obvious reluctance to push for a better agreement no doubt encouraged the company to resist the union. So, with neither the union leadership nor the company willing to move decisively, negotiations settled into a long waiting game with virtually no movement for months. A similar situation prevailed on the picket lines, at least for the first several months of the strike. CWA Local 1101, the largest union on strike with about one third of the total strikers, organized nothing but regular picket duty. Morale appeared to dwindle as some workers in other Bell System units began crossing New York Telephone workers' pickets. Nevertheless, the strikers remained determined and at their union meeting in early November voted overwhelmingly to continue the strike.[50]

The inactivity of union officials during the strike created a vacuum into which the rank-and-file organizations stepped. Activists became the leaders of the strike, building a strike committee later endorsed by the local, organizing several rank-and-file activities, and churning out a barrage of literature making their arguments about the company and the union. They rejected the wage freeze, arguing that mass action could win a better settlement despite the law. To rebuild the militancy of the strike, United Action and the BWAC proposed three areas of activity: 1) out-of-state picketing, 2) regular mass demonstrations of telephone workers, and 3) organization of the operators.[51]

---

49  Joseph Beirne to Members of the New York Plant Unit, August 30, 1971, Brent Kramer Collection.

50  I. Winkler, "The 1971 New York Telephone Strike: Celebration of Militancy or Major Defeat?" unpublished manuscript, July 10, 2003, in author's possession, courtesy of I. Winkler; New York Telephone, "Bulletin to Plant Employees," September 1, 13, 18, 1971, BK; M. Bahr, "New York Plant Strike Bulletin #3," September 27, 1972, Brent Kramer Collection; L. Johnston, "Backlog Is Huge in Phone Strike," *New York Times*, September 19, 1971, p. 53; "Phone Off the Hook," editorial, *New York Times*, September 23, 1971, p. 34; Corris, interview; "Phone Strike Continues in 20th Week," *Guardian*, December 8, 1971.

51  "End the Freeze," leaflet from coalition of rank-and-file groups in telephone, post office, taxi, and health care, DN; "Take the Initiative," UA leaflet, September 23, 1971, "Take the Offensive," UA leaflet, n.d., "Break the Stalemate," UA leaflet, n.d., all in CWA 1101 TF—UA Caucus.

Acting independently of both the rank-and-file organizations and Beirne, several CWA Local 1101 officials, including Ed Dempsey and Tom Schaefer, had come to similar conclusions. Early in the morning of December 8, they led one hundred rank-and-file strikers, including United Action members, across the Hudson River to Newark, where they set up a picket line in front of a New Jersey Bell Telephone building. Workers at the site, members of the International Brotherhood of Electrical Workers and the CWA, refused to cross the picket lines and joined the workers in a show of solidarity. Over the next several days, similar and even more successful demonstrations took place across New Jersey in New Brunswick, Hackensack, Trenton, and Paterson, as well as in Pennsylvania, Washington, D.C., and Detroit. The roving pickets drew attention to the nearly fifteen hundred out-of-state supervisors acting as strikebreakers for New York Telephone. The roving activists believed that if they could picket enough workers off the job at other Bell System units, those companies would be forced to recall their supervisors, thereby increasing the pressure on New York Telephone. The out-of-state pickets also sent a message to the union, demonstrating that the strikers had support around the country and that the union could, if it chose, call other workers out on strike to increase the pressure on New York Telephone and its parent, AT&T. Union officials had acknowledged the problem of out-of-state supervisors and complained to the company and the press, but they refused to organize any opposition. Instead, they condemned the out-of-state pickets as illegal and ineffective. Still, the activists continued their roving demonstrations off and on for several more weeks.[52]

United Action and the BWAC organized several demonstrations during the strike, including those at the homes of New York Telephone officials, at Governor Rockefeller's New York City office, and at various picket sites throughout the city.[53] A major focus of the two groups was an effort to win over New York Telephone operators to the CWA, not just for the purpose of winning the strike, but as part of the goal of one union for all telephone workers. Given the weaknesses of the operators' current organization, the Telephone Traffic Union, this should have been an easy

---

52  Winkler, "The 1971 New York Telephone Strike"; "Build the Strike," *Strike Back!* 1:9 (December 1971); "Build Out of State Picketing," "1101 Picket Supported in D.C.," *United Action* 19 (January 3, 1972); "50 Honor Bell Office Picket Line," *Bergen Record*, December 13, 1971; "Out of Town Scabs Must Go," UA leaflet, December 6, 1971, CWA 1101 TF—UA Caucus; "Win the Strike," UA leaflet, n.d., DN; Morton Bahr to Ricky Carnivale, January 27, 1972, Brent Kramer Collection.

53  "Strike Back," BWAC leaflet, January 1972, BK; "Build the Strike"; "Phone Workers Rampage—Right On! More of the Same!" *Strike Back!* 1:9 (December 1971); R. Johnson, "6 Hurt and 8 Arrested as Phone Strikers Rampage in Midtown," *New York Times*, January 13, 1972, p. 45.

task. Essentially a company union, the TTU never called strikes, simply accepted CWA pattern-setting in its negotiations, and had no grievance procedure or shop-steward system. Nevertheless, the CWA failed in several organizing drives, including one during the 1971 strike. Activists, many of whom were operators, blamed the failure on the paltry resources and careless effort put forward by CWA officials. Nor did it help that CWA officials had ordered their members to cross an operator wildcat picket line less than a year earlier. The activists also argued that, despite the failed organizing drive, the operators should be treated as if they were in the same union as the men. They publicized the CWA Local 1101 resolutions supporting the operators, invited operators to rank-and-file meetings, and argued with male telephone workers about the importance of addressing the problems of their female comrades.[54]

Many operators joined the picket lines at the beginning of the strike but returned to work once the national strike ended. Activist operators continued to support the New York Telephone strike, but not by leaving work. Then on January 31, 1972, seventy-five operators, half the workforce at New York Telephone's 108th Street central office, walked off the job "to put a stop to the continual harassment and racist and sexist practices of the New York Telephone Company." Though the wildcat violated the contract, the operators sought protection in the presence of the CWA pickets, which they claimed they were honoring. The rank-and-file groups immediately moved to support the striking operators, issuing leaflets and calling for a demonstration at the 108th Street office. But before they could organize any significant activity, their own strike began to deteriorate under rumors of a settlement. The operators soon returned to work, like the rest of New York Telephone's workers.[55]

Following months of stalemate, the CWA and New York Telephone finally reached an agreement late in January 1972. The proposal was virtually unchanged from the original, suggesting that it was the union, not the company, which had made the major concessions necessary for an agreement. The only additions in the new offer were a 15 percent premium for Saturday work and one dollar per week more for workers at top pay.

---

54   "Join Us," 2nd Avenue Traffic Women leaflet, CWA 1101 TF—New York; "Break the Stalemate Now," UA leaflet, n.d., CWA 1101 TF—UA Caucus; "Bell's Nightmare: Plant & Traffic Unite," *Strike Back!* 1:8 (August 1971); "Operators: Keep On Pushin'," *Strike Back!* 1:9 (December 1971); "Don't Just Strike—Strike Back," Bell Workers Action Committee leaflet, n.d., Brent Kramer Collection.

55   "Spread the Traffic Strike," 108th Street Committee leaflet, February 2, 1972, Brent Kramer Collection; J. Sims, "75 Women Go on Strike at Phone Plant," *Daily World*, February 4, 1972, p. 5; "Open Letter to All Traffic Women and Craftsmen," UA leaflet, n.d., and "Traffic Walks Out," UA leaflet, n.d., CWA 1101 TF—UA Caucus.

The union did get a full agency shop, but workers got no direct benefit from it.[56]

Telephone activists immediately rejected the pact, arguing that the strike could still achieve better gains. They condemned what they believed to be the union's hypocrisy in promising to fight for more but then refusing to implement any of the suggestions that could win a successful strike. As proof of the possibilities, they pointed to the success of the recent demonstrations, the operators' strike, and out-of-state picketing. These actions had been accomplished without union support, they argued, so even more could be done *with* union support. In their view, it was no coincidence that the settlement came so soon after the rebirth of militancy in December and January. "One of the reasons that Beirne and the company suddenly moved was their fear of the growing militancy and organization in 1101. He wants to stop our activities before we really threaten him, the company, or their relationship. His sellout aims to smash us." These arguments failed to sway a majority of telephone workers, who voted to accept the proposal and returned to work on February 18.[57]

As several letters by Morton Bahr demonstrated, the hostility of the CWA leadership toward the rank-and-file organizations was undeniable. After asserting that United Action, the BWAC, and other "radical groups" incited violence during the strike, Bahr wrote, "These men do not belong in any union and as President Beirne said: 'It is doubtful that they should belong to the human race.'"[58] While a desire to undermine the activity of the rank-and-file groups may have motivated CWA leaders to end the strike, the strike settlement was an outgrowth of long-term CWA leadership policy. From the beginning, Beirne believed a better settlement was unnecessary and impossible, that any effort to win one would be a waste of time, and that the New York Telephone workers were asking too much, especially when they asked other members to join the strike. The others had, after all, voted for the settlement. Beirne made his approach clear in response to criticism he received for ending the national strike before the ratification election and in violation of his own promise:

Yes, in the Task Force booklet "Let's Get it Done in '71," pages 61 and

56   D. Stetson, "Phone Workers Will Vote on Proposal to End Strike," *New York Times*, January 5, 1972, 1; Vallas, *Power in the Workplace*, p. 111; Nabach, "Telephone Strike," p. 45.
57   "Reject the Sellout—Win the Strike," UA leaflet, February 1972, CWA 1101 TF—UA Caucus; quote from "Take the Dollar and Shove It Up Their Ass," UA leaflet, February 1971, CWA 1101 TF—UA Caucus; untitled *Strike Back!* leaflet, February 1971, DN.
58   Morton Bahr, VP District 1, Letter to all CWA Members, New York Plant, March 7, 1972, CWA 1150 Box 7, Folder 3.

62, we did imply strongly that a strike could continue while ratification procedures were being followed. Yes, we state publicly that if a strike was called and we were out only 5 minutes, the strike "could" continue for at least 3 weeks after agreement was secured to allow our ratification procedures to be followed. Now this was done intentionally and was, prior to July 14th, a pressure point bargaining tool . . . We had every reason to believe that if the strike had continued while ratification through the mails was underway, the management of the System would deliberately engage in a campaign to destroy the morale of our pickets . . . Finally, it is a fact that the contract ratification and presentation committee did state that we "should" continue to strike while ratification took place. They did not say "we must," and their wisdom in carefully picking the word "should" can now be seen because it left in the hands of the Executive Board the constitutional decision to be made under these kind of circumstances.[59]

For Beirne, negotiations constituted the union's major activity and the best way to improve wages and working conditions for members. A strike was "a bargaining tool," not a weapon of class organization and struggle. It should be brandished fiercely, but used wisely, and only by union leaders. More militant tactics, like those demanded by rank-and-file activists, fell outside his repertoire of union activity, and twenty-five years of virtually constant improvement for his members had convinced him of the correctness of his course. As he saw it, in the spring and summer of 1971 the union had used the threat and then the reality of a short strike to achieve the maximum gain for the most members at the lowest cost. New York Telephone workers were impetuous and selfish to think they could win more. The settlement they achieved in the end was a good one, but they could have had it without so much pain.

## Long-Lasting Implications

The New York Telephone strike quickly became a turning point in telephone labor history.[60] Coming after several years of mounting polarization between management and labor, the strike became something of a showdown. The winner would get the upper hand in labor relations for the foreseeable future, while the loser would face a long rebuilding process. As it turned out, the result was a defeat for the workers and a

59   Joseph A. Beirne, "Task Force Report No. 15," July 29, 1971, CWA 1150, Box 14, Folder 11.
60   Newman, interview.

smashing victory for management, and both sides felt the impact for many years. One manager recalled the scene upon the strikers' return to work.

> When the union people came back, they marched into the central office in two lines, you know, to show their solidarity. And when they saw the frames looking better than before, everything looking even more neat and orderly than when they were in charge, their faces dropped to the floor! They learned that *we did not need them to run the show*.[61]

Management put its newfound confidence to work immediately. According to a history of the strike by retired New York Telephone worker Ilene Winkler, many workers faced "a reign of terror" when they returned to work. One steward found that he was the only steward for three hundred workers, because the rest "were petrified." The company fired a number of union activists, most of whom eventually got their jobs back.[62]

With the rank and file broken and discouraged, the BWAC collapsed, while United Action faded to a shadow of its former self. Rank-and-file opposition to management disintegrated. Emboldened managers took control of the shop floor, placing tight restrictions on the workplace freedoms plant workers had previously enjoyed. With the union unwilling and the rank and file unable to resist, Bell System managers accelerated the pace of automation, which effectively eliminated the conditions under which workers' job control had flourished. New electronic switching systems incorporated the information that previously only craftsmen knew, and the concentration of operations into larger offices put more workers under the direct supervision of management. The introduction of automation had long been a management policy. With their victory in the 1971–2 strike, Bell System managers had more freedom to implement their strategy.[63]

Despite the defeat, telephone workers did not come away from the strike empty-handed. The protracted conflict made company managers think twice about provoking another strike, and it encouraged them to accept national bargaining the next time around, in 1974. The result was an expansion of union power at the bargaining table, if not on the shop floor. The strike also solidified a divided CWA Local 1101, one of the most important in the country. Out of the strike, new local leaders developed. Some, like Dempsey, became longtime officials. Others, like Kramer,

---

61   Vallas, *Power in the Workplace*, p. 111. See also "Reprisals Against Phone Strikers," *Guardian*, March 22, 1972, p. 4.
62   Winkler, "The 1971 New York Telephone Strike."
63   Vallas, *Power in the Workplace*, pp. 111–36.

became stewards. A few, including Kramer and Newman, maintained small rank-and-file opposition organizations within the local for a time. Many of these activists, whether officials or not, fought hard, and often successfully, to protect telephone workers' rights on the job.

Plant workers won major improvements in wages and benefits over the ensuing years. Job loss due to automation, always a threat to operators, did not become an issue for craftsmen until the 1980s, and it was not until then that the CWA began to take the problem seriously. By that time conditions had changed dramatically, but the effects of the 1971 strike still lingered. With the workplace organization and militancy destroyed by the previous defeat, the leadership could not mount a credible effort to win a voice in technology decisions. As they had in 1971, CWA officials turned to the bargaining table. And as in 1971, they won more money, but they could not prevent the further erosion of their union's power. The supplemental income program they negotiated provided a cushion for laid-off workers, but it left the union searching elsewhere for members.[64]

---

64 Green, "The Impact of Technology on Women's Work in the Telephone Industry," chapter 11; Corris, Newman, Kramer, O'Neill, interviews.

# 10

# Rank-and-File Opposition in the UAW During the Long 1970s

## A. C. Jones

For at least four decades, between the mid-1930s and the mid-1970s, the United Auto Workers Union, along perhaps with the United Mine Workers Union, constituted the vanguard of the U.S. labor movement. As went the UAW, so went labor; its successes marked the progress of the movement, its failures its retreats. Between the mid-1930s and mid-1940s, victories by the UAW in epoch-making confrontations with the auto companies won not only recognition for the union, but, by the end of World War II, an accepted place for the labor movement in the U.S. political economy. In the subsequent high boom, between the mid-1940s and late 1950s, the UAW not only achieved unprecedented wage gains, it also pioneered what came to be known as the private welfare state, extracting from GM, Ford, Chrysler, and the others steady improvements in pensions, health insurance, unemployment insurance, vacation time, and other benefits, thereby securing for its members a historically unprecedented level of socioeconomic security. The effort required was substantial—strikes against at least one of the Big Three at the expiration of virtually every contract—and so were the costs, specifically, the ceding to management of sovereignty over working conditions on the shop floor. Nevertheless, the UAW officialdom managed for the better part of two decades to retain a certain hegemony over the union rank and file. It won widespread consent from the members to its leadership by providing them with historic improvements in their wages and living conditions, while at the same time crushing by force, when it could not co-opt, oppositions coming from below, ruthlessly employing its one-party rule and huge bureaucratic machine to do so.

But the precarious equilibrium of the golden 1950s faced a serious threat as early as the years 1958–63, when U.S. auto companies confronted the initial challenge to their monopoly of the American market and the first major hit to their profitability of the postwar epoch, at the time of the first serious economic slowdown since the 1930s. The response of the Reuther leadership to this danger to the underlying material base of its implicit arrangement with the employers—the prosperity of the American auto industry—was essentially to hold its fire. It hoped that by keeping down union demands for wages and benefits increases, allowing the companies to intensify labor on the shop floor, and corroding rank-and-file organization in those sectors of the industry where it remained most vibrant, the union could aid the recovery of corporate profitability and return to its former relationship with the Big Three. Meanwhile, the UAW hitched its fate ever more closely to the Democratic Party, which was enjoying increasingly impressive electoral and Congressional majorities during the first half of the 1960s, and looked to an expansion of the welfare state to compensate for any slowdown in the pace of benefits gains won by the union. But the fact remains that the union's concessions provoked increasing restiveness among its rank and file, especially as stagnation gave way to vigorous boom as the decade progressed. Local leaderships in particular, who were the first to feel the brunt of rank-and-file dissatisfaction, mounted strong opposition to each of the 1958, 1961, and 1964 contract settlements. Nevertheless, their failure to make much headway resulted in the ejection by the membership of no less than one third of them in the 1963 local union elections.[1]

An indication of just how far the UAW had drifted from the glory days of the 1930s and 1940s came in 1964 when Walter Reuther himself announced that the companies had never been more flush with profits, and that it was therefore time to oblige GM to finally begin to "humanize working conditions" at what he now termed the "largest, [most] glorified, gold-plated sweatshop in the world." Yet when the moment came to actually pursue this goal by striking GM, Reuther sought to detour the struggle, and the union's executive board had to compel him to call a work stoppage. Still, Reuther ended up cutting short the 1964 strike so as not to endanger a Lyndon Johnson election campaign on its way to a record landslide victory over Barry Goldwater. He showed no hesitation, moreover, in securing the membership's acceptance of the settlement by systematically isolating and brutally repressing, one at a time, individual locals fighting for improved working conditions in their own units. Although Reuther proclaimed the strike as among the most significant in the history of American labor, GM made it crystal clear that it had yielded no

---

1   N. Lichtenstein, *The Most Dangerous Man in Detroit: Walter Reuther and the Fate of American Labor* (New York: Basic Books, 1995), pp. 289–90, 295–6; S. Flaherty, "Mature Collective Bargaining and Rank and File Militancy: Breaking the Peace of the Treaty of Detroit," in P. Zarembka, ed., *Research in Political Economy* vol. 11 (1988), pp. 260–2.

significant ground, while a Ford official offered his approval of the leadership's taking "politically [the] line of least resistance" by "letting local militants learn the lessons of reality the hard way." It was an augury of things to come.[2]

What remained of the stable relationship between the auto companies and the union membership was called profoundly into question after 1965. During the first half of the 1960s, the auto companies had enjoyed a brief respite from the pressure of the foreign competition that had built up rapidly in the later 1950s. Imports had, by 1959, managed to seize 10 percent of the U.S. market, from a minimal base just a half-decade previously, thanks especially to the growing attractiveness of smaller cars, above all the Volkswagen. No doubt aided by the revaluation of the German mark in 1961, U.S. automakers managed to sharply reduce the market share of primarily German imports to just 5 percent during the first part of the 1960s. But then came the Japanese invasion. In the space of a few short years, by the early 1970s, foreign cars had come to appropriate no less than 15 percent of the U.S. market, obliging U.S. auto producers to keep prices down in order to maintain their sales. In 1973, despite record production and cars sold, GM suffered a significant fall in its profit margin compared to 1965, and its shares remained depressed.[3]

The economic problems that U.S. carmakers were obliged to confront had, moreover, no easy solution. In view of the nature of their production technology and the nature of the U.S. market, U.S. producers had for many decades geared production to larger, more luxurious cars, and had difficulty making profits on small ones. To successfully deal with the rising wave of imported small cars, they had to undertake a major reorientation of their whole business. By the early 1970s, GM and Ford had begun to make the transition to small cars with their Vega and Pinto, respectively, but they had a good distance to go technologically to compete with the Japanese, and, in any case, it would take time to make the required new investments and see them bear fruit. In the meantime, from the mid-1960s through the mid-1970s and beyond, to defend their profits, the companies had little choice but to make the best of their existing plant, equipment, and technology. This meant one thing above all—to cuts costs by way of an all-out assault on their workforce, especially through the reduction of employment and the radical speeding up of work.

---

2  Lichtenstein, *The Most Dangerous Man in Detroit*, pp. 397–401 (quotation, p. 398); and Sean Flaherty, "Mature Collective Bargaining," p. 262.

3  For this and the following paragraph, see National Academy of Engineering, *The Competitive Status of the U.S. Auto Industry: A Study of the Influences of Technology in Determining International Industrial Competitive Advantage* (Washington, DC: The National Academies Press, 1982), pp. 65–73; Emma Rothschild, *Paradise Lost: The Decline of the Auto Industrial Age* (New York: Vintage Books, 1974), pp. 3–4; Organization for Economic Cooperation and Development, *Long Term Outlook for the World Automobile Industry* (Paris: OECD, 1983), pp. 96–100.

Auto workers, for their part, were better prepared to resist than they had been in many years. The economic expansion, which had begun in 1961, was reaching record lengths, and during the years between 1965 and 1969, unemployment fell under 4 percent, from 6.7 percent as recently as 1961. The labor shortage in Detroit became so acute that by the end of the decade workers fired at one plant could go right back into another one. Commenting on the problem of absenteeism, one UAW local president remarked, "Jobs are so damn easy to get now, people don't care."[4] Auto workers' willingness to take action was no doubt enhanced by the rising number of young people within their ranks, workers under thirty constituting between 25 and 30 percent of the auto labor force in the late 1960s. Many of these youth partook of their generation's political radicalization and its revolt against hierarchies of all sorts, sympathizing with the contemporary black rebellion that was at this very moment extending itself into the factories, while opposing the Vietnam War. By 1968, the UAW as a whole was at least 30 percent African American, and at some plants, such as Chrysler's Eldon Avenue Gear and Axle plant (75 percent) or the Dodge Main plant (50 percent), the proportion was much higher.[5] After the Tet Offensive of 1968, it is likely that a majority of U.S. workers opposed the war—and were more likely to do so than college graduates and members of higher income groups.[6] Increasingly confident economically, less patient with authority than previously, and in some cases infected by the contemporary shift to the left, auto workers were ready to take matters into their own hands.

The UAW leadership was itself in a squeeze. The Big Three were on a rampage, and the UAW leadership could not itself but sympathize with the industry's problem of competitiveness, as its own relatively civilized relationship with the employers had been premised on the companies' well-being. At the same time, if the union's chiefs continued, as they had

---

4   R. Herding, *Job Control and Union Structure: A Study on Plant-Level Industrial Conflict in the United States with a Comparative Perspective on West Germany* (Rotterdam: Rotterdam University Press, 1972), p. 170.

5   For the racial composition of the UAW, see D. Georgakas and M. Surkin, *Detroit: I Do Mind Dying: A Study of Urban Revolution* (New York: St. Martin's Press, 1974), pp. 40, 102; William H. Oliver to Walter P. Reuther, April 10, 1969, in Walter P. Reuther Collection, Box 213, Archives of Labor and Urban Affairs, Wayne State University [hereafter cited as ALUA]; UAW Chrysler Department, Box 17 of 24 (unprocessed), ALUA; Steve Jefferys, *Management and Managed: Fifty Years of Crisis at Chrysler* (Cambridge: Cambridge University Press, 1986).

6   H. Hahn, "Correlates of Public Sentiment About War: Local Referenda on the Vietnam Issue," *American Political Science Review* 64 (December 1970), pp. 1186–98; H. Hahn, "Dove Sentiment Among Blue-Collar Workers," *Dissent* 17 (May–June 1970), pp. 202–5; J. E. Mueller, "Trends in Popular Support for the Wars in Korea and Vietnam," *American Political Science Review* 65 (June 1971), pp. 358–75.

since the late 1950s, to accede to the ever greater demands for concessions by the employers, especially on the issue of working conditions, they would risk losing the goodwill of the membership, which had long been the ultimate basis of its hegemony. In the event, as they proved ever less successful in delivering the goods, Walter Reuther and his successors came ever increasingly to rely on coercion, ever less on consent, to perpetuate their rule. The outcome could not but be ever more brutal conflict, not just with the companies, but especially with their own membership.

## The Rise of Auto Worker Militancy, 1965–73

With the union leadership ever more reluctant to challenge the companies' "right to manage," especially in the renewed period of company economic difficulties of the later 1960s, the UAW membership was left with little choice but to resist ever increasing company pressure on their own, and they did so in the first instance by filing increasing numbers of written grievances. Grievances had not been a problem during much of the 1950s. In 1954, so few grievances were filed against GM that committeemen used only 36 percent of their representation time to process them.[7] But starting in the latter part of the decade, the number of grievances exploded upward, as company demands increased, tension on the shop floor rose, and the union leadership assumed ever greater responsibility for enforcing order on the shop floor. A decade later, it was clear that rank-and-file workers were having their committeemen write grievance after grievance not just to redress their own particular problems, but increasingly to protest working conditions more generally. For its part, General Motors was contending that workers were abusing the system to the point where it was breaking down. Not only were greater numbers of grievances being filed, but a higher proportion were failing to be resolved by union–management negotiation in the various steps of the grievance procedure and were going up to the Umpire for arbitration. As GM complained to the union, "the procedure has become overloaded to the point where it has not been possible to schedule hearings with sufficient frequency and regularity to meet the needs of all plants." In the 1940s, no more than two hundred grievances per year went to the Umpire, and the figure fell to one hundred or fewer in the 1950s. But between 1964 and 1968, an average of no fewer than fifteen hundred grievances were going there, and the number reached 2,498 in 1969.[8]

---

7 R. MacDonald, *Collective Bargaining in the Automobile Industry: A Study of Wage Structure and Competitive Relations* (New Haven: Yale University Press), p. 331.

8 "Statement of General Motors to the UAW," July 21, 1970, in Box 2, Ernest Moran Collection, ALUA; T. St. Antoine, "Dispute Resolution Between the General Motors

GM officials protested that in many plants the whole procedure had broken down. In its view, "irresponsible" union committeemen and local officials were failing to use their influence with workers to limit the number of grievances filed. According to the company, the International's reps "should bring an independent judgment to bear on the cases rather than routinely adopt the position of the local union."[9] In fact, the UAW leadership was at one with the company in the desire to hold down grievances, and the 491 paid union committeemen who were operating in GM plants in 1969 had the explicit task of insulating union officials and the company from rank-and-file pressure. But by this time, rising resistance from below was breaking beyond the confines of the official institutions, and, as Katz observes, "both management and the UAW national leadership were struggling to reassert the more disciplined regularity that had characterized shop floor relations in the 1950s."[10]

| Written Grievances Filed in General Motors Plants, United States and Canada, 1960–9 | | |
|---|---|---|
| Year | Number of Grievances | Number Per Hundred Employees |
| 1960 | 106,000 | 34 |
| 1961 | 99,000 | 32 |
| 1963 | 115,000 | 35 |
| 1964 | 138,000 | 40 |
| 1965 | 158,000 | 42 |
| 1966 | 203,000 | 51 |
| 1967 | 209,000 | 54 |
| 1968 | 231,000 | 57 |
| 1969 | 256,000 | 60 |

Source: "Statement of General Motors to the UAW," July 21, 1970, in Ernest Moran Collection, Box 2, Archives of Labor and Urban Affairs, Wayne State University, Detroit, Michigan.

Corporation and the United Automobile Workers, 1970–1982," in T. Hanami and R. Blanpain, eds, *Industrial Conflict Resolution in Market Economies: A Study of Australia, The Federal Republic of Germany, Italy, Japan and the USA* (Deventer, Netherlands: Kluwer Law and Taxation Publishers, 1984).

9   "Statement of General Motors to the UAW."

10   H. Katz, *Shifting Gears: Changing Labor Relations in the U.S. Automobile Industry* (Cambridge, MA: MIT Press, 1985), p. 43.

From the mid-1960s, as the company demands upon them increased and their confidence, swelled by declining joblessness, rose with it, auto workers unleashed a rising torrent of wildcats strikes. At Chrysler, where the data is most complete, the average number of unofficial actions per year leaped from fifteen between 1960 and 1965, to sixty-one between 1965 and 1970, to sixty-seven between 1970 and 1973. The trend was analogous at GM, although the absolute numbers of unofficial actions was significantly lower.[11] Still, as Flaherty points out, from the late 1950s, the UAW had been more willing to authorize strikes when requested to do so by local officials, and during the period roughly corresponding to the Nixon presidency, authorized local strikes at GM rocketed, the number of worker-hours lost to the company due to authorized local strikes between 1968 and 1974 amounted to more than *double* the *total* worker-hours lost to both authorized and unauthorized intra-contractual strikes at the company during the entire postwar period up to that point.[12] Although some of these strikes were over wages, the great majority were over working conditions, a pattern that prevailed across U.S. industry in this period.

### GMAD, Gone Mad

The combination of rising international competition and increasing worker militancy was responsible for the formation and rapid expansion by General Motors of the new GM Assembly Division (GMAD). This sub-unit of the company, formed in 1965, had a very straightforward and explicit goal—to wrench ever more profit from its labor force per working minute, but without the aid of more or better plants and equipment. It sought to accomplish this by means of pure and simple speedup and de facto wage cuts, "rationalizing" production through eliminating jobs and reducing compensation per job across the division, so as to level pay per job down to the lowest rates prevailing in the GM system.[13]

Between 1968 and 1972, GMAD reorganized production in no fewer than ten of its plants and provoked work stoppages across the system. The most famous of these struggles took place in 1972 in the huge new GM assembly operation at Lordstown, Ohio, a facility more than a mile long,

---

11    Chrysler Corporation, Wage and Salary Administration, Industrial Relations Office, June 1986; S. Flaherty, "Mature Collective Bargaining and Rank and File Militancy: Breaking the Peace of the Treaty of Detroit," in P. Zarembka, ed., *Research in Political Economy* vol. 11 (1988), p. 263, Table 1b; "Letters of Intent to Authorize a Strike" in Box 26, Leonard Woodcock Collection, ALUA.

12    Flaherty, "Mature Collective Bargaining," pp. 263–4.

13    Ibid., pp. 264–5. For more detail on the GMAD transformation of the labor process and workers' resistance to it, see Rothschild, *Paradise Lost*, pp. 97–119.

adjacent to the Ohio Turnpike west of Youngstown, where the average age of the labor force at the time was twenty-five and the local was led by twenty-nine-year-old Gary Bryner.[14] "It was a young and radical work force," said Darwin Cooper, who was nineteen when the plant opened in 1966. "I really believe it had a lot to do with our country at the time. There was the Vietnam War. There were protests going on. Things were just pretty unsettled."[15] Lordstown workers had regularly shut down the production by way of wildcats—four times in November 1967 alone, for example—before the unit was incorporated into GMAD in 1971. In the ensuing productivity drive, the company literally doubled the line speed. As John Russo of nearby Youngstown State University noted, "They were trying to push 100 cars down the line an hour."[16] The Lordstown strike became the focus of national attention, symbolizing the alienation and rebellion of younger workers confronted with the latest stage of Fordist labor intensification. But UAW locals launched no fewer than eight strikes against GMAD in these years, culminating in the bitter conflict at the Norwood, Ohio plant, which lasted six months, compared to three weeks at Lordstown.

Yet the fact remains that individual locals striking on their own rarely had a hope of defeating a GM mega-corporation that could, in most cases, simply transfer work away from the struck plant and count on the passivity of the top union leadership.[17] As early as the 1964, one local leader had publicly complained that unless the union was willing to confront GM at the national level with coordinated action, resistance at individual units would have little chance of success.[18] Indeed, it was widely suspected during the later 1960s and early 1970s that the UAW's willingness to authorize local strikes represented the most convenient way to accede to GM's demands, while allowing workers to let off steam. In the latter part of 1972, at a national meeting of GMAD local officials, local union leaders finally demanded that the UAW launch a unified all-GMAD work stoppage to counter the company. But, all too symptomatically, the UAW leadership countered by implementing what it called the "Apache" strategy: a series

---

14 "Sabotage at Lordstown?" *Time*, February 7, 1972.

15 M. R. Kropko, "GM union no longer feels invincible," Associated Press online, January 19, 1999.

16 M. Ethridge, "Strikes at Lordstown seem to be original equipment," *Akron Beacon Journal*, April 16, 1996, p. B7.

17 Lordstown was actually something of an exception in this respect, as it was the only plant producing GM's new Vega compact car.

18 N. Miller, "Auto Union Ferment: Russ Alger's Problems as President of a Local Complicate GM Talks," *Wall Street Journal*, September 24, 1964, p. 10, referred to in Flaherty, "Mature Collective Bargaining," p. 262.

of weekend-long strikes, in a succession of different plants, which could not have been better organized to bring out the isolation of the locals, insure defeat, and disperse auto worker resistance. That militants across the system, some very well organized at the local level but lacking any sort of national organization of their own, were unable to effectively counter the International in the fight against GMAD spoke volumes to the central weakness of the rank-and-file revolt in auto, and industry as a whole.[19]

## League of Revolutionary Black Workers

This environment of heightened worker militancy and resistance of the later 1960s and early 1970s formed the backdrop for the emergence of independent rank-and-file organizations in the auto industry. In the UAW, the most important of these organizations were the League of Revolutionary Black Workers (LRBW) and the United National Caucus, which existed in multiple plants. But there were also single plant organizations, such as the Linden Auto Workers (LAW) in New Jersey, the United Black Brothers at the Ford Mahwah, New Jersey plant, and more informal groupings around individual militants.

The LRBW was the most celebrated oppositionist formation in the UAW in this era. A group of about thirty activists who founded a radical black monthly newspaper in Detroit in 1967, *Inner City Voice*, comprised its leadership. Some members of this collective had years of common activity, stretching back to the early 1960s. Some participated in a study group on Marx's *Capital*, led by Martin Glaberman, who had been associated with C. L. R. James in the Workers Party. By 1967–8, the Inner City Voice (ICV) group was "exploring how revolutionary ideas might be implemented in their places of work."[20] During its first year, the newspaper had an average monthly press run of about 10,000 copies.

In early 1968, the group finally gained a hearing among black auto workers when a group of nine from Chrysler's Dodge Main plant in Hamtramck joined their study group. In May of that year, the Dodge Revolutionary Union Movement (DRUM), as they called themselves, participated in their first action, a wildcat strike at the plant. This action, and the rise of the League more generally, needs to be understood within the context of rising tide of black protest at this juncture. It occurred at a time of large-scale black protest across the country, in the wake of the assassination of Martin Luther King, Jr., when, from April 4 to 11, at least 125 cities had been hit by rioting. Mike Hamlin, an ICV leader, explained their perspective:

19 Flaherty, "Mature Collective Bargaining," pp. 264–5.
20 Georgakas and Surkin, *Detroit*, p. 23.

[The May 1968 wildcat] happened at a time when many of us who had a history of radical involvement in this city for some time had just begun to develop a newspaper as a means of getting ourselves together . . . But we always had an understanding that what was necessary was that we organize black workers. And though we never had a successful entry into the plants with the workers and we really didn't know how to go about it, we attracted to us a group of nine workers from the plant just by virtue of us producing a newspaper and projecting certain ideas. We had certain radical ideas and a certain revolutionary line: that black workers would be the vanguard of the liberation struggle in this country.[21]

The immediate issue of the wildcat was speedup, and both black and white workers participated. Three weeks later DRUM held a rally of three hundred workers from the plant. They marched to the hall of UAW Local 3 to present fifteen demands to the officers, including the rehiring with full pay of all black workers fired on trumped-up charges, the establishment of a rank-and-file committee of blacks to investigate racism by the company, the handing over of a certain part of the union dues from black workers to the "Black community to aid in Self-Determination," that black workers at Chrysler subsidiaries in South Africa be "paid on an equal scale as their white racist coworkers, as well as the hiring of blacks for the positions of plant manager, foremen, general foremen, superintendents, plant doctor, plant nurses, and plant protection guards," and also the placing of an African American on the Chrysler Board Directors.[22] A stark racial divide had opened up within both the union, where there were still few leading black officials, and inside the Detroit auto plants, where virtually all foremen were white, many of them white ethnics who had made the leap to supervisor after decades on the line. The League program called at once for a rank-and-file action against speedup and the harsh working conditions in the plant and for an implacable struggle against racism in the companies and the union, while seeking at the same time to further the worldwide struggle against capitalist imperialism.

Failing to gain satisfaction on the speedup, DRUM set up picket lines the next day. "No attempt was made to interfere with whites, and the majority of white workers entered the factory. Many others honored the picket lines out of years of working-class savvy. Sympathetic or not, they

---

21 Quoted in J. A. Geschwender, *Class, Race and Worker Insurgency: The League of Revolutionary Black Workers* (Cambridge: Cambridge University Press, 1977), pp. 89–90.
22 "DRUM Demands" (July 1968), in Detroit Revolutionary Movements Collection, Box 1, ALUA.

went home. Some three thousand black workers did not go home or into the factory; they stood outside the gates as production all but halted."[23] The wildcat strike lasted three days. Although DRUM got no movement on their demands, they gained widespread recognition from their ability to attract so many supporters with militant tactics. In September 1968, DRUM ran Ron March for trustee of Local 3. He won the first ballot and then lost the two-person run-off, 2,091 to 1,386, in a campaign marked by red-baiting from local officials. That an avowed revolutionary could gain 40 percent of the vote in a local election was a measure both of the mood in the plant and the success DRUM had immediately experienced. In April 1969, Don Jackson, another DRUM member, would run for vice president of the local, and he, too, would receive nearly 40 percent of the vote.[24]

DRUM's success at Dodge Main led the ICV group to expand its activities to other plants in the Detroit area. In November 1968, black workers at Chrysler's Eldon Avenue Gear and Axle plant began passing out a single-sheet newsletter. On January 22, 1969, they held a demonstration at the headquarters of Local 961. Some three hundred second-shift workers were, as a result of their participation in this action, late for work that afternoon. The next day sixty-six of these were disciplined, receiving five- to thirty-day suspensions without pay. In protest against this discipline, ELRUM (the Eldon Avenue Revolutionary Union Movement) wildcatted on January 27. Production was totally halted, as a higher proportion of blacks participated than had been involved at Dodge Main the summer before. The plant was pivotal within Chrysler's overall production process, as it was the sole source of the metal parts for the rear axles of most of the cars built by the company.[25] Chrysler fired twenty-six workers for their involvement in this strike, hindering ELRUM activities in the months to come.[26] All but two were eventually reinstated. In the May 1969 elections in Local 961, ELRUM backed a slate wider than its own immediate grouping, and its

---

23  Georgakas and Surkin, *Detroit*, p. 47.

24  DRUM members claimed that ballots were tampered with to prevent March from winning, and Geschwender, in *Class, Race and Worker Insurgency*, p. 108, presents evidence to substantiate this claim. In March 1970, DRUM ran candidates for all officers and twenty-five delegates and alternates for the forthcoming UAW convention. They attracted one hundred workers from the plant to a special DRUM convention on February 28, 1970. But only two members of the DRUM slate even made it to the run-off in the election.

25  Georgakas and Surkin, *Detroit*, p. 102.

26  A white militant in the plant, John Taylor, argued: "I think that broke the back of ELRUM right there. I think those actions were premature. There was no way to logistically support that strike. They had no outside mobilization . . . Still, everything we ever did at the plant was premature . . ." Quoted in Georgakas and Surkin, *Detroit*, pp. 112–3.

candidate, Elroy Richardson, a relatively moderate African American, won the presidency, defeating incumbent Ed Rickard, 1,480 to 966.[27]

By early 1970, the Eldon plant was in nearly continual turmoil. Local officials charged that ELRUM was clogging the grievance procedure; ELRUM countered that local leaders were stalling on settling grievances. Then on April 15, 1970, a line worker, John Scott, was fired after a confrontation with a foreman. Workers struck the next day in protest against the firing and continued with a production slowdown until April 19. Scott was reinstated on April 20. Then, on May 1, 1970, a dozen committeemen were fired for their leadership of the April 16–19 action. Richardson, the local president, was forced to call workers out in protest of this disciplinary action. But that his only interest was to dissipate rank-and-file anger was made evident by his instruction that workers not picket, but instead go home and watch television to find out when to return. Work resumed on Tuesday, May 5, but it was September before eleven of the twelve committeemen were reinstated. The twelfth, Jordan Sims, remained fired. Later in May 1970, when a forklift driver was crushed under a machine, plant militants accused the company of running unsafe equipment and halted production with pickets.

The strength of the LRBW should be assessed on the basis of the actions it was able to stage and the number of workers who followed its lead. The organization itself was embryonic and weak. Although one militant at the Eldon Avenue plant put the number of militants who were active there in summer 1970 at about sixty to seventy, ELRUM's actual membership was smaller than this. ELRUM's loss of three central leaders in May 1970 made it impossible for the group to grow in the next few months. Throughout Detroit, the LRBW counted twelve to fifteen units at various plants. Mike Hamlin claims that, at its peak, the LRBW had about two hundred and fifty to three hundred active ("core") members in Detroit.[28] Weekly Sunday meetings for workers at Dodge Main drew up to three hundred; at Eldon up to four hundred. But many of the plant organizations consisted of only a handful of activists, and "a few bulletins or a single action might be the extent of their activities."[29]

The UAW leadership sought, from the start, to destroy the League, which was hardly surprising, as Reuther and his comrades were never able to come to terms with, let alone ally with, the series of militant black organizations that emerged throughout the period to constitute the most promising forces for progressive socioeconomic change. As early as 1964,

27   Geschwender, *Class, Race and Worker Insurgency*, p. 123.
28   Georgakas Collection, Box 1, ALUA.
29   Georgakas and Surkin, *Detroit*, p. 88.

though a supporter of the civil rights movement in many ways, Reuther made the fateful choice to ally with Lyndon Johnson against the Mississippi Freedom Democratic Party, playing hatchet man for the administration in preventing the MFDP's seating at the 1964 Democratic Party Convention. Reuther responded to the Detroit rebellion of July 1967—which saw forty-three killed, seventy-two hundred arrested, and a quarter billion dollars in property damage—by setting up a civic alliance called New Detroit, in which he partnered with the city's elite. Not only did this body accomplish little in the way of providing increased housing or jobs for the beleaguered city; in a way worse, it publicly allied Reuther with the likes of Henry Ford II, GM head James Roach, and Lynn Townsend of Chrysler—in a different class, to put it mildly, and a universe away from heavily black, working-class Detroit. As Lichtenstein points out, "DRUM's founding cohort constituted the same species of ideologically motivated [working-class] cadres who had animated the UAW in its heroic youth."[30] But from the start, Reuther labeled them a "terrorist" group and had no hesitation in completely misrepresenting their goals. An official letter sent in March 1969 by the UAW executive board to all union members charged that "A group now exists in a few plants where the UAW represents the workers which calls itself a black revolutionary union movement and whose goals are the complete separation of the races in the shop and the destruction of our Union through the tactics of violence, fear and intimidation."[31]

The UAW combined physical assault, denunciation, and cooption to defeat the League. Local officials unceasingly attacked the League's leaders in leaflets and local papers.[32] The top leadership called them dual unionist, racist, and anti-democratic. In an interview with the *Detroit News*, Emil Mazey outdid himself in asserting that "Violence by black militants in Detroit's auto factories poses a greater peril to the UAW now than Communist infiltration did in the 1930s," and calling the League's members "a group of fanatics who don't know where they are going, but whose actions are an attempt to destroy this union . . . nothing but black fascists, using the same tactics of coercion and intimidation that Hitler and Mussolini used in Germany and Italy."[33] Meanwhile, the

30   Lichtenstein, *The Most Dangerous Man in Detroit*, p. 434.

31   UAW International Executive Board Administrative Letter on Black Revolutionaries, March 10, 1969, in Detroit Revolutionary Movements Collection, Box 4, ALUA.

32   See, for example, E. Liska, "25 Workers Discharged," *Dodge Main News*, February 15, 1969, p. 1, in UAW Chrysler Department Collection, Box 1 of 24 (unprocessed), Local 3, 1968–1969, ALUA.

33   Quoted in Geschwender, *Class, Race and Worker Insurgency*, p. 114. For other statements by the UAW leadership on DRUM, see O. D. McQueen to Tony Connole, March 14, 1969, in Arthur Hughes Collection, Box 47; Bill Beckham to WPR [Walter P. Reuther],

union resorted to various dirty tricks in elections where League members stood as candidates, and mobilized the white retiree vote against them. UAW staffers physically broke the picket lines of DRUM-led strikes, while the union incited the auto companies against the League by publicly announcing that it would not protect workers who struck "with the conscious purpose of dividing our union along racial lines." To put the icing on the cake, Chrysler and other corporations quickly recruited hundreds of blacks into supervisory jobs, while top UAW officials like Douglas Fraser encouraged blacks loyal to Solidarity House to take control of the big production locals and regional directorships in Detroit.[34] The combination of the union and the company, the carrot and the stick, was more than the League could withstand, and by 1970 it had ceased to be an effective force within the plants.

It should be said that the League had serious difficulties of its own, as it was fraught with internal divisions, which always hampered its work. The weakness of the League was that it could never decide whether it was a dual union, a rank-and-file caucus within the UAW, a black nationalist organization, or a revolutionary party. All four of these perspectives existed in mutual interdependence and mutual hostility inside the League. Virtually none of the League's leaders were nationalists, but the group adapted to nationalist sentiments that were widespread within the heavily black workforces where it was active. Like the Black Panthers, it was constituted by a relatively small number of people, which stood atop a burgeoning mass movement, but without a sufficient cadre or coherent enough organization to successfully lead.[35]

## The United National Caucus

A second important rank-and-file organization within the UAW during this period was the United National Caucus (UNC). It was less militant than the League in formal political terms, but it fought on a national level and lasted longer. Dominated by skilled workers, who were overwhelmingly white men, the group's program tilted toward their concerns, but that did not prevent the UNC from attracting semi-skilled, African American, and women workers and championing their needs. Its central planks included higher wages, humane conditions, an end to discrimination against women and black workers, an innocent-until-proven-guilty grievance procedure, direct election of union leaders, and

February 13, 1969, in Walter P. Reuther Collection, Box 74, ALUA.

34  Lichtenstein, *The Most Dangerous Man in Detroit*, pp. 434–5.

35  Joel Geier, interview, August 10, 2005.

greater union presence on the shop floor. UNC activists saw their battle as threefold: against the corporations and for social justice, against the bureaucracy of the UAW, and involving larger social issues.

The UNC originated in 1966 in the Skilled Trades $1-per-hour movement, an attempt to open contracts for a wage increase for skilled workers. During 1967 contract negotiations, the group mobilized 12,000 skilled workers for a demonstration at Ford world headquarters in support of their demands.[36] Local organizations, such as the Committee for Militant Unionism at the giant Ford Local 600, soon affiliated with the UNC.[37] Starting at the 1968 convention, the UNC could pose itself as an alternative to the national UAW leadership. UNC demanded the direct election of all International Executive Board members and international representatives, opposed salary increases for full-time officials, and favored doubling strike benefits.[38]

At the 1970 convention, the UNC put forward the first rank-and-file slate for national union offices since Walter Reuther became president in 1946.[39] Its candidates stood on a platform that demanded: 1) a five dollar minimum wage, which constituted a 50 percent wage increase and met the U.S. Department of Labor definition of a moderate income for a family of four, $11,000 per year ($5.50 per hour),[40] 2) restoration of cost-of-living increases, since COLA caps had cost workers over $1,000 since 1967,[41] 3) the humanization of the plants and implementation of a real innocent-until-proven-guilty grievance procedure,[42] 4) a twenty-five-years-and-out retirement policy, and 5) referendum voting for all officers of the union.[43]

UNC leaders developed a comprehensive critique of the UAW bureaucracy. While officials did not fight hard enough to win wage

---

36  P. Kelly, "Chairman's Report," The United National Caucus 2 (April 15, 1971); "United National Caucus," introductory pamphlet, 1973, in Arthur Hughes Collection, Box 47, ALUA.

37  "The Committee for Militant Unionism Takes Its Stand" (1968), Walter P. Reuther Collection, Box 52, ALUA.

38  "United National Caucus," introductory pamphlet (1973), p. 6.

39  "United National Caucus," introductory pamphlet (1973).

40  CKLW-TV, "United National Caucus," November 8, 1970, pp. 2–3, transcript of program in Ken Bannon Collection, Box 65, ALUA.

41  "The acceptance by UAW leaders of the 1967 Cost of Living Adjustment (COLA) formula in the 1967 negotiations cost the average member $1,400. Because of this monstrous blunder, a 10-week strike at GM was needed to regain full COLA protection in 1970." The UNC took credit for pressuring the leadership to uncap COLA in 1970. "United National Caucus," introductory pamphlet (1973), p. 5. See also C. Gadson, "Dodge Local 3 Report," The United National Caucus 2 (April 15, 1971).

42  "United National Caucus," introductory pamphlet (1973).

43  "The United National Caucus Slate," leaflet for 1970 UAW convention, in Ken Bannon Collection, Box 52, ALUA.

increases, the UNC focused its criticism on working conditions, arguing that the plants were dangerous and production standards unreasonable.[44] Likewise, the UNC railed against UAW officials' failure to solve health and safety problems. Time and again UNC militants protested that issues of work standards, health and safety, and the grievance procedure were absent from national contracts.[45]

The grievance procedure was a particular source of resentment. The UNC argued that it was stacked against workers and the union. Workers accused by a foreman of violating a shop rule were automatically presumed guilty until the union proved them innocent. Workers could file grievances, but complaints often took over a year to settle.[46] As part of this struggle for better workplace justice, the UNC demanded the UAW fight an industrial system that assigned a foreman to every eight or ten workers by assigning a steward for every foreman.[47]

The UNC vociferously opposed company discrimination against both black and women workers, and held the leadership of the UAW, and its structure, responsible for the inequality. Grety Glenn, a Local 600 unit president and UNC leader, argued:

> Discrimination is . . . a serious problem in our factories today . . . It is no secret within the plant or the International Union who gets the hard, heavy, hot and dirty jobs which pay the least amount of money. It is the black workers. And it is no accident that the majority of the inspectors in the Frame Plant are white . . . In skilled trades at the Rouge, the blacks are less than 3 percent, although we are 47 percent of the total force. This makes it pretty obvious that there has not been the kind of direction, encouragement, and training that would permit our black workers the real opportunity to get into skilled trades. We work in an industrial ghetto.[48]

During several major confrontations involving black workers, UNC leaders and members played important roles in supporting the workers against attacks by both employers and union officials.

The UNC advanced sweeping proposals for union reform. These aimed to decentralize the UAW's structure, which concentrated power in the hands of the International Executive Board and crippled local independent

---

44   CKLW-TV, "United National Caucus," November 8, 1970.
45   "United National Caucus," "We Recommend a One Year Contract with Chrysler."
46   CKLW-TV, "United National Caucus," November 8, 1970, p. 8.
47   Kelly, "Chairman's Report."
48   CKLW-TV, "United National Caucus," November 8, 1970.

action. "Our union protects and isolates its bureaucracy; it gives dictatorial power to the officers and international representatives. Our 'leaders' are overpaid, insensitive to worker needs and often totally unaware of what goes on inside the plant."[49] Instead of vesting the power to appoint International Representatives in the top leadership, the UNC advocated a system of Labor Counselors, elected in the plants, to serve the locals. The UNC wanted locals to have the right to strike and for "salaries and fringe benefits of elected officials to be no higher than those of the men they represent." Officers' terms would be limited constitutionally; union functionaries would be required to return to their jobs in the plants periodically. Lastly, the UNC would restructure the dues system to diminish the International's power, in relation to the locals, and build up the strike fund.[50]

In certain locals and units, the UNC played an integral role in bargaining. At the Tool & Die Unit of Local 600, at the Ford Rouge plant, for example, the UNC led the rejection of the 1970–1 local agreement by arguing that the company's "concessions" cost no money and should have been routine during the life of the contract. In returning to the bargaining table, the unit won gains and made no concessions to the company.[51]

The UNC's largest impact was perhaps the 1973 Ford skilled trades contract rejection. The tentative contract that year included a voluntary overtime agreement, which gave the company the right to hire outside the union or promote unskilled workers to skilled positions if too many skilled workers refused overtime.[52] The UNC campaigned actively against the contract, not just the overtime question, organizing a leafleting campaign, holding press conferences, and staging a mass demonstration in front of Solidarity House.[53] While production workers accepted the pact by 105,000 to 38,000, skilled workers rejected it 20,089 to 5,943.[54]

---

49  "United National Caucus," introductory pamphlet, (1973), p. 3.

50  "United National Caucus," introductory pamphlet (1973).

51  United National Caucus, UAW Local 600, Tool & Die Chapter, "We Now Recommend Ratification," leaflet (January 1971), in UAW President's Office: Woodcock Files, Box 23, ALUA.

52  "Statement of the 24th Constitutional Convention Regarding Article 19, Section 3 of the UAW Constitution," in Ken Bannon Collection, Box 31, ALUA.

53  Independent Skilled Trades Caucus and the UNC, "Join Us in Protesting the Sell-Out 1973 Agreement," leaflet (November 1973), in Arthur Hughes Collection, Box 47, ALUA. Also see R. Poszich, Skilled Trades Committeeman, Local 228, and A. Badalamento, Skilled Trades Sergeant-at-Arms, Local 228, "An Open Letter to Tool & Die Unit—Local 600" (November 1973), in Ken Bannon Collection, Box 31, ALUA.

54  "Statement of the 24th Constitutional Convention Regarding Article 19, Section 3." A. Salpukis, in "They Can Wildcat the Union, Too," *New York Times*, November 18, 1973, sec. 4, p. 2, wrote that the "pattern of collective bargaining which despite long and bitter strikes at least had the comfort of being predictable, has been replaced by uncertainty.

In 1966, the UAW had granted skilled workers the right to ratify contracts separately, an attempt to forestall raiding activity by the Independent Society of Skilled Trades (ISST), a major rival of the UAW to represent skilled auto workers.[55] In 1973, however, faced with the first membership rejection of a nationally negotiated contract in the union's history, UAW leaders quickly changed their position. They dropped the overtime stipulation but imposed the rest of the contract, a unilateral action that infuriated rank-and-file workers. The UNC submitted the case to the UAW's Public Review Board (PRB), a quasi-judicial body of the union, but the PRB approved the actions of the IEB.[56] The 1973 Ford skilled trades conflict led the UNC leadership to focus their appeal more sharply. In 1974, they formed an Independent Skilled Trades Council (ISTC), and although its activity took place under the name of the UNC, the bulk of the organizational resources went into ISTC activity. By early 1975, the ISTC, pledging to organize skilled tradesmen as an independent force, had three thousand members.[57]

The UAW worried less about the UNC than the League, but the formation of the ISTC raised antennae at Solidarity House, in view of the enhanced leverage enjoyed by the skilled tradesmen. Documents in the Archives of Labor History show that the union devoted significant organizational resources to surveillance of the UNC and the ISTC. One officer argued that the ISTC "could possibly be a greater threat to our union than the ISST as they are working from within our structure . . ."[58]

## Auto Industry Wildcat Strikes, 1973

During 1973, especially the hot summer of that year, the rank-and-file rebellion in auto reached its zenith, and in a sense its culmination, in the revolt that took place in the old Chrysler plants in the center of Detroit. This outburst concentrated in one location all of the ingredients that had

---

And both top management and the top union leadership have been made uneasy about the future."

55 "Statement of the 24th Constitutional Convention Regarding Article 19, Section 3."
56 "Impeach Nixon and Woodcock," The United National Caucus (February 1974). United National Caucus, Local 600 UAW, Tool & Die Chapter, "Review Board Decision," April 1974, in Ken Bannon Collection, Box 31, ALUA.
57 "Skilled Trades Organize to Fight," Network 1 (February–March 1975), pp. 22–5.
58 Ken Mantyla to Ted Ogar, UAW interoffice correspondence, October 10, 1974; Ken Bannon to Doug Fraser, Skilled Trades Department to Officers and Executive Board Members, UAW (interoffice communication), June 18, 1975; Doug Fraser to Officers, Regional Directors, and Skilled Trades representatives and staff (interoffice communication), April 14, 1975; George Ryder to Jerry Dale, April 4, 1975, all in Box 65, Ken Bannon Collection, ALUA.

hitherto nourished the movement: company indifference to the basic welfare of the workers, racism, speedup, extreme safety violations, the struggle for black liberation, heightened levels of rank-and-file self-activity independent from and in opposition to the union officialdom, and the most extreme political and physical repression on the part of the UAW leadership. The economic expansion, which reached its peak in 1973–4, created conditions in which every car on the assembly line was sold even before it was put together. Since no new labor-saving plant or equipment had been introduced, the only way the company could increase production to meet demand was to intensify labor, lengthen the working day, and ignore the impact on the health and safety of the workers. It was a recipe for resistance.[59]

Speedup consumed the small margin of slack around each production worker's job. Workers' relations with foremen, who were responsible for enforcing higher production quotas, suffered most, especially as supervisors discouraged workers from using normal safety equipment if it slowed production. "If you tried to work using safety tools, you would really get ridden by the foremen . . . they could slow you down and the foremen would get angry at you."[60] Management began firing workers for failing to keep up with the pace. In September 1972 at Chrysler's Mack Avenue Plant, a bolster plate blew loose and killed a die-setter by cutting off the top of his head. When rank-and-file activists sought to get the local to establish a safety committee, the local's president ruled them out of order. In December, these workers began issuing the *Mack Safety Watchdog*.

Under such conditions, it was inevitable that conflict between workers and management would break out into the open. At Chrysler's Jefferson Avenue assembly plant, on February 28, 1973, a worker was fired for refusing to do an additional task on top of his already sped-up schedule. In support, his entire department walked out of the plant, declaring they would remain out unless he was rehired, and Chrysler acceded.[61] But on March 2, another worker, John Miller, was fired for leading that strike. Others were given reprimands. A UAW international representative promised the workers he would investigate the matter if they remained at work. But when the company had still failed to rehire Miller by March 7, both shifts left work, demanding Miller's reinstatement and amnesty for themselves. That weekend, with the workers still out, Chrysler sent discharge telegrams to eight of the strikers. The union showed itself interested in nothing but

59   J. Weinberg, *Detroit Auto Uprising: 1973* (Highland Park, MI: Network, 1974).
60   Auto worker quoted in H. A. Thompson, "Detroit: Wildcat 1973," unpublished paper, University of Michigan, 1985, p. 59.
61   Thompson, "Detroit," p. 16.

getting the strikers back on the job, and, using bullhorns, the local leadership was able to persuade enough workers to return to work by March 12 that production returned to normal.

Rank-and-file militants denounced the officials for undermining their walkout, not least by denying the strikers the right to use their own local union hall during the walkouts.

> They held one Union meeting . . . That meeting got out of hand from their point of view. Speaker after speaker stood up to denounce the Local 7 leadership. They didn't have to take a strike vote to find out how the membership of Local 7 felt—people were determined to stay out until John Miller had his job back with no penalty.[62]

Local 7 leadership replied that they had no basis for struggling against speedup. "Our hands are tied. It's company prerogative," said Sammy Bellamo, Local 7's president.[63] Instead of using the firing of eight workers to inspire workers to fight for better conditions, they warned them to "go through official channels." The March 1973 Jefferson wildcat was impressive for its length, lasting four days on both shifts, in the face of the officials' total opposition, when, normally, wildcat strikes could be sustained for only a few hours.

By July 1973, with speedup continuing, at one point there were ten wildcats going on simultaneously across the auto industry.[64] But nowhere were conditions worse than in Chrysler's large old Detroit plants, typified by Mack Avenue, where forced overtime had been continuous for months.[65] As one leaflet described the scene:

---

62    United Justice Caucus, Local 7—Jefferson Assembly, "Fight the Firings: Vote Strike," in Arthur Hughes Collection, Box 47, ALUA.

63    Weinberg, *Detroit Auto Uprising*, p. 13.

64    J. Woodward, "Rank and file action can halt sellouts," *Workers' Power* (July 1973). Dodge Main; GM Fleetwood Assembly; GMAD Norwood; Brownstown, Michigan, parts warehouse; Ford Assembly Mahwah; GM Linden; two at Lordstown, Ohio; Chevy Gear and Axle Detroit; Mack stamping.

65    "With the press room running continuously no repairs or maintenance was performed on hi-los [forklifts] and other equipment, unless they were broken down to the point of not operating . . . With scrap handling equipment broken down, scrap would pile up everywhere as the presses kept going. Oil leaks on presses would remain for months. The same leaks in high pressure air lines that gave off shrill, high-pitched screeching noises, twenty-four hours a day, seven days a week. Brakes weren't holding on most hi-los and other trucks causing accidents in the aisle ways that were clogged with stock. Press brakes were slipping and foremen resisted getting them fixed. Jobs were often set up wrong, sometimes making the work harder or leading to safety hazards . . . Accidents began to multiply." Weinberg, *Detroit Auto Uprising*, p. 31.

At least once or twice a month somebody loses a finger or a hand in a press . . . Oil drips from the presses all over your clothes. Most of the time the floors are oily and slippery. You have to work surrounded by scrap and slugs on which you can slip and fall and which can cut you . . . When it is hot outside, it is sizzling inside—particularly in the welding areas where you have to wear heavy protective clothing. The welding fumes are dangerous to health, as are the fumes from the gas hi-los. Welders are always being burned and scarred by the sparks . . . Whenever a worker refuses to place his hands under a die area or to operate an unsafe press, the foreman puts a probationary employee on the job who cannot refuse.[66]

Against this background, Isaac Shorter, a worker in the Jefferson Avenue metal shop, circulated a petition in his department to remove Thomas Woolsey, a foreman whom workers charged with racist harassment.[67] Seventy percent of the metal shop, 214 people, signed the petition. Although a committeeman passed it along to the plant management, nothing was done. According to the UAW, processing the grievance could have taken three months or more.[68] Shorter decided that was too long to wait. At 6 a.m. on July 24, Shorter and his friend Larry Carter locked themselves into the plant's power cage and demanded Woolsey be fired immediately. The plant superintendent called for maintenance to cut open the cage and remove them, but 100–150 workers surrounded the cage to protect them from removal. A steady stream of UAW officials appeared to attempt to persuade the workers to give up their protest and let the union handle the problem. Although the company sent the rest of the plant's workforce home at 10 a.m., the strike continued through the day, with hundreds of workers remaining in the plant. Senior Chrysler management was forced to hold a long meeting on Woolsey's conduct during the sit-in, concluding that Woolsey had "violated every managerial guideline and that he should be discharged immediately."[69]

Nevertheless, the UAW leadership took a strong position against the wildcatters, a UAW International representative arguing that acquiescence

66  Concerned Mack Ave. Workers, "Mack Safety Protest: The Workers' Side of the Story," leaflet in Detroit Revolutionary Movements Collection, Box 5, ALUA.

67  Workers said Woolsey "was a 'speed-up, drive your ass off, fire anyone who doesn't go along with the program' type of supervisor. His specialty was removing all the benches from the area so that workers couldn't sit down even if the line stopped. He bragged about the way he kept the workers moving all the time. He bragged about how much production increased since he took over the department." Weinberg, *Detroit Auto Uprising*, p. 10.

68  "A Precedent in Chrysler Shutdown?" *Detroit News*, July 25, 1973.

69  Interview with C. H. Eschenbach, quoted in Thompson, "Detroit," pp. 24–5.

might cause the union to lose control over workers. As C. H. Eschenbach, the plant labor supervisor, said later, "The union has an obligation to take a very firm stance with the employees with regard to the contract, and these guys did."[70] At 3:15 p.m., UAW international representative Elwood Black told workers over a bullhorn that Chrysler was terminating Woolsey and that they should leave the plant. Chrysler would deal with the strikers the next day, he said. "The auto workers surrounding the cage booed the union representatives out of the area, and Shorter said that they would not get out until both the discharge and their amnesty were put into writing."[71] The strike gained momentum at the afternoon shift change, the next shift joining out of enthusiasm and solidarity, even though they had had no contact with Woolsey.[72] At 7:15 p.m., Shorter and Carter emerged from the cage, victorious, with Woolsey fired and amnesty won. Douglas Fraser, UAW vice president in charge of the Chrysler Department, later said, "The wildcat violated our constitution, the law, the contract, and it really upset our bargaining strategy."[73]

Just two weeks later, still another major wildcat strike took place at a decrepit, ancient Detroit Chrysler factory, this time at the Detroit Forge plant, where for six months, 60 percent of the workforce had worked seven days a week, including involuntary overtime, to meet Chrysler's production schedules. On July 23, Harvey Brooks had his arm crushed on a conveyor belt.[74] Then, on August 3, a worker reported a defective crane to his steward but no correction was made. Two days later the machine severed his middle finger. "An axle flew off a conveyor belt into the chest of an auto worker and the next day (when the belt had yet to be serviced) another worker was told to resume the job. There was still blood on the equipment."[75] Finally, on August 6, 1973, the midnight shift simply refused to enter the plant. At 11 p.m. there were forty to fifty people milling outside the plant. Local 47 president Leon Klea told workers to go to work, in conformity with the contract. "I was jeered and booed and told they

70   Ibid., p. 23ff.

71   Thompson, "Detroit," p. 25.

72   "Old workers as well as young workers, white workers as well as black workers, all joined together in support. At shift change time, several hundred second shift workers entered the plant, joined the throng at the power cage, and vowed they too would stay until the demands had been met." Weinberg, *Detroit Auto Uprising*, pp. 9–10. See also David Shoemaker, "Sit-down Strike Hits Chrysler Racism," *Workers' Power* 80 (August 1973).

73   Thompson, "Detroit," p. 26.

74   "Key Chrysler Plant is Struck," *Detroit News*, August 8, 1973.

75   Jerome Scott, Thomas Stepanski, Karl Williams v. Chrysler Corporation, The United Automobile Workers and Its Local 47, State of Michigan in the Circuit Court of the County of Wayne #75-066-303 CZ, Deposition: Jerome Scott, November 14, 1977, quoted in Thompson, "Detroit," p. 34.

weren't going back to work," he said.[76] By 1:30 a.m., the whole midnight shift was on strike. One hundred and fifty people went to the union hall to discuss their grievances, demanding the reinstatement of two workers discharged after pressing safety grievances.[77]

When Doug Fraser heard that the Forge plant had been struck, he defended the company and blamed "outside agitators" for creating the problem. Personally intervening to get production restarted, he asserted that, "When specific complaints are made by workers the company has been quick to try to remedy bad conditions."[78] But plant activists charged that local officials refused to write up grievances, and on August 9, 1,397 workers were on strike. When the company obtained an injunction against the action, workers tore it up, contending that conditions in the plant were so bad that they needed no outside agitators to lead them. Bullying workers and downplaying their grievances was getting Fraser nowhere, so on August 10, he changed tactics, touring the plant and denouncing its filthy and dangerous working conditions. He threatened to call for a strike vote on August 17 if plant management failed to address the conditions, but this was evidently a ploy to get production going, as Fraser himself told the *Detroit Free Press* he would do everything in his power to get the workers back. "I've done it before," he said.[79]

At a local meeting on Sunday, August 12, workers demanded that at minimum the fired workers be rehired. As one of them put it, "These guys shouldn't get fired, they should get life-saving medals." Fraser called for a return to work, promising conditions would improve and threatening mass dismissals if workers remained out. But workers were outraged at the idea of returning to work with no change in conditions, especially given that the company had just sent eighteen discharge telegrams. For two hours, workers criticized the grievance procedure, plant conditions, and the inaction of local and national union officials. Finally, Klea called for an "informal vote" to return to work. He surveyed the crowd, determining

---

76  Ibid., p. 37.

77  "The union had instructed the workers to go back to work immediately, and the workers had no intention of doing so. They reminded the union that it had previously agreed that conditions were indeed very serious in the plant, but they were getting nowhere. Finally, the auto workers asked their elected officials to leave the meeting. After these officials left, the workers formed their own strike committee and moved to set up picket lines. The fear that the union had expressed during the Jefferson wildcat—that their control was being loosened—was fast becoming a reality when workers told them to leave their own union hall." Thompson, "Detroit," p. 38.

78  Weinberg, *Detroit Auto Uprising*, pp. 23, 25; "Key Chrysler Plant is Struck," *Detroit News*, August 8, 1973.

79  *Detroit Free Press*, August 13, 1973.

that the vote was fifty–fifty (militants claimed it was sixty–forty to continue the action), and declared the strike over. Fraser ordered workers back to work. Only about one-third of the midnight shift, 163 workers, returned to work that evening. Nevertheless, the officers persisted, threatening the strikers' jobs, and 95 percent of the day shift reported to work the next morning. Fraser's promised strike vote was not forthcoming. Conditions in the plant did not improve. Fifteen workers remained fired. Chrysler later reported: "1,397 employees lost 55,880 hours of work; all [of Chrysler's] three engine plants were forced to cut production in half; and car and truck production very nearly came to a standstill in Chrysler plants throughout the country."[80]

Conflict between union leaders and members reached new heights in a strike that started the day after the Forge strike ended. The Mack Avenue stamping plant was the scene of nearly continuous conflict during summer 1973. When die-setters engaged in a departmental strike in early June over the pace of work, they were threatened with firings. Malcolm Woods, a shop steward, tried to intervene, but was promptly fired. On June 8, 1973, workers walked out in protest of the Woods firing. The Woods dismissal would remain a focus of resistance for the rest of summer, as a group of about thirty workers met regularly to discuss a campaign to force the fight on both local and national levels for contract improvements.

Finally, on Friday, August 10, 1973, fifty second-shift workers picketed the local hall protesting inaction in the Woods case, and four days later they closed the plant with a wildcat strike. Bill Gilbreth and Clinton Smith, two members of the revolutionary organization Workers' Action Movement, precipitated the action by sitting down on the production line. But many more workers were involved than just these two, and when Chrysler closed the plant, forty-two remained inside. Jack Weinberg, a participant in the sit-down, described the action:

> Workers started gathering to find out what was going on. A number of midnight shift press room workers who had finished their jobs early but couldn't punch out until 6:30 a.m. joined the growing crowd. Three Detroit policemen strode into the plant to remove Gilbreth. Several from the crowd moved, placing themselves between the police and the . . . worker. The police withdrew, returning minutes later in a group of fifteen. This time several hundred workers stepped into their path. The police left and the workers continued standing there.[81]

---

80  Thompson, "Detroit," p. 43.
81  Weinberg, *Detroit Auto Uprising*, p. 27.

The UAW leadership had had enough. Fraser argued, "I don't think you can capitulate in a situation like this. The agitators, regardless of who they are, represent only a very tiny fraction of the total Chrysler workers." But, as Chrysler and the UAW leadership were well aware, only three of the forty-two workers inside the Mack plant were members of Gilbreth's group, and hundreds more remained outside, shouting that they would defy any police who tried to enter.[82] The sit-down strikers remained inside the whole day. When the next morning twenty-eight of them left to talk with the press, the Detroit police entered the plant and removed the remaining fourteen.

Although the sit-in was over, the strike was not. Two hundred workers and supporters went from the plant gates to the local hall, calling on the union to keep the plant closed until amnesty was guaranteed. Union officials demanded an immediate return to work, but workers established picket lines and the strike continued. By now Chrysler had fired a total of seventy-two workers, creating great animosity among a layer of workers much wider than the wildcat's organizers. Nevertheless, the union now decided upon a demonstration of their power. On August 16, 1973, the UAW bureaucracy, personally led by Doug Fraser, Irving Bluestone, Emil Mazey, and other of the UAW's very top leaders, mobilized a force of one thousand officials and loyalists and, while a hundred police looked on, forcibly removed picket signs from the militants, ushered confused workers into the plant, and physically assaulted workers who wanted to continue to picket. There could be no clearer demonstration of what the UAW had become. As Georgakas and Surkin concisely conclude, "The old guard of the UAW had once led the same kind of flying squads to keep factories shut. Now, they had come full circle and saw the task of the union as seeing that the plants remained open. The inspector of the local police precinct thanked Doug Fraser personally."[83]

Nevertheless, the struggle was still far from over. The day the UAW broke the Mack strike, the Local 3 executive board, plant committee, and stewards council held a closed meeting to discuss dealing with "troublemakers" at Dodge Main. They chased leafleters away from plant gates, continuing to enforce the UAW's new "get tough" policy.[84] But several hundred

---

82 J. Crellin, J. Burdock, P. Bernstein, and R. S. Wisler, "Chrysler Rebels Refuse to End Plant Take-Over," *Detroit News*, August 15, 1973, p. 1.

83 Georgakas and Surkin, *Detroit*, p. 230–1.

84 "[Andrew] Hardy [Local 3 president] has never written one article in the many years he has been at the Local attacking and exposing Chrysler management for the rotten conditions we face. He writes article after article attacking rank and filers. He talks about building the UAW. We disagree that that's the way you build a strong Union." "Strike Back: Which Side Are They On?" leaflet issued by Edith Fox and others, Dodge Main, UAW Local 3, n.d. (August 1973), in ALUA.

Dodge Main workers engaged in repeated wildcats in late August and early September because of heat inside the plant and forced overtime. "If the union was giving us good representation, this crap wouldn't be going on," was a common complaint.[85]

## Economic Recession and the Decline of Rank-and-File Militancy

In fall 1973, a high level of wildcat strikes continued to plague the auto industry, and rank-and-file militants considered ways to more successfully resist the companies and the union leadership. As late as spring 1974, militants at the Mack Avenue plant were regrouping to launch a slate in the local elections. But in December 1973, under the impact of rising oil prices, the boom abruptly ended. By February 1974, more than 100,000 auto workers were on indefinite layoff—an unprecedented level at this time[86]—and a year later, in January 1975, a Big Three total of 164,050 workers were in that position, nearly one-quarter of all UAW members at these firms. If one includes workers on temporary layoff, fully 50 percent were out of work.[87] Unemployment benefits helped, but were undercut by runaway inflation. The prospect of permanent joblessness cast a cloud of gloom over the auto workers.[88]

During 1974, there continued to be a high level of strikes, but they were now of a different character. Employers took a harder line in bargaining in 1974, so that three months after the approval of the national contract, 69 of 312 locals still lacked local agreements. As Irving Bluestone, head of the UAW's GM Department, said, "Where layoffs have hit hard, bargaining is not going well. I don't think there's any question that our extreme reluctance to threaten a strike has slowed progress."[89] Indeed, as early as 1974, top UAW leaders were themselves proposing concessions in response to the changed economic conditions. Irving Bluestone suggested that workers abandon part of the cost-of-living increases. The money saved could help prop up the Supplemental Unemployment Benefits fund. Doug Fraser proposed Chrysler speed up Jefferson Assembly with union approval in order to keep it open.[90] While the worst concession bargaining was still

---

85  See Dan Georgakas Collection, Box 2, ALUA.
86  Irving Bluestone to Leonard Woodcock, February 21, 1974; George B. Morris to Irving Bluestone, January 11, 1974, both in Leonard Woodcock Collection, Box 26, ALUA.
87  J. Weinberg, "UAW Response to the Economic Crisis," *Network* 1 (February–March 1975), p.15.
88  Georgakas and Surkin, *Detroit*, p. 238. I have appropriated several of Georgakas and Surkin's phrases.
89  "Heavy Layoffs Squeeze the UAW's Cast," *Business Week*, February 23, 1974, p. 84.
90  Weinberg, "UAW Response."

to come, by 1976, even with the new economic upturn, the UAW could not but recognize that the companies were in a position to bargain much harder than in the past, and were willing to withstand strikes to gain more favorable contracts. One top UAW official called an early offer by Ford in the 1976 negotiations "the worst piece of paper ever presented to us."[91]

The period between 1974 and 1978 was a time of transition. For Chrysler, 1974 and 1975 saw a significant decline in unauthorized strikes, but 1976 and 1977 were years of militancy comparable to the 1965–73 period. General Motors exhibited an essentially similar pattern. After that, however, strikes, both authorized and unauthorized, drop to consistently lower levels. Before 1974, thanks to relatively full employment, wide layers of workers could engage in unauthorized actions with impunity and were willing to entertain militants' alternative framing of their interests, which emphasized action independent from and opposed to the bureaucracy, black demands, an emphasis on safety issues, and, for some auto workers, building their own organizations, like the League of Revolutionary Black Workers or the United National Caucus. But in the years after 1973, the continual threat of joblessness turned workers' attention away from everything but the issue of job security and left them increasingly dependent upon the union. As William Bean, a UAW Local 51 steward, put it:

> The people really weren't ready for the massive layoffs. They were in a position where they thought they had security. They found out they didn't have any. Now they're back. And after layoffs, most people think that the people become stronger. But they don't. They're worried. About their jobs and how long it will last . . . So they're not stronger. They are weaker. And they accept a lot of things they wouldn't ordinarily accept.[92]

But the worst was yet to come. In 1979, the era of all-out concession bargaining began, when the Carter administration demanded that the workers provide major givebacks to the company as the price of bailing out the Chrysler corporation. By 1980–1, the U.S. auto industry was in perhaps the worst crisis in its history, hit simultaneously by the worst downturn of the postwar era, a rising wave of competition from Japanese imports, and a shift in consumer preferences toward small cars. Literally hundreds of thousands of people had lost their jobs. Communities dependent on the auto

---

91  Elissa Clark, "Could Ford's offer be so bad that even Woodcock turns it down?" *Workers' Power*, September 6, 1976, in Detroit Labor Papers, Box 2.
92  C. Williams, "Auto fight starts now," *Workers' Power*, August 21–September 3, 1975, in Detroit Labor Papers, Box 2.

industry suffered devastating losses in employment and financial resources. All the domestic producers had experienced big financial losses and had permanently closed a number of large facilities.[93] The situation called for a strategic thinking on the part of the UAW, and labor more generally, of a qualitatively different sort from anything undertaken previously. But a labor officialdom that had been unable to stir itself against the companies at the peak of auto profitability and prosperity in 1964 could not, in this moment of crisis for the automakers, begin to break itself from the pattern of adapting to the requirements of the industry. Since the auto rank and file, even at the height of its militancy and creativity, had been unable to carry the union beyond its commitment to the reproduction of the bureaucracy and business unionism, it was in no position to offer an alternative.

---

93   National Academy of Engineering, *The Competitive Status of the U.S. Auto Industry*, p. 10.

# American Petrograd: Detroit and the League of Revolutionary Black Workers

## Kieran Taylor

One year after the Detroit Rebellion and four weeks after Martin Luther King, Jr.'s assassination, a series of wildcat strikes rocked the Chrysler Corporation's Dodge Main plant, leading to the formation of the Dodge Revolutionary Union Movement (DRUM)—a militant black worker organization.[1] To jittery city leaders, plant managers, and union officials, the workplace protests and the emergence of DRUM appeared as a spontaneous outburst of rage, but they were the result of years of planning by a group of African American working-class intellectuals who built the organization upon deep feelings of anger and desperation among black workers in the Motor City.[2] Beginning in the mid-1960s, the automakers responded to rising demand and foreign competition by maximizing productivity through assembly-line speedups that caused enormous strain

---

[1]  The author thanks David Cline, Erik Gellman, Jacquelyn Hall, Sarah Nyante, and Heather Thompson for their good criticisms of this chapter, and Jennifer Coombs for her hospitality during my visits to Detroit. General Baker, Rich Feldman, Ron Glotta, Mike Hamlin, Marian Kramer, Jim Jacobs, Frank Joyce, David Riddle, and Wendy Thompson were generous with their time and insights, and patient with my questions. All of the interview recordings and transcripts are located in the Southern Oral History Program Collection #4007, Southern Historical Collection, Wilson Library, University of North Carolina at Chapel Hill.

[2]  The unrest in the plants was mirrored by the discontent in black neighborhoods, where housing choices for African Americans were tightly constrained by discriminatory realty, banking, and insurance practices. For decades, white neighborhood associations also re-enforced rigid patterns of housing segregation through grassroots political organizing and acts of intimidation and terror. The Detroit Police Department, in the minds of many young African Americans, was "an army of occupation." (Ed Vaughn, interviewed by Kim Hunter for *Against the Current* in 1997. For the best overview of Detroit in the postwar era, see T. Sugrue, *The Origins of the Urban Crisis: Race and Inequality in Postwar Detroit* [Princeton, NJ: Princeton University Press, 1996].).

on the workforce, particularly the young African American workers who were relegated to the hardest, dirtiest, and most dangerous jobs. The United Auto Workers (UAW), while supportive of the mainstream civil rights movement, did little to challenge the industry's racist employment practices, which kept most black workers out of management and the skilled trades. The union's staff and the leadership of many UAW locals also remained overwhelmingly white, even though African Americans made up a fourth of the workforce and a majority at many of the plants in the city.

Within a few months, revolutionary union movements sprung up at dozens of other plants and industries across the city. By 1969 these groups had formed an umbrella group—the League of Revolutionary Black Workers, which at its height gave voice to the demands of young African American workers for an end to job discrimination and unsafe working conditions, while it organized around issues well beyond the workplace. Propelled by a boundless sense of possibility, League members battled police brutality, advocated local control of schools, and provided legal counsel to defendants in several high-profile political trials. They also launched a publishing house and film production company to encourage the formation of revolutionary union movements outside of Detroit, and they attracted attention from some of the country's most prominent radical activists. Though the League ultimately failed to transform itself into an ongoing labor-based organization, its brief existence represented the high point of a more than ten-year drive to fuse the energy of Detroit's student and civil rights movements with the growing discontent of black workers. These efforts preceded the League's formation by several years, continued well into the 1970s, and inspired hundreds of similar alliances of radical activists and workers.[3]

Young, working-class African Americans with links to the full spectrum of the city's vibrant left stood at the center of the Detroit black workers' movement. General Baker, Jr. had deep ties to the black nationalist community and was a member of both the Garveyist African Nationalist Pioneer Movement and a rifle club inspired by the self-defense gun clubs of the fugitive black activist Robert F. Williams.[4] Though Baker's

---

3   The best overviews of the black worker protests in Detroit include D. Georgakas and M. Surkin, *Detroit: I Do Mind Dying* 2nd ed. (Cambridge, MA: South End Press, 1998); J. A. Geschwender, *Class, Race and Worker Insurgency: The League of Revolutionary Black Workers* (Cambridge: Cambridge University Press, 1977); and H. A. Thompson, *Whose Detroit?: Politics, Labor, and Race in a Modern American City* (Ithaca: Cornell University Press, 2001). See also E. Allen, "Dying From the Inside: the Decline of the League of Revolutionary Black Workers," in D. Cluster, ed., *They Should Have Served that Cup of Coffee* (Boston: South End Press, 1979), pp. 71–109.

4   The Pioneers were led by Dominican-born New Yorker Carlos Cooks. Baker joined

nationalist mentors fed his growing intellectual curiosity with black history books and pamphlets, he came to regard them as "weekend militants who wanted to sit up and talk black shit on Saturday and Sunday and go kiss ass all week."[5] As a student at Highland Park Community College and Wayne State University—an urban campus with a strong tradition of radical activism—Baker joined protests against police brutality and the war. He also traveled to Cuba in 1964 with a delegation of radical youth. There he played baseball with the heroes of the revolution—Fidel and Raul Castro and Juan Almeida Bosque—and met with Che Guevara and dozens of other revolutionaries from around the world. Baker's discussions with these radicals challenged the narrowness of his black nationalism and pushed him in the direction of multinational Marxism-Leninism. "I just had to go stay in a hotel a couple of days just trying to regroup," he recalled. "Everything you thought you used to know was gone out the window."[6] Upon returning to Detroit in the fall, Baker drifted away from the black nationalists but continued to study and organize, as well as work a new job on the line at Dodge Main.[7]

Mississippi native and former U.S. Army sergeant Mike Hamlin brought to the movement a strong commitment to conflict mediation, organization building, and the development of outside allies. After attending high school in Ecorse, just outside of Detroit, and doing a stint in the Army, Hamlin

---

the organization shortly after hearing Malcolm X address a February 1962 police brutality protest rally at Detroit's Olympia Stadium. He also worked at the Pioneers' bookstore and participated in their reading groups (Baker, interview by author, May 24, 2004). Through informers and spies, the Detroit Police Department maintained a close watch on Baker and his associates in the Fox and Wolf Hunting Club (see The Black Power Movement, Part 4; The League of Revolutionary Black Workers Papers, 1965–1976, Reel 2, Intelligence Bureau Files General Baker, 1 and 2). Baker was also affiliated with the clandestine Revolutionary Action Movement (see The League of Revolutionary Black Workers Papers, 1965–1976, Reel 2, Detroit Police Files, Index Cards). North Carolina NAACP leader and advocate of armed self-defense, Robert Williams was chased from the state by the police and the FBI following a near race riot in his hometown of Monroe in 1961. He fled with his wife Mabel to Cuba. For more on Williams, see T. Tyson, *Radio Free Dixie: Robert F. Williams and the Roots of Black Power* (Chapel Hill: University of North Carolina Press, 2001).

5  Baker, interview by author, May 24, 2004.

6  Ibid. Baker was among a group of eighty-four students who defied the U.S. State Department ban on travel to Cuba. The trip was sponsored by Progressive Labor, an early 1960s offshoot of the Communist Party. While in Cuba, Baker also spent time at the home of Robert and Mabel Williams, who in exile were becoming important figures in the growing Black Power movement.

7  During this period, Baker and some of his comrades attended presentations at Debs Hall sponsored by the Socialist Workers Party, and they developed ties with older Detroit radicals like James and Grace Lee Boggs and Martin Glaberman, all of whom had been close associates of Trinidadian Marxist C. L. R. James.

returned to the city in 1960 "greatly frustrated, alienated, and disaffected by the conditions" facing African Americans.[8] Were it not for his friendship with precocious and eccentric black radical John Watson, Hamlin suspects he might have become a "suicidal revolutionary," perpetrating acts of violence against white people or self-destructing.[9] Watson was eight years younger than Hamlin, but had attended Detroit's preeminent public high school—Cass Technical High School—and developed contacts with intellectuals and left-wing activists as a teenager in the late 1950s. As they worked together in the distribution department at the *Detroit News*, Watson encouraged Hamlin to study Marxism and convinced him that through organizing the working class he could help make positive change. Both men were active with the mainline civil rights groups, including the NAACP and the Congress of Racial Equality (CORE), and they were impressed by the Socialist Workers Party's and the Communist Party's rhetorical commitment to class struggle. But ultimately they felt that neither the civil rights organizations nor the Old Left communist parties had developed a program to match the rising militancy of Detroit's black workers.

Hamlin and Watson were joined at the *Detroit News* by Ken Cockrel, a charismatic law student who became the League's best-known figure. Cockrel was born just outside of Detroit in 1938 and raised in the city by his aunt and uncle after his parents died when he was twelve. He dropped out of high school and joined the Air Force in 1955, but earned undergraduate and law degrees from Wayne State after his discharge. At campus rallies, Cockrel delivered fiery speeches against racism and the war in the early days of the antiwar movement. A sharp talker by all accounts, Cockrel quickly made a name for himself as an impressive orator and a combative debater.

Marian Kramer, who was one of just a handful of women among the leaders of the black workers' movement, had a more traditional civil rights pedigree than her male counterparts. She had served as a CORE field organizer in her native Louisiana before relocating to Detroit in 1964. There she found work as a secretary for the Hotel Employees and Restaurant Employees Union (HERE), while devoting much of her political energies to the growing welfare reform movement and the West Central Organization (WCO), a community group that represented the interests of the poor and working-class residents of neighborhoods bordering the

---

8   "BWC Leader Looks at Past, Sees New Stage of Struggle," *Guardian*, February 28, 1973.

9   Mike Hamlin, interview by author, June 19, 2004. In an earlier interview, Hamlin elaborated on his state of mind as a young man: "I was interested in terrorist kind of activities. It was a response to frustration. A lot of people at that time talked about kamikaze or suicidal attacks. You would end your pain and you would strike a blow." (See R. Mast, *Detroit Lives* [Philadelphia: Temple University Press, 1994], p. 85.)

ever expanding Wayne State.[10] The organization was a locus for various groups of Detroit activists, including white organizers, black nationalists, neighborhood leaders, liberal clergy, and radical students and professors.

By the mid-1960s this group of black radicals had attended college classes, campaigned to end the war, participated in Marxist study groups, and worked in factories together. They had shared apartments and an occasional jail cell. Each had also attracted the interest of the Detroit Police Department's Red Squad—a special unit that had tracked the activities of "subversive" organizations and individuals since the 1930s.[11] While these young radicals were committed to the black freedom struggle, they were critical of the existing protest organizations and the unions, none of which seemed able to connect to black workers and youth. The Old Left political parties offered theoretical rigor but had few activities beyond educational programs, and had only casual ties to black workers in the late 1960s. The city's white youth and student-based radical groups distrusted and at times disdained the working class and geared their efforts toward the swelling movement on college campuses. The UAW they dismissed as hopelessly racist. Given these limitations, Hamlin, Baker, and their associates decided that they would have to "create the kind of thing we needed, a new avenue of struggle, a new method of dealing with oppression and exploitation."[12]

Their formation of a black student group—UHURU (the Swahili word for freedom)—at Wayne State in 1963 marked one of their earliest efforts to create such an organization. UHURU members published and distributed *Razor* for students and the worker-oriented *Black Vanguard*, which included essays urging readers to form a "League of Black Workers," and featured excerpts from Robert Williams's account of his flight from North Carolina and contributions from auto workers describing their shop-floor experiences with racism.[13] Longer theoretical articles argued that because

---

10   Marian Kramer, interview by author, May 19, 2004. Kramer's work in the South came to an end in 1964 when she married a white CORE organizer. Believing it was too risky to live and work together in Louisiana, they moved to Detroit.

11   Baker's and Cockrel's Red Squad files include detailed accounts of meetings and demonstrations, information gathered from informants and spies, and employment records. Though sometimes heavily redacted, the files suggest that the police had tracked Cockrel, Baker, Watson, and other comrades for several years, and that informants had penetrated some of the radical groups to which they belonged. For Cockrel's Red Squad files, see Box 2, Folders 9–17, Kenneth V. and Sheila M. Cockrel Collection, the Walter P. Reuther Library of Labor and Urban Affairs, Detroit (hereafter Reuther Library). For Baker's police, FBI, and IRS files, see The Black Power Movement, Part 4, The League of Revolutionary Black Workers Papers, 1965–1976, Reels 2–3.

12   "BWC Leader Looks at Past," *Guardian*, February 28, 1973.

13   Williams's book was popular among black militants in the 1960s. See R. Williams, *Negroes With Guns* (Detroit: Wayne State University Press, 1998).

black workers were clustered at the center of basic industry, they would play a strategic role in a larger revolutionary struggle by disrupting capitalist production. This was a theme to which they would continually return over the next several years. The tone of the publications was deliberately provocative, frequently denouncing the "white crackers," the "brutes in blue," and Uncle Toms, who posed "the greatest menace to the black freedom struggle." The editors believed the incendiary tone accurately reflected the anger and despair of young African Americans in Detroit.[14]

In addition to producing the publications, UHURU members protested Detroit's failure to pass an open housing ordinance by disrupting a 1963 torch-passing ceremony promoting the city's bid to host the 1968 Olympic Games. Baker, Watson, and four others were arrested for booing during the national anthem and taunting the torch bearer—an African American medal winner.[15] Two years later, Baker and his associates posted dozens of signs around Detroit promising a major "smash the draft" protest at his upcoming draft hearing. The police kept close tabs on Baker in the weeks before the promised protest, and they were relieved when fewer than a dozen supporters showed up at the Fort Wayne Induction Center on the city's southwest side. Baker attended his hearing and was rejected by the draft board, to whom he had issued a statement accusing the U.S. military of having on its hands the blood of Angolan and South African freedom fighters, Patrice Lumumba, Medgar Evers, and the "defenseless women and children burned in villages from Napalm jelly bombs."[16]

UHURU attracted relatively little attention beyond that of the Detroit Police Department, but the Detroit Rebellion opened up new possibilities

---

14   See, for example, "Traitors," *Black Vanguard*, August 1965, Reel 1, The Black Power Movement, Part 4, The League of Revolutionary Black Workers Papers, 1965–1976.

15   The UHURU protests were part of a larger NAACP demonstration. The accused were later acquitted. See "Five Bias Foes Acquitted in Jeering of National Anthem," *Detroit Free Press*, February 24, 1966.

16   Detroit Police observers noted that only nine protesters attended the rally, which followed several weeks of buildup during which Baker and his friends posted inflammatory signs, such as: "Damn the draft—to hell with whities' army. Join the Sept. 10 movement." See The Black Power Movement, Part 4, The League of Revolutionary Black Workers Papers, 1965–1976, Reel 2, Detroit Police Files, Index Cards; for the text of Baker's statement to the draft board, see Baker, "Fight for Freedom," *Inner City Voice*, 1970, Detroit Revolutionary Movements Collection, Reuther Library. Baker later reported that the idea had been to scare the police into believing the protest would be much larger, though he had hoped for more support from his friends in the black nationalist community: "It was a lonely trek down there that day because all these nationalists . . . and all these assholes that I done come up through this. They were scared. The reason they didn't come is because they was chicken shit. They were scared. They were halfway scared of us and damn sure halfway scared of what we were saying." (See Baker, interview by author, May 24, 2004.)

for the kind of mass movement that the black radicals had envisioned. On July 23, 1967, vice officers raided an after-hours party at Twelfth Street and Clairmount Avenue on the near west side. A crowd soon gathered and began hurling rocks and smashing windows. The incident spread quickly to the east side and erupted into a citywide rebellion, during which thousands of African Americans took to the streets, attacking the police and looting stores. The National Guard and the US Army 82nd Airborne Division quelled the violence, but after five days of fighting, more than forty people had been killed and more than one thousand were injured. According to many accounts, it was the most destructive urban upheaval of the 1960s.[17]

General Baker was among the seven thousand people, mostly young and black, who were rounded up and jailed in the midst of the turmoil. For two weeks he was held at Ionia State Penitentiary, where he witnessed generalized feelings of despair and anger transformed into political consciousness among the other prisoners.[18] "People had seen the naked role of the state, and they hated these goddamned police," he later remarked. "My cellblock looked like the damned assembly line. It had so many people I worked with that were arrested too." As black workers returned to the plants after the Rebellion, the anger and militancy carried over into the factories. Workers fashioned the bullet casings that littered the city streets into necklaces and wore them as a symbol of resistance. Back at his job at Dodge Main, Baker recalled that "people came back in that plant with their hair grown out [in afros], and fifty caliber bullets around their neck and it was a sight to see. They weren't taking any more shit."[19]

By the time of the Rebellion, *Razor* and *Black Vanguard* had dissolved. Watson, Hamlin, Baker, and the other black activists who had been frequenting the West Central Organization office responded to the rising mood of militancy with a new newspaper—the *Inner City Voice*. They hoped the *Voice*, like the earlier publications, could serve as the tool around which they might "build an organization of black workers, black students both in high schools and colleges, and ultimately to create a black Marxist-Leninist

---

17 For more on the Rebellion, see S. Fine, *Violence in the Model City: The Cavanaugh Administration, Race Relations and the Detroit Riot of 1967* (Ann Arbor: University of Michigan Press, 1988); F. R. Harris, I. Wicker, comp., *The Kerner Commission Report: The 1968 Report of the National Advisory Commission on Civil Disorders* (Washington, DC: GPO, 1968); and "The 43 Who Died," *Detroit Free Press*, September 3, 1967.

18 Baker was arrested on a curfew restriction—a violation of the terms of his parole related to an earlier arrest during what was known as the Kercheval mini-riot of 1966. See R. Bragaw, "2 in Kercheval Race Case Get 5-Year Probation Terms," *Detroit Free Press*, March 29, 1967.

19 Baker, interview by author, May 24, 2004.

Party."[20] But beginning with its inaugural issue in September 1967, *Voice* editors made it more accessible than its predecessors, and it quickly found a wider audience. Like *Razor* and *Black Vanguard*, it included coverage of incidents of police brutality and discrimination in the plants, but the longer theoretical pieces gave way to articles on the national antiwar movement and local news of interest to African Americans.

Those involved with the new newspaper had held industrial jobs intermittently and had long discussed the need for organizing workers at the point of production, but, as Hamlin admitted, they "had never had a successful entrée into the plants with the workers" and "really didn't understand how to go about it."[21] Nevertheless, by early 1968, General Baker had begun to attract a small following of black workers at Dodge Main, which employed about nine thousand mostly African American workers. For several weeks, Baker met with a small group of his coworkers to discuss *Voice* articles, racial discrimination, and conditions on the shop floor. To prevent any participant from being fingered as a ringleader by company spies, Mike Hamlin, who was not a Dodge employee, chaired the meetings.

Their opportunity to move from discussion to action came unexpectedly a month after Martin Luther King, Jr.'s assassination. In May 1968 workers at Dodge Main carried out several spontaneous wildcat strikes over production-line speedups. Though the strikes had been instigated by both white and black workers, the focus of the struggle shifted quickly when Dodge laid most of the blame for the strikes on the black workers. Baker and another worker were fired, and dozens more black workers were suspended. The UAW declined to defend the fired workers.[22]

It was at this point that Baker and a group of about ten black workers vowed to fight the dismissals and suspensions. They adopted the name Dodge Revolutionary Union Movement to make it clear that theirs was not a reformist approach to change. As Hamlin put it, "we had certain radical ideas and a certain revolutionary line: that black workers would be the

---

20   According to Watson, who served as editor, they believed the newspaper would also serve as the "focus of a permanent organization, it could provide a bridge between the peaks of activity. It creates an organization and organizes the division of labor among revolutionaries. Revolutionaries do something, not just a meeting on Sundays, making speeches and passing resolutions. It creates the kind of division of labor needed not just for the newspaper but for a revolutionary organization." See "Black Editor: An Interview," *Radical America*, July–August 1968.

21   "Our Thing Is DRUM," reprinted from *Leviathan*, June 1970, Box 1, Folder 6, Detroit Revolutionary Movements Collection, Reuther Library.

22   The UAW may have been at odds with local union leaders, who together with Chrysler wished to get rid of DRUM. See Geschwender, *Class, Race and Worker Insurgency*, p. 90.

vanguard to the liberation struggle in this country."[23] Right away, DRUM leaders made two critical decisions. Because their point of unity was the company's racist application of discipline and the union's unwillingness to defend black workers, they decided to remain exclusively black. DRUM hoped "to prove to black workers that they alone had enough strength to control the productive capacity inside the shop." DRUM also committed to closing "the communications gap," which had been an important barrier to organizing in the enormous ten-story facility. Workers seldom had access to reliable information regarding incidents and conditions outside of their own departments. By distributing leaflets at both ends of the plant, DRUM aimed to "consolidate the people around the same issues."[24]

Over the next several weeks, DRUM issued a series of provocative newsletters and leaflets blasting Chrysler and UAW racism. These charges resonated with young black workers, who began looking to DRUM for leadership. "You can only agitate for so long [before] people start demanding that you do something because I guess you've done perked their consciousness enough so that they've moved further from where they used to be and now they want action," Baker remembered. "By the time you put out leaflets about eight or nine weeks people started saying 'You're talking shit. Now what you going to do?'" As a test of strength, DRUM issued a flier urging a boycott of the convenience stores and restaurants across from the plant that had refused to hire African Americans. The surprising success of the boycott indicated to Baker that "these people are ready."[25]

Those early efforts led to larger rallies and demonstrations and culminated in DRUM's first strike. On July 8, DRUM called for a walkout of black workers at the plant. In order to avoid further retaliation against its leaders, DRUM arranged for student and community supporters to distribute fliers at the plant gates.[26] DRUM later boasted that 70 percent of the black workforce stayed out of the plant, crippling Chrysler's production for the better part of three days. Fearing additional wildcat strikes, Chrysler obtained an injunction against DRUM that prevented Baker and other leaders from further picketing. This proved to be a critical blow to the movement, and its impact continued to be felt for months, as Baker was the DRUM leader with the most organizing experience and the strongest relationship to the workers.

---

23   "Our Thing Is DRUM," reprinted from *Leviathan*.

24   Baker, interview by author, May 24, 2004.

25   Ibid.

26   The flier included the following slogans: "Strike your blow against racism do your part no work today" and "Black workers strike Only racist honkies and Uncle Tom's Traitors work today." DRUM, flier, July 1968, Box 1, Folder 6, Detroit Revolutionary Movements Collection, Reuther Library.

With Baker no longer working at Dodge Main and DRUM leaders prohibited from picketing, some DRUM members began arguing that they should capitalize on the momentum of the strikes and shift focus to vying for power within Local 3. DRUM had initially viewed the union, UAW Local 3, as hopelessly compromised by its racism and complacency. Ron March was a DRUM activist who had supported an earlier multiracial reform caucus within Local 3, but he and other black radicals believed that the UAW had used their group to "unify black workers behind sell out candidates" for office who failed to confront Chrysler's racist practices and the union's racist culture.[27] After considerable deliberation, DRUM launched a campaign to elect March union trustee in September 1968. His success in a preliminary election stunned UAW leaders, who responded quickly to prevent his advance to the run-off. Local 3 members ripped DRUM literature from walls and solicited the help of the police, who spied on black workers and disrupted their political and social gatherings. On election day, black workers reported that they had been prevented from voting after being detained by the police for routine traffic violations.[28] March lost in the run-off after Local 3 mobilized a large numbers of white working members as well as retirees, many of whom did not normally vote in union elections. Local 3, often with UAW international support, used similar tactics to defeat DRUM candidates again in 1969 and 1970.[29]

As news of DRUM spread, black workers formed Revolutionary Union Movements at other Detroit-area auto plants, as well as at Blue Cross and Blue Shield, United Parcel Service, Henry Ford Hospital, and the *Detroit News*. These efforts quickly outstripped DRUM's organizational capacity, so Hamlin, Baker, Cockrel, and their comrades formed the League of Revolutionary Black Workers in early 1969 to coordinate the

---

27   He dismissed the reform effort as "a bourgeois social thing. It created divisions which led into opportunism among some of the members." Excluding whites gave DRUM "a sense of togetherness" and prevented "the kinds of division we had experienced," according to March. See Donna Shoemaker, "Drum Beat," *The Fifth Estate*, October 17–30, 1968.

28   When DRUM supporters inquired about those arrested, they were forcibly turned away from the police station, so they moved across the street to their union hall, where they were soon joined by the mayor and a police commissioner. A short while later, a white union official led the police into the hall, where they again attacked black workers with clubs and mace in an effort to liberate the city officials who they claimed were being held captive. See DRUM, "Victory, victory," September 1968, Box 1, Folder 8, Detroit Revolutionary Movements Collection, Reuther Library.

29   For a detailed account of DRUM's failed electoral efforts in Local 3, see Thompson, *Whose Detroit?* pp. 160–70. For Baker's account of the Ron March campaign, see H. Harris and L. Stiefel, "Dodge Revolutionary Union Movement (DRUM): A Study Through Interviews," September 15, 1969, Box 1, Folder 10, Enid Eckstein Collection, Reuther Library.

various workplace-based activities. Marian Kramer and other women were also instrumental in the formation of the League—a reflection of their growing importance within the movement. Women had performed many of the behind-the-scenes duties, including clerical work, leaflet editing, and literature distribution, and they had assumed leadership roles on picket lines and at demonstrations in order to shield male workers from plant discipline.[30] Those responsibilities provided women a platform from which they pushed the League to include within its umbrella the grassroots community organizing many of them had been doing since before DRUM's formation. The League's culture, nevertheless, remained strongly masculine to the end. Kramer recalled that "male supremacy was rampant and we never got proper credit" for fighting urban renewal and police brutality, and defending the rights of tenants and welfare recipients.[31]

Over the next year, the League and its various affiliates pulled off a string of audacious protest activities, including additional wildcat strikes, a year-long takeover of the student newspaper at Wayne State University, electoral campaigns on behalf of black militants seeking union office, demonstrations at UAW headquarters, and high-profile legal defense activities on behalf of black workers and other fellow radicals. Other activities included the operation of a book discussion club, an education reform coalition, a Black Student United Front for high school students, and a national outreach effort to establish Revolutionary Union Movements in other cities.

The League's efforts at Chrysler's Eldon Avenue Gear and Axle—representing its most sustained organizing at one worksite—illustrates some of the strengths and limitations of the organization's work. In November of 1968, just four months after the formation of DRUM, black workers at Eldon Avenue—who made up about 60 percent of the plant's four thousand workers—formed ELRUM and began distributing flyers and a newsletter. Within two months, ELRUM had built up enough support among black workers to launch its first action—a meeting at the union hall, where they confronted their union president and presented him with a list of grievances. The following day, dozens of these workers who had taken

---

30   The presence of women at League demonstrations is highlighted in the reports of plant security officers: "One female demonstrator was dressed in bright colored kimono, seemed to be leading the others." The same report notes that twelve of twenty-five demonstrators were women. See H. Archambeau, "Demonstration March in front of General Office building, Highland Park," July 12–13, 1968, Box 4, Folder 31, Detroit Revolutionary Movements Collection, Reuther Library.

31   Mast, *Detroit Lives*, p. 104. For more on the experiences of women within the League, see Edna Ewell Watson's reflections in Georgakas and Surkin, *Detroit: I Do Mind Dying*, pp. 221–7, and Kramer, interview by author, May 19, 2004.

part in the meeting received written reprimands and suspensions of up to one month for being away from work without authorization.[32]

Shortly after 5 a.m. on January 27, ELRUM supporters—including students and other community allies to protect workers from further reprisals—formed pickets of ten to thirty protesters at each of three plant entrances and asked black workers to stay home for one day to protest the suspensions. Hundreds of black workers honored the picket lines, and the strike crippled production at the plant. As Eldon was Chrysler's sole supplier of axles, the disruption had a ripple effect throughout Chrysler's Detroit area plants. The company's response was swift and severe. Twenty-six workers were discharged for their participation in the work stoppage, including an ELRUM cofounder and other key members. Nearly one hundred other black workers were suspended. As at Dodge Main, the dismissals undermined the Revolutionary Union Movement's ability to sustain momentum by separating the leaders from their base. Working ELRUM members, now reduced to a handful, kept a low profile for much of the rest of the year, until a new round of shop-floor conflicts erupted.[33]

In April 1970, a confrontation between a black worker and his white supervisor triggered another series of unauthorized strikes; ELRUM members again took a leading role in these wildcats, but this time they were joined in an uneasy alliance by other radical groups who had also been organizing within the plant. When Chrysler retaliated by suspending many of the union stewards who had called their workers out, ELRUM members formed the Eldon Safety Committee along with white radicals and some of the stewards. After being instructed by their lawyers that workers were not obligated to work under abnormally dangerous conditions, Safety Committee members believed they had found a strategy for carrying out legal work stoppages without fear of violating the law or risking company injunctions. They initiated an extensive research program to document plant conditions and to force the company to make improvements by threatening safety strikes.[34]

---

32  ELRUM, "Calling Black Workers Everywhere!" (1969), Box 1, Folder 15, Detroit Revolutionary Movements Collection, Reuther Library.

33  Plant security reports from the January 27 protest indicated that picketers, including General Baker, who was battling his dismissal from Dodge Main and restricted from activity there, carried placards with signs such as: "Long live heroic black power struggle," "All racist honkies and Toms out of the plant," and "Be a man strike back only uncle Toms and aunt Susies work today." See H. Engelbrecht, "Incident Report," January 27, 1969, and H. G. Phipps, "ELRUM pickets," January 27, 1969, Box 2, Folder 25, Detroit Revolutionary Movements Collection, Reuther Library.

34  John Taylor interview, August 25, 1972, Box 3, Folder 17, Dan Georgakas Collection, Reuther Library.

But events in the plant soon provided evidence of the poor safety conditions that was far more compelling than any list of unsafe practices and faulty machinery. On May 26, Gary Thompson died when his faulty jitney malfunctioned and he was buried under three thousand pounds of scrap metal. A twenty-two-year-old black veteran, Thompson had survived Vietnam "only to be crushed" under a pile of steel at Eldon.[35] Thompson was preceded in death by two black women on the line. Two weeks before Thompson's death, Mamie Williams had been ordered to work despite her physician's recommendation that she stay home. She was rushed from the plant in an ambulance before dying that evening. Rose Logan, a janitor, was struck in the leg by an overloaded jitney and developed a fatal blood clot.[36]

The day after Thompson's death, the Eldon Safety Committee and ELRUM organized picket lines around the plant urging workers to stay out. This strike, while not as successful as the earlier wildcats, nevertheless crippled Chrysler's axle production for a day. Once again, in retaliation, Chrysler fired three key ELRUM leaders, as well as John Taylor, a white Appalachian worker on the Safety Committee who had worked closely with ELRUM members.

ELRUM never regained a solid presence within the Eldon plant due primarily to the dismissals of key members, its inability to protect its leaders from company discipline, and its failure to develop a structure to support workers' struggles over the long haul. Eldon workers continued to battle for better union representation and safe working conditions, but, for the most part, ELRUM remained on the sidelines, according to Taylor, who grew critical of ELRUM during this period for disregarding workers who could have been potential allies. Those ELRUM members still in the plant occasionally attended union meetings, but they were "into a program of disruption" that "was insulting to those workers who had come to the hall in good faith to take care of whatever business they thought important."[37] Older black workers, as well as white members who may have agreed with ELRUM's criticisms, found their style and rhetoric alienating. The second issue of the ELRUM newsletter, for instance, explained that the exclusion of "stupid ass Honkies" was necessary due to "past traitorist acts

35  See ELRUM Workers Safety Committee, "ELRUM Speaks" (1970), Box 3, Folder 14, Detroit Revolutionary Movements Collection, Reuther Library; and Thompson, *Whose Detroit?* p. 107.

36  See Georgakas and Surkin, *Detroit: I Do Mind Dying*, p. 87, and Thompson, *Whose Detroit?* pp. 106–7.

37  John Taylor interview, August 25, 1972, Box 3, Folder 17, Dan Georgakas Collection, Reuther Library.

and because of their present mental condition."[38] While that rhetoric may have attracted angry young African American workers and given ELRUM some early momentum, it arrested the organization's growth when it needed to articulate a long-range strategy for change.

Those weaknesses became especially apparent as ELRUM ventured into union politics. In the spring of 1969, Jordan Sims, a black militant who had worked at Eldon since 1948, ran for the presidency of UAW Local 961. Over the years, Sims had participated in various reform efforts within the local and had built up a strong base of support among black and white workers. During the wildcat strikes of 1970, he was among the principals in the Eldon Workers Safety Committee and was among those fired for their leadership of the protests. Sims sympathized with much of ELRUM's critique of Chrysler and the UAW, and he provided the organization with material for its newsletter. Though he was assumed to be an ELRUM member by management and many white workers, Sims never officially joined, believing that some of the group's rhetoric and practices were counterproductive.[39] Moreover, he disagreed with ELRUM's blanket dismissal of the UAW and its disinterest in sustaining a radical caucus within the union. "I would tell them I got this union thing," he recalled. "They would say, 'Man, hell with the union.' I would say, 'Well give me something better.'"[40]

By 1971 ELRUM's power at Eldon had been reduced to such an extent that Sims considered their support more of a liability than an asset. In May of that year, Sims ran for union president and succeeded in advancing to the run-off before losing by thirty-six votes. Shortly before the election, he asked ELRUM members to refrain from publicly endorsing his candidacy, fearing their support would alienate him from whites and older black workers. "They promised me they would," Sims recalled to an interviewer

38  The newsletter continued: "For the most part their plan has worked on the stupid ass Honkies in the plant. These fools are getting fucked over almost as badly as the Black workers (almost). But a disease called racism has poisoned their stupid little pea brains beyond help. They would rather receive pitiful little hand outs as a reward for helping keep you down than work with you to better the over all conditions and in the long run would better off themselves. For this reason elrum has taken the position that . . . there is no room for honkies in the present Black workers revolution." See "Honkies," ELRUM, vol. 1, no. 2, Detroit Revolutionary Movements Collection, Reuther Library.

39  Political opponents attempted to smear Sims by alleging that he was "the owner and organizer of ELRUM." See "Concerned Eldon Avenue Employees," January 1970, Reel 2, Intelligence Bureau Files—ELRUM, The Black Power Movement, Part 4, The League of Revolutionary Black Workers Papers, 1965–1976.

40  Jordan Sims, Eddie Barksdale, and Carla Cooke, interview with Georgakas and Surkin, August 19, 1972, Box 3, Folder 18, Dan Georgakas Collection, Reuther Library.

the following year. "They didn't, so I lost."[41] Sims nevertheless challenged the election, contending that UAW armed guards had intimidated voters and that dozens of ballots had been improperly invalidated. The UAW belatedly agreed with some of Sims's charges and ordered a new election, which Sims lost again, before at last winning the union presidency in May of 1973.[42]

Just as their presence in the plants declined, however, League-affiliated attorneys pulled off the organization's most high-profile victory—the successful legal defense of thirty-five-year-old James Johnson, an Eldon line worker who had murdered two foremen and a coworker shortly after being suspended in July of 1970. Just hours after his suspension over an allegation of insubordination, Johnson returned to the plant and shot and killed two foremen and a coworker. Leading Johnson's defense, League attorney Ken Cockrel announced that he would "put Chrysler on trial for damages to this man caused by his working conditions."[43] Framing the murder in the context of a violent workplace culture created by Chrysler's racism and callous drive for profits, Cockrel explained to the jury that Chrysler had failed to invest in updating the plant and equipment at Eldon, so that by the mid-1960s working conditions had deteriorated significantly, causing frequent injuries and even deaths. Cockrel argued that as Chrysler's sole supplier of gears and axles, management had pushed Eldon workers, including James Johnson, to the breaking point.

Cockrel took the jury, which included several auto workers and auto workers' wives, to Eldon Avenue, so that they could observe for themselves the conditions that had driven Johnson to murder his coworkers. The trip was effective for the defense. Though Chrysler had shut down the line and cleaned and painted the walls for their visitors, jury members were moved by expressions of solidarity from Johnson's former coworkers. The jury found him not guilty by reason of insanity.[44] A year later, Ronald Glotta, a League-affiliated lawyer, made a similar argument at Johnson's workman's compensation trial and won $75 per week dating from the day of the murder.

The League's legal defense efforts—formalized in the spring of 1971 as the Labor Defense Coalition—grew out of the need to fight police brutality and to protect Revolutionary Union Movement members facing

---

41  Ibid.

42  See "UAW Recount Set for Chrysler Local," *Detroit Free Press*, June 8, 1971; and Ralph Orr, "UAW Election Bias Charged at Eldon," *Detroit Free Press*, November 20, 1971; Georgakas and Surkin, *Detroit: I Do Mind Dying*, p. 103.

43  Georgakas and Surkin, *Detroit: I Do Mind Dying*, p. 86.

44  See "Hell in the Factory," *Time*, June 7, 1971, and T. Ricke, "Jurors, Slayer Visit Factory Where 3 Died," *Detroit Free Press*, May 15, 1971.

discharges, injunctions, and other legal reprisals stemming from their political activity.[45] Cockrel and other Coalition lawyers believed that well-publicized and politically charged trials offered an opportunity to radicalize thousands of people beyond the factory gates, including the middle class. At the same time, good legal work could put the companies on notice and secure much needed reforms for workers. In the Johnson cases, Cockrel and Glotta transformed their courtrooms into classrooms, using the trials to show how Chrysler's policies had taken their toll on employees, even to the point of killing some of them. Cockrel later used a similar strategy to successfully defend a man accused of killing Detroit police officers from the elite anti-crime unit STRESS (Stop the Robberies, Enjoy Safe Streets). STRESS was feared in the black community because it had killed an astounding number of young black suspects and had a horrifying record of civil rights abuses. Just as he had done to Chrysler, Cockrel put STRESS on trial, exposing the public to its racist practices. Detroit's first black mayor, Coleman Young, made the dismantling of STRESS a key issue in his 1973 election.

During a 1970 conference on police repression, Cockrel elaborated on the significance of the League's legal work, boasting of its ability to keep members out of jail. He compared the League's record favorably to that of the Black Panthers, which had been destroyed by costly criminal trials and its inability to defend itself from government attacks. Cockrel argued that League leaders understood their "principle responsibility" and "obligation to conduct themselves in such a way as to avoid incarceration." Moreover, the alliances that the League had so painstakingly developed with white radicals, black high school students, and other black progressives served as an effective shield against numerous legal complaints and grand jury investigations: "We've got a highly sophisticated black community in the city of Detroit and . . . we relate in such a way as to make it impossible for the MAN to frame us on jive chicken shit charges."[46]

Even as Cockrel boasted of the League's legal defense capabilities, however, the group's base among Detroit workers was disintegrating, due in no small part to the dismissals of most of the key leaders in the plants.[47]

---

45    "Black Coalition Asks Abolition of Detroit Police Spy System," *Detroit News*, May 4, 1971. For the most complete account of the Johnson case and other League-affiliated legal struggles, see Thompson, *Whose Detroit?* chapters 5, 6.

46    Cockrel, "From Repression to Revolution," *Inner City Voice* (1970), Detroit Revolutionary Movements Collection, Reuther Library.

47    Several years later, League attorney Ron Glotta, suggested that Cockrel preferred high-profile cases to mundane workers' defense cases that "carried no glamour." See Glotta to Dan Georgakas, May 25, 1975, Box 13, Folder 22, Detroit Revolutionary Movements Collection, Reuther Library.

League leaders recognized these weaknesses, but their personal and strategic differences grew almost as rapidly as their programs, which by 1971 included the operation of a bookstore, a publishing company, and a printing press.

In an effort to impose much needed discipline and structure on the organization, Mike Hamlin persuaded civil rights leader James Forman to relocate to Detroit to assist with some managerial, fundraising, and educational needs. Forman, who had been the executive secretary of the Student Nonviolent Coordinating Committee (SNCC) during its heyday and had served briefly as the minister of foreign affairs for the Black Panther Party, had a reputation within the movement as a talented administrator and political tactician. Forman also had connections to many elements of the American left and had recently secured financing from several mainline protestant churches.[48] For his part, Forman had been so impressed by what he had seen of the League that he accepted the invitation to move to Detroit. In the League, Forman saw an opportunity to develop a black revolutionary movement that would join black workers from the urban north with African Americans in the South. In a note he wrote for colleagues in New York, Forman argued that black radicals in the 1970s needed to concentrate their efforts on "those cities where black workers are strategically situated near the centers of mass production of the essentials of any industrialized society, steel, coal, automobiles and oil." The civil rights movement, he asserted, had "concentrated too much on the middle class," and that "most of the gains except the long range political consciousness have resulted in the middle class of the black community entrenching itself further."[49]

In his enthusiasm for the League, Forman was typical of many black and white radicals who had endured the demise of the Students for a Democratic Society (SDS) and SNCC, and the fragmentation of the antiwar, civil rights, and student movements into an endless array of political activities, including electoral campaigns, international solidarity work, and community organizing. The Detroit factory protests and the League's legal defense campaigns captured the American left's political imagination as few other locally based protest movements had done since the height of the Southern black freedom struggle. Moreover, a renewed sense of militancy among American workers, who set records for the numbers of strikes in

---

48   In the spring of 1969, Forman had participated in the Black Economic Development Conference in Detroit, where he delivered his "Black Manifesto," which included demands for reparations from white churches and synagogues. See "Black Manifesto," April 26, 1969, Box 4, Folder 9, Kenneth V. and Sheila M. Cockrel Collection, Reuther Library. Georgakas and Surkin, *Detroit: I Do Mind Dying*, pp. 78–81.

49   J. Forman, "Ten-year Plan," December 21, 1969, from *The Political Thought of James Forman* (Detroit: Black Star, 1970).

1969 and again in 1970, seemed to signal the potential for creating two, three, or many Detroits.[50]

Many young radicals learned of the League through *Finally Got the News*, a 1970 documentary film that featured jarring black-and-white footage of production and picket lines, rendered in a deliberately intimate and frenetic style.[51] Others read about the League in the pages of *The Movement, Radical America*, or the *Guardian*, which devoted a special section to Detroit's "black worker insurgency" in March of 1969. The *Guardian* correspondent declared that the city's "black workers movement is the most important revolutionary action in the country," and that "all the elements are here. The vanguard is here. The workers are here. The guts of monopoly capitalism's production are here. And the conditions are worsening in Detroit's auto plants."[52]

The response to the flattering press and the film was immediate. Speaking invitations, requests for literature, and calls for film showings poured into the League offices from across the country. Graduate students at Pennsylvania State University who were in the midst of a union organizing drive requested *Finally Got the News* to show at their labor arts festival, noting that the failure of teaching assistants to identify with the working class had been one of their "major obstacles to organizing."[53] Members of the Mother Jones collective in Baltimore and the Haymarket collective in Los Angeles ordered League pamphlets for their bookstores and study sessions, while dissident workers in a Portland box factory requested guidance in establishing a rank-and-file caucus within their union.[54]

Cockrel, Hamlin, and Watson handled much of the outreach. Watson in particular spent increasing amounts of time outside of Detroit, meeting with sympathetic radical groups in the United States, Europe, and the Middle East. During trips abroad to sell copies of *Finally Got the News*, Watson established ties to Palestinian liberation groups, Italian extra-parliamentary organizations, and other European supporters of the black

---

50   Almost 2.5 million workers went out on strike in 1970 alone, including national strikes of postal workers, General Electric employees, and coal miners. Thousands of other workers, including members of the United Mine Workers of America, the United Steelworkers of America, and the International Brotherhood of Teamsters, participated in efforts to oust corrupt and entrenched labor leaders and to democratize their unions.

51   Black Star Productions, *Finally Got the News*, 1970.

52   R. Dudnick, "Black Workers on the March: Special Supplement on Black Worker Insurgency in Detroit," *Guardian*, March 8, 1969.

53   Edward F. Bontempo to Black Star Productions, April 2, 1971, Box 1, Folder 8, Dan Georgakas Collection, Reuther Library.

54   Mack Faith to League of Revolutionary Black Workers, April 6, 1971; Rachel Bishop to Norman Engelsberg, March 9, 1971; and "To comrades," February 27, 1971, all located in Box 1, Folder 8, Dan Georgakas Collection, Reuther Library.

freedom movement. Sympathetic academics and high-profile friends, such as actress Jane Fonda, provided additional links to Asian and South American radicals, though a proposed series of League-sponsored films never materialized, despite long discussions between Watson, Cockrel, Fonda, and the actor Donald Sutherland.[55]

A number of young radicals were so inspired by the League that they relocated to Detroit, which they referred to only half-jokingly as the American Petrograd—the city in which workers and their intellectual allies would lead a socialist revolution. In 1969, David Riddle, an SDS-affiliated journalist, moved from Berkeley to Detroit after hearing of the city's political movements. "I was part of that generation of '60s radicals who saw Detroit as a very significant place," said Riddle, who worked in several Detroit auto plants before becoming a Teamsters Union activist. "People looked at themselves, almost consciously, as Narodniks—the young Russian student intellectuals who wanted to bring the world of revolution to the peasant masses."[56]

In 1970 Richard Feldman arrived in Detroit with thirty-five University of Michigan comrades from nearby Ann Arbor. Their decision to move to Detroit followed weeks of intensive study and discussion regarding how to make their campus-based politics "more real, where you could make a revolutionary movement or be part of one because that's where the real people lived."[57] Before choosing Detroit, they sent members to various industrial cities to scope out the organizing terrain and meet with local activists. They settled into a large old house not far from Wayne State University. Though the group quickly split over various political and personal differences, many of them continued to organize in Detroit, focusing their energies on the labor, antiwar, and women's liberation movements.[58]

That same year, the International Socialists (IS), a small Trotskyist student group based in Berkeley and New York, relocated their headquarters to Detroit—a decision that coincided with their plans to refocus their activity from organizing on college campuses to building rank-and-file caucuses within industrial unions. After viewing *Finally Got the News*, University of Southern California student Wendy Thompson moved to Detroit to

---

55  See Fonda to Cockrel, April 26, 1972, and Cockrel to Fonda, May 8, 1972, Box 1, Folder 22, Kenneth V. and Sheila M. Cockrel Collection, Reuther Library.

56  Mast, *Detroit Lives*, p. 325.

57  Richard Feldman, interview by author, May 19, 2004.

58  Members of the "Ann Arbor 35" also joined various communist groups like the Workers World Party, Revolutionary Communist Party, and the October League. Feldman helped produce a radical newspaper, *Red Times*, and secured work in an auto plant, where he remained active in the UAW for many years.

help produce the IS newspaper, while hoping to secure a job in an auto plant so that she might work with the League. She soon found a job at Chevy Gear and Axle and became active in the union, but like many of the young radicals who flocked to Detroit in the early 1970s, Thompson was disappointed to learn that the League had ceased to have any meaningful presence in the auto plants.[59]

Strategic differences and an unrelenting hostility toward the UAW had undermined the League leadership's ability to transform the Revolutionary Union Movements into a viable labor organization. In June of 1971, Cockrel, Watson, and Hamlin resigned from the League and issued a thirty-page polemic detailing their differences with the organization's "petty bourgeois opportunists" and "backward reactionary-nationalist lumpen-proletarians."[60] They explained that their strategy for the League—the necessary and correct broadening of the factory-based struggle—had been undermined by constant criticism and even sabotage from those who felt they were diverting resources from the workers. Cockrel, Watson, and Hamlin argued that far from being diversionary efforts, their recruitment of allies from among the black middle class, white radicals, and supporters outside of the city had accrued critical resources to the League and built up its defensive capacity. The legal defense work, the book club, the publishing house, and the documentary film drew additional resources into the organization and helped protect workers from reprisals.

Beyond the strategic differences, Cockrel, Watson, and Hamlin also raised strong objections to anti-white tendencies within the organization and the behavior of some members that they believed was "wholly inconsistent with continuance in the ranks of a revolutionary organization." They asserted that some League members had chased away white film crew members during the filming of *Finally Got the News* and had sometimes rejected the assistance of white lawyers, journalists, and other supporters. For Mike Hamlin, who was the key to keeping the core group of leaders together, the League's continuing failure to reign in the "outrageous acts" committed by some of its members represented the final straw. Reflecting on the experience over thirty years later, Mike Hamlin acknowledged that DRUM's achievements in the summer of 1968 required "some pretty reckless folks" to stand outside the factory gates, facing harassment and intimidation from "reactionary workers" and the police: "To stand

---

59   Wendy Thompson, interview by author, June 14, 2004; see also F. Coodin, "Interview with a Local Union President: The First Woman to Do This and the First Woman to Do That," *Labor Notes*, October 2002.

60   Hamlin, Watson, and Cockrel, "The Split in the League of Revolutionary Black Workers: Three Lines and Three Headquarters" (June 1971), Box 1, Folder 19, Detroit Revolutionary Movements Collection, Reuther Library.

up against them and say that you were a revolutionary and you were a Communist. You had to be willing to stand there and be prepared to do battle with them."[61] Many of those initially attracted to the League were also drawn by the opportunity to fight white workers, but as the leadership began thinking about a long-range strategy for change, those "undisciplined elements in the organization" became a liability. They alienated too many potential supporters and put the organization even further on the defensive.[62] Hamlin, Watson, and Cockrel pledged to continue their efforts through the Black Workers Congress, a national organization intended as an extension of the League, and a vehicle through which other cities might establish their own Revolutionary Union Movements. The Black Workers Congress drew heavily on James Forman's SNCC networks, but it, too, was short-lived.[63]

Those who remained in the League of Revolutionary Black Workers, including Baker and Kramer, considered the departures an opportunity to consolidate their work around the "organization of black workers," and to "remedy the erroneous tendency . . . to consider it only a part of our general activities."[64] From their perspective, the "splitters" had become too removed from the worker base; Watson's filmmaking and foreign travel, Hamlin's unceasing networking and organization building, and Cockrel's speechmaking had diverted resources from the factory struggles. By refocusing the League's resources on the worker organizing, they hoped to re-establish their base within the auto plants.

The League also viewed the split as an opportunity to develop new leadership for the organization from among the workers—a task that they had largely failed to accomplish. According to Baker, that flaw was built into the League at its inception:

It was built out of duress. It was built as a defensive mechanism under attack. Therefore it wasn't ever really built right. It should've had worker representatives from each one of those groups on it. It didn't have that.

61 Hamlin, interview by author, June 18, 2004.

62 Hamlin, interview by author, June 19, 2004, and Hamlin, "Toward the Organizing of Revolutionary Union Movements," May 1–2, 1971, Box 4, Folder 14, Kenneth V. and Sheila M. Cockrel Collection, Reuther Library.

63 On the activities and demise of the Black Workers Congress, see Georgakas and Surkin, *Detroit: I Do Mind Dying*, pp. 131–50, and Geschwender, *Class, Race and Worker Insurgency*, pp. 203–4.

64 League of Revolutionary Black Workers, "On Splits" (July 1971); see also John Williams, Rufus Burke, and Clint Marbury to Brothers and Sisters (August 1971); both documents Box 7, Folder 9, Ken Kenneth V. and Sheila M. Cockrel Collection, Reuther Library.

It had a group of us around *Inner City Voice* on it as its leadership, which was improper. But we were the most skilled political people at that time to help consolidate and keep the rest of it together.[65]

In the rush to sustain the protests and protect black workers from further reprisals, the League founders had failed to cultivate rank-and-file leaders. The decision-making powers within the organization rested largely with the intellectuals and activists who had founded the group.

As a corrective measure, Baker and the others still loyal to the League embarked on a program to educate members and promote new workers to leadership positions. In January of 1972, following a meeting of the policy committee, the League decided to "go into an organizational strategic retreat." This would allow members to engage in intensive study, while the leadership restructured the League along Leninist principles of democratic centralism. They believed this shift was necessary to control the breakdown in organizational discipline.[66] The League, however, never really re-emerged from the retreat. Individual activists, notably Baker and Kramer, continued to organize within the labor movement and in a host of other political struggles. Periodically, Detroit area workers assumed the Revolutionary Union Movement mantle, but these groups usually had little or no connection to DRUM or the League.

Significant changes in Detroit and in the auto industry within a few short years obviated the need for a League of Revolutionary Black Workers, at least as it had been originally established. Black auto workers in the 1970s continued to face racism, line speedups, and treacherous working conditions, but they had more resources at their disposal for battling racism and exploitation on the job. A growing body of civil rights law gave black workers "a different framework to fight," while both the automakers and the UAW managed the League's disruptions with a combination of brutal opposition and tactful accommodation.[67] As ambitious as the DRUM and ELRUM demands had been in the late 1960s, the automakers and the unions quietly adopted many of them within the first few years of the new decade.[68] Chrysler and the other automakers began opening hundreds of

---

65   Baker, interview by author, May 24, 2004.

66   See Karl Williams, "On the Rationale for Strategic Retreat," January 1972, and League of Revolutionary Black Workers, Agenda, General Meeting, January 2, 1972, Box 1, Folder 25, Detroit Revolutionary Movements Collection, Reuther Library.

67   Baker, interview with author, May 24, 2004.

68   Workers carried out various protest activities over the next few years in the name of the League of Revolutionary Black Workers, but their connections to the League founders varied. Regarding the wave of 1973 plant protests, see Thompson, *Whose Detroit?* pp. 184–91, 199–203.

skilled and managerial positions to African Americans; the UAW hired and appointed new black representatives and officials, and dozens more were elected to union offices. "Who would've thought?" asked Baker many years later. "We asked for fifty black general foremen. We were just blowing shit out. A black on the board of directors of Chrysler Corporation. You know, they gave us all of that." [69]

The years of careful planning, close personal relationships, and resource development could not save the League of Revolutionary Black Workers from the same splits that plagued much of the left in the 1960s. In the final analysis, the League, like many of the 1960s protest movements, proved to be more effective as a disruptive force and less successful as an ongoing organization. League leaders never achieved a method for harnessing the dynamism, optimism, and spontaneity of a strike or demonstration while simultaneously developing an institution to provide stability, resources, and leadership for a continuing struggle to build workers' power.

Beyond their ability to secure reforms within the UAW and the industry, the League of Revolutionary Black Workers and its host of constituent groups alerted New Left and civil rights movement activists to the potential for an alliance between young radicals and the working class. Over the course of the 1970s, thousands of these activists took jobs in steel mills, hospitals, auto plants, and truck barns. They rented rooms in working-class districts and immersed themselves in community life. They organized on job sites, from the salmon canneries in Alaska to the lumber mills of Mississippi, and within unions as influential as the United Auto Workers of America and as obscure as the Glass and Bottle Blowers Association. But it would be left to each of the individuals and radical groups who made this turn to the working class to resolve important unresolved issues—to define their relationship to their unions, to develop a means of sustaining their efforts over the long haul without losing their sense of movement, to be deliberate about the centrality of gender and race, and to nurture new leadership from among the working class. These were among the unfinished tasks of the League of Revolutionary Black Workers.

---

69    Baker, interview with author, May 24, 2004.

# 12

# "A Spontaneous Loss of Enthusiasm": Workplace Feminism and the Transformation of Women's Service Jobs in the 1970s

## Dorothy Sue Cobble

An upsurge of collective activity among women service workers in the United States took place during the 1970s. Much of this activity took place outside the traditional labor unions, and although it did not result in large numbers of new collective bargaining contracts, it helped fundamentally transform the gender, class, and racial norms governing millions of women's service jobs. Three groups of female service workers—flight attendants, clericals, and household workers (or, according to 1970s terminology: stewardesses, secretaries, and maids)—experienced significant collective organization on a national basis for the first time in this period. In the 1970s, women composed 95 percent of flight attendants, 97 percent of secretaries (the largest group of office workers), and 97 percent of domestic workers.[1] Not surprisingly, the organizations they created were almost exclusively female.

The heightened militancy among women service workers in the 1970s drew on decades of prior struggle for racial, class, and gender justice. In addition to the civil rights movement, they drew on less visible efforts of a network of female reformers, such as those who called for an economic

---

1  This is an abridged version of the author's article "'A Spontaneous Loss of Enthusiasm': Workplace Feminism and the Transformation of Women's Service Jobs in the 1970s," *International Labor and Working-Class History* 56 (Fall 1999), pp. 23–44. Women's Bureau of the US Department of Labor, 1975 Handbook on Women Workers, Bulletin 297 (Washington, DC, 1975), pp. 96–8, 276; Bureau of Labor Statistics, Perspectives on Working Women: A Databook, Bulletin 2080 (Washington, DC, 1980), pp. 10–1; B. Gutek, "Women in Clerical Work," in A. Stromberg and S. Harkess, eds, *Women Working: Theories and Facts in Perspective* (Mountain View, CA: Myfield Publishing Co., 1988), pp. 225–8.

and political agenda that was partially realized in the establishment of the Presidential Commission on the Status of Women and the Equal Pay Act of 1963.[2] The passage of the 1964 Civil Rights Act brought long-simmering disagreements over the support of sex-based state protective laws into the open. In 1969, the Equal Employment Opportunities Commission ruled that most sex-based state protective legislation conflicted with Title VII and hence was illegal. Virtually overnight, the principal basis for a half century of opposition to the Equal Rights Amendment (ERA)—defense of protective laws—disappeared. The collapse of this cornerstone of the older labor feminism made possible the emergence of a new, transformed, workplace-based feminism.[3]

In this new environment, blue-collar factory women in the late 1960s embraced a new vision of gender equality and for the first time rejected en masse the sex-typing of jobs as discriminatory. Rank-and-file union women flooded the Equal Employment Opportunity Commission (EEOC) offices with sex discrimination claims in the 1960s and forced the agency to take the issue seriously. Once stirred into action, the EEOC sought and won major court decisions designed to end sex segregation and discriminatory practices by such prominent employers as AT&T and U.S. Steel.[4]

Working women relied on workplace-based organizing as well as the courts to advance gender equality. Both non-professional and professional women organized workplace caucuses that took up issues of affirmative action and employment discrimination.[5] They also sought to transform the bargaining and legislative agenda of the labor movement. By 1974, union women had established the Coalition of Labor Union Women (CLUW). A self-consciously feminist organization, CLUW supported the Equal Rights

---

2   D. S. Cobble, "Recapturing Working-Class Feminism: Union Women in the Postwar Era," in. J. Meyerowitz, ed., *Not June Cleaver: Women and Gender in Postwar America, 1945–1960* (Philadelphia: Temple University Press, 1994), pp. 57–83; Kathleen Laughlin, "Backstage Activism: The Policy Initiatives of the Women's Bureau in the Postwar Era, 1945–1970" (PhD Diss., Ohio State University, 1993).

3   D. S. Cobble, *The Other Women's Movement: Workplace Justice and Social Rights in Modern America* (Princeton: Princeton University Press, 2004).

4   N. Gabin, *Feminism in the Labor Movement: Women and the United Auto Workers, 1935–1975* (Ithaca: Cornell University Press, 1990); D. Deslippe, "Organized Labor, National Politics, and Second Wave Feminism in the US, 1965–1975," *International Labor and Working-Class History* 49 (Spring 1996), pp. 143–65; R. Rosenberg, *Divided Lives: American Women in the Twentieth Century* (New York: Hill and Wang, 1992), p. 217; Venus Green, "Race and Technology: African-American Women in the Bell System, 1945–1980," *Technology and Culture* vol. 36:2 (April 1995), pp. 128–36.

5   N. Maclean, "The Hidden History of Affirmative Action: Working Women's Struggles in the 1970s and the Gender of Class," *Feminist Studies* vol. 25:1 (Spring 1999), pp. 43–78.

Amendment as well as women's reproductive rights, and the founders' goals included moving women into union leadership, increased attention to organizing women workers, and an end to sex segregation and other discriminatory workplace practices based on sex.[6]

What is less known, however, is the activism among women in female-dominated jobs during this period, and the ways in which their reform movements changed the longstanding familial and paternalistic norms governing female-dominated service jobs. These women took older reform traditions and reworked them to suit their own realities as woman service workers. They built upon the past, but they broke with it as well. They expanded the vocabulary of workplace rights, made a public and political issue of the gendered construction of women's jobs, and invented new forms of workplace representation.

### "Sex Objects in the Sky Unite"[7]

In 1972, a group of tired stewardesses tried to explain their concerns to the incredulous male transit union officials who led their union. No, the primary issues were not wages and benefits, they insisted, but the particular cut of their uniforms and the sexual insinuations made about their occupation in the new airline advertisements. Their words fell on deaf ears. Despite their commonalities as transportation workers, the gender gap separating the two groups was simply too wide to cross. Indeed, male subway drivers could not understand why the stewardesses would object to their glamorous sex-object image. Deeply held gendered notions of unionism and politics also stood in the way of communication. For even if the complaints of stewardesses were accepted as "real," to many male union leaders they seemed petty, matters not deserving of serious attention, let alone concerted activity.

Unlike most women in the female service ghetto, the majority of flight attendants had joined unions in the 1940s and 1950s, including the Stewards and Stewardesses (S&S) division of the Air Line Pilots Association (ALPA), the Teamsters, and the Transport Workers Union. These unions had secured moderate advances in wages, hours, and working conditions for flight attendants, and under growing pressure from the flight attendants themselves and the impetus of new anti-discriminatory legislation, they had helped undermine the airline policies restricting the occupation to

---

6  D. Balser, *Sisterhood and Solidarity: Feminism and Labor in Modern Times* (Boston: South End Press, 1987), pp. 151–210.

7  P. Kane, *Sex Objects in the Sky: A Personal Account* (Chicago: Follett Publishing Co., 1974).

white, young, single, and childless women. Airlines hired a small number of minority women as attendants in the late 1950s, and by the end of the 1960s, flight attendants could marry, have children, and work past age thirty-two.[8]

But by the early 1970s, flight attendants wanted more: They wanted economic rights and opportunities equal to men, as well as the right to control and define their own sexuality and "personhood."[9] To secure these rights, flight attendants put increasing pressure on their male-dominated unions and formed the first all-female national organization of flight attendants, Stewardesses for Women's Rights (SFWR). As Sandra Jarrell—a twenty-seven-year-old former Eastern flight attendant, University of Maryland Women's Studies student, and cofounder of SFWR—explained, "the most obvious tool available for remedying the injustices we are subject to are [sic] the unions. Unfortunately, unions do not have the reputation of representing the interests of women." The male leadership, she continued, blamed stewardesses, but they "will obtain rank and file support only if they stop limiting [themselves] . . . to economic issues."[10] Instead of building cross-gender coalitions with working-class men, SFWR turned to closer partnerships with middle-class women, including airline women in managerial and supervisory positions. At least initially, they had friendlier relationships with organized feminism than with organized labor.[11]

The emergence of this new militancy among flight attendants in the

---

8   On the history of flight attendants, see G. P. Nielsen, From *Sky Girl to Flight Attendant: Women and the Making of a Union* (Ithaca: ILR, 1982); F. Rozen, "Turbulence in the Air: The Autonomy Movement in the Flight Attendant Unions," (PhD Diss., Pennsylvania State University, 1988); K. Barry, "'Coffee, Tea—But Not Me!': Stewardesses for Women's Rights: Flight Attendant's Construction of a Feminist Professional Identity in the 1970s," (manuscript, New York University History Department, 1996); L. Van Gelder, "Coffee, Tea, or Me," *Ms.* (1973), pp. 86–91, 105; K. Lukas, "The Evolution of the Flight Attendant in the United States," n.d. (c. 1980), Box 2, Folder 52, Stewardesses for Women's Rights Records, 1963–87, Tamiment Library, Wagner Archives, New York University (hereafter cited as SFWR Records); Independent Union of Flight Attendants Collection (Pan Am), Tamiment Library, Wagner Archives, New York University (hereafter IUFA Collection).
9   The reference to "personhood" is from Cynthia Glacken, letter, October 1, 1975, Box 2, Folder 50, SFWR Records.
10   S. Jarrell, "Keynote Address at First SFWR Conference," SFWR Newsletter vol. 1:2 (May 1973), Box 2, Folder 51, SFWR Records.
11   Heenan, "Fighting the Fly-Me Airline," SFWR Newsletter vol. 1:7 (December 1973), Box 2, Folder 51, SFWR Records. Gloria Steinem and other middle-class feminists profiled the organization and the problems of flight attendants in *Ms.* magazine and at numerous New York City feminist conferences. Feminist leaders and organizations also spoke at conferences, provided legal counsel, and helped with fundraising, office space, and getting media attention for SFWR.

1970s was spurred in part by the new feminist sensitivity to employment discrimination, and to male control over female sexuality. Flight attendants, however, were as much feminist leaders as followers. They helped invent the new feminism in the 1960s, and they were instrumental in the 1970s in demonstrating the power of these ideas when applied to women's jobs.

The rise of activism among flight attendants was also a product of the transformation of the occupation and the kind of women who entered it. By the early 1970s, for the first time, the majority of flight attendants were married and expected to stay in their job longer than the earlier average of eighteen months. Moreover, working conditions had deteriorated. Flight attendants' real wages fell as higher fuel costs and recession-related declines in business travel cut into airline profits.

But most galling, the occupation was sexualized as companies came to rely upon female sexuality to sell seats. The fantasy image of flight attendants in the 1950s had been the fresh-faced girl next door—the kind you wanted to marry. By the early 1970s, however, the image had shifted to the "playmate in the sky, available for sex," or the "flying geisha girl," there to entertain and please.[12] Airlines routinely required flight attendants to wear hot pants and other sexually alluring uniforms. National's rules called for all stewardesses to wear "Fly Me" buttons. The company maintained with a straight face that no sexual innuendo was intended, despite their ad campaign featuring stewardesses panting, "Hi, I'm Linda, and I'm going to FLY you like you've never been flown before." Continental learned from National's success. In 1972, they aired ads in which stewardesses promised that we "really move our tail for you." As one airline executive explained: "It's the sex thing, pure and simple. Put a dog on a plane and twenty businessmen are sore for a month."[13]

Historically, attendants had taken pride in their appearance and the company's celebration of their attractiveness, but the more crass approach was objectionable to many. The new sexy image encouraged harassment by male passengers; it also meant that the women had become less respectable. As one explained: "It represents a lack of respect for hostesses. We have always projected pride, a class kind of image, and this slogan is barroom talk. We're professional career women and mothers . . . not fly girls."[14]

12   Kane, *Sex Objects in the Sky*, pp. 11–63,102–3. For "geisha girl" label, see p. 19.

13   K. Heenan, "Fighting the Fly-Me Airlines," *The Civil Liberties Review* (December 1976–January 1977), pp. 48–53; A. Sweeney, "The Turn of the Screwed," SFWR Newsletter vol. 2:5 (May 1974), pp. 6–7, Box 2, Folder 52, SFWR Records; F. J. Prial, "The Great Girl Shortage in the Sky," *New York World Telegram*, August 25, 1965 (part 1), p. 25, and August 26, 1965 (part 2), p. 17.

14   B. Liddick, "Tail Slogan Hits Bottom, Say Stews," *Los Angeles Times*, January 25, 1974, pp. E1, 9, in Box 2, Folder 64, SFWR Records.

Others objected to any gendered image being uniformly imposed. Why should stewardesses be asked to speak and look alike when other workers weren't treated this way? Former stewardess and popular author Paula Kane claimed the "new militancy" arose because stewardesses wanted "to free themselves from the prison of the female role" and assert their own individual identities.[15]

Flight attendants initially took their concerns to the three chief unions that represented them, but they made little headway. In exasperation and somewhat reluctantly, stewardesses began organizing in opposition to their unions as well as their employers. Not only did they form their own national organization in 1972, SFWR, but by the end of the 1970s they had deserted the male-dominated transportation unions in droves, setting up a bewildering array of independent flight attendant unions.[16]

The SFWR dedicated itself to "fighting the policies of the airlines which strip us of our individuality and dignity" and "stigmatize us as sex objects." They rejected the airlines' manipulation of the flight attendant's sexual image.[17] The SFWR attacked the problem from a number of angles. They picketed films that depicted flight attendants as hypersexual women. They filed lawsuits against Continental and National alleging that their airline ads created a hostile work environment. They distributed buttons reading "Go Fly Yourself," as well as "National, Your Fly is Open" bumper stickers.[18]

And they initiated an elaborate media campaign to publicize their alternative image of the flight attendant as a career woman and professional. The campaign culminated in the release of a "countercommercial" aimed at ending what they called "sexploitation." In it, they defined themselves as professionals responsible for passenger safety, not passenger sexual titillation. "The sexpot image is unsafe at any altitude," the script proclaimed, because "people do not obey the safety orders of their sexual fantasies." Or, as one SFWR leader put it in a letter to *Time* magazine: "We're in the business of saving tails, not serving them. The airlines are ass-king for pecuniary returns with a part of my anatomy that is not for sale."[19]

---

15   Kane, *Sex Objects in the Sky*, pp. 11–5, 52–63, 155; S. Pratt, "They're in a Stew about Discrimination," *Chicago Tribune*, September 17, 1973, pp. 2, 6; E. Cray, "The Barbie Dolls Revolt," *Air Fair*, April 1975, pp. 16–9.

16   Neilsen, *From Sky Girl to Flight Attendant*, pp. 117–36; Rozen, "Turbulence in the Air."

17   SFWR Newsletter vol. 1, no. 1 (1973), Box 2, Folder 51, SFWR Records.

18   Box 1, Folders 7, 15–17, 22–25, and Box 2, Folders 51–54, SFWR Records; unidentified news clipping, Box 2, Folder 64, SFWR Records; R. Fulman, "Get Off My Back, Don't 'Fly Me,'" *New York Daily News*, September 13, 1974.

19   In SFWR Records, see in particular C. Ivy, "Stews Organized Against Sexism," Box 2, Folder 64; H. Leith, "'Sexpot' Stereotype Angers Stews," unidentified undated clipping,

Although the SFWR took the lead in this campaign, they were joined by some union officials, particularly those leading the Association of Flight Attendants (AFA), the former S&S Division of ALPA which had decided to go independent in 1973.[20] SFWR and the AFA worked to change the rules governing appearance, demanding that airlines change stewardesses' uniforms and abolish their archaic grooming and weight requirements. While SFWR kept up its flurry of lawsuits and media pressure, the unions threatened strikes, sick-ins, and the old Industrial Workers of the World tactic of slowdowns—what Kelly Rueck, the strong-willed AFA president, described as a "spontaneous loss of enthusiasm" for the job.[21] SFWR and union pressure helped convince airlines to let flight attendants choose their own makeup and hair style.[22] They also made progress in addressing other issues, such as promotional opportunities for stewardesses, workplace health and safety, and the end of mandatory layoffs during pregnancy.[23]

But the airlines drew the line at weight: Thinness was the one non-negotiable aspect of female attractiveness. Airlines weighed attendants weekly, held them to weight standards which were detrimental to their health, refused to adjust requirements as women aged, and fired more flight attendants for violations of weight regulations than for any other reason. The SFWR argued that such rules were discriminatory since only female attendants were required to be pencil thin, that the airline "appearance supervisors" used highly arbitrary standards, and that the only acceptable work rules an employer should impose were those related to a person's ability to perform his or her assigned job.[24]

The SFWR made a splash despite its brief organizational life. It captured media headlines.[25] It also moved new issues of control over one's body and personality into the center of union politics, ultimately reinvigorating unionism among flight attendants.

---

Box 2, Folder 64; SFWR Newsletter vol. 2:9 (September–October 1974), pp. 1–2, Box 2, Folder 52; letter from Cynthia Glacken to *Time* magazine, February 14, 1974, Box 1, Folder 22. See also "Coffee, Tea, or Tails," *Newsweek*, February 11, 1974, p. 10.

20   Press release from Association of Flight Attendants, June 25, 1974, Box 1, Folder 22, SFWR Records; Association of Flight Attendants Papers, Dallas Collection, 1952–1980, Archives of Labor and Urban Affairs, Wayne State University.

21   C. Childers, "Stews Challenge Airlines," *Christian Science Monitor*, n.d. (c.1974–5), Box 2, File 64, SFWR Records; Nielsen, *From Sky Girl to Flight Attendant*, pp. 106–16.

22   Prial, "The Great Girl Shortage," p. 25; Cray, "The Barbie Dolls Revolt," pp. 16–9, Box 2, Folder 61, SFWR Records.

23   "Press Release, July 19, 1973, S&S Division, ALPA," Box 1, File 16, SFWR Records; "Press Release, Association of Flight Attendants, June 25, 1974," Box 1, File 22, SFWR Records; Prial, "The Great Girl Shortage," and Cray, "'The Barbie Dolls Revolt," Box 2, File 61, SFWR Records; Nielsen, *From Sky Girl to Flight Attendant*, pp. 97–9.

24   Box 1, Folders 15–17, SFWR Records.

25   Box 2, Folder 64, SFWR Records.

When the SFWR folded in 1976, many former SFWR activists turned full-time attention to union work. A number ran for union office and won. In their new capacity as union officers and activists, they continued the flurry of lawsuits and press releases. By the end of the 1970s much had changed. Weight restrictions were lifted; new, more dignified uniforms appeared; and flight attendants no longer looked like mass-produced life-size Barbie dolls.

## Raises and Roses

Like flight attendants, clericals' working conditions were declining as their needs and expectations rose, spurring protest. Clerical work had been in decline since the late nineteenth century as female workers replaced male, and wages, status, and promotional opportunities plummeted. But conditions deteriorated further in the post–World War II decades. As larger, more bureaucratic organizations became the norm and new office technologies spread, many secretaries found themselves reorganized into office clerical pools. Others saw their jobs downgraded to a monotonous routine of typing and filing. Accompanying this decline was a shift in the needs and expectations of the women employed as clericals. The majority were married (as they had always been), but a growing proportion were single or heads of families without a partner. They spent more years at work and felt frustrated by their "secondary earner" wages and the lack of promotional opportunities.[26]

The messages of the new feminism also stirred discontent. If flight attendants did not take kindly to being seen as mistresses, many secretaries no longer found solace in their role as "office wives." Not only did they have to attend to the bosses' personal needs, but like housewives their labor was rarely acknowledged or respected. And since few job descriptions for secretarial positions existed, there were no protective boundaries, emotional or otherwise. Of course, secretaries did have their one day of token recognition, National Secretaries Day, begun in 1951.[27] Being taken

---

26 For the historical transformation of clerical work, see H. Braverman, *Labor and Monopoly Capital: The Degradation of Work in the Twentieth Century* (New York: Monthly Review Press, 1974); M. Davis, *Women's Place Is at the Typewriter: Office Work and Office Workers, 1870–1930* (Philadelphia: Temple University Press, 1982); and A. Kwolek-Folland, *Engendering Business: Men and Women in the Corporate Office, 1870–1930* (Baltimore: Johns Hopkins University Press, 1994). For analysis of more contemporary conditions, see J. Tepperman, *Not Servants, Not Machines* (Boston: Beacon Press, 1976); M. Benet, *The Secretarial Ghetto* (New York: McGraw Hill, 1973).

27 C. Snyder, "Secretaries Week: Area Office Professionals Look Back Over the Changes and Challenges of the Past 5 Years," *Princeton Packet*, April 21, 1998, pp. 1B–2B.

out to lunch and given roses by the boss once a year was supposed to compensate for poor working conditions the rest of the year.

Organized clericals set out to change this state of affairs. Public-sector clericals had organized along with teachers, maintenance workers, and others in the 1960s; now the focus shifted to the millions of unrepresented office workers in the private sector.[28] Margie Albert, a twenty-five-year office veteran and a steward for the Distributive Workers of America, spoke of a "new spirit" sweeping America's secretaries in a 1973 *New York Times* opinion editorial piece; New York Congresswoman Bella Abzug had it read into the Congressional Record.[29] Albert claimed the movement erupted in 1969 when employers imposed a "no pants, dresses only" rule on office staff. Women rebelled, she reported, signing petitions, organizing delegations to the boss, and threatening mass walkouts.[30] Albert may have exaggerated the extent of the discontent, but certainly the acceptance of conventional office etiquette was eroding.

Within the next few years, over a dozen independent office-worker organizations sprang up, perhaps the most effective being 9to5. Launched in 1973, 9to5 grew quickly from its origins as a luncheon gripe session for Harvard secretaries (led by fellow University of Chicago refugees Karen Nussbaum and Ellen Cassedy) to a citywide organization with hundreds of members.[31] Similar groups emerged in Chicago (Women Employed), New York (Women Office Workers), San Francisco (Women Office Employees), and elsewhere. By the end of the decade, twelve local groups (with a total membership of some ten thousand) had united under the umbrella of the National Association of Working Women.[32] Like flight

---

28  On public-sector organizing, see D. Bell, "Unionized Women in State and Local Government," in R. Milkman, ed., *Women, Work, and Protest: A Century of U.S. Women's Labor History* (Boston: Routledge & Kegan Paul, 1985), pp. 280–99; T. Brooks, *Toil and Trouble: A History of American Labor* (New York: Delacourte Press, 1971), chapter 23; R. Freeman, "Unionism Comes to the Public Sector," *Journal of Economic Literature* vol. 24:1 (March 1986), pp. 41–86.

29  M. Albert, "Something New in the Women's Movement," editorial, *New York Times*, December 12, 1973, editorial; Congressional Record, December 12, 1973, 41255.

30  Albert, "Something New"; P. Foner, *Women and the American Labor Movement: From Colonial Times to the Eve of World War I* (New York: The Free Press, 1979), p. 557.

31  D. S. Cobble and A. Kessler-Harris, "Interview with Karen Nussbaum," in M. S. Hartman, ed., *Talking Leadership: Conversations with Powerful Women* (New Brunswick, NJ: Rutgers University Press, 1999), pp. 135–55; J. Hoerr, *We Can't Eat Prestige: The Women Who Organized Harvard* (Philadelphia: Temple University Press, 1997), p. 47.

32  For a fuller discussion of the various organizations and their issues, see Foner, *Women and the American Labor Movement*, pp. 556–7; N. Seifer and B. Wertheimer, "New Approaches to Collective Power: Four Working Women's Organizations," in B. Cummings and V. Schuck, eds, *Women Organizing* (Metuchen, NJ: Scarecrow Press, 1979), pp. 152–83; J. Sealander and D. Smith, "The Rise and Fall of Feminist Organizations in the 1970s:

attendants, clericals wanted higher wages and promotions; they also wanted their occupation professionalized and upgraded. The objectionable quality of interpersonal relationships in the office or "insulting male behavior," however, angered women the most.[33]

As Karen Nussbaum remembered it, the "most powerful motivator was the issue of respect. Women did not want to feel they were office wives. They were real workers with real jobs." They also wanted their personhood acknowledged. Nussbaum recalled with chagrin her experience of being looked "dead in the eye" and asked, "Isn't anybody here?"[34] Other clericals spoke bitterly of being "invisible," of having people not "really look at you as a person," and of the indignity of the "servant role."[35] In short, clericals rejected being an "office maid" as well as an "office wife."

The office-worker movement looked to modernize and depersonalize the boss–secretary relationship. They called for evaluations based on more objective criteria, such as skills in typing, office management, and budget administration, rather than on a pleasing personality or good looks. More "precise job descriptions," some thought, would limit the almost total discretion bosses had over them.[36] At the same time, the office-worker movement also believed that bureaucratization and depersonalization were not the ultimate solution. Rather than banish the personal, they sought to transform it. They hoped to rewrite the cultural scripts governing office relationships and change the larger cultural norms that underlay the "micro-inequities" of daily office encounters.[37]

To effect these ends, office-worker groups relied on a range of tactics: lawsuits, petitions, pickets, as well as more unorthodox tactics—described by one reporter as a combination of "street theatre and Madison Avenue hype." Their public relations skills served them particularly well in their

---

Dayton as a Case Study," *Feminist Studies* 12:2 (Summer 1986), pp. 321–41; Tepperman, *Not Servants*, pp. 63–84; R. Wyper, "Secretaries Dictate New Images," *Worklife* (September 1976), pp. 29–31; S. M. Evans, *Born for Liberty: A History of Women in America* (New York: The Free Press, 1989), pp. 299–300; "Rebellion Behind the Typewriter," *Business Week*, April 28, 1980, pp. 86, 89–90; D. Plotke, "Women Clerical Workers and Trade Unionism; Interview with Karen Nussbaum," *Socialist Review* 49 (January–February 1980), pp. 151–9.

33  Hoerr, *We Can't Eat Prestige*, pp. 47–51.

34  Cobble and Kessler-Harris, "Interview with Karen Nussbaum," pp. 138, 140.

35  Hoerr, *We Can't Eat Prestige*, p. 52; Tepperman, *Not Servants*, pp. 2, 15, 63; J. Moscato, "Hard Day at the Office: The Pitfalls and Promise of Clerical Organizing," *Union* (December 1988–January 1989), pp. 22–6.

36  For quote, see Wyper, "Secretaries Dictate New Images," pp. 29–31. See also Tepperman, *Not Servants*, pp. 40, 84; Cobble and Kessler-Harris, "Interview with Karen Nussbaum."

37  Hoerr, *We Can't Eat Prestige*, p. 52.

attempt to "repossess" National Secretaries Day. Their demand for an office-worker "Bill of Rights" and their slogans "Respect, rights, and raises" and "Raises not roses" instigated a public debate over the working conditions of clericals and the cultural norms governing boss-and-secretary interaction. Their call for secretaries to refuse participation in such a longstanding and widespread public ritual as National Secretaries Day set off confusion in offices nationwide.[38] Did secretaries really prefer raises to roses? As with the male union officers who had represented flight attendants, few male bosses could understand why their female support staff would want to reject what many saw as flattering forms of male attention. But for a significant segment of the clerical workforce, National Secretaries Day represented an outmoded paternalism perfectly symbolized in the demeaning rituals of one-way gift-giving.[39]

9to5 and other groups also devised innovative tactics to draw attention to the non-job-related duties often required of clericals—the duties, as one secretary explained, "that have no purpose but to make the boss seem, and feel, important." They held "worst boss contests" to publicize the most outrageous requests bosses made of secretaries, and on occasion they picketed individual bosses. Karen Nussbaum tells the story of one secretary whose boss screamed at her because the corned beef sandwich she brought him was on white bread rather than rye. When she refused to give up her own lunch hour and go back out in the rain for a different version of the sandwich, he fired her. She contacted 9to5, and forty women turned out to picket his office, carrying placards reading, "Boss Says Rye Bread or No Bread." The woman never got her job back, but as Nussbaum remarked years later, that "was one satisfied secretary."[40]

Office-worker groups, like the SFWR, had an impact way beyond their small numbers. By the end of the 1970s, the movement had helped win millions of dollars in back pay and equity raises, spurred the development of employer affirmative-action plans, turned National Secretaries Day into a contested ritual, and inspired a hit "9 to 5" song, movie, and TV show.[41]

---

38  "Rebellion Behind the Typewriter," pp. 86, 89–90; Cobble and Kessler-Harris, "Interview with Karen Nussbaum"; Plotke, "Women Clerical Workers"; Tepperman, *Not Servants*, p. 81; Evans, *Born for Liberty*, pp. 299–300; 9to5 and the National Association of Working Women, *Anniversary Celebration Commemorative Journal* (New York, 1988).

39  For a discussion of how one-way gift-giving reinforces hierarchical relationships, see J. Rollins, *Between Women: Domestics and Their Employers* (Philadelphia: Temple University Press, 1985).

40  "Rebellion Behind the Typewriter," pp. 86, 89–90; Sealander and Smith, "Rise and Fall," pp. 246–52; Cobble and Kessler-Harris, "Interview with Karen Nussbaum," p. 141.

41  9to5 and the National Association of Working Women, *Anniversary Celebration*; J. Klemesrud, "Jane Fonda to Office Workers: 'Organize'," *New York Times*, September 26,

Ultimately, the office-worker movement helped transform the daily office encounters that had done so much to humiliate and demean secretaries. As *Business Week* noted in 1980, 9to5 changed public "notions of fairness," of "what a boss may fairly ask a[n] office worker to do." Personal errands, coffee-making, and numerous other requests were no longer acceptable business practice in most offices.[42]

These gains, as significant as they were, left problems unresolved. Many clericals, particularly those who occupied the lower rungs of the occupation—typing, filing, and processing forms in huge faceless offices— still faced low wages and poor working conditions.[43] Office-worker groups turned to unionization as a way of broadening the movement and addressing the particular concerns of the lower echelons of the clerical sector.

9to5, through its new sister organization Local 925 (later Service Employees International Union District 925), focused on organizing women in insurance and banking, because, as Nussbaum explained, it was "the heart of the clerical work force—some 30 percent," and "the majority came from working-class neighborhoods."[44] District 65 and other unions also targeted clericals in banking and insurance as well as publishing, legal offices, and universities.[45]

Employers fought with every weapon available, particularly in the insurance and banking sector. "We never knew what hit us," Nussbaum remembered some fifteen years later. "We got smashed over and over. These businesses [insurance and banking] had not traditionally been unionized, and they were damned if they were going to be the first ones in the new wave."[46] After a hard-fought organizing and contract victory at the Syracuse offices of Equitable Life, the company closed its Syracuse branch and laid off all its unionized workers.[47] Union density actually fell in the 1980s in the banking industry.[48] The major successes were among university clericals, especially

---

1979, p. C12; Seifer and Wertheimer, "New Approaches to Collective Power," pp. 156–7.

42   "Rebellion Behind the Typewriter," pp. 86, 89–90; Tepperman, *Not Servants*, p. 172; Moscato, "Hard Day at the Office," p. 25; Cobble and Kessler-Harris, "Interview with Karen Nussbaum."

43   S. H. Garfinkle, "Occupations of Women and Black Workers, 1962–1974," *Monthly Labor Review*, November 1975, p. 31.

44   *AFL-CIO News*, March 7, 1981; Tepperman, *Not Servants*, p. 89.

45   Foner, *Women and the American Labor Movement*, p. 562; R. Hurd, "The Unionization of Clerical Workers in Colleges and Universities," in J. M. Douglas, ed., *Power Relationships on the Unionized Campus* (New York: National Center for the Study of Collective Bargaining in Higher Education and the Professions, 1989), pp. 40–9.

46   Cobble and Kessler-Harris, "Interview with Karen Nussbaum," p. 145.

47   Moscato, "Hard Day at the Office," p. 25.

48   D. S. Cobble, "The Willmar, Minnesota, Bank Strike of 1977–1979," in R. Filippelli, ed., *Labor Conflict in the United States: An Encyclopedia* (New York: Garland Press, 1990),

at prestigious schools such as Harvard, Yale, Vassar, and Columbia. It took many years to overcome the intransigence of these privileged institutions, but some 70 percent of the campaigns among university clericals conducted in the 1970s and 1980s emerged with union contracts.[49]

By the end of the 1980s, office-worker unionization (16 percent) was comparable to the workforce as a whole (17 percent).[50] The 1980s did not witness the reversal of union decline—one that began for the private-sector workforce in the 1950s—but the fault cannot be laid at the door of office workers.

## "Taking the 'Mammy' Out of Housework"[51]

The household-worker movement also burst into public view in the early 1970s. In 1971, some six hundred mostly black and middle-aged women gathered for the first national conference of household employees. Under the banner "Pay, protection, and professionalism," they applauded enthusiastically as speaker after speaker spoke of a new day for domestics. The conference received extensive press coverage, encouraging hope that a fundamental shift in the employment relations governing domestic work was under way.[52]

Prior to the 1960s, organized efforts to reform domestic work, largely led by middle-class white reformers, had been sporadic.[53] Local organizations of household employees—inspired by the civil rights and poor people's movements—began forming in the late 1960s. In the 1970s, for the first time, a national movement organized primarily by household workers arose.

---

pp. 571–4; R. Perras, "Effective Responses to Union Organizing Attempts in the Banking Industry," *Labor Law Journal* 35:2 (February 1984), pp. 92–102; Sealander and Smith, "The Rise and Fall of Feminist Organizations in the 1970s," pp. 244–6.

49   On Harvard, see Hoerr, *We Can't Eat Prestige*; R. Hurd, "Organizing and Representing Clerical Workers: The Harvard Model," in D. S. Cobble, ed., *Women and Unions: Forging a Partnership* (Ithaca: Cornell University Press, 1993), pp. 316–36.

50   Moscato, "Hard Day at the Office," p. 25.

51   Quote from D. A. Sragow, "Taking the Mammy Out of Housework," *Civil Rights Digest* (1971), pp. 34–8.

52   For coverage of conference, "Domestics Uniting for More Pay and Respect," *New York Times*, July 18, 1971, pp. 1, 43; J. Smyth, "Household Workers Organize," *Detroit News*, July 22, 1971; "Farewell to Dinah," *Newsweek*, August 2, 1971, p. 67.

53   R. D. G. Kelley, "'We Are Not What We Seem': Rethinking Black Working-Class Opposition in the Jim Crow South," *Journal for American History* 80:1 (June 1993), pp. 75–112; P. Palmer, *Domesticity and Dirt: Housewives and Domestic Servants in the United States, 1920–1945* (Philadelphia: Temple University Press, 1989), pp. 111–35; idem, "Outside the Law: Agricultural and Domestic Workers Under the Fair Labor Standards Act," *Journal of Policy History* 7:4 (1995), pp. 416–40.

Dorothy Bolden, a veteran community and civil rights activist who had started cleaning houses in 1935 at the age of twelve, founded a domestic-workers organization in Atlanta with the aim of improving working conditions and building "respect for the women in this low-income field of labor." Bolden wrote: "I have been a maid all my life, I have rocked cradles and given guidance to little boys. Now we're going to give them some guidance when they are grown."[54] Similar groups organized in some two dozen other cities across the country. As one participant explained, "The garbage men have been upgraded to sanitation workers, with all the benefits, and that's just what we have to do. If you're tough enough to talk back to your big man on Sunday, don't tell me you're afraid of Miss Suzy on Monday."[55]

By the early 1970s, the majority of local domestic worker organizations joined in a loose national movement headed by the National Council of Household Employees (NCHE). The NCHE, formed in 1965 under the auspices of the Women's Bureau, grew out of the longstanding commitment of labor feminists, like former Women's Bureau director Esther Peterson, to revalue household labor. With funding from the Department of Labor and the Ford Foundation, the NCHE initially focused on training household employees and fostering minority contractors in the private household-services sector. In the early 1970s, under the leadership of Edith Sloan, a young African American woman with legal training as well as experience as a domestic worker, the NCHE redefined itself as an advocacy organization promoting the interests of female domestic workers first and foremost. Instead of fostering small businesses, which were usually owned by minority men, the NCHE put its energy into building a national movement of household workers.[56]

---

54  National Domestic Workers Union Records, 1965–79, Southern Labor Archives, Georgia State University (hereafter cited as NDWU Records); "Dorothy Bolden Portrait," in N. Seifer, ed., *Nobody Speaks for Me! Self-Portraits of American Working-Class Women* (New York: Simon and Schuster, 1976), pp. 136–77; "Dorothy Bolden Interview With Gerda Lerner," in G. Lerner, ed., *Black Women in White America: A Documentary History* (New York: Vintage Books, 1972), pp. 234–8; "Dorothy Bolden Interview with Chris Lutz," Atlanta, Georgia, August 1995, Special Collections, Georgia State University; D. C. Yancy, "Dorothy Bolden," in D. C. Hine et al., eds, *Black Women in America: An Historical Encyclopedia*, (Bloomington, IN: Carlson Publishing Inc., 1993), pp. 144–5. Quote from newspaper clipping, *Nashville Tennessean*, March 13, 1972, NDWU Records, Box 1633, Folder 181.

55  "Domestics Uniting," pp. 1, 43; C. Lesi, "Maids Say Days of Slavery Are Over," *Washington Post*, September 8, 1968.

56  E. Peterson, *Restless: The Memoirs of Labor and Consumer Activist Esther Peterson* (Washington, DC: Caring Publishing, 1995), pp. 79–80, 100–1; US Department of Labor Press Release (February 11, 1965), Esther Peterson Collection, Schlesinger Library, Radcliffe College, File 975; Frieda Miller Papers, 1909–73, Schlesinger Library, Radcliffe

The household-worker movement differed in many respects from those of flight attendants and clericals. Household workers were older, and much more likely to be women of color and single heads of household. They worked alone in private homes, supervised almost wholly by women, and the norms governing these highly privatized encounters were rooted as much in racial and class prejudices as in gender. Hence, the movement relied upon different tactics than did the others, and it drew its inspiration more from traditions of race and class justice than from gender. Indeed, rather than attack the gender status quo, at times the household-worker movement used traditional gender values to justify their assaults upon the oppressive norms under which they worked.[57]

Nevertheless, all three movements had remarkably similar goals. Like flight attendants and clericals, household workers sought to upgrade and professionalize their occupation. They wanted their skills as cooks, caretakers, and cleaners recognized. They sought dignity and respect for their person as well as concrete economic benefits. And at the heart of the movement was the effort to transform the nature of interpersonal relations at work.

Household workers, however, faced far greater obstacles than flight attendants and clericals. They were denied the basic statutory protections governing wages, hours, and working conditions afforded other employees. Their average yearly incomes were below poverty level, and many domestics still worked from sunup to sundown. Despite the formal end of slavery some one hundred years earlier, the relationship between mistress and maid was often reminiscent of slavery. As a worker in the big house, the domestic still was seen as part of the white family, despite her own outside household. As one NCHE official asserted, "In no other industry is the modern day worker so completely at the mercy of her employer."[58]

---

College, Box 12, Folder 253 and Box 13, Folder 254; US Department of Labor Press Release (March 13, 1968), Katherine Ellickson Collection, Pt. 1, Box 9, Folder 44, Archives of Labor and Urban Affairs, Wayne State University; NCHE, "Employer Training Manual" (n.d.), NDWU Records, Box 1629, Folder 116; Women's Bureau of the US Department of Labor, Report of a Consultation on the Status of Household Employment (Chicago, 1967), California Department of Industrial Relations Collection, Box 31, Labor Archives and Research Center, San Francisco State University; Palmer, "Outside the Law," pp. 429–30; "Domestics Uniting," pp. 1, 43; NCHE News, vol. 1, no. 1 (November 1970–September 1971), Box 2, Folder 11, Mary Upshaw McClendon Collection, Wayne State Labor Archives (hereafter cited as McClendon Collection).

57 For a similar argument based on the union campaigns among African American hospital workers, see K. Sacks, Caring by the Hour: Women, Work, and Organizing at Duke Medical Center (Urbana: University of Illinois Press, 1988), p. 3.

58 Sragow, "Taking the Mammy Out of Housework," p. 34–8.

Household workers faced different expectations than flight attendants and clericals. Domestics had to meet the psychosocial needs of female employers rather than those of male bosses or customers. Female bosses did not need sexually attractive subordinates; indeed, they preferred older, more matronly figures with whom one could develop intimacy. At the same time, and in part due to this emotional connection, household employees were expected to reinforce the unequal power dynamic by displaying deference. Domestics became adept at "learning people," as one expressed it. They knew when to be invisible, when to be the best friend and spiritual guide, and when childlike obedience was required.

The consequences of "misreading" one's employer, or "sassin'," could be severe. Maids who strayed from the familiar scripts found themselves without a job, or worse. When Dorothy Bolden refused an order to wash dishes and walked out, her employer had her arrested for insubordination. "They said I was mental because I talked back . . . I was in jail five days." She was only released after her uncle hired two psychiatrists who testified to her mental health.[59]

Like clericals, household workers wanted their tasks and their compensation more formalized. "We want to be treated like an employee," explained one maid. "Everyone tells you you're in the family and then they won't even give you a holiday." Household workers wanted compensation in cash rather than in gifts of old clothes and food; they wanted their job to be defined as a set of discrete tasks that they themselves could manage. Like other service workers, they wanted occupational criteria that revolved around objective skills rather than the more subjective criteria of personality and the right attitude.[60]

Household workers wanted to be adults, to be treated with "the respect due any human being"; they objected to the "common use of first names, and uninvited familiarity by employers."[61] They wanted to replace the oppressive one-way personalism with a relationship that was "a two-way street," one with "promptness, integrity, and courtesy" from both parties.

The dilemma for the reform movement was how to bring about these changes and push domestic work, "the last holdout against modernization,"

---

59    "Dorothy Bolden Portrait," 142; G. Coleman, "Domestic Work Now a Virtue Because of Dorothy Bolden," *Atlanta Daily World*, March 23, 1975; J. Tyson, "Black Women Discuss Their Plight," *Atlanta Journal and Constitution*, January 29, 1976.

60    "Farewell to Dinah," *Newsweek*, August 2, 1971, p. 67; Geraldine Roberts interview, Twentieth Century Trade Union Woman Oral History Project, University of Michigan, 1977; "Dorothy Bolden Interview by Chris Lutz," n.p.; National Domestic Workers of America, Inc., "Proposal to Implement a Training Program for Household Management Technicians in Metro Atlanta" (June 26, 1974), Box 1625, Folder 52, NDWU Records.

61    "Domestics Uniting," pp. 1, 43.

into the twentieth century.[62] Some groups, such as a statewide organization in Massachusetts, focused primarily on extending state protective statutes to household workers.[63] Others, like the Detroit Household Workers Organization (HWO) and the Atlanta-based National Domestic Workers Union (NDWU), acted as a combination "lobby group, training program, placement service, and grievance committee."[64]

Dorothy Bolden, head of NDWU, spent much of her time staffing the union's employment placement service, accepting requests from employers who would agree to abide by the union's wages and working conditions. She also leafleted maids at bus stops to spread the word about the new standards: fifteen dollars a day plus carfare. "After we set the price," she explained, "you had to teach these women how to ask for it. You had to learn how to communicate with the lady and tell her about the cost of living." In their career center program, the NDWU offered "human relations training on how to handle employee–employer relationships including 'rap' sessions with employer volunteers." The NDWU, like the Detroit HWO, sought to improve the bargaining power of individual women by fostering self-esteem, creating "an awareness of the value of their labor," and upgrading household workers' skills and marketability.[65]

In 1970, Bolden initiated one of the NDWU's most successful projects, what she called "Maid's Honor Day." She organized the event with the aim of recognizing "those who toil in the home without recognition," and honoring "outstanding women in the field of domestic labor for their professional skills, great common knowledge," and their ability to "mastermind two households."[66] Despite Bolden's intentions, however, the annual affair became for many whites an occasion to reinforce their own expectations of loyalty, sacrifice, and self-abnegation from their

---

62   Sragow, "Taking the Mammy Out of Housework," p. 38; "National Domestic Workers of America," pamphlet (n.d. [c. 1975]), p. 9, Box 1628, Folder 102, NDWU Records; J. Smyth, "Union Maid: A Two-Way Street," *Washington Post*, July 17, 1971.

63   "Domestics Uniting," pp. 1, 43.

64   With the help of the Grosse Point Junior League, the HWO achieved some success in persuading employers to honor a model contract by disseminating a pamphlet to employers entitled "You and Your Household Help," which discussed "good employment practices." See Box 1, Folders 23 and 29, and Box 2, Folder 5, McClendon Collection.

65   Minutes, 1968–78, Box 1633, Folder 173, NDWU Records; "Dorothy Bolden Portrait," p. 161; "Proposal to Implement a Training Program for Household Management Technicians in Metro-Atlanta"; News Release (December 12, 1973), Box 1633, Folder 183, and Box 1626, Folders 66–9, NDWU Records; "Bolden Interview by Chris Lutz"; "Dorothy Bolden interview with Gerda Lerner," pp. 237–8.

66   "History" (n.d.), Box 1628, Folder 97; "National Domestic Workers," pamphlet (n.d. [c. 1975]), p. 9, Box 1628, Folder 102; and Box 1627, Folder 77, all in NDWU Records.

maids. Atlanta's mayor established July 15, 1970, as "Maid's Day," and
called on city dwellers to honor their maids because of their "admirable
record of devotion and loyalty," their "significant and notable contribution
to family life," and their assistance in giving "mothers and other women
more opportunity to add their creativity and energy to Atlanta's growth."[67]
Presumably it was white mothers who had been freed from the home, and
white family life that had been sustained.

The thousands of letters sent to Bolden between 1970 and 1977 from
employers nominating maids for the award reveal the family-like bonds
between maid and mistress in all their excruciating contradictions. Letter
writers describe their maids as "a very dear part of us," "a devoted family
friend," a "second mother," and "a loving and sincere person who always
puts 'her people' [referring to the family of the employer] ahead of herself."
Other letters praise maids for their spirituality and self-sacrifice, their
emotional nurturing, and their loving care. One explained simply: "She's
remarkable . . . I love her. I'm so proud to call her mine!"[68]

Bolden herself and many of the other domestic workers who
participated in this ritual also claimed for themselves the role of stand-
in mother, spiritual adviser, and caretaker.[69] Yet, at the same time, they
rejected the possessive and demeaning overtones in many of the employer
accolades, and they used these well-worn maternal roles to challenge the
status quo rather than reinforce it. Moreover, the point for Bolden was
to honor the domestic work of these women in their own community as
well as in the white family, a nuance almost completely lost on the white
community.

But not everyone in the household-workers movement embraced
Bolden's maternalist rhetoric. Neither did they see an emphasis on "self-
sacrifice" and "love" as the best tactic for improving the lot of household
workers. Indeed, for many, it was precisely the "'personal' aspect of
the existing relationship" that had to be eliminated. Real change could
only come through unionization, Edith Sloan of the NCHE asserted,
or by imposing a third party—a contractor—between the employer and
employee. Otherwise, she promised to loud cheers at the first national
conference of domestic workers in 1971, "'Madam' is going to have to

---

67    Proclamations from Atlanta Mayor Sam Massell (July 15, 1970, reissued 1971, 1972),
Box 1633, Folders 184–5, NDWU Records.
68    Entry Blanks for Maids' Honor Day, 1970–6, Box 1627, Folders 79–90, NDWU
Records.
69    K. Light, "Love Jobs, Say Maids," *Atlanta Constitution*, July 22, 1970; J. Tyson, "Maids
Day Slated, Honor Yours," *Atlanta Journal and Constitution*, April 11, 1971; "Message" from
Dorothy Bolden in "Programme: First Annual Maids' Honor Day" (1970), and "Message
from the President" (1972), Box 628, Folder 97, NDWU Records.

clean her own house and cook and serve her own meals because everyone is going to quit."[70]

By the end of the 1970s, the NCHE and most of its affiliates were in decline, but the movement could claim some crucial victories. The lobbying of grassroots domestic workers, combined with pressure from female legislators such as Shirley Chisholm, Yvonne Burke, and Patsy Mink, forced the inclusion of domestic workers under the Fair Labor Standards Act provisions for the first time in 1974. A few states also added domestic workers to their minimum wage, unemployment insurance, and workers' compensation coverage.[71] In addition, although wages for household employees remained unconscionably low, significant economic gains were made in some key regional labor markets.[72] And, as Geraldine Roberts, longtime civil rights and later household-worker activist explained in 1977, "We thought that we needed them to make a living, but we learned that they needed us, that we were important."[73]

While many private domestic jobs still involve the oppressive one-on-one personalism and deference of the past, household cleaning is increasingly done by teams of workers from agencies or by individual workers who contract on a fee-for-service basis.[74] Moreover, many of the domestic functions once performed by individual women in the home have shifted into the commercial realm. African American women in particular moved into these newly commercialized "domestic" jobs of hotel maid, home healthcare aide, janitor, day care, and kitchen worker.[75] And during the late 1970s and 1980s, they and their coworkers built strong unions in many of these "public household" occupations. Indeed, some of the most important union breakthroughs in the 1980s occurred precisely in these sectors.[76]

---

70  Sragow, "Taking the Mammy Out of Housework," pp. 34–8; For Sloan's plans to form a national union and the growing ties between black unionists and NCHE, see Box 1629, Folder 116, NDWU Records; Coleman, "Domestic Work Now a Virtue"; J. Tyson, "Walks the Streets; Good Maids Hard to Find," *Atlanta Journal*, March 3, 1975; "Domestics Uniting," pp. 1, 43.

71  National Organization for Women (NOW) Legal Defense and Education Fund, *Out of the Shadows: Strategies for Expanding State Labor and Civil Rights Protections for Domestic Workers* (New York: NOW Legal Defense and Education Fund, 1997), pp. 1–2, 20; Sylvia Porter, "1.4 Million Domestic Workers Have Big Stake in Pay Bill," *Miami Herald*, August 24, 1973.

72  J. Kennedy, "Household Help Upgraded," *Washington Star*, January 30, 1976.

73  Geraldine Roberts interview, 94.

74  M. Romero, *Maid in the USA* (New York: Routledge, 1992), chapter 6. Household workers are now more likely to be immigrant women from Latin America or the Caribbean than African Americans. Idem, "Household Workers," in W. Mankiller et al., eds, *The Reader's Companion to U.S. Women's History* (Boston: Houghton Mifflin, 1998), pp. 260–3.

75  Garfinkle, "Occupations of Women and Black Workers, 1962–74," pp. 27, 31; Romero, "Household Workers," pp. 260–3.

76  J. Sweeney, *America Needs a Raise* (Boston: Houghton Mifflin, 1996), pp. 22–7; D. S. Cobble and M. Merrill, "Collective Bargaining in the Hospitality Industry in the 1980s,"

## Conclusion

The movements of flight attendants, clericals, and household workers were about degendering women's jobs, about dismantling the gendered structures and norms around which these occupations had been created. In short, flight attendants, clericals, and household workers sought escape from the gender constraints of their work. They wanted to be treated as human beings and "real workers," not as sex objects, office wives, or "mammies." Women service workers subjected these age-old scripts to public scrutiny and brought them into the arena of labor–management negotiation.

Race and class norms infuse women's jobs as well, and intersect with gender expectations in complicated ways. Flight attendants, often young, white, single women, faced heightened sexualization at work, but it was tempered by competing notions of flight attendants as respectable and potential marriage partners. Similarly, the elite of the clerical workforce, secretaries and administrative assistants, also benefited from being white and having some college education. In contrast, household workers, mainly poor women of color, had no such shields. Dismantling the "mammy" stereotype, with its expectations of self-sacrifice and deference, required an assault against multiple ideologies of domination.

Of course, men's jobs also bear the mark of gender. But for most men, gendered labor has meant higher wages, status, and more autonomy. Thus, dismantling gender constructs has not been a prime concern of collective action among men. Indeed, typically men have relied upon the dominant gender ideology as an aid to their advancement.

Nevertheless, the experiences of women service workers in the 1970s suggested that the old industrial vision of one big union based on class identity and class solidarity must give way to a new ideal, one in which psychological and cultural as well as economic issues are paramount, one in which control over one's emotional terrain is as central as control over one's mind and body. This new ideal must recognize the multiple constructs of domination and the variety of collective movements that will arise in response.

in P. Voos, ed., *Contemporary Collective Bargaining in the Private Sector* (Madison: Industrial Relations Research Association, 1994); S. Mosle, "How the Maids Fought Back," *New Yorker*, February 26 and March 4, 1996.

# 13

# The Enduring Legacy and Contemporary Relevance of Labor Insurgency in the 1970s

## Steve Early

Some students of American labor history may regard the preceding essays on labor insurgency in the 1970s as a mere snapshot in time, and find the whole collection to be just a "family album" by and for aficionados of rank-and-file movement-building. Even Mike Davis, a veteran of post-1968 labor activism and a sympathetic left-wing observer, minimizes the impact of the upsurge:

> In contrast to Western Europe, where the insurgencies of 1968–1973 led to profound upheavals that set new agendas for the labor movement and recomposed its activist leadership, the American rank-and-file struggles did not succeed in re-orienting the new unions towards "qualitative" demands, nor did they produce a distinct new layer of worker-militants. As often as not, the defeat of local insurgencies, or, conversely, their immediate cooptation in the status quo, only left enduring legacies of frustration and demoralization.[1]

At first glance, workplace eruptions during "the long decade" do seem disconnected from the relatively quiescent condition of American labor today. Juxtaposed with the militancy of shop-floor activity three to four decades ago, contemporary challenges to management or union authority appear tame, not to mention far more infrequent. Nevertheless, for many radicals whose labor activism—then and now—was originally sixties-inspired, the long 1970s constituted a second defining moment. The political orientation and organizing lessons derived from what Stan Weir called the "new era of labor revolt" were not simply forgotten and discarded. Despite frustration

---

1  M. Davis, *Prisoners of the American Dream: Politics and Economy in the History of the U.S. Working Class* (London: Verso, 1986), p. 127.

and defeats, drop-outs and defections, the passage of time and changing conditions, veterans of the 1960s social movements and their militant worker allies accomplished a lot, not just during the long 1970s, but over the subsequent decades.[2] Many continued to promote left-wing political causes within the labor movement, organize union reform campaigns, establish alternative labor education and media projects, and support successful union-organizing drives that have changed the face of some local and national unions, as well as the AFL-CIO itself. Simply put, the rank-and-file struggles of the 1960s and 1970s continue to influence the labor movement in important ways right into the present—through the institutions they created, the reforms they won within unions, the continued participation of many of their leading militants, and the continuing relevance of their ideas.

My own initial union activity in the 1970s involved miners, steelworkers, and Teamsters. I worked for the UMW after the MFD's 1972 election victory, Ed Sadlowski's "Steelworkers Fightback" campaign for the presidency of the USWA in 1976–7, and the Professional Drivers Council, a dissident truck drivers group that merged with TDU in 1979. The UMW, USWA, and IBT bureaucracies were dangerously calcified forty years ago. The union officialdom was inaccessible and unresponsive, often incompetent, and, in the case of the Mine Workers and Teamsters, prone to corruption, violence, and intimidation. Working members paid the heaviest price for this organizational decay, since it was they, not any big employers, who were being muscled by the union leadership and staff. Many miners and Teamsters had long relied on larger-than-life figures like John L. Lewis or Jimmy Hoffa to deliver the goods at contract time. Belatedly, they discovered that these business unionist demigods, not to mention their benighted successors like Tony Boyle or Frank Fitzsimmons, had left them defenseless in the face of mounting management attacks when the economy changed for the worse, between 1965 and 1975.

The employers' offensive resulted in deteriorating job safety and health, increased employment insecurity, eroded pension and medical benefits, stagnant pay, and labor–management cooperation schemes that undermined unionism itself. When dissidents organized to counter these threats, they often focused not just on management, but on union practices and policies, because this was the only way open to them to turn their unions into effective institutions for struggle against the boss. Within the UMW, USWA, and IBT, rank-and-file rebels raised hell about rigged elections and union benefit fund rip-offs, the abuse of international union trusteeship powers, undemocratic (or even non-existent) procedures for ratifying contracts and

---

2  S. Early, "A New Generation of Labor Leftists," *The Nation*, May 5, 1984, pp. 543–6. See also S. Lynd and A. Lynd, *The New Rank-and-File* (Ithaca: Cornell University Press, 2000).

electing union representatives, and restrictions on the ability of workers to strike over unresolved grievances or even at contract expiration.[3] But even unions widely hailed as "progressive" during this era—like the UAW and UFW—operated as top-down autocracies with little pretense of internal democracy, with the consequence that militants who wished to fight the employers effectively had no choice but to confront their "liberal" leaders and attempt to transform the union.[4]

In the 1970s, fights within unions over leadership and programs were thus an indirect form of worker struggle against management; rank-and-file demands for greater democracy expressed workers' immediate economic self-interest vis-à-vis employers. Left-wing "colonizers," along with other political radicals who offered support from outside, took a central part in many reform struggles. Yet what made the grassroots labor insurgency of the later 1960s and 1970s so significant, and gave it its power, was the active participation of tens of thousands of workers who were *not* initially motivated by ideology or personal idealism, although there was no shortage of the latter, along with great personal courage. The union dissidents I met during this period learned the hard way that workers who lose their voice in the union are unable to maintain it for very long at work. None that I know would have agreed with SEIU president Andy Stern that "it's hard to make the argument that unions with direct elections better represent their members."[5] Among the lasting achievements of these rank-and-file struggles were new constitutional rules and voting procedures in the UMW and IBT, which made national union leadership more accountable to the membership. These changes not only improved the quality of union representation regardless of who was in office, but opened the way to historic victories for reformers in both unions in the 1980s and 1990s.

## Lessons and Legacies of the Long '70s

The grassroots organizing that built TDU starting in 1975–6, and which has continued into the present, played an indispensable part in laying the groundwork for the successful campaign for Teamsters president Ron Carey in 1991. Without TDU, this first-ever referendum vote on IBT national

---

3  S. Early, "Union Democracy in Mineworkers, Steelworkers, and Teamsters Unions," *Proceedings of San Fernando Valley College of Law Symposium on Labor Law and Industrial Relations* (Sepulveda, CA: San Fernando Valley Law Review, 1978), pp. 41–53.
4  See N. Lichtenstein, *The Most Dangerous Man in Detroit: Walter Reuther and the Fate of American Labor* (New York: Basic Books, 1995), and S. Ferriss and R. Sandoval, *The Fight in the Fields: Cesar Chavez and the Farmworkers Movement* (New York: Harcourt Brace, 1997).
5  As quoted in S. Early, "Reutherism Redux: When Poor Workers' Unions Wear the Color Purple," *Against the Current* (September/October 2004), p. 35.

officers and executive board members would never have been held. Carey's election made it possible for the bottom-up contract campaigns—long promoted by TDU—to become part of the union's official approach to bargaining. During Carey's administration, and with a decisive contribution by TDU at the grassroots, the Teamsters conducted a nationwide strike at UPS in 1997 that produced the most important victory for the IBT and the entire labor movement in more than twenty years.

In the run-up to the UPS strike, many months of intensive education, discussion, and internal communication within the union's newly created "member-to-member networks" built a broad consensus about union bargaining goals and how best to articulate them. The IBT's main objective was to create more full-time jobs by thwarting management's strategy of converting to a predominantly part-time workforce. The Teamsters' ability to frame this dispute to strike a chord with the broader public, along with a tremendous outpouring of picket line support for drivers and package handlers, was crucial to the victory. As the union put it in innumerable research reports, press releases, and rank-and-file interviews, "Part-Time America Doesn't Work!"

The union's victory not only beat back the UPS's demands for concessions, but also opened the way for the creation of more full-time jobs. It became a rallying point for everyone concerned about the impact of part-timing, with its accompanying erosion of job-based benefits. The strike thus demonstrated how much broader the appeal of unions can be when they are perceived to be fighting for the interests of all workers. As AFL-CIO president John Sweeney observed soon after the settlement: "You could make a million house calls, run a thousand television commercials, stage a hundred strawberry rallies [for the United Farm Workers], and still not come close to doing what the UPS strike did for organizing."[6]

Ron Carey's TDU-aided election victory in 1991 had the further effect of changing the balance of forces on the AFL-CIO Executive Council. It thereby facilitated Sweeney's own election as federation president. In 1995, Sweeney, then the leader of the SEIU, challenged Tom Donahue, the heir to the old conservative leadership of Lane Kirkland and George Meany. Sweeney's election was the first victory over an incumbent in one hundred years. His Teamster-backed "New Voice" slate included Rich Trumka, who came to power in the UMW, much like Carey in the IBT, thanks only to the organizational changes implemented by a rank-and-file movement of the 1970s—in his case, MFD, which defeated Tony Boyle in

---

6 M. Witt and R. Wilson, "Part-Time America Won't Work: The Teamsters' Fight for Good Jobs at UPS," in J. Mort, ed., *Not Your Father's Union Movement: Inside the AFL-CIO* (New York: Verso, 1999), p. 183.

1972. Trumka was elected president a decade later and was able to thwart a resurgence of the conservative Boyle faction. Like Teamsters, UMW members changed the direction of their union in the 1980s and beyond, thanks to the power they built at the base through the militant action of the 1960s–70s.

Sweeney's "New Voice" administration ushered in what many hailed as a new era of labor glasnost, if not perestroika as well. Where open discussion and criticism of union problems was once verboten under the Meany-Kirkland regimes, Sweeney—to his credit—let a hundred flowers bloom. "New Voice" headquarters staffers and central labor council leaders included numerous veterans of sixties activism, who were independent union organizers in the 1970s or participants in rank-and-file caucuses and movements. A group of left-wing academics with similar backgrounds formed a high-profile labor support group call Scholars, Artists, and Writers for Social Justice (SAWSJ), which pledged to assist the federation's "remobilization" of its affiliates. Like SAWSJ, most left-liberal commentators gave the AFL-CIO, under Sweeney, high marks for its campus outreach, media savvy, progressive coalition-building, sensitivity to diversity issues, and purge of cold warriors from labor's international programs (which continued to be funded by the U.S. government). During the World Trade Organization meeting in Seattle in 1999, members of AFL-CIO-affiliated unions joined students, environmentalists, and anti-globalization activists in a historic protest against one of the most powerful governing bodies of international capitalism. Most of the Teamsters in the streets were members of TDU-led Local 174 in Seattle. The social movement unionism that gave rise to this alliance of "Teamsters and Turtles" had its roots in the 1970s reform struggles that brought new leadership to power, in Seattle and other centers of Teamster conservatism.

Another important manifestation of the new political climate within the AFL-CIO was the success of labor-based organizing against U.S. military intervention by sixties peace activists. In 1967, the federation's national convention rejected an anti–Vietnam War resolution by a margin of two thousand to six.[7] In 2005, thanks to lobbying by U.S. Labor Against the War, AFL-CIO convention delegates in Chicago called for an end to America's occupation of Iraq. Federation policy on immigration has also changed for the better from the days when unions supported deportation of undocumented workers and legal sanctions against employers who hired them. During heated Congressional debates about "immigration reform" in 2006–7, the AFL-CIO took a strong stand against punitive measures

---

7  R. Zeiger, *American Workers, American Unions* (Baltimore: Johns Hopkins University Press, 1986), p. 172.

sought by the Bush administration, and also opposed a new "guest worker" program that would further undermine labor standards in agriculture and other industries.

Unfortunately, neither Sweeney's AFL-CIO nor Change to Win (CTW), the rival group formed by federation defectors in 2005, has been able to successfully address the labor movement's fundamental problem—the long-term decline of the unions. It is conceivable that labor's current stasis is just a prelude, as sociologist Dan Clawson optimistically argues, to its next mass upsurge, like the 1920s was vis-à-vis the 1930s. But if that's to be the case, a lot of preliminary organizing must take place in the interim, for no eventual reassertion of workers' power—on the job and in politics—can be expected to take place in a purely spontaneous manner.[8] As the sine qua non for successful and broad-ranging labor resistance, organizational seeds must first be planted and cultivated, horizontal networks created, and obstacles to direct action overcome, just as they were in the '30s. This is a task that an impressive layer of activists has taken upon itself, both outside and within the official labor movement, many with roots in the 1960s and 1970s.

The decay of established unions has become so advanced that some younger activists—unlike their counterparts of earlier eras—no longer consider organized workplaces to be promising arenas for "colonization" and the revival of "class struggle unionism." Like *Monthly Review* editor and author Michael Yates, they actively question whether "existing labor unions and leaders" can ever "be the vehicle through which unions become relevant again."[9] With only 12 percent of today's total workforce unionized, many left-wingers have shifted their attention to unorganized sectors of the economy. There, millions of foreign-born workers toil under terrible conditions in low-wage jobs, thanks especially to a restructuring of the world economy which has put the survival of organized labor very much in question.

Although some AFL-CIO and CTW unions have welcomed and defended undocumented workers, they are clearly failing to meet the day-to-day needs of enough immigrants and their families. That's why more than 135 community-based "workers centers" have emerged around the country to provide the foreign-born with legal advice, leadership training, organizing support, and a vehicle for public advocacy. Some of the earliest of these centers date back to the late 1970s. One of the first was the Chinese Staff and Workers Association, which aided independent union organizing by restaurant workers, who were neglected by HERE in New York City's

---

8    D. Clawson, *The Next Upsurge* (Ithaca: Cornell University Press, 2003).
9    S. Early, "Can Workers Centers Fill the Union Void?" *New Labor Forum* vol. 15:2 (Fall 2006), p. 116.

Chinatown. In North Carolina, Black Workers for Justice was formed in 1981 to defend African American workers at Kmart and other non-union firms that mainstream unions had ignored. Meanwhile, along the Texas border, La Mujer Obrera—an organization of Mexican American women—grew out of a garment workers strike at Farah Clothing in 1981.[10]

By the spring of 2006, building on these efforts, a new generation of workers centers spread across the country, strategically positioned to aid an escalating series of marches and rallies protesting the proposals for "immigration reform" of the Bush administration and Congress. These unprecedented demonstrations ultimately involved millions of workers and led to the largest work stoppage in U.S. history over a political issue since the eight-hour-day walkouts of the 1880s. The historic job stay-away on May 1, 2006—dubbed "The Day Without Immigrants"—developed a mighty momentum all its own and took place despite the warnings and reservations of some community leaders, local union officials, and equally cautious Catholic clergy.[11]

Many militant organizers have continued throughout recent decades to focus their efforts on the existing unions, including an indispensable core of socialists who had been radicalized in the movements of the 1960s and entered the labor movement in the early 1970s. A group of these veterans of the rank-and-file struggles formed the Detroit-based Labor Education and Research Project (LERP) in 1979; no labor-related institution, large or small, has done more to promote grassroots activism. The founders of LERP, which publishes *Labor Notes*, correctly anticipated the heightened need for resistance and solidarity from below in a period of ever greater concessions on the part of official union leaders. Soon after *Labor Notes* got started, the avalanche of labor defeats began: PATCO, Phelps-Dodge, Greyhound, Hormel, Eastern Airlines, and International Paper, followed later by the *New York Daily News*, *Detroit Free Press*, Staley, and Caterpillar. National and local union leaders proved ineffective, preferring to focus their resources and activities ever more obsessively on elections and the Democratic Party, at the expense of membership mobilization around contracts, strikes, or boycotts.

Fortunately, the resulting vacuum was filled, at least in part, by a network of unofficial solidarity committees. These left-led ad hoc groups organized

---

10 K. Moody, *US Labor in Trouble and Transition: The Failure of Reform from Above, the Promise of Revival from Below* (New York: Verso, 2007), p. 217.

11 See N. V. Lopez, "The Battles Before Us: Strategy and Tactics for Immigrants Rights in 2007," *Against the Current* (March/April 2007), pp. 4–9. Also see K. Moody, "Changing Face of Unionism: The Harvest of Empire," *Against the Current* (May/June, 2007), pp. 33–8, and D. La Botz, "The Immigrant Rights Movement: Between Political Realism and Social Idealism," *New Politics* (Summer 2007), pp. 145–54.

mass picket lines and rallies, conducted plant-gate collections and solidarity
tours, and encouraged the "adoption" of strikers' families. *Labor Notes* played
a key role in helping these groups link up, coordinate, and publicize their
activities around the country. LERP's work of coordination, education,
and information, which continues vigorously to this day, remains a lasting
product of the rank-and-file activism of the long 1970s—and represents an
important strain of political continuity between that period and the current
era. Every two years, the *Labor Notes* network holds a national conference,
which brings together one thousand or more union and worker-center
activists from the United States and abroad. As a monthly publication, *Labor
Notes* continues to reach about seven thousand hard-copy readers, and
thousands more via its website. For militant shop stewards, local officers,
organizers, and other rank-and-file-oriented union reps, there is still no
other place to find all the news and analysis that the official labor press
doesn't see fit to print.

Through its series of book-length publications—including *Working
Smart: A Union Guide to Participation Programs and Reengineering*; *Democracy Is
Power: Rebuilding Unions from the Bottom Up*; and *A Troublemaker's Handbook
2: How to Fight Back at Work and Win*—*Labor Notes* has made unique
contributions to the ongoing debate about how labor should "change to
win." Each book illuminates aspects of management strategy, while offering
models of working-class organizing that promote rank-and-file leadership
development, the day-to-day fight to improve job conditions, and the
formation of lasting community-labor coalitions like Jobs with Justice.
*A Troublemaker's Handbook 2* includes many case studies of contemporary
strikes, boycotts, job actions, and organizing campaigns that successfully
employed tactics and strategies utilized in the 1970s (and earlier periods
of labor insurgency).[12] These volumes have been widely used in union-
sponsored shop-steward training and *Labor Notes*–backed "Troublemakers'
Schools" around the country.[13]

Through vehicles like TDU, *Labor Notes*, Jobs with Justice, and workers
centers—as well as by virtue of institutional changes within labor caused
by the influx of social movement activists from the 1960s—the struggles
from below of the long 1970s continue to make themselves felt in the new
millennium. Perhaps the most important legacy of labor's last period of
upsurge is the bottom-up perspective it embodied. As in the 1930s, there

---

12   J. Slaughter, ed., *A Troublemaker's Handbook* 2 (Detroit: Labor Notes, 2005), and
other *Labor Notes* books are available from Labor Education and Research Project at 7435
Michigan Ave., Detroit, Michigan, 48210. (See www.labornotes.org.)
13   See, for example, C. Kutalik, "Troublemakers Find Their Way to San Jose," *Labor
Notes* (June 2007), p. 2.

was strong validation of the idea that workers experience, every day on the job, relentless pressure from employers that adversely affects their working conditions and standard of living, thus motivating them to fight back. At the same time, it is in the workplace—more than any other arena—that hourly or salaried workers are most able to form the bonds of solidarity necessary for offensive and defensive struggles. To be effective, therefore, any union must root itself in the shop floor and build countervailing power from the bottom up by mobilizing its rank-and-file base. Unfortunately, the experience of unionized workers in the postwar era was often just the opposite. In both its conservative and more liberal forms, bureaucratic business unionism proved unresponsive to the needs of the membership, leading to widespread alienation between the rank and file and the full-time leadership and staff.

This is why the most successful rank-and-file movements of the long 1970s (and beyond) rooted themselves in the workplace and tried to unite members in contract campaigns and day-to-day fights against the boss, while also attempting to gain control over union structures so the latter could facilitate rather than impede rank-and-file struggles. Where they have flourished, groups like TDU provide a critical forum for democratic debate and decision-making often missing from the internal life of unions themselves. As the TDU-inspired 1996–7 UPS contract fight demonstrated, no union can tap the full potential power of a mobilized membership without keeping the rank and file informed about and involved in all aspects of campaign planning and implementation. Internal union democracy is not just a luxury—nor, as traditionally believed, a liability—because confrontations with management require military-style discipline on the union side. On the contrary, strong mechanisms for membership control and leadership accountability are indispensable components of real union power—and the greater political influence working people can have when their unions are run by and for the members.[14]

### A Way Forward from the Top Down?

But the fact remains that more than a decade into John Sweeney's reign, less than 8 percent of all private sector workers were covered by collective bargaining agreements, down from a high of 35 percent in the early 1950s. Management opposition to unionization remains as strong as ever, generating hundreds of National Labor Relations Board (NLRB) cases every year, involving threats, intimidation, discriminatory firings, and other forms of

---

14   For a further discussion of "the rank-and-file strategy" for building workplace power, see Moody, *US Labor in Trouble and Transition*, pp. 177–9.

illegal conduct. Individual employers fiercely resist both alternative and traditional union organizing efforts aimed at securing private agreements that would require employer neutrality and recognition of new bargaining units based on "card checks" rather than representation elections. In 2007 the Democratic-controlled Congress failed to enact an "Employee Free Choice Act" that would require employer recognition of unions based on signed authorization cards instead of NLRB votes—legislation that would have been vetoed by George Bush. So far in 2009, similar legislation has met the same fate, despite even greater Democratic majorities in Congress and a Democratic president.

In the public sector, about a third of the workforce is organized, but public employee unionization is largely confined to the coasts and the upper Midwest. Elsewhere, twenty states still deny public employees the right to negotiate binding labor agreements—even though many workers there have joined unions and are lobbying for full collective bargaining rights. To make matters worse, recent decisions by the NLRB have stripped millions of workers of their status as employees, because they are undocumented, hired through temp agencies, work as so-called "independent contractors," or function as "supervisors" according to management's expansive definition. The combined impact of these statutory prohibitions and case-law exclusions is staggering. A 2002 General Accounting Office study estimated that no fewer than 32 million public and private sector workers today lack legal protection for collective activity aimed at securing union recognition and the right to bargain with their employers.

By 2004, the unions' continuing failure to grow was leading to a second upheaval within the AFL-CIO, as some of the original backers of John Sweeney's original "New Voice" slate had grown increasingly frustrated by the slow pace of change under his leadership. Andy Stern, president of SEIU, along with John Wilhelm and Bruce Raynor, presidents respectively of HERE and UNITE, formed what was initially called the "New Unity Partnership" to provoke debate about the need for union restructuring and greater investment in membership recruitment. In Stern's words, it was time "to transform the AFL-CIO or build something new." NUP secured the backing of the Laborers and Carpenters Unions, but it could not win majority support for its proposals for reconfiguring the federation prior to the AFL-CIO's 2005 convention, or sufficient votes to unseat Sweeney. The NUPsters therefore decided to boycott the convention and precipitate a formal split in the AFL-CIO in order to create a rival federation, Change to Win, which ultimately included the Teamsters, United Farm Workers, and United Food and Commercial Workers, as well as the Laborers and Carpenters.

Some observers have likened this breakaway to the emergence of the

Congress of Industrial Organizations (CIO), the militant grassroots alternative to craft union conservatism in the mid-1930s. But, rhetoric aside, there were few actual similarities to the earlier rift. SEIU and the Carpenters have both embraced "market share recovery" strategies that aim to increase their own membership "by just about any means necessary."[15] In so doing, they have downplayed the rank-and-file initiative, shop-floor militancy, and democratic decision-making by workers themselves that played such a central part in the formation of the CIO, relying instead on the labor–management cooperation, bureaucratic consolidation, and top-down control so characteristic of the old AFL. Union democracy, in particular, is currently viewed by key CTW unions—and their academic boosters—as irrelevant at best, or, at worst, an impediment to much-needed centralization, modernization, and membership growth. According to CTW-oriented academics like University of California professors Kim Voss and Ruth Milkman, successful union transformation today—unlike in the 1970s—is "typically orchestrated from the top down, contrary to the romantic view that only the rank-and-file can be the fount of democratic change."[16]

Stern himself argues that the purpose of transforming union structures is not, in any case, to bring more democracy. It is not "to make it easier or harder to elect or re-elect leaders," but "for workers to be able to unite, fight, and win together"—as if there were no connection between union effectiveness and the ability of union members to hold their leaders accountable. "Workers want their lives to be changed," he insists. "They want strength and a voice, not some purist intellectual, historical, mythical democracy" that, according to Stern, is only of concern to "progressives" and "intellectuals." To Stern and SEIU strategist Steven Lerner, the question of internal democracy will become relevant again only when a much larger portion of the U.S. labor force gets organized. Until then, they contend, for the vast majority without bargaining rights, "union democracy" is a moot point.[17] One wonders how this proposition would have sounded to the radicals and militants who built the CIO at a time when the percentage of industrial workers in unions was far lower, but nonetheless insisted on union democracy from day one.

Stern, Lerner, and their allies, such as Bruce Raynor, argue, in addition, that organized labor is hopelessly hamstrung by its own Lilliputians: the AFL-CIO has too many small unions, lacking sufficient "industry focus" and without the bargaining strength or political clout necessary to deal

---

15  L. Featherstone, "Andy Stern: Savior or Sell-Out?" *The Nation*, July 16, 2007, pp. 8–10.

16  From the introduction to R. Milkman and K. Voss, eds, *Rebuilding Labor: Organizing and Organizers in the New Union Movement* (Ithaca: Cornell University Press, 2004), p. 6.

17  As quoted in Early, "Reutherism Redux," p. 35.

with employers effectively. To launch an organizing offensive on the scale of 1930s, the federation's fifty-eight separate unions should ideally consolidate themselves into fifteen or twenty much larger entities, each concentrating on its own core industries, with more resources and less overlapping jurisdiction.[18] In Stern's view, labor organizations should mirror the market scope and corporate structure of business—at the local, regional, and international levels. Smaller-scale union bodies—no matter how participatory—have become an anachronism "in an era of corporate mergers," he argued. A traditional "local union structure" may have "made sense years ago," but "now does more to handicap workers than it does to help."[19]

SEIU's approach has attracted so much attention, from academics and trade unionists alike, because of the union's apparent success. SEIU is America's second-largest union and the fastest growing, with more than 1.4 million members at the time of the AFL-CIO split. Stern challenged the AFL-CIO "to organize or die," while offering his own union up as a model for organizational streamlining throughout the labor movement. Under Stern's presidency, SEIU healthcare, building services, and public sector members were reorganized into separate entities. Local unions were then consolidated into huge statewide or multi-state "mega-locals," with as many as 85,000 to 300,000 members. More than forty SEIU affiliates— about 14 percent of the total—were in turn put under International Union trusteeships, so that new leaders could be installed from Washington, D.C., to implement SEIU's "New Strength Unity" program. As sociologists Kim Voss and Rick Fantasia observed admiringly in their 2004 book *Hard Work: Remaking the American Labor Movement*, much of SEIU is now run by a new breed of "senior managers" and college-educated field-staffers recruited, in large numbers, from outside the union. Holding "appointed rather than elected positions," these agents of change are, they say, "trying to build a new labor movement in the shell of the old." According to Voss and Fantasia, SEIU operatives may "give off an air of arrogance and exclusivity," they may be "brash and overconfident," and their style of work may resemble that of "Silicon Valley entrepreneurs," but what nonetheless makes them successful is that they have "zero tolerance" for locals or elected local officials who fail to organize.[20]

---

18    See S. Lerner, "An Immodest Proposal: A New Architecture for the House of Labor," *New Labor Forum* vol. 12:2 (Summer 2003), pp. 9–30.

19    Ibid., p. 14.

20    K. Voss and R. Fantasia, *Hard Work: Remaking the American Labor Movement* (Berkeley: University of California Press, 2004), p. 244. See also Voss and R. Sherman, "Breaking the Iron Law of Oligarchy: Union Revitalization in the American Labor Movement," *American Journal of Sociology* vol. 100:2 (September 2000), pp. 303–49. Applauding the "visionary" use

Of course, organizing growth—or increased "density" as it's called in SEIU—requires more than just signing up new members and petitioning for NLRB representation elections. Unions operating in the private sector must find ways to neutralize employer interference that often makes it impossible to win such elections and negotiate a first contract. Management's success in rendering the National Labor Relations Act nearly useless should have led, by now, to wider union embrace of alternative recognition strategies. To their credit, SEIU janitorial service organizers helped pioneer comprehensive, community-based campaigns that "bypassed the Board" more effectively than many other unions have been able to do. The union's Justice for Janitors (JFJ) campaigns targeted building owners who were the real power behind cleaning service contractors and secured negotiated procedures for employer neutrality and "card check." As Milkman describes in *L.A. Story: Immigrant Workers and the Future of the U.S. Labor Movement*, "Justice for Janitors originated as part of a strategic union rebuilding effort. It was conceived by SEIU's national leadership and relied heavily on research and other staff-intensive means of exerting pressure on employers." Yet, as Milkman makes clear, in the original 1990 JFJ campaign in Los Angeles, and in subsequent efforts in many other cities, "rank-and-file mobilization played a critical role in its success."[21]

JFJ thus represents a hybrid model, combining elements of bottom-up militancy with top-down leadership control and direction. SEIU janitorial union campaigns have employed direct-action tactics, built strong ties with immigrant communities, and presented the workers' causes in a way that elicits sympathy and support from the broader public concerned about social justice and fair treatment of oppressed minorities. By persisting in its building services campaigns over an extended period of time, SEIU has forced recalcitrant employers to accept collective bargaining in a sector that was headed for de-unionization. Nevertheless, new collective power and contract protection on the job has not always translated into a leading role for immigrant janitors in conducting the affairs of their own SEIU locals. After the 1990 JFJ campaign in Los Angeles, for example, the newly organized workers became members of Local 399. A number of the sophisticated and resolute Latino shop-floor activists, who emerged from

---

of trusteeship powers by SEIU and other unions affiliated with CTW, the authors describe how international unions which "favor innovation" have installed new non-member "leaders" in their locals (i.e., staffers "with activist experience outside the labor movement who interpret the decline of labor's power as a mandate to change"). According to Voss and Sherman, "It is commonly believed that only democratic movements from below can vanquish bureaucratic rigidity. Our research challenges this view . . ."

21   R. Milkman, *L.A. Story: Immigrant Workers and the Future of the U.S. Labor Movement* (New York: Russell Sage Foundation, 2006), p. 159.

the union recognition struggle, were soon complaining about the local's out-of-touch leadership, its neglect of day-to-day workplace issues, and the lack of rank-and-file participation in union decision-making. Relying on their existing networks, the janitors took part in a successful electoral insurgency, led by the "Multiracial Alliance Slate." The SEIU national leadership quickly nullified the Alliance's election victory by throwing the local into trusteeship and eventually moving L.A. janitors into a much larger, regional building services local.

Even a JFJ observer as sympathetic as Milkman acknowledges that there was "widespread criticism" of the union's response to this "outbreak of factionalism that, at least on the surface, appeared to involve rank-and-file rebellion against the local SEIU officialdom."[22] The effect of the trusteeship was to disperse and dilute the energy, organization, and collective experience of the janitors who had carried out the struggle for union recognition. A SEIU critic believes this had a negative impact on subsequent collective bargaining, which produced wage gains of 12.3 percent between 1990 and 1995, and another 6 percent between 1995 and 2000. In the decade after their 1990 victory,

> LA janitors with the best conditions saw their real wages fall 10%. In this same period, average real hourly wages in the U.S. rose by 4.8%. It is just possible that had the LA janitors been in their own local instead of statewide Local 1877, with its low wages, minimal benefits, and long contracts, they could have pressured the industry for more and set a better pattern for others.[23]

In Stern's 2006 book, *A Country That Works*, which recounts the achievements of JFJ in L.A. and elsewhere, he expresses a strong preference for bargaining relationships established without even the tactical use of "rank-and-file mobilization." A student activist in the late 1960s at the University of Pennsylvania, Stern became a welfare case worker after graduation and joined the Pennsylvania Social Service Union (PSSU), an independent union which later affiliated with SEIU. There—like many of the 1960s–1970s "troublemakers" described in this collection—he was "part of an opposition movement" in PSSU, which staged a three-day wildcat strike in an effort "to reject a statewide contract as a 'sell-out.'"[24] Now older and wiser, Stern says that "going out on strike at the first sign of trouble is a losing

---

22    Ibid., p. 159.
23    Moody, *US Labor in Trouble and Transition*, p. 195.
24    A. Stern, *A Country That Works: Getting America Back on Track* (New York: The Free Press, 2006), p. 46.

strategy."[25] Instead, organized labor should, like SEIU under his leadership, shed the "old class struggle mentality" that is a "vestige of an earlier, rough era of industrial unions."[26] "Our members go to work every day wanting to solve problems," he explained to the *Chicago Tribune*. "They don't want to create problems for their employer. They don't want someone to come in and turn things upside down."[27] Instead of engaging in such counter-productive workplace troublemaking, modern labor organizations should, according to Stern, be more sensitive to "employers' competitive reality and attempt to create or add value to their business models."[28] As he told the *Wall Street Journal*, "we want to find a twenty-first century new model [of unionism] that is less focused on individual grievances, more focused on industry needs."[29] After visits to the United Kingdom to promote this "new model" there, Stern has even been "quoted or paraphrased as telling his British counterparts that shop stewards are a bad idea."[30]

Skeptics about Stern's approach wonder, of course, how a union can appeal to employers' interests when its putative objective is to improve wages, benefits, and working conditions, all of which cost them more money. Not surprisingly, SEIU's "value-added partnerships" have been most successful in building dues-paying membership in publicly funded healthcare, long-term care, and related areas. In these sectors, the union has greater ability to deliver the goods for management as a pre-condition for organizing rights. It has demonstrated its worth as a partner by lobbying for more government financing of hospitals, nursing homes, and agencies or programs providing home-based childcare or elder care. In states with labor-friendly governors or legislatures—who can be showered with union political donations—new SEIU bargaining units have been created for an estimated 400,000 home-based care providers previously classified as "independent contractors."[31] This has resulted in the formal unionization of a low-paid, often part-time, high-turnover workforce, which is predominantly non-white and female, and which includes many

---

25  R. Kirkland, "The New Face of Labor," *Fortune*, October 16, 2006, p. 128.

26  Stern, *A Country That Works*, p. 90.

27  As quoted in interview by B. Rose, "Leader Has New View For Unions," *Chicago Tribune*, October 15, 2006, p. 27.

28  Stern, *A Country That Works*, p. 58.

29  As quoted in interview with K. Maher, "Are Unions Relevant?" *Wall Street Journal*, January 22, 2007, page R5.

30  Moody, *US Labor in Trouble and Transition*, p. 194.

31  J. Fine, "Does the Labor Movement Have a 'Plan B'?" *New Labor Forum* vol. 16:2 (Spring 2007), p. 41. See also E. Boris and J. Klein, "'We Were the Invisible Workforce': Unionizing Home Care," in D. S. Cobble, ed., *The Sex of Class: Women Transforming American Labor* (Ithaca: Cornell University Press, 2007), pp. 177–93.

"workfare" program participants. The organizing model developed by SEIU in this sector—in high-profile campaigns in California and Illinois—has since been copied, with varying degrees of success, in other states, by other unions, including its leading competitor in the field, AFSCME, along with CWA, AFT, and the UAW. Like SEIU, several of these unions have partnered with the community organization ACORN in the card-signing stage of their campaigns, utilizing its youthful door-to-door canvassers and inner-city base of neighborhood activists who are also daycare or home-care providers. Home-based workers now represent the biggest single source of membership growth in the labor movement.

But the ability of SEIU, or any union, to offer employers material incentives for the acceptance of union organization—while, at the same time, extracting from them costly gains for workers—is obviously very limited, especially across much of the private sector, where it is far more difficult to offer "value added" to employers as a quid pro quo for union recognition and improved compensation. Even in the new bargaining units created for home healthcare aides and childcare providers, SEIU and other unions have accepted, in return for union recognition, legislation or executive orders that exclude these workers from standard public sector healthcare and retirement coverage. A fundamental danger of top-down deal-making in these cases is therefore that the interests of workers may be sacrificed to the drive for greater "market share," particularly where existing and/or prospective members have little or no say, due to their lack of control over or even involvement in the union or the organizing process. Initial bargaining gains for these newly organized groups have been modest at best, leaving them with wages that still "rarely exceed the poverty level."[32] As Karlyne Mills—an SEIU 1199 member and thirteen-year home-care aide, who still makes only $8.30 an hour in New York City with no family health insurance—says: "It's getting a little frustrating waiting [for a raise to $9] because we're working hard. From the time that I became a home health aide, I always wondered why this job is so important and our pay is so low."[33]

The fact that the "non-traditional workplace" of most of these caretakers is their own or someone else's home only heightens the temptation for unions to shirk the formidable, ongoing "internal organizing" challenge of building real union organization, connections between members, and even a functioning steward system. Several years after SEIU's big home-

---

32   R. Fitch, *Solidarity for Sale: How Corruption Destroyed the Labor Movement and Undermined America's Promise* (New York: Public Affairs, 2006), p. 308.
33   As quoted by P. McGeehan, "Health Care Drives Job Growth in Region, but With Many Jobs That Pay Poorly," *New York Times*, May 25, 2007, p. C13.

care workers victory in Southern California, for example, 60,000 out of the 80,000 workers in the unit involved were still agency fee payers, never having been signed up as members—a weakness exploited by the National Right to Work Committee in a lawsuit that forced their local to refund $8 million it had collected and spent on political action aimed at improving their pay. Within SEIU, there has also been an all too frequent readiness to ditch patients and consumers in return for management favors—or to do a particular "union friendly" employer a favor. This tendency was most pronounced in the union's past lobbying, alongside California HMOs, to restrict patient lawsuits, as well as its opposition, alongside the state's nursing home industry, to a nursing home residents' bill of rights.[34]

In 2007, shortly after the publication of Stern's book, there was a wave of negative publicity, followed by unprecedented internal criticism, about where his partnership strategy was headed in the nursing-home industry. First, a *Seattle Times* article described a ten-year deal negotiated by SEIU Local 775 in Washington which promised "no strikes and agrees to let the nursing-home operators—not the union or workers—decide which homes are offered up for organizing," and agreed "not to try organizing more than half of a particular company's non-union homes."[35] Then *San Francisco Weekly* publicized details of "employer-friendly" model contracts in California, which specify that "the union is not allowed to report healthcare violations to state regulators, to other public officials, or to journalists, except in cases where the employees are required by law to report egregious cases of neglect and abuse to the state." According to this report, "the agreements also prohibit unionized workers from picketing, and negotiating improvements in health care or other benefits," and "prohibit the workers from having a say in their job conditions."[36]

In a *Dissent* magazine interview and in a critique simultaneously distributed to former national executive board colleagues, Jerry Brown, retired longtime president of the Connecticut and Rhode Island 20,000-member healthcare local SEIU 1199, questioned several aspects of these "institutional peace

---

34   See, for example, April 11, 2007 press release from the California-based Foundation for Taxpayer and Consumer Rights, entitled "Internal Documents Show How Andy Stern Sold Out Nursing Home Workers and Patients." Issued in response to reporting by the *San Francisco Weekly* (see footnote 36 below), the release quoted FTCR president and well-known consumer advocate Jamie Court as follows: "Nursing homes are a sector where caregivers are the eyes, the ears, and the witnesses when there is patient abuse . . . I've never seen a labor union except for the SEIU enter into a top-down, industry-friendly agreement that binds the hands of the workers. To tie their hands and tie their tongues is to let people die."
35   R. Thomas, "Union, Nursing Home Alliance Team Up," *Seattle Times*, March 5, 2007, p. B-1.
36   M. Smith, "Union Disunity," *San Francisco Weekly*, April 11, 2007, p. 1.

pacts" under which SEIU offers "political help in leveraging public money" in exchange "for the employer's help in allowing the union to organize employees and collect dues." The problem, said Brown, is that "even when we are then allowed to organize, unbeknownst to the members, there is often a pattern agreement or 'template' in existence which hinders or even makes impossible the growth of a workplace organization that can make decisions for itself." According to Brown, what SEIU should be asking itself is whether such "methods can produce a real, democratic workers organization"—or will they just lead to a membership alienated from the union? He warned that a workplace situation in which workers view themselves, correctly, as a "third party"—in a relationship brokered by labor and management bosses—is "the very antithesis of true rank-and-file unionism." Brown argued that SEIU must address this problem "if we really believe in the fundamental dignity of union members"—plus do far more to "preserve effective democratic processes" within its recently created regional or multi-state locals.[37]

In California, meanwhile, SEIU state leaders voiced concerns similar to Brown's and took the issue of internal democracy, leadership accountability, and worker self-activity directly to the membership. In May 2007, the executive board of 150,000-member United Healthcare Workers-West (UHW) accused SEIU of "negotiating employer agreements that may hinder healthcare workers from advocating effectively on behalf of the people they serve, significantly limit the scope of workers' collective bargaining rights, and frustrate healthcare workers' rights to participate in negotiations and vote on agreements that affect them." UHW board members demanded that SEIU meet three conditions: First, in any new organizing agreements, "healthcare workers' ability to make their voices heard on matters of patient/resident/consumer care . . . must be furthered, not frustrated." Second, "to advance workplace democracy," the rank-and-file "must have a seat at the bargaining table," be "fully informed of the terms and conditions of any proposed agreement," and have the right to ratify or reject it. Third, any agreement that deprives healthcare workers of "full collective bargaining rights, including the right to engage in concerted action" must be very limited in duration.[38]

In a follow-up letter to thousands of home-care workers, President Sal Rosselli and other local officers informed them that "UHW nursing home members and elected representatives" had been excluded from the negotiating process in their industry by the SEIU International—and

---

37  J. P. Brown, unpublished review of Stern's *A Country That Works*. See also Brown quotes in J. McNeill, "Work in Progress: The State of the Unions Two Years After the AFL-CIO Split," *Dissent* (Summer 2007), p. 36.

38  United Healthcare Workers Executive Board resolution, May 19, 2007.

warned that UHW home-care workers might be disenfranchised next. "If we cannot ensure that our nursing home members have a voice at work, it's only a matter of time before we, as home-care workers, lose our voice and ability to negotiate contracts that move us forward," the letter said. To prevent this from happening, the leadership urged members to sign petitions, distributed by UHW stewards, demanding "a voice for quality care," "union democracy," and "full collective bargaining rights."[39] Within a month, Stern responded to the clamor by announcing that he had terminated "the controversial agreement with a number of California nursing homes . . . that gave SEIU the right to organize in exchange for meeting 'political benchmarks'" tied to increasing Medi-Cal reimbursement rates and making legislative progress on "tort reform" limiting patients' right to sue.[40]

Such stirrings of discontent—including growing public criticism of SEIU's strategy—will, it is hoped, legitimize wider membership debate and lead to more formal organizational opposition, perhaps on the model of "Service Employees for Democratic Reform," a mid-1990s grouping that included both Brown and Rosselli. Despite SEIU's singular track record of growth, its ongoing internal restructuring is clearly generating a grassroots backlash.[41] As *The Nation* reported in July of 2007, based on interviews with a number of "committed SEIU staff members," the union's "emphasis on consolidating small locals into larger organizations" is making it "harder for workers to find their union rep or file a simple grievance. If union members don't feel the union is serving them, organizers say, they begin to ask why they are paying dues."[42] Thus, just as in the 1970s, questions related to contract bargaining and strike strategy, shop-floor initiative, relationships with the community, union transparency and financial accountability, and, ultimately, membership control are all coming to the fore again in a nascent political challenge to what Kim Moody calls "bureaucratic corporate unionism."[43]

---

39  SEIU United Healthcare Workers leadership letter to home-care members, May 29, 2007. See also M. Smith, "Stern Reprimand: SEIU Members in Northern California Challenge the National Boss," *San Francisco Weekly*, June 13, 2007, p. 12.
40  Stern left the door open for later renegotiation of the deal, saying SEIU would return to the table if the nursing-home chains "have some new ideas." See M. Amber, "SEIU Terminates Controversial Agreement With Nursing Home Chains in California," Bureau of National Affairs Labor Report, June 14, 2007, and M. Brenner, "Service Employees End Nursing Home Partnership," *Labor Notes* (July 2007), pp. 8–9.
41  W. Johnson, "Service Employees Union Mergers Lead to Conflict in California," *Labor Notes* (June 2007), pp. 8–9.
42  Featherstone, "Andy Stern: Savior or Sell-Out?" p. 9.
43  Moody, *US Labor in Trouble and Transition*, p. 193.

## Creating Alternative Models

Before, during, and since organized labor's 2005 split, critics of SEIU and CTW advocated other ways of rebuilding unions, from the bottom up, with a broader social vision and a greater commitment to independent political action. Among those differing with Stern's approach were leaders of smaller left-leaning independent unions like the California Nurses Association (CNA) and UE, prominent labor educators and historians, and, of course, rank-and-file activists and local officers long associated with *Labor Notes* and TDU.[44] These skeptics noted that SEIU and its CTW allies seemed largely oblivious to the lessons of labor history (including those learned in the '70s): namely, that real union power can only be created through democratic workplace organization, membership mobilization, strike activity, cross-border solidarity, and strong links between labor and other social movements. In a wide range of settings, progressive activists—some of whom have won positions of influence within local or national labor organizations—continued to demonstrate that "another world is possible" in the realm of union revitalization and reform.

## CWA Mobilization

A very vocal group of CWA activists has played a role in changing their national union, over twenty-five years, by "engaging rank-and-file workers in the project of labor revitalization" and creating a culture of "grassroots mobilization" rooted in strengthened workplace steward structures.[45] This group includes CWA national president and a past *Labor Notes* contributor Larry Cohen. Like Stern, Cohen is a product of sixties' campus activism and then human-services worker organizing in Pennsylvania and New Jersey. But their parallel public sector origins did not lead to similar views on union democracy, labor–management relations, or how to rebuild the labor movement thirty-five years later.[46]

---

44   Within the Teamster reform movement, Stern's credibility suffered from his warm embrace of "old guard" IBT president James Hoffa, who is far more interested in media spin and saving millions of dollars in AFL-CIO per capita dues than helping the IBT "change to win" in its dealings with employers like UPS. For an illustrative account of Hoffa's handling of the Teamsters 2007 negotiations with UPS, see *TDU Convoy-Dispatch* (October 2007), pp. 6–7.

45   H. Rosenstein and B. Master, "No Short-Cuts: Mobilization and Politics Must Drive Labor's Revival from the Bottom Up," unpublished paper (March 2006), p. 2. See also S. Early, "Labor Debates How to Rebuild Its House," *Tikkun* (May/June 2005), pp. 45–8, and Jeff Crosby, "Democracy, Density and Transformation: We Need Them All," unpublished paper (March 17, 2005), p. 13, available from jcrosby@local201iuecwa.org.

46   See, for example, CWA Executive Board resolution drafted by Cohen, "Democracy in the Workplace—CWA Proposals For the AFL-CIO," January 2005. Also R. Wilson,

Attempts to institutionalize "CWA mobilization" began in the mid-1980s—inspired, in part, by the example of grassroots contract campaign activity by 35,000 newly organized New Jersey state workers.[47] Prior to a ten-day strike at NYNEX over healthcare cost shifting in 1986, CWA District 1 (covering New Jersey, New York, and New England) distributed 10,000 copies of a *Labor Notes* and TDU-inspired "contract campaign guide" that encouraged one-on-one recruitment of workplace activists, collective action on the job, and extensive strike preparation to fend off the management demands for concessions that, by then, had become widespread in the wake of PATCO's defeat. To implement this program at the local union and job-site level, District 1 urged the formation of "large rank-and-file contract mobilization committees" and began preparing, in 1988–9, for another showdown with NYNEX, the "Baby Bell" company that then employed 60,000 CWA and IBEW members in the northeast.

This campaign drew on the experience of the 1971 technicians strike in New York, which was fraught with internal tensions and divisions between a militant rank-and-file, various company unions that sat out the strike, and a reluctant, even obstructionist CWA national leadership. Eighteen years later, under new and actively supportive regional leadership, all unionized workers struck together in every department—plant, operator services, accounting, and commercial marketing. To win their battle against medical benefit cuts, CWA and IBEW members turned to tactics of militant mass mobilization that have since proven indispensable in telecom strikes or contract campaigns in the same region in 1998, 2000, and 2003 (by which time NYNEX had become Verizon). The 1989 NYNEX walkout featured mobile and mass picketing, civil disobedience, and sabotage, plus a CWA-aided revolt by strikers in Boston against an IBEW official who tried, unsuccessfully, to end IBEW participation in the struggle with a secretly negotiated divide-and-conquer "me too" deal with management.

At the same time, workers enhanced the impact of their strike and its political message by forging new labor and community relationships. They distributed tens of thousands of stickers calling for "Health Care For All, Not Health Cuts At NYNEX." They formed alliances with the Rainbow Coalition, National Organization for Women, Citizen Action, Physicians for a National Health Program, and other healthcare reform groups. In Boston, weekly mass meetings featured speakers from these

---

"Cohen's Call for 'Stewards Army' Opens Door for New Labor Activism," *Labor Notes* (January 2007), p. 6.

47  S. Early, "Building a New Public Employee Union," *National Lawyers Guild Labor Update* (October–November 1982), p. 5–9, and "CWA Grass Roots Organizing Drive Proves Popular With Jersey Workers," *Labor Notes*, March 25, 1981, p. 6.

groups, including Rev. Jesse Jackson, fellow strikers from Pittston and Eastern Airlines, plus innumerable public officials, labor, and community supporters. Strike-related rallies and publicity all emphasized the common bond between union and non-union, insured and uninsured workers and their mutual need for national health insurance. The four-month NYNEX fight ended in a rare union victory during the grim decade of lost strikes, lock-outs, and concession bargaining that followed the "long seventies."[48] Within the CWA and IBEW, this protracted struggle helped revive and legitimize 1970s-style shop-floor activism, and the community-labor solidarity organizational form deployed in Boston and many other cities via the campaigning of Jobs with Justice, a CWA-initiated national network of workers' rights activists that continues to unite non-labor groups with militant local unions, regardless of their AFL-CIO or CTW-affiliation.[49]

Important NYNEX strike lessons were summed up internally—and applied, where possible, in subsequent private or public sector campaigns— through the widespread use of a CWA stewards' manual, called "Mobilizing To Build Power."[50] This union-building guide—updated regularly over the last two decades—projects a model of workplace education, action, and local union functioning in which "internal organizing" around shop-floor issues and recruitment of non-union workers are closely linked.

Instead of creating a false dichotomy between "organizing" and "servicing," the CWA mobilization strategy posits that "individual grievances" are no less important than membership growth or grappling with other "big picture" issues and challenges. But a union can respond to workers' day-to-day problems either by encouraging '70s-style collective activity on the job or by relying instead on the slow, legalistic, staff-dominated process of grievance handling and arbitration. Within CWA, the former approach is actively promoted, if not yet embraced in all (or even most) locals. Where fully implemented, however, CWA mobilization has built a network of "worker militants" whose on-the-job activities have better equipped them to enforce

---

48   For more on the NYNEX strike, see S. Early, "Holding the Line in '89: Lessons of the NYNEX Strike," a sixty-page report published by the Labor Resource Center (Somerville, MA: 1990) available from the author; "Political Lessons of NYNEX Strike," *Boston Globe* (November 26, 1989); S. Early and M. Calvey, "A Labor Perestroika," *Boston Globe*, September 4, 1989, p. 28; "Striking NYNEX," *Labor Research Review* #17 (1990); or "The NYNEX Strike: A Case Study in Labor–Management Conflict Over Health Care Cost Shifting," in *Proceedings of NYU Annual National Conference on Labor* (New York: Little, Brown & Co., 1991).

49   S. Early and L. Cohen, "Jobs With Justice: Mobilizing Labor-Community Coalitions," *WorkingUSA* (November/December 1997), pp. 49–57.

50   "Mobilizing To Build Power," CWA Mobilization Manual, available from CWA Education Department, 501 3rd St. NW, Washington, DC 20001.

contracts, understand and deal with the "big picture" in their industry, and function as political activists as well. Membership mobilization around contracts and workplace issues has also helped create a pool of committed, experienced rank-and-file activists who can function as effective "member organizers" in recruitment drives among non-union workers.[51]

## Longshore Rebellion

A wide-ranging solidarity campaign by dissident longshoremen—launched from the heart of the anti-union South—provides another illustration of what can be accomplished with a rank-and-file orientation. International Longshoremen's Association (ILA) Local 1422 in Charleston, South Carolina, waged a successful international campaign against a big Danish shipping company, whose union-busting activity was aided and abetted by state authorities. In the process, the largely African American leadership of the local also dared to challenge the entrenched corruption, nepotism, and treachery of the ILA national union leadership.

Local 1422's fight began in December 1999, when industry giant Nordana switched to a non-union stevedoring outfit to unload its ships in Charleston. In response, Local 1422 mobilized a series of local picket lines and demonstrations which managed to prevent one Nordana ship from sailing with all its cargo. Hoping to increase the impact of their campaign and stop Nordana elsewhere, Local 1422 leaders Ken and Leonard Riley reached out to international union officials. But ILA headquarters did nothing to discourage other ILA members from handling Nordana ships in ports up and down the East Coast. Then, in January 2000, six hundred South Carolina state police attacked a much smaller group of Local 1422 pickets with tear gas and smoke grenades. At least ten people involved in the melee ended up in the hospital, and five ILA members were indicted on trumped-up criminal rioting charges. A local judge dismissed the case, but South Carolina attorney general Charles Condon—hoping to win higher office with a racist law-and-order campaign—convened a grand jury, which indicted the five again and placed them under house arrest.

Local 1422 immediately launched a campaign to "Free the Charleston Five" that resonated around the world. Drawing on civil rights traditions, longshoremen reached out to the local African American community, which protested the racist attack on black workers. The union had credibility with the community because it had taken a prominent role in

---

51 For more on the role of rank-and-file activists in union organizing, see S. Early, "Membership-Based Organizing," in G. Mantsios, ed., *A New Labor Movement for the New Century* (New York: Monthly Review, 1998), pp. 85–7.

the movement to remove the Confederate flag from the state capitol. Local 1422 also appealed to other labor organizations throughout the United States and, more importantly, dockworkers' unions around the world. In a few months, the campaign raised $300,000 for legal defense costs and held demonstrations by more than five thousand people at the state capitol, seeking dismissal of the felony charges.

While top officials of the ILA still refused to take action against Nordana, dockers in other ports understood the importance of solidarity. The International Transport Workers Federation put pressure on the company to settle its dispute in Charleston—and Spanish dockers refused to handle Nordana ships until it did. In April of 2000, the company agreed to use a stevedoring company employing Local 1422 members. Strengthened by this victory on the docks, the campaign to free the Charleston Five continued, as Local 1422 leaders, members, and supporters lobbied and petitioned to get the criminal charges dropped. Leading up to the scheduled November 2001 trial of the Charleston Five, their union-backed defense campaign mounted new demonstrations, and dockworkers around the world prepared for a day of job actions. Shortly before the trial date, attorney general Condon faced such political pressure for his overzealous prosecution that he was forced to remove himself from the case. The charges were reduced to misdemeanors, carrying a $100 fine, and the Charleston Five were free.

In the aftermath of the campaign, Local 1422 president Ken Riley became one of the founders and leaders of the Longshore Workers Coalition (LWC), a rank-and-file organization trying to reform the ILA. The LWC believes that the ILA leadership is not accountable to the membership, negotiates concessionary contracts, and has failed to organize—leading to a serious erosion of jurisdiction and the proliferation of shipping companies using non-union labor. The LWC is campaigning for the direct election of international officers by the membership, instead of the current system of voting only by delegates at conventions. Direct elections, the group contends, will force the leadership to be more responsive and fight management more aggressively. The LWC also organizes for better contracts, to protect workers on the job, and to expand the rights of dockers. Over the years, Riley and his comrades have built the LWC into an active network of reform-minded members and local unions around the country. Like the Teamsters in the late 1980s, the gangster-ridden ILA is faced with the threat of a federal civil racketeering suit. LWC may be in a position, like TDU before it, to push for membership control over the ILA instead.[52]

---

52   For a full account of the Charleston Five defense campaign, see S. Erem and E. P. Durrenberger, *On the Global Waterfront: The Fight to Free the Charleston Five* (New York: Monthly Review, 2008).

## Transit Workers' Struggle

In December 2005, 38,000 New York City transit workers, members of Transit Workers Union Local 100, stopped all subway and bus operations for three days—and then, in an echo of contract rejections more common in the 1970s, narrowly voted down a controversial agreement negotiated by Local 100 leaders. This brave stand against healthcare cuts came at great cost to the membership, thanks to the draconian penalties of the state's Taylor Act, which prohibits public employee strikes. Strikers lost two days' pay for each day they struck, while the union was fined, its president was briefly jailed, and the TWU's right to collect dues via payroll deduction was suspended.

Many years of workplace organizing laid the basis for the impressive display of rank-and-file solidarity during the strike and contract vote which followed. New Directions—the longtime vehicle for reform efforts in Local 100—originated in the mid-1980s with a small group of left-wing activists who "industrialized" as transit workers. Taking inspiration from TDU, New Directions supporters put out a newsletter, *Hell On Wheels*, which exposed the Transit Authority's (TA) abusive management practices and unsafe working conditions. Where it could, the group also helped workers defend themselves—in the absence of effective Local 100 representation—through collective protests on the job.

During the late 1980s and 1990s, New Directions evolved into a membership caucus and expanded its presence in the local, becoming a more influential and politically diverse organization. Its growth and influence came from work in three related areas: workplace organization, contract campaigns, and union electoral politics. The focus on workplace activity arose from the group's belief that the primary source of the union's power was in the collective action of its members on the job. By defending workers' interests at work, New Directions would win adherents and, eventually, union power. In one example in 1991, New Directions supported a subway slowdown that protested scheduling changes designed to undermine seniority. The action lasted over a week and, in the end, under the cover of arbitration, the TA backed down.

New Directions' contract campaign work grew out of its shop-floor presence and organization. Every three years, its activists would push for greater membership involvement in bargaining and in activity designed to pressure the Metropolitan Transportation Authority. *Hell on Wheels* would put out information about contract issues and suggest various strategies and tactics for winning workers' demands. Often, the caucus launched "vote no" campaigns when the union officials offered up concessionary contracts. In 1992, the campaign, which built momentum through rallies, large marches across the Brooklyn Bridge and into Midtown, job actions, and an extensive distribution of literature, resulted in the first-ever contract rejection in Local 100. At the height of the 1999 contract campaign, New Directions forced union officials to hold the first local-wide union meeting in a generation. At that meeting, when union officials abandoned the stage after reading a court injunction against striking to the four thousand transit workers in attendance, New Directions leader Tim Schermerhorn called for a strike authorization vote, in violation of the injunction, and received overwhelming support from the gathered members. Though the union did not strike, the pressure created by New Directions–led activity resulted in a larger wage increase than other public employees had received in recent bargaining.

The workplace organization and contract campaigns raised the profile of New Directions and built its reputation as a group that fought for transit workers. This translated into electoral success in subsequent campaigns. In 1988, Schermerhorn, an African American train operator, ran for president of the local and received 22 percent of the vote, while the New Directions slate won three executive board seats. In 1994, Schermerhorn received 45 percent of the vote and New Directions won fifteen seats on the executive board. In 1998, in a re-run of a disputed election the year before, Schermerhorn received 49.5 percent of the vote and lost by some six hundred votes, out of about 18,500 cast, but New Directions won twenty-two of the forty-six executive board seats.

New Directions' biggest breakthrough finally came two years later, but at a price. Internal tensions had always existed between activists who stressed the organization of the rank and file and those who focused on winning union office. As New Directions moved closer to taking power, these differences increased. For its presidential candidate in the 2000 election, New Directions nominated Roger Toussaint, a leader in the track maintenance division, instead of Schermerhorn. In contrast to previous New Directions campaigns—which had stressed the need for bottom-up membership involvement in the union—Toussaint's campaign took a top-down approach that emphasized how his new leadership would rebuild Local 100. Facing incumbents who were discredited by their poor performance in the 1999 contract campaign and weakened by their own infighting, Toussaint and New Directions won an overwhelming majority vote, sweeping all three local-wide positions, all four vice presidencies in the subways (including Schermerhorn), one of three vice presidents in the buses, and a total of forty-one out of forty-seven seats on the executive board.

Unfortunately, this long-awaited electoral victory did not translate into the type of rank-and-file-led union originally envisioned by New Directions' founders. During his first term as Local 100 president, Toussaint consolidated power in his own hands, distanced himself from New Directions (which is now dissolved), and limited membership involvement in the affairs of the union. In the wake of the 2005 contract negotiations, which ultimately resulted in healthcare concessions, Toussaint faced opposition from multiple candidates and won re-election with less than 45 percent of the vote. In December, 2009, however, Local 106 reformers, including ex-New Directions activists, made a strong comeback when the "Take Back Our Union" slate was elected on a platform of restoring democracy and fighting concessions more effectively.[53]

## Teachers Union Transformation

One of the most impressive recent examples of union reform in the public sector involves 45,000-member United Teachers of Los Angeles (UTLA), the second-largest teachers union in the nation. Running on a program of union militancy, teacher empowerment, labor and community coalitions, and authentic school reform, the United Action (UA) slate swept the 2005 UTLA election, defeating the incumbent leadership, taking a large majority of the union's Board of Directors, and winning all three of the seven full-time officer positions for which it contested. UA had refrained from seeking a majority of the top officer jobs, on the theory that it did not yet have an active enough rank-and-file base to support its program. Yet, as it turned out, dark horse presidential candidate A. J. Duffy, an independent endorsed by UA, also won. Upon election, Duffy immediately joined UA, giving its slate control over the direction of UTLA.

The 2005 election mandate was the culmination of many years of patient rank-and-file work. Beginning in 1992, several union activists launched a newsletter, *A Second Opinion*, which became the alternative voice of UTLA members and was distributed in many of L.A.'s seven hundred or more public schools. Throughout the years, *A Second Opinion* presented progressive viewpoints on all the major issues relevant to teachers—from the need for organized union chapters in every school and a mobilized membership to support for bilingual education, affirmative action, teacher/parent/student alliances, and solidarity with other district

---

53  For a detailed history of the Toussaint years, see Steve Downs, *Hell on Wheels: The Success and Failure of Reform in Transport Workers Local 100*, a Solidarity pamphlet, published in 2008, available at http://www.solidarity-us.org/hellonwheels. For an account of the "Take Back Our Union" slate victory, see Steve Early, "NYC Reformers Rise Again—In Transit and Teamsterdom," Working In These Times, December 9, 2009. (http://www.inthesetimes.com/working/entry/5283/nyc_reformers_rise_againin_transit_and teamsterdom/).

unions. At times, depending on the capacity of the progressive forces within UTLA, the newsletter functioned as the organ of an opposition caucus which attempted to pressure the leadership into organizing around contract demands and workplace issues. Between 1992 and 2005, UTLA was governed by officers who balked at mobilizing members during contract negotiations. They agreed to salary and work rule concessions, plus offered no resistance to the test-driven mandates imposed by "No Child Left Behind," federal legislation that robs teachers of their academic freedom and students of their right to a broad, enriched, and engaging educational program.

By 2002, several contributors to *A Second Opinion* were winning important regional leadership positions within UTLA. In 2004, *A Second Opinion* coalesced with other union activists to form Progressive Educators for Action (PEAC), which initiated, among other things, rank-and-file education and agitation around contract issues neglected by the leadership. While other union progressives tended to focus just on winning office or passing motions at UTLA meetings on external political issues, the radical teachers in PEAC understood the need for long-term rank-and-file base building at school sites. This work culminated in UA's election upset in 2005. But that victory soon presented PEAC with a set of difficult challenges that it continues to grapple with several years later.

While UA candidates held four out of seven full-time officer positions, the other three could not be relied upon to carry out UA's ambitious new organizing program. Also, UTLA's field staff was more oriented toward servicing—its traditional role—than organizing, and thus resistant to change. Finally, and perhaps most problematic, the burdens and distractions of their new union roles led to a post-election breakdown in communication between UTLA officers and board members who ran on the UA slate, and the rank-and-file activists in PEAC who campaigned for them. This disconnect became painfully obvious soon after the election when the union leadership—attempting to head off Mayor Antonio Villaraigosa's takeover of L.A. schools—negotiated a compromise agreement with City Hall on school reform. The deal was concluded in secret with Villaraigosa, a former UTLA staff member, and bypassed the union's governing body, creating a serious breach within the UA coalition that was difficult to repair. Over time, however, improved internal communication between reform leaders, their key supporters, and the broader membership has helped to dispel the initial atmosphere of distrust created by a flawed negotiating process.

UA's elected officials first regained their footing within UTLA by working closely with parents, teachers, and students at the predominantly African American Crenshaw High School to reverse the retaliatory transfer of a key teacher activist—an administrative sanction now curbed by new contract language. Then, in 2006–7, they waged a year-long drive for a new contract, ratified by a 90 percent margin, that provided a 6 percent first year pay raise, maintenance of healthcare benefits, and, most important, an unprecedented reduction in class sizes via a new class-size cap. As UTLA officers Josh Pechthalt and Julie Washington report, "the contract campaign was as unconventional as the contract itself." It featured previously unheard of workplace solidarity actions, combined with a radio advertising campaign which showed that teachers were "championing the needs of students, not just themselves." Almost three hundred school chapters actively participated in the development of contract demands. In December 2006, "over 10,000 UTLA members poured into the streets . . . for the largest demonstrations in UTLA history."[54]

In 2008, based on their contract success, UA slate members swept to electoral victory once again and set about organizing and mobilizing the teacher rank and file to confront a number of challenges, including school reform, standardized testing requirements, the rapid growth of charter schools, and budget cuts. As part of this process, socialists active in the union and allied organizations in the African American and Latino communities have been meeting together since the fall of 2006 to develop more coherent strategies for seeking educational justice for the L.A. school system's huge and diverse student body. One result has been the participation of parents and students in school-wide protests and hungers strikes against layoffs in the spring of 2009, including several cases where students went on "strike" because the teachers faced severe penalties if they walked out.

## Conclusion

For telephone workers, teachers, longshoremen, or transit workers, putting 1970s-style "movement back in the labor movement" is obviously easier said than done. The political and economic context is quite different today than it was three or four decades ago. Union members are, on average, much older now. And too often, the experience of participation in sixties social upheavals has become a nostalgic memory for "progressive union" baby boomers, rather than a continuing inspiration for direct action and participatory democracy in unions today. The contemporary discourse of "union reform"—even among proponents of "rank-and-file power"—reflects the shrunken aspirations of the current period. Thirty-five years ago, membership frustration with grievance-handling delays and setbacks—in the UMW, UAW, Teamsters, and other unions—produced wildcat

---

54   J. Pechthalt and J. Washington, "How Los Angeles Teachers Won A Year Long Contract Campaign," *Labor Notes* (May 2007), pp. 8–9.

strikes and, among miners, even a series of strikes *over being able to strike!* This led to a wide-ranging debate in left labor and legal circles about the need for "open-ended" grievance procedures that would permit selective walkouts over contract violations during the life of a collective bargaining agreement.[55]

In 2008, the backlog of contract grievances is no smaller in most unions, and the pace of their resolution is probably no less glacial. Yet who today in labor is arguing, as many did in the 1970s, that the way to settle more individual or group grievances quickly and effectively is to get out from under the legal straitjacket of binding arbitration and "no strike" clauses? In an era when striking—even at contract expiration—has become increasingly rare, perhaps only the UE continues to call, officially, for the right to strike over unresolved midterm contract disputes. (Both the UE and IUE-CWA do retain the ability to strike during the life of the contract at one major employer, General Electric—a right that was exercised in 2003, when 18,000 GE workers walked out for two days over contested medical plan changes.)

To boost labor's strike capacity at contract expiration—if not over grievances as well—CWA promoted, in 2004–5, the idea of creating a system of "national strike insurance for all AFL-CIO unions." This concept was based on CWA's own $380 million Member Relief Fund, created after the NYNEX walkout bankrupted an earlier and inadequately funded CWA defense fund. Under CWA's plan, all strikers in any union would be guaranteed to receive at least $200 per week, and these benefits would be funded from AFL-CIO per capita dues (with rebates for unions with equivalent or, like CWA, greater coverage of their own). Such a fund could even have eased the financial pain suffered by New York City's transit strikers as a result of their brave flouting of the Taylor Act. Unfortunately, this proposal received little serious consideration before the Change to Win split made its implementation even more unlikely. Representatives of SEIU—which has no national strike fund—were particularly dismissive. In SEIU's view, building strike capacity is like encouraging union democracy. It's just an impractical distraction from what should always be the central task of unions today—membership recruitment and related lobbying and political spending designed to facilitate it.

In conclusion, I would like to return to those "stirrings of discontent" in SEIU referred to above. In less than a year's time, this discontent became rebellion—and revealed what may well be the best opportunity "to put the movement back in the labor movement" in a generation. By mid-summer

---

55   See, for example, S. Early, "The Right-To-Strike: Why It's Needed in the '79 Freight Contract," *The PROD Dispatch* (September/October 1978) p. 7.

2008, UHW was leading a full-blown assault on the entire scandal-ridden SEIU paradigm—frontally challenging the top-down, authoritarian style of Stern and his regime as well as his backroom deals and the corruption of his lieutenants—that is, its bureaucratic corporate unionism.[56]

The dispute inside SEIU became public in March 2008 when the *San Francisco Chronicle* disclosed: "SEIU Leader Moves To Oust West Coast Dissident."[57] The dissident, Sal Rosselli, had resigned from the SEIU's International Executive Board, citing conflicts with the majority on issues including membership rights, union democracy, corruption, and the SEIU's nursing home "alliance" strategy. More than a hundred UHW activists and SEIU dissidents attended the *Labor Notes* conference in Dearborn that spring, which was marred by a failed SEIU invasion. Next, the dissidents presented reform proposals to the June 2008 SEIU International Convention in Puerto Rico, which received support from 10 to 15 percent of the delegates, a decent showing given how tightly Stern controlled the convention.[58]

Inside the union and out there was widespread opposition to the prospect of an SEIU trusteeship—akin to a hostile takeover—of UHW. Its 150,000 members made it larger than many national unions. UHW had deep roots in Northern California, where it began in 1934 as an offshoot of the San Francisco General Strike, when longshoremen inspired a transformation of industrial relations on the Pacific Coast. In the aftermath of a strike at San Francisco General Hospital, SEIU Local 250 was organized, the first hospital union in the country.

In 2005, Local 250 merged with Southern California healthcare workers Local 399 to form UHW, which was an industrial union that represented all classifications of healthcare workers in hospitals, nursing homes, clinics, and home-health agencies, as well as home-care workers. It was one of the fastest growing unions in the nation. In the period of the merger, Locals 250 and 399 added more than 75,000 new members, chiefly in hospitals, more than any other SEIU local. The majority of UHW members were women, mostly people of color; more than fifty languages were spoken by its members.

UHW was a force for reform. It opposed war and supported social justice. Its support for universal healthcare dated back to the 1980s, when it supported Proposition 186, the single-payer healthcare initiative

---

56  One of the most offensive episodes of this period was the SEIU raid, in alliance with the island's governor, on the Puerto Rican teachers union, the largest and most militant of Puerto Rican unions. This adventure, as remains the case with much of this history, has largely been ignored by U.S. academics and progressive labor observers. See Juan Gonzalez, *Democracy Now!*, June 3, 2008.

57  *San Francisco Chronicle*, March 27, 2008.

58  Steve Early, "Showdown in Puerto Rico," *CounterPunch*, June 3, 2008.

in California. It was a founding member of US Labor Against the War (USLAW) in Iraq. It led, with the California teachers, the trade union fight against Proposition 8, the anti-same-sex marriage referendum, which was narrowly passed in November 2008. Rosselli is a past Grand Marshall of San Francisco's annual Gay Pride Parade.

Protests quickly followed the threat of trusteeship. Labor councils throughout California supported UHW, as did Mike Casey, president of UNITE-HERE Local 2 in San Francisco. More than one hundred labor educators, writers, and intellectuals signed a May Day open letter to Andy Stern published in the *New York Times*. Signers of the letter, which urged caution, included Noam Chomsky, Howard Zinn, David Montgomery, Mike Davis, Elaine Bernard, Adolph Reed, Francis Fox-Piven, Jennifer Klein, Vijay Prashad, Marcus Rediker, and Nelson Lichtenstein.[59] Bill Fletcher, Jr., speaking to Juan Gonzalez on *Democracy Now!*, described the SEIU maneuvers as "absurd."[60] In response, SEIU denied any threat to place UHW in trusteeship—"the only talk of trusteeship has come from UHW itself." SEIU vice presidents Eliseo Medina and Gerry Hudson personally chastised the concerned labor educators. As late as mid-July, SEIU spokesman Stephen Lerner called the threat of trusteeship a "myth."[61]

Nevertheless, SEIU prepared to retaliate, despite warnings from its own staff. The danger, wrote Bill Ragen in an email to other officers, was that trusteeship could become like the U.S. occupation of Iraq—"easy to get into, then a slog . . . Implosion would be a better outcome."[62] Sworn testimony would reveal that as early as November 2007, top SEIU officials, including Stern, Secretary-Treasurer Anna Burger, and Stephen Lerner, held a "war council" where plans were developed to dismantle UHW.[63]

Simultaneously, apparently, SEIU considered "implosion" and trustee-ship: the dust, however, on the trusteeship front had barely settled when down came a new gauntlet. UHW was informed that 65,000 Southern California home-care workers—nearly half the UHW membership—were to be removed arbitrarily from UHW and reassigned to Tyrone Freeman's Los Angeles–based Local 6434. Freeman, then a Stern appointee and favorite, spoiled this plan. In a series of exposés, Paul Pringle of the *Los Angeles Times* revealed massive corruption within Local 6434—$1 million paid out to relatives, lavish golf tournaments, Ford Explorers for

59   *New York Times*, May 1, 2008.

60   Bill Fletcher Jr. on *Democracy Now!*, September 19, 2008.

61   "SEIU: Debating Labor's Strategy," www.MRZine.org, July 14, 2008.

62   Ray Marshall, "Report and Recommendation to the International President on Whether a Trustee Should Be Appointed at SEIU United Healthcare Workers-West," January 21, 2009 , p. 62.

63   Ibid., p. 6.

the staff, even second cars for some.[64] Freeman, facing federal criminal charges, was quickly removed, and Local 6434 was placed in trusteeship, putting a majority of California's SEIU's membership under International union control. Associated scandals were exposed in Michigan and again in California, where Annelle Grajeda, chair of SEIU's California State Council and also a Stern appointee, was forced to resign, charged with funneling union funds to a boyfriend. Collapse in Southern California demanded strategic retreat; the "implosion" plan was shelved, temporarily.

SEIU settled on trusteeship, and to put a legal gloss on the hostile takeover it held hearings in September and November 2008 chaired by eighty-year-old Ray Marshall, former Secretary of Labor under President Jimmy Carter. Marshall delivered his findings in mid-January. While he ruled against UHW on several issues, he recommended *against* trusteeship, unless UHW refused to transfer its home-care workers to Local 6434.[65] This gave Stern the opening he wanted. He issued an ultimatum to UHW: give up the home-care workers or face trusteeship. UHW countered with an offer to accept the transfer *if it were put to a vote by the members involved.* Knowing such a vote would not succeed, Stern used Marshall's ruling as cover to implement the trusteeship. With the help of police, SEIU leaders seized UHW facilities, fired UHW's elected officers, and evicted the hundreds of members who had occupied all of UHW's California offices.[66] They then dismantled the vast and active shop-floor organization UHW had built over decades.

SEIU believed that once trustees were installed, the "war" would be won. They were wrong. In the months running up to the trusteeship, despite an avalanche of mailings, "spam," robo-calls, personal visits, threats, and offers, tens of thousands of UHW members and supporters took to the streets in a spectacular counter-offensive. They packed meetings and petitioned, wrote letters, sent emails, and made phone calls, all not just in defense of UHW, but also demanding membership participation in democratic unions, membership participation in bargaining, membership rule in the union. They opposed the SEIU's centralism, its sweetheart contracts with employers, and its backroom deals with politicians.

The UHW response was extraordinary, involving rank-and-file mobilization unparalleled in this period. This uprising, involving tens of thousands of members, erupted first in March 2008 in reaction to

---

64 *Los Angeles Times*, January 17, 2009.

65 Ray Marshall, "Report and Recommendation to the International President on Whether a Trustee Should Be Appointed at SEIU United Healthcare Workers-West," January 21, 2009 , p 103.

66 Cal Winslow, "Stern's Gang Seizes UHW Union Hall," *CounterPunch*, February 2, 2009.

the Stern trusteeship letter, when UHW members packed the local's Oakland headquarters. In July in Manhattan Beach (Southern California), six thousand members overwhelmed "jurisdictional hearings" held to justify the removal of home-care workers from UHW. On September 6, following the UHW's rank-and-file leadership conference, five thousand members marched rebelliously through San Jose's center, chanting "Hands off our union!" Then, on September 26, eight thousand members greeted the trusteeship hearings in San Mateo. Inside the hearing, held in a grim exhibition hall, more than a thousand members sat for hours, enduring two days of tedious pseudo-legal wrangling in sweltering heat, to have their say. In the hour allotted, seventy members spoke in defense of their union, often with emotion, all with dignity and great strength in their beliefs.

In December, SEIU proposed an election, but with a catch-22 choice for UHW members: either option would dismantle the union. The results were an unqualified repudiation of the SEIU leadership. Out of 309,000 eligible voters (all California healthcare locals were involved) approximately 24,000 members cast ballots. Some 91 percent of eligible members boycotted the election. Just as important, members presented the election officer with petitions protesting the election signed by 80,000 members, accompanied by 40,000 formal letters of protest. UHW members presented these letters and petitions in sacks weighing hundreds of pounds. It was an astonishing outpouring of opposition, organized in less than one month.

How did this happen? UHW leaders responded that its hospital members had the highest standards in the industry in the nation: wages, benefits, rights in staffing, workplace safety, and patient care standards. Its contract with Kaiser was referred to as the "gold standard." At the same time, even in this storm, UHW won dramatic victories, including successful negotiations with Catholic Healthcare West. The union also won elections at O'Connor Woods, Stanford, Marian Medical Center, Sacramento Medical Foundation Clinic, and St. Francis Center, winning more hospital workers than the rest of SEIU combined. In late December, UHW ratified contracts at ten nursing homes operated by Kindred Healthcare. The Kindred settlement was the fourth major breakthrough contract in the nursing home industry, part of a decades' long campaign to line up contracts to make significant gains in the nursing-home and hospital sectors. UHW was in bargaining for 75,000 people in 2008.

The healthcare industry has been, and remains, harshly contested industrial terrain. Unions frequently face fiercely anti-union employers, and victories rarely come easily. UHW campaigns relied on strikes and the threat of strikes. UHW's 2005 triumph at Sutter in San Francisco was the result of a knock-down, hard-fought, sixty-day strike. UHW has led strikes at Catholic Healthcare West, Daughters of Charity, HCA (formerly

Hospital Corporation of America), and against numerous nursing-home chains.

Angela Glasper, an ousted elected vice president of UHW, now a spokesperson for the new National Union of Healthcare Workers (NUHW), explained the basis of this success:

> In our organization, workers made all the major decisions in the organization. So the workers in a department had the right to elect whom their steward would be. They also had the right to un-elect the stewards, if the stewards didn't represent their interests. The stewards, together in a facility, comprised a Stewards Council. The Stewards Council made policy and other types of decisions at the facility level. The stewards who were part of the facility Stewards Council at least quarterly came together as a part of a divisional Stewards Council. All the stewards in the union gathered together at least once per year at a leadership conference to determine the direction of the union overall for the coming year, to review what accomplishments, what the successes and failures had been in the preceding twelve months, and to lay out a vision for the next twelve months or longer.
>
> Our executive board was comprised of a rank-and-file body, a rank-and-file-dominated executive board. Roughly one hundred people, of which a super, super majority were elected by a constituency of about fifteen hundred, so that the membership was able to have direct communications with their executive board member and have an ability to ensure that the person who's representing them on the executive board was someone whom those workers believed in and supported . . . That way the information in the union flowed not just from the top down, but more importantly from the bottom up. And the stewards at all levels of the organization were in positions to help make decisions about the direction, coordination, and strategy of the union.[67]

Stern, by contrast, does not believe in shop stewards. SEIU has begun setting up Membership Resource Centers, which are glorified call centers. He sees the strike as archaic, counterproductive: "It's not good for America when people fight," he told the *Wall Street Journal*.[68] Interviewed on National Public Radio, he confessed, "I don't think anymore the power of unions comes from its ability to strike. I think it comes from its ability to participate in the political process and to change America in issues that

---

67   Unpublished interview with John Borsos, March 12, 2009, in author's possession.
68   M. Kaminski, "Let's 'Share the Wealth,'" *Wall Street Journal*, December 6, 2008.

we've been talking about, like healthcare."[69] The full irony of this position became apparent in Chicago in December 2008, when the workers at Republic Windows and Doors emerged triumphant from their magnificent sit-in strike, facing down, among others, the Bank of America.

The trusteeship of UHW began on January 27, 2009. The NUHW, following the mass meetings involving five thousand elected shop stewards and activists, formed on January 28. Five days later the union filed decertification petitions with the National Labor Relations Board covering more than fifty nursing homes and a dozen hospitals, a total of 10,000 healthcare workers. Four days later, another 15,000 healthcare workers filed petitions with the NLRB or the comparable public sector labor boards. In little more than a month, petitions were filed representing the overwhelming majority of UHW members, more than 100,000 workers. Thus far, however, the NLRB, pressured by SEIU's management-style campaign of challenges, has allowed no elections, keeping UHW members as virtual hostages.

NUHW confronts enormous obstacles. Amassed against it is one of the largest, fastest-growing unions in the country. It commands great financial and organizational resources and spends freely. It is reported to have expended $85 million supporting Obama and the Democrats in this past election. Its leadership is ruthless and highly centralized. Still, SEIU's leaders are by no means invulnerable. There are, in fact, sparks of dissent throughout the union, including those connected with SMART (SEIU Members for Reform Today). NUHW's greatest challenge will be keeping its workplace organizations together, at least until 2010 when the NLRB will no longer be able to hold off elections in key bargaining units.

SEIU's attack on UHW/NUHW is not its only union-vs.-union fight. In the summer of 2009, SEIU bankrolled what was essentially a raid on another union, CTW partner UNITE-HERE, a union formed in 2004 by the merger of garment (UNITE) and hotel (HERE) workers' unions. Stern directed his union's resources to support a split from UNITE-HERE led by Bruce Raynor, former UNITE head and former UNITE-HERE co-president. With Stern's money and personnel, Raynor unilaterally declared the UNITE-HERE merger a failure, led several locals out of the union, and formed a new union called Workers United, which immediately affiliated with SEIU.

John Wilhelm, UNITE-HERE president, condemned the SEIU intervention at his union's June convention in Chicago and received vocal support from virtually the entire labor movement. Presidents of both AFL-CIO and CTW unions wrote a letter to Stern condemning the "raid" in the strongest possible terms. At the same time, the convention delegates rewrote the union's constitution and dedicated themselves to what they described as

---

69    "Profile," National Public Radio, August 4, 2008.

"member-driven" democratic unionism. In the presence of the AFL-CIO and CTW leaders, Wilhelm led delegates in a stinging rejection of the SEIU corporate model. Under the new constitution, the union's governing bodies will be composed of a voting majority elected locally and regionally. The constitution provides strong guarantees of local and joint board autonomy, including that no local or joint board can be forced to merge with another affiliate unless the members of each of the merging affiliates vote separately in favor of the merger. "I am proud of our union's new constitution. It stands in stark contrast to the top-down, autocratic manner in which SEIU has approached our union and its own members," Wilhelm noted. Then, in a press conference immediately following the convention, he praised NUHW as "the harbinger" of a "new beginning for labor."[70]

NUHW, then, is a central test. The survival, much less revival, of unions depends on the labor movement's ability to champion the rights of all workers and reliably support other groups identified with the "public interest" and common good. If, in the pursuit of sectoral membership growth, unions make political endorsements or pursue "partnerships" with employers at the expense of their relationships with environmental, consumer, civil rights, or student groups, the short-term gain may not outweigh the long-term damage to community-labor coalition building.[71]

Unions cannot effectively advocate for social and economic justice if, at the same time, they continue to behave like—and reinforce their negative image as—a "special interest group." Nor will they be able to make workers rights' struggles—and the campaign for labor law reform, which is critical—the object of greater public sympathy without better responding to the problems of members and allies alike, based on the old IWW adage that "an injury to one is an injury to all."

If the material in this collection does nothing more than dust off and disseminate relevant lessons from the "era of revolt," it will have made its own contribution to critiquing strategies for union restructuring and growth that undermine what the labor movement should really be doing, on the job and in the community, from the bottom up, to become a force for fundamental change once again.

---

70   Conference call with John Wilhelm, July 1, 2009.
71   See S. Early, "New Politics Not on the CTW Agenda," in "Turmoil in the AFL-CIO: A Dollars & Sense Roundtable," *Dollars & Sense* (September/October 2005), pp. 20–2.

# List of Contributors

**Frank Bardacke** teaches at a public adult school in Watsonville, California. Working for seven years in the field in the Salinas Valley, in an otherwise all-Mexican labor force, he served as a crew shop steward under the first United Farm Workers contract. In the off-season, he taught agricultural history at the UC Santa Cruz. In 1979, he loaded trucks at the local frozen-food plants, where he helped start a Teamsters for a Democratic Union chapter. He is the author of *Good Liberals and Great Blue Herons: Land, Labor and Politics in the Pajaro Valley* (Center for Political Ecology, 1994) and a translator of *Shadows of Tender Fury: The Letters and Communiqués of Subcomandante Marcos and the Zapatista Army of National Liberation* (Monthly Review Press, 1995).

**Aaron Brenner** is a senior research analyst at the Service Employees International Union and president of Rank & File Enterprises, a labor and financial research firm. He is the editor of *The Encyclopedia of Strikes in American History* (ME Sharpe, 2009) and a contributing author of *A Troublemaker's Handbook 2* (Labor Notes, 2005). His articles have appeared in *Labor Notes*, *Labor's Heritage*, *New Labor Forum*, and *Against the Current*, among others. He holds a PhD in American history from Columbia University.

**Robert Brenner**, Professor of History at UCLA, is the author of *The Boom and the Bubble: The US in the World Economy* (Verso, 2002) and *The Economics of Global Turbulence* (Verso, 2006). He is the director of the Center for Social Theory and Comparative History.

**Dorothy Sue Cobble** is Professor of Labor Studies, History, and Women's/Gender Studies at Rutgers University. Her recent books include *The Sex of Class: Women Transforming American Labor* (Cornell University Press, 2007), *The Other Women's Movement: Workplace Justice and Social Rights in Modern*

*America* (Princeton, 2004), which won the 2005 Philip Taft Book Prize for the best book published in American labor history in 2004, as well as other awards, and *Dishing It Out: Waitresses and Their Unions in the Twentieth Century* (University of Illinois, 1992).

**Steve Early** was a Boston-based international union representative and organizer for the Communications Workers of America between 1980 and 2007. During the 1970s, he was a staff member of the United Mine Workers and assisted union reform movements in the Steelworkers and Teamsters. He serves on the editorial advisory board of *Labor Notes* and has written about labor issues for *The Nation, The Progressive, In These Times, New Labor Forum, WorkingUSA*, and many other publications. He is the author of *Embedded With Organized Labor: Journalistic Reflections on the Class War at Home* (Monthly Review, 2009).

**Mike Hamlin**, a founder of DRUM and the League of Revolutionary Black Workers, is a clinical social worker, crisis manager, and employee assistance professional with employees of the Big Three auto companies and over 350 other employers. Over the last sixteen years, Mike has been affiliated with Wayne State University, teaching in the Labor Studies Center and the Black Studies Department.

**A. C. Jones** (a pseudonym) is a labor writer and activist based in Washington, D.C. She holds a PhD in political science from the University of Chicago and is the author or editor of several books on politics and labor. She can be reached at acjones0324@gmail.com.

**Dan La Botz** is a Cincinnati-based teacher, writer, and activist. He was formerly a truck driver in Chicago and a founding member of Teamsters for a Democratic Union. He has written books on labor and politics in the United States, Mexico, and Indonesia. He is currently working on a book on Tijuana.

**Kim Moody** was a cofounder and for many years director of *Labor Notes*. He has written widely on labor and political issues and is the author of four books: *An Injury to All* (Verso, 1988), *Workers in a Lean World* (Verso, 1997), *From Welfare State to Real Estate: Regime Change in New York City, 1974 to the Present* (The New Press, 2007), and *U.S. Labor in Trouble and Transition* (Verso, 2007). He is currently a Senior Research Fellow at the Centre for Research in Employment Studies at the University of Hertfordshire in the UK.

**Marjorie Murphy** is a Professor of History at Swarthmore College, an expert on teachers unions, and the author of *Blackboard Unions: The AFT and the NEA, 1900–1980* (Cornell University Press, 1990), which traces the history of the unionization of public school teachers. She writes on the past and future of American public education, American labor history, public sector unionism, and women's history.

**Paul J. Nyden** is an investigative reporter and editorial writer for the *Charleston Gazette* in Charleston, West Virginia. A *Charleston Gazette* reporter since 1982, Nyden has won thirty newspaper awards. He taught at the University of Pittsburgh and other colleges from 1972 to 1978, did research for federal agencies from 1979 to 1981, and, since 1994, has taught courses in Sociology and Labor History at the West Virginia University Institute of Technology.

**Judith Stein** is a Professor of History at the Graduate Center and City College of the City University of New York. She is the author of *The World of Marcus Garvey* (Louisiana State University Press, 1986), and *Running Steel, Running America* (University of North Carolina Press, 1998). Her book *Pivotal Decade: How the United States Traded Factories for Finance,* was published by Yale University Press, 2010.

**Kieran Taylor** is the Associate Director of the Southern Oral History Program at the University of North Carolina at Chapel Hill. He is the coeditor of volumes IV and V of *The Papers of Martin Luther King, Jr.* (University of California Press, 2000, 2005) and *American Labor and the Cold War* (Rutgers University Press, 2004).

**Cal Winslow** is a Fellow in Environmental Politics at the University of California, Berkeley. He coauthored *Albion's Fatal Tree* (Penguin and Pantheon, 1975) with Edward Thompson and others, edited *Waterfront Workers: New Perspectives on Race and Class* (University of Illinois Press, 1998) and is the author of *Labor's Civil War in California: The NUHW Healthcare Workers' Rebellion* (PM Press, 2010). He is the Director of the Mendocino Institute.

# Index

9to5, 119, 343, 345–46

ABC News, 86
Abel, I. W., 90, 126, 183–84
Abzug, Bella, 343
accidents, 71, 190, 208, 300n65
Ackley, Gardner, 61
ACORN, 372
Addonizio, Hugh J., 241, 243
AFA (Association of Flight Attendants), 341
AFL, 41, 109, 114, 135–36, 205, 367
and CIO, 39–40
AFL–CIO, 3, 16, 24–25, 29, 31, 34, 90–91, 100, 117–19, 158, 183, 193, 199, 202–3, 224, 239, 358, 360–62, 366–68, 378, 386, 392–93
conservatism, 17
vs Iraq war, 361
African Americans. See blacks
African Free School, 243
AFSCME, 19, 22, 29, 117, 127, 235, 246, 372
AFT (American Federation of Teachers), 15, 117, 136, 229–32, 239–40, 242, 245, 248, 372
expansion, 231
growth of, 16
racial disputes, 16–17
Agricultural Labor Relations Act (ALRA), 161–62
Agricultural Workers Organizing Committee (AWOC), 158–59
airline mechanics, 8, 19, 24
Air Line Pilots Association (ALPA), 337
airline workers, 133. See also flight attendants
air traffic controllers (PATCO), 7, 34–35, 142, 363, 377
Akron, 40
Alabama, 106, 173
Alaska, 333
Albert, Margie, 343
Alinskyism, 150, 156, 159
All in the Family (TV), xii–xiii
Amalgamated Clothing Workers, 109, 193
Amax, 182
American Petrograd, 329
Anderson, Jack, 188, 234n8
Antal, Lou, 185, 190n20

anti-war movement, xii–xiii, xvi– xviii, 4, 21, 33, 141, 145, 200, 221, 229, 252, 265–66, 314, 318, 327, 329
Antle, Bud, 159–60
Appalachia, 6, 33, 173–74, 176–77, 179, 181, 183, 186, 192, 195, 197, 323
Arab-Israeli war, 93
Arkansas, 196
Armstrong, R., 133n77, 134n82
Aronowitz, S., 230n1
AT&T, 251–55, 257–59, 261, 264, 272, 274, 336
racial and gender inequality, 264
Atlanta, 22, 223, 234, 348, 352
Atlantic City, 155
automation, 123, 132, 207, 278–79
See also mechanization; technology
auto workers, 5, 8, 10, 13–14, 19, 21, 40, 50, 52, 56, 60–61, 116, 121, 124, 129–30, 133, 138–39, 141, 143, 219, 231, 265, 281–308passim
black, 289–91, 296, 307, 311–33passim
crisis, 307–8
firings, 292, 306–7, 323
forced to work, 305
foreign competition, 283
golden age for, 281–82
grievance explosion, 285–86
jailed, 317
job ease, 284
strike symbolizes alienation of, 288
weak rank and file, 289
wildcat torrent, 287

Bachowski, Walter, 183
Bahr, Morton, 268–69, 273n50, 274n52, 276
Baker, General, vii, 312–13, 315–20, 322n33, 331–33
Balanoff, Elizabeth, 256n10
Baldanzi, George, 90
Ball, George W., 82
Balser, D., 15n61, 119n34, 337n6
Baltimore, 235, 328
Bank of America, 392
Banker, Howard, 267, 269
Baraka, Amiri, 16, 242–44, 248
Baran, xiii

Barbash, Jack, 9, 10n40, 61n40
Barry, Jack, 131
Batres, Berta, 164
BCOA, 19
Beame, Abraham, 245
Bean, William, 307
Beck, Dave, 114, 201, 206
Beirne, Joseph, 267, 268n37, 269–74, 276–77
Belgium, 81
Bellamo, Sammy, 300
Bell and Howell, 90
Bell System, 252–54, 253, 257–60, 258–60, 262–66, 263–66, 268–70, 269–70, 273–74, 278
Bellush, J., 127n63, 234n8
benefits, 19–20, 26–27, 45, 48, 50, 60, 114–15, 117, 121–22, 127, 137, 140, 161, 163, 176, 186, 188, 190, 192, 194, 199–200, 202–3, 205, 208, 212, 221–22, 226, 251–52, 260, 270–72, 279, 281–82, 371, 373, 390
Benson, Herman, 214
Bergsten, Fred, 89
Berle, Adolph, 95
Bernard, Elaine, 388
Bernstein, Irving, 109
Best, "Curly," 212, 215
Betheil, R., 48n13, 50n15, 60n35, 140n94
Bethlehem Steel, 139
The Bicycle Thief (De Sica), 79
Bituminous Coal Data, 181n9
Bituminous Coal Operators Association (BCOA), 19, 173, 176, 187, 189–91, 194, 196
Black, Elwood, 302
Black Caucus, 96
black liberation, vii, xvii, xix, 26, 138, 140, 145, 266, 299
Black Lung, xi, 106, 137, 141, 179–80, 183–84, 186, 196, 215
Black Lung Association, 179–80, 183–84, 186, 196, 215
black movement, 4, 7, 12–15, 22, 33, 106, 140, 209, 221
black nationalism, 22, 145, 237–39, 243–44, 265, 294, 312–13, 315, 316n16
Black Panthers, 5–6, 138, 209, 234, 294, 326–27
Black Power, xii, xviii, 13, 33, 106,

119, 145, 155, 200, 229, 234, 236, 242, 252, 313n6
blacks, vii, xiii–xiv, xvi–xvii, 6, 14, 16–18, 90–91, 106, 115–20, 138–41, 154, 159, 184, 188, 196, 205, 229, 231–32, 252, 262, 284, 347–49, 353, 379, 382, 384–85
  Ad Hoc Committee for Concerned Black Steelworkers, 139
  auto workers, 289–91, 296, 307, 311–33passim
  as communists, 293
  confront teachers, 232–48passim
  liberation badges, 26
  rank and file inspired by, 144–45, 265
  recruited as supervisors, 294
  telephone workers, 262–64
  vs UFT, 234–40
  and unemployment, 22, 96
  See also DRUM; LRBW
Black Vanguard, 315, 317–18
Black Workers for Justice, 363
Blair, James E., 188
Blue Cross and Blue Shield, 320
Bluestone, Irving, 305–6
Boeing, 29
Bolden, Dorothy, 348, 350–52
Bommarito, Peter, 127
Bosque, Juan Almeida, 313
Boston, 10, 16, 235, 377–78
bottom-up, 186, 360, 364–65, 367, 369, 382, 393
boycott, 28, 46, 161, 163–64, 166–67, 184, 201–2, 204, 233, 271, 319, 366, 390
  grape, 153–57, 159–60
Boyle, Tony, 5, 19, 173, 177–79, 182–83, 186, 188, 196, 215, 358, 360–61
Bracero Program, 152, 158–59, 161, 163, 169
Braverman, Harry, 26, 342n26
Brazil, 83
Brecher, J., xviiin2, 21n91, 115n19
Brenner, A., xviiin2, 3n15, 10n44, 11n45, 138n88, 208n16, 214n24, 230n1, 251n1, 260n24
Brenner, Johanna, 117
Brenner, R., 4n16, 12n50, 38n1, 85n14, 120n38, 129n70
Bretton Woods, 73, 77, 80, 88, 91–92
Bridges, Harry, 115, 123
Brody, D., 2n4, 6
Brookings Institution, 108
Brooks, Harvey, 302
Brooks, T. R., 255n8, 256n9&10
Brophy, John, 174
Brown, H. Rap, 243
Brown, Jerry, 161–62, 373–75
Bruce Church Inc., 167
Bryner, Gary, 10, 288
Brzezinski, Z., 98n38
Buckley, William, 86
Buder, L., 232n5, 233n6, 238n15&16, 239n18, 242n24, 247n33
Buffalo, 235
Buhle, P., 230n1
Bundy, McGeorge, 236–37
Bunker, Archie, xiii
Burdon, George, 129
bureaucracy. See unions and unionism, bureaucratization
Burger, Anna, 388
Burke, James, 90

Burke, Yvonne, 353
Burke-Hartke bill, 90–91
bus drivers, 19
Bush, G. W., 94, 362–63, 366
Business Roundtable, xv, 99, 101, 143
business unionism, xv–xvi, xix, 5, 12, 33, 107, 114–15, 117–18, 120, 122–24, 126, 135–37, 140–44, 204, 211, 213, 308, 365
  isolation of, 140, 144
  purpose of, 122
  rank and file stuck with, 308
  workers' control vs, 141
Business Week, 125, 131, 181, 192, 223, 346
Bustamante, Chava, 164
Bustamante, Mario, 164, 167
Butterfield, F., 244n28, 245n29
BWAC (Bell Workers Action Committee), 260–62, 264–66, 269, 271–74, 276, 278

Cadell, Pat, 99
California, 15, 17, 29, 33, 118, 138, 149–70passim, 182, 211, 329, 367, 372–76, 387–90, 388–89
California Agricultural Labor Relations Act (ALRA), 161–62
Camarata, Pete, 138, 217, 223
Cambodia, 11, 93, 215
Cambridge, 235
cannery workers, 28–29, 138, 221
Canton, 29
Capital (Marx), 289
capital, 6, 38, 62, 70, 73–74, 78, 90, 98, 142
  and labor, 11, 41, 50, 55, 58, 62, 87, 94, 97, 120–21, 129
  power of, xv
  vs strike, 7
  vs workers, 31
capitalism, xiii, 6, 30, 77, 79, 114, 141, 214, 290, 328
Carey, James, 126–27
Carey, Ron, 25–26, 223–25, 359–60
car haulers, 29, 138, 205, 221–23
Carmichael, Stockley, 155, 234–35
Carson, Robert Sonny, 234, 237, 239, 248
Carter, Jimmy, 2, 24, 30, 77, 93, 96–102, 141, 143, 173, 191–93, 222, 307, 389
Carter, Larry, 301–2
Casey, Mike, 388
Cassedy, Ellen, 343
Castro, Fidel, 313
Castro, Raul, 313
Caterpillar Tractor, 83, 101, 363
Charleston, 13, 188, 379–80
Chatfield, LeRoy, 149–50
Chávez, César, 149–50, 154–57, 159, 162–69, 180
Chávez, Helen, 157
Chevy, 330
Chicago, 10–11, 15, 22, 27, 131, 193, 203, 207, 209, 211, 215, 224, 235, 241, 361, 392
Chicago Tribune, 371
China, 82, 93
Chiquita Banana, 163–65
Chisholm, Shirley, 353
Chomsky, Noam, 388
Chrysler Dodge, vii, xvi, 14, 21, 34, 40, 49, 60, 106, 111, 116, 123, 139, 142–43, 281, 284, 287,

289–94, 298–99, 301–2, 304–7, 311, 324, 332–33
  bailout, 307
  deaths at, 323, 326
  Eldon, vii, 14, 139, 284, 291–92, 321–25
    extreme conditions, 300, 325–26
  Main, vii, 14, 106, 284, 289, 291–92, 305–6, 311, 313, 317–18, 320, 322
    racism, 319–20, 325
Church, Sam, 196
Cincinnati, 130, 183, 187, 193, 234–35
CIO, 38, 105, 107–12, 114, 118, 123, 126, 219, 367
  and AFL, 39–40
  counter-offensive fruits, 40–41
  UMW behind, 176
  and union "stabilization," 42–43
civil rights, 6, 13, 14n58, 21, 33, 90, 97, 106, 117, 119, 145, 145, 154–55, 178, 200, 205, 209, 223, 229, 232, 234, 238, 247–48, 252, 266, 293, 312, 314, 326–27, 332–33, 335, 347–48, 379
Civil Rights Act, 336
Clark, Paul, 5n23, 176n6, 178
class struggle, vii, 4, 74, 120, 176, 204, 214, 314
  vestige of old, 371
class war, xv, 31, 44, 74
Clawson, Dan, 362
Clean Air Act, 88, 96
clerical workers, 119, 342–47
  getting organized, 343
  National Secretaries Day, 342, 345
  race-class-gender, 354
  respect, 344
  and unions, 346–47
  working conditions, 342–43
Cleveland, 10–11, 25, 119, 193, 203, 213, 215–16
Clinton, Hillary, 97
CLUW (Coalition of Labor Union Women), 15, 23, 336
CNA (California Nurses Association), 376
coal
  economy, 181
  industry, concentration, 181–82
  necessity of, 194
  power, 177
  production, record high, 180–81
  See also energy
Coal Employment Project, 119
Coalition of Black Trade Unionists (CBTU), 118
Coalition of Labor Union Women (CLUW), 118–19
coal miners. See miners
Cobble, D. S., 336n2&3, 343n31, 344n34&36, 345n38&40, 346n42&46&48
Cockrel, Ken, 314, 320, 325–26, 328–31
Cohen, Jerry, 168
Cohen, Larry, 376, 378n49
Cold War, 82, 84, 89, 93, 107, 178
Communist Party, 175, 224, 314
community control, 209, 229, 234, 236, 238–41, 239–41, 247–48
  See also sexuality control; workers, control
Condon, Charles, 379–80
confederate flag, 380

Congress of Racial Equality (CORE), 234, 236–37, 240–41, 314
Connally, John, 92, 95
Connecticut, 10
*Conquering Goliath* (Ross), 149
conservatism, xiii, xvi, 5, 17, 32–33, 85, 95, 200, 206, 361, 367
construction workers, 128–29, 133
consumer movement, 96
Continental (Air Line), 339–40
Continental Oil, 181
Contreras, Rufino, 164
*Convoy*, 138, 220, 225
Coontz, Stephanie, 116, 117*n*25
Cooper, Darwin, 288
Coors Brewing, 28, 184
corporations, 30, 39–40, 48, 59, 88, 101, 106, 110, 120, 122, 129, 131–32, 145, 174, 180–81, 207, 209, 214, 294–95
    avoid unions, 121
    few liberals oppose, 91
    and labor, 56
    power of, 31, 33
    profit push, 43
    and unions, 42–44, 50
    US support for, xv
    *See also* multinationals
Corris, Charles, 253–54, 259, 273*n*50, 279*n*64
Cost of living adjustments (COLA), 59, 131, 134, 137, 190–91, 271–72, 295, 306, 351
*A Country That Works* (Stern), 370
Cray, E., 340*n*15, 341*n*22&23
Crowe, K. C., 138*n*89, 224*n*39
Cruz, Juan de la, 160
CTW, 367, 376, 378, 392–93
CWA (Communication Workers of America), 136, 193, 218, 252, 255, 258–61, 263–64, 267, 269–75, 279, 372, 377–78, 386
    and other movements, 252
    racial and gender inequality, 264
    rank and file hostility, 276
    sexism, 256

Dalrymple, Sherman, 110
Dalton, Dennis, 215
Daly, D. J., 52*n*20, 68*n*46
Davis, Mike, 39*n*2, 56*n*29, 121*n*39, 122*n*44, 357, 388
Davis, William, 110
Dawes, Kenneth, 185
Dayton, 29
Delano, 154–55, 157, 159–61, 160, 165
Delaware, 235
DeLury, John, 246
democracy, xiii, xiv, 5, 6–7, 27, 30, 32, 39, 101, 109, 112, 114, 136–37, 180, 187, 200, 206, 209, 213–14, 224–26, 266–67, 359, 367, 374–76, 383, 385
    as fetter, 101
*Democracy Is Power*, 364
*Democracy Now!*, 388
Democrats, xv–xvi, 3, 24, 38, 40–45, 56, 77, 84–87, 90–91, 94–97, 100, 102, 112, 124, 143, 150, 156, 162, 217, 222, 224, 241, 245, 282, 293, 363, 366–67, 392
Dempsey, Ed, 274, 278
Denby, C., 129*n*68, 139*n*92

Denver, 10, 223
depression, 38, 48, 51, 78–80, 84, 106
desegregation, 229, 232, 234, 236
De Sica, Vittorio, 79
Detroit, vii, 10, 13–14, 22–23, 25, 34, 60, 106, 116, 118–19, 130, 138–39, 193, 202–3, 207, 212, 216, 231, 234, 265, 274, 284, 289–94, 298, 300, 302, 304–5, 311–16, 320, 322, 326–30, 332, 351, 363
    as American Petrograd, radicals move to, 329
    Rebellion, 13, 293, 311, 316
    Treaty of, 49
*Detroit Free Press*, 303, 363
*Detroit News*, 293, 314, 320
Detroit Rebellion, 13
Deukmejian, George, 169
Dietsch, Paul, 5
Di Giorgio Corporation, 154
direct action, 3, 6, 9, 32, 49, 111, 128, 186–87, 369, 385
    movements legitimate, 209
discrimination, 116, 118, 196, 261, 264–65, 270, 272, 294, 296, 312, 318, 336, 339
Dobbs, Farrell, 201
Dodge. *See* Chrysler Dodge
*La Dolce Vita* (Fellini), 79
Dolson, Gail, 15
Donahue, Tom, 360
Dorosh, Walter, 130
Drake, Jim, 154
Draper, Hal, 214
DRUM (Dodge Revolutionary Union Movement), vii, 14, 106, 138, 289–91, 293–94, 311, 318–21, 330, 332
    first strike, 319
    vs UAW, 320
Duffy, A. J., 383
Duke Power, 182
Dunne, Joe, 263, 264*n*30

Early, Steve, 1*n*1, 200*n*1, 225*n*42, 358*n*2, 359*n*3&5, 362*n*9, 376*n*45, 377*n*47, 378*n*48–49, 379*n*51, 383*n*53, 386*n*55, 387*n*58, 393*n*71
*Economist*, 10
economy, xiv, 2, 4, 18, 20–22, 46, 50, 77–102*passim*, 122, 130–31, 133–34, 141, 143, 176, 202, 218, 221, 245, 251, 257, 282–83, 285, 306–7, 358
    deregulation, 102, 199–200, 222
    downturn, 51–56, 106, 220
    infinite expansion, 44
    profitability decrease, 62–64, 69, 73
    regulation, 77, 201
    state intervention, 77–83*passim*, 98
    turnaround, 62
    *See also* depression; exports; free market; imports; nationalization; recession
Edwards, P. K., 128*n*66, 129*n*68
Eisenhower, 52, 56–57, 86
electrical workers, 61, 128–29, 133, 274
Ellis, Georgia, 29
ELRUM, 14, 291–92, 321–24, 332
Elwood, 29
*The Emerging Republican Majority* (Phillips), 85
emotional issue, 23

Employee Free Choice Act, 366
employer-friendly labor, 373
employers' offensive, xvi, 4, 12, 32, 37–38, 55–62, 70–74, 105, 120, 124, 129, 137, 200, 207–9, 222–23, 251, 283, 358
energy, 18, 30, 92–93
Engle, Clair, 159
environmental movement, 96
Environmental Protection Agency (EPA), 88, 96
Equal Employment Opportunity Commission (EEOC), 336
Equal Rights Ammendment (ERA), 17, 119, 336
Eschenbach, C. H., 302
ethnicity, 150, 157, 262
Ethridge, M., 288*n*16
Europe, 67, 78, 80–83, 91, 93, 97, 136
    unions, vs US, 3
    welfare state, vs US, 45
European Economic Community (EEC), 82, 84
Evans, S. M., 344*n*32, 345*n*38
Evers, Medgar, 316
Experimental Negotiating Agreement (ENA), 27–28, 143
exports, 37, 52–53, 55, 62, 65–69, 82, 88–89, 91–92, 98

Fair Labor Standards Act, 353
Fantasia, Rick, 128*n*66, 368
Farah, 28, 154, 363
farm workers, 19, 29, 33, 105, 149–70*passim*
    elections, 161–62
    harvest power, 151–53
    historical corrective, 149–53
    vs industrial workers, 152
    isolation of, 153
    strikes, 158–68
    teach UFW, 152
    union bureaucracy, 156–57, 162
FCC, 257, 261
Featherstone, L., 367*n*15, 375*n*42
Feldman, Richard, 329
Fellini, Federico, 79
feminism, 106, 118–19, 145, 229, 266, 338, 348
    transformed, 336, 339
*The Fifth Wheel*, 215–16
*Finally Got the News* (film), 328–30
Fiorito, Frank, 243
firemen, 19
Fitch, R., 214*n*24, 372*n*32
Fitzgerald, Albert, 180
Fitzsimmons, Frank, 25, 137, 206–7, 210–12, 216–17, 221–22, 358
Flaherty, S., 49*n*14, 50*n*15, 60*n*37&38, 282*n*1, 283*n*2, 287, 288*n*18, 289*n*19
Fletcher, Bill, 388
flight attendants, 117, 337–42
    race-class-gender, 354
    as sex objects, 337–40
    campaign against, 340–42
    sexuality control, 338–39
    weight of, 341–42
    *See also* airline workers
Flint, 40
FLOC (Farm Labor Organizing Committee), 29
Florida, 257, 272
Floyd, Anise, 196
Fonda, Jane, 329

Foner, P., 116*n*21, 118*n*32, 135*n*84, 343*n*30&32, 346*n*45
Ford, 49, 60, 111, 116, 130, 134, 138, 281, 283, 289, 295, 297–98, 307, 388
Ford, Gerald, xiii, 77, 88, 93–95
Ford, Henry, 293
Ford Foundation, 236–37, 240, 348
Foreign Trade and Investment Act, 90
Forman, James, 327, 331
*Fortune*, 49, 133–34, 192, 195
Foster, William Z., 136
Fox, A., 206*n*13, 213
Fox-Piven, Francis, 388
France, 2, 79, 81, 214
Franklin, Ben A., 195
Fraser, Douglas, xv, 31, 74, 139, 294, 302–6
Fraternal Association of Steel Haulers (FASH), 5, 137, 210–11
Freeman, J. B., 22*n*94, 59*n*34, 71*n*51, 132*n*76, 231*n*4, 234*n*8, 247*n*33
Freeman, R. B., 57*n*31&32, 343*n*28
Freeman, Tyrone, 388–89
free market, 78–80, 92–93, 102
free trade, 80
Fremont, 138
Friedman, S. R., 208*n*15, 211*n*21
*From the Horse's Mouth*, 216
FRUM, 14
Frye, Carol, 29
fuel crisis, 18

G-7, 67, 92
Gabin, N., 336*n*4
Galamison, Reverend Milton, 238
Galbraith, John Kenneth, 87
Ganz, Marshall, 164–65
Garfinkle, S. H., 346*n*43, 353*n*75
garment workers, 136
Garnes, William, 130
gas crisis, 18
GATT, 80–83
Gelder, L. Van, 263*n*28&29, 338*n*8
General Electric, 57, 127, 130, 132–33, 386
General Motors (GM), 8, 10, 18, 31, 40, 60, 106, 112, 116, 133–35, 138, 281–82, 285–88, 293, 306–7
record sales, profits fall, 283
strikes explode, 287
General Tire, 40
Georgakas, D., 14*n*56, 132*n*76, 284*n*5, 289*n*20, 291*n*23&25–26, 292*n*29, 305, 306*n*88, 312*n*3, 321*n*31, 323*n*36, 324*n*40, 325*n*42&43, 326*n*47, 327*n*48, 328*n*53&54, 331*n*63
Germany, 52, 55, 61–62, 67–68, 79, 91, 97–98
Geschwender, J. A., 140*n*95, 290*n*21, 291*n*24, 292*n*27, 293*n*33, 312*n*3, 318*n*22
Gibson, Kenneth A., 243
Gilbreth, Bill, 304
Glaberman, Martin, 289, 313*n*7
Glacken, Cynthia, 338*n*9, 341*n*19
Glasper, Angela, 391
Glenn, Grety, 296
globalization, 46, 78, 82, 88–89, 121
Glotta, Ronald, 325–26
GMAD (General Motors Assembly Division), 287–89
gold, 91–92

Goldfield, M., 46*n*9, 47*n*10, 57*n*32, 72*n*53
Goldwater, Barry, xiii, 282
Golin, S., 242*n*24, 243*n*25
Golodner, D., 239*n*18, 240*n*21
Gompers, Samuel, 135
Gonzalez, Juan, 387*n*56, 388
Goodrich, 40
Goodyear, 29, 40
Gotbaum, Victor, 127, 246
Govea, Jessica, 168
Graham, Katharine, 23
Grajeda, Annelle, 389
grape boycott, 153–57, 159–60
*The Grapevine*, 216
Graves, Carole, 242–44, 248
Great Britain, 2, 67, 79, 81
Great Depression, 38, 48, 51, 78–80, 106
Green, J., xviii*n*2, 119*n*36, 132*n*76
Green, V., 256*n*10, 262, 263*n*28&29, 264*n*31, 279*n*64, 336*n*4
Greene, David, 30*n*129, 197*n*32
Greenspan, Alan, 89*n*22, 94–95
*Guardian*, 328
Guevara, Che, 313
Guilt, Tom, 210
Gulf Oil, 191
Guzman, Cleofus, 164

Hack, John, 210
Hall, Burton, 214
Hamlin, Mike, 289, 292, 313–15, 317–18, 320, 327–28, 330–31
Hard-Hatted Women, 119
*Hard Work* (Voss & Fantasia), 368
Harlem, 106
Harriman, W. Averell, 79
Harris, W. H., 12*n*51, 13, 22, 24*n*105
Hartke, Vance, 90
Haughton, Ronald, 125
Hawthorne, 124
Hayden, T., 231*n*4, 241–42
healthcare, 190, 371–73, 377–78, 381, 383, 385, 387, 390, 392
healthcare workers, 15, 353, 368, 372–75, 387, 389–93
health and safety, 6, 19–21, 26, 45, 48, 132, 137, 139, 176–77, 179, 187, 190–91, 194, 199–200, 202, 205, 208, 261, 281, 296, 299, 301–2, 307, 322–23, 358, 373, 390
Heenan, K., 338*n*11, 339*n*13
*Hell On Wheels*, 381
Henry Ford Hospital, 320
HERE, 366, 388, 392
Heritage Foundation, 101, 184
Higgins, J., 132*n*76, 192
highway system, 121, 201
*See also* technology
Hillman, Sidney, 39, 109–10
Hoerr, J. P., 27*n*116, 343*n*31, 344*n*33&35&37, 347*n*49
Hoffa, James, Jr., 225
Hoffa, Jimmy, 8, 137, 200–203, 206–10, 212, 216, 358
Honey, Michael, 13
hospital workers, 19, 117, 193
household workers, 347–54
Maid's Day, 351–52
organization, 348
personal to commercial, 353
race-class-gender, 354
read people, 350
slave-like, 349

and unions, 351–52
working conditions, 348
Household Workers Organization (HWO), 351
Hudson, Gerry, 388
Huerta, Dolores, 157, 168–69
Humphrey, Hubert, 95
Humphrey-Hawkins bill, 24, 96
Humphrey-Javits, 98
Hurd, R., 346*n*45, 347*n*49
Hyman, Richard, 2, 3*n*10, 8*n*32, 23*n*102, 30, 34

IBM, 90
IBT (International Brotherhood of Teamsters), xiii, 1, 25, 31, 34, 138, 143–45, 199, 201–4, 206–11, 213, 216–23, 226, 358–60
failures, 200
first national strike, 216
TDU as opposition within, 199
IBT (International Brotherhood of Teamsters)
*See also* Teamsters
Illinois, 29, 185
ILWU, 123, 136
IMF, 80, 99
immigration, 361, 363
Imperiale, Anthony, 241–42
imperialism, 91, 266, 290
Imperial Valley, 158–59, 161–64
imports, 69, 82–83, 88, 90, 92, 98, 283, 307
India, 83
Indiana, 29, 231
Indianapolis, 26, 213
industrialization, 33
industrial relations, 7, 11, 14, 44, 108, 120, 124, 135, 387
strikes repudiate, 1
industrial work, to service sector, 15
Industrial Workers of the World (IWW), 153*n*6, 341, 393
industry
suppresses personality, 7
workers' control, 32
*The Inner City Voice*, vii, 289, 291, 317, 318, 332
International Association of Machinists (IAM), 57, 131
International Executive Board (IEB), 183, 295–96, 298
International Longshoremen's Association (ILA), 9, 128, 379–80
International Socialist Organization (ISO), 219*n*31
International Socialists (IS), 200, 213–21, 225, 266, 329–30
crisis in, 220
International Union of Electrical Workers (IUE), 57, 126–28
Iran, 93, 99
Iraq, 361, 388
Island Creek, 181, 194
isolation, 33, 140, 144–45, 153, 174, 240, 248, 289
ISST (Independent Society of Skilled Traders), 298
ISTC (Independent Skilled Traders Council), 298
Italy, 2, 79, 89, 214

Jackson, Don, 291
Jackson, Henry, 3
Jackson, Jesse, 378

Jackson, Maynard, 22
Jackson State, 215
Jacob, Jesse, 244
James, C. L. R., 289, 313*n*7
Japan, 52, 55, 61–62, 66–69, 78, 80–82, 91, 93, 97–98
JARUM, 14
Javits, Jacob, 82, 95
Jennings, Paul, 127
Jim Crow, 22
Jobs with Justice, 364, 378
*Joe* (film), xii
John Birch Society, 184
Johnson, James, 325
Johnson, Lyndon B., 56, 77, 85, 87–88, 93, 130, 282, 293
Johnson, R., 244*n*27, 274*n*53
Jones, D. R., 210*n*18&19
Jones, LeRoi. *See* Baraka, Amiri
Jorgenson, D. W., 69
Joyce, William, 211
J. P. Stevens, 28
justice, 6, 29, 130, 209, 235, 266–67, 295–96, 335, 338, 349, 369, 385, 387, 393
Justice for Janitors (JFJ), 369–70

Kaier, 390
Kane, Paula, 337*n*7, 339*n*12, 340
Kansas City, 133, 235
Katz, H., 286
Kennedy, John F., 56, 77, 82, 84–85, 87–88, 158*n*8, 230
Kennedy, Robert, 203
Kennedy, Ted, 222
Kennedy Round, 82, 90–91
Kent, 138
Kent State, 11, 18, 25, 215, 217
Kentucky, 29, 176, 182, 188, 193, 195
Kessler-Harris, A., 343*n*31, 344*n*34, 345*n*38&40, 346*n*42&46
Keynesianism, 78–80, 84–86, 88, 93–94, 97–98, 100–102
*Keystone Coal Industry Manual*, 181
Kihss, P., 237*n*14, 238*n*15
King, Martin Luther, Jr., 12–13, 21, 235, 238*n*15, 240*n*20, 247–48, 289, 311, 318
Kirkland, Lane, 34, 100, 360, 371*n*25
Kissinger, Henry, 89–90, 92–93, 97
Klea, Leon, 302–3
Klein, A. J., 56*n*28, 57*n*31
Klein, Jennifer, 388
Kmart, 363
Knight, A. O., 127
Kochan, T. A., 56*n*28, 57*n*31
Koontz, Elizabeth, 17
Korean War, 48, 51, 55, 62, 73, 120, 237
Kramer, Brent, 254, 261*n*25, 265–66, 267*n*35, 278–79, 331–32
Kramer, Marian, 314, 315*n*10, 321
Ku Klux Klan, 183–84
Kuroda, M., 69
Kusley, William, 210

labor, 5, 7, 10, 56, 61, 72–73, 78–79, 96, 124, 126, 135–36, 143, 145–46
broken by business, 123
bureaucracy, 140
and capital, 11, 41, 50, 55, 58, 62, 87, 94, 97, 120–21, 129
catastrophe for, 35
and civil rights, 248

and corporations, 56
costs, 52–53, 61–62, 68
decline of, xviii
defeat of, 34
vs Democrats, 24, 44
eruption, 70
glasnost, 361
government attacks, 142
honeymoon for, 37
institutionalization, 146
international division of, 66
needs organization, 362
new movement, 368
new workers (women & minorities), 115–20
officialdom eschews militancy, 112
organization, 364–75*passim*
employer-friendly, 373
productivity, 58, 63, 65, 67–68, 85
quiescent today, 357
revitalization, 376
segregation, 118
unions depend on, 393
vs union in strike, 45, 277
upsurge, 136
*See also* workers
Labor Against the War, 388
Labor Education and Research Project (LERP), 363–64
Labor Management and Reporting Disclosure Act, 204
*Labor Notes*, 119, 363–64, 376–77, 387
La Botz, D., xviii*n*2, 25*n*108, 138*n*88&89, 210*n*19, 225*n*41, 363*n*11
Landrum-Griffin Act, 204, 215
Laos, 93
La Paz, 162, 164–65, 167–69
*LA Story*, 369
Las Vegas, 213, 216–17
Latinos, 6, 18, 106, 117, 138–39, 145, 205, 221, 223, 237, 252, 369, 385
Leavitt, Jim, 210
Ledbetter, L., 263*n*28
Lens, Sidney, 113, 136*n*85, 214
Lerner, Steve, 367, 368*n*18, 388
Less Developed Countries (LDCs), 83
Lester, Richard, 107–8
Lewis, John L., 5, 19, 39, 109–10, 114, 118, 136, 176, 178, 358
Lichtenstein, Nelson, 6, 43*n*7, 46*n*8&9, 49, 50*n*15, 57*n*33, 60*n*36&38, 61*n*41, 110*n*9, 111, 112*n*11, 282*n*1, 283*n*2, 293, 294*n*34, 359*n*4, 388
Lindbeck, A., 63*n*43, 98*n*39
Linden Auto Workers (LAW), 289
Lindsay, John, 245
Linwood, 29
List, Frederick, 79
Little Steel, 40–41
living standards, 4, 74, 114, 122, 130, 174, 176, 200, 222, 252, 281
Livingston, David, 180
Logan, Rosa, 323
longshoremen, 2, 9, 13, 61, 133, 153, 174, 193, 379–80, 385, 387
Lordstown, 10, 12, 18, 29, 106, 141, 287–88
Los Angeles, 10–11, 22, 154, 159, 206, 211–12, 215–16, 222, 241, 328, 369–70, 383–85, 388
*Los Angeles Times*, 388
LRBW (League of Revolutionary Black Workers), vii–viii, xv–xvi,

14, 139, 289, 292, 298, 307, 312, 320–21, 327–33
legal victories, 325–26
vs UAW, 292–94
Lucy, William, 235
Luddite, 23*n*102
Lumumba, Patrice, 316
Luxemburg, Rosa, 7
Lyddon, D., 2*n*9, 4*n*16, 15
Lynd, S., 28*n*120, 39*n*2&3, 40*n*4, 358*n*2

machinists, 29, 57, 61, 90, 125
International Association of Machinists (IAM), 131
*Mack Safety Watchdog*, 299
Madar, Olga, 23
Magarelli, Pat, 131
Mage, Judy, 117
Mahwah, 138
Maid's Day, 351–52
Maier, M. H., 3*n*11, 10*n*44, 14, 15*n*59, 117*n*29, 245*n*30
*The Making of the English Working Class* (Thompson), 7
Mandel, Ernest, 141*n*96
Manpower Development and Training Act, 84
Mansfield, 8
manufacturing, decline, 52
Marable, Manning, 14*n*56, 22
March, Ron, 291, 320
Marcuse, Herbert, xiii
marriage, same-sex, 388
Marshall, Ray, 389
Marshall Plan, 81
Marx, Karl, 79, 289
Marxism, 313–14, 317
Mast, R., 314*n*9, 321*n*31, 329*n*56
Matles, James, 132*n*76, 180
Matusow, Alan, 86
Mazey, Emil, 135, 293, 305
McBride, Lloyd, 184
McCarthy, vii, 107
McClellan, John, 204
McCoy, Rhoady, 237–39
McDonald, David, 59, 122, 126
McNiff, Joseph, 268*n*37, 272*n*48
McQueen, O. D., 293*n*33
Meany, George, 3, 100, 118, 158, 360
meat cutters, 13
meat packing, 121, 223
mechanization, 176–77
*See also* automation
Medicare, 87
Medina, Eliseo, 388
Mellon Scaife, 184
Memphis, 13, 29, 235, 247
Meredith, Vince, 27
MES (More Effective Schools), 233–34
metal workers, 136
Metropolitan Transportation Authority, 381
Metzgar, J., 121*n*40, 123, 124*n*49
Mexico, 83
Michels, Robert, 107–8
Michigan, vii, 329, 389
Middle East, 93
Milkman, Ruth, 367, 369–70
Miller, Arnold, 5, 20, 173–74, 180, 184–89, 191, 194–96
Miller, George, 264
Miller, John, 299–300
Mills, C. Wright, 109, 112, 214

Mills, Karlyne, 372
miners, 2, 6, 8, 18–20, 24, 29–33, 39, 61, 106, 128–29, 132–33, 136–37, 141, 144, 173–97*passim*, 176–77, 215, 358
  free speech revoked, 197
  isolation of, 174
  job gains, 177–78
  job loss, 176–77
  killed, 174
  vs law, 192
  refuse Taft-Hartley, 194
  support for, 193–94
  uniqueness of, 175, 178, 186
  *See also* strike, miners
*A Miner's Life* (Brophy), 174
Miners for Democracy (MFD), 5, 19, 28, 136–38, 140, 144, 173, 179–80, 182–83, 185, 189, 215, 224, 358, 360
  dismantling of, 185
  racial unity in, 184
Miners' Right to Strike Committee (MRTSC), 19–20, 184
Mink, Patsy, 353
Minneapolis, 10, 40, 153
Mississippi, 182, 333
Mississippi Freedom Democratic Party, xvi, 155, 293
Mitchell, D. J. B., 56*n*29, 73*n*54
Modernization and Mechanization Agreement, 115
Mojica, Hermilo, 164
Moldea, D., 210*n*17&19, 216*n*27
*Monopoly Capital* (Baran & Sweezy), xiii
Montgomery, 106
Montgomery, David, 1, 3*n*13, 4, 11*n*48, 14*n*58, 109*n*7, 136*n*85, 388
Montgomery, Oliver, 139
*Monthly Review*, 362
Moody, K., xviii*n*2, 5*n*21, 12*n*49, 16*n*65, 28, 31*n*131, 107*n*4, 115*n*17, 119*n*35, 137*n*87, 138*n*89, 142*n*98, 143*n*101, 363*n*10–11, 365*n*14, 370*n*23, 371*n*30, 375
Moscato, J., 344*n*35, 346*n*42&47, 347*n*50
Motor Carrier Act, 201
Moundsville, 8
*The Movement*, 328
movements, 106, 141, 144–45, 169–70, 178, 200, 209, 219, 221, 225, 229, 252, 265–67, 312, 327, 347
  decline of, 225, 251
  legitimate direct action, 209
  and workers, 4
  *See also* anti-war; black; consumer; DRUM; environmental; Revolutionary Union Movement; Telephone Revolutionary Movement; women's
multinationals, 82–83, 88, 91, 101
  in dictionary, 89
  *See also* corporations
Murphy, Marjorie, 15–18, 230*n*1, 233*n*6, 237*n*14
Murray, Philip, 39, 50, 109–10

NAACP, 314
Nabach, Joseph, 272*n*48, 276*n*56
Nader, Ralph, 100, 138, 212–13, 222*n*35

*The Nation*, 375
National (Air Line), 339–40
National Association of Working Women, 343
National Guard, 11, 18–19, 30, 34, 199, 210–11, 242, 317
nationalization, 30*n*129, 79, 164*n*10, 192, 197
National Labor Relations Act, 46
National Public Radio, 391
National Master Freight Agreement (NMFA), 202, 206, 208–11, 216
National Miners Union (NMU), 175
National Recovery Act, 95
*National Review*, 86
National Secretaries Day, 342, 345
NCHE (National Council of Household Employees), 348–49, 352–53
NCUP, 241–42
NDWU (National Domestic Workers Union), 351
NEA (National Education Association), 9, 15, 29, 31, 229, 232
  growth of, 16
  racial disputes, 17
Negro American Labor Council (NALC), 13, 118
neo-liberalism, 78
neo-liberalization, xvii
Nestlé, 154
Newark, 229, 234–35, 245, 274
  teacher struggle, 241–44
New Deal, xiii, xiv, 11, 38, 77, 100, 145–46
New Directions, 381–83
New Jersey, 10, 29, 133, 138, 211, 229, 234, 242, 253, 265, 272, 274, 289, 376–77
Newman, Dave, 266, 270*n*43, 277*n*60, 279
New Mexico, 176
Newport News, 29
newspaper workers, 14, 23–24
New York, 10, 16, 18, 25–26, 94, 117, 131, 133, 143, 193, 203, 207, 229–37, 239–40, 242–43, 245–46, 253, 255, 257–60, 262–65, 267–68, 271, 327, 362, 372, 377, 381, 386
  phone service (1969), 256
*New York Daily News*, 363
New York Telephone, 10, 252, 254, 256–63, 265, 267, 271–75, 277–78
*New York Times*, 5, 9, 11, 15, 22–23, 60, 98, 195, 233, 256, 268, 271, 343, 388
Nicholas, Donald, 243
Nielsen, G. P., 117*n*30, 338*n*8, 340*n*16, 341*n*21
niggermarn, 139
Nixon, Richard, xiii, 2, 11, 18, 73, 77, 85–94, 97, 137, 145, 160, 272
NLRA, 120
NLRB (National Labor Relations Board), 38, 47, 57, 127, 142, 365–66, 369, 392
NMFA, 137–38
No Child Left Behind, 384
Nordana, 379–80
Normal, 29
North American Aviation, 138
North Carolina, 363

Northrup, H. R., 53*n*22, 56*n*29, 122*n*44, 264*n*31
nuclear workers, 29, 128
Nunley, Donald, 195
nurses, 15, 22–23
Nussbaum, Karen, 119, 343–46
Nyden, P., 2*n*7, 19*n*84, 24*n*106, 27*n*117, 30*n*125, 115*n*16, 132*n*76, 139*n*93
NYNEX, 377–78, 386

Oakland, 265, 390
Obama, 392
Occidental Petroleum, 181
Occupational Safety and Health Administration (OSHA), 88
OECD, 66
office workers, 15
Ohio, 1, 8, 10–11, 18–20, 25, 28–29, 138, 181–82, 206, 288
oil, 177, 181, 202
oil crisis, 18, 73, 92–93, 99
oil prices, 88, 101–2, 306
oil workers, 127–28
Old Ben Coal, 181
Olympic Games, 316
*One-Dimensional Man* (Marcuse), xiii
Operation Dixie, 46
Organization of Negro Education (ONE), 244
Organization of Petroleum Exporting Countries (OPEC), 92
Ortiz, Frank, 164
Otabe, K., 81

Padilla, Gilbert, 157, 168
Paff, Ken, 201*n*1, 220
painters, 19, 136
paper workers, 29, 125
Paris Spring, 2
Parrish, Richard, 232, 238*n*17, 239–40, 248
Patrick, Harry, 180, 184, 188, 196
Patterson, Lee Roy, 183–84, 188
Peabody Coal, 181, 194
PEAC (Progressive Educators for Action), 384
Pechthalt, Josh, 385
Peick, Louis, 211
Pennsylvania, 1–2, 8, 18, 25, 173, 175–76, 179–80, 182–83, 193, 196, 272, 274, 376
Perlmutter, E., 256*n*11, 272*n*48
Perry, C. R., 2*n*6, 20*n*85, 30*n*128, 187*n*15
Perry, Jack, 185
Peterson, Esther, 348
Peterson, Peter, 90
Peurto Ricans' Young Lords Party, 209
Phi Beta Kappa, 265
Philadelphia, 8–10, 29, 133, 241
Phillips, Kevin, 85
*Picket Line*, 215
Piketown, 29
Pittsburgh, 1, 5, 10, 14*n*58, 27, 119, 179–80, 185, 193, 215–16, 231
*Pittsburgh Post-Gazette*, 185
Pittsburg and Midway Coal, 191
Plotke, D., 344*n*32, 345*n*38
Podair, J. E., 233*n*6, 240*n*19
*Political Parties* (Michels), 107
postal workers, 3, 10, 29, 129, 132–33, 141
Powell, Helen, 196

Prashad, Vijay, 388
pre-huelga, 165–66
Presidential Commission on the Status
    of Women and the Equal Pay
    Act (1963), 336
Presser, Jackie, 138, 222–23
Presser, William, 206
Prial, F. J., 339n13, 341n22
Pringle, Paul, 388
privatization, 102, 247–48
Professional Drivers Council
    (PROD), 138, 212–13, 217, 220
The Protester, 138
Provenzino, Andrew, 212
PSSU, 370
public workers, 230, 245, 248, 366, 381

race, 150, 154–55, 205, 354
racism, 6, 32–33, 116–18, 139–40,
    144, 180, 183–84, 232, 234, 237,
    239, 245, 261–62, 264–65, 267,
    269, 275, 290, 293–94, 299, 301,
    312, 314–15, 319–20, 324n38,
    325–26, 332
Racketeer Influenced and Corrupt
    Organizations Act (RICO), 223
Radical America, 23, 328
Ragen, Bill, 388
railroad workers, 24, 29, 133, 136
Randolph, A. Philip, 118
rank and file, 3, 5, 7, 9–10, 19–21, 25,
    27–32, 34, 39–42, 44, 50, 59–61,
    70, 72, 74, 77, 105–46passim,
    110, 156, 158, 169–70, 173–74,
    180–81, 184–87, 195–96,
    199–200, 203, 206–9, 211–18,
    220–21, 224–25, 229, 251,
    260, 262, 265–69, 271, 275–79,
    281–82, 285–86, 290, 292,
    294–95, 298–99, 328, 332, 300,
    306, 336, 360–61, 364–65, 367,
    369–70, 374, 376–77, 379–85,
    389–91
    blacks inspire, 144–45, 265
    emergence, 37–38
    emerge in unions, 106, 136
    lack organization, 140–41
    propmpts union overturnings, 127
    renew unions, 129
    repression of, 109–10
    sacrificed, 45
    still influential, 358
    stuck with business unionism, 308
    vs unions, 11, 42–43, 49, 70–71,
        109–10, 125, 135, 143, 156–57,
        162, 210, 251–52, 262, 267–68,
        273, 277, 359
    weak in auto industry, 289
    weaknesses, 33
Ranzall, Richard, 260
Raskin, A. H., 193n24, 195
Rauh, Joseph, 179
Raynor, Bruce, 366, 392
Razor, 315, 317–18
Reagan, Ronald, xvii, 19, 21, 56, 78,
    95, 100–102, 142
    defeats labor, 34
recession, 38, 46, 48, 52, 67, 69, 73,
    77, 84–85, 94, 99–100, 102, 106,
    120, 130, 133, 141–42, 197, 200,
    221, 225, 260, 339
Rediker, Marcus, 388
Reed, Adolph, 388
Republicans, xv, 45, 56, 86–87,
    94–96, 137, 217, 224

Republic Windows and Doors, 392
retail clerks, 13
Reuther, Victor, 112
Reuther, Walter, 10, 49, 60, 112,
    123, 155, 218, 282, 284n5, 285,
    292–93, 295
Revolutionary Union Movements,
    118, 138–39, 265, 293, 320–22,
    325, 330–32
Reyes, Sergio, 164
Ricardo, David, 80–81
Richardson, Elroy, 292
Richmond, 29
Rickard, Ed, 292
Riddle, David, 329
Riley, Ken, 379–80
Riley, Leonard, 379
Rinaldi, M., 205n8, 217n29
Roach, James, 293
Roberts, Cecil, 30n129, 195, 197n32
Roberts, Geraldine, 353
Roberts, Lillian, 117
Robert Treat School, 243
Rockefeller, David, 91, 93, 97
Rockefeller, John D., 188
Rockefeller, Nelson, 95, 274
Roosevelt, Franklin D., 40–41, 85–86,
    95, 97, 109
Ross, Fred, 149–50
Rosselli, Sal, 374–75, 387–88
Rozen, F., 338n8, 340n16
rubber workers, 40, 61, 115, 121, 133
Rueck, Kelly, 341
Rumsfeld, Donald, 87
Russian Revolution, 136
Russo, John, 288

Sadlowski, Ed, 28, 139–40, 183–84,
    218, 358
safety. See health and safety
Safeway, 29
Salinas, 160–62, 164–69
San Francisco, 10, 40, 153–54, 159,
    215–16, 387–88, 390
San Francisco Chronicle, 387
San Francisco Weekly, 373
sanitation workers, 19, 235, 247
San Jose, 390
San Mateo, 390
SAWSJ, 361
scabs, 152, 159–60, 163–66, 182,
    195, 211
Scammon, Richard, 85–86
Schaefer, Tom, 274
Schatz, R., 121n41, 127n60
Schermerhorn, Tim, 382
Schultze, George, 99–100
scientific management, 255
Scott, John, 292
SDS (Students for a Democratic
    Society), xiii–xiv, 209, 241,
    265–66, 327, 329
Sealander, J., 343n32, 345n40, 347n48
Seattle, 22, 29, 215–16, 361
    Battle of, 225
The Seattle Semi, 216
Seattle Times, 373
A Second Opinion, 383, 385
segregation, 233, 245
Seifer, N, 346n41, 348n54
SEIU (Service Employees
    International Union), 19, 359–60,
    366–75, 386–87, 390–93
    antithesis of rank and file, 374
    attention grabbing, 368

corruption, 388–89
    first hospital union, 387
    vs healthcare workers, 389
    oblivious to labor history, 376
    restructuring, 375
Selden, David, 230n1, 231
Serrin, W., 8n32, 60n36, 72n52,
    112n11, 115n18, 135
services, industry to, 15
sexism, 117–18, 256, 261–62, 264–66,
    269–70, 275, 337
sexuality control, 338–39
    See also community control;
    workers, control
SFWR (Stewardesses for Women's
    Rights), 338, 340–42, 345
Shabecoff, P., 271–72n47
Shachtman, Max, 214
Shanker, Albert, 230, 238–40, 245–46
Shapp, Milton, 2
Sheridan, W., 203n6, 206n14
Shoemaker, Donna, 302n72, 320n27
Shorter, Isaac, 301–2
Sikorski, J. C., 206n45, 213
Silk, Leonard, 99
Simkin, W. E., 61n40, 120n37, 125
Simon, William, 94, 239n18, 240, 248
Sims, Jordan, 139, 275n55, 292,
    324–25
slavery, 349
Slichter, Sumner, 108, 110
Sloan, Edith, 348, 352
Smith, Clinton, 304
Smith, D., 343n32, 345n40, 347n48
Smith, Floyd, 90
Smith, G., 256n11, 257n15
Smith, Howard K., 86
Smithsonian Agreements, 69
Smyth, J., 347n52, 351n62
SNCC, xvi, 155, 164, 235–36, 241,
    243, 327, 331
socialism, 7, 136, 192, 214, 220, 266
    fear of, 217–18
    See also International Socialists
social justice. See justice
Social Security, 87
Social Services Employees Union, 117
Sohmen, E., 53n21&22, 55n26
Solidarity Day, 34
South Africa, 290
South Carolina, 13
Southern University, 17
Soviet Union, 81, 84, 93
Sovine, Red, 193–94
Spain, 89
speed, 21, 43, 50, 58, 60, 71, 105, 110,
    121, 129, 132, 139, 163, 190, 207,
    253, 269, 283, 287, 290, 292,
    299–300, 306, 311, 318, 332
Sragow, D. A., 347n51, 349n58,
    351n62, 353n70
Standard Oil, 181–82
Stanley, D., 193n25
Stearns, 29
steel industry, 39, 50, 52, 56, 59–61,
    96, 116, 122, 143
    decline of, 27–28
    women in, 119
steel workers, 5, 19, 27–28, 108–9,
    115, 125, 132, 138–39, 143–44,
    175, 184, 209–10, 219, 221, 358
Steelworkers Fight Back, 28, 138–40,
    142, 144, 218
Steelworkers Organizing Committee
    (SWOC), 41, 109

Stein, Herbert, 87, 95
Stein, J., 46n9, 52n19, 56n30, 84n12,
      90n25
Steinem, Gloria, 338n11
Stepan-Norris, J., 46n9
Stern, Andy, 359, 366–68, 370–71,
      373, 375–76, 387–92
   on strikes & unions, 370–71, 391
Stewards and Stewardesses (S&S), 337
St. Joe Minerals, 182
STRESS, 326
strike, 21, 28–29, 38, 40, 47, 49–50,
      60–61, 70, 72, 107, 117, 121, 123,
      125, 127–29, 131–35, 137, 139,
      145, 153, 204, 229, 327–28, 364,
      370, 376, 390–92
   airline mechanics (1966), 8
   auto workers (1973), 14
   auto workers, 8, 10, 48, 282, 292,
      294, 299–300, 302–7, 319–20,
      322–23
   decline, 307
   ensure security, 281
   explode, 287
   as national symbol, 288
   banned, 143
   Black Lung, 137
   Britain (1972), 2
   vs capital, 7
   car haulers (1979), 29
   decrease of, 30–31
   drop-off in, 142
   eschewed, 59
   everywhere (1976–9), 24
   farm workers, 29, 151–52, 157–68,
      223
   firefighters (1978), 29
   flight attendants, 341
   Ford, 49
   France (1968), 2
   General Electric, 57, 127
   GM (1945), 112
   GM (1970), 134
   isolation of, 144
   Italy (1969), 2
   and labor movement, 7
   labor vs union in, 45, 267
   longshoremen (1968), 9
   longshoremen (1971), 2
   miners (1974–75), 2
   miners (1978), 2, 144, 173–74, 180,
      182, 189–90, 192–95, 197
   miners, 8, 19–20, 24, 29–31, 175,
      178–79, 184, 187–88
   most important, 179
   newspapers, 23–24
   New York (1970), 10
   nuclear workers, 29
   nurses (1974), 15
   nurses (1976), 22–23
   paper workers (1978), 29
   pledge not to, 45, 50, 59, 110–11,
      121, 230, 373
   postal workers, 3, 10, 29, 141
   problem of, 34
   prohibition of, 230, 242, 381, 386
   railroad (1978), 29
   rare today, 386
   reluctance, 221
   as repudiation, 1
   right to, 19–20, 24, 27, 270
   rise and fall of, 8–9
   sanitation workers (1968), 12
   sanitation workers (1977), 22
   sanitation workers, 235

   as self-defense, 4, 7
   steel workers (1959), 27, 56–57, 126
   steel workers (1979), 29
   steel workers, 48
   teachers (1966), 9
   teachers, 16–18, 29, 231, 233, 235,
      238–39, 241–44, 385
   failure of, 245–48
   telephone, 10, 218, 252, 258–61,
      267–78
   first national, 260
   traded for wage increase, 134
   truckers (1965), 8–9
   truckers (1974), 2
   truckers, 11, 18, 25, 199, 201–2,
      208–11, 216, 221
   understandings of, 7–8
   vs union, 11
   United Aircraft Corporation, 57
   universities, 29
   UPS (1973), 1
   UPS (1997), 25, 31, 224, 360
   as vestige of old, 370–71, 391
   See also boycott; walkouts; wildcat
      strike
Strike Back!, 260–61
Student League for Industrial
      Democracy, xiii
Sullivan, John M., 201
Sun Harvest, 163, 165, 167, 169
Surkin, M., 14n56, 132n76, 284n5,
      289n20, 291n23&25–26, 292n29,
      305, 306n88, 312n3, 321n31,
      323n36, 324n40, 325n42&43,
      327n48, 331n63
Sutherland, Donald, 329
Swados, Harvey, 124
Sweeney, John, 224, 353n76, 360–62,
      365–66
Sweezy, xiii

table grape boycott. See grape boycott
Taft, Philip, 9
Taft, Robert, 88, 173
Taft-Hartley Act, xv, 2, 24, 30, 46, 57,
      123, 141, 173, 191–94, 204
Tampa, 234
taxi drivers, 133
Taylor, John, 322n34, 323
Taylor Act, 381, 386
Taylorism, 26, 124
TDC (Teamsters for a Decent
      Contract), 25, 137–38, 216
TDU (Teamsters for a Democratic
      Union), 25, 137–38, 140, 142,
      144, 200, 211, 213, 216–22,
      224–26, 358–61, 364–65, 376–77,
      380–81
   opposition within IBT, 199
   and socialism, 217
   turned inward, 225
teachers, 9, 15–19, 29, 31, 105, 133,
      141, 229–48passim, 383–85
   attacked, 244
   Black Power confronts, 229
   vs community control, 234–40
   control, 233
   identified with establishment, 234
   Newark struggle, 241–44
   strike failures, 246–47
   vs unions, 246
   and urban unrest, 232–48
   as villains, 246–47
   See also AFT; strike, teachers
Teamsters, xv, 8, 16, 19, 25, 29, 34,

      114, 129, 133–34, 137–38, 144,
      159–62, 193, 199–226passim,
      329, 337, 358–61, 366, 380,
      385. See also IBT (International
      Brotherhood of Teamsters)
   bureaucracy, 204–7, 213
   flextime, 208
   and movements, 209, 219, 225
   organized crime, 203–4, 207
   power, 201–3
      job security, 202–3
   reform, 209–26passim
      TDU and IS, 213–21
   rise in militancy, 200
   roll back, 221
   and Turtles, 225, 361
Teamster United Rank and File
      (TURF), 137, 211–12, 215
technology, 26–27, 54, 58, 67, 77,
      82–84, 108, 114, 123, 132, 137,
      154, 199, 207, 255, 258, 279,
      283, 342. See also automation;
      highway system
Telephone Revolutionary Union
      Movement, 262, 265–66
telephone workers, 15, 19, 33, 129,
      132, 218–19, 251–79passim, 385
   demographic trends, 262–64
   inequality, 264
   electro-mechanical equipment,
      254–55, 278
   equality and justice, 267
   job control, 254, 256, 258, 261
   job freedom, 253
   and other movements, 252, 265–67
   out-of-towners, 267–69
   phone service, 256–57
   racial and gender inequality, 264
   and radical change, 266
   unionized, 254–56
   See also strike, telephone
Tennessee, 13, 29, 182, 196
Tepperman, J., 342n26, 344n32&35,
      345n38, 346n42
Terkel, Studs, 5, 10
Texas, 363
textile workers, 40, 90, 174, 193
Theodus, Sam, 223
third party, 40
Third World, xiii, 93, 265
Thompson, Edward, 7
Thompson, Gary, 323
Thompson, H. A., 140n95, 299n60–
      61, 301n69, 302n71&73, 303n77,
      304n80, 312n3, 320n29, 323n35,
      326n45
Thompson, P., 124n52, 140n95
Thompson, Wendy, 329–30n59
Time, 340
tire builders, 153
Tobin, James, 79
Toledo, 18, 28, 40, 153, 211–12
Toussaint, Roger, 382–83
Townsend, Lynn, 293
trade
   balance, 55, 62, 80, 91, 98
   barriers, 81, 83, 90
   crisis, 69
   deficit, 88–89, 98
   free, 80–81, 83, 85, 91
   growth, 66–67
   international, 81, 90
   See also exports; imports
Trade Union Educational League
      (TUEL), 136

transit workers, 381, 385–86
Transport Workers Union, 337
Trbovich, Mike, 180, 182–83, 196
Treaty of Detroit, 49
Trenton, 235, 274
Trilateral Commission, 97
Trotsky, Leon, 214
*A Troublemaker's Handbook*, 364
Troy, L., 57*n*32, 142*n*99
truckers, 2, 6, 8–9, 18, 24–25, 125,
    133, 153, 202, 211, 216, 222,
    358
    golden age, 201
    *See also* IBT; Teamsters
Truman, 46
Trumka, Rich, 360–61
TTU (Telephone Traffic Union), 261,
    269, 274–75
Tugwell, Rexford, 95
Tyson, T., 313*n*6, 350*n*59, 352*n*69,
    353*n*70

UAW (United Auto Workers), 9–10,
    23, 34, 40, 48–49, 57, 60–61,
    74, 91, 108, 111–15, 123, 128,
    130, 134–35, 138–40, 143–45,
    193, 206, 218, 281–308*passim*,
    312, 315, 318, 321, 324–25, 330,
    332–33, 359, 372, 385
    awash in profits, 282
    bureaucracy, 297
    crisis, 307–8
    vs DRUM, 320
    forces work, 305
    grievance explosion, 285–86
    vs LRBW, 292–94
    racism, 290, 315, 319–20
    represses resistance, xv–xvi
    UNC critiques, 295–97
    unprecedented security of, 281
    women in, 119
UFT (United Federation of Teachers),
    231–33, 245
    vs blacks, 234–40
UFW (United Farm Workers), 359,
    366
UHURU, 315–16
UMW (United Mine Workers), xvi,
    19–20, 30–31, 33, 39, 109, 114,
    137, 145, 173–97*passim*, 215,
    223–24, 281, 358–59, 361, 385
    behind CIO, 176
    fails miners, 177
    and USW, 183
    virtual disappearance, 175
UNC, 139, 144, 294–95, 298, 307
    vs UAW, 295–97
unemployment, 20, 22, 41, 48, 51–52,
    55, 58, 60, 63, 71, 77–79, 84–85,
    90, 94, 102, 123, 130, 132, 141,
    200, 232, 237, 241, 251, 255, 271,
    284, 306, 353
unions density, xv, xvii, 31*n*131,
    46–47, 142, 182, 221, 346
    erosion of, 182
*Unions Mature* (Lester), 108
unions and unionism, 4–6, 13–18,
    20, 23, 29, 31–35, 39–40, 42,
    61, 72–73, 100, 133, 140, 145,
    159–60, 202, 277, 386
    anti–, 260, 390
    as big business, 12, 114
    bottom-up, 365
    or top-down, 367, 369, 372,
        382, 387

bureaucratization, 41, 45, 107–15,
    156–57, 204–7, 297, 358–59, 375
    spurs revolt, 115
changed direction (1980s), 361
clerical workers, 346–47
conservative role, 122
co-opted, 38, 59
and corporations, 42–44, 50
    corporations avoid, 121
decline of, 220, 362
defeat of, 46
depend on labor movement, 393
difficulties for, 57
employers resist, 366
Europe vs US, 3
as fetters, 101
flight attendants, 341
hospital, 387
and household workers, 351–52
insensitivity of, 105
and job control, 254
jurisdictional maze, 144
vs labor in strike, 45
membership drops, 142
new workers (women & minorities),
    115–20
vs non-unions, 163, 182, 222
officials vs workers, 41–42, 74,
    109–10, 143, 156–57
overturnings in, 126
passivity of, 61
vs profit, 181
rank and file emerge in, 106, 136
rank and file renew, 129
vs rank and file, xvi, 11, 42–43, 49,
    70–71, 109–10, 125, 135, 143,
    162, 210, 251–52, 262, 267–68,
    273, 277, 359
real, 261, 376
regeneration, 47–50
respond to workers, 378
restrictions on, 204
vs strike, 11
strike reluctance, 221
and urban rebellion, 248
vestige of old, 371, 391
weakening, 123–24
and women, 336–38, 340
wreckers of, 183
Union WAGE, 118
UNITE, 366, 388, 392
United Action, 262, 265–66, 268–74,
    276, 278, 383–85
United Aircraft Corporation, 57
United Black Brothers, 138, 289
United Electrical Workers, 126–27,
    193
United Farm Workers (UFW), 12, 28,
    149–70*passim*
    bureaucracy, 156–57
    confusion by, 149–50
    defeat of, 169–70
    grape defeat, 161
    history of leaders, 157
    learns from workers, 152
    paid reps, 168
    strikes, 158–60
    strikes precede, 152
    two souls, 156, 162
    union structure established, 153
    *See also* grape boycott
United Fruit, 163, 165, 167
United Kingdom. *See* Great Britain
United National Caucus, 140, 289
United Nations, 97

United Parcel workers, 14
United Press, 11
United Rubber Workers (URW), 40,
    110, 127
United States, 61–62, 67–69, 97
    blacks and poverty, 22
    and capitalism, 6
    class struggle, 4
    coal necessity, 194
    confederate flag, 380
    conservatism, 5, 32, 85, 95
    crisis, 86, 91, 93–94
    divided, 33
    domestic investment deterred, 54
    economic dominance, 81, 84
        diminished, 92
        first critique of, 90
    economic shift, 21
    energy, 92–93
    exchange rate renounced, 92
    first hospital union, 387
    foreign dependence, 92
    foreign investment, 37, 53–54,
        82–83, 88–90, 100–101
    free market vs state intervention,
        78–80, 89, 98
    import growth, 69
    largest armed confrontation, 175
    largest labor organization in, 31
    longest strike wave, 251
    longest waterfront strike, 2
    manufacturing decline, 52, 70
    miners killed, 174
    miners unmatched struggle, 178
    mine seizures, 176
    private-sector union, 202
    production avoids unions, 121–22
    socialism declines, 136
    support for corporations, xv
    third party, 40
    unions compared with Europe, 3
    welfare state, vs Europe, 45
    wildcat strikes, 1
    workers obscured, 7
    workers' power, 18
    working-class uniqueness, 116
UPRUM, 14
UPS (United Parcel Service), 1, 6,
    25–26, 31, 137–38, 207, 216–17,
    222–24, 320, 360, 365
UPSurge, 25–27, 137, 216
URW, 136
US Labor Against the War, 388
US Steel, 31, 194, 336
USW (United Steelworkers), 27–28,
    48, 50, 57, 109, 119, 122, 126,
    128, 134, 136, 139, 143, 145, 183,
    190, 193, 206, 358
    and UMW, 183
UTLA (United Teachers of Los
    Angeles), 383–85
UTW (United Telephone Workers),
    261

Vallas, S. P., 254*n*6, 255*n*8, 260*n*23,
    263*n*28, 276*n*56, 278*n*61&63
Vatter, H. G., 51*n*17, 55*n*27
Velasquez, Baldemar, 29
Verizon, 377
Vestal, Don, 212
Veviaka, Rose, 263*n*28, 267*n*35
Vietnam War, xii, xvi, 2, 11, 17, 21,
    88, 93, 106, 155, 178–79, 209,
    221, 229, 232, 236, 284, 288
Villaraigosa, Antonio, 384

violence, 11, 34, 184, 210, 235, 276, 293, 314, 317, 358
Virginia, 182, 232
Volcker, Paul, 89, 98–99
Volkswagen, 283
Voss, Kim, 367–68
Vranesh, George, 183

Wage Labor Board (WLB), 110, 112
wages, 6, 19, 22–24, 26, 37, 45–47, 51–54, 56, 58–61, 63–64, 68, 71–73, 84–85, 98, 112, 114–15, 117–18, 121–23, 127, 130–34, 137, 141–42, 150–53, 158–59, 161–62, 167, 176–77, 182, 186, 190, 192, 200, 202–3, 208–11, 213, 221–23, 229, 233, 246, 251–52, 258, 260, 262, 267, 270–73, 277, 279, 339, 342, 353–54, 362, 370–72, 390
    blacks vs whites, 116
Wagner, Robert, 230
Wagner Act, 57
walkouts, 49–50, 127, 129, 133, 158, 210–11, 259–60, 267, 271, 275, 300, 319, 343, 363, 386
Wallace, George, xiii, 145, 188
*Wall Street Journal*, 78, 83, 95, 191–92, 371, 391
Wanger, E. D., 56n28, 57n31
Washington, D.C., 18, 131, 188–89, 193, 235, 274
Washington, Julie, 385
*Washington Post*, 23–24
Watergate, 94–95
Watson, Edna Ewell,, 321n31
Watson, John, vii, 314, 316–17, 328–31
Watsonville, 138, 223
Wattenberg, Ben, 86
Watts, M., 5n20, 6n27, 32
Wayne State, 315, 321, 329
Weinberg, Jack, 21, 34n134, 299n59, 300n63&65, 302n72, 303n78, 304, 306n87&90
Weir, Stan, 8, 61n39, 105, 124, 127n61, 128n65, 214, 357
Wertheimer, B., 343n32, 346n41
West Coast Farms, 167, 169
Westmoreland Coal, 186
West Virginia, 8, 18, 20, 137, 173, 175, 178–82, 184–85, 187–88, 192–93, 196
white backlash, 145
whites, viii, xii–xiii, 13–14, 22, 24, 32–33, 85, 106, 116–17, 140, 145,

156–57, 184, 202, 204–5, 232, 236–37, 240–41, 245, 247–48, 252, 262–64, 290, 294, 296, 312, 314–16, 318, 320, 322–24, 326–28, 330–31, 338, 347, 349, 351–52, 354
wildcat strike, 2–5, 8–10, 14, 19, 24–25, 29, 40, 50, 61, 71, 105, 111, 121, 129, 133, 135–41, 143, 179, 182, 187, 195, 199, 208–11, 215–16, 260–61, 269, 275, 287–91, 300–301, 304, 306, 311, 318–19, 321–24, 370, 385
    defined, 1
    largest, 11
    reject authority, 128
Wilhelm, John, 366, 392–93
Williams, Eunice, 135
Williams, Mamie, 323
Williams, Raymond, 23n102
Williams, Robert F., 312, 313n6, 315
Williams, Roy, 222
Wilson, R., 224n41, 360n6
Winkler, I., 273n50, 274n52, 278
Winslow, C., 18n81, 230n1, 389n66
Wise, Helen, 17
Withorn, A., 15n61, 23
Witt, M., 224n73, 360n6
Witwer, D., 203n6, 205n9&10, 206n14
Wobblies, 153n6
women, 6, 15, 18, 26, 32, 106, 115–20, 141, 196, 205, 221, 252, 255, 262, 264–65, 275, 294, 321, 335–54*passim*, 371
    Hard-Hatted Women, 119
    sex objects, 337–40
        campaign against, 340–42
    and unions, 336–38, 340
    work composition (1970s), 335
women's movement, 4, 7, 22–23, 119, 252, 329
Woods, Malcolm, 304
Woolsey, Thomas, 301–2
workers, 7, 10, 18, 59, 111, 123–24, 132, 145, 214, 221, 223, 367
    assault on, 55
    auto strike symbolizes alienation of, 288
    blue-collar, depictions of, xii–xiii
    vs capital, 31
    and capitalism, 6
    challenge authority, 6, 299
    control, 32, 60, 121, 141, 163, 199–200, 202, 207, 226, 251, 278
        reduced, 207, 252, 254–56, 258, 261, 372–73
    divided, 33

foreign trade costs jobs, 90
golden age for, 47
informal networks, 124–25
isolation of, 140
and Martin Luther King, 12–13
necessity of, 170
need workplace, 365
new generation (women & minorities), 115–20
obscured in US, 7
vs officials in unions, 41–42, 74
and other movements, 4
power not spontaneous, 362
and prosperity, 130–31
pushed to brink, 105, 125
strength of, 30
strike reluctance, 221
unionized today, 362
unions depend on, 393
unions respond to, 378
union vs non-union, 73, 378
US power of, 18
on warpath, 72
women as, 344
*Workers' Control in America* (Montgomery), 1
*Workers' Power*, 19, 218
Workers' United, 392
working class, dissipating power of, 38–46
working conditions, 4, 21, 43, 49, 60, 74, 115, 123, 127, 139–40, 158, 176, 190, 222, 229, 251, 255, 262, 277, 281, 285, 287, 290, 296, 300, 302–4, 312, 322–23, 325, 332, 337, 339, 342–43, 346, 348–49, 362, 371, 373, 381
Working Smart, 364
Working Women, 119
World Bank, 80
World Trade Organization, 225, 361
Worthington, Bill, 186
Wurf, Jerry, 127, 246
Wyper, R., 344n32, 344n36

X, Malcolm, 313n6

Yablonski, Jock, xv, 5, 34, 137, 179–80
Yellow Freight, 222
Young, Coleman, 326
Young Americans for Freedom, 86
Youngstown, 28–29, 235, 288

Zambrano, Aristeo, 164
Zander, Arnold, 127
Zinn, Howard, 388